AGRICULTURAL POLICY, AGRIBUSINESS, AND RENT-SEEKING BEHAVIOUR

Costing billions of dollars annually, international trade in agricultural products is impactful and influenced by several factors, including climate change, food policy, and government legislation. The third edition of *Agricultural Policy, Agribusiness, and Rent-Seeking Behaviour* provides comprehensive economic analyses of the policies that affect agriculture and agribusiness in Canada and the United States.

Looking at current agricultural policies, the third edition includes new chapters on food pyramids, climate change, and GMOs, while also highlighting the effect of international policies on Canadian trade, including the problematic US ethanol policy. The new edition addresses current issues, including how the COVID-19 pandemic has negatively affected agricultural value chains and played a hand in the ongoing growth in opioid use.

Including a number of key findings, and discussing current debates on topics including foreign ownership of Canadian farmland, *Agricultural Policy, Agribusiness, and Rent-Seeking Behaviour* will appeal to students in agricultural economics and policy, as well as policymakers, agricultural firms, energy companies, and readers wishing to reduce their nation's carbon footprint.

ANDREW SCHMITZ is a Ben Hill Griffin Jr. Eminent Scholar and professor of food and resource economics at the University of Florida.

CHARLES B. MOSS is a professor of food and resource economics at the University of Florida.

TROY G. SCHMITZ is an associate professor in the Morrison School of Agribusiness and the W.P. Carey School of Business at Arizona State University.

G. CORNELIS VAN KOOTEN is a professor of economics and Canada Research Chair in Environmental Studies and Climate at the University of Victoria.

H. CAROLE SCHMITZ is a freelance journalist writing on economics.

Agricultural Policy, Agribusiness, and Rent-Seeking Behaviour

Third Edition

ANDREW SCHMITZ, CHARLES B. MOSS, TROY G. SCHMITZ, G. CORNELIS VAN KOOTEN, AND H. CAROLE SCHMITZ

UNIVERSITY OF TORONTO PRESS
Toronto Buffalo London

ISBN 978-1-4875-2280-3 (paper)
ISBN 978-1-4875-1841-7 (EPUB)
ISBN 978-1-4875-1840-0 (PDF)

Library and Archives Canada Cataloguing in Publication

Title: Agricultural policy, agribusiness, and rent-seeking behaviour / Andrew Schmitz, Charles B. Moss, Troy G. Schmitz, G. Cornelis van Kooten, and H. Carole Schmitz.
Names: Schmitz, Andrew, author. | Moss, Charles B. (Charles Britt), author. | Schmitz, Troy Gordon, author. | Van Kooten, G.C. (Gerrit Cornelis), author. | Schmitz, H. Carole, author.
Description: Third edition. | Includes bibliographical references and index.
Identifiers: Canadiana (print) 20220132763 | Canadiana (ebook) 20220132828 | ISBN 9781487522803 (paper) | ISBN 9781487518417 (EPUB) | ISBN 9781487518400 (PDF)
Subjects: LCSH: Agriculture and state – Canada. | LCSH: Agriculture and state – United States. | LCSH: Agriculture and state – European Union countries. | LCSH: Agriculture – Economic aspects – Canada. | LCSH: Agriculture – Economic aspects – United States. | LCSH: Agriculture – Economic aspects – European Union countries.
Classification: LCC HD1787 .S37 2022 | DDC 338.1/8 – dc23

We welcome comments and suggestions regarding any aspect of our publications – please feel free to contact us at news@utorontopress.com or visit us at utorontopress.com.

Every effort has been made to contact copyright holders; in the event of an error or omission, please notify the publisher.

We wish to acknowledge the land on which the University of Toronto Press operates. This land is the traditional territory of the Wendat, the Anishnaabeg, the Haudenosaunee, the Métis, and the Mississaugas of the Credit First Nation.

University of Toronto Press acknowledges the financial support of the Government of Canada and the Ontario Arts Council, an agency of the Government of Ontario, for its publishing activities.

ONTARIO ARTS COUNCIL
CONSEIL DES ARTS DE L'ONTARIO
an Ontario government agency
un organisme du gouvernement de l'Ontario

Funded by the   Financé par le
Government   gouvernement
of Canada   du Canada

Contents

Introduction

This book is for readers who have a basic understanding of microeconomics and an interest in agricultural policy. Although this may include students in disciplines such as history and political studies, our target audience is undergraduate and graduate students in general economics, agricultural economics, and agribusiness. This may not be a book many students wish to read from cover to cover, so we have structured it in such a way that chapters may be used individually. For advanced students, we have included appendices to many of the chapters; these contain more rigorous developments of selected topics.

The focus of this book is on agricultural policies in the United States, Canada, and the European Union. The scope is much broader and more current than the book by Schmitz, Furtan, and Baylis (2002). Since then, the United States has passed a new farm bill in 2008, Canada has introduced a new safety-net program, and the European Union has moved towards a more developed farm program. Also, European Union policy is covered in depth along with the litany of arguments as to why agriculture should be protected. New topics have emerged that we cover in this book, including biofuels and genetically modified organisms (GMOs).

Several important books discuss various aspects of agricultural policy; we include them in our extensive reference list, which may be used as a guide to supplemental reading. For example, more in-depth analyses on the history of US policy are contained in several volumes, including those by Benedict (1953), Cochrane and Runge (1992), Cochrane and Ryan (1976), Gardner (1987), and Tweeten (1970). Other policy books (e.g., Helmberger and Chavaz 1996; Knutson, Penn, and Flinchbaugh 1998) cover some of the same topics we do in this volume, but their focus is largely restricted to US policy. We include additional important topics, such as the impact of agricultural policy on agribusiness, and we provide an economic framework for analysing policy options. Ours is not a detailed analysis of the development of US agricultural policy and its implementation; the design, support, and implementation of US farm policy are discussed by Orden, Paarlberg, and Roe (1999). Rather, our book considers contemporary agricultural policy worldwide. Our framework employs aspects of several economic theories, including welfare economics, public choice, transaction-cost theory, and the economics of regulation. Combined, these approaches broaden the understanding of agricultural policy. Our focus is not only on producers (farmers), but also on the various entities that comprise the agribusiness sector. We discuss policy in the context of vertical market structures.

CHAPTER ONE

Food and World Agriculture: Trade, Agricultural Policy, and Agribusiness

Without a prosperous agriculture, there is no prosperity in America ...

– Dwight Eisenhower

If money could have solved the farm problem, we would have solved it a long time ago ...

– Ronald Reagan

1.1 THE SCOPE OF FOOD AND AGRICULTURAL POLICY

Historically, books on agricultural policy have restricted the discussion to farm programs that impacted the agricultural industry. But agriculture is impacted by many forces outside the purview of farm programs. For example, US agriculture was impacted greatly by US energy policy that provided subsidies to produce ethanol from corn. Further, food policy that restricts the consumption of certain foods impacts agricultural resource use. Trade also has a major impact on agriculture worldwide, and agricultural policy is highly intertwined with trade. Thus, for example, US tariffs on Chinese goods and China's response to such tariffs have targeted the US farm sector, causing many US commodity prices to plummet. At least part of the hurt felt by US farmers has been offset by US farm policy programs (Swinnen 2019).

1.2 FOOD POLICY

The influence of consumer demand upon food production and food policy has increased substantially over time and has changed the landscape of food policy in the United States. For example, organic food production and demand have grown significantly.

Furthermore, as United States Department of Agriculture (USDA) health and nutritional guidelines have evolved, food policy designed to mitigate obesity and its health effects has emerged. For example, many cities in the United States and the European Union have instituted a tax on sugar-sweetened beverages. As with genetically modified organisms (GMOs) and gluten-free products, heightened consumer awareness and demand for lower sugar content in both beverages and food have already prompted unofficial added labelling. Partly due to these factors, the US sugar industry has seen a decrease in domestic sugar sales.

The connection between food policy and food waste must also be considered, especially in the context of global food security. Some geographical areas suffer from severe undernourishment (starvation), while other areas suffer from overnourishment (obesity). Many programs are successfully addressing malnutrition in areas where consumers lack purchasing power but changing the behaviour of consumers who make poor diet decisions is not a simple task. Debates continue about what types of policy best address this behaviour. Another problem occurs when food products that could feed the malnourished are used to create non-food commodities, such as the conversion of corn to ethanol.

CHANGING FOOD TRENDS

- Consumer food preferences are shifting more towards convenience, with more companies outside of agriculture participating in retail marketing (such as Amazon, Blue Apron, etc.).
- Organic foods have become mainstream.
- Micropropagation of tissue-cultured food crops is expanding.
- Customized agricultural animal gene breeding has implications from farm to table.

1.3   AGRICULTURAL POLICY AND BUDGETARY OUTLAYS

Agricultural policy, which has provided significant income support to farmers, reflects the ways that governments influence agriculture and how the agricultural sector, in turn, influences government. In some countries, such as the United States, agricultural policy is set via legislation. The United States is required to pass a farm bill every five to six years. Since the first US farm bill was passed in 1933, agricultural policy has shifted markedly. For example, the US 1996 Federal Agriculture Improvement and Reform (FAIR) Act eliminated target prices and acreage set-aside requirements, but these were later reinstituted.

In Canada, several new safety-net programs were instituted for grain and oilseed producers every few years, while the European Union (EU) made drastic changes to its Common Agricultural Policy (CAP) by introducing a single-farm payment scheme (SFPS) consisting of decoupled farm payments which, in theory at least, do not influence production decisions.

Many developed countries allocate large sums of money to government programs that indirectly impact the farm sector. For example, in the United States, the USDA heavily supports the US school lunch program and the Supplemental Nutrition Assistance Program (SNAP). As a result, in 2018 only 30 per cent of the USDA budget was devoted to farm programs.

A newer area of agricultural policy deals with aquaculture, which is the commercial farming of all types of seafood products in marine and freshwater environments for human (and animal) consumption. Over time, aquaculture has become a major agricultural industry worldwide. In the global aquaculture market, China is a major exporter, and the United States is a major importer of aquaculture products (Asche, Anderson, and Garlock 2019).

As agricultural markets expand globally, agricultural policy must take into account the World Trade Organization (WTO), which governs the rules of trade between nations at a global or near-global level. The WTO is a rules-based, member-driven organization, in which all decisions are made by the member governments, and the rules are determined by negotiations among members. The WTO began on 1 January 1995, but its trading system is half a century older. Since 1948, the General Agreement on Tariffs and Trade (GATT) has provided the rules for the system. The agricultural sector has been an obstacle to the resolution of multilateral trade negotiations, and farm programs are often in violation of WTO guidelines. As of 2021, the WTO consisted of 164 member countries. Sometimes member states' individual programs conflict with their international obligations as members of the WTO (Sumner 2005).

WTO COMMITMENTS

"There is a strong argument that the United States has been and will be in violation of its WTO commitments regarding the overall level of trade-distorting subsidies ... US farm programs for a variety of commodities may be suppressing market prices in violation of the WTO Agreement on Subsidies and Countervailing Measures ... US subsidies depress world corn prices by 6 to 9 per cent and world rice prices by 4 to 6 per cent ... US programs need a major overhaul to bring them into conformity with international obligations" (Sumner 2005, 1).

Figure 1.1. Total producer subsidy equivalents (PSEs) for selected countries, 1986–2018

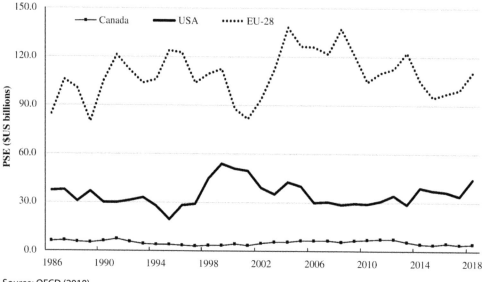

Source: OECD (2018).

Agricultural legislation has provided substantial support for the farm sector worldwide, including the European Union, the United States, and Canada. The European Union leads the pack, followed by the United States (based on producer subsidy equivalents [PSEs] as measured by the Organisation for Economic Co-operation and Development [OECD]). Support for EU agriculture increased significantly between 1985 and 2018. For example, the European Union alone transferred almost US$140 billion to producers in 2004 (Figure 1.1).

EU farmers receive large subsidies under the Common Agricultural Policy (CAP), which was established in 1962. For example, the EU agricultural budget was European currency unit (ECU) 22.9 billion in 1986, €40.5 billion in 2000, €56.7 billion in 2010, and €58.1 billion in 2018 (Figure 1.2). Anderson and Josling (2007, 1), who are critical of the CAP, observe that:

> The CAP, born of painful political compromise, proved an inflexible instrument for the encouragement of modern agriculture. Costs continued to grow relative to benefits throughout the 1970s and beyond. Costs were imposed not only on EU consumers, taxpayers, and non-agricultural industries, but also through its depressing impact on international food prices on farmers in many other parts of the world. Starting in the early 1990s, the CAP evolved in a significantly different direction ... The 1992 reforms, followed by further changes in 1999 and 2003, shifted the main focus of support in two important ways: to direct payments, which were less distortionary, and to the encouragement of the production of higher quality food, for which affluent consumers in Europe and abroad were able to pay a premium.

Figure 1.2. Changes in CAP spending for selected years, 2000–18

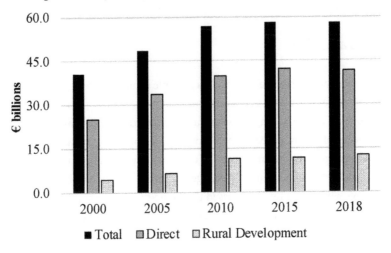

Source: European Commission (2021).

1.4   AGRICULTURE AND ITS CHANGING NATURE

1.4.1   Importance of Agriculture

In most developed countries, the importance of agriculture has declined in terms of its share of gross domestic product (GDP) – a measure of the monetary value of the goods and services produced by a nation through economic activity – and in terms of its proportion of the labour force. Agriculture does, however, play an important role in some sectors, including trade. In 2016, for example, Canada was the largest exporter of canola and third largest exporter of wheat in the world after Russia and the United States, but it accounted for about 47 per cent of the international durum wheat market and slightly more than half of the world canola/rapeseed market. In 2019, the agricultural and food sector accounted for 11 per cent of Canada's GDP and almost 10 per cent of Canada's total merchandise trade. Although less than 3 per cent of the Canadian labour force is directly involved in agricultural production, food processing is the country's largest manufacturing employer by far, supporting more than 250,000 jobs across the country. Although in many countries agriculture is decreasing in economic importance and the number of farms is declining dramatically, considerable debate persists about what to do with the farm sector. In some countries, government support for agriculture has not diminished – rather, it has increased.

1.4.2   Agriculture Continues to Change

Many changes have occurred in agriculture, and these must be considered when designing farm policy. For example, technological change has enabled individuals to operate large farms.

Consequently, farm size has increased dramatically since the early days of European land settlement in North America.

1.4.3   Who Is a Farmer?

Before we can discuss the farm problem and its possible solutions, we need to define a *farmer*. A farmer may be anyone – a doctor, lawyer, or accountant – who owns and/or is a partner of the person who used to be the single owner and operator of a family farm. The term *farmer* includes producers of many different products and, accordingly, many different producer groups, so sweeping generalizations about the effects of any given agricultural policy are impossible. The structure of agriculture has changed dramatically and has become more diverse. Gone are the days when most farmers passed their land on to their sons and daughters in anticipation that they would become the next generation of farmers. When examining the impact of agricultural policy, it is important to recognize that land transferred to heirs is often rented by farm operators who may actually own very little farmland themselves.

The farming community consists of many types of farmers, ranging from the wealthy to those living below the poverty level. This, too, makes policy design difficult. Whom should agricultural policy target? Should it be aimed at poverty-level farmers? Should policy facilitate the exit of low-income farmers from agriculture? Should policy be targeted at all?

One of the most striking structural changes in the agricultural sector is the increase in farm families' off-farm income. For example, despite record low grain prices in 2000, farm bankruptcies in North America were relatively low, mainly due to farmers who used off-farm income to offset their farm losses. Off-farm income accounted for nearly 77 per cent of total average farm income in Canada in 2013 (Statistics Canada 2018). In 1996, off-farm income in the United States constituted more than 60 per cent of the average farm-family income (Hoppe et al. 1996), which increased to 95 per cent in 2000 and then fell to 80 per cent of total average farm income of US$117,918 by 2016 (Schnepf 2017, 23–4). Off-farm income has the effect of both increasing and stabilizing farm-family income.

The profile for agriculture depends on the definition of the term *farmer*. If so-called hobby farmers are included in the definition (i.e., those whose income from farming is small relative to their total income), average US farm household income will equal or exceed the national average household income of non-farm families (Offutt 2000). However, if a narrower definition of the term *farmer* is used, in which farm households include only those whose major source of income is farming, this may no longer be true. This distinction may affect the extent to which farm programs target specific types of farmers.

1.4.4   Who Owns Farmland?

Farmland is an asset worth billions of dollars. The price of farmland in the United States, as in other parts of the world, has increased significantly over time. For example, US farmland

Table 1.1. Tenure of operators of Iowa farmland, 1982–2017 (percentage of farmland)

Ownership Type	1982	1992	2002	2007	2012	2017
Sole owner	41%	38%	28%	29%	25%	38%
Joint tenancy	39%	38%	37%	35%	32%	38%
Tenancy in common	7%	7%	12%	10%	8%	7%
Partnership	<1%	2%	2%	3%	3%	2%
Estates	4%	3%	4%	3%	3%	3%
Trusts	1%	5%	8%	10%	17%	5%
Corporations	8%	8%	7%	9%	7%	8%
Limited liability company	N/A	N/A	1%	1%	5%	N/A
Government/institutions	N/A	N/A	1%	1%	>1%	N/A

Source: W. Zhang, Plastina, and Sawadgo (2018, 11).

was valued at US$2.687 trillion in 2018. Land values are affected by agricultural policies, with economists arguing that the owners of farmland are major beneficiaries of farm bills.

As farming evolves over time, ownership of farmland has become increasingly separated from the farm operator. Farm operators who do not own the land provide labour for a set price under a rental contract with the farmland owner, who receives the agricultural supports and gleans the financial benefits or losses based on crop prices.

In the United States, not all of the farmland is owned by actual farmers. For example, in 1982 in the United States, 41 per cent of Iowa farmland was owned solely by the farm operator (Table 1.1). By 2017 this had decreased to 38 per cent, and the decline continues (W. Zhang, Plastina, and Sawadgo 2018). Many argue that any attempts to support farm income through price supports will fail because the benefits will be passed to the landowner and not to the actual farm operator. The increasing separation between landowners and farm operators is one of the major stumbling blocks for policymakers when they try to design farm policy.

1.4.5   Farm Consolidation

Farms have become fewer in number and larger in size. In Canada, for example, in the late 1930s the number of farms exceeded 700,000; since 1996, this number fell from 270,000 to less than 200,000 today (Figure 1.3). Corresponding to the decrease in farm numbers has been the increase in farm size. Since 1996, farm size has increased by nearly 40 per cent. The United States is experiencing this same type of consolidation. At the same time, wage rates have increased and capital has continued to substitute for labour. In the 1980s and 1990s, for example, many grain farmers changed their technology in favour of four-wheel-drive tractor units and the corresponding complement of larger machinery. This increased the productivity of farm labour by roughly 50 per cent (e.g., in 1950 one farmer in the North American Grain Belt could plant between 80 and 100 acres of wheat per day; by 1999 this same farmer could easily plant over 300 acres per day).

Figure 1.3. Farm numbers and farm sizes in Canada, 1996–2016

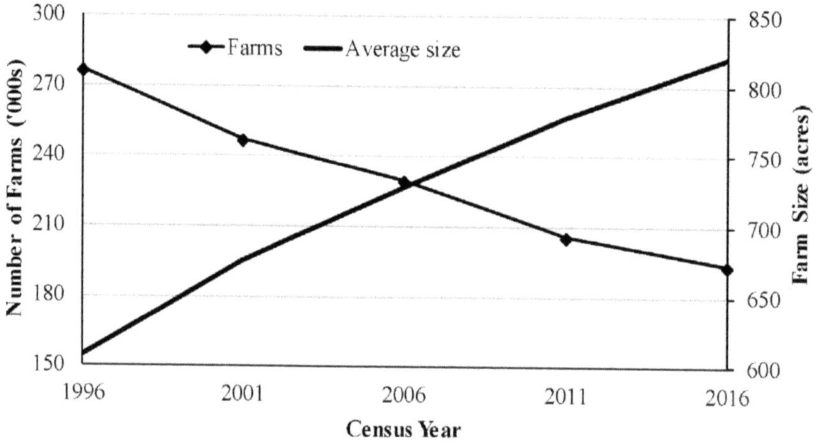

Source: OMAFRA (2016).

US FARM CONSOLIDATION

How extensive is the wave of consolidation sweeping US agriculture? Just after the Second World War there were nearly six million farms in the United States. By 2018 that number dropped by two-thirds to 2.03 million farms. Between 2011 and 2018, the number of farms fell by 4.8 per cent, with average farm size increasing from 429 acres to 443 acres. The decline in farm numbers continues, but at a slower pace. Of course, the rate of decline might have been faster if hobby farmers and retirees were excluded from the data, as farms with annual sales of $10,000 or less (indicative of hobby farms) constitute about half of total farm numbers. Within agriculture, some sectors are undergoing more dramatic consolidation. The hog industry is a good example. Since 1970 the United States has lost about 85 per cent of its hog farms. In this case, the decline appears to be continuing as strongly as ever. The decline in the number of hog farms has nothing to do with a decline in pork production; indeed, pork production has increased dramatically (see, for example, Lamb 2000, 23–4).

Despite such consolidation, net farm income before farm subsidies are taken into account has been negative for extended periods in Canada and the United States. In Canada, net farm income peaked at more than C$6 billion in the early 1970s, and then fell to an all-time low of less than C$2 billion in 1991 (Figure 1.4). In the United States, net cash farm income peaked at US$80 billion in the mid-1970s, and then fell to an all-time low of roughly US$30 billion in 1999. Farm subsidies in both countries have increased to offset falling farm incomes, with

Figure 1.4. Canadian net farm income, 1981–2007

Net Farm Income, Canada, 1981 to 2007

Source: Statistics Canada (2007).

subsidies in Canada much lower than those in the United States, as indicated in Figure 1.1. Canadian farm support no longer provides direct payments (Vercammen 2013), with policies focused only on subsidized business risk management programs (see Chapter 8). US programs are also relying more on subsidized crop insurance (Chapter 7).

1.4.6 Water and Urban-Rural Land Use Conflicts

Water used in agriculture is in short supply and the allocation of water among farmers is highly controversial. As Mark Twain reportedly said: "Whiskey is for drinking; water is for fighting over." This still holds true today. Irrigated agriculture is widespread throughout the United States and without irrigation many crops would not be grown. For example, cotton would likely not have been grown in California or Arizona without the development of irrigation. Water is in extremely short supply, and competition for it has intensified because, at least in the United States, water for agriculture is subsidized. Water subsidies are partly responsible for alleged trade distortions caused by US farm policy. Agricultural water use competes with the demand for water from urban-residential areas. Thus, there is a conflict between urban development and land for agriculture. Moreover, more and more farmland is priced for urban real estate development.

1.4.7   Climate Change and Carbon Sequestration

Climate change and its effect on various sectors, including agriculture, is debated on both the social and scientific level nationally and internationally. In agriculture, carbon sequestration is linked to climate change. Some farmers, for example, have already sequestered considerable carbon in soils by adopting measures such as reduced tillage, continuous cropping, conversion of annual cropland to perennial grasses, and tree planting. Estimates vary on the amount of carbon sequestration generated from agriculture (van Kooten 2005). Continuous cropping and reduced tillage could sequester up to 0.5 tonnes of carbon per acre per year, although a more realistic average is around 0.2 to 0.3 tonnes. For Saskatchewan alone, given the roughly forty million acres of farmland used for annual crops, the sequestration potential could be more than twenty million tonnes per year. This subject is discussed further in Chapter 14.

1.4.8   Genetically Modified Organisms

The daily diets of more and more people include genetically modified (GM) foods (Chegini and A. Schmitz 2021). While more and more US agricultural products are genetically modified (GM), the growth in the adoption of GM plant varieties has slowed considerably. Significantly, major US crops used for human consumption, such as wheat and rice, are not genetically modified. In parts of the world plagued by plant diseases – for example, the US state of Florida, where citrus production has declined drastically due to citrus greening – many plant breeders believe that the only solution is to use at least partly GM citrus varieties, which could be produced by combining biotechnological conventional and transgenic (GM) breeding (Grosser and Dutt 2017). This view presents problems for companies that rely on international sales in countries where GM products are banned (Zilberman et al. 2019). The economic implications of the genetic engineering of agricultural crops are considered in more detail in Chapter 18.

1.5   INSTABILITY AND UNCERTAINTY IN AGRICULTURE

Farm commodity prices and incomes are highly variable, mainly because of changes in weather and agricultural policies that affect international supply and demand. For an example of price variability and declining real commodity prices: the price of Canadian wheat was C$446 per

Figure 1.5. US wheat prices, 1999–2021

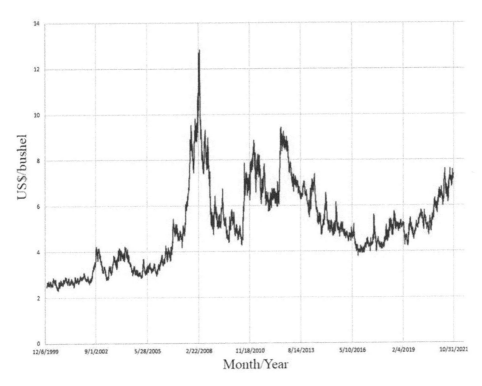

Source: Macrotrends (2021a).

tonne in 1917 (measured in 1981 deflated dollars), falling to below C$10 per tonne in the early 1930s, increasing to roughly C$350 per tonne in the mid-1970s, only to fall to below C$10 per tonne in 1998. The real price of wheat fell throughout most of the twentieth century.

From 1972 to 1979, in the United States, crop prices were four to ten times more variable than between 1955 and 1963. Prices were relatively stable throughout the 1990s and into the 2000s. However, instability returned in 2005, as corn and wheat prices roughly tripled between 2006 and 2008, only to collapse at the end of 2008. The price of wheat rose again through 2010 to 2012, before falling to a lower level for the period up to 2019, and then began rising sharply (Figure 1.5). This is true not only for corn and wheat, but also for high-value crops such as canola. For example, in 2021, the price of canola was roughly twice what it was in 2019.

The vagaries of weather produce extreme variability in crop yields, which is a major cause of the fluctuation in farm income. Crop insurance schemes were first introduced in Canada in 1961, with the objective of providing producers some form of yield insurance (see Chapter 8). Annual crop insurance payouts vary due to price and yield variabilities.

In 2021, parts of the United States and Canada, as well as other areas around the globe, experienced the worst drought since the Great Depression. The 2021 drought had a significant effect on crop yields. For major crops, such as canola and wheat, yields were over 50 per cent lower than long-term averages. The impact on prices was astronomical. Never before had prices escalated to the extent that they did in 2021. As examples, canola prices more than doubled and durum wheat prices roughly tripled (Figure 1.5).

RISK MANAGEMENT

"An important issue in the policy debate concerns the proper role for government policy ... that helps deal with the sizeable production risk existing in agriculture. The management of risk is an important tool for farm producers, but risk-management techniques cannot deal with the secular decline in commodity prices. That trend largely reflects a declining production cost because yields have increased and mechanization has made labour more productive.

Risk-management strategies can help producers deal with the substantial weather-related risk of crop yields but, in such strategies, the appropriate role for government intervention is far from clear. There is the substantial problem of insuring farmers against certain types of production risk. In particular, risk which does not affect all producers in a large geographical area (what economists call idiosyncratic risk) is difficult to insure against. The government is no better at solving the moral-hazard and adverse-selection problems than the private markets are. Indeed, the effects of credit schemes, which were designed to assist the rural areas of both the United States and Canada, have shown that governments are less successful when dealing with these problems than the private markets are" (Lamb 2000, 26).

1.6   BOOM-BUST CYCLES: THE IMPORTANCE OF WEALTH

The boom-bust nature of agriculture is an important phenomenon that plays havoc with sound government policy design. For example, the wealth created in the 1970s boom period could not be sustained during the bust period of the late 1980s. The boom facilitated excessive capitalization of assets in agriculture, particularly in land. In his Waugh Lecture on boom-bust cycles within the agricultural sector, A. Schmitz (1995a) states that, during a boom period, farm income does not need to track land values, which are not necessarily tied to production or revenue. For example, in the 1970s and early 1980s, farm income was actually decreasing while farmers' wealth (of which land is a major source) was increasing. Thus, the agricultural sector looked financially sound when, in fact, it was experiencing only a temporary growth in wealth through increased land values. Because a farmer's ability to borrow money is related to the banker's perception of the farmer's net worth (Shalit and Schmitz 1984), farmers were able to borrow large sums of money during the boom of the 1970s and early 1980s because the high value of their land increased their net worth. (Many of the loans could not be supported by cash flow from the actual farm operations.) This excess capitalization phenomenon shows up clearly in Canadian farm financial data. For example, agricultural debt in Saskatchewan was roughly C$2.1 billion in 1977 and C$6.1 billion in 1986. Net farm income, however, remained relatively flat. During the bust period, bankers' estimates of wealth became more conservative, which resulted in decreased lending and the recall of farm loans that created the farm debt crisis of the 1980s (A. Schmitz 1995a).

The lesson for policymakers is that *farm income* must be distinguished from *farm wealth*. This distinction manifests itself during the boom periods, where wealth plays a much greater role in farm financing and restructuring than does farm income.

BOOM-BUST CYCLES

In his 1995 Waugh lecture entitled "Boom/Bust Cycles and Ricardian Rent," A. Schmitz (1995a, 1110) states that "critical to understanding the boom-bust phenomenon are the dynamic changes in wealth as distinguished from net realized farm income. During the peak of the US-Canada agricultural boom period in 1981 to 1982, the value of farm real estate in the United States exceeded US$800 billion – more than double the 1974 value – only to drop in 1987 to US$597 billion. The changes in Saskatchewan, Canada, were even more dramatic. Between 1972 and 1982 the value of land and buildings increased by a factor of roughly 7.0, from C$3.6 billion to C$27.1 billion ... Realized net farm income, however, did not grow nearly as rapidly as did asset values."

During periods of farm prosperity, interest in farm policy matters dwindles. However, when the farm economy collapses, policymakers scurry to come up with a new farm policy. This is evidenced by the formation of the US Commission on Twenty-First Century Production Agriculture, set up during a period of depressed farm prices and income with a mandate to lay the groundwork for the 2002 US Farm Bill.

> **AGRICULTURE AS THE *TITANIC***
>
> "The RMS Titanic represents the current state of agriculture very well. Imagine the huge, majestic ocean liner sailing merrily across the North Atlantic, unaware and unwilling to recognize danger. The crew and passengers believed that the Titanic was so big, strong, and powerful that nothing could stop it. But an iceberg – a sudden, dramatic, and terrifying phenomenon of nature – took it to the bottom of the sea, with several hundred lives lost. Today, the worldwide food-production system resembles the Titanic as it sails along.
>
> Politicians and the general public ignore, to their peril, the economic conditions of agriculture. Only during turbulent times – in periods of food shortages or economic crises – does agriculture get broad policy attention. Policy that only reacts to crises is not generally the policy needed to sustain an industry" (Quigley 2000).

1.7   AGRIBUSINESS AND CONTRACT FARMING

Unlike many treatises on agricultural policy, this book emphasizes the interface between agricultural policy and agribusiness. Rent-seeking behaviour by stakeholders, including agribusiness (who spend large amounts of money lobbying politicians), helps steer policy in a particular direction. Some interpret the word *agribusiness* narrowly, taking it to mean only very large or conglomerate producers within the agricultural sector. But agribusiness is more than large corporations in basic production agriculture. J.H. Davis and Goldberg (1957) define *agribusiness* much more broadly to include the total of all operations involved in the manufacture and distribution of farm supplies; production operations on the farm; the storage, processing, and distribution of farm commodities; and the items made from the farm commodities. Many agribusinesses are large corporate giants that buy and sell agricultural outputs and inputs worldwide.

> **GRAIN COMPANIES' PROFITS SOAR**
>
> "At the same time parts of the world are facing food riots, Big Agriculture is receiving huge profits. Archer-Daniels-Midland Company (grain-processing) has reported a large increase in net income in its unit that stores, transports, and trades grains such as wheat, corn, and soybeans. Monsanto Company (seeds and herbicides), Deere and Company (tractors, combines, and sprayers), and Mosaic Company (fertilizers) have reported similar windfalls" (Kesmodel, Etter, and Patrick 2008, A1).

Policy analysts often disregard the influence of agribusiness on policy decision-making. Yet the influence of agribusiness is growing. For example, Monsanto's 1966 annual report noted that US farm policy was shifting from surplus control to increased production, a move that might have increased the demand for farm chemicals. Company goals included more production, lower farm product prices, and fewer farmers. These goals were in direct conflict with those of farm policy (Levins 2000, 43).

LEVEL THE PLAYING FIELD

One cannot overemphasize that "as policy economists, we have lagged behind in developing language that would help us formulate realistic solutions in the New Generation of Power. We speak of farm program benefits being capitalized into land values without thought that agribusiness may be taking its share, too, or that active farmers own less and less of US farmland. We talk of large farmers doing in small farmers, with virtually no consideration that powerful agribusiness interests may be doing in both.

"We must begin by recognizing that the 1996 Farm Bill, popularly known as Freedom to Farm, is completely wrongheaded. The farm sector was to be freed from troubling public restrictions and allowed to compete on a level playing field. The playing field to be leveled was that of trade barriers between farmers in the United States and those in other countries ... Meanwhile, the multinational processors and input suppliers went on about their business of mergers and acquisitions in an all-out effort to become less competitive. If the government's goal is to strengthen the farm sector, it set out to level the wrong playing field. Competition lowers profits while economic concentration has the opposite effect" (Levins 2000, 45).

Contract farming is growing rapidly in North America and is part of the agribusiness complex. Contract farming involves producers signing fixed-price contracts with processors and other upstream corporations. In certain cases (e.g., US poultry), producer control is even more limited because the processor controls the output of the producer. Levins (2000) indicates that US production contracts covered about US$60 billion in agricultural products by 1997, which is almost one-third of the farm-level crop and livestock sales. In 2002, production contracts exceeded US$70 billion, and the value of contracts kept increasing.

OLD MACDONALD'S FARM

Levins (2000) observed that "old MacDonald's farm" is being absorbed into what might be called "new MacDonald's farm." In other words, farming has begun to re-semble the corporate world. The operator buys the supplies and the equipment from the brand-name company and produces to its uniform specifications.

This sophisticated corporate system for food production is in the process of creat-ing new pockets of poverty across prosperous America – places where people with-out much income or influence dwell in an environment that is ruined both physically and socially (Greider 2000, 26).

Often large factory farms and packing houses are located in isolated rural com-munities. According to T. Johnson (2000, 16), "the food factories will operate with the most advanced technologies, yet local public services, especially education, will be minimal. Incomes will be significantly lower, populations stable or declining, the tax base weak and eroding. These communities will rival inner cities as the primary destination of international immigrants ... These immigrants will largely work at close to minimum wages for value-added agricultural processing or other manufacturing firms. The pattern is already visible in rural backwaters and on Indian reservations – sites are chosen by agribusiness on the assumption that very poor people will not object to anything that promises even a little income."

1.8   LACK OF COUNTERVAILING POWER

One policy issue related to the growing degree of concentration of agribusiness firms that remains important to farmers worldwide is the imbalance of market power. Generally, small independent farmers express concern that they have no market power when they bargain with large agribusiness firms.

DAVID VERSUS GOLIATH

Farmers lack countervailing power against industries that are highly organized in nature. This frustration was summarized one hundred years ago by Ed Partridge (founder of United Grain Growers) from Sintaluta, Saskatchewan, when he said, "At present we are but pigmies attacking giants. Giants may compete with giants, pig-mies with pigmies, but pigmies with giants – never" (Schwartz 1959, 7).

The increased concentration of input suppliers and processors is a growing concern among producers. There remain only a few manufacturers of large tractors and grain harvesters, and the processing sector has become highly concentrated. Farmers have had little success in bargaining with input dealers or with processors (Fowke 1957). If there is only one processor in a region, a producer's options will be limited. The degree to which the producer is captive to a processor will depend on the producer's cost of moving his or her product to an alternative processor. This varies not only with the distance travelled to any one processor, but also with the expense involved. Producers who have the same costs to move their products to either of two delivery points have some ability to negotiate price. Once the commodity is at a specific processing facility, however, producers have expended a certain amount of cost which, of course, they prefer not to forfeit. This leads to the potential for market power to be exerted on the producer by the processing or marketing firm. Many agricultural regulations and programs have been constructed to address the imbalance of bargaining power between farmers and the companies selling inputs to them, and between farmers and the companies buying their products. For example, the Canadian federal government's revenue cap on the movement of western Canadian grain mitigated the market power of the railroads. In 1986, the Canadian federal government introduced the Competition Act, which was intended to limit the use of market power by firms. The Competition Act is seen as having little influence when protecting farmers from the market power of input and processing firms. This leaves farmers with few options other than government regulation.

1.9 FARM POLICY, GOVERNMENT SUPPORT LEVELS, AND EFFECTIVE LOBBYING

Government support for agriculture varies by commodity and country. Government support for grain farmers in Canada is much less than it is for the supply-managed sector, primarily dairy and poultry. Likewise, US dairy supports are higher than those for grains and oilseeds. Government support for grain farmers in the United States is much higher than it is in Canada, while support in the European Union is higher than it is in the United States (see Figure 1.1). In 1999, for example, North Dakota wheat producers received 85 per cent of their net farm income from government transfers; in Saskatchewan, however, transfers made up less than 10 per cent of net farm income (Moss and Schmitz 2000). Reasons for this discrepancy include the following:

1 Grain farmers in the United States are much better represented in the US Congress than Canadian grain producers are represented in the Parliament of Canada.
2 The western Canadian grain lobby is divided in its intent, so it is unable to bring political pressure to bear on the federal government.

3 There are constitutional differences between the United States and Canada. Unlike in the United States, farm policy in Canada involves both federal and provincial jurisdictions. The provinces are roughly 50 per cent responsible for financing farm programs, but some provinces in Canada do not have a broad tax base. This creates financial difficulties for any major agricultural province experiencing a farm crisis.

4 Politicians are not overly generous with farm payments unless there is a political payoff. This is clearly visible in western Canada because, at times, the political stripes of the governments of Saskatchewan and Manitoba are different from those of the federal government (A. Schmitz 2000). Also, policy favours Ontario and Quebec because of the large number of voters in these provinces compared to western Canada.

5 Because of Canada's small population, relative to the size of its agricultural exports, it does not use price supports nor export subsidies.

6 Relative to the United States and the European Union, Canada may be adhering to a much narrower interpretation of the WTO's Green Box category that defines trade-distorting policies.

1.10 TARGETING FARM SUBSIDIES

Debate continues as to whether farm subsidies should be targeted to low-income farmers. A report by Offutt (2000), administrator of the United States Department of Agriculture, Economic Research Service Division (USDA/ERS), provides an income profile of US farmers and demonstrates what might happen if policy is targeted to low-income farmers. The net cost of the program does not change significantly if targeting occurs, but the distributional effects are very different. However, the report by the US Commission on Twenty-First Century Production Agriculture (2001) seems to sidestep the issue of whether or not policy should be targeted; rather, the commission focused on (1) production of an abundant supply of high-quality agricultural products at reasonable costs; (2) maintenance of a prosperous and productive economic climate for the farmer producers; (3) maintenance of the family-farm organization as a dominant part of the production system; and (4) realization of a high quality of life for all individuals living in rural areas. These goals do not include targeting. In fact, the conclusion of the commission supports increased subsidies for a broad range of agriculture.

CAPPING FARM PAYMENTS
In 2009 the Obama administration pushed for coordination within federal agencies to strip direct farm payments from thousands of farmers. The USDA and the Internal

Revenue Service (IRS) teamed up to prevent payments from going to millionaires. The 2008 US Farm Bill ruled out direct payments to those with a US$500,000 per year average for three years of farm income and an average of US$350,000 per year of adjusted gross income. Beginning with the 2009 crop year, the USDA required farmers and other entities receiving payments to sign a separate form that grants the IRS the authority to provide income information to the USDA for verification purposes (Schuff 2009).

1.11   RURAL COMMUNITIES

Many rural communities flourished in the early 1900s only to disappear in the late 1900s. The most important reason why this happened is technological advancement. During the early agricultural settlement of western Canada, the horse and wagon was the major mode of transportation. Farmers had to haul their grain in horse-drawn wagons to the closest elevator located on a rail line. The maximum distance a farmer could be expected to travel with a grain-loaded wagon was approximately seven miles. Elevators were built about every seven miles along the railway track, which then became the location for a new farm community. As new roads and vehicles became available and farmers could haul their products farther, some of the elevators were removed, which gradually caused the communities that had grown up around these elevators to disappear.

DYING COMMUNITIES
"And every time a light goes out, this country is losing something. It is losing the precious skills of a family-farm system that has given this country [the United States] unbounded wealth. And it is losing free men" (Kotz 1976, 41).

Furthermore, with the development of larger tractors, including four-wheel-drive units, farm owner-operators can farm increasingly larger tracts of land more efficiently; consequently, farm size has increased dramatically since the early 1900s. In 1950 it was not uncommon for farmers to plant a crop with an eight-foot, one-way disk that was pulled by a small tractor. By 2001 crops were planted using sixty-foot air drills pulled by large, four-wheel-drive units. Technological advancement has displaced farm families as fewer people are needed to farm larger tracts of land efficiently.

Politicians often defend agricultural programs on the grounds that they bolster rural communities. However, from an analytical viewpoint, the link between farm programs and rural communities has not been established. In many cases, the available evidence suggests that agricultural programs have been unable to stop the collapse of rural communities. For example, the closure of many country elevators was neither the result of, nor could it have been averted by, agricultural policy; rather, grain elevator companies shut down many of their elevators simply to maximize profit.

The survival of rural farming communities depends on the number of farm families, which is decreasing. It is an open question as to whether or not governments should interfere with this outward movement of people. Some argue that assistance packages should be provided to help farmers exit the agricultural sector rather than to support dying communities. One of the limitations of this book is that it does not delve into the issue of whether policy could save rural towns, or even if it should. Many economists argue that rural community development requires its own policies and cannot depend on agricultural policy alone.

1.12   COMMISSIONED REPORTS

Numerous commissions have studied various dimensions of the farm problem. For example, in 1969, the Canadian federal government commissioned a report on agriculture entitled *Canadian Agriculture in the Seventies* (Cambell et al. 1969). The report argues that there are too many resources in agriculture and that adjustment is required. In essence, it claims that there are too many farmers in Canada, and that two-thirds of them need to leave the industry so that the remaining one-third can make a decent income from farming. This report reflects a changing federal government view of primary agriculture that lacks enthusiasm about the agricultural sector.

Despite the commission's conclusions, successive governments introduced programs to prop up farm income, hoping to slow down the out-migration of people from agriculture. Supply management programs were introduced for dairy, eggs, and poultry. Prior to 1970, Canadian farmers received virtually no direct payments from government (Fulton, Rosaasen, and Schmitz 1989). Beginning in the mid-1980s, government support for farmers increased dramatically.

The US government, too, commissioned numerous studies on the future of agriculture. These studies concluded that too many resources are committed to agricultural production and that there is an urgent need for farm consolidation.

1.13   TRADE AND TRADE POLICY

Agricultural trade is an important income component for farmers, processors, and distributors. Trade has increased significantly, especially with the change in its composition. For example, seafood has become an important component of agricultural trade. Between 2010 and 2019, the amount of seafood traded was 39 per cent of seafood production.

While we spend a considerable amount of time on the discussion of trade instruments such as tariffs, quotas, and export taxes, the effect of these instruments cannot be analysed without recognizing the interface of agricultural and trade policy. For example, a price support policy increases production and lowers world prices. This is a benefit to importers because they pay lower prices for food and food products. Even so, this constitutes an export subsidy, and is a result of farm policy.

1.14   SUMMARY AND CONCLUSIONS

- Agriculture is a highly complex and dynamic industry. The catch-all term *farming* has grown from simply referring to family farms to include hobby farms; small, medium, and large farms; *factory* farms; and agribusiness corporations, which makes creating effective farm policies extremely difficult.
- Changes in consumer food preferences, including the popularity of organic foods, have altered food production.
- Food crops continue to be used for non-food purposes, such as ethanol production, despite the persistence of undernourishment as a public health concern.
- Food policy is an integral part of agricultural policy, particularly through its impacts on trade and through the effects and regulation of technological advances.
- Agriculture is susceptible to producer risk and to disruptive market patterns. While risk-reducing strategies such as contract farming do exist, agriculture is highly unstable, which exposes producers to high risk. In addition, boom-bust phenomena create difficulties for policymakers.
- Producers and agribusinesses are able to engage effectively in rent-seeking behaviour for government subsidies. Lobbyists and politicians generally circumvent the complexity of the farm industry by neglecting to define agriculture. Often, the goals of agricultural policy are simply stated in terms of unstable and low farm incomes.
- Politicians are reluctant to target farm subsidies to benefit those in need.
- Rent-seeking behaviour arguments help explain the levels of governmental farm support. In the United States and the European Union, government farm support is high. This is also true in Canada, where support for the supply management sectors is higher than support for grains and oilseeds.

CHAPTER TWO

Agricultural and Food Policy

2.1 EFFECTIVE LOBBYING: FARM POLICY AND GOVERNMENT SUPPORT LEVELS

Government support for agriculture varies by commodity and country. Take the grain sector, for example, where EU government support for its grain farmers is higher than that in the United States or Canada, and US government support is higher than that in Canada (Moss and Schmitz 2000). There are many reasons for this discrepancy.

Agricultural policy is a definite course of government action selected from available alternatives to guide and determine present and future conditions in agriculture. The debate over the extent to which government should be involved in agriculture is heated (Tweeten 1970, 1983; W.W. Cochrane 2000). Agricultural policy has changed along with technology. For example, earlier agricultural policies focused on land settlement, with direct income transfers from government to producers being minimal (A. Schmitz, Furtan, and Baylis 2002). Beginning with the twentieth century, agricultural policies began relying more on income transfers to producers from the government and consumers assumed a greater voice in policymaking.

AGRICULTURAL POLICY

Agricultural policy is a complex web of interventions covering output markets, input markets, trade, public goods investments, renewable and exhaustible natural resources, regulation of externalities, education, and marketing and distribution of food products. At the federal level, these interventions have resulted in enormous

budgetary costs, huge surpluses of farm products, major disputes with other countries, distorted international markets, and benefits to special interests. The same programs, however, have been part of an agricultural sector whose productivity over
much of the past century has been spectacular (Rausser 1992, 133).

2.1.1   What Is the Goal of Agricultural Policy?

Often, agricultural policy design is ill-conceived because the farm problem itself is not well
defined. Can you imagine target practice without a target? First, one must define the goal and
objectives of agricultural policy. That is extremely difficult in view of the complex nature of
agriculture (see Chapter 1). D. Paarlberg (1964, 55) puts it well when he states that a problem
well defined is a problem half-solved, which applies nowhere with more force than it does
in agriculture. Economists can suggest many ways to solve any farm problem, but progress
towards a solution rests clearly on the definition of the objectives (Tweeten 1970). Frequently,
the experts do not agree on what the farm problem is or why it persists. Politicians tend to use
agricultural policy to address the crisis of the day or to create the image that there is a farm
crisis when there may be none. This perception is consistent with rent-seeking behaviour by
politicians but is not necessarily consistent with lobbying efforts by farmers or agribusiness.
Thus, agricultural policy is often developed in the absence of defined objectives, which leads
to many possible solutions to the farm problem and to increased confusion. Adding to the
confusion is the often-stated sentiment: "The farm problem is what politicians want it to be!"
The quandary over the farm problem remains. Knutson, Penn, and Flinchbaugh (1998) divide
the farm conundrum into two categories: the old farm problem and the new farm problem.

WHAT IS THE FARM PROBLEM?
Agricultural policy is a difficult subject. While a number of economists have written
on the subject, they have disagreed over the cause of the continuously low returns
to agriculture.

Willard Cochrane (1958, 96) argues that agricultural output has a completely inelastic supply curve and that output expands because farmers utilize the new technology, which shifts the supply curve to the right. After a short-run increase in income,
the average farmer is right back where they started as far as their income position is
concerned. Thus, the average farmer is on a treadmill with respect to technological
advances.

Glenn L. Johnson (1958) claims that once resources, such as capital, are brought into the agricultural sector, they become fixed. When commodity prices decline, it is not economically feasible to transfer these resources to the non-agricultural sector. Johnson describes how this affects the supply curve: when commodity prices increase, new resources are added and the supply curve shifts outward; when commodity prices decrease, resources are fixed and the output levels remain constant. The supply curve is elastic for price increases and inelastic for price decreases; this snares agriculture in an overproduction trap.

Don Paarlberg (1964) argues that government involvement in agriculture is intrusive and unnecessary. If left alone, agricultural markets would clear, and returns to agriculture would equal those in the non-agricultural sector. His view can be summarized as follows: because price supports and production controls never really worked, let's get rid of them.

Lamb (2000, 26) argues that agricultural production is very integrated, with production tightly linked from the farmers' fields to the consumers' tables (from farm to table). Production is consolidating into the hands of fewer, but larger, producers. Policy debate is driven by short-run weaknesses, not by the long-run forces reshaping agriculture. What is the appropriate policy for the farm economy? Lamb emphasizes that the rule of policy should resemble the Hippocratic oath taken by doctors, which states: First, do no harm.

Susan Offutt (2000, 1) argues that development of a solution to the farm problem is hindered both by imprecision in the definition of the problem itself and by the lack of recognition of the diversity that exists across farm households. In the past, the farm problem was the disparity between the incomes of farm and non-farm households. Today, average farm income equals or exceeds the national average income of non-farm families. Problem solved? Apparently not.

OLD FARM PROBLEM

Chronically low farm prices and incomes are symptoms of chronic excess capacity, which has decreased since the 1960s. Off-farm income has helped to increase and stabilize farm-family income. Reduced farm numbers are a positive sign of adjustment and a result of technological change. With regard to market power, agribusiness has been far more helpful than harmful. Despite cases where agribusiness has become a dominant or monopolistic force, the clear record is that of a highly competitive structure (Knutson, Penn, and Flinchbaugh 1998, 240).

NEW FARM PROBLEM

Instability: Farm incomes remain highly unstable, making operations more difficult to support on narrow income margins. Diversity and changing farm structure: How do you design farm policy to help farmers when they include the whole gamut from well-established owner-operators to renters, beginning farmers, and agribusiness? Food security: As governments stop stockpiling food, concerns about food security surface. Resource scarcity and agricultural externalities: As concern about the environment mounts, and as agricultural production techniques intensify, resource use will become an increasingly important issue to farmers, environmentalists, and farm policymakers (Knutson, Penn, and Flinchbaugh 1998, 241).

2.1.2   The Scope of Agricultural Policy Analyses

As a field of study, agricultural policy will not lose its importance any time soon: it will remain at the forefront of deliberations on the future of agriculture. A sound framework for decision-making must underlie the policy process. This book offers such a framework. It provides a summary description of agricultural programs and policies that have been or could be implemented within Canada, the European Union, and the United States, together with quantitative and qualitative assessments of the economic impacts of these programs and policies. History, institutions, and constitutions play an enormous role in the moulding of agricultural policy; and within their given context, farm lobby groups and agribusiness entities spend significant sums of money to garner political support for their cause. This leads to our central thesis: Agricultural policy is influenced by rent-seeking behaviour, and because agricultural policy affects both producers and agribusiness, generally these rent-seeking activities occur on many different fronts.

AGRICULTURAL POLICY, TWENTY-FIRST CENTURY STYLE

"Contemporary agricultural policy extends well beyond simply price and income support programs. It includes trade, conservation, agricultural research, animal and plant health, food safety and human health, and other programs" (US Agricultural Secretary Ann Veneman, as quoted in Schuff 2009).

2.1.3   Ever-Changing Commodity Markets

Agricultural policy has to be viewed in the context of continuously changing market conditions. For many years, the blame for the farm problem was aimed at commodity surplus and low prices, but how this has changed! In an earlier version of this book, A. Schmitz, Furtan, and Baylis (2002) point out the pervasiveness of farm surpluses.

FARM SURPLUSES

Farm surpluses can fuel farm-price woes and add to the debate on farm aid. US Department of Agriculture (USDA) economists do not expect to see lower food prices at the retail level; pleas for short-term relief are certain to push government spending on farm aid upward. Surpluses can complicate government efforts to open up more foreign markets (Ingersoll 2000, B6)

Commodity prices fluctuate widely. Take for example, US corn and wheat prices between 2010 and 2019. At the time of the 2017 US Farm Bill, commodity prices had dropped significantly, triggering government payments to farmers.

2.2   POLITICS AND POLITICAL INSTITUTIONS

Often what is overlooked in policy debates is the role of special interest groups that participate in rent-seeking activities with the aim of obtaining government subsidies. We present traditional arguments about why governments intervene in an economy and how rent-seeking activities can lead to paths that are not supported by the theory of optimal government intervention. In addition, we present arguments from the theory of public choice, in which rent-seeking behaviour plays a key part. As we demonstrate, not all agricultural policies coming out of rent-seeking behaviour result in large inefficiencies of resource use.

Many factors have a significant influence on the development of policy (W.W. Cochrane and Ryan 1976; A. Schmitz, Furtan, and Baylis 2002). The type of institution influences the ability of special interest groups to set the farm policy agenda. While the United States and the European Union have implemented agricultural policies, Canadian farmers rely heavily on ad hoc programs.

The nature of a country's policies is the outcome of a range of social, economic, political, and institutional factors (I. Roberts et al. 1989, 149). Government support and polices are determined through political and administrative mechanisms. These mechanisms, and the institutional frameworks within which they operate, differ significantly between countries (ibid., 150).

The governing structure of Canada, the United States, and the European Union is set out in their constitutions. All three have a bicameral system: Canada has a Senate and House of Commons, the United States has a Senate and House of Representatives, and the European Union has a Parliament and Council. Canada is a constitutional monarchy; under the British North America Act of 1867, the prime minister and his or her appointed Cabinet have the power to enact law, to tax, and to spend money. The British monarch (Crown) is the head of state and is represented in Canada by the governor general, who is appointed by the British monarch upon the advice of the Canadian prime minister. Canadian citizens elect representatives to the House of Commons by geographical region or constituency; each constituency has approximately the same number of voters, though exceptions are made for remote, northern seats and for Prince Edward Island, which have smaller numbers of voters. The leader of the political party that has the most seats in Parliament is asked by the governor general to form the government. If this leader can get the support of the majority of the elected members of Parliament, he or she will become the prime minister. The Senate, however, is not elected; members are appointed by the prime minister.

The US Congress has both an elected House of Representatives and an elected Senate. Seats in the House of Representatives are allotted by population, while each state gets two seats in the Senate, regardless of population. This gives regional concerns a voice at the federal government's policy table. As well, US citizens elect the president through the Electoral College, meaning that the president does not necessarily have a majority of support in Congress. Thus, important policy decisions, such as the creation of farm bills, are generally bipartisan, unlike in Canada, where the party in power can usually get its bills passed into legislation without multiparty support.

In the United States, three branches of government determine federal policies: the legislative branch (Congress, which is made up of the Senate and House of Representatives); the executive branch (the president); and the judicial branch (the Supreme Court). The development of agricultural legislation rests primarily with the Senate and the House agricultural committees and their subcommittees. The executive branch implements and administers the legislation enacted in Congress. The Cabinet department primarily responsible for agriculture is the United States Department of Agriculture (USDA), whose secretary is appointed by the US president and confirmed by the Senate (I. Roberts et al. 1989; Skogstad 1987).

The European Union (EU) has a different political process than either the United States or Canada. It has several bodies that influence agricultural policy, including the Agricultural Commission, the European Parliament, and the EU Council. The primary policy body is the Agricultural Commission, made up of representatives from several countries, each with a five-year appointment. The agricultural commissioner plays a key role in setting and administering agricultural policy. The European Parliament comprises members elected in the member countries for five-year terms. They amend and vote on legislation and approve the appointments to the EU Commission. The EU Council is made up of the heads of state of the twenty-seven member countries. There is also an Agricultural Council, made up of the agricultural ministers of each of the twenty-seven member countries. The EU Agricultural Commission has the sole right to propose policy. Proposed policy is voted on by the European Parliament and by the EU Council. In the case of agricultural policy, however, the European Parliament has a limited role, and it only gives its opinion to the EU Council on the Agricultural Commission proposals.

EU AGRICULTURAL POLICY CHANGE

Three major policy changes in the European Union (Chapter 7) are the Agenda 2000, MacSharry, and Fischler reforms. The broader political context of EU agricultural policymaking changed ... which made agricultural trade subject to stricter rules and set the scene for a new round of trade negotiations in the WTO. However, the change of the international context of the CAP (Common Agricultural Policy) cannot in itself explain the nature of CAP reform. The EU institutional setting within which reform is negotiated and settled also plays a crucial role ... The two most substantial reforms of the CAP, the MacSharry and Fischler reforms, were decided by farm ministers, while the modest Agenda 2000 reform was adopted by the European Council (Daugbjerg and Swinbank 2007, 19).

In a must-read treatise on the rent-seeking behaviour of the EU CAP, Swinnen (2008a; 2008b), expanding on the works of Grant (1997), Josling (2008), Moyer and Josling (2002), Olper (1998), Pappi and Henning (1999), and Ritson and Harvey (1997), argues that the Fischler Reform was not a result of pressure for change from the EU farm groups. Rather, key politicians played an important role, including President Chirac of France.

THE FISCHLER REFORM AND POLITICS

Three large countries (France, Spain, and Germany) controlled a blocking minority. Unexpectedly, the Iraq war played a decisive role. It initially made allies out of Chirac and Schröder in the opposition to the reforms – despite Germany's earlier demand for reforms. But EU Agriculture Commissioner Franz Fischler used the Iraq alliances to manoeuvre Spain out of the anti-reform group through British Prime Minister Blair's links with Spanish Prime Minister Aznar. Fischler paid a price in having to drop the capping of the subsidies (for Blair's support for his strategy) and by allowing regional instead of historically based payments (to secure the German votes later).

President Chirac played an important role, but in ways differently than intended. First, Chirac's intervention at the 1999 EU Council in Berlin initially looked like a major political victory, but ultimately allowed a review of agricultural policies in 2003 – something that otherwise would not have been the case. Second, it made Fischler anticipate any potential obstacle and strategy in order to avoid the economic and environmental costs associated with the Agenda 2000 reform. Third, it reinforced Fischler's resolve with reforms. Fourth, his earlier successes in blocking reforms may have caused him to become complacent. In combination, Chirac's earlier interventions opposing CAP reforms contributed to the most radical reform of the CAP (Swinnen 2008b, 35–6).

2.3   CONSEQUENCES OF THE POLITICAL PROCESS

For agriculture legislation, Canada uses ad hoc programs, the United States uses farm bills, and the European Union uses the Common Agricultural Policy (CAP). Canada's political structure makes it difficult for Canadian farmers to bring their concerns to the attention of policymakers. This is one of the reasons that federal economic support levels (producer subsidy equivalents, or PSEs) often have been much lower in Canada than they have been in the United States or the European Union (Table 2.1).

Canadian farmers have difficulty making their concerns known to the federal government for reasons including the following:

1 *Power rests with the prime minister.* Much of the political power in Canada rests in the hands of the prime minister, which makes lobbying difficult.
2 *Lack of regional representation.* Seats in the House of Commons and in each of the provincial legislatures are distributed by population. Members are not elected by region, therefore regional concerns do not have a guaranteed voice in the political process of Canada. Because agricultural concerns are usually regional, they receive unequal treatment.
3 *Federal-provincial coalitions.* In provinces where agriculture comprises a large part of the economy, government support often depends on coalitions between the provincial and federal governments.

2.4   RATIONALE FOR GOVERNMENT INTERVENTION IN A MARKET

To understand why agricultural policy exists, one needs to understand why governments intervene in markets. Traditionally, economists have viewed the role of government in terms of

Table 2.1. Producer subsidy equivalents (PSEs) for wheat: EU, US, and Canada, 1988 and 1998

	PSEs	
Country	1988	1998
European Union	50	65
United States	39	43
Canada	41	18

Source: OECD (1998).

its ability to mitigate the effects of market failures. Market failures arise from the existence of externalities (benefits or costs not captured by the market). Externalities produce a market solution that is not optimal because the full costs or benefits of an activity are not included in its price. While optimal government intervention may move the market equilibrium closer to the societal optimum, government inefficiencies may outweigh the inefficiencies of the market.

Coase (1937) pioneered the concept that market failure results from misspecified property rights. The idea is that if an externality can be assigned property rights, a market can be created for that externality. For example, if government could assign ownership to carbon dioxide emissions and set a quota for these emissions, a market for emissions could be established. (Such a market has been created in the United States for sulphur emissions.) The result would be that a firm must purchase the right to pollute, effectively assigning a cost to pollution. Thus, it would create an incentive for firms to reduce their emissions. Following Coase's (1937) logic, one does not need direct government intervention to address market failure; rather, one needs only to change how property rights are defined.

Often, in the literature on agricultural economics, one comes across the phrase *getting the institutions right*. An example of an institution is property rights (North 1981). Misspecifying them may result in inefficient markets, so getting the institutions right may be an important role for government.

In his Canadian Economic Association presidential address, Boadway (1997) argues that there are three basic reasons for government intervention: (1) efficiency, (2) stabilization, and (3) income redistribution.

1 *Efficiency.* To maximize efficiency, the efficiency branch of government introduces policies, programs, and expenses with the objective of making markets more efficient. It includes the subsidization of public goods (such as some form of public research), the limiting of externalities (including Pigouvian taxes), and regulations that limit market power.
2 *Stabilization.* The stabilization branch of government attempts to stabilize the economy. Boadway (1997) refers to the creation by a government of macro-institutions, such as the US Federal Reserve and the Bank of Canada, as the means to stabilize currency.

3 *Redistribution.* Another function of government is to redistribute income among groups in society. Economists recognize that markets may produce an efficient optimum without regard to distribution among the members of its society. Therefore, society may have social goals that precipitate the redistribution of resources or outputs.

A number of agricultural programs have more than one objective. First, consider storage. A storage policy can be welfare-improving since it improves efficiency. It can also bring about increased stabilization and the redistribution of income. Second, consider crop insurance. Under crop insurance schemes, the government provides subsidized crop insurance to producers. Crop insurance programs guarantee a per acre yield in cases of damage caused by natural events that include weather and destruction by wildlife. Crop insurance is made available by the government because the market does not provide an efficient quantity or quality of all-risk crop insurance to producers. Thus, there is an efficiency component underlying crop insurance. It is intended to mitigate the swings in yield that result from factors beyond the producer's control. Hence, crop insurance is intended partially to stabilize income for the farm sector. Because there is a significant amount of public funding supporting crop insurance, at times the income redistribution component is significant.

Why would governments want to redistribute income? One traditional explanation is that governments want to maximize some aggregate welfare function, whereby different weights are attached to each individual's function. These weights may give rise to the desire to redistribute income to maximize the societal-objective function. An alternative hypothesis, which fits into the theory of public choice, is that economic rents exist and can be transferred among individuals, creating the incentive for groups to organize to capture these rents. Because of the lobbying of special interest groups, for example, policies may be introduced that facilitate the transfer of economic rents among members of society.

2.5   GOVERNMENT FAILURE AND POLICY UNCERTAINTY

While governments may have laudable objectives for intervening in the marketplace, government policies can also fail because governments are limited in their ability to maintain long-term contracts with farmers. Thus, farmers make production and marketing decisions under policy uncertainty. One example of government failure is the 1991 Gross Revenue Insurance Program (GRIP) in Canada, which, though it was promoted to farmers as a long-term program to stabilize income, quickly ended for political and economic reasons, leading to farmers facing increased government-induced uncertainty. This government failure was costly to farmers who committed resources to their farms based on promises made under the 1991 GRIP program.

> **GOVERNMENT AND MARKET FAILURE**
>
> One argument that favours government intervention is that there is a need to reduce resource misallocation, societal losses, and market failure resulting from the fixity of agricultural assets. M.A. Johnson and Pascur (1982), however, have cast doubt on the efficacy of government intervention for this purpose. They argue that where institutions of the real world are concerned, government failure is as inevitable as market failure. Consequently, market failure does not warrant public intervention unless it can be demonstrated that there would be a superior outcome after allowing for the likely degree of government failure (I. Roberts et al. 1989, 150).

2.6   THE THEORY OF PUBLIC CHOICE AND AGRICULTURAL POLICY

Public-choice theory begins with the premise that governments themselves have objectives they seek to realize, paramount of which is retaining power. In a democracy this means securing votes for re-election. In such an environment, governments will curry the favour of particular groups whose support they need by providing these groups with regulations, taxes, or subsidies that enhance their economic position. The interest groups promote this process by spending their money on such things as informing politicians of their wishes, making campaign contributions to politicians, and obtaining positive media exposure for the causes of the interest group. In other words, there is a political market in which governments provide farmers with subsidies in exchange for party support.

Public-choice theory focuses on voting and on politics through which people maximize their utility from political outcomes. Politicians supply services that respond to public demands, and political behaviour must be analysed as if each person involved (voter, politician, or bureaucrat) is maximizing his or her own utility (Buchanan and Tullock 1974). The theory of public choice is related to rent-seeking activity that may be undertaken by an individual or group of individuals (e.g., farmers) to obtain transfers from government, either through a direct subsidy or through favourable regulations (Krueger 1980). Bureaucrats also engage in rent-seeking behaviour. Niskanan (1968) argues that bureaucracies employ rent-seeking activities to increase employment and employment-related benefits. Rent-seeking activities may have either positive or negative impacts on the efficient allocation of resources (Rausser 1992).

Politicians may not necessarily entertain policies that are efficient. A policy can be extremely inefficient yet be supported by politicians if it garners a large number of votes. At the extreme, politicians rank policies by voting criteria, not by efficiency criteria. In certain cases, politicians may well choose the most economically inefficient program. For example,

Table 2.2. Political rent-seeking activity and policy choice

Policy	Economic Efficiency Choice	Number of Votes	Political
		Rankings	
A	A	D	D
B	B	C	C
C	C	B	B
D	D	A	A

Source: Authors' compilation.

in Table 2.2, Policy A is ranked as the first choice using efficiency criteria. However, Policy D is ranked first using voting criteria. Under the public-choice framework, politicians, at the extreme, may select Policy D over Policy A.

2.7   RENT-SEEKING BEHAVIOUR

Farm groups and others have successfully lobbied governments for support. The US Congress passed the Food, Conservation, and Energy (FCE) Act in 2008. This act was the second farm bill of the twenty-first century, following the Farm Security and Rural Investment (FSRI) Act of 2002, which President Bush signed into law on 13 May 2002. The FCE Act follows most of the policy instruments of the FSRI Act; however, both represent a significant departure from the market-oriented reforms enacted in the Federal Agriculture Improvement and Reform (FAIR) Act of 1996. The Agricultural Market Act Transition Payments (AMTAPs) under the FAIR Act were replaced with countercyclical payments (CCPs) reminiscent of the early price deficiency payments. There was a gradual reduction in government payments that affected production decisions under the FAIR Act. However, government payments increased with the passage of both the FSRI and the FCE Acts.

The above Acts came into being due to *rent-seeking behaviour*, which is the activity of influencing the political process to obtain favourable outcomes or to avoid unfavourable ones (Krueger 1974). In other words, groups in search of economic benefits offer incentives to politicians or bureaucrats to provide these benefits (Downs 1957). Politicians, in turn, respond positively if it is in their own best interests to do so (Babcock, Carter, and Schmitz 1990; Gardner 1996). In addition, governments can act in their own best interests. Political rent-seeking activities, for example, may occur when politicians decide on certain policies that support their chances for re-election.

There are additional components to rent-seeking behaviour. First, bureaucrats are involved in the policy process, and they may or may not facilitate policy change. Second, employees may exhibit rent-seeking behaviour for the maintenance of well-paying jobs once a policy is in place. An example of this is evident in the Canadian Agricultural Income Disaster Assistance

(AIDA) Program, introduced in 1998 as a response to low grain prices. AIDA requires that a file be kept for every farmer in the program and that it be reviewed a number of times by a bureaucrat. This produces the need for government personnel and for personnel hours to keep the program running. Third, there is the notion that bureaucrats employ rent-seeking behaviour for a particular policy outcome. An example of bureaucratic rent-seeking behaviour is when agricultural experiment stations support the licensing of GMOs because they have a formal or informal agreement with large multinationals. No empirical analysis has been conducted on the relationship between bureaucratic rent-seeking behaviour and agricultural policy, though the Niskanan (1968) model of rent-seeking behaviour has been applied to state-trading enterprises (STEs) (Carter and Loyns 1996; Fulton, Schmitz, and Gray 2000). In addition, there have been numerous studies written about the impact of bureaucratic rent-seeking behaviour for non-agricultural projects (A. Schmitz and Zerbe 2008a, 2008b).

The payoff to rent-seeking behaviour varies among commodities and also among countries. Based on information provided in this volume, producers and agribusinesses in the United States seem to be more successful than those in Canada. We present many reasons why this happens. In this discussion, one cannot overlook the fact that many US farmers may have received from the government large income transfers that facilitate rent-seeking behaviour.

POLICY OBJECTIVES AND RENT-SEEKING BEHAVIOUR

Defining a country's objectives for agriculture – as is true in most policy areas – is not straightforward. One approach is to examine statements by politicians and administrators and to examine declarations in preambles to legislation; in this way, the stated goals can be ascertained. It will not be surprising to find mention of characteristics that virtually every country would like for its agriculture. These include plentiful, wholesome food at reasonable and stable prices, family-farm ownership and operation, equality of rural and urban income, and conservation of land and water resources. These objectives are likely to be expressed in any statement of agricultural policy intent (D. Paarlberg 1984, 9).

To achieve an appreciation of the policy objectives that are really important to legislation, one needs to go beyond these universally desired aims, because the real objectives often remain unstated. Tangerman (1985, 85) points out that many policy objectives are implicit and may be recognizable only through analysis of the policies themselves and of the motivations of the policymakers at the time they introduce the legislation. In this context, D. Paarlberg (1984, 9) observes that there are two goals of US agricultural policy that never appear in the preambles to legislation and are rarely mentioned in public meetings. These goals are to support agriculture in the manner to which it has become accustomed and to elect or re-elect certain persons to public office. Paarlberg (ibid.) concludes that to discuss commodity programs without acknowledging the importance of these two goals is to deal with the form rather than with the substance of the issue (I. Roberts et al. 1989, 92).

One cannot overemphasize the importance of rent-seeking behaviour in policy formulation. Much of the early work on the subject, including that by Krueger (1974), suggests that rent-seeking activities are costly to society in that they cause misallocations of resources. However, not all rent-seeking activities result in inefficient resource use.

2.7.1   Productive versus Predatory Rent-Seeking Behaviour

Rent-seeking behaviour is generally viewed as a wasteful activity (Tullock 1967). Interest groups or firms will take resources from other productive endeavours and spend them on lobbying or other rent-seeking activities, decreasing overall economic efficiency, which can cause problems when governments rely on interest groups for information to determine the social desirability of policy. Presumably, there is an asymmetry of information between the government and interest groups with respect to public preferences or the specific effects of certain regulations. Thus, some rent-seeking activities may actually increase overall welfare. A distinction can be drawn between productive and non-productive rent-seeking behaviour. Some expenditures may be transaction costs incurred to inform government (productive rent-seeking behaviour), but other expenditures may be attempts to influence political outcomes independent of broader welfare implications (non-productive rent-seeking behaviour).

If an economy has no distortions, any rent-seeking activity will result in inefficiencies. However, if distortions do exist, it is possible that rent-seeking activity can improve economic efficiency. Rausser (1992) splits rent-seeking behaviour into two categories: rent-seeking behaviour that is purely an economic transfer, which he calls political-economic-seeking transfers (PESTs), and rent-seeking behaviour that seeks to correct some market distortion, which he calls political-economic-resource transactions (PERTs). Governments must balance the interests of different groups in the provision of PESTs and PERTs in their attempt to acquire or to maintain political power. Rausser (1992) estimates PESTs and PERTs for selected US agricultural commodities (Table 2.3). For example, Rausser reports that US government transfers from trade protection are 77 per cent of total US sugar beet revenue. Of this 77 per cent, Rausser estimates that 92 per cent are PESTs and 8 per cent are PERTs. The authors of this book did the same analysis for Canada. The producer subsidy equivalent for total Canadian sugar

Table 2.3. PERTs, PESTs, and PSEs, US and Canada, selected commodities, 1982–6 (average as % of unit values)

Commodity	PSEs[a]		PSEs (PERTs)[b]		PSEs (PESTs)[c]	
	US	Canada	US	Canada	US	Canada
Wheat	36.5	33.0	13.5	20.8	86.5	79.2
Corn	27.1	16.4	17.7	22.8	82.3	77.2
Barley	28.8	45.0	20.9	13.1	79.1	86.9
Canola	N/A	26.8	N/A	30.0	N/A	70.0
Soybean	8.5	12.2	74.3	42.1	25.7	57.9
Sugar beets	77.4	38.0	7.9	14.0	92.1	86.0
Milk	53.9	71.2	7.8	6.0	92.2	94.0
Beef	8.7	18.0	55.5	73.3	44.5	26.7
Pork	5.8	16.6	82.5	83.7	17.5	16.3
Poultry	8.3	26.0	65.0	27.5	35.0	72.5
Eggs	N/A	26.6	N/A	24.2	N/A	75.8

Source: Rausser (1992) for the US calculations; A. Schmitz, Furtan, and Baylis (2002) for the Canadian calculations, utilizing Rausser's methodology.
[a] PSEs = producer subsidy equivalents.
[b] PERTs = political-economic-resource transactions.
[c] PESTs = political-economic-seeking transfers.

beets is 38 per cent. Of the total PSEs, the authors of this book estimate that 86 per cent are in the PEST category and 14 per cent are in the PERT category.

PRODUCER SUBSIDY EQUIVALENTS

Rausser (1992) uses PSEs as a measure of government intervention in different agricultural sectors. The PSEs he uses are the percentages of the total value of a commodity made up by government transfers. He divides government intervention into PERTs (e.g., research and development [R&D] that increases producer surplus through a shift in the supply curve) and PESTs (e.g., an import tariff that raises producer surplus by taxing consumers). From these, a measure of whether rent-seeking behaviour is increasing or decreasing the efficiency of the sector, and by how much, is calculated.

Rausser points out that in the United States, commodities with the most inelastic demand curves and inelastic supply curves have the most unproductive rent-seeking behaviour. The Canadian numbers support Rausser's conclusions. Supply-managed commodities protected by tariffs and import quotas have mostly PEST rent-seeking behaviour, while commodities traded on the world market more closely fit the PERT category (Rausser 1992).

2.7.2   Conflicting Rent-Seeking Behaviour

There are many special interest groups involved in agricultural policymaking other than just farmers and farm organizations. Agribusiness, which includes input dealers and processors, is also involved, but the interests of these groups can conflict with those of farmers. For example, the Canadian supply management system restricts output through production quotas, but this might not be in the best interest of processors, who may prefer a larger volume of output.

Given that various interest groups can have objectives counter to the interests of agricultural producers, rent-seeking behaviour by agricultural groups may be needed to counter other lobbying efforts. Consider, for example, the question of the disposition of Canadian government-owned, grain hopper rail cars. In 1995 the federal government of Canada made it clear that it wanted to sell its grain hopper rail car fleet. The federal agriculture minister organized a group comprised of industry representatives to decide the future of the fleet and to determine a method for rail car allocation. A number of farm groups formed a coalition to gain possession of the rail cars. In this case, the rent-seeking behaviour by the producers offset the rent-seeking behaviour by the railways and the elevator companies, and as a result, the federal government of Canada decided to retain its ownership of the cars.

2.8   COALITIONS AND LOGROLLING

Part of the above discussion on rent-seeking behaviour involves coalitions and logrolling. Coalitions are made up of individuals or groups who band together to seek a common end. For example, the American Sugar Alliance (ASA) is a coalition made up of many groups, including sugar producers, corn growers, and high fructose corn syrup (HFCS) manufacturers. Logrolling occurs when commodity groups band together to lobby governments for subsidies that benefit their groups. For example, Stratmann (1992) shows that one commodity group traditionally combines forces with another commodity group which, in turn, combines forces with yet another commodity group to lobby effectively for US farm programs. Viewed in this context, it is easy to see why US farmers receive sizeable farm subsidies under federal farm bills.

We use producer subsidy equivalents for seven US commodities (Table 2.4) to show how logrolling influences US farm programs (OECD 2000). These figures show the overall decline in agricultural subsidization in the first year of the US Federal Agriculture Improvement and Reform (FAIR) Act of 1996. Table 2.4 indicates that between 1986 and 1997 the PSEs fell for every commodity (OECD 2000). The largest reductions were for maize (corn) and rice, which fell 63 per cent and 81 per cent, respectively. The smallest decline was for sugar, which fell only 24 per cent. PSEs for commodities have increased as their prices have declined. The PSE for maize increased 93 per cent in 1998 over the 1997 level. In addition, the PSEs for other crops, such as oilseeds, grew at a phenomenal rate.

Table 2.4. US producer subsidy equivalents (PSEs), selected commodities, 1986–99

Commodity	PSE Level by Year					PSE Growth by Year		
	1986–8	1997–9	1997	1998	1999	1986–97	1997–8	1998–9
Wheat	49	37	25	39	46	−49.0	56.0	17.9
Maize (corn)	38	24	14	27	30	−63.2	92.9	11.1
Other grains	40	34	23	40	40	−42.5	73.9	0.0
Rice	52	17	10	15	26	−80.8	50.0	73.3
Oilseeds	8	15	4	15	25	−50.0	275.0	66.7
Sugara	58	56	44	56	68	−24.1	27.3	21.4
Milk	60	54	45	61	57	−25.0	35.6	−6.6

Source: OECD (2000).

2.9   AGRICULTURAL AND FOOD POLICY

The above discussion on agricultural policy should be linked to what has become known as food policy, as well as to international trade. Also, there are policies outside the jurisdiction of agriculture that have significant impact on agriculture. One example is the use of corn for biofuels. This was initiated by the US Department of Energy rather than the US Department of Agriculture.

By definition, food policy involves the agricultural farm-to-table process (i.e., how food is produced, processed, distributed, and purchased). Food policies are designed to influence public policies and are linked to agricultural policy and trade (W.A. Ker 2017; A. Schmitz, Seale, and Chegini 2019). The interface between international policy and trade is taken up theoretically in Chapter 5.

2.10   SUMMARY AND CONCLUSIONS

- Agricultural policy is a complex web of interventions, including output markets and public goods. Farm programs have been part of an agricultural sector whose productivity has been spectacular.
- The goal of farm policy is widely debated, in part because of the so-called *farm problem* – the question of what constitutes a farm and the variety of entities that engage in farming. For example, a *farm* can refer to a small family dairy operation or a huge factory farming complex/conglomerate, which makes targeting policies towards appropriate beneficiaries extremely difficult.
- The United States is no longer producing food surpluses, marking a significant shift in its agricultural policy needs.

- Wide fluctuations in commodity prices contribute to the level of risk in agriculture operations.
- Special interest groups play a major role in the design of farm policy through the theory of public choice, rent-seeking behaviour, and logrolling.
- Agricultural policy has faced major changes of late, especially in the European Union, which has moved away from direct payments to producers.
- The rationale for government policy intervention is to create efficiency, stabilization, and redistribution.
- The theory of public choice helps explain some types of policies that exist today. Policy designs based on public choice may differ markedly from those based on neo-classical economics, where efficiency plays a key role. These policies based on efficiency considerations are often not implemented for political reasons.

CHAPTER THREE

Theoretical Considerations

3.1 ECONOMIC EFFICIENCY AND INCOME DISTRIBUTION

Economics is the study of allocating scarce resources among competing ends. Economic efficiency is achieved when the maximum social economic benefit is produced at the minimum social cost. The maximum social benefit is attained when supply (social marginal costs) is equal to demand in all markets. If all markets are perfectly competitive there will be no concern over efficiency issues.

Arriving at an optimal income distribution, however, is still a problem. This requires a social welfare function and developing such a function is virtually impossible. An economy can allocate resources efficiently, such that a first-best solution is achieved, but this situation may not be optimal. There are many first-best bundles, each with a particular income distribution. There is no objective way of determining which of the many first-best bundles is optimal. An economy can be highly efficient, yet because of a skewed income distribution, its members can be miserable. Since certain policies are put in place with the aim of redistributing income at a minimum cost in favour of the farm sector, income distribution issues are a focus of this book.

To have perfect competition in a market, there needs to be (1) complete information, (2) a large number of buyers and sellers, (3) a homogeneous product, (4) perfect divisibility of output, (5) no transaction costs, and (6) no externalities. (This scenario assumes that all the required institutions are in place.) Economists are interested in measuring both the loss of efficiency that can result from government failure and the gains that are associated with a productive government policy.

In this chapter, we present a methodology to evaluate farm policies. In certain cases, a particular methodology may be appropriate for policy analysis. In other cases, a combination of methodologies might be more appropriate. We start with the basic principle of neo-classical economics – that is, the Pareto Principle – which allows for the comparison of two or more states (i.e., two or more bundles of goods, each distributed differently among consumers). Standard welfare analysis is then reviewed, including the fundamental assumptions underlying the framework of consumer and producer surplus. (The latter framework is a very powerful tool for analysing policy.) We then discuss imperfect markets and contestable market theory. Information theory, transaction-cost theory, and regulation theory are discussed briefly within the context of agricultural policy questions.

3.1.1   Pareto Conditions and Pareto Optimality

Pareto conditions state the requirements for maximum economic welfare. To derive the equilibrium conditions for a Pareto optimum, economists combine households and firms to determine the level of consumption and production of all goods and services in the economy. Consumers and producers are brought together through exchange, which determines the prices of all inputs and outputs. A Pareto optimum occurs when the prices for the goods and services reflect their true production scarcity and their value to consumers. The conditions for a Pareto optimum can be derived from the Edgeworth-Bowley Box (Appendix 3A).

There are three Pareto conditions. Under the first condition, the rate of exchange of one good for another must be equal for all consumers. Two consumers will trade until the marginal rate of substitution (MRS) between the two goods is equal. The second condition deals with production inputs. To achieve Pareto production optimality, the marginal rate of technical substitution among inputs must be equal for the many goods produced. The third Pareto condition links production and consumption. Optimality is achieved when the marginal rate of substitution in production is equal to the marginal rate of substitution in consumption.

The fundamental theorem of welfare economics states that when a competitive equilibrium exists, it attains Pareto optimality (R.E. Just, Hueth, and Schmitz 2004, 24). The point is that if the price of inputs and outputs are set such that the markets are in equilibrium, then the competitive equilibrium is also a Pareto optimum. This raises the question: What is the definition of a competitive equilibrium? Looking forward towards the second fundamental theorem of welfare economics, we define a competitive equilibrium as that set of input and output prices where the supply of each product (both inputs and outputs) equals the demand for each product. In addition, we assume that the price paid by the consumer is equal to the price received by producers (hence, there are no tax or information wedges). Given these two conditions, market prices have been determined such that the marginal rate of substitution is equal for all consumers and between the input and output markets. In general equilibrium terms (i.e., taking the set of all input and output prices and quantities simultaneously), this implies that input and output prices have been determined such that the excess demand for every commodity is equal to zero.

The second fundamental theorem of welfare economics then conjectures that competitive markets are sufficient to generate this equilibrium (R.E. Just, Hueth, and Schmitz 2004, 28). This result is somewhat more difficult to demonstrate. The simplest proof of the second fundamental theorem of welfare economics is the derivation of the competitive equilibrium through Walrasian tatonnement. In this process, a fictional auctioneer announces a price vector and all the producers and consumers announce the quantities of goods that they will demand and supply. Given this set of quantities demanded and supplied, the Walrasian auctioneer then increases the price of commodities where the demand exceeds the supply and reduces the price of commodities where the supply exceeds demand. As long as supply curves are upward sloping and demand curves are downward sloping, a sequence of price bids exists which will generate a competitive equilibrium. Finally, any prospective Pareto equilibrium can be generated by redistributing the initial resources.

3.1.2 Economic Surplus Framework

The concepts of consumer and producer surplus are widely and legitimately used by economists to measure the impact of policy change (R.E. Just, Hueth, and Schmitz 2004, 2008). These concepts date back to the very beginnings of economics. Models based on consumer and producer surplus are used widely for policy purposes because they can be estimated using real world data. As a result, the surplus framework provides more than theoretical niceties. Numbers that are useful to policymakers can be generated (Currie, Murphy, and Schmitz 1971; see Appendix 3B and Appendix 3C for more details).

Measures of consumer and producer surplus can be represented graphically. In Figure 3.1, the consumer surplus is the area above the price line P_0 and below the demand curve D, while the producer surplus is the area below the price line P_0 and above the supply curve S (see also Appendix 3B and Appendix 3C). Given demand D and supply S, the total surplus is (acb) of which (aP_0b) is consumer surplus and (P_0cb) is producer surplus. In the absence of externalities, for price P_0 and quantity Q_0, the total surplus is at a maximum under competition.

The legitimacy of the concepts of producer and consumer surpluses is grounded in Harberger's Postulates. Harberger (1971) developed a set of empirically tractable criteria that is consistent with competitive equilibrium (i.e., Pareto optimality). As will be discussed later, Harberger's analysis supports using the concept of economic surplus to measure the size and distribution of gains and losses from a policy change (A. Schmitz and Zerbe 2008a, 2008b). Harberger's (1971, 795) three basic postulates are as follows:

1 The competitive demand price for a given unit measures the value of that unit to the consumer; that is, the price a consumer is willing to pay for a good is equal to its value to that consumer.
2 The competitive supply price for a given unit measures the value of that unit to the supplier; that is, the price at which a good is supplied is the marginal cost (MC) of producing that good.
3 When evaluating the net benefits or costs of a given action (project, program, or policy), the costs and benefits accruing to each member of the relevant group (e.g., a country)

Figure 3.1. Consumer and producer surplus

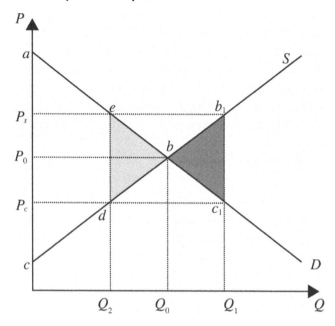

should be added without regard to the individual(s) to whom they accrue; that is, the marginal value of a dollar is assumed to be constant, no matter who receives it.

3.1.3   The Harberger Tax and Monopoly Power

As a further illustration of the use of economic surplus measures, Harberger (1971) shows the effects of a consumer tax, the "Harberger tax" (Figure 3.2). Competitive equilibrium price and quantity are P_e and Q_e, respectively. Suppose a per unit tax $(P_1 - P_2)$ is imposed on a good such that the price consumers pay for the good no longer equals its cost of production, and (acb) measures the loss in economic welfare, which is the deadweight loss (DWL), or the Harberger triangle. Tax policy will redistribute economic surplus between consumers and producers and will cause a loss that is not captured by anyone (DWL). Harberger (1971) shows that only the competitive market price P_e and quantity Q_e meet all three of his postulates, thus resulting in the maximum social surplus. Therefore, because of government policy or market failure, any deviation from the competitive equilibrium will result in a loss of economic welfare.

Monopolies may exist in a contestable market; therefore, they will price their product at average cost to deter the entry of others into the market. The existence of a monopoly is not Pareto optimal because the demand price and marginal cost are different. Monopolies charge higher prices by reducing the amount of output placed on the market. A monopoly, like a

Figure 3.2. Monopoly pricing

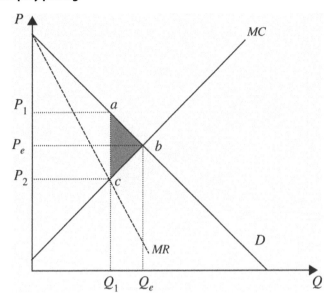

tax, results in a loss of economic efficiency; therefore, the removal of the monopoly can be welfare-improving.

The effects of monopoly power can also be represented in Figure 3.2. The firm's profit-maximizing output is determined by setting its marginal revenue (MR) equal to its marginal cost (MC). The monopolist charges price P_1 and produces Q_1. The per unit marginal cost of production is P_1. Consumer surplus is reduced by an amount equal to (P_1P_eba), while the welfare of the monopolist increases by $(P_1P_2ca - P_eP_2cb)$. As a result of the monopoly, the DWL is (acb).

3.2   INCOME TRANSFERS

When governments have the objective to redistribute income, there are a number of policies they can use to transfer income between groups. In the case of agriculture, two possible policies are deficiency payment schemes and production quota systems. The deficiency payment program was introduced by Brannan (1949) and the production quota system was proposed by W.W. Cochrane (1959). Wallace (1962) compares the efficiency of a deficiency payment scheme with a production quota system as a vehicle for transferring income to producers. The deficiency payment scheme has been used extensively in the United States, except for the 1996 Farm Bill (the deficiency payment scheme was central to the 2002 and 2008 Farm Bills). Likewise, the production quota system underlies many of the supply management programs still in existence.

Figure 3.3. Price supports and production quotas

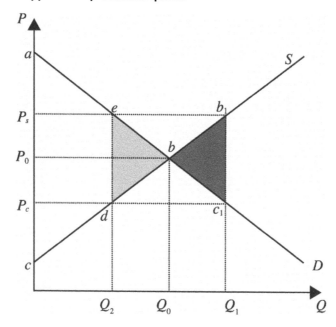

3.2.1   Deficiency Payment Program

A deficiency payment scheme makes use of a government-support price, which is set at some level above the competitive market price (Figure 3.3). As a result, producer output increases and consumer price decreases. Governments use deficiency payments to make up the difference between what producers receive and what consumers pay.

Consider a price support P_s in Figure 3.3, given a supply curve S and a demand curve D. Output expands from Q_0 to Q_1. Consumer prices drop from P_0 to P_c. Producers gain ($P_sP_0bb_1$). Consumers gain (P_0P_c c_1b). The government deficiency payment to producers is (P_s P_c c_1b_1). Thus, even though both producers and consumers gain from price supports, society loses (bc_1b_1). Given price support P_s, Pareto optimality is not achieved. The move from competitive equilibrium to price supports satisfies neither the Pareto Principle nor the Compensation Principle.

3.2.2   A Production Quota System without Trade

Under a production quota system, production is limited through the use of quotas, which are established for individual producers. Through quotas, producers (farmers) are limited in the amount of a commodity they can sell. Because of quotas, production is restricted below competitive levels. In Figure 3.3, assume that a production quota system, rather than a deficiency payment scheme, is used to support farm income. A quota will restrict output to Q_2, with an associated net cost. In this case, there is a net cost to society from the quota equal to (*edb*). The production quota system, like the deficiency payment scheme, results in net welfare costs. Both programs meet neither the Pareto test nor the Compensation test. However, unlike the deficiency payment scheme, the production quota system does not involve government payments. Instead, income is transferred directly from the consumer to the producer through increased food costs.

AGRIBUSINESS

There is a very important difference between target-price schemes and production quota systems when viewed through the eyes of agribusiness. Both programs support producer prices at P_s (Figure 3.3). However, the quantity produced differs substantially under each program. The deficiency payment program results in quantity Q_1, which is much greater than the production quota output Q_2. Agribusiness prefers target-price programs to production quotas because it is able to process and market greater volumes of product. From the agribusiness perspective, output is greater under a deficiency payment scheme. Thus, processors and marketers handle a larger output, and this is good for business.

3.2.3   The Pareto and Compensation Principles

In policy discussions, reference is often made to the Pareto and Compensation Principles. By the Pareto Principle, a new policy is desirable if no individual in the economy is made worse off while at least one person is made better off. The Pareto criterion is one of efficiency, and as such does not address the question of optimal income distribution. Conversely, the Compensation Principle (Hicks 1939; Kaldor 1939) states that State B is preferred to State A if there is an improvement in the efficiency of resource use, such that all could be made better off if the gainers were to compensate the losers. Unlike the Pareto Principle, the Compensation Principle does not require the actual payment of compensation; it requires only that the potential for compensation exists. In other words, a policy is welfare-improving if it is capable of producing a large enough increase in efficiency so that the gainers could compensate the losers and still be better off.

When a policy change is introduced, there are both gainers and losers. Policymakers at times adhere to the Compensation Principle, rather than to the Pareto Principle, when designing and implementing policy. Take, for example, the Canadian grain transportation subsidy (the Crow Benefit), which was removed in 1995. Canadian Prairie grain farmers received only partial compensation – approximately 20 per cent of the subsidy's value – even though everyone could have been made better off from the added efficiencies introduced by having the Crow Benefit disappear. Politicians argued that the Prairie economy would benefit from an expanded livestock sector, and the resulting economic growth would more than make up for the loss of the Crow Benefit subsidy. The benefits from the policy change, however, flowed to the livestock producers, and not to the grain producers who had given up the Crow Benefit.

THE TOMATO HARVESTER AND THE COMPENSATION PRINCIPLE

Since the early days of the Industrial Revolution, workers have had concerns about being displaced by technological changes. A. Schmitz and Seckler (1970) estimate the costs and benefits that resulted from the development of the mechanical tomato harvester in the 1960s, and its effect on agricultural labourers in the United States. They estimated the annual gross social returns resulting from the development of the harvester to be between US$43 million and US$59 million. Given the cost of developing the harvester, this investment yields a 929 per cent to 1,282 per cent rate of return. However, this ignores the unemployment cost of lost jobs due to mechanization. The harvester displaced approximately ninety-one hours of labour per acre of tomatoes harvested, for a total loss of 19.4 million hours of labour per year. If workers were totally compensated for lost wages, the net rate of return to the tomato harvester still would have been around 700 per cent, which would have benefited everyone (ibid.).

One cannot overemphasize the role that compensation plays in policy design. For example, many Canadian producers of supply-managed products, such as dairy, may be willing to give up supply management if, in so doing, they would be fully compensated for the loss in value of their production quota. With changes in farm policy at the beginning of the twenty-first century, US tobacco and peanut growers were fully compensated for the loss in quota values when the tobacco and peanut production-based quota programs were removed. Otherwise, these programs likely would have remained if buyout packages had been unavailable to growers. But there are cases in which the payment of compensation is not feasible. This does not, however, invalidate the use of the surplus framework discussed above as a basis for policy analysis (A. Schmitz and Zerbe 2008a, 2008b). A primary purpose of the welfare economic framework is to determine the losers and gainers of a policy change in the absence of compensation.

Figure 3.4. Production quotas and trade

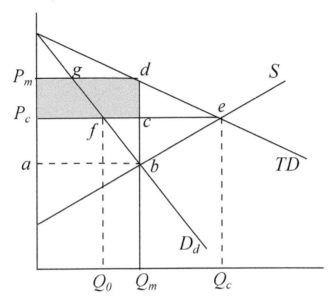

3.2.4   Producer Subsidy Equivalents and Welfare Economic Measures

The concept of a producer subsidy equivalent (PSE) and its use in ranking countries according to the degree of agricultural support was popularized by the Organisation for Economic Co-operation and Development (OECD). The PSE is a percentage of the total value of a commodity made up by government transfers.

With reference to Figure 3.3, consider the effect of the price support system. The total government transfer is $(P_s\ P_c\ c_1\ b_1)$, which would be labelled the PSE attached to this program. However, note that the producer gain from the subsidy is only $(P_s\ P_0\ bb_1)$. The producer gain is much less than the PSE amount. Thus, by using a PSE, rather than a welfare measure of the producer gain from the distortion, one overestimates the losses implied from producer price supports. For a quota, there is no government transfer to producers, as producers receive the additional benefits from quotas through an increase in consumer price. Therefore, in this case, there is a consumer tax equivalent, which is less than a consumer subsidy equivalent measure.

3.2.5   Agricultural Policy in the Presence of Trade

The previous models are within a closed economy framework. Below we discuss an example of the effects of a production quota in the presence of trade (Figure 3.4). In Figure 3.4, we incorporate quotas in the presence of exports. The total demand is given by *TD*, the domestic

Figure 3.5. Effects of technological change

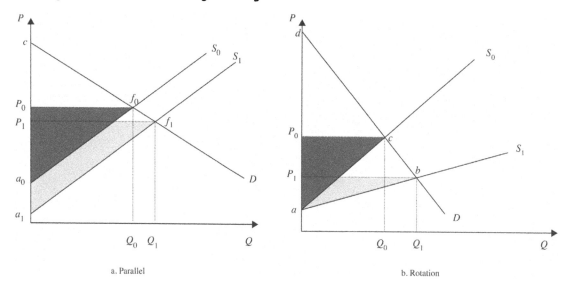

a. Parallel   b. Rotation

demand is D_d. The domestic supply is given by S. Under free trade, price is P_c, and quantity is Q_c. Exports total Q_0Q_c. Consider the implementation of a production quota that cuts production from Q_c to Q_m. The price increases to P_m. Unlike in the previous model, the producers in the exporting country gain $\{P_m\,P_c\,cd - cbe\}$, while domestic consumers lose $(P_c\,abf)$. Note that now the importers lose $(gfed)$ from the quota. As a result, the net loss from the two countries taken together as a result of a production quota is (dbe). However, there may or may not be a loss for the exporting country as it depends on whether or not $(P_m\,P_c\,cd)$ is greater than $\{cbe + P_c\,abf\}$. P.R. Johnson (1965) shows that under the US production quota tobacco program, there could be net gains to the United States from imposing production quotas.

3.2.6 Technological Change

Within this framework, consider the effects of technological change (Figure 3.5). The supply curve shifts in a parallel fashion from S_0 to S_1. The increase in economic surplus is equal to $(a_0\,a_1f_1f_0)$. Of this surplus, the gain to consumers is $(P_0\,P_1f_1f_0)$ and the gain to producers is $(P_1\,a_1\,f_1 - P_0\,a_0f_0)$, In this example, a technological change results in a Pareto improvement. The new price P_1 and quantity Q_1 represent a Pareto-superior move because both producers and consumers gain. The price and quantity corresponding to the new Pareto optimum are P_1 and Q_1.

As illustrated in Figure 3.5a, producers were made better off through a shift in the supply curve caused by technological change. Consider the situation in which technological change causes a shift in the supply curve that makes producers worse off from a welfare analysis standpoint (Figure 3.5b). Suppose a technological change causes the supply curve to pivot from S_0 to S_1. In this scenario, consumer surplus increases from $(dP_0 c)$ to $(dP_1 b)$. Therefore, this technological change makes consumers better off. However, producer surplus decreases from $(P_0 ac)$ to $(P_1 ab)$. As a result, producers are now worse off with the technological change. (Comparing the results illustrated in Figure 3.5a and Figure 3.5b, one can conclude that producers are not always better off under technological change.) In Figure 3.5b, after technological change occurs, the price and quantity at the new Pareto optimum are P_1 and Q_1. Unlike in Figure 3.5a, technological change is preferred to no change on the basis of the Compensation Principle. However, the Pareto Principle is not satisfied.

3.3   EFFICIENCY OF INCOME TRANSFERS

Governments often transfer income among individuals and groups in society. This transfer of income may cause distortions in markets. (One exception is when government forces a move between two Pareto-efficient points, as mentioned above.) These distortions may give rise to inefficiencies, the cost of which can be measured using consumer and producer surplus. Often what is at issue is how to minimize the associated economic costs, not whether the transfers should occur.

Governments transfer income to producers for many reasons, including rent-seeking behaviour. What is the most efficient means of transferring money to farmers? This question has drawn considerable interest because of the large money transfers that have historically gone to producers (farmers) from taxpayers and consumers.

Wallace (1962) and Gardner (1983) illustrate the welfare costs associated with various methods of income transfer. They begin with the premise that the sole purpose of government policy is income redistribution. In this context, the objective function of the regulator takes into account the consumer, producer, and taxpayer surpluses such that the producer surplus has the highest welfare weight (i.e., producer surplus is valued more highly by government than is either consumer surplus or taxpayer surplus).

3.4   POLICY COMPARISONS

We compare production quotas versus price supports using only the surplus framework. Consider Figure 3.6, where production quotas are compared to price supports with deficiency payments (see A. Schmitz et al. 2010 for an alternate comparison methodology). Given S and D, the competitive price is P_c and output is Q_c. Consider a production quota Q_m (a monopoly solution) where marginal revenue crosses supply for a price of P_m. As discussed earlier, the producer gain from a quota is $(P_m P_c\ da) - (dbf)$.

Figure 3.6. Production quota versus producer compensation

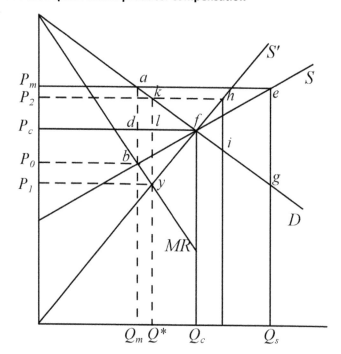

The corresponding efficiency loss from the quota Q_m is the Harberger triangle *(abf)*.

Instead of a quota, a price support yields very different results. For a price support of P_m, output is Q_s. The producer gain is much larger than from a production quota as $\{(P_mP_cfe) > (P_mP_cda - dbf)\}$. But now the size of the Harberger triangle associated with the price increases to *(fge)*, which is greater than *(abf)*.

Consider now supply S' that generates prices P_1 and P_2. In this case, the producer gains are different from the above. With supply S', the producer gains $(P_2P_clk - lyf)$. The producer gain from a price support still exceeds that for a quota, but now the Harberger triangle inefficiency effect is smaller as *(kyf)* > *(fih)*. Under a price support, the Harberger triangle is reduced to *(fih)*. But note that the producer gain is reduced to (P_2P_cfh).

3.5   AGRICULTURAL POLICY AND THE CONNECTION TO INTERNATIONAL TRADE

In the above analysis, trade does not enter the picture. Consider Figure 3.7, where supply is S, and domestic demand is D. With no trade, price is P_1 and quantity is Q_1. In the context of international trade for an exporting country, total demand is given by TD, price increases to

Figure 3.7. International trade and the connection to agricultural policy

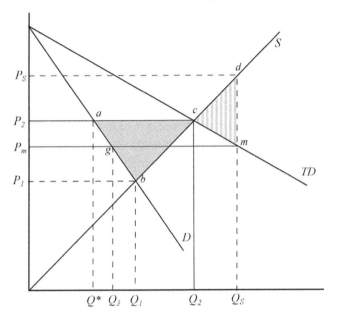

P_2, and exports total Q^*Q_2. Consumer rent in the exporting country decreases by (P_2P_1ba), while producers gain (P_2P_1bc). The net effect of trade in the exporting country is a gain of the Harberger triangle (abc).

3.6   TRADE WITH PRICE SUPPORTS

Now consider the effect of a price support in the context of international trade for the same exporting country. A price support of P_s is put into place. Output increases to Q_s, the export price decreases from P_2 to P_m, and domestic consumption increases to Q_3. Exports total Q_3Q_S. There is a total deficiency payment of (P_sP_mmd). As such, producers in the exporting country gain P_sP_2cd, consumers in the exporting country gain P_2P_mga. Importing consumers gain $(agmc)$. On net, the exporting country loses $(agmdc)$. Taken together, there is a net loss of the Harberger triangle of (dcm).

3.6.1   Input Subsidies

Water, a major subsidized input in US agriculture, has a number of competing uses, including industrial, residential, recreational, and agricultural uses, and for the generation of hydroelectric power. The allocation and cost of water to the agricultural sector have been strongly influenced by government policy and, in turn, by rent-seeking behaviour. The magnitude of water subsidies varies by state and California farmers are the largest recipients of water subsidies.

WATER SUBSIDIES

"In much of the western United States, land was granted to farmers in conjunction with water rights, which gave producers access to long-term supplies of water at low cost. Thus, farmers in states such as Nevada and Arizona are often in conflict with urban developers over who has the right to the use of available water supplies" (A. Schmitz, Furtan, and Baylis 2002, 416).

In Chapter 5, we explore the effects of input subsidies with and without trade. In addition, we consider a combination of input and production subsidies with and without trade.

3.7 THE THEORY OF REGULATION

Agriculture has a preponderance of regulations. Originally, regulation was seen as a good produced at no cost by government that was used as a response to some market failure. This view assumes that government is benign and that the political process will respond automatically to need. In his Nobel prize–winning work, George Stigler (1971) proposes an alternative view of regulation as a form of rent-seeking behaviour that has since changed the way many economists model the government.

Regulation is often used to limit the market power of firms because market power can lead to inefficient resource allocation (Stigler 1975; Strick 1990). At times, governments have introduced regulations that have forced firms with market power to price as if the firms were in a competitive industry. However, price regulation has not been without difficulty.

It is possible for the regulators to be captured by the regulated. This is called interest-group theory, a situation in which concentrated groups of individuals affected by legislative decisions have an incentive to influence those decisions. Interest groups then spend resources to lobby policymakers (Becker 1983). Stigler (1971) proposes that the only people willing to spend large sums to present information to policymakers are those who stand to benefit directly from certain policy decisions. The greater the potential benefit, the more funds the interest group is willing to spend, and the more influence it can have. Likewise, because garnering information is costly, regulators will not necessarily hear counterarguments. Thus, Stigler (1971) put forward the hypothesis that special interest groups will have more influence over the regulators than will the general public because of their targeted lobbying efforts. This is the thesis of regulatory capture.

Stigler's (1971) hypothesis has been applied to supply management in Canada (A. Schmitz 1995b). Federal and provincial governments regulate the marketing activities of the Canadian supply management boards. For certain industries, prices are set by a cost of production (COP) formula agreed on by the regulators using information supplied by the producers. At times, the COP formula overstates producer costs, and often these costs are not challenged by regulators. Stigler's framework fits the rent-seeking arguments presented in Chapter 2. In the above example, effective rent-seeking behaviour is possible when the regulator is captured by producers.

3.8   PRODUCER COMPENSATION AND DISTRIBUTIONAL IMPACTS

Many issues surrounding agricultural policy concern the degree to which producers will be compensated for losses in the event that a particular policy is terminated. Consider two US policies: the peanut program and the tobacco program. A key element of both policies was the use of production quotas. In 2004 both the US tobacco and peanut programs were eliminated. In both cases, producers were compensated for their losses. This was also true in Canada, where the tobacco program ended in 2014.

3.9   SUMMARY AND CONCLUSIONS

- The Pareto Principle for maximum economic welfare states that a policy is Pareto superior if it makes at least one person better off and no one worse off. The Pareto Principle does not consider optimal income distribution.
- The Compensation Principle states that a policy is desirable if it creates sufficient welfare so that the gainers could potentially compensate the losers. Compensation, however, is not actually made. Often policy does not contain a compensation package for the losers.
- In the absence of externalities and under the assumption that the marginal value of a dollar is constant, Harberger's (1971) three postulates suggest that one can use welfare measures to calculate the efficiency or deadweight loss (DWL) of policies.
- The welfare effects of a policy will vary with the assumptions of market structure. If a distortion exists in the market, ex ante forecasts will remain uncertain about the impacts of government intervention on efficiency.
- The efficiency of income transfers can be determined using welfare measures in the framework developed by Wallace (1962) and Gardner (1983). Many argue that US farm policy is efficient in redistributing income because the associated *net cost* is small.

- The cost of information is an important component of farm programs, and its availability often determines the success of a program. In many cases, the cost of getting information can be prohibitive.
- Agriculture is highly regulated; as such, it creates opportunities for regulatory capture and for rent-seeking behaviour.
- Income stabilization is a main goal of farm policy, but the degree to which farm policy results in such stability varies greatly by country and region.
- Stabilization programs often act as an income floor, causing producers to prefer greater variation in income, given that they are protected from downturns but can gain from upturns.

APPENDIX 3A: GRAPHICAL DESCRIPTION OF THE CONDITIONS FOR A PARETO OPTIMUM

The Pareto conditions give the requirements for a Pareto optimum. If we have two consumers, A and B, and two products, Q_1 and Q_2, with two inputs, x_1 and x_2, the following equilibrium conditions can be derived. At a Pareto optimum, the following conditions apply:

1 $MRS^A_{Q_1 Q_2} = MRS^B_{Q_1 Q_2}$ Thus, the marginal rate of substitution (MRS) between products must be equal for all consumers.

2 $MRS^{Q_1}_{x_1 x_2} = MRTS^{Q_2}_{x_1 x_2}$ The marginal rate of technical substitution ($MRTS$) of inputs must be equal for any two outputs.

3 For production and consumption together, $MRT_{Q_1 Q_2} = MRS^A_{Q_1 Q_2} = MRS^B_{Q_1 Q_2}$. This condition implies the price ratio from production that is equal to the marginal rate of transformation (MRT) must equal the price ratio from consumption that is equal to the marginal rate of substitution.

Condition (1) for a Pareto optimum states that the marginal rate of substitution between two goods must be equal for all consumers. The Pareto optimal points of consumption can be illustrated using an Edgeworth-Bowley Box (Figure 3.A1). In this situation, we have only two consumers, A and B, and two goods, Q_1 and Q_2.

At point z, A consumes Q_1^0 and Q_2^z and B consumes Q_1^z and Q_2^z. Consumer A is on the indifference curve I_A^1 and Q_2^z and consumer B is on the indifference curve I_B^1. A is indifferent among points z, x, and w, or the consumption bundles (Q_1^0, Q_2^2), (Q_1^1, Q_2^1), and (Q_1^2, Q_2^0). Thus, we know that at point z, A is willing to forego $(Q_2^2 - Q_2^1)$ of Q_2 to get an extra (Q_1^1, Q_1^0) of good Q_1 and move from point z on this indifference curve to point w. Meanwhile, we know that at point z, B is willing to trade $(Q_1^2 - Q_1^y)$ of Q_1 for $(Q_2^y - Q_2^z)$ of Q_2, which will move B from point z to point y on this indifference curve. From the diagram we can see the amount of Q_2 that B is willing to trade is equal to the amount of Q_2 that A is willing to take, thus $(Q_2^2 - Q_2^1) = (Q_2^y - Q_2^z)$. But if

Figure 3.A1. Pareto optimal points of consumption in an Edgeworth-Bowley Box

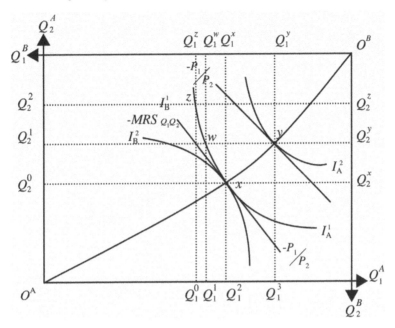

A is willing to give more Q_1 for Q_2, then B needs to remain indifferent to the transaction. Thus, at point z the marginal rate of substitution of good Q_1 for good Q_2 of consumer A is greater than that for consumer B (i.e., $MRS^A_{Q_1Q_2} > MRS^B_{Q_1Q_2}$). The welfare of consumers A and B can be increased by trade until they reach a point on the contract curve between points x and y.

The contract curve is a subset of the Pareto optimal set and depends on the initial endowment. The contract curve is the set of all Pareto optimal points that are Pareto superior to the initial allocation (e.g., in Figure 3.A1, at point z, the contract curve is the Pareto set between and including x and y). At all points on the Pareto optimal set (i.e., on the locus of Pareto optimal points between O^A and O^B), the relative preference for A and B between the two goods is equal ($MRS^A_{Q_1Q_2} = MRS^B_{Q_1Q_2}$); thus, there are no gains from trade. In other words, on the Pareto optimal set, neither party can be made better off without making the other worse off; therefore, they are at a Pareto optimum. Note that at the points on the Pareto optimal set (e.g., x and y), the slope of the line tangent to the indifference curves of both parties is the same. The slope of this line is ($-MRS_{Q_1Q_2}$) that also equals the relative price ratio ($-P_1/P_2$).

Condition (2) for Pareto optimality is that the marginal rate of technical substitution of inputs must be the same for any two outputs. First, note that all Pareto optimal points must occur on the production possibility frontier (PPF). If production is within the frontier, then more of one good can be produced without producing less of another. On the PPF, production efficiency is maximized for all inputs. For the Pareto optimal points of production, consider

Figure 3.A2. Pareto optimal points of production in an Edgeworth-Bowley Box

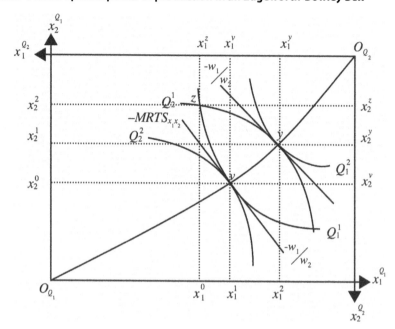

another Edgeworth-Bowley Box (Figure 3.A2) where we illustrate the production of outputs Q_1 and Q_2 using two inputs x_1 and x_2. In this case, the isoquants represent levels of production of either Q_1 or Q_2, thus the isoquants labelled represent the combinations of x_1 and x_2 that can produce quantity Q_1^1 of Q_1.

The logic used here is the same as that used above. The manufacturer will substitute inputs between the products until there is no longer a benefit from substitution. This will occur at any point along the curve O_{Q_1}, O_{Q_2}. At point v in Figure 3.A2, quantities Q_2^2 of output Q_2 and Q_1^1 of output Q_1 are produced given the fixed quantity of inputs x_1 and x_2. At this point, the line tangent to both isoquants has a slope equal to the negative rate of technical substitution ($-MRTS_{x_1 x_2}$).

In terms of Condition (3), note that the maximum social welfare will occur where the production possibility frontier is tangent to the highest possible social indifference curve I_2 at point a (Figure 3.A3). For the price ratio to hold under a Pareto optimum, the price ratio for production has to equal the price ratio of consumption. The price ratio that occurs at any point along the PPF is equal to the marginal rate of transformation between Q_1 and Q_2 (Figure 3.A2), thus ($-P_1/P_2 = -MRT_{Q_1Q_2}$). Equally, the price ratio that occurs at any point along the indifference curve is equal to the marginal rate of substitution between Q_1 and Q_2 (Figure 3.A1); that is, ($-MRS_{Q_1Q_2} = -P_1/P_2$). If only quantity is produced (e.g., because of the existence of a monopoly in the production of Q_2), society will be at point b (Figure 3.A3), and welfare will not be

Figure 3.A3. Price ratio under a Pareto optimum

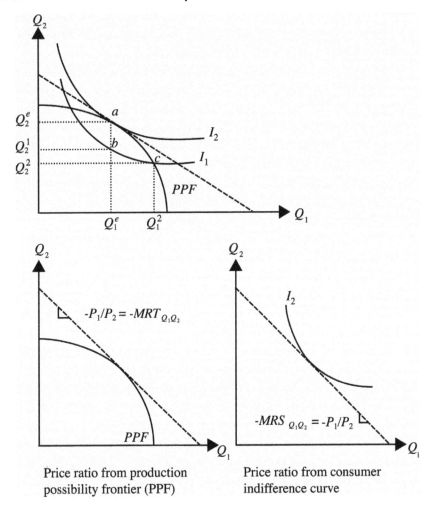

Price ratio from production   Price ratio from consumer
possibility frontier (PPF)   indifference curve

maximized. Equally, if production occurs at point c, giving a combination of Q_2^2 and Q_1^2, even though production is maximized (because c is on the PPF), utility is not. Society can move to a higher level of utility at point a, going from indifference curve I_1 to I_2.

APPENDIX 3B: CONSUMER SURPLUS

The notion of consumer surplus dates back to Dupuit (1844) and was popularized by Marshall (1920) who, in the 1930s, was one of the first economists to use the concept. Consumer surplus is an approximation of the change in consumers' economic welfare. It was not used extensively in economics until the 1940s, and even now some economists reject the idea that aggregate welfare measures are useful; nevertheless, they are still used extensively as empirical measures (Willig 1976). Currie, Murphy, and Schmitz (1971) present a thorough review of the theory and application of consumer and producer surplus measures.

Consumer surplus is the area above the price line and below the demand curve. It is "the excess of the price which [the consumer] would be willing to pay rather than to go without the [good], over that which he actually does pay" (Marshall 1920, 124). To estimate consumer surplus, Marshall assumes that the marginal utility of money is approximately constant, implying that all consumers place an equal value on an extra dollar of income. Later, Hicks (1939) argues that the change in consumer welfare should be measured using a demand curve that removes the effects of income changes, which became known as the Hicksian compensated-demand curve. The change in consumer welfare measured using the Hicksian compensated-demand curve is known as the true measure of economic welfare.

The debate over the utility of consumer surplus arises from the fact that economists use these two different demand relationships: Marshallian demand and Hicksian compensated demand. (Another, perhaps more important, debate over the use of consumer surplus is the aggregation of surplus across individuals. Some argue that when consumer surplus areas for different individuals are aggregated, an implicit weight is assigned to each individual. If the weights are incorrect, the aggregated consumer surplus will not reflect true social welfare.) Hicksian compensated demand allows for a true measure of change in economic welfare, because the Hicksian compensated-demand curve holds the level of utility constant before and after a price change. The Marshallian demand curve allows for both the price of the good and the level of the income to change. However, we can estimate only the Marshallian demand, which provides an approximation of the true change in consumer welfare from market prices and quantities. Therefore, the difference in the measurement of welfare comes from the way in which change in income resulting from the change in price is incorporated. If the income effects from the policy change are zero, the measures of change in consumer surplus will be identical (the change in Hicksian consumer surplus will equal the change in Marshallian consumer surplus). This difference is important when the policy change (price change) is large enough to actually have a perceived income effect on the consumer.

There are policy situations in which the income effect from a price change is large enough that the Marshallian demand curve is insufficient to measure the change in economic welfare. If the price change is the result of a broad-based tax, the change in income may be large. For agricultural economists, a similar situation may occur within developing countries in which food costs make up a large portion of the family income. A change in the price of a staple food may result in a large change in real family income. However, in developed countries, most price changes, if small enough, are not likely to cause a large error in the estimate of change in consumer surplus.

Figure 3.B1. Consumer surplus under a change in price and income

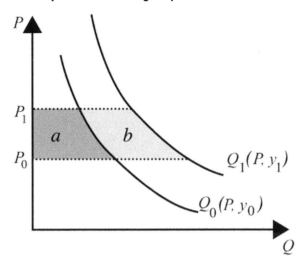

Using the Hicksian demand curve, one can calculate compensating or equivalent variation. Compensating and equivalent variations are useful welfare measures when calculating the effect of multiple-price changes or price-and-income changes because they are independent of ordering (i.e., they give you the same answer no matter which price you change first.)

Consider Figure 3.B1, which illustrates consumer surplus under a change in price and income. The (Marshallian) demand is affected by both an increase in a good's price and an increase in the consumer's income. The Marshallian demand, before the income change, is denoted as $Q_0(P,y^0)$ and after the income change is $Q_1(P,y_1)$ where P is the price vector and y is the level of income. If one assumes that the price change occurs first, then the measure of the change in consumer surplus is equal to the change in consumer surplus measured under the initial Marshallian demand (a) because of the increase in price, plus the change in income Δy. However, if one assumes the income change occurs first, the change in consumer surplus is measured by the change in income Δy plus the change in consumer surplus, which is ($a + b$), measured under the new Marshallian demand curve. These two measures are the same only when there is no income effect; that is, when ($b = 0$).

The argument is similar when using consumer surplus to measure the effect of a change in the price of two (substitutable) goods. Figure 3.B2 depicts consumer surplus when the price increases for good 1 and good 2. If the price of good 1 changes first, the difference in consumer surplus will be measured in the market for good 1 plus ($a + d$) in the market for good 2. If the price for good 2 increases first, the change in consumer surplus will be (a) in the market for good 2 plus ($b + c$) in the market for good 1. These two measures will be the same only if the income effect of a price change in the other good is equal for both goods; that is, if (c) = (d).

Figure 3.B2. Consumer surplus with a price change in two goods

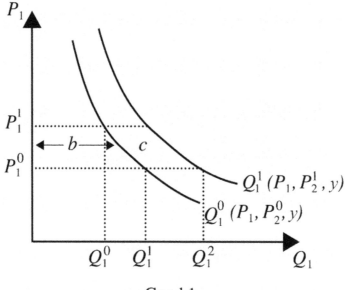

Good 1

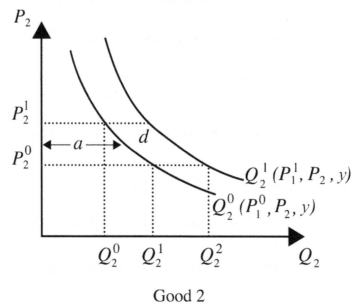

Good 2

Figure 3.B3. Different welfare measures

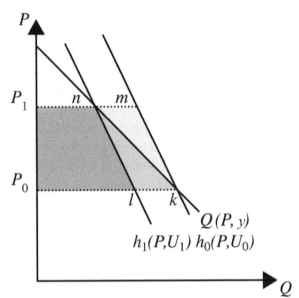

One way to address the consumer surplus problem is to use measures of welfare change under the Hicksian demand curves that keep the level of utility constant over the price change (Figure 3.B3). The area between the two prices under the initial Hicksian demand $h_0(P, U_0)$, where P is the price vector and U is the level of utility, is the compensating variation and is illustrated as $(P_1 P_0 km)$. The area between the two prices under the resulting Hicksian demand $h_1(P, U_1)$ is the equivalent variation and is illustrated as $(P_1 P_0 ln)$. The change in consumer surplus is that area between the new price P_1, the old price P_0, and the area under the Marshallian demand curve $Q(P, y)$, where P is the price vector and y is the level of income equal to $(P_1 P_0 kn)$.

Like consumer surplus, compensating variation and equivalent variation have intuitive definitions. Compensating variation is the change in the amount of income the consumer needs to remain at the same level of utility as before. Equivalent variation is the change in the amount of income the consumer needs at the old prices to get to the new level of utility.

Consider the compensation principal mentioned earlier in this chapter. If a policy change is introduced that raises price from P_0 to P_1, consumers are compensated an amount equal to compensating variation, so that they are not worse off from the change.

The primary difference in the use of equivalent variation and compensating variation comes from their different units of measurement. Since equivalent variation measures the change in income needed at the initial prices, it is a better measure of change in welfare when comparing two possible policy options, since the units of measurement remain consistent.

APPENDIX 3C: PRODUCER SURPLUS AND ECONOMIC RENT

Producer surplus is a notion similar to consumer surplus and exists for the production of goods. Producer surplus is the area above the supply curve (i.e., only the marginal cost curve above the minimum average cost) and below the price line. It represents the excess income the firm earns over that required to keep the factors of production at this level of activity (R.E. Just, Hueth, and Schmitz 1982).

In the short run, the producer surplus is the quasi-rent that accrues to some quasi-fixed factor. In the long run, if all firms are operating at the minimum point on their average cost curve, no (quasi) rent can be found. Therefore, by definition, no surplus could exist. But economists believe that some rents do exist in the long run. This is the notion of Ricardian rents, in which the return is to some fixed factor, like land, that remains scarce in the long run. Ricardian rent is different from excess profit. For firms operating at the minimum of their average cost in the long run, the long-run average-cost curve (LRAC) must include these rents. Thus, if there is a fixed factor of production, there may be Ricardian rent if the LRAC includes the rent and equals the marginal cost.

The concept of producer surplus is built on the idea that different qualities of land are used in the production of the same product. The land with the highest quality (i.e., the most productive with the greatest output for the least input) will be brought into production first. To increase production, land of lower quality will be used, but the return on all land (of both high and low quality) will be based on the price of the commodity produced. Thus, the more productive land will earn a rent, which will be reflected in its higher price. Land of higher quality will be worth more than land of lower quality producing the same product. This difference in price is caused by the Ricardian rent. According to Currie, Murphy, and Schmitz (1971), the area above the supply curve and below the price line is relevant, provided the supply curve is based on the marginal cost curve that excludes rents, and is based on the LRAC that includes rents.

One of the major agricultural policies of government is funding research and development, which results in increased agricultural productivity (e.g., through higher-yielding crop varieties and more feed-efficient animals). Increased productivity lowers the marginal cost of production, which shifts the supply curve down and to the right. The benefit, if any, for farmers, can be measured by comparing producer surplus before and after the technological change. To attribute the change in producer surplus to the farmer, we must assume that the producer is the owner of the scarce resource (i.e., the farmland is owned by the farmer, who does not rent his or her land).

CHAPTER FOUR

Farm and Food Policy, Agricultural Trade, and Macroeconomic Policies

4.1 AGRICULTURAL TRADE

Agricultural trade is extremely important for many countries and is limited by sometimes sizeable tariffs and by other non-tariff barriers. International trade is also affected by institutions, agricultural programs (such as commodity price supports or subsidies), and macroeconomic variables. The United States and the European Union (EU) both have agricultural programs such as domestic price supports and, at times, export subsidies that affect world prices and trade volumes. Likewise, both use trade policies such as import quotas or tariffs that affect domestic producers, marketers, processors, and consumers. In his book, *World Agriculture in Disarray*, D. Gale Johnson (1973) argues that many of the distortions in agricultural markets are caused by trade barriers.

In this chapter, we first discuss the theoretical foundation of international trade in agricultural goods and services. We examine the various policy instruments that have been created, such as tariffs and export subsidies. We also highlight the role of multinational firms because these large agribusinesses conduct most of the international trade in agricultural products. We focus on the key government policies that distort trade and show examples of how these have been dealt with in the realm of international trade. Finally, we discuss macroeconomic variables such as interest and exchange rates to examine how these variables impact agriculture.

4.2 INTERNATIONAL TRADE THEORY

Many theories have been developed to explain patterns in international trade. In 1817, David Ricardo proposed the law of comparative advantage in his essay *Principles of Political Economy and Taxation*. His theory states that even if one nation is less efficient at producing all goods than another nation (i.e., it has an absolute disadvantage), both nations can still benefit from trade as long as each nation has a comparative advantage in the production of one commodity. The nation with the absolute disadvantage should produce the goods for which its disadvantage is smallest. In 1933, Bertil Ohlin formulated a comparative advantage theory around resource endowments, arguing that a country will export commodities produced from its relatively abundant factors. A more modern theory of trade developed by Krugman and Obstfeld (1991) focuses on trade and specialization resulting from economies of scale. A usable theoretical treatment of trade theories is given in Devadoss and Luckstead (2019).

4.2.1   Gains from Trade

Adam Smith (1776), in his well-known treatise *The Wealth of Nations*, stressed the importance of trade, and argued that freer trade is superior to protected trade. Many economists still agree. The gains from trade depend on several factors, including whether or not a country can affect the world price of a commodity by changing the quantity supplied or demanded. Under the small-country assumption, world prices are not affected by producers' production decisions or by consumers' consumption decisions. In the large-country case, prices are affected by changes in output or consumption.

     The gains from trade can be illustrated graphically. In Figure 4.1, a hypothetical country has a price ratio of $(-P_2/(P_1 = \beta_0)$. At this price, without trade (point A), Q_1^0 of good 1 and Q_2^0 of good 2 are produced, where the price line is tangent to the production possibility frontier (PPF), at which it reaches the social utility level U_1. What happens if the country opens up its borders to trade? If its trading partner is more efficient at producing good 1 than it is at producing good 2, the country modelled in Figure 4.1 will trade good 2 for good 1. If the new price ratio of good 1 to good 2 is β_1 where $(\beta_1 = -P_2^*/P_1^*)$, the country will produce Q_1^S of good 1 and Q_2^S of good 2 at point β. But consumption is not yet a factor. Consumption will take place where the indifference curve is tangent to the new price line at point c, with the country consuming Q_1^d of good 1 and Q_2^d of good 2. Hence, the country exports $(Q_2^s - Q_2^d)$ at some new exchange price for (P_2^*) and imports $(Q_1^d - Q_1^S)$ at a new exchange price (P_1^*). This exchange allows it to increase its consumption of both goods relative to the situation before trade, giving it a higher level of social utility U_2.

     For policy purposes, the gains from trade can be cast in a supply and demand curve framework. To illustrate this, we will first derive an excess supply curve. In Figure 4.2, price P_a is determined where domestic supply S equals domestic demand D. The excess supply is the horizontal subtraction of domestic demand from domestic supply, which shows the supplies available for export for prices above P_a.

     Likewise, the excess demand ED is the horizontal subtraction of domestic demand D from domestic supply S. It shows the amount imported for prices below P_a. At a world price of P_w, the country consumes Q_d, produces Q_s, and exports Q_x.

Figure 4.1. Gains from trade

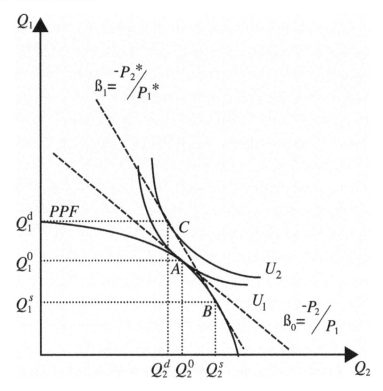

Figure 4.2. Derivation of excess supply and demand curves

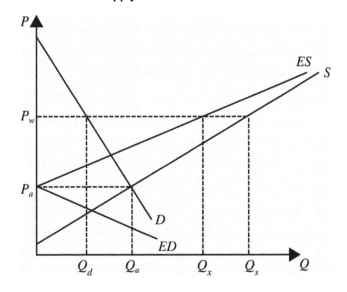

Figure 4.3. Gains from trade: two countries, one commodity

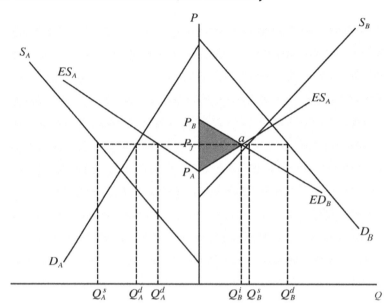

4.2.2   Gains from Trade: The One-Commodity Case

In Figure 4.3, we assume two countries – a large-country exporter and a large-country importer – and one commodity; thus, both countries can affect world price. Assume country A produces cattle at a low cost. Country A's supply curve is S_A and its domestic demand is D_A. The supply curve for cattle in country B is S_B while its domestic demand is D_B. The free trade price is P_f, which is determined by the intersection of the excess supply curve ES_A with the excess demand curve ES_B. At P_f, country B imports Q_B^i from country A. Under free trade, production in country A is Q_A^s and consumption is Q_A^d. In country B, production is Q_B^s, and consumption is Q_B^d.

The total net gain from trade is $(P_B P_A a)$. Of this total, $(P_B P_f a)$ is the net gain to country B, while $(P_f P_A a)$ is the net gain to country A. Even though there are net gains from trade for both countries, there are also net losses from trade. Producers in country A gain from trade, while consumers lose. For country B, consumers gain from trade and producers lose. (An example of negative gains from trade is given in Appendix 4A.)

4.2.3   Gains from Trade: The Two-Commodity Case

In Figure 4.4, we expand the above analysis and consider the gains from trade for two countries and two commodities. In our example, Canada exports beef to the United States, and

Figure 4.4. Gains from trade: two countries, two commodities

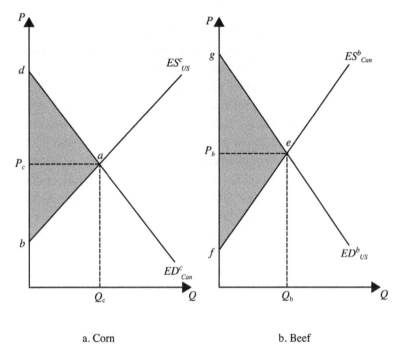

a. Corn   b. Beef

the United States exports corn to Canada. The excess supply curve of US corn is ES^c_{US}, while the Canadian excess demand curve for US corn is ED^c_{Can}. The excess supply curve of beef in Canada is ED^b_{Can}, while the excess demand curve of the United States for Canadian beef is ES^b_{US}. Free trade in beef will occur at price P_b, and the quantity of beef exported from Canada to the United States will then be Q_b. The quantity of corn exported from the United States is Q_c at a price P_c. The net gain from trade for both countries taken together is ($dba + gfe$). Of this total, the net gain to the United States is ($P_cba + gP_be$) and the net gain to Canada is ($dP_c a + P_b fe$).

4.3   TRADE POLICY INSTRUMENTS

Both developed and less-developed countries use trade policy instruments that include tariffs, export subsidies, and import quotas. Selected trade instruments are discussed below. For broader coverage of this topic, see A. Schmitz and T.G. Schmitz (1994b); T.G. Schmitz and A. Schmitz (2014); T.G. Schmitz, Zhu, and A. Schmitz (2016a, 2016b); A. Schmitz and Sheldon (2019).

4.3.1   Import Tariffs

Import tariffs are a common trade barrier. These tariffs, such as Canadian tariffs on dairy products and US tariffs on beef imports, allow governments to protect their domestic industries. There are two kinds of import tariffs: (1) a specific tariff based on per unit cost, and (2) an ad valorem tariff based on a percentage of the price of the product.

   Tariffs are a long-standing practice with an eventful history (A. Schmitz, Furtan, and Baylis 2002). For example, in the United States, tariffs of 5 per cent were established as early as 1789 and increased to between 15 and 20 per cent in 1816. After 1870, support for tariff reform in the United States grew rapidly but faced constant resistance, resulting in a series of back-and-forth hikes and cuts. In 1872, the Dawes Bill lowered tariffs by 10 per cent; however, the McKinley tariff of 1890 gave the United States the highest protection afforded by any of the previous tariff acts. After a brief move to lower tariffs in 1913, the United States returned to a protectionist policy in 1921. The most dramatic increase in US tariffs came with the introduction of the Smoot-Hawley tariff in 1930. Canada immediately responded by placing its own higher tariffs on US imports, which increased Canada's trade with Britain even more than after the well-known removal of the British Corn Laws in 1820. Canada remained a significant agricultural exporter to Britain until the end of the Second World War (Marchildon 1998).

4.3.2   Specific Tariffs

Figure 4.5 below shows the effects of a specific import tariff on different groups, including producers and consumers. In Figure 4.5a, the small-country case, the domestic supply schedule is S, while the domestic demand schedule is D. The free trade price is P_w. If tariff T is introduced, the internal price in the small country will increase to P_1 and imports will be reduced to $(Q_2 - Q_1)$. The net loss from the tariff is ($acb + dfe$). Producers will gain ($P_1P_w\,ca$). Consumers will lose ($P_1P_w\,ed$), and the government will collect ($abfd$) in tariff revenue.

   Now, consider Figure 4.5b, the large-country case. The free trade price P_w is set in the world market where excess supply ES equals excess demand ED_0. Suppose tariff T is again introduced. This tariff will shift the excess demand curve downward from ED_0 to ED_1. The internal price will increase to P_1, and the import price (world price) will fall to P_0. In this case, the large country sees a net gain from the use of a tariff in the amount of [($bhgf$) – ($acb + dfe$)]. If $bhgf$ > ($acb + dfe$), then the tariff will actually result in a net gain for the large country.

4.3.3   Optimal Welfare Tariffs

Optimal welfare tariffs have a long history in international economics. The optimal welfare tariff is welfare-improving for the importing country, but these tariffs create a net loss when all countries are taken into account. In Figure 4.6 the excess supply curve of country A is given

Figure 4.5. Import tariffs in a small country and in a large country

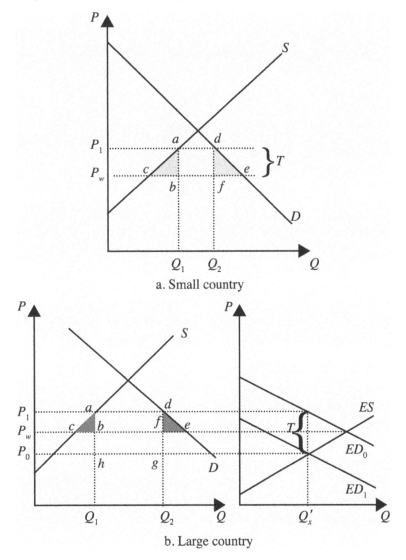

a. Small country

b. Large country

by ES_A, and the excess demand curve of country B is ED_B. The free trade price is P_w. The optimal welfare tariff $(P'_B - P'_A)$ is determined where the marginal outlay curve MO intersects the marginal revenue curve MR_{ED}. (The marginal outlay curve MO is the marginal cost of buying additional imports, while the marginal revenue curve MR_{ED} is the revenue generated from the sale of the last unit of the product sold.) If country B imposes an optimal import tariff $(P'_B - P'_A)$, it acts as a monopsonist on the buying of imports from country A. The total tariff collected will be $(P'_B P'_A ba)$. Consumers lose from the tariff while producers gain.

Figure 4.6. Optimal welfare and revenue tariffs

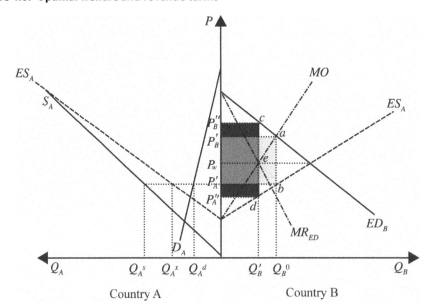

Country A   Country B

4.3.4   Optimal Revenue Tariffs

Governments use revenue tariffs to collect revenue from imports. These types of tariffs have been used by the Japanese Food Agency and by the European Union (Carter and Schmitz 1979; A. Schmitz, Firch, and Hillman 1981). Conceptually, these tariffs are set so the government can exploit both exporters and domestic consumers. The optimal revenue tariff is determined at point e where MO and MR_{ED} intersect in Figure 4.6 above. The optimal revenue tariff is $(P_B'' - P_A'')$ per unit of import. The tariff revenue collected is $(P_B'' P_A'' dc)$. Note that imports will be Q_B', which are below those under the optimal welfare tariff.

4.3.5   Optimal Byrd Tariffs

The US Continued Dumping and Subsidies Offset Act (CDSOA) of 2000 enabled US producers and processors who successfully petition the US government to impose antidumping (AD) or countervailing (CV) tariffs on competing imports to keep the proceeds of those tariffs, which previously went to the US government (A. Schmitz and T.G. Schmitz 1994b). The CDSOA is commonly referred to as the Byrd Amendment because it was sponsored by Senator Robert Byrd of West Virginia. Under the Byrd Amendment, producers and processors can gain from tariffs. These tariffs include an optimal Byrd producer tariff (T.G. Schmitz and Seale

Figure 4.7. Optimal processor tariff

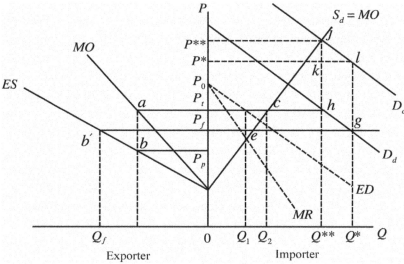

2004), an optimal processor tariff (A. Schmitz, Seale, and T.G. Schmitz 2006), and an optimal producer-processor joint tariff (T.G. Schmitz, A. Schmitz, and Seale 2009). These models are important for policy purposes, since they focus on producers as well as on economic activities beyond the farm gate.

To show the effect of tariffs in a vertical market structure, we select the optimal processor tariff model. Consider a group of processors, referred to as the processing industry, who buy inputs for processing from abroad and from domestic producers. The excess supply curve of an input for processing for the exporter is ES (Figure 4.7). The importer's domestic supply schedule for producing the same input is S_d. The demand curve for the processor's output is D_c. The processor's derived-demand curve for the input is D_d. The free trade price for the input is P_f and exports are Q_f.

Under free trade, the raw-product processor will purchase Q_f from abroad at price P_f and will purchase Q_1 domestically at price P_f. The total outlay for the raw product will become $(P_f Q_f + P_f Q_1)$. In essence, the processor's input totals $(Q_f + Q_1)$, which is Q^*. A portion of the processed input comes in the form of imports, and the remainder is produced domestically. Under constant processor costs, given the consumer demand for the final product D_c, the processor will produce Q^* of the final product for sale at price P^*.

Now, suppose the processor is effective when lobbying for a tariff on the raw product of size $(P_t - P_p)$ (Figure 4.7). The processor now imports only Q_t of the input to be processed at price P_t. Under the Byrd Amendment, tariff revenue (abP_pP_1) will be reimbursed to the processor; hence, its effective outlay on imports will be reduced to (P_pQ_t). Conversely, raw product processor expenditures on domestic inputs will increase from (P_fQ_1) to (P_tQ_2). Combining these two effects, total expenditures by the processor on purchases of both imports and the domestic raw products will actually decrease when the tariff revenue is rebated to the processor. When compared with free trade, a tariff of size $(P_t - P_p)$ will cause the processor to process Q^{**} of the input for sale at price P^{**}.

The optimal processor tariff is derived where the marginal outlay curve MO intersects the marginal revenue curve MR at the excess derived-demand curve ED shown in Figure 4.7. Thus, the optimal processor tariff is $(P_t - P_p)$. Imports for the profit maximizing processor under the tariff are represented by Q_t, for which the processor pays producers in the exporting country price P_p. Producers in the importing country now will receive a higher price of P_t, but consumers will also be charged a higher price. Export producers will lose $(b'bP_pP_f)$, import consumers will lose $(P_tP_f gh)$, domestic producers will gain $(P_tP_f ec)$, and processors will gain $(abP_pP_t gh)$.

At the optimal tariff $(P_t - P_p)$, processor profits are at a maximum. Essentially, the government tariff policy will create non-competitive rents for the processor. A processor under the Byrd Amendment will gain (abP_pP_t) from the tariff relative to free trade, which is exactly equal to the tariff revenue rebated to the processors by the government and is also equal to the optimal tariff revenue. To see this, note the following:

$\Delta\pi$ (processor $= \Delta TR - \Delta TC +$ TRevenue)

$\Delta TR = \{(P^*O_q^*l) - (P^{**}O_q^{**}j)\}$

$= -(kq^{**}q^*l) + (p^{**}P^*kj)$

$\Delta TC = (kq^{**}q^*l) - (P^{**}P^*kj)$

ΔTRevenue $= (abP_pP_t)$

Therefore, $\Delta\pi = (abP_pP_t) =$ Tariff revenue rebated to the processor.

4.4   TRADE DISTORTIONS CAUSED BY MARKET POWER

Trade distortions can occur when market power is exercised through various means, including import-export cartels, voluntary export restraints, and producer marketing boards. For example, the United States uses suspension agreements for trade between the United States and Mexico for tomatoes and sugar, which take the form of import-export cartels or voluntary export restraints (see, for example, Bredahl, Schmitz, and Hillman 1987; T.G. Schmitz and Lewis 2015; Asci et al. 2016).

4.4.1   Voluntary Export Restraints

The use of voluntary export restraints (VERs) requires that exports be restricted below free trade levels. This practice is quite widespread. Examples include voluntary export restraints on beef exports to the United States (Allen, Dodge, and Schmitz 1983) and tomato exports into

Figure 4.8. Voluntary export restraints

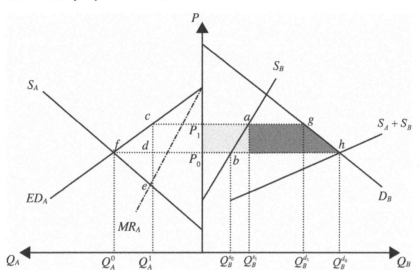

Source: Bredahl, Schmitz, and Hillman (1987).

the United States (Bredahl, Schmitz, and Hillman 1987). This voluntary reduction in exports can increase the welfare for producers in both the exporting and importing countries. In 1987, Bredahl, Schmitz, and Hillman modelled this scenario for Mexican winter tomatoes entering the United States. (This model was used in the tomato-dumping case between the United States and Mexico in the mid-1990s, and their cooperative solution result was the basis of the resolution.)

In Figure 4.8, under free trade, Mexico exports Q_A^0 of winter tomatoes to the United States for price P_0. To simplify the model, Bredahl, Schmitz, and Hillman (1987) assume that all Mexican winter tomatoes are produced for the export market. At this price, the United States produces $Q_B^{S_0}$ of tomatoes and consumes $Q_B^{d_0}$ of tomatoes. If Mexican producers voluntarily restrict exports to increase price, they will set the voluntary export restraint at Q_A^1, where the marginal revenue curve MR_A of US excess demand ED_A is equal to Mexican supply S_A. The decreased quantity exported will raise the price of tomatoes in the United States to P_1, encouraging domestic producers to increase their production to $Q_B^{S_1}$. In this case, the US producers will gain $(P_1 P_0 ba)$, the Mexican producers will gain $(cdP_0 P_1 - fed)$ and the US consumers will lose $(P_1 P_0 hg)$.

Voluntary export restraints have the added attraction of benefiting the producers in the importing country; thus, VERs are sometimes put in place by an exporter trying to avoid trade sanctions. For example, after numerous trade battles with the United States over their softwood lumber imports, Canada put a VER in place for 2×4s being exported to the United

Figure 4.9. Export tax

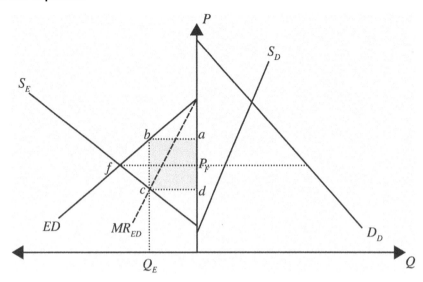

States. As another example, Australia put a VER on its exports of beef to the United States in the 1970s. In both cases, VERs were instituted to lower trade tensions and to circumvent retaliatory actions.

4.4.2   Export Taxes

Agricultural export taxes are used by many countries, including Argentina, Venezuela, and Russia. With export taxes, usually the government gains and producers in the exporting country lose. An export tax is equivalent to a voluntary export restraint, but the distributional effects are very different. Under an export tax, the producers in the exporting country lose, which is opposite to the voluntary export restraint model.

In Figure 4.9, the free trade price is given by P_F. The optimal tax is determined where S_E crosses the marginal revenue demand curve MR_{ED} at point c given the excess demand curve ED. Unlike the VER case, the optimal export tax revenue collected by the government is given by $(bcda)$. Producers in the exporting country lose $(fcdP_F)$. However, producers in the importing country gain from the optimal tax.

4.4.3   Producer Import-Export Cartels

Figure 4.10 shows a model of a producer import-export cartel. Producers in both countries join together to restrict supply and to increase price. The producer supply curve in the exporting

Figure 4.10. Producer import-export cartel

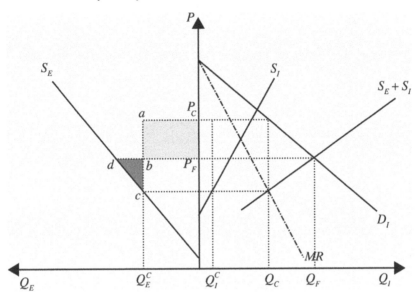

country is S_E (for simplicity, assume no domestic demand). The demand and supply schedules in the importing country are D_I and S_I. The free trade price is given by P_F. If producers in both countries form a cartel, joint profits will be maximized where the marginal revenue curve MR intersects the combined supply schedule $(S_E + S_I)$. The cartel quantity is Q_c and the price earned by producers in both countries is P_c. The quantity produced in the importing country will be Q_I^c, while the quantity produced in the exporting country will be Q_E^c. Producers in both countries will gain by the cartel. For example, the net gain to the producers in the exporting country will equal $(abP_FP_c - dcb)$.

4.4.4 Export Subsidies

Like tariffs, export subsidies create trade distortions. The use of export subsidies can result from government domestic farm programs that support the incomes of the producers. This linkage is shown in a simplified model of price supports and export subsidies (Figure 4.11). Domestic supply is S_d, total demand is TD, and domestic demand is D_d. At the free trade price P_f, quantity $(Q_f - Q_w)$ is exported.

Suppose a country introduces a price support program that supports producers at P_S. Output will expand to Q_S, the export price will fall to P_c, and domestic consumption will increase to Q_c. As a result of the price support program, the government will clear the market by providing an export subsidy of the amount of $(adcb)$. This type of farm program is not decoupled, since it is

Figure 4.11. Price supports and export subsidies

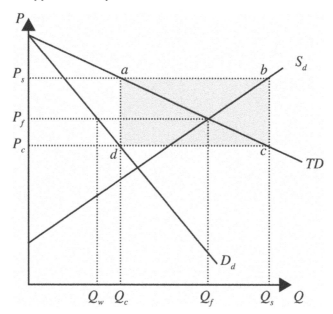

paid on a per unit of production basis and distorts trade. The value of exports under free trade $P_f (Q_f - Q_w)$ is less than the value of exports with export subsidies $P_S (Q_S - Q_c)$. (Note that the total government deficiency payment is $(P_S P_c\ cb)$, of which $(adcb)$ is an export subsidy.)

4.4.5   Transportation

Transportation is an integral part of trade. Many traded commodities are transported over long distances. The cost and availability of transportation remains an important agricultural policy issue, but unfortunately, it receives very little attention in formal economic analysis. High oil prices have brought a renewed interest in the impact of increasing transportation costs. Railroads, in particular, have a long history as a key component of transportation (A. Schmitz, Furtan, and Baylis 2002). The US government provided funding to railroad companies for construction and granted railway companies land and government loans (Benedict 1953). To this end, in 1887, the US government passed the Interstate Commerce Act. The Interstate Commerce Commission was also created, with the purpose of regulating freight and passenger rates. Like the US government, the Canadian federal government provided assistance for railway construction. The Canadian Pacific Railroad was completed in 1885, with government support of C$62.8 million, substantial land grants in western Canada, and tax exemptions (Innis 1956; Fowke 1957).

4.5   MACROECONOMICS, TRADE, AND EXCHANGE RATES

A variety of factors have contributed to the difficulties experienced in the US agricultural sector (Reed and Saghaian 2019). One factor is the effect of macroeconomic variables on agricultural trade through the exchange rate market. In a seminal paper, Schuh (1974) argues that US agriculture suffered because of an overvalued US dollar. One standard conjecture is that, as the economy develops, agriculture looks increasingly towards export markets for its growth. The implications of Working's model (Working 1943; Theil, Chung, and Seale 1989) are consistent with this storyline, but it is important to realize that colonial economies were predicated largely on the *export* of agricultural outputs (e.g., cotton, tobacco, and sugar) to the home country. In many cases, these trading patterns were dictated by laws, such as the Navigation Ordinance of 1651 and the Molasses Act of 1733, which restricted trade between English colonies and other European powers. However, the issues that arose in the twentieth century revolved around the terms of the exchange rate.

The Bretton Woods Agreements in 1944 created a variety of organizations, including the International Monetary Fund (IMF). One of the results of these organizations was the establishment of fixed exchange rates managed in terms of gold. This regime of fixed exchange rates held until the collapse of the agreements in the early 1970s. Following the collapse of the Bretton Woods Agreements, countries were left to their own devices to manage their exchange rates. Countries could opt to fix their exchange rate to another currency (e.g., the US dollar) by purchasing or selling the base currency as the value of each currency varied. Alternatively, the country could allow its currency to float freely or attempt to conduct monetary policy in order to meet certain monetary targets. However, the monetary policy actions required to manage exchange rates are largely the same monetary and fiscal policy variables used to manage the domestic economy.

Typically, the international impacts of monetary policy are divided into two accounts: (1) the current account, and (2) the capital account. The current account depicts the international purchase and sale of goods and services, and the capital account depicts the international transactions involving investment. Economic theory holds that net exports are a decreasing function of aggregate income and the exchange rate. Relatively, we demand more foreign goods than we supply as aggregate income increases, which results in downward pressure on the exchange rate. However, growth in the domestic economy leads to an increased interest rate, which causes the exchange rate to increase as foreign investors demand domestic currency to invest in the domestic economy.

In the early 1970s, agriculture in the United States and Canada experienced a golden period with the growth in international demand for grains. Thus, throughout the 1970s, the future of agriculture was tied to increases in international trade. However, the escalating exchange rates increased the relative prices of US grains on the international market. This upward pressure on prices, coupled with increased real interest rates and reduced inflation, helped create a "perfect storm" that contributed to the onset of financial stress for much of the commercial agriculture in the US Midwest into the 1980s.

4.5.1 Exchange Rates

Exchange rates have a major impact on the competitiveness of agriculture. When Canada and the United States sell wheat to Japan, the price is quoted to the Japanese in US currency. As a result, the competitiveness of Canadian and American wheat producers is determined in part by the Canada/US exchange rate. To examine the effect changes in exchange rates have on agricultural production and trade, we turn to the trade model presented in Figure 4.12. The domestic supply curve is S_D, while domestic consumers' demand is D_D. The excess supply relationship is ES. In the foreign market, the aggregate demand curve is D_F and the aggregate supply curve is S_F, which results in an aggregate excess demand curve of ED. The intersection of the excess supply curve and the excess demand curve results in a free market price of P, quantity produced in the domestic market of Q_D^S, quantity consumed in the domestic market of Q_D^D, and a quantity exported of $(Q_D^S - Q_D^D)$.

Next, suppose the US dollar becomes devalued with respect to other currencies. The foreign demand curve for corn, another US commodity exported around the world, will shift upward from S_F to S_F', while the demand curve will shift upward from D_F to D_F'. The excess demand curve for corn from the rest of the world will shift outward from ED to ED'. This will result in an increase in the world price of corn from P to P'. In the United States, production will increase from Q_D^S to $Q_D^{S'}$, while the domestic demand for corn will fall from Q_D^D to $Q_D^{D'}$. The net impact will then be an increase in the quantity of corn exported to the rest of the world from $(Q_D^S - Q_D^D)$ to $(Q_D^{S'} - Q_D^{D'})$. Internationally, the quantity of corn consumed in the rest of the world will increase from Q_F^D to $Q_F^{D'}$, while the quantity of corn produced in the rest of the world will fall from Q_F^S to $Q_F^{S'}$.

Exchange rates among major trading nations can fluctuate greatly. How does devaluation affect, for example, US corn producers? To answer this question, we construct a weighted average per cent change in the exchange rate (the change in the natural logarithm of each exchange rate) in which each weight is the share of US corn imported by each country. The value of the US dollar fell by 10.9 per cent in comparison with other countries purchasing US corn.

We assume that the market price for corn in the United States is US$3.50 per bushel. We assume that the elasticity of demand in the rest of the world is -0.40, with an elasticity of supply of 0.45. In addition, we assume that the elasticity of demand in the United States is –0.25, with a supply elasticity of 0.45. Given these assumptions, deflation of the US dollar will cause the price of corn to increase to US$3.74 per bushel, with the domestic supply increasing to 13,472 million bushels and domestic demand decreasing to 10,469 million bushels. US corn exports will increase to 3,003 million bushels. Foreign demand will increase to 20,514 million bushels, while foreign production will decrease to 17,511 million bushels.

Figure 4.12. Effect of exchange rates on imports

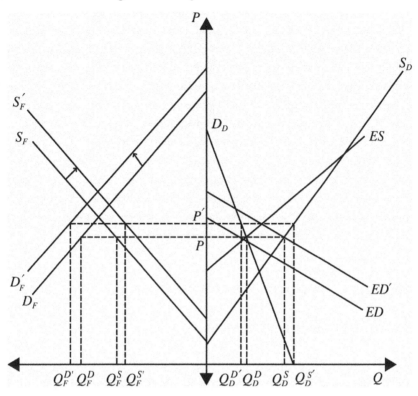

4.5.2   Macroeconomics

Most research into the effect of macroeconomics on agriculture and agricultural policy during the latter part of the twentieth century focused mainly on the effect of monetary and fiscal policy on exchange rates. However, as presented in Appendix 4B, a recession in the broader economy can have a variety of effects on the agricultural sector. While the effect of changes in aggregate income will most likely have only small impacts on the demand for agricultural products, the associated impacts of these changes in money and equity markets may have dramatic effects on agricultural investment and, hence, the supply.

The recession that began in 2008 is an example of these relationships. The housing collapse in 2008 led to a dramatic decline in the liquidity of the banking system. The response was the passage of the Troubled Asset Relief Program (TARP) in the late summer of 2008. Policies similar to TARP continued into 2009 as attempts to increase the liquidity of the banking sector and to increase aggregate demand in the face of growing recessionary pressures. The net impact of these programs on agriculture has been complicated by three forces. First, the additional liquidity has dramatically reduced the nominal interest rate. Second, given the fact that food is a necessity whose value is relatively insensitive to fluctuations in aggregate income (at least in the United States), the aggregate demand for food has created little downward pressure on agricultural prices. Thus, we may expect a small decline in the price of food, with an increased quantity produced if the reduction in interest rates will encourage agricultural investment. This effect may be dampened by the potential negative effect of declining home prices on farmland values. However, the dampening effect of home price declines may be regional. Farmland values in Florida have declined, partially in response to the decrease in the urban building sector (Clouser et al. 2009). However, the negative impact has probably been fairly small in states like Iowa. The long-term effect of these policies will depend on the effect that the recovery packages have on inflation. If these recovery packages spawn long-term increases in inflation, farmland may provide an inflationary hedge (Feldstein 1980) that may yield higher farmland prices. Third, weakening input demand in other sectors that are more sensitive to aggregate income may produce lower variable costs in the farm sector.

4.6   POLICY DECOUPLING, GATT, AND THE WTO

4.6.1   Policy and Decoupled Production

Global interdependence in the digital age has resulted in the creation of many new and important trade linkages, associations, agreements, and disputes. The latter are exemplified by the separate cases that Brazil has brought to the World Trade Organization (WTO) against the US cotton industry and against the EU sugar policy (Powell and Schmitz 2005), both of which were won by Brazil on the grounds that US and EU domestic farm policies were distorting trade. The WTO decisions have important implications for future US farm bills. Because of its high-profile defeat at the WTO, debate over the US cotton program has been reignited in academic circles, with the subsequent examination of the alleged economic inefficiencies and rent-seeking behaviour resulting from trade-distorting agricultural policies. Part of the agricultural policy debate centres on the degree to which a specific policy is decoupled from production (Chambers and Voica 2017).

> **DECOUPLING AND AGRICULTURAL SUPPORT**
> Decoupling agricultural support from production decisions has become one of the central issues in agricultural policy, both nationally and internationally. The need to minimize international trade distortions associated with support to the agricultural

sector was a key element in the principles for agricultural policy reform adopted by OECD ministers in 1987. This same issue dominated much of the debate leading to the adoption of the Uruguay Round Agreement on Agriculture (URAA) in 1994. Since the opening of the new WTO round of multilateral trade negotiations in December 1999, it has been clear, from the debate and the proposals being put forward, that decoupling remains an important aspect of the negotiations on agriculture (OECD 2005).

4.6.2   Policy Categories and Decoupling[1]

The WTO has several responsibilities, including administering trade agreements, acting as a forum for trade negotiations, settling trade disputes, and performing other supervisory duties. Prior to the creation of the WTO, the General Agreement on Tariffs and Trade (GATT) was signed in 1948 by twenty-three countries, including Canada, the United States, and some European countries. Agriculture was not included until the seventh round of negotiations. These negotiations began in Uruguay in 1986 and resulted in a 1994 agreement that created the WTO in 1995. The WTO now oversees the GATT as well as the General Agreement on Trade in Services (GATS) and the Agreement on Trade-Related Aspects of Intellectual Property Rights (TRIPS). Many countries' policies are designed with the WTO rules in mind. For example, Canadian dairy policy has been modified through WTO rulings, as has US cotton policy.

As a result of the Uruguay Round Agreement, farm programs have been separated into multiple box categories – blue, green, amber, or red – according to their trade-distorting impacts. Green Box policies are not actionable for countervailing duties or other GATT challenges during the implementation period. Ultimately, Green Box criteria ensure that policies and programs in the category are production and trade neutral.

The WTO regulates domestic support policies, which are divided into two types, those that are subject to reduction commitment and those that are exempt. Exempt policies include Green Box programs and Blue Box programs.

4.6.3   Green Box Policies

Two basic criteria apply in Green Box policies: (1) support must be government funded, and (2) the money cannot provide price support. Categories fitting the Green Box criteria include research, inspection, extension and training, marketing and promotion, public stock holding for food security, domestic food aid, decoupled income support, income insurance and safety net programs, structural adjustment assistance, regional assistance, and environmental aids.

4.6.4   Blue Box Policies

Blue Box policies include program payments received under production-limiting programs that are based on fixed area and yields, a fixed number of head of livestock, or on 85 per cent or less of the base level of production. Those programs that do not fit these three categories are subject to reduction commitment. For these non-exempt programs, a quantitative measure of the level of intervention is calculated using an aggregate measure of support (AMS).

4.6.5   Amber Box Policies

Amber Box policies are trade-distorting domestic support programs such as market price support and input subsidies that are subject to reduction commitments.

4.6.6   Red Box Policies

Red Box policies are prohibited. Since there is no agreement on how to apply the "stop" red light to any domestic policy, the "Red Box" has been empty.

4.6.7   Discussion

During the Uruguay Round of trade negotiations, a number of authors attempted to classify domestic support policies based on the degree to which they distort trade; however, certain policies do not fit neatly into the categories. For example, it is difficult to assign the Canadian Net Income Stabilization Account (NISA) program a precise spot within the green part of the green-red spectrum. The program is not entirely neutral, because additional government contributions can be obtained through additional sales. The US Production Flexibility Contract (PFC) program is also hard to categorize. Concerns surrounding the PFC program stem from the large dollar amounts of the payments, the expectation that production may now be required for a future program, and the recent use of the program to provide additional ad hoc transfers to producers. Also, the original EU compensatory payments cannot be considered *green*.

Although Green Box policy programs are more benign than other forms of support, it is clear that large ongoing payments, by their size and permanence, attract and keep resources in agriculture. As the Green Box becomes a more popular avenue for governments to provide domestic support, the expenditure envelope will expand, and the potential distortions will increase accordingly. Moreover, although programs may be designed to be production neutral, they are not always so in practice. Even though a program may be only marginally distorting, large program expenditures may turn a small distortion into a big impact. This raises the need for a cap on total Green Box spending, possibly combined with a cap on each element in the Green Box.

4.7   SUMMARY AND CONCLUSIONS

- Most countries are dependent on agricultural trade. Some agricultural products (e.g., grain and, to a lesser degree, livestock) have become export staples, whereas other products (e.g., some horticultural production and the industries under supply management) have been oriented towards the domestic market. Therefore, no single trade policy meets the interests of all the producers, and rent-seeking behaviour is pursued by both pro-trade and anti-trade producers.
- The theory of international trade clearly shows positive gains from trade in the absence of distortions.
- The gains from trade can be shown in both a partial and general equilibrium setting.
- Subsidies and quotas can cause negative gains from trade.
- Free trade has been shown to maximize welfare in a competitive market. Distortions brought about by the use of trade instruments such as tariffs usually result in net welfare losses, even though certain sectors can gain from protectionism. Two common tariffs include the optimal revenue tariff and optimal welfare tariff.
- Distortions caused by market power and voluntary export restraints also impact trade.
- Export taxes are widely used by countries such as Russia, Argentina, and Venezuela. These taxes often impose heavy burdens on domestic producers.
- Export subsidies and transportation costs are a major component in the pricing of traded commodities.
- The WTO has emerged as a force in the resolution of trade disputes among countries.
- Trade agreements and the WTO have attempted to limit the use of trade-distorting measures, with the view that more liberalized trade increases societal welfare. In theory, Green Box policies are non-trade distorting; however, finding actual Green Box policies that meet these criteria is difficult.
- Tariff theory is critical to understanding why governments enter into suspension agreements, such as the one regulating fresh tomatoes from Mexico (exporter) into the United States (importer).
- Macroeconomic variables, such as exchange and interest rates, affect trade flows and, thus, farm income. Further, some argue that US agriculture at times has not been competitive in world markets because of an overvalued US dollar.

APPENDIX 4A: NEGATIVE GAINS FROM TRADE

The concept of negative gains from trade (NGT) originates in the presence of trade and price supports. NGT occur when the net welfare costs of price supports are greater than the classic gains from trade, when the comparison is made between free trade and no trade.

Consider Figure 4.A1, where S_d is domestic supply, D_d is domestic demand, and T_d is total demand. Under no trade, the price is P_1 and output is Q_1. In a world of free trade, however, the price rises to P_2 and output increases to Q_2. Exports equal $(Q_2 - Q_3)$. The net gains from free trade equal (acb). Producers gain (P_2P_1cb) while domestic consumers lose a lesser amount equal to (P_2P_1ca).

Now compare the free trade and no trade situations with trade in the presence of a price support P_S. Given P_S, output expands to Q_S and exports expand to fe. The domestic prices fall to P_3. The net effects are

1 Producers gain relative to free trade (P_SP_2bd)
2 Domestic consumers gain (P_2P_3fa)
3 The Treasury provides subsidy payments of (P_2P_3ed)
4 The net welfare cost of the price support is $(afedb)$

For NGT to occur, $(afedb)$ must be greater than the classic gains from trade (acb), which is clearly the case in Figure 4.A1. Thus, no trade is preferred to trade under price supports. Note, however, that one can construct a model in which this will not be the case. The result depends on several factors, including the height of the price support, the percentage of the product exported, and the demand-price elasticities.

Put another way, what will be the net gains when moving from trade under a price support of P_S to no trade?

1 The Treasury saves (P_SP_3ed)
2 The domestic consumers gain (P_3P_1cf)
3 Producers lose (P_SP_1cd)

As a result, there are negative gains from trade $(dge - fcg)$.

What happens when free trade cannot be achieved? Suppose total demand shrinks from T_d to T_D' because of subsidies abroad (Figure 4.A2). The trade price will be P_t and output will be Q_t. In the presence of a price support of P_S, the net cost associated with the price support will be $(gcebf)$. However, do we see negative gains from trade? Note that the gain from trade in the presence of foreign subsidies will be only (gcf), which is smaller than (acb) that exists if free trade takes place in the absence of foreign subsidies. Since $(gcebf)$ is greater than (gcf), we see net gains from trade totalling (bce).

Figure 4.A1. Negative gains from trade without foreign subsidies

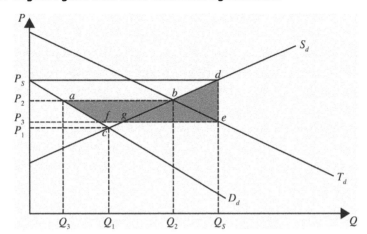

Figure 4.A2. Negative gains from trade with foreign subsidies

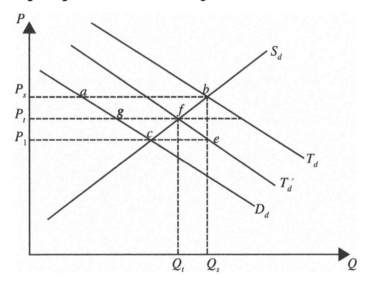

The same result can be obtained by comparing the no trade situation P_1 with the price support P_S. The Treasury will save (P_SP_1eb), producers will lose (P_SP_1cb), and consumers will be unaffected. Hence, the net gain from trade at a price of P_S to that of no trade is (*bce*). No trade is better than price-supported trade in the presence of foreign subsidies.

APPENDIX 4B: EFFECT OF MACROECONOMIC VARIABLES ON AGRICULTURE/AGRICULTURAL POLICY

Macroeconomic policy affects the agricultural sector through the aggregation of commodities in aggregate income. Specifically, we know that aggregate income and consumption include agricultural output. However, does economic theory give any guidance on whether the agricultural sector benefits more or less than any other sector of the economy? Likewise, we know that the agricultural demand for credit is one component of the overall money market demand [$L(Y, i)$], but is there reason to suspect that agriculture as a sector benefits more from monetary policy than do other sectors? To examine some of these questions, we begin with a profit function for agriculture

$$\Pi_{ag} = p_{ag}\,y + \tau(G) - C(y) - Di, \qquad (4.B1)$$

where π_{ag} is the profit accruing to the agricultural sector, p_{ag} is the price of agricultural output, y is the level of agricultural output, $\tau(G)$ is the level of transfer payments to agriculture, $C(y)$ is the cost of production, and D is the level of agricultural debt. Next, we begin by differentiating Equation 4.B1 with respect to government spending

$$\frac{d\Pi_{ag}}{dG} = \left[\frac{dp_{ag}}{dy} - C'(y)\right]\frac{dy}{dY}\frac{dY}{dG} + \tau'(G) + \left[\frac{dD}{di} + D\right]\frac{di}{dG}. \qquad (4.B2)$$

Equation 4.B2 provides the basic parameters for our discussion of the effect of macroeconomic policy on the farm sector. Several questions need to be answered. Do increases in macroeconomic variables, such as government spending, increase the demand for agricultural output (or is $dy/dY > 0$)? What part of aggregate government spending focuses on agriculture (what is the nature of $\tau'(G)$ relative to overall government spending)? Is the debt response of the agricultural sector different from other sectors? The questions posed by monetary policy (as opposed to fiscal policy) are similar:

$$\frac{d\Pi_{ag}}{dG} = \left[\frac{dp_{ag}}{dy} - C'(y)\right]\frac{dy}{dY}\frac{dY}{dM} + \left[\frac{dD}{di} + D\right]\frac{di}{dM}, \qquad (4.B3)$$

although the discussion of monetary policy has followed a slightly different approach that focuses on the effect of macroeconomic policy on trade.

One of the most important factors affecting the interaction between the general economy and the agricultural sector is the effect of macroeconomic policy on the demand for agricultural outputs (dy/dY). We hypothesize that the demand for normal goods increases as income increases. Thus, we conjecture that $dy/dY > 0$. However, certain characteristics of food may have implications for the relative increase in the demand for agricultural output as aggregate income increases. Specifically, Seale and Theil (1986) provide empirical support for Working's

Law, which states that the share of consumers' expenditures of food declines as the natural logarithm of income increases. Mathematically,

$$\frac{y}{Y}=a+b\ln(Y)\Rightarrow dy=\left[\frac{y}{Y}+b\right]dY \text{ or } \frac{dy}{y}=\left.\left[\frac{y}{Y}+b\right]\middle/\frac{y}{Y}\right.\frac{dY}{Y}, \tag{4.B4}$$

where a and b are fixed parameters. Working's Law implies that $b < 0$ for food. In the United States, expenditures are the greatest for housing, followed by transportation and food.

Theil, Chung, and Seale (1989) compute the percentage change in expenditures on housing, transportation, food, and fuel. They find that while increases in aggregate income lead to increased demand for food, food represents a declining portion of the aggregate economy. Stated slightly differently, as the aggregate economy expands, the increase in income causes a relatively smaller increase in agricultural demand (or those increases in income are less impactful to the farm sector). Thus, dy/dY is small for highly developed countries such as the United States, Canada, and the European Union. (However, this derivation focuses only on the role of food and agricultural products in the domestic economy.)

To determine the effect of macroeconomic policy on the debt market, we focus on the magnitude of $dD/di + D$. While the aggregate debt-to-asset levels in agriculture since the 1960s have been quite modest (typically less than 0.25), the sector's access to capital has caused some significant difficulties in the sector. For example, the farm debt crisis of the mid-1980s was linked to macroeconomic fundamentals beginning in the 1970s (Harl 1990). In October 1979, the Federal Reserve Board made the decision to restrain the growth in money supply to dramatically reduce inflation in the US economy. However, reducing the inflation rate also resulted in significantly higher real interest rates. The combination of lower inflation rates and higher real interest rates led to lower asset values, which reduced sector solvency and helped create the financial difficulties of the mid-1980s. This discussion is appropriate for analysing the effect of macroeconomic policies from the 1980s through 2019. The US economy has gone through major changes; for example, in 2019, the farm debt-to-asset ratio reached an all-time low partly because of historically low interest rates and rising land values (see Chapter 7).

The historical evidence suggests that domestic macroeconomic policies have affected the farm sector primarily through capital markets. While macroeconomic policies may have affected aggregate income, Working's model indicates that increases in aggregate income will result in relatively small changes in agriculture's share of the overall economy. However, historical events, such as the collapse of the credit market following the panic of 1830 and the financial crisis of the 1980s, have suggested that the agricultural sector is affected dramatically by changes in the nominal and real interest rates that result from changes in either the monetary or fiscal policy.

CHAPTER FIVE

The Interface between Trade, Food, and Agricultural Policies

5.1 INTRODUCTION

A main goal of this book is to emphasize the critical interrelationship between agricultural and food policy and trade. The extent to which a country imports and exports agricultural goods is tied to the magnitude of its agricultural policy. For example, a country's exports can be greatly enhanced by the country's agricultural producer subsidies, even in the presence of tariffs. The opposite is true for an importing country, where the magnitude of trade is not only a function of tariffs and quotas, but also a function of domestic producer support within that country.

5.2 PRODUCTION QUOTAS

5.2.1 Zero Trade

The impact of production quotas, assuming no trade, is analysed in Figure 5.1a. Demand and supply are given by D and S. Marginal revenue and marginal cost are given by MR and MC. The competitive equilibrium price and quantity are p and q_2. This is not the case if production is restricted through quotas. If producers collectively act as monopolists, they set the price, for example, at p_1 and produce quantity at q_1. The price increase gives rise to a gross quota rent value of (p_1p_2ab). The quota results in a consumer loss of (p_1pcb), whereas, on net, producers gain $[(p_1peb)(eac)]$. This net welfare gain to producers is less than the value of the quota (p_1p_2ab). Also, a quota gives rise to a net efficiency loss of (bac). This is often referred to as deadweight loss, or the Harberger triangle.

Figure 5.1. Production quotas: Export goods

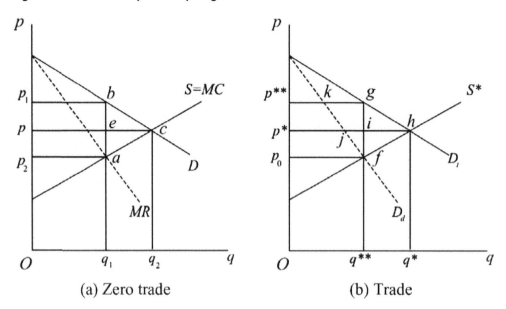

(a) Zero trade   (b) Trade

5.2.2   Export Goods

In the classic example of the US tobacco program (see Chapter 7), where part of the production was exported, production quotas were key to maximizing producer returns. In an analysis of the impact of tobacco quotas, both domestic and export markets must be taken into account. P.R. Johnson (1965) emphasized the importance of exports in the presence of exporter monopoly power and concluded that the United States can achieve net gains from the tobacco quota program.

For illustrative purposes, the impact of trade on an export good under a production quota is shown in Figure 5.1b. Total demand is given by D_t, whereas domestic demand is D_d. The competitive equilibrium price and quantity are p^* and q^*, and exports total $j\,h$. If a production quota is set at q^{**}, the price will rise to p^{**}. As a result of the quota, producers gain $[(p^{**}p^*ig)$ $(if\ h)]$. The loss to consumers in both the exporting and importing countries is $(p^{**}p^*hg)$, where domestic consumers lose $(p^{**}p^*jk)$ and foreign consumers lose $(kj\ hg)$.

5.2.3   Import Goods

Production quotas also play a major role in the functioning of the Canadian supply management system for dairy, eggs, broilers, and turkeys. However, unlike the tobacco example above, production quotas in Canada operate at an import-competing basis, whereas the United States would export to Canada in the absence of supply management. This was an issue under

Figure 5.2. Domestic production quotas and import concessions

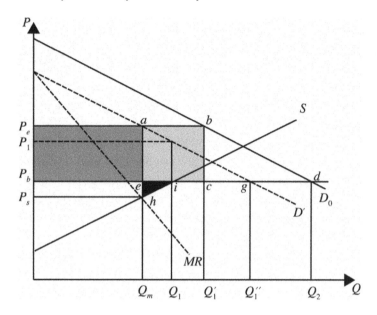

President Trump's renegotiation of NAFTA (which became the USMC Agreement in 2020), and in concessions where Canada liberalized trade in dairy products.

Vercammen and Schmitz (1992) consider quotas in the context of an import good by analysing Canadian agricultural supply management in the presence of two distortions: domestic production controls and import tariffs. They show the impact of supply management programs on Canadian producers and consumers given producer maximization of profits subject to tariff-constrained imports; however, they do not analyse the impact of removing production quotas.

Under supply management, both production controls and import quotas enhance returns to producers of supply-managed products (Vercammen and Schmitz 1992). Both of these policy instruments are modelled in Figure 5.2. Domestic demand is given by D_0 and domestic supply is given by S. Under free trade, the domestic (border) price is P_b, domestic production is Q_1, and domestic consumption is Q_2. Imports total $(Q_2 - Q_1)$.

Only an agreed-upon quantity of imports set in the Minimum Access Commitment are given tariff-free access to the Canadian market. Imports are restricted to $(Q_2 - Q_1'')$. Now domestic producers face the demand curve D'. Because of the nature of demand, the pricing structure for milk is much more complicated than that presented in Figure 5.2. For example, there are many demands for milk, including fluid milk, milk products, and demand by industrial milk users. An expanded version of Figure 5.2 should include at least two demand curves: one that is inelastic (demand for fluid milk) and one that is elastic (demand for milk products). Producers will maximize profit for any given level of output by practising price discrimination in different dairy-related markets. Because of the nature of demand and the allocation of the output to various markets, conflicts often arise between producers and industrial processors.

For the domestic producers to maximize profits, the production quota is set where the marginal revenue curve MR equals the supply curve S, which results in domestic production Q_m. Producers gain ($P_e P_b\,ea - ehi$). The quota value for any producer will be the discounted value of ($P_e - P_s$) per unit of quota. The total approximate quota value for the industry will be the discounted value of ($P_e P_s\,ha$). Moschini (1984) uses this methodology to calculate quota values for Ontario dairy production.

In Figure 5.2, consumers lose ($P_e P_b\,db$) and importers gain ($aecb$). The availability of import quotas gives importers (many of whom are also domestic food retailers) incentives for rent-seeking behaviour, because import quotas have value equal to $\left[(P_e - P_b)(Q_i' - Q_m)\right]$ or ($aecb$). This value arises because importers buy the product at P_b and sell it in the domestic market at P_e. Producers challenged the right of importers to capture these rents in the courts; however, the decision ruled in favour of the importers.

In Figure 5.2, triangle (bcd) is referred to as the deadweight loss (DWL), which can also be stated as $[P_e P_b\,db - (P_e P_b\,ea + aecb)]$ and it is the net cost of the supply management program. The smaller the deadweight loss, the greater is the efficiency with which income can be transferred from consumers to producers. Thus, the size of the income transfer can be large, while the DWL triangle can be small.

MODELLING SUPPLY MANAGEMENT

One of the most important considerations when modelling supply management is deciding at what level to set the production quota. McCutcheon and Goddard (1992) start with an arbitrary quota level, while A. Schmitz and T.G. Schmitz (1994a) use an example in which the domestic production quota is set at the monopoly solution, which gives the maximum producer revenue, given a fixed level of imports. In the above model, we use the monopoly rule to set the domestic production quota, even though it is not likely the case in the application of the supply management policy. One can easily work out different solutions if quotas are not set at the monopoly level. For example, in Figure 5.2, suppose that production is set at Q_1, which gives rise to a domestic price of P_1. In this case, producers gain less from supply management than they do under the monopoly case. The cost to consumers is also less.

Moschini (1984) calculated the quota amounts that would give rise to maximum producer profits using supply and demand estimates for Canadian milk. Due to the inelastic nature of demand, milk production (under the production quota system) in Canada far exceeds that which would occur if producers acted as pure monopolists.

Figure 5.3. Price supports

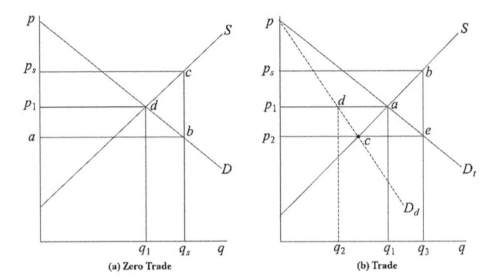

(a) Zero Trade   (b) Trade

5.3   PRICE SUPPORTS

5.3.1   Price Supports without Trade

In Figure 5.3, we consider the case where price supports are used in a closed market setting. Given supply S and demand D, the price and quantity in the absence of price supports are $p_1 q_1$. However, this is not the case if the government introduces a price support of p_s. Because of the price support, producers gain ($p_s p_1 dc$), consumers gain ($p_1 abd$), and the government incurs a deficiency payment cost of ($p_s abc$). On net, the price support generates a net cost of (dbc).

5.3.2   Price Supports with Trade

The model for price supports with trade is more complicated than the situation discussed above. We introduce two demand curves – total demand D_t and domestic demand D_d. Given domestic supply S, the free trade price and quantity are $p_1 q_1$. Of the total amount produced q_1, $q_1 q_2$ is exported.

Now consider the effect of a price support p_s that causes production to increase to q_3 and the consumer price to fall to p_2. Producers gain ($p_s p_1 ab$) and domestic consumers gain ($p_1 p_2 cd$). Consumers in the importing country gain ($dcea$) and government deficiency payments total ($p_s p_2 eb$). On net, the exporting country suffers a loss from the price support of ($dceba$).

Figure 5.4. Japanese beef tariffs and domestic price supports

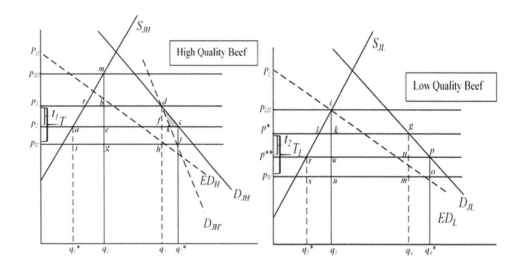

5.4   JAPANESE BEEF

The Japanese beef sector is highly protected through tariffs on beef imports from the United States and Australia. There is continuing dialogue about having these tariffs lowered, and research continues on what the effects would be. A. Schmitz, Seale, and Chegini (2019) show that the effects of Japanese protection depend critically on the extent to which Japanese beef producers are compensated, through price supports and other means, for losses incurred from freer trade.

Consider Figure 5.4, where S_{JH} is the supply of Japanese high-quality beef and D_{JH} is the aggregate Japanese demand. The excess demand is ED_H. The world price for high-quality beef is p_w. A tariff of T causes prices in Japan to rise from p_w to p_1. In the presence of a producer price support p_{SH}, domestic production is q_1. At p_1, Japan imports $q_1\,q_2$ of high-quality beef. In the event that Japan lowers the tariff by t_1, the internal price falls to p_2. With no compensation, producers lose $p_{SH}\,p_2am$, consumers gain p_1p_2cd, and the change in tariff revenue is {(aige) + (fhjc) – (befd)}.

Japan was prepared to compensate producers for losses incurred due to freer trade under the Trans-Pacific Partnership (TPP) agreement (A. Schmitz, Zhu, and Zilberman 2017). If the producers are compensated through a deficiency payment scheme with a producer price support p_s, then producers are unaffected by the tariff at the expense of the government in the form of additional deficiency payment of the amount p_1p_2be. Production will remain at q_1, and imports increase from q_1q_2 to $q_1q_2{}^*$. Consumers gain p_1p_2cd. The government sees a change in tariff revenue of {fhjc – befd}, which does not necessarily offset the extra deficiency payment cost of $p_1 p_2 be$. On net, when producers are fully compensated through deficiency payments, the welfare effect is $\{dfc + fhjc\}$.

However, the above deficiency payment compensation scheme assumes that production is not decoupled from prices. In the case where compensation payment is at least partially decoupled, such as in a decoupled producer lump sum buyout, the welfare gains to Japan from lowering tariffs would be larger than in the case of complete coupling.

Under full compensation through lump sum buyout, the Japanese government would pay producers $p_{SH} p_2 am$. Under the assumption of decoupling, production falls to $q_1{}^*$ and imports increase to $q_1{}^* q_2{}^*$. Under lump sum buyout compensation, the net welfare gain from tariff reduction is $\{(aem) + (dfc) + (aige) + (fhjc)\}$.

The effect of Japanese beef tariffs must be put in the context of Japanese imports of both high- and low-quality beef. We now discuss tariffs within the context of low-quality beef (Figure 5.4b) and then discuss the two classes of beef within an aggregate market structure. In Figure 5.4b, the demand for low-quality beef is given by D_{JL}. The supply in Japan of low-quality beef is S_{JL}. The excess demand is ED_L. The world price is Pw. For a tariff of T_L, the Japanese low-quality beef price is p^*, where imports total $q_3 q_4$. The net gains from freer trade are $\{gnp + nmop\}$ if producers are compensated through deficiency payments. If producers are compensated through a lump sum buyout, the net gains are greater in value, at $\{irw + rsuw + nmop + gnp\}$. If producers receive no compensation, the net efficiency is the same as the lump sum buyout scenario; however, the distribution of gains is significantly different.

Per the TPP, Japan agreed to lower tariffs on both high-quality beef from the United States and low-quality beef from Australia (A. Schmitz, Zhu, and Zilberman 2017). Unlike the A. Schmitz, Zhu, and Zilberman (2017) study, beef is assumed to be heterogeneous in the following argument. Consider Figure 5.4b, where tariffs are lowered by t_1 for high-quality beef and by t_2 for low-quality beef. Since the percentage tariff reductions apply equally to both types of beef, the relative prices remain unchanged. Therefore, one can rule out major substitutional effects between the two types of beef. As a result, for high-quality beef, the proposed tariff reduction of 11 per cent in the original TPP agreement gives rise to the following result: consumers gain $(p_1 p_2 cd)$, while producers in Japan lose $(p_{SH} p_2 am)$ in the absence of compensation from the Japanese government. In the low-quality beef market, consumers gain $(p^* p^{**} pg)$, while producers lose $(p_{LH} p^{**} ri)$.

Because Japan was prepared to pay Japanese beef producers for losses incurred from freer trade, a decrease in tariff price to p^{**} (Figure 5.4b), with price supports of p_{LH} remaining intact, could give rise to a government cost of $(P_{LH} p^{**} wi)$. Along with the price support, imports become $(q_3 q_4{}^*)$. This gives rise to a change in government tariff revenue of $\{(nmop) - (kwng)\}$.

Table 5.1 gives the results of freer trade in beef, where Japan lowers its beef import tariffs. If Japan lowers its tariffs without compensating its domestic beef producers, the net gains from freer trade range between US\$810 million and US\$935 million. At the other extreme, if Japan fully compensates its beef producers, the net gains fall drastically to between US\$93 million and US\$214 million.

Table 5.1. Beef tariff reductions* in Japan under *homogeneous beef* and *small-country* assumptions *without and with government support*

	Case I $(\varepsilon_{ED} = -0.5)$	Case II $(\varepsilon_{ED} = -1.2)$
A. Economic impacts without full support (US$)		
Consumer surplus gain	591,385,040	612,218,277
Government deficiency savings	2,453,429,656	2,453,429,656
Without support: producer loss	2,182,229,681	2,182,229,681
Government tariff revenue change	52,768,747 (loss)	51,397,438 (gain)
Net gain from free trade	**809,816,270**	**934,815,690**
B. Economic impacts with full support under deficiency payment program (US$) (Ps = US$15.29)		
Consumer surplus gain	591,385,040	612,218,277
Government tariff revenue loss	266,813,555	165,947,370
Gov't incurred extra deficiency payment	231,986,185	231,986,185
Net gain from free trade (deficiency payment)	**92,585,300**	**214,284,722**
C. Economic impacts with partial producer support under deficiency payment program (US$) (Ps = US$11.80)		
Consumer surplus gain	591,385,040	612,218,277
Government tariff revenue change	170,829,082 (loss)	66,662,897 (loss)
Producer surplus loss	1,121,713,976	1,121,713,976
Government deficiency savings	1,244,444,136	1,244,444,136
Net gain from free trade	**543,286,118**	**668,285,540**
D. Economic impacts with partial producer support under deficiency payment program (US$) (Ps = US$8.31)		
Consumer surplus gain	591,385,040	612,218,277
Government tariff revenue change	71,544,609 (loss)	32,621,576 (gain)
Producer surplus loss	2,033,426,248	2,033,426,248
Government deficiency savings	2,300,871,049	2,300,871,049
Net gain from free trade	**787,285,232**	**912,284,654**

*11% reduction in snapback tariffs as outlined by the TPP
Source: A. Schmitz, Seale, and Chegini (2019).

5.5   ECONOMICS OF INPUT AND OUTPUT SUBSIDIES

5.5.1   Input Subsidies without Trade

Input subsidies are widespread – especially in countries such as the United States – yet relatively little attention has been paid, at least theoretically, to their impact. Water, a major subsidized input in US agriculture, has a number of competing uses, including industrial, residential, recreational, hydroelectric power, and agricultural. The allocation and cost of water to the agricultural sector have been strongly influenced by government policy and, in turn, by rent-seeking behaviour. The magnitude of water subsidies varies by state, with California receiving the most water subsidies for its farmers.

Figure 5.5. Input subsidies without trade

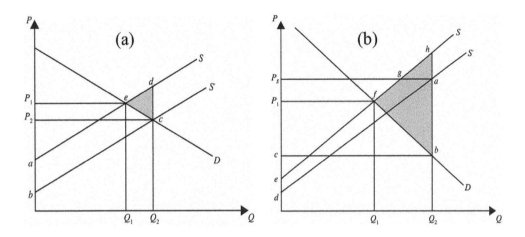

To examine the impact of subsidies in a closed model where trade is absent, consider Figure 5.5a, where S is the supply schedule and D is the demand schedule. In the absence of an input subsidy, the price is P_1 and the quantity is Q_1. Now consider an input subsidy that results in a shift in supply from S to S'. What is the effect? Consumers gain ($P_1 P_2 ce$), while producers gain ($P_2 bc - P_1 ae$). The input subsidy costs a total of ($abcd$). The net welfare cost of the input subsidy is (dec).

5.5.2   Combined Input and Output Subsidies without Trade

In Figure 5.5b, we show what happens when an input subsidy exists in the presence of commodity price supports. Demand is D and the subsidized supply curve is S'. A commodity price support is represented by P_s. The two subsidies combined have the following impacts: consumers gain ($P_1 cbf$) and producers gain ($P_s P_1 feda$). The input subsidy costs total ($edah$), while the Treasury costs for the price support total ($P_s cba$). The net welfare cost of the two input and output subsidies combined is represented by (hfb). Note that for a given input subsidy, the welfare costs of adding price support payments increase as the size of the price support increases.

5.5.3   Input Subsidies with Trade

What happens to subsidy impacts in the presence of trade? The welfare effects of the subsidies discussed above are no longer represented by a triangle. Consider Figure 5.6, where the domestic demand is D_d and the total demand is T_D. The net cost of the input subsidy that shifts supply from S to S' is given by ($cdeab$). The cost is greater than (bea) because of the slippage effect ($cdeb$), which is the cost of subsidizing importers.

Figure 5.6. Input subsidies with trade

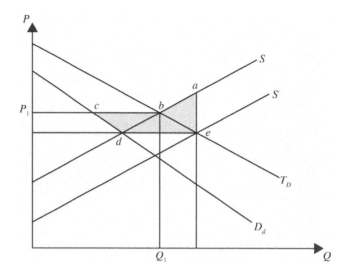

5.5.4   Input and Output Subsidies with Trade: Multiplicative Effects

Input subsidies are often used in conjunction with production or output subsidies. Here we focus on the interaction of price supports, which for our purpose include both countercyclical payments (CCPs) and loan rate payments (LRPs), as well as input subsidies. We analyse these instruments taken together as well as individually and demonstrate that they operate in a multiplicative rather than an additive manner.

5.5.4.1   THE EXPORTER CASE

Figure 5.7 presents a combined input subsidy and price support payment model. In addition, this figure explicitly represents each policy program instrument separately. In the model, S and S' represent, respectively, the supply curve with and without the water subsidy. The domestic demand curve is D_d and T_d is the total demand curve.

Under the multiplicative effects (ME) scenario given, the support price for cotton is P_S, the water-subsidized supply curve is S', output quantity is q^*, and the world price is P_w. Domestic producers receive $(P_S P_f fmno)$ as a net gain, while domestic consumers gain $(P_f P_w cd)$. Also, $(dcbf)$ is referred to as slippage, representing rents received by importing countries. The cost to the government for the input subsidy is $(mnoa)$, while the cost of the government price support payments equals $(P_S P_w bo)$. Therefore, the combined net domestic cost to society of the two subsidies applied together is $(dcbaf)$. The net cost comparison is made with reference to point f, where P_f and q_2 are free from distortions. In this model, the relative magnitude and

Figure 5.7. Input and output subsidies and price supports for an export good

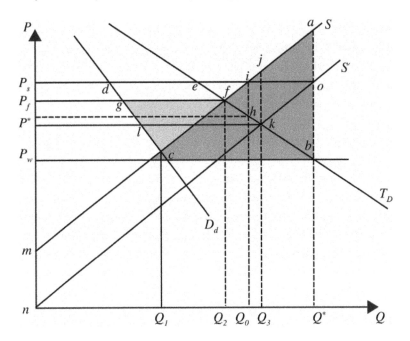

distribution of the rents depend largely on the demand and supply elasticities, the amount of exports, and the per unit cost of the water subsidy. For example, the more elastic the supply, the greater the deadweight loss (DWL); likewise, the higher the proportion of domestic production that is exported, the greater the net cost of the combined subsidies. Using this model framework, T.G. Schmitz, A. Schmitz, and Dumas (1997) theoretically and empirically show negative gains for the United States from trade in cotton (NGT).

For the theoretical ME model, depicted in Figure 5.7, domestic cotton producers gain more rents from the water subsidy (*mnoi*) than from the price support payments ($P_S P_f$ i) although most of the price support payments from the government go to domestic consumers (P_f Pwcd) and to foreign countries (*dcbf*) rather than to producers. However, the actual distribution of these rents is an empirical matter that illustrates how parameter changes affect the calculation and distribution of the subsidy rents and welfare losses.

A combination of the two subsidies distorts output more than when each acts alone, causing the multiplicative effects of the two instruments to be greater than a mere summation of the individual effects. For example, in Figure 5.7, the production quantity Q^*, is established where the target price P_S intersects the input-subsidized supply curve S' at point *o* instead of at point *i* (associated with quantity Q_0), where it would otherwise be given only a price support. Thus, adding the water input subsidy to the price support increases production from Q_0 to Q^*. In addition to increased output, the world price decreases significantly, falling to P_w. Both of these effects increase the price support payments made by the government, and in conjunction with price supports, the aggregate size of the input subsidy is greater than in the absence of price supports. Therefore, we refer to Figure 5.7 as the multiplicative effects (ME) model.

One can also observe the individual effects of input subsidies and price supports. In Figure 5.7, the net cost of the price support is given by (*dghif*). The net cost of the input subsidy is (*dlkjf*). Note that the diagrammatical shape of the two instruments is the same, and in addition, each has the same shape as the combined impact.

5.5.4.2 THE IMPORTER CASE

Consider Figure 5.8 for an import good. Demand is D and supply is S. Under the small-country assumption, the world price is P_w, where imports total Q_1Q_w. Assume that two distortions exist: (1) a price support P_S, and (2) a per unit water subsidy. The price support results in a price increase from P_w to P_S, while the water subsidy causes supply to shift from S to S'. There is no effect on consumers under the small-country assumption. The producers gain $\{(P_sP_wfg) + (debg)\}$. The cost to the government of the water subsidy is (*debc*), the government cost for the price support is $P_S P_w$ *ab*, and the net cost of the two government programs is (*cfa*).

5.6   TRADE REMEDY ACTIONS: COUNTERVAILING AND DUMPING CASES

The United States often imposes duties on imported products. Most of these cases involve action brought against foreign countries by US domestic producers. These cases are either of a countervailing or a dumping nature. In the case of countervailing measures, duties are imposed if an exporter ships to the United States a product whose production is subsidized by the government in the exporting country (see subsidy models above). In dumping cases, anti-duty dumping duties are imposed if an exporter sells a product in the United States below fair market value.

For international subsidies, the World Trade Organization (WTO) allows countervailing and anti-dumping duties as trade remedy actions. Here, we examine WTO trade remedies for the United States. In both cases, two conditions must be met to qualify for remedies. Under the WTO agreement, countervailing duties can be imposed when these conditions are met. First, the US Department of Commerce determines that a government of a country or a public entity within a county provides countervailing subsidies on exports sold in the United Sates. Second, the US International Trade Commission determines that an industry in the United States may suffer injury from the sale of imported goods. The WTO identifies three types of actionable subsidies: (1) subsidies that provide advantages over rival exporters in a third-country market; (2) subsidies that benefit the domestic market over exporters to that country; and (3) subsidies that damage the domestic market in the importing country.

Figure 5.8. Input subsidies and price supports for an import producer

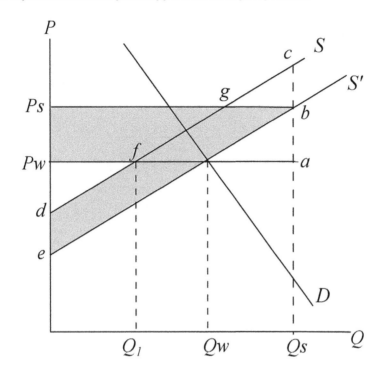

Under the WTO agreement, dumping actions can be imposed when the following two conditions are met. First, the US Department of Commerce determines that foreign goods may be selling at less than fair value. Second, the US International Trade Commission determines that an industry in the United States may suffer a verified injury from the sale of the goods. Often, a dumping action involves charging extra import tariffs to bring the price closer to normal value (i.e., the price in the domestic market). Normal value can be calculated three different ways: (1) comparing the export price with the price in the exporter's domestic market; (2) comparing the export price with the price charged in a third-country market; or (3) a combination of the exporter's production costs, expenses, and normal profit.

5.7   PRICE SUPPORTS AND STORAGE

Many policy analysts argue that agricultural policies that provide both price and income stability should be supported. Price stability is discussed with reference to commodity storage, recognizing that there are additional avenues to generate stability, such as optimal hedging strategies (Feder, Just, and Schmitz 1980). The general conclusion is that society may well prefer stability to instability, but this need not be the case under price certainty (A. Schmitz 2018a, 2018b).

Figure 5.9. Storage under price supports and loan rates

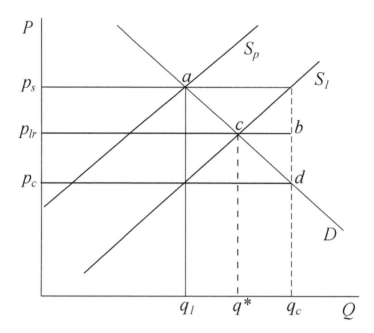

In analysing the impact of commodity storage, the interaction of storage and other policy instruments has to be taken into account. For example, the United States had two policy instruments for grains: target price and loan rate. In the 1990s, these policies contributed to a massive accumulation of stocks. Figure 5.9 incorporates both a price support and a loan rate policy instrument. In period 1, the equilibrium price and quantity in the absence of government are p_s and q_1, respectively. In period 2, the equilibrium price and quantity are p_{lr} and q^*, respectively. Now suppose the government supports price at p_s and sets the loan rate at p_{lr}. What is the effect of a supply shock that shifts supply from S_p to S_1? In the absence of the loan rate, the market would clear at price pc. However, with the loan rate in place, storage of $q_c q^*$ is required, which is equal to the amount cb.

5.8   SUMMARY AND CONCLUSIONS

- Agriculture, food policy, and trade are critically interdependent. Quotas, subsidies, and other price supports factor into these relationships.
- This chapter presents models with domestic production quotas in place for both export and import goods.
- The gains and losses from producer subsidies are likewise given for export and import goods.

- Producers generally gain from production quotas and price support subsidies, while consumers generally lose from production quotas but gain from subsidies.
- From an international trading perspective, a country can gain from production quotas, as in the case of the US tobacco production quota program.
- The Japanese government supports its domestic beef industry through tariffs and price supports. The gains from removing Japanese tariffs are greatly reduced if Japan keeps domestic producer price supports in place.
- Countries often use both input and output subsidies in the production of a given commodity.
- Trade models become increasingly complicated when the impact of both input and output subsidies are taken together in determining gains from trade. They become even more complicated when storage is added.

CHAPTER SIX

Disruptions in the Value Chain

6.1 INTRODUCTION

Decision makers are often interested not only in the direct welfare impacts of policies, but also in their potential effects on other sectors of the value chain. Lobbying of policy makers by input suppliers and processors can have an effect on farm policy. For example, grain companies such as Cargill are interested primarily in shipping and handling, which means that they prefer policies that facilitate greater production. Meanwhile, insurance companies lobby for government subsidization of crop yield and revenue insurance premiums, and direct payments to cover the administrative and operating costs of providing protection against risks (Chapter 8). In addition to concerns about efficiency and income distribution, legislators are concerned about employment in upstream and downstream sectors of the economy, especially when such sectors are located in a legislator's home district. In this chapter, therefore, we examine how welfare impacts are measured in vertical (and horizontal) markets, with particular focus on disruptions in the value chain.

6.2 DISRUPTIONS IN THE FOOD VALUE CHAIN

The US beef industry provides the basis for food value chain analysis. We begin with a discussion of the link between beef production and a major feed component (corn).

6.2.1 The Link between Beef Production and Corn

The US beef industry is discussed in Figure 6.1a. The United States exports Q_1Q_2 of beef at price P_1, given supply function S. Correspondingly, in Figure 6.1b, at price P_0, the United States will export Q^*Q_0 of corn, a major ingredient for US beef production.

Figure 6.1. Disruptions in the food value chain

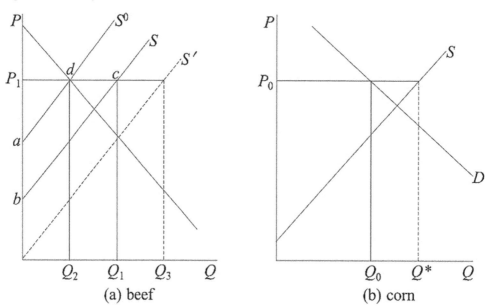

(a) beef

(b) corn

Now consider two different types of disruption. As a historical example, China shut its border to corn imports from the United States (T.G. Schmitz 2018). This lowers the internal corn price in the United States, causing the US supply of beef to shift from S to S'. At a fixed price P_1, exports of beef from the United States increase by Q_3Q_1. Second, as an alternative, consider the US policy of using corn for ethanol production. The price of corn increases, making beef production costlier for the United States, and so the US beef supply curve shifts to S^0. At price P_1, beef exports cease, and US beef producers lose (*abcd*).

Beef production is affected by rising corn prices, in part caused by corn-based ethanol. The beef sector typically operates through three markets that occur around approximate weight classes. First, cow-calf operators sell their cattle at a weight of 400–600 pounds as stocker cattle to backgrounders, who either pasture or feed the cattle until they reach a weight of 700–800 pounds. These stocker cattle are then marketed as feeder cattle to feedlot operators, who fatten the cattle to a finished weight of over 1,100 pounds. The fattened cattle (of which corn is a major input) are then sold to packing plants that butcher the cattle and sell the meat for human consumption. Partial equilibrium analysis can demonstrate how increased ethanol prices affect these three cattle markets in the vertical channel prior to increased ethanol production (T.G. Schmitz, A. Schmitz, and Moss 2005a).

In the beef value chain, the supply curve for cow-calf operators before any disruptions in the value chain is S_R (Figure 6.2). The marginal cost for backgrounding cattle is given by S_F,

Figure 6.2. Beef cattle chain

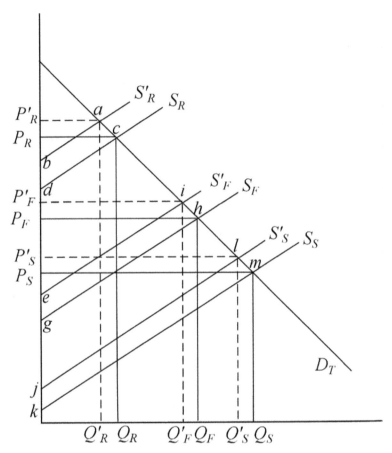

while the marginal cost for producing fat cattle is S_S. The demand curve for all beef is given by D_T. In this situation, the prices for feeder cattle, stockers, and fat cattle are P_R, P_F, and P_S, respectively. The quantities produced are Q_R, Q_F, and Q_S. The corresponding rents are $P_R dc$ (for feeder cattle), $P_F gh$ (for stockers), and $P_S km$ (for fat cattle). Therefore, the total industry rents, not including packing and retailing, are the sum of three rents above.

6.2.2   Market Disruption: Ethanol Production from Corn

Consider the introduction of the US ethanol program, where subsidies to corn ethanol manufacturers caused corn to be used to produce ethanol. The increase in ethanol production caused corn prices to rise roughly 15–20 per cent. In turn, this price increase has disrupted the supply chain for beef since corn is a major feed ingredient for livestock.

Initially, higher corn prices create an additional cost for feedlot operators who produce fat cattle, which in turn influences the price for stockers and cow-calf operators. The additional cost is introduced into the model as an inward shift in the supply curve for fat cattle from S_s to S'_s (Figure 6.2). Consumers of beef produced from fat cattle lose ($P'_S P_S\, ml$) in consumer surplus due to increased prices. Even though the price that feedlots receive for sales of fat cattle rises to P'_S, because the quantity of fat cattle sold decreases to Q'_S, feedlot operators lose $[(P_S mk) - (P'_S lj)]$. Also note that the supply of feeder calves shifts to S'_R and the supply of stockers shifts to S'_F Therefore, the sector that produces stocker cattle loses $[(pfgh)-(P_F\, ei)]$. Correspondingly, the cow-calf operators lose $[(P_R\, P'_F\, c) - (P'_R\, da)]$. Therefore, the impact of the US ethanol program on the cattle-producing sector is the sum of the changes in rents to each sector.

6.2.3   Market Disruption: BSE (Mad Cow Disease)

Figure 6.3 illustrates the effect in the beef supply chain from the presence of bovine spongiform encephalopathy (BSE), commonly known as mad cow disease. Initially, the demand for beef is given by D_T, but the effect of BSE causes a shift in demand to D'_T. Using the same logic as above, the loss to the feedlot sector is ($P_S P'_S xm$), the loss to the stocker sector is ($P_F P'_F yh$), and the loss to the cow-calf operators is ($P_R P'_R zc$). Therefore, the total loss from BSE is $[(P_S\, P'_S)+(P_F P'_F yh)+(P_R P'_R zc)]$.

6.2.4   Market Disruption: Price of Feeder Steers and Slaughter Animals

To add empirical content to the above model, we use ordinary least squares (OLS) to estimate the price of Oklahoma City feeder steers (med. No. 1, 600–650 pounds) as a linear function of the price of Nebraska slaughter steers (choice 2–4, 1,100–1,300 pounds) and the average corn price received by farmers in the United States. Data on cattle and corn are taken from the United States Department of Agriculture (USDA) and the United States Department of Agriculture, National Agricultural Statistics Service (USDA-NASS), respectively.

The following relationship is derived using ordinary least squares: (Feeder Steer Price) = −0.64 + 1.46 (Slaughter Steer Price) − 8.40 (US Corn Price). The R-square associated with the regression is 89 per cent, and both variables are significant at the 99 per cent level. Thus, corn prices negatively affect feeder cattle prices. The more inelastic the supply curve facing the feeder cattle sector, the greater the loss in economic rents from an increase in corn prices triggered by the expansion of ethanol production.

6.3   TRADE IN VALUE CHAINS

Value chain analysis is also important when discussing food sectors, such as the beef sector, in the context of international trade. Figure 6.4 represents the beef sector example in a trade context.

Figure 6.3. The effect of BSE for cattle producers

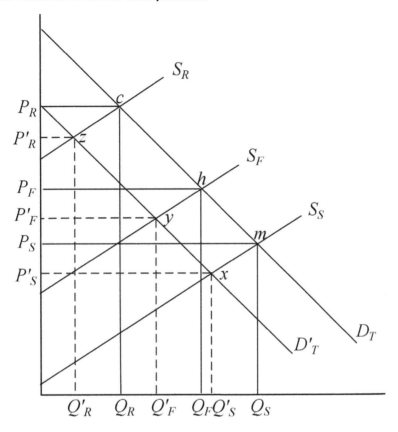

Without trade: In Figure 6.4, S_m is domestic supply for the importer and D_m is domestic demand. When trade is not a factor, the domestic price is P_m, output is Q_0, and for the exporter, D_T is demand under no trade. The supply of feeder cattle is S_R, S_F for stockers, and S_S for fat cattle, with corresponding prices of P_R, P_F, and P_S. Under no trade, the three sectors earn the following rents: (abc), (def), and (ghi).

With trade: With trade, the free trade price is P'_m, where imports total Q_1Q_2. Trade causes the demand in the exporting country to change from D_T to D'_T, where exports Q_3Q_4 equal Q_1Q_2. The prices for S_R, S_F, and S_S increase to P'_R, P'_F, and P'_S, respectively. Along with the price increase, corresponding rents also increase. For example, the rents to the fat cattle sector increase by $(lgij)$. Thus, under freer trade, total rent to the fat cattle sector becomes (lhj). Free trade increases the total rents from all sectors to $[(lgij) + (kdfp) + (vacq)]$. As a result, one must account for changes in rents across all beef-production sectors that would result from a change in trade barriers.

This example demonstrates that when examining the impact of freer trade on an exporting country, one can only calculate accurate gains or losses by accounting for rent shifts in all

Figure 6.4. Value chain analysis and trade

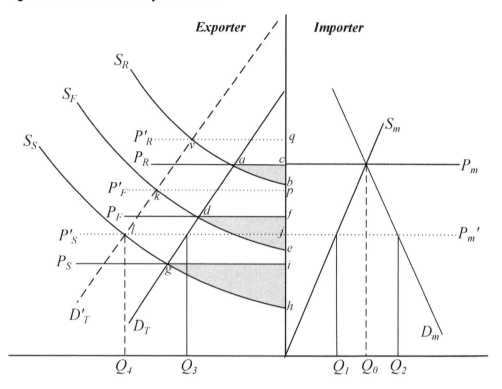

market segments. Gains will be understated if one considers the increase in rent to only one market (for example, fattened cattle).

6.4 SWEETENER VALUE CHAIN AND CORN FOR ETHANOL PRODUCTION

The United States sweetener market provides another interesting example of complex value chains, partly because sugar is tied to corn, due to high fructose corn syrup (HFCS) production and the ethanol program. The market for US sugar production and consumption is given in Figure 6.5a, where the no-trade price and quantity are p_0 and q_0. At the free trade world price p_w, the US imports $q_1 q_2$ of sugar. Below we discuss two potential disruptions to this value chain: sugar import quotas and the emergence of corn-based ethanol.

Disruption 1: The United States imposes quotas on sugar imports. For a quota of $q_3 q_4$, the internal US price is p'_w. How does this price increase affect related markets? One of sugar's major competitors is HFCS (Figure 6.5b). Prior to the sugar import quota, the HFCS price is

Figure 6.5. (a) US sugar market; (b) US HFCS market; (c) US corn market

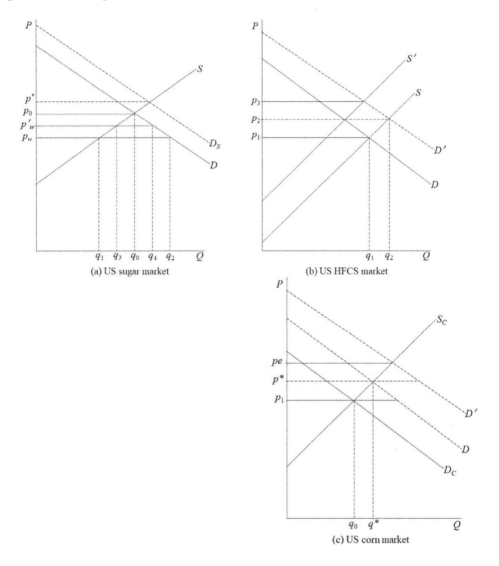

(a) US sugar market

(b) US HFCS market

(c) US corn market

p_1 and quantity is q_1. The sugar import quota increases the price of HFCS to p_2. In addition, the price of corn increases from p_0 to p^* due to the increased demand for corn.

Disruption 2: Now consider the effect of the US corn ethanol program. The demand for corn shifts to D^e with an increase in corn prices to p^e (Figure 6.5c). This increases the price of corn for US HFCS refiners, causing the supply of HFCS to shift leftward to S' (Figure 6.5b). In the case of no trade, at price p_3, because of the substitution between sugar and HFCS, the price of sugar increases to p^*. However, when trade is possible, sugar quotas lead to significant gains for US sugar producers.

6.5   SLEEPY CREEK LANDS

Disruptions to supply chains may come from several sources, including entrepreneurial innovations and environmental policies. An example of one such disruption is the case of Sleepy Creek Lands (formerly Adena Springs Ranch) in Marion County, Florida (Moss and Schmitz 2013). In August of 2012, Sleepy Creek Lands requested permission from the state to pump 13.267 million gallons of water per day (mgd) from the springshed (part of the Floridian aquifer) to Silver Springs, located in north Florida, for their large, grass-fed cow-calf operation. After acquiring consumptive water permits to pump only 1.46 mgd, they submitted a new request to pump greater amounts of water from the aquifer for future expansion of their cattle ranch. This value chain would replace the standard marketing channel in which Florida produces stocker cattle that are backgrounded and fed in the plains.

The attempt by Sleepy Creek Lands to produce and market grass-fed cattle in Florida can be analysed in our value chain model. The aim of Sleepy Creek Lands cattle ranch was to remove their portion of the aggregate feeder calf supply curve (S_R) and market these cattle as grass-fed, based on the assumption that more money can be made marketing grass-fed cattle than grain-fed cattle.

However, the gains from the innovation towards grass-fed beef tell only part of the story. Environmental groups contend that the massive quantity of water being pumped at the springshed by Sleepy Creek Lands threatens the environmental quality of the springs in the area. This debate has intensified after the renewed request by Sleepy Creek Lands to pump even more water from the springshed.

6.6   MEASURING WELFARE IMPACTS IN RELATED MARKETS[1]

The measurement of welfare impacts is complex and poses a problem for economists whenever policies that are implemented in one market impact related markets. Suppose that a policy affects some market, denoted as A. Markets related to A could be upstream or downstream from A, and thus part of a vertical chain, or they might be horizontal markets of goods that are complements or substitutes for A. An example of a vertical chain is the market for logs, which are then processed into lumber that is subsequently used in the construction of buildings or the manufacture of furniture. Upstream from the market for logs are markets for logging trucks, harvesting equipment, diesel fuel, and so on. A policy that restricts the harvest of logs will have an impact on the market for harvesting equipment (e.g., chainsaws) because the log restriction shifts inward the derived demands for chainsaws and diesel fuel for use in harvest operations.

Consider a different example. A vertical chain of markets might begin with fertilizer used to grow wheat that is used to make food products, such as bread and pastries. A regulation that requires farmers to use less fertilizer will affect the supply of wheat, thereby affecting both the market in which wheat is traded and the markets for bread and pastries. To measure the welfare changes that occur because of restrictions on logs and fertilizer requires that economists take into account the upstream (diesel fuel) and downstream (bread/pastry) markets.

Not only do the welfare impacts on upstream and downstream markets need to be taken into account, impacts on horizontal markets must also be considered. For example, if a restriction on logs raises the price of lumber (as fewer logs are available to produce lumber), construction companies will be inclined to substitute aluminum for lumber in building construction.

The question that faces the economist is this: to what extent can one measure welfare impacts in the market directly affected by a policy change or disruption such as a wildfire that destroys a large amount of commercial timber or a drought that affects agricultural crops? It would be an onerous task to consider all of the markets that might be impacted. In addition, it would be too expensive, and perhaps impossible, to measure the welfare changes of a policy/disruption across all potential vertical and horizontal markets that might be affected.

Fortunately, economic theory enables us to impose limits on what needs to be measured in other related markets. Under certain restrictive assumptions, all measurements of welfare changes can occur only in the market directly affected by the change in policy or some other disturbance. The theory of welfare measurement in these circumstances can be found in seminal publications by Boadway and Bruce (1984) and R.E. Just, Hueth, and Schmitz (2004). We provide a brief summary of the main points below.

6.6.1   Measuring Welfare across Vertical Markets

The most difficult aspect of welfare measurement concerns vertical chains. As noted, a disruption in one market will affect upstream and downstream markets. Suppose there is a disruption in market A. The producer surplus (area above the supply function and below price) in market A will likely change, but it can be measured directly in market A. It can also be measured as a consumer surplus in the upstream market, say market A_U, because the suppliers of good A have a derived demand for input A_U. As long as the price in market A_U is unaffected by the disruption in downstream market A, and A_U is the only input used to produce A, the change in consumer surplus in A_U due to a shift in demand for A_U will be identical to the change in producer surplus in A. Further, the assumption that the price in the input market remains unchanged implies that the supply function is horizontal, in which case there is no change in the surplus accruing to suppliers of input A_U because of the disruption in market A.

It should be noted that if there are multiple inputs, then the changes in consumer surplus across all input markets need to be summed across those markets, and the restriction that the price in market A_U be unchanged must hold for all upstream markets. For technical details pertaining to welfare measurement within vertical chains and across horizontal markets, see van Kooten and Voss (2021, 27–38).

Now consider the downstream market in which good A is a final consumer good or an input into yet another good farther downstream. Denote the market downstream of A as A_D.

The demand function for goods in market A are derived demands by suppliers in market A_D. As noted above, one can measure the changes in the producer surplus in market A_D as the consumer surplus in market A. However, given that the disruption in market A also might affect the consumer surplus in downstream market A_D, it is necessary to impose a restriction on the demand function in market A_D – the demand function must be infinitely elastic (horizontal) so the price in market A_D is unaffected by the disruption in market A. In that case, there is no change in consumer surplus in downstream market A_D.

It is possible to measure all the welfare changes of a disruption or policy affecting market A in that market alone. By assumption, there is no producer surplus to measure in upstream market A while the consumer surplus in that market can just as well be measured as the producer surplus in market A. Likewise, by assuming no price changes in the downstream market A_D, there is no change in consumer surplus in that market. The change in producer surplus in market A_D can be measured as the change in consumer surplus under the derived demand functions in market A. Thus, by imposing some (perhaps restrictive) assumptions, it is possible to confine the measurement of changes in welfare due to a disruption or policy affecting a market in that market only. Given the multitude of upstream and downstream markets in a vertical chain, these assumptions enable economists to estimate the costs and benefits in markets directly affected by disruptions and policies.

6.6.2   Markets for Complements and Substitutes: Horizontal Markets

What about markets for goods that are complements or substitutes of a commodity affected by a disruption? Economic theory indicates that welfare measurement in these horizontal markets needs to be accounted for only if there is a distortion in any market for complements or substitutes. A distortion implies that price exceeds marginal cost – that the demand price exceeds the supply price. If price equals marginal cost (supply equals demand) in a distorted market, then there is no need to take into account welfare measures in those horizontal markets. However, if price exceeds marginal cost, then all that needs to be determined is the extent to which a disruption in market A will change purchases in a horizontal market.

Let A_C denote commodities that are complements of A, and let A_S denote substitutes of A. Further, assume that these two markets are distorted so that price (which represents the marginal benefit) exceeds marginal cost. A disruption or policy that increases the price of A will reduce demand for the complementary good A_C but increase demand for the substitutionary good A_S. Given the distortions in A_C and A_S, it will be necessary to measure the changes in welfare those markets brought about by the disruption/policy affecting A. That is, in addition to measuring the welfare changes in market A, it will be necessary to take into account the welfare changes in markets A_C and A_S. A correct measure of these welfare changes would require that we determine the supply and demand functions in the complementary and substitutionary markets, and measure the changes in the surpluses accruing to consumers and producers.

However, one can approximate the total welfare changes by determining the changes in purchases of complements A_C and substitutes A_S.

An increase in the price of A will reduce purchases of the complementary good A_C and increase the purchase of the substitute A_S. If these are the only horizontal markets affected by the disruption in market A, then an approximate welfare measure is the following (Boadway and Bruce 1984):

$$\Delta W_H = \Delta Q_C(P_C - MC_C) + \Delta Q_S(P_S - MC_S),$$

where ΔW_H represents the change in welfare in distorted horizontal markets. ΔQ_C and ΔQ_S refer to the changes in purchases in the complementary and substitutionary markets, respectively, and $P_C - MC_C$ is the difference between the price and marginal cost for the complementary good and $P_S - MC_S$ is the difference between price and marginal cost for the substitute good.

6.6.3   Export Taxes: The Use of Excess Supply and Demand Curves

Countries use trade policy to protect domestic suppliers or to collect rents that would otherwise accrue to a foreign entity. For example, the United States imposes tariffs (export taxes are prohibited in the United States) on Canadian softwood lumber to protect their own lumber manufacturers. In the past, the Canadian government had negotiated the use of an export tax in lieu of a US import duty. An export tax imposed by Canada on exports of softwood lumber to the United States is, in principle, no different from a tariff applied by the United States on Canadian imports. The only difference concerns the party collecting the tax. If Canada imposes an export tax, Canada collects the revenue; if the United States imposes a tariff, it collects the revenue. In either case, US lumber producers are protected against competition from Canada.

There is an alternative to export taxes and import tariffs. Canada's lumber producers could restrict exports so that they would equal US imports of softwood lumber that would occur under a tariff – there would be a quota on exports of Canadian lumber to the United States. Canadian producers do not gain welfare via a revenue instrument but, rather, collect the artificially created quota rent. The only problem with a quota regime is the need for Canadian lumber exporters to form a cartel that can exercise monopoly power.

A theoretical framework for finding the optimal export tax is provided in Figure 6.6, where we employ excess supply and demand curves. The excess supply curve for logs and lumber is ES_{log} and the excess demand is ED_{log}. At price P_L, log exports total Q_L. The corresponding equilibrium in the lumber market is given in panel (b). The excess demand and supply functions for lumber are given by ED_{lum} and ES_{lum}. At price P^*_L, lumber exports are Q_L^*. The optimal export tax on logs in panel (a) is $(P_C - P_P)$, where the government collects tax revenue of $(P_C P_P ba)$. Log exports are reduced to Q_C with the exporter gaining $(P_C P_L da - dbe)$ from the tax. However, this

Figure 6.6. Export tax

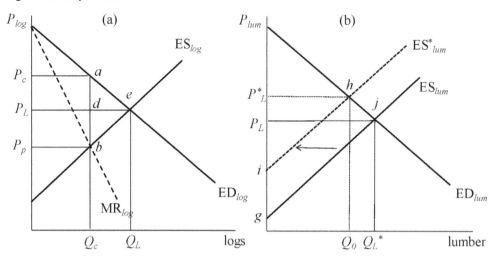

is not the case when lumber exports are taken into account. The tax on logs causes the excess supply curve of lumber to shift left from ES_{lum} to ES^*_{lum} (as shown by the arrow). The lumber price increases to P_L^* from P_L and exports fall to Q_0. The tax on log exports creates a loss in the lumber sector of ($P_Lgj - P_L^*ih$). (One can also use this framework to consider the effects of an optimal tax on lumber exports rather than on logs, or a tax on both logs and lumber.)

As an example, consider the case where Russia imposed an export tax on logs that was as high as 25 per cent (Simeone and Eastin 2012). What are the welfare impacts of such an export tax? As noted above, since logs and lumber are in the same vertical chain, and we assume downward sloping supply of logs, it is necessary to measure welfare in both the log and lumber markets, while avoiding double counting (e.g., producer surplus in the lumber market equals consumer surplus in the log market). Due to World Trade Organization (WTO) negotiations, the log export tax is converted to a quota on what Russia exports. The changes in welfare caused by the Russian policy were investigated by van Kooten and Johnston (2014), who developed a numerical trade model with several global regions to investigate the welfare impacts of removing the 25 per cent export tax that Russia had imposed on log exports that went mainly to China. A summary of the findings is provided in Table 6.1. Notice that the supply of logs is an upward sloping function, whereas the demand function is downward sloping. While we measure the change in producer surplus in the log market, we do not measure the change in consumer surplus in the log market. The reason for the latter is that the demand function in the log market is a derived demand, with the surplus area under the derived demand in the log market identical to the producer surplus in the upstream lumber market (as noted above). Since the demand for lumber is downward sloping and not horizontal, we also measure the welfare impact of liberalizing Russian log exports on the consumers of lumber (even though these might not be the final consumers but further processors, such as construction companies).

Table 6.1. Annual welfare implications of removing a Russian export tax on logs (US$ million)

Country	Log Market Δ in producer surplus	Lumber Market Δ in consumer surplus	Lumber Market Δ in producer surplus	Total Δ in total welfare
Canada	+92.1	−79.9	+780.8	+183.0
United States	−64.5	−326.6	+280.0	−111.1
China	−56.1	−161.2	+117.2	−100.1
Russia	+2,304.3	−51.6	+313.8	+1,938.9

Removal of the disruption in the supply chain caused by the Russian tax on log exports has ramifications beyond Russia and its Chinese trading partner. Removal of the tax on log exports raises the price of logs in the domestic Russian market, leading to a large increase in log production and increase in producer surplus accruing to Russian loggers (essentially landowners). They gain nearly US$2 billion per year. The increase in Russian log exports reduces prices of logs elsewhere, with US loggers losing US$65 million per year and Chinese loggers some US$56 million as they both import more logs. Despite the lower cost of logs, lumber production in all markets, and especially Russia, declines as the lower cost of logs leads to less log production in all jurisdictions, except Canada. In Canada, exports of logs decline, with logs now destined for the domestic market; log output increases by more than three million cubic metres, thereby accounting for the increase in producer surplus in the log market. As the world's lowest-cost producer, Canada's exports of lumber rise accordingly, displacing domestic production of lumber in other regions. Surprisingly, global output of lumber declines somewhat because of the lower log production in most countries. These results indicate the intricacies of liberalizing global markets—low-cost producers benefit at the expense of high-cost producers, with impacts spread across countries in unexpected ways.

6.7   MARKET CONFUSION: CORONAVIRUS PANDEMIC

At the end of 2019, a deadly coronavirus was identified which caused a global pandemic. Millions of people worldwide have died due to the respiratory illness COVID-19, which is caused by the virus severe acute respiratory syndrome coronavirus 2 (SARS-CoV-2).

In the United States, supply chains for many commodities were disrupted by the pandemic. A major disruption occurred in shipping and transportation (Voiland 2021). For two of the busiest US ports (Port of Los Angeles and Port of Long Beach in Southern California), the number of cargo ships waiting to be unloaded reached a record high of seventy-three on 19 September 2021. Before the pandemic, cargo ships rarely waited to unload cargo.

Ship backlogs at ports were not just limited to the United States. Ports in Malaysia, Singapore, Hong Kong, and Shanghai all had ten or more cargo ships waiting in mid-October 2021.

CARGO SHIPS: WAITING TO UNLOAD

"Booming demand for consumer and goods, labor shortages, bad weather, and an array of COVID-related supply chain snarls are contributing to backlogs of cargo ships at ports around the world" (Voiland 2021).

The supply chain of many commodities was disrupted by COVID-19. For example, the gas-oil complex was seriously disrupted by the pandemic. Other examples discussed below include meat (beef, pork, and poultry), canola, wheat, corn, oats, and cotton.

Keep in mind that these data do not necessarily identify the impact due to the pandemic. There are many factors that could have affected market changes in addition to the pandemic. To calculate the economic impact of the COVID-19 pandemic separately from other factors, the theoretical models presented earlier would have to be empirically estimated to identify the impact caused solely by the pandemic.

COST OF THE PANDEMIC IN 2020

"The COVID-19 crisis created large economic losses for corn, ethanol, gasoline, and oil producers and refineries both in the United States and worldwide. Schmitz and Moss estimate within a welfare economic cost-benefit framework that, at a minimum, the producer cost due to COVID-19 in the United States for these four sectors totals US$176.8 billion for 2020. For US oil producers alone, the cost was US$151 billion. When world oil is added, the costs are much higher, at US$1055.8 billion. The total oil producer cost is US$1.03 trillion, which is roughly 40 times the effect on US corn, ethanol, and gasoline producers, and refineries. If the assumed unemployment effects from COVID-19 are taken into account, the total effect, including both producers and unemployed workers, is US$212.2 billion, bringing the world total to US$1266.9 million" (A. Schmitz et al. 2020, 1).

The pandemic negatively impacted the economic sectors of many countries on a global scale. The US agricultural and food sectors were among those. The meat industry, which is a major component of the US food supply chain, experienced widespread shutdowns due to large numbers of meat processing employees contracting COVID-19. McLean (2020) states that pork processing plants were hit especially hard, with three of the largest in the United States going offline in the long term: Smithfield in Sioux Falls, South Dakota; JBS in Worthington, Minnesota; and Tyson in Waterloo, Iowa.

According to John Tyson of Tyson Foods, "the food supply chain is breaking. US farmers don't have anywhere to sell their livestock. Millions of animals – chickens, pigs, and cattle – will be depopulated because of the closure of our processing facilities. There will be limited supply of our products available in grocery stores until we are able to reopen our facilities that are currently closed" (McLean 2020).

6.7.1   Beef, Pork, and Poultry

In the United States, the meat sector was severely impacted by the pandemic. The major impact occurred at the packing plant level.

> **TYSON FOODS: WARNING ABOUT FOOD SUPPLY CHAIN PROBLEM**
> Tyson Foods has issued a warning that "millions of pounds of meat" will disappear from the US food supply chain as the coronavirus (COVID-19) pandemic pushes meat processing plants to close, leading to product shortages in grocery stores across the United States (McLean 2020).

To highlight the discussion above, consider Figure 6.7, where D is the demand for meat produced by the processing sector whose marginal cost is MC and average total cost is ATC. These existed prior to the COVID-19 pandemic. The amount of meat sold is q_0 at a price p_0.

The pandemic impacted the meat processing sector in the following manner. Because of the shutdown of processing plants due to the virus, costs shifted upward to ATC' and MC'. The price of beef increased to p_1 and output was reduced to q_1. The processing sector lost as a result of the virus, as did consumers. The consumer loss is given by $(p_1 p_0 ab)$. This situation also has negative effects on, for example, the beef production chain from the cow-calf sector to fat cattle production.

Figure 6.8 shows the retail price of USDA choice sirloin steak from September 2019 to September 2021. Retail price peaked in June 2020 at US$10.42/lb. Comparatively, Figure 6.9 show the price of feeder cattle. Over the same period that retail beef prices were rising significantly, the price of feeder cattle dropped substantially. From the beginning of 2021 onwards, prices of both retail beef steak and feeder cattle have recovered past their 2020 values.

Some would argue that monopoly pricing on the part of the meat packers was part of the cause for the instability in cattle prices. Others, like Azzam and Dhoubhadel (2021), argue otherwise.

US pork (swine) prices are given in Figure 6.10 for October 2016 to October 2021. A historically low price of US$0.40/lb correlated with the onset of the pandemic in April 2020. The price of pork/swine recovered and more than doubled by June 2021 with a high price of US$1.16/lb. An interesting component of the increase in pork/swine demand is the increase in

Figure 6.7. Meat processors and COVID-19

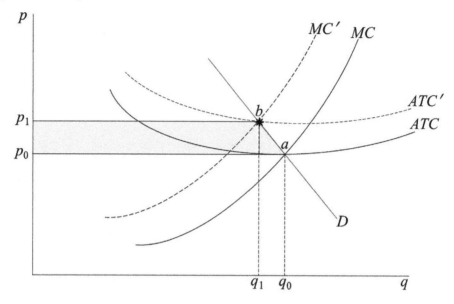

Figure 6.8. US retail price for beef sirlon USDA Choice (US$/lb), September 2019–September 2021

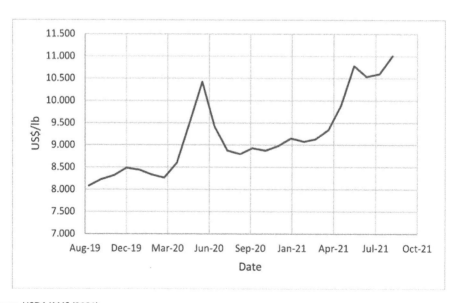

Source: USDA/AMS (2021).

Figure 6.9. US feeder cattle price (US$/lb), October 2016–October 2021

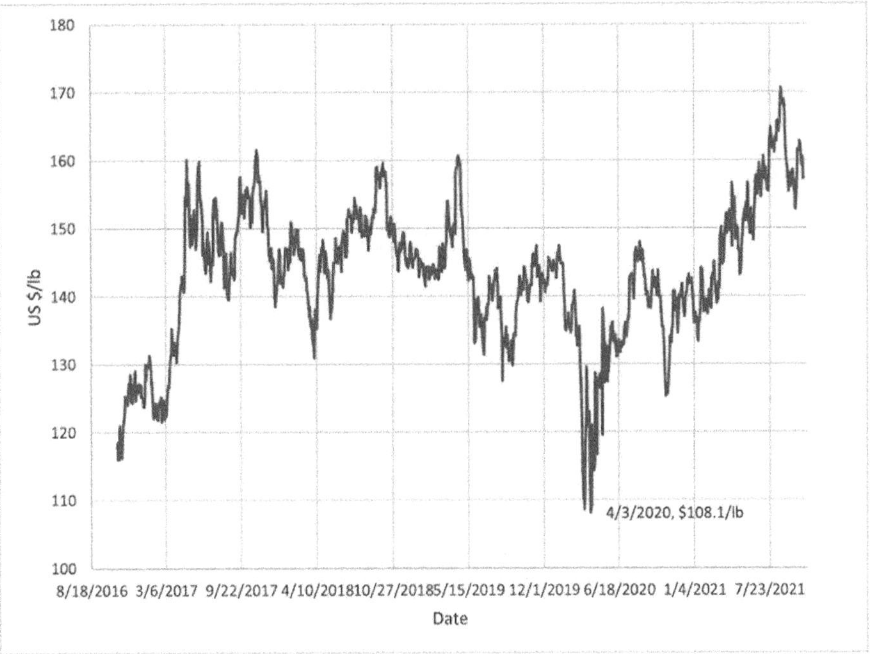

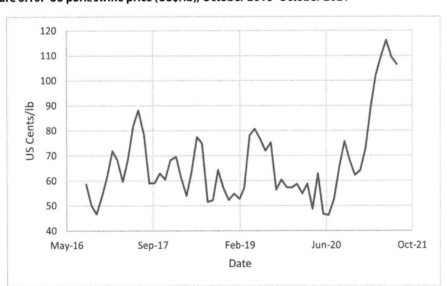

Source: Nasdaq (2021).

Figure 6.10. US pork/swine price (US$/lb), October 2016–October 2021

Source: CME Group (2021).

Figure 6.11. US live poultry price (US$/kg), October 2016–October 2021

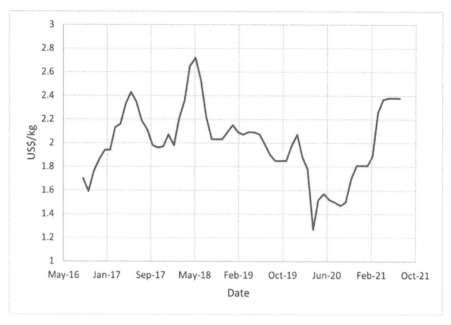

Source: USDA/AMS (2021).

the retail price of bacon. According to the USDA, the price of bacon increased from US$5.35/lb to US$7.22/lb in September 2021.

Figure 6.11 shows the price of live poultry in the United States from October 2016 to October 2021. From the period of onset of the pandemic in March 2020, the price of live poultry dropped by 78 per cent from US$1.78/kg to US$1.27/kg month over month to April 2020.

6.7.2   Canola and Durum Wheat Prices

The price of two major crops, canola and durum wheat, reached all-time highs in October 2021. Prices of canola more than doubled and prices of durum wheat tripled since March 2020. This was a historically unprecedented price increase. The price of canola reached over C$20/bu (per bushel) while the price of durum wheat reached C$21/bu.

> **HIGH PRICES IN SASKATCHEWAN, CANADA, 2021**
> These are elevator prices for canola and durum wheat received by producers in Saskatchewan in October 2021. The commodity prices paid by Richardson International (canola) and Canada Limited (durum wheat) were at historic highs.

Figure 6.12. US corn price (US$/lb), January 2000–October 2021

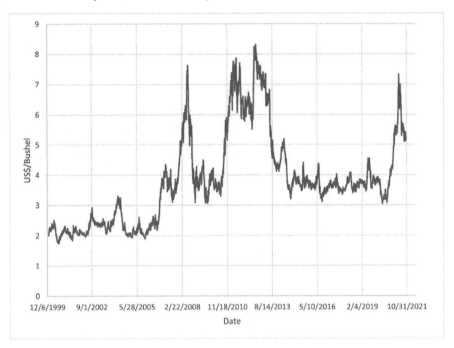

Source: USDA/NASS (2021).

RICHARDSON

Richardson International

SETTLEMENT DOCUMENT

Account: Schmitz Ranch

Receipt Date	Product	Price/Net MT
10/20/21	SK Canola	$927.37 CAD

G3 Canada Limited

SETTLEMENT DOCUMENT

Account: Schmitz Ranch

Receipt Date	Product	Price/Net MT
10/21/21	SK Durum	$771.62 CAD

6.7.3   Corn

Figure 6.12 shows the price of corn in the United States from January 2000 to October 2021. From April 2020 to May 2021, the price of corn almost doubled from US$3.07/bu to US$7.89/bu. From May 2021 to October 2021, the price of corn fell from US$7.80/bu to US$5.25/bu.

Figure 6.13. US oats price (US$/bu), January 2000–October 2021

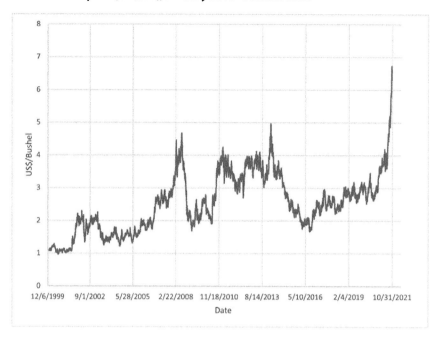

Source: Macrotrends (2021b).

Figure 6.14. US cotton price (US$/lb), October 2019–October 2021

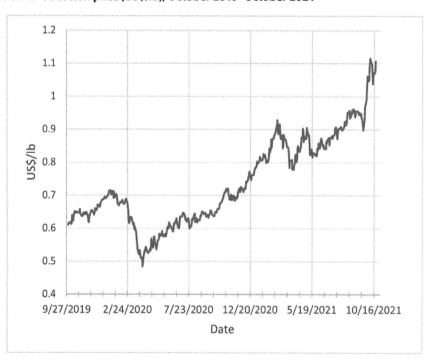

Source: Macrotrends (2021c).

6.7.4   Oats

Figure 6.13 shows the price of oats in the United States from January 2000 to October 2021. From March 2020 to October 2021, the price of oats more than doubled from US$2.53/bu to a historic twenty-year high of US$6.56/bu.

> **OAT PRICE VOLATILITY**
> During the month of October 2021, oat prices increased sharply. The contract price for oats (according to Lyle Funk, oat farmer in Canada) for January 2022 delivery was set at C$10.50/bu.

6.7.5   Cotton

Figure 6.14 shows the price of cotton in the United States from October 2019 to October 2021. From March 2020 to October 2021, the price of cotton doubled from US$0.48/lb to US$1.11/lb.

6.8   SUMMARY AND CONCLUSIONS

- Value chain analysis is important for quantitative research in trade.
- Disruptions in the food value chain are many, including animal diseases, pandemics, and subsidies to produce biofuels from crops.
- In value chain analysis, it is possible to work out the effect of a policy that directly affects one of the components in the value chain.
- The analysis of lumber clearly illustrates the complexities associated with comparing different market structures.

CHAPTER SEVEN

United States Agricultural Policy

7.1 US STABILIZATION: POLICIES AND DIRECT FARM SUBSIDIES

Agricultural commodity and conservation legislation in the United States has its roots in the Agricultural Adjustment Act of 1933. Since that time, the United States has passed more than a dozen farm bills spaced five to seven years apart. This chapter presents the key components of several of the farm bills and analyses some major US crops (corn, wheat, barley, cotton, oilseeds, and rice) along with the US dairy and sugar programs. In an earlier edition (A. Schmitz, Furtan, and Baylis 2002), a detailed discussion was presented on the peanut and tobacco programs, which have changed dramatically through quota buyouts (discussed briefly in this chapter).

Agricultural difficulties in the late 1920s led to a dramatic reorientation of agricultural policies in the United States that focused on directly supporting agricultural prices. Previous agricultural policies focused on the developmental aspects of the farm sector, including land settlement. Important agricultural legislation before 1920 included the Homestead Act (1862), the Morrill Act (1862), the Hatch Act (1887), and the Smith-Lever Act (1914), which augmented the human capital resources in agriculture and the rural economy (Benedict 1953).

7.2 US AGGREGATE FARM BILL EXPENDITURES

US farm programs have generated considerable controversy partly due to the public's perception that too much taxpayer money is spent on agricultural commodity programs. The agricultural commodity programs and agricultural subsidy titles accounted for only 5.6 per cent of the actual 2018 United States Department of Agriculture (USDA) budget expenditures (US$11,983

Table 7.1. USDA agricultural budget, 2017–20 (US$ million)

| | Actual | | Estimate | Budget |
	2017	2018	2019	2020
Farm production and conservation	48,586	45,355	65,383	58,081
Farm Service Agency	35,219	29,819	46,796	40,128
Risk Management Agency	8,847	10,333	13,476	12,726
Natural Resources and Conservation Service	4,520	5,202	5,110	4,960
Farm Production and Conservation Business Center		1	1	267
Trade and foreign agricultural affairs	4,032	4,032	7,957	6,098
Rural development	40,604	41,327	43,902	38,710
Food, nutrition, and consumer services	108,323	105,126	103,421	99,168
Food safety	1,279	1,071	1,071	1,059
Natural resources and environment	6,076	7,290	6,324	7,570
Marketing and regulatory programs	2,621	2,862	3,037	2,130
Research, education, and economics	3,088	3,231	3,323	3,094
Departmental activities	426	2,793	422	723
Total USDA spending	215,035	213,087	234,840	216,633
Farm Services Agency	35,219	29,819	46,796	40,128
Farm loan and grant programs	8,003	8,006	8,048	7,674
Conservation programs	1,886	1,955	2,089	2,106
Commodity programs	17,830	11,983	28,644	22,570
Commodity Credit Corporation Export Programs	5,936	5,926	6,466	6,467
Salaries and expenses	1,516	1,520	1,520	1,307
Other programs	48	429	29	4

Source: USDA (2019, 2020).

million of US$213,087 million) and were budgeted for 12.1 per cent of the 2019 expenditures (US$28,644 million of US$234,840 million) (Table 7.1). In contrast to expenditures on agricultural commodities, expenditures on nutrition programs decreased from US$108.3 billion in 2017 to US$103.4 billion in 2019. Economic growth, measured by a reduction in the unemployment rate, which fell from 4.7 per cent in January of 2017 to 4 per cent in January of 2019, undoubtedly contributed to the decline in expenditures on nutritional programs.

USDA FOOD ASSISTANCE PROGRAMS

About one in five Americans participate in at least one of USDA's fifteen food assistance programs at some point during the year, and federal outlays for these programs account for over one-half of the USDA total budget. The Economic Research Service of USDA (USDA/ERS) studies and evaluates many aspects of these programs, including their outcomes and effects on vulnerable populations, their operations and integrity, their role in food security, and their relationship with the general economy (USDA/ERS 2008).

Table 7.2. US agricultural policies, 1929–2018

Year	Title	Overview
1929	Agricultural Marketing Act	Created Federal Farm Board to lend to cooperatives to stabilize prices through orderly marketing
1933	Agricultural Adjustment Act of 1933	Introduced the concept of parity; moved to "federalize" the cooperative stocks introduced by the Federal Farm Board for cotton, and introduced direct lending titles
1938	Agricultural Adjustment Act of 1938	Formalized the acreage allotments and parity and introduced the concept of a non-recourse loan (Section 302(h))
1948	Agricultural Act of 1948	Provided a sliding parity level for price support
1949	Agricultural Act of 1949	Formed basis for most of the permanent agricultural legislation
1954	Agricultural Act of 1954	Added trade specifications; allowed disposal of dairy surpluses
1956	Agricultural Act of 1956	Created Soil Bank, which removed agricultural land from production
1965	Food and Agriculture Act	Included voluntary acreage diversion programs for feed grains
1970	Agricultural Act of 1970	Set the maximum payment to any individual at US$55,000; broadened the acreage diversion to the set-aside program
1973	Agricultural and Consumer Protection Act	Lowered maximum payment to US$20,000 and introduced target prices and deficiency payments
1977	Food and Agriculture Act	Established the Farmer Owned Reserve; continued flexible production controls
1981	Agriculture and Food Act	Set specific target prices for the four-year life of the bill
1985	Food Security Act	Implemented loan deficiency payments
1990	Food, Agriculture, Conservation, and Trade Act	Continued to set the loan rate at 85% of the Olympic average price with a floor specified by the law
1996	Federal Agriculture Improvement and Reform Act	Replaced deficiency payments with production flexibility contracts; decoupled these payments from production
2002	Farm Security and Rural Investment Act	Introduced direct payments and transformed the production flexibility contracts into countercyclical payments
2008	Food, Conservation, and Energy Act	Continued the payments in the 2002 Act with minor changes
2014	Agricultural Act of 2014	Allowed producers to choose between agricultural risk coverage and price loss coverage
2018	Agricultural Improvement Act of 2018	Expanded programs for trade and energy

7.3   A HISTORY OF AGRICULTURAL POLICY IN THE UNITED STATES

There are many excellent books on the history of US agricultural policy. The early farm programs are discussed in detail in volumes including W.W. Cochrane and Ryan (1976), Tweeten (1970), Gardner (1981), and Knutson, Penn, and Flinchbaugh (1998). In addition, A. Schmitz et al. (2010) provide a benefit-cost analysis of several US farm programs up through 2008. What follows is a very short discussion of the history of the US farm program.

There have been many farm programs implemented in the United States (Table 7.2). These include the Agricultural Marketing Act of 1929, the Agricultural Act of 1949, the Food and Agriculture Act of 1977, the Farm Security and Rural Investment Act of 2002, and the Agricultural Improvement Act of 2018. From a historical perspective, the election of Franklin D.

Roosevelt in 1932 led to more direct policy involvement in the farm sector. The first task of the Franklin D. Roosevelt administration was to end the Federal Farm Board by transferring the Board's lending to cooperatives to the newly created Farm Credit Administration (Benedict 1953, 280). Roosevelt's New Deal also would involve direct benefits to farmers.

Below we examine the various farm programs and their effect on US agriculture over time. First, we give an overview of the farm programs, followed by a discussion of several of the farm programs enacted between 1929 and 2018 by the United States government.

AGRICULTURAL MARKETING ACT – 6 JUNE 1929

Section 1(a). That it is hereby declared to be the policy of Congress to promote the effective merchandising of agricultural commodities in interstate and foreign commerce, so that the industry of agriculture will be placed on a basis of economic equality with other industries, and to that end to protect, control, and stabilize the currents of interstate and foreign commerce in the marketing of agricultural commodities and their food products

1 By minimizing speculation.
2 By preventing inefficient and wasteful methods of distribution.
3 By encouraging the organization of producers into efficient associations or corporations under their own control for greater unity of effort in marketing and by promoting the establishment and financing of a farm marketing system of producer-owned and producer-controlled cooperative associations and other agencies.
4 By aiding in preventing and controlling surpluses in any agricultural commodity, through orderly production and distribution to maintain advantageous domestic markets and prevent such surpluses from causing undue and excessive fluctuations or depressions in prices for the commodity (Public Law 71-10 [1929, 11]).

AGRICULTURAL ADJUSTMENT ACT OF 1938

Section 302(h). No producer shall be personally liable for any deficiency arising from the sale of the collateral securing any loan [the corn, wheat, or cotton supporting the loan] under this section unless such a loan was obtained through fraudulent representation.

Section 322(a). Whenever in any calendar year the Secretary determines from available statistics of the Department, including the Crop and Livestock Estimates of the Bureau of Agricultural Economics of the Department that the total supply of corn as of October 1 will exceed the normal supply thereof by more than 10 per centum, marketing quotas shall be in effect in the commercial corn-producing area for the crop of corn grown in such area in such calendar year, and shall remain in effect until terminated in accordance with the provision of this title.

Section 332(b). The Secretary shall determine, on the basis of the estimated average yield of corn in such area for such crop, the acreage in such area which the Secretary determines would make available for the marketing year beginning October 1 a supply of corn (together with the estimated production of corn in the United States outside such area) equal to the normal supply. The percentage which the number of acres so determined is of the total number of acres of the acreage allotment under section 328 shall be proclaimed by the secretary (Public Law 75-430 [1938, 44]).

- The **Agricultural Adjustment Act of 1933** provided for direct payments to farmers in return for reduced plantings. Also, the Secretary of Agriculture was given the power "to provide for a reduction in the acreage or reduction in the production for market, or both, of any basic agricultural commodity, through agreements with producers or by other voluntary methods, and to provide rental or benefit payments in connection therewith or upon that part of the production of any basic agricultural commodity required for domestic production, in such amounts as the Secretary deems fair and reasonable, to be paid out of any moneys available for such payments ... " (Public Law 73-10, 48 Stat. 31 [1933]).
  - As described by Benedict (1953, 307), the wheat program of the Agricultural Act of 1933 involved signing a contract to reduce the amount of wheat planted by 54 per cent for payments of US$0.30 per bushel produced. In addition, the 1933 Act provided for government storage of excess commodities. The Agricultural Adjustment Act of 1933 represented a dramatic departure from the Agricultural Marketing Act of 1929.
- The **Agricultural Adjustment Act of 1938** included soil conservation payments. It also included non-recourse loans. The loan program specified a market price where farmers were given a payment if, at harvest time, the market price was less than the declared loan price. If the market price for the crop exceeded the loan price plus the interest accrued at any time during the marketing year, the farmer could reclaim the loan and sell the crop. However, if the market price never exceeded the loan rate plus accrued interest, the farmer would simply forfeit the output to the government. Given these operations, the loan rate provided a price floor for major commodities (e.g., corn, cotton and wheat). The Commodity Credit Corporation (CCC) was the government entity charged with the loan rate and often accumulated stocks of excess commodities under the terms of 1938 Act.

- The **Agricultural Act of 1948** was intended to support prices received by producers of cotton, wheat, corn, tobacco, rice, and peanuts marketed before 30 June 1950. The 1948 Act also provided for changes in the structure of the support levels in the Agricultural Adjustment Act of 1938.
- The **Agricultural Act of 1949** together with certain provisions of the Agricultural Adjustment Act of 1938 formed the basis of permanent agricultural legislation. For example, the payments and provisions for the Agricultural Improvement Act of 2018 are the marketing years 2019 through 2023. If the 2018 Act had expired without being replaced by a similar public law, agricultural program payments and provisions would have reverted to the permanent legislation under the Agricultural Adjustment Act of 1938 and the Agricultural Act of 1949. This reversion would have required the imposition of acreage allotments following the 1938 Act coupled with much higher price supports linked to the historical parity. Table 7.3 gives estimated price supports under permanent legislation.
- The **Agricultural Act of 1956** created the Soil Bank (Title I) to reduce the production of basic crops, maintain farm income, and conserve soil. The program had two components: The Acreage Reserve Program (ARP) which was intended to reduce the supply of wheat, corn, cotton, tobacco, rice and peanuts in the short run, and the Conservation Reserve Program (CRP), which attempted a permanent shift from farmland to pasture, range, forest, or wildlife uses.
- The **Food and Agriculture Act of 1965** introduced the concept of acreage reductions (e.g., normal crop acres not planted) in place of acreage allotments. The basic concept was to decrease the supply of feed grains to increase the price received by farmers by diverting cropland into conservation, including summer fallow.
- The **Agricultural and Consumer Protection Act of 1973** created a new payment system referred to as deficiency payments based on target prices. The deficiency payment was the difference between the target price and either the five-month average market price (after harvest) for the supported crop or the loan rate (whichever was higher) times the historic program yield on the farmer's allotted acres. The target price for wheat in the 1973 Act was US$2.05/bushel (bu) while the target price for corn was set at US$1.38/bu. The loan rate for wheat under the 1973 Act was US$1.37/bu, while the loan rate for corn was US$1.10/bu. The introduction of deficiency payments introduced a two-part program. At one level the loan rate, which provided a basic price floor, was retained. However, the target price represented an income support payment that was somewhat less tied to current production decisions. In the vernacular of economics, the effect of the loan rate was coupled to production decisions while the deficiency payments were more decoupled.
- The **Federal Agriculture Improvement and Reform Act of 1996** represented a significant move towards a more market-oriented agriculture. The Act transformed the deficiency payments introduced in the 1973 Act into a series of fixed production flexibility contract (PFC) payments, which declined slightly over time.

Table 7.3. Support prices under permanent legislation (US$)

Commodity	Description of Payment	Parity Price	Minimum Support	Farm Price (July 2018)	2018 Farm Bill
Milk (cwt = hundredweight)	Purchase milk and butterfat products at 75%–90% parity	52.10	75% parity = 39.08	15.40	Margin-based
Wheat (bu = bushel)	Non-recourse loans and direct purchases. Acreage allotments. Loan rate at 75%–90% parity	17.60	75% parity = 13.20	5.00	5.50
Upland cotton (lb)	Non-recourse loans and direct purchases. Acreage allotments. Loan rate at 65%–90% parity.	2.00	65% parity = 1.30	0.741	
Rice (cwt)	Permanent authority repealed by 1981 farm bill but restored by 1996 farm bill. Loan rate at 50%–90% parity.	40.00	50% parity = 20.00	13.70	14.00
Corn (bu)	Non-recourse loans and direct purchases. Acreage allotments not authorized. Loan rate at 50%–90% parity	13.20	50% parity = 6.60	3.47	3.70
Sorghum (bu)	Support for sorghum, barley, oats, and rye based on feeding value with respect to corn	22.40	50% parity = 11.20	6.79	3.95
Barley (bu)		14.90	50% parity = 7.45	4.52	4.95
Oats (bu)		8.59	50% parity = 4.30	2.61	2.40
Rye (bu)		18.50	50% parity = 9.25	4.50	
Honey (lb)	Purchase honey at 60–90% parity	5.15	60% parity = 3.09	2.06	

- The **Farm Security and Rural Investment Act of 2002** represented a move away from the market-oriented reforms of the 1996 Act. The 2002 Act included direct payments on harvested crops. For example, the direct payment for wheat was US$0.52/bu and for corn was US$0.28/bu. The PFC payments were replaced with countercyclical payments (CCPs). The CCP paid 85 per cent of the reference price less the market year average price or the loan rate (whichever was greater) times the base acres times the base yield.
- In the **Agricultural Improvement Act of 2018**, the longest-lasting provision of agricultural policy is the commodity loan rate, which has been used since the 1938 Act to set a price floor for most agricultural commodities.

7.4   THE AGRICULTURAL ACT OF 2014

A recent formulation of agricultural policy is the Agricultural Act of 2014, which made minor modifications to the Food, Conservation, and Energy (FCE) Act of 2008. The largest change is that farmers have a choice of payment mechanisms. The traditional payment mechanism is the

Table 7.4. Program prices under 2014 and 2018 US agricultural programs

Crop	Loan Rate		Reference Price
	2014	2018	
Wheat (US$/bu)	2.94	3.38	5.50
Corn (US$/bu)	1.95	2.20	3.70
Grain sorghum (US$/bu)	1.95	2.20	3.95
Barley (US$/bu)	1.95	2.50	4.95
Oats (US$/bu)	1.39	2.00	2.40
Long grain rice (US$/cwt)	6.50	7.00	14.00
Medium grain rice (US$/cwt)	6.50	7.00	14.00
Soybeans (US$/bu)	5.00	6.20	8.40
Peanuts (US$/ton)	355.00	355.00	535.00

price loss coverage (PLC), which provides payments to farmers based on market prices. The alternative payment mechanism is the agricultural risk coverage (ARC) program, which makes payments based on a farmer's total revenue (i.e., price times yield).

The 2014 Act can be seen as the heir to historical agricultural programs. First, the PLC makes payments based on "base acres and yields" for program crops. In this case, each farm's base acres could be determined by (1) historical base program acres and yields, or (2) proven commodity acres and/or yields based on recent plantings. If the market year price is less than the reference price, the PLC payment is then defined as 85 per cent of the difference between the lesser of either the reference price (Table 7.4) minus the market year average or the reference price minus the loan rate for each commodity, times base acres, times base yield. For example, suppose that a farmer in Oklahoma historically planted 320 acres of wheat with a proven program yield of 40 bushels per acre. If the market year average price for 2016 was US$5.00/bu, because (reference price – market year average price) < (reference price – 2014 wheat loan rate), the PLC payment would be 0.85 x (5.50 – 5.00) x (320 x 40) = US$5,440.00. If instead of US$5.00/bu, the market year average wheat price had been US$2.50, the PLC payment would have been 0.85 x (5.50 – 2.94) x (320 x 40) = US$27,852.80, because (reference price – 2014 wheat loan rate) < (reference price – market year average price). Payment is decoupled from production decisions.

The agricultural risk coverage (ARC) alternative is based on the comparison between observed revenue and a target revenue. Consider the historical soybean price and yield data for Tippecanoe County, Indiana (Table 7.5). To determine the ARC payment amount for 2018, it is necessary to calculate the ARC target revenue, the ARC coverage rate, and the observed revenue. The ARC target revenue per acre is calculated by multiplying the baseline yield/acre by the Olympic average price/bushel (or other weight measurement quantity). The ARC coverage rate will cover 86 per cent of the target revenue. The observed revenue is the actual revenue received per acre on a given year. To calculate the ARC, we first assume that the farmer updated his or her baseline yield in 2014 at 50.61 bushels per acre. Next, we construct the Olympic average price for 2018, which is defined as the average price for the period 2013 through 2017, with the high and low prices dropped: (10.20 + 9.69 + 9.61)/3 = US$9.83/bu. Therefore, the 2018 ARC target revenue is ($497.50/acre = 50.61 bu/acre x $9.83/bu). The 2018 ARC revenue coverage rate is 86 per cent of the target revenue = ($427.85/acre = 0.86 x $497.5/ acre). For this example, assume that the market year price for soybeans in 2018 is US$9.07/ bu and the observed yield per acre in Tippecanoe County is 46.0 bu. As such, the observed revenue would be US$417.22/acre. The ARC payment will be the lesser of either the ARC revenue coverage minus the observed revenue (i.e., the revenue loss) or 10 per cent of the ARC target revenue, whichever is smaller. For this example, the (ARC revenue coverage – observed revenue) = ($427.85/acre – $417.22/acre) = ($10.63/acre). Ten per cent of the target revenue = (0.10 x $497.50/acre) = ($49.75). In this case, the ARC payment will be $10.63/acre, the smaller of the two values.

Alternatively, assume that the market price for soybeans in Tippecanoe County fell to US$8.00/bu, instead of the previous $9.07/bu, with yield remaining at 46.0 bu/acre. The ARC target revenue and ARC revenue coverage remain the same from the original calculation, but the observed revenue would fall to $368.00/acre. The difference between ARC revenue coverage ($427.85) and the observed revenue changes to $59.85/acre. However, unlike the previous example, in this case 10 per cent of the target revenue ($49.75) is less than the difference between ARC revenue coverage and the observed revenue. As such, the ARC payment is limited to the lesser value of $49.75/acre. Therefore, at any market price and production yield, the maximum attainable ARC payment will be 10 per cent of the target revenue.

The ARC program is implemented at two levels. Farmers can choose to (1) collect ARC payments based on individual yields (ARC-IC); or they can (2) collect ARC payments based on county-level yields and prices (ARC-CO).

The discussion of PLC and ARC is from an ex post perspective (i.e., the amount of each payment paid to the farmer after the price/quantity outcome is known). However, the policy impact of each program is ex ante (i.e., before the price/quantity outcome becomes known). From this perspective, PLC is a free price insurance policy, while ARC is a free revenue insurance policy. The ex ante dimension is an important consideration when producers choose between the two policy alternatives. Table 7.6 presents an ex ante distribution for soybean prices and production in Tippecanoe County, Indiana, based on historical distribution from Table 7.5. Given that the market price is US$2.864/bu, the PLC pays US$2.20/bu (or the US$8.40/bu reference price for soybeans less the US$6.20/bu loan rate). We assume that the PLC pays on 85 per cent of the base yield (i.e., 0.85 x 51.47 = 43.75), yielding a PLC payment per base acre of US$96.25/acre. When the soybean price increases to US$7.428/bu, the PLC payment decreases to US$42.52/acre. That is, the PLC payment per bushel falls to US$0.972/bu if the soybean market year average price increases to $7.428/bu (e.g., US$8.40/bu – US$7.428/bu). When the market year price increases above

Table 7.5. Historical soybean price and yield data for Tippecanoe County, Indiana, 2000–17

Year	Price (US$/bu)	Yield (bu/acre)	Year	Price (US$/bu)	Yield (bu/acre)
2000	4.61	46.4	2009	9.80	51.5
2001	4.42	49.3	2010	11.50	53.8
2002	5.55	51.7	2011	12.70	49.5
2003	7.67	36.1	2012	14.70	40.5
2004	5.66	52.4	2013	13.20	55.8
2005	5.78	53.0	2014	10.20	61.9
2006	6.53	54.5	2015	9.16	50.1
2007	10.20	49.2	2016	9.69	61.1
2008	10.20	53.5	2017	9.61	56.1
Mean	8.95	51.47			

US$8.20/bu, the PLC payment becomes zero. We can compute the expected value of the PLC program given data in Table 7.5:

$$\left[PLC\right] = \sum_{i=1}^{5}\sum_{j=1}^{5} Prob_{ij}PLC_{ij} = 24.563 \tag{1}$$

where $Prob_{ij}$ is the probability for price i and quantity produced j and PLC_{ij} is the price loss coverage payment for the same combination of prices and quantities produced.

The same basic approach can be used to compute the expected value of the ARC program. Again, starting with the second entry in Table 7.6, a soybean price of US$2.864/bu and a yield of 48.351 bu results in a revenue of US$138.48/acre. Given our discussion of the ARC program, this results in an ARC payment of US$49.75/acre (e.g., 10 per cent of the ARC benchmark revenue). Following the same procedure in Equation 1, the expected value of the ARC program is US$18.02/acre.

Table 7.7 presents the historical ARC payments for corn in four selected counties. In general, the ARC payments for corn have declined over time. Focusing on the payments in traditional corn growing areas (Fayette County, Ohio, and Tippecanoe County, Indiana), the yields are relatively high in these counties (183.25 bu/acre for Fayette County and 181.50 bu/acre for Tippecanoe County). In fact, the yield is only substantially lower than the benchmark yield in Tippecanoe County in 2015. In these counties, the ARC payment is relatively large in 2014 and declines over time. Most of this decline is due to a general decline in corn's benchmark price (falling from US$5.29/bu in 2014 to US$3.95/bu in 2017). While not in the corn belt, the corn yields in Chicot County, Arkansas, are similar to the corn belt counties. In addition, the payments more or less mirror those in the corn belt counties. The results for Alachua County, Florida, are included to highlight the breadth of the impact of commodity program payments.

The ARC payments for wheat in our four selected counties show the same general pattern as the corn payments (Table 7.8). Payments tend to be larger in 2014; however, the observed

Table 7.6. Ex ante distribution of soybean production and prices for Tippecanoe County, Indiana

Price (US$)	Yield (bu/acre)	Probability	PLC Payment (US$/acre)	Revenue (US$/acre)	ARC Payment (US$/acre)
				Per Acre Amounts	
2.864	38.993	0.00127	96.25	111.68	49.75
2.864	48.351	0.04267	96.25	138.48	49.75
2.864	51.470	0.01198	96.25	147.41	49.75
2.864	54.589	0.02794	96.25	156.34	49.75
2.864	63.947	0.00379	96.25	183.14	49.75
7.428	38.993	0.07787	42.52	289.64	49.75
7.428	48.351	0.08404	42.52	359.15	49.75
7.428	51.470	0.06189	42.52	382.32	45.53
7.428	54.589	0.09049	42.52	405.49	22.36
7.428	63.947	0.06494	42.52	475.00	0.00
8.950	38.993	0.01189	0.00	348.99	49.75
8.950	48.351	0.04942	0.00	432.74	0.00
8.950	51.470	0.05265	0.00	460.66	0.00
8.950	54.589	0.04425	0.00	488.57	0.00
8.950	63.947	0.01711	0.00	572.33	0.00
10.472	38.993	0.00889	0.00	408.34	19.52
10.472	48.351	0.07133	0.00	506.33	0.00
10.472	51.470	0.05847	0.00	538.99	0.00
10.472	54.589	0.08445	0.00	571.66	0.00
10.472	63.947	0.01062	0.00	669.65	0.00
15.036	38.993	0.00733	0.00	586.30	0.00
15.036	48.351	0.02817	0.00	727.01	0.00
15.036	51.470	0.05336	0.00	773.90	0.00
15.036	54.589	0.02299	0.00	820.80	0.00
15.036	63.947	0.01217	0.00	961.51	0.00

Table 7.7. County-level agricultural risk coverage payments per acre for corn, selected counties

	2009	2010	2011	2012	2013	2014	2015	2016	2017
National Prices (US$/bu)									
Benchmark price						5.29	5.29	4.79	3.95
National price			6.22	6.89	4.46	3.70	3.61	3.36	3.36
Chicot County, Arkansas *[yield(bu/acre), revenue & payment (US$/acre)]*									
County yield	137	156	154	188	186	189	188	175	181
Benchmark yield						165	177	187	187
Benchmark revenue						872.85	936.33	895.73	738.65

(Continued)

Table 7.7. Continued

	2009	2010	2011	2012	2013	2014	2015	2016	2017
Guarantee revenue						750.65	805.24	770.33	635.24
Maximum payment						87.29	93.63	89.57	73.87
Actual revenue						699.30	678.68	588.00	608.16
Difference						51.35	126.56	182.33	27.08
Payment rate						51.35	93.63	89.57	27.08
Alachua County, Florida *[yield(bu/acre), revenue & payment (US$/acre)]*									
County yield	152	155	156	166	169	133	164	158	151
Benchmark yield						159	159	162	163
Benchmark revenue						841.11	841.11	775.98	643.85
Guarantee revenue						723.35	723.35	667.34	553.71
Maximum payment						84.11	84.11	77.60	64.39
Actual revenue						492.10	592.04	530.88	507.36
Difference						231.25	131.31	136.46	46.35
Payment rate						84.11	84.11	77.6	46.35
Tippecanoe County, Indiana *[yield(bu/acre), revenue & payment (US$/acre)]*									
County yield	179	175	160	117	185	207	146	200	180
Benchmark yield						171	173	164	177
Benchmark revenue						904.59	915.17	785.56	699.15
Guarantee revenue						777.95	787.05	675.58	601.27
Maximum payment						90.46	91.52	78.56	69.92
Actual revenue						765.90	527.06	672.00	604.80
Difference						12.05	259.99	3.58	0.00
Payment rate						12.05	91.52	3.58	0.00
Fayette County, Ohio *[yield(bu/acre), revenue & payment (US$/acre)]*									
County yield	187	172	184	128	180	184	176	175	191
Benchmark yield						179	179	180	177
Benchmark revenue						946.91	946.91	862.2	699.15
Guarantee revenue						814.34	814.34	741.49	601.27
Maximum payment						94.69	94.69	86.22	69.92
Actual revenue						680.80	635.36	588.00	541.76
Difference						133.54	178.98	153.49	0.00
Payment rate						94.69	94.69	86.22	0.00

Table 7.8. County-level agricultural risk coverage payments per acre for wheat, selected counties

	2009	2010	2011	2012	2013	2014	2015	2016	2017
National Prices (US$/bu)									
Benchmark price						6.60	6.70	6.70	6.12
National price						5.99	4.89	3.89	4.72
Otero County, Colorado									
[yield(bu/acre), revenue & payment (US$/acre)]									
County yield	44	65	75	63	39	47	56	69	63
Benchmark yield						57	58	55	55
Benchmark revenue						376.20	388.60	368.50	336.60
Guarantee revenue						323.53	334.20	316.91	289.48
Maximum payment						37.62	38.86	36.85	33.66
Actual revenue						281.53	273.84	268.41	297.36
Difference						42.00	60.36	48.50	0.00
Payment rate						37.62	38.86	36.85	0.00
Ford County, Kansas									
[yield(bu/acre), revenue & payment (US$/acre)]									
County yield	40	51	33	37	26	25	37	66	51
Benchmark yield						37	32	32	34
Benchmark revenue						244.20	214.40	214.40	208.08
Guarantee revenue						210.01	184.38	184.38	178.95
Maximum payment						24.42	21.44	21.44	20.81
Actual revenue						149.75	180.93	256.74	240.72
Difference						60.26	3.45	0.00	0.00
Payment rate						24.42	3.45	0.00	0.00
Beckham County, Oklahoma									
[yield(bu/acre), revenue & payment (US$/acre)]									
County yield	17	28	17	33	17	6	21	34	26
Benchmark yield						21	21	19	24
Benchmark revenue						138.60	140.70	127.30	146.88
Guarantee revenue						119.20	121.00	109.48	126.32
Maximum payment						13.86	14.07	12.73	14.69
Actual revenue						35.94	102.69	132.26	122.72
Difference						83.26	18.31	0.00	3.60
Payment rate						13.86	14.07	0.00	3.60
Wheeler County, Texas									
[yield(bu/acre), revenue & payment (US$/acre)]									
County yield	13	29	13	25	13	9	23	15	27

(Continued)

Table 7.8. Continued

	2009	2010	2011	2012	2013	2014	2015	2016	2017
Benchmark yield						17	17	17	17
Benchmark revenue						112.20	113.90	113.90	104.04
Guarantee revenue						96.49	97.95	97.95	89.47
Maximum payment						11.22	11.39	11.39	10.40
Actual revenue						53.91	112.47	58.35	127.44
Difference						42.58	0.00	39.60	0.00
Payment rate						11.22	0.00	11.39	0.00

county-level yields in 2014 are significantly below the benchmark yields. For example, in Beckham County, Oklahoma, the county-level yield in 2014 was 6 bu/acre which is 15 bu/acre below the benchmark. Hence, larger relative ARC payments for wheat were due to lower yields. This situation had reversed by 2017, when the county-level yields were as much as 58 per cent above the benchmark yield, but the wheat market year average price was significantly lower than the benchmark price (e.g., US$4.72/bu market year average price compared with a benchmark price of US$6.12/bu). The result of this tradeoff is that ARC payments of US$3.60/acre were made in Beckham County, Oklahoma.

To compare the election between ARC and PLC, we start by examining the market year average (MYA) price for the marketing years 2000/1 through 2016/17 for corn and soybeans with the reference prices and loan rates for each commodity presented in Table 7.9. The MYA price was less than the reference price for the marketing years 2002/3 through 2005/6 for corn while the MYA price for soybeans was less than the reference price in marketing years 2002/3, 2004/5, and 2005/6. Hence, throughout the duration of the 2002 Act there were several times that countercyclical payments (the forerunner of PLC) were made on each commodity. However, beginning with the 2006/7 marketing year, the MYA price exceeded the reference price; hence, no countercyclical or PLC payments were made. Table 7.10 presents the computation of the PLC payments per bushel and Table 7.11 presents the PLC yields for our selected sets of counties.

In general, how do the returns under the ARC election compare with the PLC option? Table 7.12 presents the PLC and ARC payments per acre for corn and wheat in our selected counties. The first point to notice is that the MYA price for all three commodities (corn, wheat, and soybeans) was above the reference price in 2014; hence, there were no PLC payments for these crops in 2014.

Agricultural prices have been supported through the loan rate program since the Agricultural Adjustment Act of 1938. As it was initially implemented, the non-recourse feature of the loan produced a price floor for agricultural commodities. In Figure 7.1, the supply of corn is S while the demand for corn is D. We assume that the US policy has provided a loan rate of p_L

Table 7.9. Market year average prices, reference prices, and loan rates for corn and soybeans

Marketing Year	Corn (US$/bu)			Soybeans (US$/bu)		
	MYA Price	Reference Price	Loan Rate	MYA Price	Reference Price	Loan Rate
2002/3	2.32	2.60	1.98	5.53	5.80	5.00
2003/4	2.42	2.60	1.98	7.34	5.80	5.00
2004/5	2.06	2.63	1.95	5.74	5.80	5.00
2005/6	2.00	2.63	1.95	5.66	5.80	5.00
2006/7	3.04	2.63	1.95	6.43	5.80	5.00
2007/8	4.20	2.63	1.95	10.10	5.80	5.00
2008/9	4.06	2.63	1.95	9.97	5.80	5.00
2009/10	3.55	2.63	1.95	9.59	5.80	5.00
2010/11	5.18	2.63	1.95	11.30	6.00	5.00
2011/12	6.22	2.63	1.95	12.50	6.00	5.00
2012/13	6.89	2.63	1.95	14.40	6.00	5.00
2013/14	4.46	2.63	1.95	13.00	6.00	5.00
2014/15	3.70	2.63	1.95	10.10	6.00	5.00
2015/16	3.61	2.63	1.95	8.95	6.00	5.00
2016/17	3.36	2.63	1.95	9.47	6.00	5.00

Table 7.10. Price loss coverage payments per bushel, 2014–18 (US$/bu)

	2014	2015	2016	2017	2018
Corn					
Reference price	3.70	3.70	3.70	3.70	3.70
MYA price	3.70	3.61	3.36	3.36	3.60
Loan rate	1.95	1.95	1.95	1.95	1.95
PLC effective price	3.70	3.61	3.36	3.36	3.60
PLC payment	0.00	0.09	0.34	0.34	0.10
Soybeans					
Reference price	8.40	8.40	8.40	8.40	8.40
MYA price	10.10	8.95	9.47	9.33	8.60
Loan rate	5.00	5.00	5.00	5.00	5.00
PLC effective price	10.10	8.95	9.47	9.33	8.60
PLC payment	0.00	0.00	0.00	0.00	0.00
Wheat					
Reference price	5.50	5.50	5.50	5.50	5.50
MYA price	5.99	4.89	3.89	4.72	5.15
Loan rate	2.94	2.94	2.94	2.94	2.94
PLC effective price	5.99	4.89	3.89	4.72	5.15
PLC payment	0.00	0.61	1.61	0.78	0.35

for corn so that instead of an equilibrium price and quantity of p^* and q^*, farmers produce q_P and consumers demand q_C. In this equilibrium, through the Commodity Credit Corporation (CCC), the government would purchase and hold stocks of $q_P - q_C$. Notice that in recent years the market price for corn has been well above the loan rate so that no forfeitures would occur.

At this point, we can derive the economic costs and benefits of a historically important agricultural policy. Starting with the change in consumer surplus, the non-recourse loan

Table 7.11. Price loss coverage yields for selected US counties

	Corn (bu)	Peanuts (lb)	Sorghum (bu)	Soybeans (bu)	Wheat (lb)
Alachua County, Florida	92	3270	38	19	38
Beckham County, Oklahoma	73	3453	33	9	26
Chicot County, Arkansas	143		49	37	42
Ford County, Kansas	161		67	51	39
Fayette County, Ohio	146		106	44	58
Otero County, Colorado	146		66	36	64
Tippecanoe County, Indiana	151		64	47	56
Wheeler County, Texas	123	2032	34		21

Table 7.12. Price loss coverage and agriculture risk coverage, 2014–17 (US$/bu)

	2014	2015	2016	2017
Corn				
Chicot County, Arkansas				
PLC (143 bu)	0.00	10.94	41.33	41.33
ARC	51.35	93.63	89.57	27.08
Alachua County, Florida				
PLC (92 bu)	0.00	7.04	26.59	26.59
ARC	84.11	84.11	77.60	46.35
Tippecanoe County, Indiana				
PLC (151 bu)	0.00	11.55	43.64	43.64
ARC	12.05	91.52	3.58	0.00
Fayette County, Ohio				
PLC (146 bu)	0.00	11.17	42.19	42.19
ARC	94.69	94.69	86.22	0.00
Wheat				
Otero County, Colorado				
PLC (64 bu)	0.00	33.18	87.58	42.43
ARC	37.62	38.86	36.85	0.00
Ford County, Kansas				
PLC (38 bu)	0.00	19.70	52.00	25.19
ARC	24.42	3.45	0.00	0.00
Beckham County, Oklahoma				
PLC (26 bu)	0.00	13.48	35.58	17.24
ARC	13.86	14.07	0.00	3.60
Wheeler County, Texas				
PLC (21 bu)	0.00	10.89	28.74	13.92
ARC	11.22	0.00	11.39	0.00

program reduced consumer surplus by the area $p_L a c p^*$. Specifically, by "purchasing" additional commodity through the non-recourse loan program, the policy increases the price paid by consumers from p^* to p_L. In response, consumers reduce their purchases of the commodity from q^* to q_C. On the other hand, the additional "purchases" through the non-recourse loan program increase producer surplus by $p_L b c p^*$. Whether the net social effect is positive or negative depends, in part, on the assumptions that one makes about the disposition of the stocks. The total value of stocks accumulated by the CCC in the production year is area ($a b q_p q_c$) or

Figure 7.1. Effect of commodity loan rate

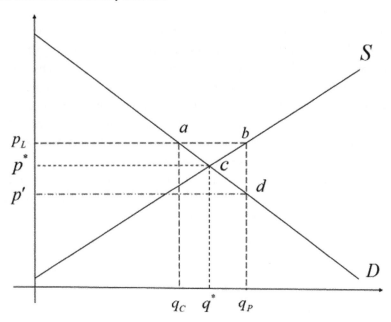

p_L x $(q_p - q_c)$. While several possible outcomes are possible, let us start with the best possible outcome. Let us assume that there is either an outward shift in demand in the next year, or negative shock to supply. In this case, we could assume that the price of the commodity in the next year is higher than the loan rate in this year (i.e., $p'' > p_L$). In this case the stocks accumulated in this period are sold for a higher price next period. To complicate this formulation slightly, we assume a discount rate of r and a holding or storage cost of ϕ per unit. The net gain from holding CCC stocks then becomes

$$\left(\frac{1}{1+r}p'' - p_L - \phi\right) \times (q_P - q_C) \tag{7.1}$$

which could be either positive or negative. Let us assume for the moment that the value in Equation 7.1 is zero (e.g., the discounted future price is exactly high enough to pay for the original loan rate and the cost of storage). In this case, there is no cost to the non-recourse loan program. Unfortunately, this scenario was relatively rare.

The non-recourse loan was a factor contributing to the accumulation of government stocks (i.e., CCC holdings). In most cases, the law specified market conditions such that the stocks could be released for sale (i.e., in one case, stocks could be sold when the market price exceeded 105 per cent of parity). However, over several periods of the non-recourse loan programs, the US farm program has resulted in significant accumulation of a variety of stocks. These accumulations raise several difficulties. First, it is often costly to hold government stocks. In the past, the agricultural program has included funds for the CCC to build storage facilities. In addition, the quality or usability of a variety of commodities declines over time (by loss or wastage), or the government stocks may depress agricultural prices in the long term. Because of both of these difficulties, the federal government has tried several mechanisms to reduce the holding of stocks. Several of the Great Depression-era nutritional programs were basically surplus distribution programs – the government gave food to the poor. In a similar vein, Public Law 480, also known as the Food for Peace Initiative, which was passed in 1954, initially provided for the distribution of surplus commodities overseas to address food needs in developing countries. A further example, the Payment-in-Kind program of 1982 distributed stocks that accumulated under the Farmer Owned Reserve program.

Given the difficulties of holding stocks, the non-recourse loan program was transformed into loan deficiency payments (LDPs). The LDP pays the farmer an amount that would be roughly equivalent to the farmer forfeiting output to the CCC. As a starting point, consider the loan formulation in Figure 7.1 where the producer produces q_P based on the loan rate of p_L. Suppose that the producer sells his or her production on the market resulting in a market clearing price of p'. The producer would be indifferent between making this market transaction and receiving a payment of p_L-p–0 for each unit produced (i.e., bushel of corn) and placing the crop into a traditional non-recourse loan program. So, LDP would be a payment of $(p_L$-p–$0) \times q_P$. The producer and consumer gains from this program are the same as a traditional subsidy program. As before, producers would gain $p_L bcp^*$, but consumers now gain from increased consumption at lower prices ($p^* cdp'$). The additional cost is borne by the Treasury (i.e., the USDA commodity payments) – ($p_L bdp'$).

To complete our picture of the LDP program, a posted county price (PCP) is computed for each county. This price is the prevailing price for a thirty-day period. The PCPs for each of the selected corn-producing counties are presented in Table 7.13. In 2017, the PCPs were higher than the county loan rates so no LDPs were made. However, the derivation of the PCPs and loan rates in Table 7.13 provides several points of discussion. First, county-level prices for most agricultural commodities vary. This variation is largely explained by transportation costs to the closest market. For example, the highest price for wheat in the 1970s was typically the export port of Galveston, Texas. Hence, the county-level price for wheat typically fell as it got farther away from Galveston as the distance implied higher trucking costs. However, this relationship was distorted by access to large train facilities in certain areas, such as Enid, Oklahoma. This difference between local prices and prices at central markets is typically referred to as *basis*. The PCP calculations in Table 7.13 provide two alternative basis calculations for determining local prices. For example, the two markets considered for Chicot County, Arkansas, are the Gulf of Mexico and Memphis. The price on the Gulf in the past thirty days was US$4.22/bu. Next, assuming a standard basis between Chicot County prices and the Gulf market of -0.62/bu, this yields an implicit Chicot County price of US$3.60/bu. Note that the county-level loan rates also include implicit basis adjustment.

Table 7.13. Posted county prices for selected counties, 2017 (US$/bu)

	30-Day PCP	Terminal Market	Terminal Price	Adjustments	Price after Adjustment	Alternative PCP	County Loan Rate
Chicot County, AR	4.18	Gulf	4.22	−0.62	3.60	3.60	2.11
		Memphis	3.91	−0.39	3.52		
Alachua County, FL	3.38	Cincinnati	3.74	−0.04	3.70	3.71	2.22
		Gulf	4.22	−0.51	3.71		
Tippecanoe County, IN	4.06	Gulf	4.22	−0.78	3.44	3.46	1.99
		Kansas City	3.69	−0.23	3.46		
Fayette County, OH	4.10	Cincinnati	3.74	−0.26	3.48	3.48	2.02
		Toledo	3.66	−0.18	3.48		

To determine the cost and benefits of the 2018 program, Table 7.14 presents the estimated market year price received for corn for marketing years 2018/19 through 2020/21. These results suggest that the price of corn will be slightly lower than the reference price for the 2018/19 marketing year (i.e., a MYA price of US$3.60/bu compared with a reference price of US$3.70/bu). However, it appears extremely unlikely that the corn price for 2018/19 will fall below the loan rate of US$2.20/bu. Figure 7.2 presents the corn market equilibrium under this policy scenario. Under this set of assumptions, the price and quantity of corn is determined by the intersection of the supply and demand curve (e.g., the price of corn is p^* while the quantity of corn produced is q^*). This equilibrium depends on two assumptions. First, the loan rate (p_L) is below the equilibrium price, so it does not affect production decisions. Second, the production decisions are not affected by the reference price (p_R). The farmer receives PLC payments based on historical yields and program base acres. In this case, the consumer surplus is (abp^*). The producer surplus comes from two sources. First, the market generates a producer surplus of (p^*bc). Second, the government makes PLC payments to farmers based on the market price. To derive this payment, assume that ARC does not exist (e.g., deficiency payments are made as PLC). Under this scenario, payments are made on q_{PLC} bushels (e.g., 85 per cent of program yields on base acres). In this case the PLC payment will be ($p_R dep^*$). Given our projections, this payment will be fairly small (slightly less than US$0.10 per bushel).

One of the unique characteristics of the 2014 and 2018 Acts was the selection of payment contracts. Intuitively, the total payment under PLC can be represented in terms of Figure 7.2. ARC as developed above is a form of revenue insurance that pays off under certain combinations of price and production given a historical benchmark. However, we can depict the effect of the choice between PLC and ARC in Figure 7.2. As stated in the preceding paragraph, we initially assumed that q_{PLC} bushels represent 85 per cent of base acres for program yields (e.g., the quantity of bushels paid the deficiency payment if all acres signed up for PLC). Next, we assume that only bushels are eligible for PLC payments. The acres for the

Figure 7.2. Effect of price loss coverage on commodity market

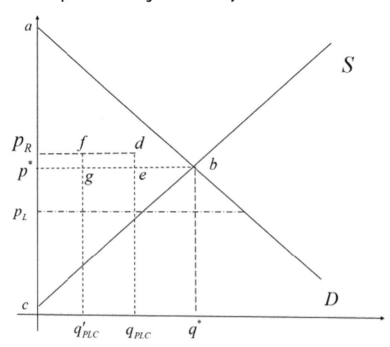

Table 7.14. Quantity and price range for corn in the United States, 2018–20

	Lower Bound	Mean	Upper Bound
Corn Quantity (billion bushels)			
2018/19	12.551	14.900	17.249
2019/20	12.681	15.153	17.624
2020/21	12.995	15.489	17.982
Corn Price (US$ per bushel)			
2018/19	2.324	3.606	4.888
2019/20	2.466	4.059	5.651
2020/21	2.797	4.574	6.351

q^* acres that have been enrolled in ARC. Under these assumptions, the PLC payment is smaller ($p_R fgp^*$). Table 7.15 presents the PLC/ARC choice for corn by state. In total, 121,526 farms chose PLC while 1,240,419 chose ARC. Hence, 91 per cent of farms chose ARC. In terms of total acres, 6,388,066 acres were enrolled in PLC while 90,380,379 acres were enrolled in ARC (or 93 per cent of corn base acres were enrolled in ARC). Given these statistics, we expect the PLC payments to be very small (e.g., not only due to the fact that PLC payments will only be US$0.10 per bushel, but also since only 7 per cent of corn acres are enrolled for

Table 7.15. Price loss coverage/agricultural risk coverage election by state (US$)

		PLC	ARC	Total			PLC	ARC	Total
AL	Acres	75,083	167,876	242,960	NE	Acres	417,281	10,161,792	10,579,073
	Farms	5,155	9,581	14,736		Farms	3,895	77,102	80,997
AZ	Acres	40,417	2,967	43,384	NV	Acres	442	1,519	1,961
	Farms	545	19	564		Farms	20	54	74
AR	Acres	32,070	197,809	229,879	NH	Acres	902	11,296	12,198
	Farms	830	4,437	5,267		Farms	27	383	410
CA	Acres	166,020	174,383	340,403	NJ	Acres	7,388	73,184	80,573
	Farms	2,739	1,815	4,554		Farms	226	2,025	2,251
CO	Acres	412,615	1,078,347	1,490,963	NM	Acres	58,622	87,559	146,181
	Farms	2,974	5,902	8,876		Farms	765	437	1,202
CT	Acres	6,178	18,347	24,525	NY	Acres	15,780	1,013,909	1,029,689
	Farms	217	571	788		Farms	357	21,469	21,826
DE	Acres	5,856	161,747	167,603	NC	Acres	32,377	910,484	942,861
	Farms	147	3,460	3,607		Farms	1,957	47,077	49,034
FL	Acres	11,899	49,688	61,586	ND	Acres	55,749	3,025,961	3,081,710
	Farms	507	1,937	2,444		Farms	1,301	25,360	26,661
GA	Acres	57,931	358,690	416,621	OH	Acres	81,181	4,080,599	4,161,780
	Farms	3,123	16,037	19,160		Farms	2,084	89,569	91,653
ID	Acres	98,416	103,050	201,466	OK	Acres	56,957	226,382	283,339
	Farms	1,681	1,461	3,142		Farms	1,400	2,411	3,811
IL	Acres	257,720	12,957,672	13,215,392	OR	Acres	17,420	46,144	63,564
	Farms	3,951	159,772	163,723		Farms	522	777	1,299
IN	Acres	144,860	6,573,290	6,718,150	PA	Acres	54,643	703,970	758,613
	Farms	2,374	104,878	107,252		Farms	1,629	25,107	26,736
IA	Acres	422,434	15,148,095	15,570,529	RI	Acres	110	717	826
	Farms	4,983	148,025	153,008		Farms	3	55	58
KS	Acres	590,065	3,936,996	4,527,061	SC	Acres	23,940	340,992	364,932
	Farms	8,350	40,155	48,505		Farms	1,044	14,888	15,932
KY	Acres	84,448	1,593,310	1,677,758	SD	Acres	113,283	5,812,014	5,925,297
	Farms	3,965	38,767	42,732		Farms	1,062	47,371	48,433
LA	Acres	32,720	279,821	312,541	TN	Acres	11,961	846,920	858,882
	Farms	998	5,555	6,553		Farms	448	27,579	28,027
ME	Acres	122	31,908	32,031	TX	Acres	991,040	1,244,409	2,235,449
	Farms	4	1,144	1,148		Farms	20,552	10,347	30,899
MD	Acres	26,079	452,431	478,510	UT	Acres	9,067	50,816	59,883
	Farms	571	10,922	11,493		Farms	443	1,586	2,029
MA	Acres	0	17,633	17,633	VT	Acres	492	87,828	88,319
	Farms	0	853	853		Farms	29	2,321	2,350
MI	Acres	96,087	2,660,940	2,757,027	VA	Acres	51,203	403,013	454,216
	Farms	2,011	49,937	51,948		Farms	2,955	19,145	22,100
MN	Acres	107,614	8,727,939	8,835,554	WA	Acres	63,805	49,125	112,929
	Farms	1,573	91,052	92,625		Farms	871	688	1,559
MS	Acres	18,703	346,873	365,576	WV	Acres	756	63,066	63,822
	Farms	723	11,398	12,121		Farms	118	2,360	2,478
MO	Acres	1,472,378	2,013,459	3,485,837	WI	Acres	80,553	3,971,390	4,051,943
	Farms	28,934	32,829	61,763		Farms	2,029	81,348	83,377
MT	Acres	62,899	28,893	91,792	WY	Acres	20,500	85,126	105,626
	Farms	1,434	453	1,887		Farms	442	955	1,397

Figure 7.3. Effect of a significant increase in supply on price loss coverage and agricultural risk coverage payments

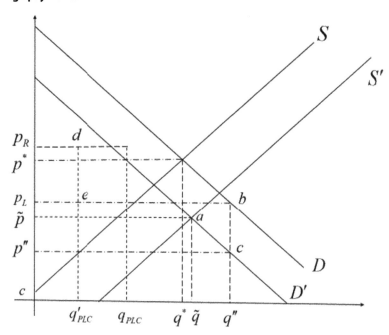

PLC payments). For slightly different reasons we also expect that the ARC payments will be small barring major weather events.

The policy scenario depicted in Figure 7.2 assumes that the price of corn will remain above the loan rate. Figure 7.3 assumes a significant supply increase (e.g., a shift from S to S' coupled with a reduction in demand from D to D'). The result would be a new equilibrium at a lower price ($\tilde{p}$) and a larger quantity ($\tilde{q}$). Given that the price is lower than the loan rate (p_L), the government will make LDPs on all corn that is produced by farmers who participate in the farm program. Since the loan rate is p_L, farmers will produce q'' bushels of corn. Again, since we assume that the government will make LDPs instead of accumulating stocks, the LDP payment will be (p_L-p'') per bushel or (p_L bcp'') in total. Under this scenario consumers gain ($\tilde{p}acp''$) while producers gain ($p_L ba\tilde{p}$). These producer and consumer gains added to the Treasury cost yields the classic deadweight loss of (bca). In addition to these market-based transfers, the farmers will also receive a PLC payment of ($p_R dep_L$). The net impact of these changes in supply and demand on ARC payments are a little more difficult to determine without additional information. It would depend in part on whether the shift in supply and demand occurred slowly over a time in which the benchmark revenue had also crept downward due to falling prices and increasing yields. We could approximate the benchmark revenue as ($p^* \times q^*$) and the observed revenue as ($p_L \times q''$), so the question is whether ($p_L \times q'' \leq 0.86\ p^* \times q^*$).

SETTING LOAN RATES AND TARGET PRICES

Typically, agricultural policy before the 1970s retained the objective of setting loan rates and target prices based on the parity concept. Early legislation attempted to guarantee prices that would return 100 per cent of parity while later acts resulted in less ambitious targets (e.g., 90 per cent of parity in the Agricultural Act of 1948). The 1996 FAIR Act set more flexible targets. However, the most recent agricultural programs have set loan rates (and target prices) without reference to either market conditions or parity.

7.5 CONSERVATION RESERVE PROGRAM

The Conservation Reserve Program (CRP) was established by the Food Security Act of 1985. To get support for the 1985 US Farm Bill, a provision to retire highly erodible lands for ten to fifteen years was included. While the primary environmental objective of the CRP was to reduce soil erosion, one of the secondary objectives was to reduce the supply of certain program commodities so as to increase the farm gate price and to bolster net farm income.

To reduce the impact of the Conservation Reserve Program on rural communities should too much cropland be removed in any one area, each county was limited to removing 25 per cent of its total cropland from production. Each year farmers received a per acre payment for their land that was enrolled in the CRP, up to a per person limit of US$50,000. The intent of the CRP was to reduce crop acreage by forty to forty-five million acres. By 1991, thirty-eight million acres of land had been placed in the CRP by contract holders (Knutson, Penn, and Flinchbaugh 1998). In 2000, the USDA estimated that about thirty-four million acres of land were in the CRP (USDA/FAS 2008).

Most of the land placed in the CRP under the 1985 Food Security Act was in the Great Plains. To make the program more attractive to farmers in the Midwest, the 1990 Food, Agriculture, Conservation, and Trade (FACT) Act placed its emphasis on improving water quality for both agriculture and the environment. In the 1996 FAIR Act, the preservation of wildlife habitat became one of many criteria for placing land in the CRP. Thus, the emphasis of the Conservation Reserve Program has changed over time.

From a worldwide perspective, this may be one of the most important components of US farm policy. In 2008 there were roughly thirty-two million acres in the CRP (only about one-half of which were suitable for agricultural production). Because of the high crop prices in 2007 and 2008, the United States considered removing some of the acreage from the CRP, but it did not. If the United States had removed fifteen million acres from the CRP, the impact on commodity prices would have been significant.

> **ENVIRONMENTAL BENEFITS OF CRP**
>
> Since 1990, criteria of acceptance to the CRP have been broadened to include envi-
> ronmental indicators, such as water quality and wildlife habitat. A significant amount
> of the land entering the CRP after 1990 was devoted to the production of row crops
> such as corn and soybeans. Extensive row-crop production is known to be detrimen-
> tal to many wildlife populations; it also increases the rate of soil and water erosion.
> By converting row-crop lands into grasslands, the CRP could positively affect wildlife,
> increase the quality of water, and reduce soil erosion.

7.6   DAIRY, SUGAR, TOBACCO, AND PEANUTS

7.6.1   US Dairy Policy and Marketing Orders

The dairy industry is one of the most highly regulated agricultural sectors in the United States
(Manchester 1983). Dairy programs are intended to (1) stabilize dairy farm income, (2) lessen
the seasonal instability in milk prices, and (3) bring about orderly marketing. These policy
objectives have historically been met using a variety of policy mechanisms. First, milk is marketed under an agricultural marketing order. These orders are basically producer agreements
for the orderly marketing of some agricultural product.

7.6.1.1   THE US DAIRY PROGRAM BEFORE 2014

Figure 7.4 depicts the effect of the two-price milk program on the quantities supplied and
on demand, and the relative price for each grade of milk. The figure starts with two different
demand curves for milk: the demand for fluid milk (D_F) and the demand for milk processed
into other products such as cheese and butter (D_P). Summing these two demand curves hori-
zontally yields the total demand for milk (D_T). To solve for the market equilibrium, we assume
that the demand curve for fluid milk is

$$q_F = 150.00 - 2.78 p_F \tag{7.2}$$

while the demand curve for milk to be used in the production of processed milk products is

$$q_P = 92.50 - 2.36 p_P . \tag{7.3}$$

To solve for the equilibrium price, we assume that the price for fluid milk and processed milk
is the same and equate the sum of the two demand functions with the supply function for milk

$$q_S = 82.5 + 3.75 p \tag{7.4}$$

Figure 7.4. Market equilibrium for fluid and processed milk market

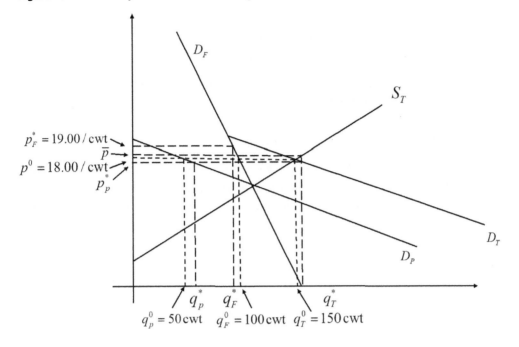

$q_p^0 = 50\,\text{cwt}$ $q_F^0 = 100\,\text{cwt}$ $q_T^0 = 150\,\text{cwt}$

yielding an equilibrium price for milk of US$18.00/cwt and a total quantity demand of 150 cwt (as depicted in Figure 7.4).

The basic design of the traditional milk program is to exploit the differences in the elasticity between the demand curves. In the current example, the demand curve for fluid milk is more inelastic than the demand curve for processed milk (e.g., -0.50 compared with -0.85). The basic concept is to increase the average or blended price by raising the price in the fluid milk market (reducing the quantity of fluid milk consumed) and increasing the supply of processed milk (decreasing its price). As an example, suppose that we increased the price in the fluid milk market to US$19.00/cwt. This would decrease the quantity of fluid milk consumed to 97.22 cwt. The result would be a blended milk price

$$\bar{p} = \frac{19.00 \times 97.22 + p_P q_P}{97.22 + q_P}. \tag{7.5}$$

This system is solved by introducing the supply function for denominator in Equation 7.5. The quantity of processed milk produced at equilibrium $\left(q_P^*\right)$ is 53.33 cwt (i.e., the quantity of processed milk produced increases), the equilibrium price in the processed milk market declines to US$16.59/cwt, and the blend price increases to US$18.15.

While the two-price plan increases farmer income, an additional level of price support was introduced by government purchases of milk to create butter and cheese. To demonstrate this program, we start by introducing government purchases of milk to produce butter and cheese (q_G) the new blend price can then be written as

$$\bar{p} = \frac{19.00 \times 97.22 + p_p(q_p + q_G)}{97.22 + q_p + q_G}. \tag{7.6}$$

We will assume that the policy goal is a blended price of milk of US$18.25/cwt. Given this objective, the price of processed milk becomes

$$p_p = \frac{18.25 \times q_T^* - 19.00 \times 97.22}{q_p + q_G}. \tag{7.7}$$

Next, we note that if the blended price of milk is set at US$18.25/cwt, the total supply of milk will be 150.94 cwt (from the supply function in Equation 7.4). This total supply also determines the private demand for milk for processed products and the amount of milk purchased for government uses:

$$q_P + q_G = 150.38 - 97.22 = 53.71. \tag{7.8}$$

Substituting the total production of milk and the amount of milk used for processing into Equation 7.7 yields a processed milk price of US$16.89/cwt. At this price, the private milk processors will demand 52.61 cwt of milk (using Equation 7.3) and the government purchase of milk is determined as 1.10 cwt.

7.6.1.2   MARGIN PROTECTION PROGRAM FOR DAIRY

The political support for the traditional milk program waned over time, in part due to the significant quantity of butter and cheese accumulated by the government. As a result, the Margin Protection Program for Dairy (MPP) was introduced in the 2014 Farm Bill. This program provides for an insurance payment per hundredweight (cwt) of milk sold if the dairy margin, defined as the milk price minus feed cost, drops below a specified level. Table 7.16 presents the margins and cost of protection in the 2018 Act. As an example, suppose that a farmer has 150 cows producing 22,000 pounds of milk per cow, or 3,300,000 pounds of milk. This individual is a "Tier I" producer. Next, we assume that the producer completely covers production at US$7.50 coverage, 0.300 * 3,300,000/100 = US$9,900. If the milk margin declined to US$7.25, the farmer would collect (7.50 – 7.25)*3,300,000/100 = US$8,250.

DAIRY PROGRAM COSTS

The net cost of the dairy program was sizeable in the early 1980s because the government purchased large quantities of milk products. However, in the 1990s, the cost of the dairy program was greatly reduced because the milk support price was

Table 7.16. Margin protection program premiums per hundredweight (cwt)

Margin	Tier I Less Than Five Million Pounds	Tier II Greater Than Five Million Pounds
$4.00	0.000	0.000
$4.50	0.000	0.020
$5.00	0.000	0.040
$5.50	0.009	0.100
$6.00	0.016	0.155
$6.50	0.040	0.290
$7.00	0.063	0.830
$7.50	0.067	1.060
$8.00	0.142	1.360

well below the market price. For example, throughout 1999, average market prices exceeded support prices by US$2 per cwt. From 1977 to 1991, the US government purchased from 5 per cent to almost 10 per cent of domestic production, although this quantity dropped substantially after the 1996 US Farm Bill (Sumner 1999).

7.6.2   US Sugar Rate and Tariff Rate Policies

The US sugar program is a perennial point of discussion in the arena of agricultural policy (A. Schmitz and Christian 1993). The program supports the price of sugar in the United States through the operation of a tariff rate quota (TRQ). The TRQ on sugar in the United States is set to guarantee a domestic sugar price of US$0.18 per pound on raw sugar and US$0.23 per pound on sugar refined from sugar beets.

The tariff rate quota is based on two different quota rates (Figure 7.5). The first quota rate t_0 is relatively low and allows for a basic minimum access to the domestic market (Figure 7.5b). The second rate t_i is typically prohibitive. Figure 7.5a is the supply and demand of sugar produced in foreign countries. Subtracting the foreign demand D_F from the foreign supply S_F yields the excess supply of foreign sugar into the US market before the tariff ES_F (Figure 7.5c). The excess demand from the United States is ED_{US}. Figure 7.5b depicts the tariff rate. The lower (first level) tariff t_0 is charged on all imports below the minimum access quantity $\tilde{Q}_E$. Above the minimum access quantity $\tilde{Q}_E$, any imports into the US market are charged a higher tariff t_i. Figure 7.5c depicts the excess supply and excess demand. The effective excess supply curve ES_F' (the discontinuous line [abcd]) is derived by adding the tariff to the excess supply curve from foreign suppliers. The effective excess supply curve is discontinuous at the minimum access quantity resulting in the domestic market price of $\tilde{P}$. The goal of the US sugar program is to generate a domestic market price higher than US$0.18 per pound for raw cane sugar. In Figure 7.5a, the foreign market price

Figure 7.5. Tariff rate quota program for US sugar, 1995–2008

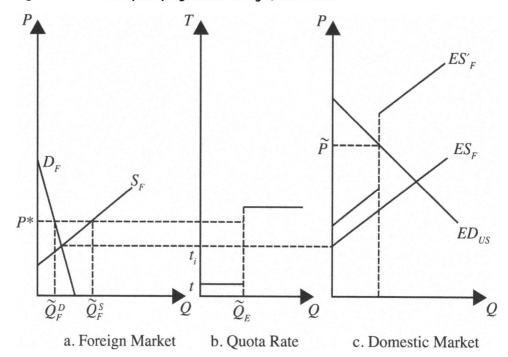

a. Foreign Market   b. Quota Rate   c. Domestic Market

of sugar $\tilde{P}^*$ is equal to that price, balancing supply and demand in overseas markets after the minimum access quantity of sugar has been exported to the United States. In Figure 7.5a, $\tilde{Q}_F^S$ pounds of sugar are produced in the foreign market and $\tilde{Q}_F^D$ pounds of sugar are consumed in the foreign market. The quantity of sugar exported to the United States is $\left(\tilde{Q}_F^S - \tilde{Q}_F^D\right)$.

In addition to the tariff rate quota, the Food, Conservation, and Energy (FCE) Act of 2008 includes a non-recourse loan program to provide a floor for domestically produced raw sugar from sugar cane. The operation of this particular loan program is complicated by the Dole Amendment of the 1985 US Farm Bill, which requires that the sugar program be conducted at no cost to the US Treasury (Messina and Seale 1993). One result of the Dole Amendment is that payments under the loan rate provisions for sugar will be typically made using payments-in-kind.

WORLD SUGAR

Many of the studies that have been critical of both the EU and US sugar policies base their analyses on world sugar prices. These are generally below the US domestic support levels. The American Sugar Alliance argues that the world price of sugar would be roughly the same as the internal support price if production subsidies in countries such as India were removed.

7.6.3   Peanuts

Historically, the US peanut policy consisted of a volume (poundage) quota system in which production was regulated for the domestic edible market (A. Schmitz, Furtan, and Baylis 2002). Quota peanut production exceeded domestic edible demand in the mid-1990s, about the same time that the North America Free Trade Agreement (NAFTA) and World Trade Organization (WTO) agreements began to loosen the import restrictions that had been necessary to implement the price support (Dohlman and Livezey 2005). To balance the market, the 1996 US FAIR Act lowered the peanut loan rate. Other changes followed with the passage of the 2002 Farm Security and Rural Investment Act. For example, US peanut policy includes linking direct and countercyclical payments to historical production levels on specific "peanut base acres" (similar to those for grains and cotton) – thus introducing greater flexibility and market incentives to peanut producers (ibid.).

The US peanut quota buyout program was terminated in 2002, and producers were compensated for losses from removal of the program. Compensation was based on the quota owner's 2001 quota. The unit value of this program was worth US$220 per ton and was offered in annual installments between 2002 and 2006 or was offered as a lump sum payment in the fiscal year of the owner's choice. The dollar amount of the US peanut buyout was based on the production quota values (A. Schmitz and T.G. Schmitz 2010) According to Dohlman and Livezey (2005), compliance with international trade agreements (e.g., NAFTA and WTO) was a source of concern that influenced the demise of the peanut marketing quota system in 2002.

7.6.4   Tobacco

The federal tobacco program dates back to 1938 and was designed to stabilize the US tobacco market and ensure fair prices for tobacco farmers. Marketing quotas and price supports were the two basic elements of the US tobacco program (A. Schmitz, Furtan, and Baylis 2002). Tobacco farmers were allocated an annual acreage-based quota, limiting the quantity of tobacco that quota owners could place on the market. Initially, tobacco quotas were allotted to each producer on the basis of historical tobacco production. Over time, most of the tobacco produced in the United States was converted from acreage-based production quotas to poundage-based marketing quotas. Annual quotas were set on the basis of a formula that included the purchase intentions of domestic tobacco manufacturers, a three-year average of exports, and a stock adjustment giving the US secretary of agriculture limited flexibility for quota adjustments.

As the quantity and quality of foreign-grown tobacco increased over time, lower-priced imported tobacco began to displace significant quantities of domestic tobacco used in manufacturing, and there was limited ability to adjust domestic prices within the constraints of the program. Other problems also emerged that put pressure on the tobacco price support program. For example, domestic tobacco manufacturers began to bypass traditional auction markets in favour of direct contracts with producers (A. Schmitz, T.G. Schmitz, and Rossi 2006).

In response, tobacco producers supported a tobacco quota buyout. In October 2004 the US Congress included the Fair and Equitable Tobacco Reform Act (the tobacco buyout) as part of larger corporate tax reform legislation. Beginning with the 2005 crop, the tobacco quota buyout: (1) terminated the federal tobacco price support and supply control programs; (2) made compensation payments to tobacco quota owners and to active tobacco growers for the elimination of the tobacco quota asset; and (3) provided for the orderly disposal of existing Commodity Credit Corporation (CCC) tobacco pool stocks. Payments to tobacco quota owners and growers totalled US$9.6 billion by the end of the 2005 crop year, with annual payments being spread evenly over the following ten years. Additional funding for handling CCC tobacco pool stocks and administration costs brought the total buyout package to US$10.14 billion, which was funded entirely by tax assessments on tobacco product manufacturers and tobacco product importers. Since 2005, farmers have had no restrictions on the amount or location of tobacco production. Similarly, they can sell tobacco to anyone they want, at any price.

A. Schmitz, Haynes, and T.G. Schmitz (2016b) estimated that the payments made to tobacco growers and tobacco quota owners were generous in that the buyout payments exceeded the true value of the producer gain from the use of quotas. The payments appeared to be based on the value of the quota, which can be far greater than the value of the net producer gain from quotas. In the Canadian case, compensation to Canadian tobacco growers for terminating the tobacco program was based on quota levels established in the 1950s (A. Schmitz, Haynes, and T.G. Schmitz 2016a).

7.7   IN PERSPECTIVE

The support of agricultural commodity prices in the United States has a long history dating back to the Agricultural Marketing Act of 1929. Early mechanisms attempted to increase agricultural income by providing higher prices through "orderly marketing" of agricultural products. During the Great Depression, these efforts focused on the allotment of the right to grow certain commodities coupled with a price support mechanism referred to as the commodity loan rate. Interestingly, several of these commodity mechanisms were integrated into the 2018 Farm Bill. Specifically, the 2018 Farm Bill still incorporates a commodity loan rate in the guise of the loan deficiency payment, and the price support mechanism initially referred to as the price deficiency payment still exists as the price loss coverage (PLC) program. However, there have been changes, such as the transition from traditional price-based programs to programs that reduce production risk through insurance-like programs (such as the ARC program).

Regardless of the movement towards more insurance-based agricultural program payments, commodity prices have been above most of the program targets over the past decade. Figure 7.6

Figure 7.6. Comparison of corn price with loan rate and reference price

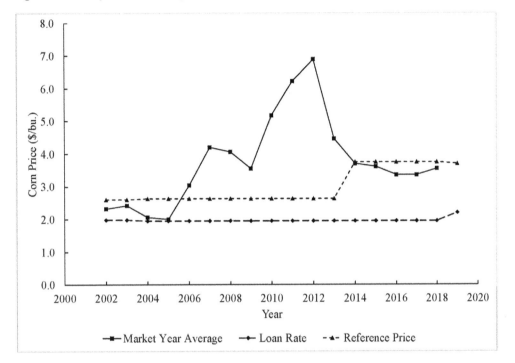

depicts the MYA price for corn compared to the loan rate and reference price for corn. In general, the corn price exceeded both the loan rate and reference prices from 2006 through 2014. After 2014, the market corn price was higher than the loan rate but lower than the reference price. Empirically, there were no countercyclical payments (the forerunner of PLC) between 2006 and 2014, with a small PLC payment in recent years. Figure 7.7 depicts the same pattern for soybean prices in the United States. These figures demonstrate that the commodity payments have been small in recent years. However, as will be discussed in the chapter on biofuels, much of the increase in commodity prices can be traced to biofuels (e.g., ethanol production).

Regardless of the low commodity payments from 2006 through 2018, the overall decline in recent years suggest that program payments may increase in the near future. Specifically, Figures 7.6 and 7.7 illustrate that the PLC program payments may increase, but more dramatic changes will have to occur before commodity prices fall to the loan rate.

Debate continues about the overall effect of farm programs. To what extent are farm programs of a political-economic-resource transaction (PERT) nature or of a political-economic-seeking transfer (PEST) nature? Empirically estimating the effect of farm programs is extremely time consuming, and this is perhaps why few empirical estimates about the impacts of policy are available, except, for example, in the cases of Canadian supply management and the US tobacco program.

Figure 7.7. Comparison of soybean price with loan rate and reference price

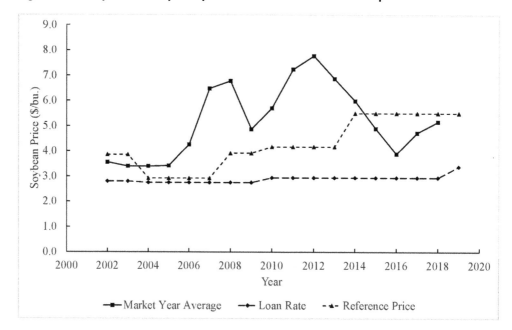

MOVING FORWARD

With the increased emphasis on business risk management and the increased prominence of subsidized crop insurance programs in several countries, one can ask whether any farm programs are still needed at all since farm incomes and wealth have increased significantly after the programs were introduced during the Great Depression. There is work to be done to ensure the continued evolution and improvement of farm policies worldwide (van Kooten, Orden, and Schmitz 2019, 373).

7.8   SUMMARY AND CONCLUSIONS

- Agricultural policies in the United States have shifted from policies that promoted the development of agricultural resources towards the support of agricultural prices.
- Historically, farm policies attempted to increase farm income by increasing the price received by farmers.
- Early programs attempted to increase farm prices using a two-pronged approach. First, programs reduced production output by allotments that limited the farmer's acreage in

program crops, and thus limited the amount of product the farmer produced. Second, the programs allowed for a variety of direct and indirect payments to farmers.

- Starting in the 1980s, a variety of policy innovations were implemented to make commodity programs more market oriented. Market orientation culminated with the passage of the Federal Agricultural Improvement and Reform Act of 1996, which implemented several policy instruments that attempted to decouple commodity supports from production decisions. The passage of the Farm Security and Rural Investment Act of 2002 represented a return to more traditional instruments of commodity programs. More recent Acts (e.g., the Agricultural Act of 2014 and the Agricultural Improvement Act of 2018) have moved towards more market-oriented policies by the introduction of risk-reducing agricultural policies akin to subsidized insurance products such as ARC program.
- The United States is a net importer of sugar. The domestic sugar price is supported with a tariff rate quota that restricts the amount of imported sugar.
- The peanut and tobacco production quota programs were terminated through buyouts wherein the future rents under the program were purchased by the federal government.
- Farm programs contribute to the value of farmland, but the debate about their necessity is ongoing.

CHAPTER EIGHT

Canadian Agricultural Programs

8.1 INTRODUCTION

Canadian agricultural policy involves the constitutional assignment of powers among the levels of government. Canada's Constitution requires that the federal government act in conjunction with the provinces in planning agricultural policies and programs, with the eventual mix of policies and programs an outcome of bargaining between the provinces and the federal government. Included in this policy-setting framework is the issue of equalization payments, which amount to a transfer of monies from the "have" provinces to the "have-not" provinces so that *fiscal capacity* is somewhat equal across the provinces. While fiscal capacity refers to the ability of provinces to raise taxes, equalization payments are simply a mechanism to transfer wealth from one province to another. Agricultural payments are one important means to make such transfers.

In Canada, there is some division of power in areas of economic, agricultural, and social activities between the provinces and the federal government. While individual provinces have ownership of their natural resources (e.g., coal, oil, and gas resources), there are exceptions, including resources originating from federal lands, such as national parks, private lands granted to the Canadian Pacific Railway, and lands allocated to Indigenous peoples. For the most part, agriculture is a *shared jurisdiction* between the provincial and federal governments, where the federal government's authority originates from its spending power (viz., equalization payments); its control over interprovincial and international trade, navigation, and fisheries; and its constitutional provisions, such as its spending and taxing ability, emergency power, and declaratory power (van Kooten and Scott 1995). How the federal government uses these options, in conjunction with provincial governments, determines the extent to which income is redistributed along with the associated costs.

Costs associated with agricultural programs in Canada can be funded by the following entities:

1 Provincial and federal governments plus producers (referred to as *tripartite programs*).
2 Provincial and federal governments.
3 One level of government and producers (becoming less common).
4 One level of government only (e.g., many provinces fund their own livestock programs).

As a result of shared jurisdiction and different lobbying groups in provincial legislatures, Canadian agricultural policies and support levels can also differ between provinces. Provinces can create their own farm support programs, and they individually bargain for federal funding (within the framework of federal equalization policies). Due to this balance of power and Canada's lack of fiscal and political ability to maintain high farm support levels, Canadian agricultural policies also differ greatly from those in the United States and the European Union (EU).

AGRICULTURE AND THE PROVINCES

The size and makeup of an agricultural sector varies greatly across provinces. For example, the grain-producing provinces of Alberta, Saskatchewan, and Manitoba face similar risks, so all three provinces will bargain for similar programs, and such programs generally include British Columbia's grain growing region in the northeast; these programs are rarely extended to grain farmers elsewhere in Canada. Nonetheless, a rich province such as Alberta may choose to support premium subsidies at a higher level.

8.2   AGRICULTURAL SUPPORT IN CANADA: BACKGROUND

To provide some indication of the degree to which Canada supports its agricultural sector, we first compare support for agriculture across sectors and countries using the Organisation for Economic Co-operation and Development's (OECD) producer support estimate (PSE) and the nominal rate of assistance (NRA). As indicated in Figure 8.1, Canada's 2016 rate of assistance to agricultural producers (policy transfers as a share of gross farm receipts) is much lower than the OECD average (10.7 per cent versus 18.9 per cent). As Figure 8.2 illustrates, Canada's rate of assistance has fallen from approximately 40 per cent in 1986 to slightly more than 10 per cent in 2016. Its rate is lower than that of the European Union and is now comparable to the rate of the United States.

Figure 8.1. Rates of assistance to agriculture based on producer support estimates, selected countries/regions, 2016

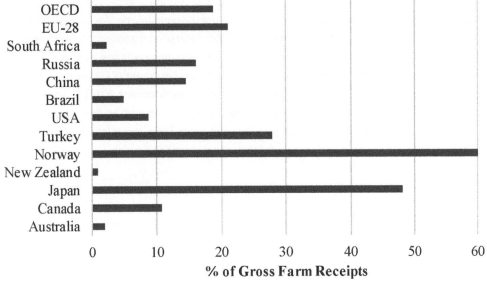

% of Gross Farm Receipts

Source: OECD (2018).

Figure 8.2. Rates of assistance to agriculture based on producer support estimates, Canada, China, EU-28, and United States, 1986–2016

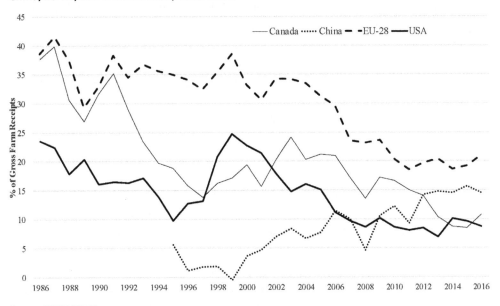

Source: OECD (2018).

MEASURING AGRICULTURAL SUPPORT ACROSS COUNTRIES

To compare support for agriculture across sectors and countries, Anderson and Nelgen (2013) and Anderson, Rausser, and Swinnen (2013) use the *nominal rate of assistance* (NRA). The NRA is the percentage by which the domestic producer price is above (or below if negative) the border price of a similar product, net of transportation costs and trade margins.

A similar alternative measure is the *producer support estimate* (PSE) produced by the Organisation for Economic Co-operation and Development (OECD). The PSE measures "policy transfers to agricultural producers, measured at the farm gate" (Greenville 2017) and is "expressed as a share of gross farm receipts" (OECD 2018). These measures are both estimates of direct government policy intervention.

Canada's NRA tracks higher than that of the United States and other comparable countries due to the role of supply-managed sectors, especially dairy. Supply management began in Canada with the passage of the Farm Products Agency Act in 1972, with effective quota regimes established in 1974 (van Kooten 2019; van Kooten, Orden, and Schmitz 2019). As indicated in Figure 8.3, nominal rates of assistance since the early 1970s have ranged from near zero to more than 80 per cent for eggs, and zero to 50 per cent for poultry. However, after implementation of supply management in dairy, NRAs increased from about 35 per cent to as much as 480 per cent, averaging nearly 200 per cent thereafter. Meanwhile, NRAs and PSEs in the grain and livestock sectors (excluding supply-managed poultry and low levels of subsidized maize production) are currently well below 5 per cent.

Illustrated in Figure 8.4 are annual direct agricultural program payments as a proportion of annual total farm cash receipts and of net farm income for the period 1980–2017. Except for 2004, real program payments exceeded net farm income between 2001 and 2007. When prices rebounded after 2007, the share of direct program payments declined dramatically, while net farm income grew. However, the ratio of direct payments to net farm income averaged 0.17 from 2013 to 2017, while averaging 0.75 from 2000 to 2017. Meanwhile, the ratio of direct payments to real total cash receipts remained relatively constant over the entire period 1980–2017.

In Figure 8.5, direct payments are allocated by type of program. Crop insurance benefits and those provided by hail insurance are considered separately, as are payments provided by various provincial government programs. Payments related to AgriInvest are combined with those of a predecessor program, the Net Income Stabilization Account (NISA); similarly, AgriStability payments are combined with those of its Gross Revenue Insurance Program (GRIP) predecessor. (AgriInvest and AgriStability are discussed in section 8.4 on business risk management.) Finally, Western Grain Stabilization payments, pre-supply management dairy payments, and other government transfer payments are summed together under *Other*. Annual total program payments rose during much of the 1980s, then decreased and plateaued

Figure 8.3. Nominal rates of assistance to agriculture, Canada's supply-managed sectors, 1962–2011

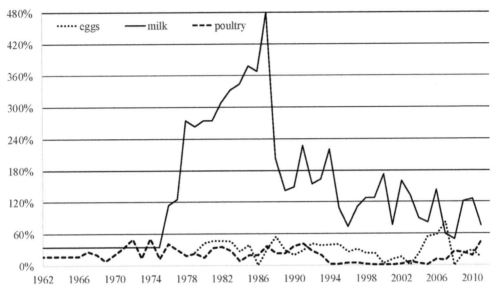

Source: Anderson and Nelgen (2013).

Figure 8.4. Ratio of government direct agricultural program payments to net farm income and to total cash receipts, Canada, 1980–2017

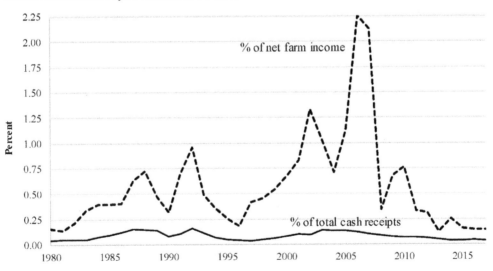

during the 1990s, when total payments averaged C$(2017)3.0 billion; however, total payments averaged C$4.1 billion during the period 2000–17 (values are in Canadian currency [C$] throughout this chapter unless otherwise indicated).

Figure 8.5. Government direct program payments by type of program, Canada, 1980–2017 (C$ billion)

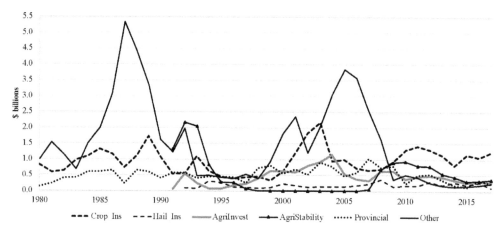

Direct payments from a variety of provincial and "other" programs have historically been an important source of revenue for farmers. For example, in the 1980s, major funding for grain farmers came via the Western Grain Stabilization Act and the Special Canadian Grains Program (part of the "other" category), and in 2007 provincial programs provided farmers with nearly C$(2017)1 billion with "other" federal government programs providing more than C$3.5 billion.

Figure 8.6 illustrates a compilation of total payments from different direct-payment programs in Canada for the period 1981–2010 (Vercammen 2013). During that period, individual Canadian programs had an average weighted lifetime of 8.7 years and provided an annual average payment of C$48.7 million, with 27 programs providing an average of about C$282 million per year. Business risk management programs account for approximately 60 per cent of all payments to agricultural producers over the period 1981–2010. Income support programs, including the Special Canadian Grains Program, feed freight assistance, input rebates, and direct payments from provincial programs, account for the remaining transfers.

8.3   CANADIAN AGRICULTURAL SUPPORT PROGRAMS

8.3.1   Agricultural Price Stabilization Legislation

The first agricultural price stabilization legislation in Canada was the 1958 Agricultural Stabilization Act (ASA). It was fully funded by the federal government, guaranteed farmers 90 per cent of a three-year moving average price for all commodities, and covered grain and

Figure 8.6. Number of programs and total direct payments to Canadian farmers, 1981–2010

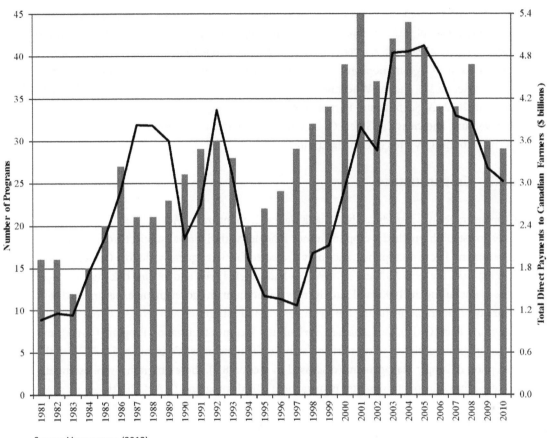

Source: Vercammen (2013).

livestock commodities in all provinces. Payouts under this legislation remained low until 1975 when they rose rapidly. In 1976, the Western Grain Stabilization Act (WGSA) removed grains produced in the northern Great Plains from the ASA. Dairy, eggs, and poultry were also removed from the ASA when their respective supply-management programs were introduced in the early 1970s. During this time, to support Canadian farmers against low world prices resulting from EU and US agricultural subsidy programs, tripartite payments, special Canadian Grain payments, and other provincial subsidies were implemented as needed. These were abandoned when an Agreement on Agriculture was struck in 1994 at the conclusion of the Uruguay Round of General Agreement on Tariffs and Trade (GATT) negotiations, coming into effect on 1 January 1995, with the establishment of the World Trade Organization (WTO), which replaced the GATT.

8.3.2   Canadian Wheat Board (CWB)

State trading through the Canadian Wheat Board (CWB) began in 1935; the CWB was a single-desk seller of western Canadian grains, playing an integral role in Canada's approach to agricultural stabilization for seventy-five years. However, due to increasingly negative farmer sentiments, the CWB monopsony over output ended with the Marketing Freedom for Grain Farmers Act (2011), and the Wheat Board ceased to be the sole marketer of western wheat and barley in 2012 (A. Schmitz and Furtan 2000). It was subsequently privatized in 2015, when a joint venture, known as the Global Grain Group, purchased a 50.1 per cent stake and changed the name of the CWB to G3 Canada Limited.

8.3.3   Crop Insurance

Crop insurance was introduced in Canada via the Crop Insurance Act of 1959. It allowed provinces to establish provincial crop insurance schemes with financial support from the federal government. Because crop insurance only protected farmers against yield loss (targeting production risk), the 1958 ASA and 1976 WGSA had targeted price and income risk. As these were phased out during the 1990s and into the new millennium, the government experimented with a variety of programs, including the Net Income Stabilization Account (NISA), Gross Revenue Insurance Plan (GRIP), the Canadian Agricultural Income Stabilization Program (CAIS), and other programs designed to support and stabilize farm incomes (Vercammen 2013). With the exception of supply management (discussed in section 8.5), these programs were essentially replaced by a suite of business risk management (BRM) programs (AAFC 2021b).

8.3.4   Subsidized Transportation Programs

Two subsidized transportation programs, the Crow's Nest Pass Agreement of 1897 and the Feed Freight Assistance program of 1941 became part of the Canadian agricultural stabilization policy. To facilitate the extension of the Canadian Pacific Railway (CPR), the Crow's Nest Pass Agreement provided lower freight rates for grain in exchange for a C$3.4 million subsidy to the CPR for building a rail link from Alberta to British Columbia. The freight rate on grain sold through Lake Superior ports was also lowered by 20 per cent. Then, the Railway Act (1925) made the freight rate statutory in perpetuity and extended the Crow Rate to the Canadian National Railway, with 1927 legislation extending the statutory rate to cover more agricultural exports.

As the costs of transporting grain increased over time, the railways no longer invested in transportation infrastructure because returns from moving grain were too low. Despite stopgap measures, such as government subsidies, the statutory Crow Rate could not survive. The Crow subsidy was finally eliminated in 1995, with a one-time payment of C$1.6

billion to compensate farmers for lost land values, and C$300 million to offset some adjustment costs. In the end, the Crow Rate was the longest running agricultural subsidy program in the world.

The Feed Freight Assistance program, fully funded by the federal government, provided a subsidy for feed grains shipped from the Prairies to livestock producers in British Columbia and central and eastern Canada. It distorted the location of the livestock producing and processing sectors by increasing the price of feed grains at the farm gate while reducing them near the population centres (Toronto, Montreal, and Vancouver).

MAJOR MILESTONES RELATED TO THE CANADIAN AGRICULTURAL SECTOR

1897 Crow's Nest Pass Agreement
1925 Railway Act
1935 Canadian Wheat Board (CWB)
1941 Feed Freight Assistance Program
1958 Agricultural Stabilization Act (ASA)
1959 Crop Insurance Act
1970 Supply management established for dairy, eggs, poultry
1976 Western Grain Stabilization Act (WGSA)
1994 Agreement on Agriculture (completed Uruguay Round of the GATT)
2008 Growing Forward business risk management programs implemented
2011 Marketing Freedom for Grain Farmers Act
2015 CWB becomes G3 Canada Limited
2020 US-Mexico-Canada Trade Agreement (USMCA) [replaced NAFTA]

8.4 CANADIAN AGRICULTURAL BUSINESS RISK MANAGEMENT PROGRAMS

Canada is shifting away from agricultural support programs towards agricultural business risk management (BRM) programs as the primary mechanism for protecting farmers' incomes. To bring all the BRM programs together, a five-year federal/provincial/territorial agricultural agreement, known as Growing Forward (GF), came into effect in 2008. The agreement focused on the following areas: (1) competitiveness, (2) innovation, (3) environment, and (4) business risk management. Programs were overhauled and subsumed under Growing Forward to provide agricultural risk protection for farmers through four programs:

1   *AgriInvest* is a government-matched savings account intended to address "shallow" reductions in net farm income – to help producers protect their margin from small declines. Under GF, individual producers could deposit up to 1.5 per cent of their allowable net sales (ANS) into the AgriInvest account annually, which is matched by a government contribution. ANS is limited to C$1.5 million, with the largest matching annual government contribution equal to C$22,500. Further, the account balance is limited to 25 per cent of a producer's average ANS.

2   *AgriStability* is a margin-based, whole-farm program that protects against larger income losses than under AgriInvest – it provides "deep" protection. Indemnities under AgriStability are based on the difference between the realized gross margin in any year and a reference historical margin, with payments triggered when a producer's realized gross margin falls 85 per cent or more below the reference margin. The reference margin is determined as an Olympic average (lowest and highest margins removed) of realized gross margins over the last five years. Under GF, funds from AgriInvest are meant to cover the first 15 per cent by which the realized margin falls below the reference margin. After that, the coinsurance (what the producer pays) is 30 per cent when the realized margin is between 70 and 85 per cent of the reference margin, but is only 20 per cent when it is less than 70 per cent. Producers pay no premiums.

3   *AgriRecovery* provides relief in the case of disasters, permitting governments to fill risk gaps not covered by other government programs. This disaster-relief program is offered by the federal, provincial, and territorial (FPT) governments to assist producers with extraordinary costs of recovering from natural disasters.

4   *AgriInsurance* provides protection to producers from production losses for specified perils, including economic losses arising from natural hazards, such as drought, flood, wind, frost, excessive rain or heat, snow, losses from uncontrollable disease, insect infestations and wildlife – it is production insurance. AgriInsurance is an extension of subsidized multi-peril crop insurance that has been available to Canadian farmers since 1959, although the range of products covered has increased over time. AgriInsurance does not cover livestock producers, although on-farm feed production can be insured. Compared to AgriStability, which is whole-farm and margin-based, AgriInsurance is commodity-specific and yield-based.

With some modifications, this suite of BRM programs remains in place and constitutes, along with supply management, the primary form of support for Canada's agricultural sector (Table 8.1). Growing Forward (GF), in effect from 1 April 2008 through 31 March 2013, was replaced by Growing Forward 2 (GF2) from 1 April 2013 through 31 March 2018, which was replaced by the Canadian Agricultural Partnership (CAP) beginning 1 April 2018 and ending in 2023.

Table 8.1. Agricultural programs providing direct net payments to Canadian farmers, 2011–17, and average annual payments (C$ million)

Program	2011	2012	2013	2014	2015	2016	2017	Average
Crop insurance	660.2	496.7	251.2	112.6	455.5	328.5	493.3	399.7
AgriInvest	424.9	452.3	418.6	321.0	268.9	297.3	281.4	352.0
AgriStability	740.8	726.1	517.4	432.9	295.7	311.0	356.5	482.9
AgriRecovery	292.9	49.7	0.6	1.3	4.1	2.7	9.0	51.5
Provincial stabilization programs	259.3	331.6	169.2	115.5	75.8	254.4	213.2	202.7
All other programs[a]	133.92	231.36	193.34	156.26	190.57	207.26	249.43	194.6
Total government funded programs	2,512.1	2,287.8	1,550.4	1,139.5	1,290.5	1,401.2	1,602.7	1,683.4

Source: Statistics Canada (2018).
[a] Includes Agri-Quebec (average C$80 million); Self-Directed Risk Management program (C$20 million); Crop Loss Compensation (C$14 million); two programs focused on waterfowl and other wildlife damage to crops (C$16 million); two livestock loss programs (C$7 million); and the remainder on flood assistance (not included in AgriRecovery), remnants of discontinued programs (e.g., CAIS) and temporary (three years or less) programs.

MARGINS

A margin simply refers to the difference between a producer's revenue and costs. Costs are difficult to calculate because some are variable (e.g., fuel for tractors, fertilizer), while others are fixed and one-time (land purchases) or are encountered every few years (equipment purchases). For the purpose of determining costs associated with agricultural program payments, the government specifies which types of costs are eligible. Since not all costs are eligible, the term "gross margin" is employed: the gross margin equals a farmer's sales revenue minus predetermined eligible expenses. The problem is that the income tax system is required to determine the cost side of the gross margin.

8.4.1   Shift from Growing Forward (GF) to Growing Forward 2 (GF2)

As a result of dissatisfaction with the AgriStability program, agricultural BRM programs were subsequently revised to change two programs – AgriInvest and AgriStability. Under AgriInvest, the producer contribution limit was increased from 1.5 per cent of allowable net sales to 100 per cent of ANS, but only 1 per cent (down from 1.5 per cent) was matched by the government, although a provincial government could act to increase the matching contribution. Further, the government's annual matching contribution was limited to C$15,000, down from a maximum of C$22,500 under the former program, although the balance limit that could be held in a farmer's AgriInvest account was increased from 25 per cent of historical average ANS to 400 per cent.

The changes to AgriInvest were required partly because of the changes made to AgriStability. GF2 simplified the AgriStability payment calculation by harmonizing multi-tier compensation rates under GF to a single level (70 per cent), but the level of program margin necessary to trigger a payout was reduced from 85 per cent of the reference margin to 70 per cent, with a 30 per cent gap rather than 15 per cent now to be covered by AgriInvest. These changes were made to comply with WTO rules under the Agreement on Agriculture. Under GF2, the coinsurance component was 30 per cent (payouts based on 70 per cent of the coverage of the eligible decline) regardless of the degree to which income falls (as was the case with GF). Again, producers could employ AgriInvest to cover shallow losses. Also, under GF2, a reference margin limit (RML) was imposed for calculating indemnities under AgriStability – the reference margin was set at the lesser of the historic average program margin (as previously determined) and the historical average of allowable expenses (determined for the same three years used to calculate the reference margin).

For livestock producers who grow feed grains and participate in crop insurance, there is a Western Livestock Price Insurance Program (WLPIP) that cattle and hog producers can use to manage the risk of falling prices in Canada's four western provinces. WLPIP protects producers against an unexpected drop in cattle and hog prices over a period of time. In essence, it protects against market volatility by providing a floor for cattle and hog prices. Program premiums are determined much like option prices, with the premium depending on the strike price, current price, period, and amount of coverage desired. It does not appear that a similar program exists outside the four western provinces.

PROTECTION FOR LIVESTOCK PRODUCERS (EXAMPLES)

A producer in Red Deer, Alberta, could take out a ten-month insurance contract on 28 August 2018 to protect the future (June 2019) price from falling below C$136/100kg (C$172/100kg), paying a premium of C$4.38/100 kg (C$18.72/100kg). This is much like a futures contract, but with more options for length of contract and level of protection. Premiums change daily. Poultry producers are not covered because of supply management (Livestock Price Insurance 2021).

A problem occurs with AgriStability. Suppose the price of cattle falls by 25 per cent while that of feed grain increases by 35 per cent. A producer who purchases feed grain will undoubtedly receive a payout under AgriStability as revenue falls and costs increase. Contrariwise, a producer of the same size, except dependent on their own stocks of feed grain, sees a loss on the revenue side but an increase in the value of inventories that offsets all or part of the loss on cattle sales, and might not be eligible for a payout. Is this fair?

8.4.2   From Growing Forward 2 to the Canadian Agricultural Partnership (CAP)

According to Agriculture and Agri-Food Canada's (AAFC) website, "the *Canadian Agricultural Partnership* is a five-year, C$3 billion investment by federal, provincial and territorial governments to strengthen the agriculture and agri-food sector" (Government of Canada 2021). The main changes from GF2 were meant to simplify and streamline BRM programs and make them easier to access. In particular, AgriStability employed the federal income tax system to determine eligibility and payments to producers. Unfortunately, reliance on tax forms and the tax system leads to a great deal of uncertainty for participating producers regarding indemnities and delays in receiving payments because the calendar (tax) year often differs from a producer's fiscal year (Ference & Company Consulting, Ltd. 2016). Therefore, AgriStability was modified so that participants with non-calendar fiscal year ends could now apply for AgriStability when their fiscal year ends, thereby providing earlier access to program benefits. Unlike AgriInsurance, AgriRecovery is not listed as a CAP program, primarily because farmers cannot register to participate; it is typically administered at the provincial/territorial level, but with federal funding.

Two additional changes were made to the AgriStability program. First, the RML was modified to ensure that producers from all sectors would have improved access to support, regardless of their cost structure. Under the modification, the RML could not reduce the reference margin by more than 30 per cent. Thus, if a farmer's historical average of allowable expenses fell below 70 per cent of the reference margin, the RML would equal 70 per cent of the reference margin rather than the lower value determined from the historical average expenses. Second, a late participation mechanism was introduced to ensure that all producers could access AgriStability support should a significant decrease in revenue threaten the viability of their farm. The late participation mechanism would be triggered at the provincial/territorial level in response to "significant events," with program benefits subsequently reduced by 20 per cent.

In going from GF2 to CAP, the maximum allowable net sales eligible under AgriInvest was reduced from C$1.5 million to C$1.0 million, while the annual matching contribution from government was lowered to C$10,000 from C$15,000. The producer contribution limit under AgriInvest was increased from 1.5 per cent of allowable net sales to 100 per cent of ANS, but only 1 per cent (down from 1.5 per cent) was matched by the government. Further, the government's annual matching contribution was now limited to C$10,000, down from C$15,000 under GF2. Canadian policymakers tweaked various components of the BRM suite to achieve various objectives (van Asseldonk et al. 2019).

In addition to the four main programs of Canada's BRM suite, there are an additional twelve programs that constitute the CAP: AgriRisk (three separate initiatives), AgriScience (two programs), AgriMarketing (two programs), AgriAssurance (two programs), AgriCompetitiveness, AgriDiversity, and AgriInnovate (AAFC 2021d). Except for farmers and farm cooperatives, for-profit organizations are only eligible to participate in three programs – one AgriScience program, one AgriMarketing initiative, and AgriInnovate; the remaining programs are directed at academic and not-for-profit entities. If the above programs are included, there are now forty-one different programs that are designed to provide aid to Canada's agricultural sector (AAFC 2021d). Programs are designed to do such things as fund research into clean technologies, innovations throughout the food chain, marketing, and product diversity, among other things. Two new research initiatives under AgriRisk provide small grants (C$25,000/year for upward of three years) to fund academic research addressing issues relevant to BRM in Canada's agriculture sector, and much larger grants to facilitate development and adoption of private risk management tools that would then be paid for by the agricultural producers.

Fifty-three agricultural programs have been terminated, although thirteen of these continue via some successor program (AAFC 2021c). For example, the federal government has an Advance Payments Program (APP) that complements but is not a part of the suite of BRM programs described above. The APP helps crop, livestock, and other agricultural producers with cash flow (including producers whose principal activity may not be farming), which provides flexibility for marketing of commodities (e.g., a farmer can decide to sell product based on market conditions and not just need for cash flow). The APP provides a loan to producers of up to C$400,000, of which C$100,000 is interest free, depending, however, on the size of their enterprise. Producers can take out the loan at any time but must repay it within eighteen months (twenty-four months for cattle and bison producers).

8.4.3   Impact on Farmers of BRM Programs and Changes to Programs

What has been the impact of the federal BRM suite of programs on farmers' incomes? Jeffrey, Trautman, and Unterschultz (2017) calculated the expected net present values (NPV) of a representative Alberta farm enterprise under no BRM programs, and then under GF and GF2. Without BRM, the net annual earnings were estimated to be C$71.97 per hectare (ha) (net farm worth equal to C$931,960/ha) with the coefficient of variation (CV) equal to 0.40. Under GF, expected annual earnings increased to C$110.07/ha (net worth of C$1,425,386/ha) with a CV of 0.27, falling to C$106.69/ha (C$1,381,693/ha) with slightly higher CV of 0.29 under GF2. Upon examining representative farms in six regions of Alberta and looking at only the changes in AgriStability from GF to GF2, Liu, Duan, and van Kooten (2018) found that gross margins fell between 0.6 and 1.1 per cent depending on the region, thereby confirming the results of Jeffrey, Trautman, and Unterschultz (2017).

Liu, Duan, and van Kooten (2019) examined the impact of introducing a reference margin limit in the AgriStability program. This had a negative effect, which was greater for farmers with the lowest costs, as expected. Further, the choice of late participation does offer farmers some flexibility in enrolment, but the researchers found that all farmers would be better off in terms of expected gross margins if they participated in AgriStability every year.

8.4.4   Program Funding and the Role of Provinces and Territories

When it comes to funding, the two levels of government (federal and provincial/territorial) budgeted C$2 billion for the BRM component of GF2 (an increase of 50 per cent from Growing Forward). CAP relies on bilateral agreements between individual provinces or territories and the federal government – there is no widespread, sweeping legislation covering all levels of government simultaneously; the agricultural BRM programs are cost-shared 60:40 with the provinces and territories, who contributed C$0.8 billion (AAFC 2017). In addition, under GF2, the federal government was the sole funder, to the tune of C$1 billion, of programs that aim to facilitate economic growth in the agricultural sector (AgriInnovate, AgriCompetitiveness, and AgriMarketing). Overall, therefore, the federal government spent C$1.2 billion on BRM programs, plus another C$1 billion on marketing, competitiveness, and innovation, over the five-year period ending 31 March 2018. As noted above, governments expect to spend C$3 billion on CAP (an increase of 50 per cent from GF2) over the period 2018–23, again split 60:40 between the two levels of government. Annual expenditures are estimated to run at C$600 million, not including expenditures on non-CAP programs.

The amount paid by farmers is difficult to determine as it depends on uptake or enrolment in various BRM programs. To participate in AgriStability, farmers must pay C$4.50 annually for every C$1,000 of reference margin protected (where reference margin in this case is 70 per cent of the contribution reference margin); in addition, there is an annual administrative fee of C$55. As an example, if the farmer's reference margin is C$70,000, the fee will be C$220.50 (= C$4.50/$1,000 × 0.7 × C$70,000) plus C$55 (AAFC 2021a). The introduction of a fee might explain why the participation rate for AgriStability fell from 57 per cent under GF to 42 per cent under GF2 – producers did not pay a premium under GF. However, as noted above, Liu, Duan, and van Kooten (2019) find that farmers who participate in AgriStability can expect to be better off.

In British Columbia, Alberta, Saskatchewan, Ontario, Quebec, and Prince Edward Island, AgriStability is delivered by the respective provincial government, while the federal government delivers these programs elsewhere in Canada. AAFC provides seven examples to illustrate how AgriStability works in conjunction with AgriInvest and AgriInsurance to protect a farmer against price and yield risk (AAFC 2021d). Examples consist of both production and price risk for cattle producers, potato farmers, and grain growers, and yield risk for an apple grower. Only a grain producer experiencing yield loss due to flooding receives a benefit from AgriInsurance. Of course, the indemnities are based on participation in all three programs and depend on the amount of funds the agricultural producers have in their AgriInvest accounts.

Production insurance (AgriInsurance) is a tripartite program because it is funded by both levels of government and the producers (AAFC 2021c). The allocation of funding for premiums and administration is shown in Table 8.2. In addition, the federal government provides a reinsurance pool for provinces; a province can insure against an insurance claim that could bankrupt its crop

Table 8.2. Tripartite sharing of responsibility under AgriInsurance

Level of Government	Premium[a]	Administration
Federal	36%	60%
Provincial/territorial	24%	40%
Producer	40%	

[a] There are some special program options that are cost-shared at different rates but the vast majority of premium costs are shared at this level.

insurance agency. Such a "too big" crop insurance claim can be the result of an adverse weather event, for example, that affects a large proportion of the farmers in a province. The provincial crop insurance bodies are responsible for the design and administration of AgriInsurance, absorbing all underwriting gains and losses (which is why they often employ reinsurance).

AgriRecovery is best considered to be complementary to AgriInsurance, since it protects producers against catastrophic losses due to massive floods, animal diseases, etc. Expenditures under AgriRecovery are paid by the federal government and farmers are not required to enrol (as noted earlier). Since most major commercial crops in Canada are currently insured against deep losses under AgriInsurance, AgriRecovery is called upon only in unusual circumstances of extremely deep losses. Meanwhile, the great majority of farmers are also covered for shallow losses via AgriInvest, whereby the federal government contributes 1 per cent of whatever a farmer deposits into a savings account, up to a total annual subsidy of C$10,000.

Many provincial governments created Crown corporations to operate agricultural financial services as a cost-cutting budgetary measure. A study by A. Ker et al. (2017) indicates that the Crown corporations act too much like private insurance companies as opposed to public delivery agents. These authors argue that these Crown corporations rely too much on private reinsurance while holding too many reserves. Alberta, Saskatchewan, Manitoba, Ontario, and Prince Edward Island paid C$108 million in premiums to private reinsurance companies in 2014, while holding C$3.65 billion in reserve. Reserves as a percentage of liabilities averaged more than 23 per cent in 2014 for the six provinces with Crown corporations, from a high of 46 per cent in Alberta to a low of 8 per cent in Manitoba. Using Monte Carlo simulation, the authors estimated that it would take more than 8,000 years to deplete the reserves held by Crown corporations in Alberta and Ontario (A. Ker et al. 2017). Given that the agricultural sector is small relative to the rest of the economy, there is no reason whatsoever for provinces to rely on private reinsurance, especially given that the federal government already provides a reinsurance program for pooling risks.

Not surprisingly, A. Ker et al. (2017) also argue that the public sector can provide crop insurance to farmers more efficiently than the private sector. Governments are risk averse, require lower rates of return, and can use various policy levers to incentivize farmers to engage

PROVINCIAL CROP INSURANCE

Provinces are responsible for administering AgriInsurance, AgriInvest, and AgriRecovery. These BRM programs are delivered at the regional level through provincial Crown corporations or directly by the province's ministry of agriculture. A provincial Crown corporation is a publicly owned enterprise created by an Act of the legislature that shields it from government intervention; these corporations are supposed to operate at a profit, just as a private sector company, unless otherwise directed by the legislature that created them. Agricultural risk management Crown corporations operate in Alberta, Saskatchewan, Manitoba, Ontario, Quebec, and Prince Edward Island, with remaining provinces vesting this function within their ministries of agriculture. In Saskatchewan, delivery occurs through the Saskatchewan Crop Insurance Corporation (SCIC) – a provincial Crown corporation; in Manitoba, it is known as the Manitoba Agricultural Services Corporation (MASC); in Alberta, the Agriculture Financial Services Corporation (AFSC); in Ontario, AgriCorp; in Quebec, le Programme d'Assurance Stabilisation des Revenus Agricoles; and, in Prince Edward Island, Agricultural Insurance Corporation.

in on-farm, risk-reducing activities. Indeed, public provision of AgriInsurance can be made more effective by introducing coinsurance into the program, as is done in the AgriStability program. Finally, these authors reiterate complaints others have voiced about the AgriStability program. It leads to uncertainty regarding the indemnity a farmer might expect to be paid and to delays before payment is received and is viewed as an obstacle to on-farm diversification. Therefore, AgriStability should be replaced by commodity-specific revenue insurance as revenue is much easier to measure and track than is gross margin. Calculation of gross margin requires knowledge of input use and costs, and these can only be determined from a farmer's tax receipts – the tax system is needed to resolve the payments a farmer would receive, which leads to delays and uncertainty.

8.4.5   Private Market Agriculture Insurance Alternatives

While governments promote a greater role for private sector involvement in the provision of BRM tools (see below), this is very difficult because, in Canada, the Crown corporations have a monopoly, and they provide subsidized products. As a result of subsidies, therefore, any private sector offering cannot compete. However, research summarized by V.J. Smith (2017) indicates that there would be little uptake of private sector crop insurance in the absence of government subsidies because few farmers would be willing to pay the full premium of the insurance product plus administration and operations costs. This creates a situation where there really are no private sector tools that are commercially viable. One exception is hail insurance, which is currently the only payment listed in Statistics Canada farm accounts as a separate BRM payment to agricultural producers; here the private sector has succeeded because hail insurance does not suffer from moral hazard (producer decisions cannot influence outcomes) or adverse selection (premiums are unaffected by participation rates), and costs of providing this product are lower than with other forms of crop insurance.

Another possible success is a product called Global Agricultural Risk Solutions (GARS). GARS is a relatively new production cost insurance product offered to grain producers in western Canada. It is delivered by the private sector and premiums are not subsidized. The product provides basic insurance coverage for three major input costs, including fertilizer, seed, and chemicals, plus enhanced coverage for qualifying producers for a specific amount of revenue per acre. GARS is a whole-farm revenue insurance product that provides coverage when net production income is less than insured net crop production. It pays indemnities based on farm-specific production income, and not an index. While GARS provides coverage for input costs, as well as for a specific amount of revenue per acre for qualifying producers, GARS has a number of unique features:

- Premiums are based on a producer's specific circumstances and financial records. Therefore, at least five years of accrual financial statements are needed, which farmers must provide. Producers using cash financials must convert to accruals.
- "Enhanced" coverage levels of C$25, C$50, C$75, C$100, or C$125 per acre are available only to qualified producers based on an analysis of financial records. Consequently, insurance is only offered to a limited number of producers who are financially sound – adverse selection in reverse.
- GARS does not insure individual crops.
- Claim payments can be delayed, however, since 60 per cent of the indemnity is paid after an interim harvest report from an accountant is provided. The remaining 40 per cent of the indemnity is withheld until after 1 May, the inventory cut-off date.
- GARS coverage levels are determined based on an average of the producer's production history. Therefore, farm performance (i.e., profitability) from previous years impacts the insurance coverage in the current year.

GARS is successful because it is able to select only the top agricultural producers and penalize them in subsequent periods if they "shirk," or perform below expectation. Unfortunately, little is known about uptake of GARS, although, based on its staffing level, it is clear that the company serves a small clientele. Besides the fact that GARS only appeals to top producers, some crop producers might shy away from this product because participation requires farmers to make their financial transactions available to the insurer. It is unlikely that this product could operate in anything but a small niche market.

In addition to GARS, some private companies provide over-the-counter, index-based insurance products. Index-based insurance is considered a good alternative to crop insurance because individual loss characteristics of the producer cannot influence the underlying index – adverse selection and moral hazard no longer applies. However, uptake of such products has not proven very good so far, partly because private insurance companies are unable to compete with highly subsidized public corporations that protect farmers' incomes and subsidize high premiums. It is unlikely that index-based insurance will be attractive to farmers without subsidy (V.J. Smith 2017).

CLIMATE CHANGE, AGRICULTURE, AND CARBON TAXES

Agriculture is responsible for about 15 per cent of total anthropogenic greenhouse gas (GHG) emissions (FAO 2009). Given that farmers benefit from government programs, it is unlikely that carbon taxes will be imposed on agricultural activities to the same extent as in the rest of the economy. This still needs to be determined, but Canada already has an agricultural program in place to help farmers reduce greenhouse gas emissions in the areas of livestock systems, cropping systems, agricultural water use efficiency, and agroforestry. Beginning 1 April 2019, the Government of Canada levied a carbon tax of C\$20 per tonne of CO_2 (tCO_2), or C\$0.044 per litre of gasoline (US\$0.125 per US gallon), in provinces that do not already have their own carbon pricing schemes. This tax is expected to rise to C\$50/tCO_2 (C\$0.11per litre, US\$0.31 per gallon) by 2022. However, the future of the carbon tax, how it might be implemented in the agricultural sector, and the development of new programs to help farmers mitigate climate change or simply cope with economy-wide efforts to reduce GHG emissions are to be determined (see Chapter 14).

8.5 SUPPLY MANAGEMENT

Perhaps the most controversial feature of Canada's agricultural programs is supply management (SM). The enabling legislation for SM in agriculture is the Farm Products Agency Act of 1972. It led to the establishment of SM boards in dairy in 1974, although the Canadian Dairy Commission had started to "intervene" in the milk sector several years earlier. SM was also established in eggs (1973), turkey (1974), chicken (1978), and chicken hatching eggs (1986) – the "feather industries." Although SM remains the identifying characteristic of these sectors, the focus is usually on dairy because it receives the largest support of any agricultural commodity in Canada (Figure 8.3). Dairy SM was a major impediment to Canada's renegotiation of the North American Free Trade Agreement (NAFTA), which resulted in a new trade agreement – the United States-Mexico-Canada Agreement (USMCA) (van Kooten 2019).

TRADE AND CANADIAN AGRICULTURE

When conclusion of the Doha round of trade negotiations under the auspices of the World Trade Organization appeared imminent, Canadian agricultural economists asked "whether the current supply-managed system should be realigned only to be consistent with the new trade rules [that had yet to be determined], or if more funda-mental changes should be undertaken to better position the industry for the future" (Barichello, Cranfield, and Meilke 2009, 205). While the Doha round of multilateral trade negotiations has still not yet been concluded, regional trade negotiations took over the agenda, impacting Canada's supply-managed sector – the limit on imports of cheese has been increased somewhat, while imports of ultra-fine filtered milk are unrestricted. Canada's trading partners have made inroads into its SM sectors, pri-marily by raising Canada's tariff rate quotas (T.G. Schmitz and Seale 2019). In addition, trade disputes between China and the United States over genetically modified corn have negatively affected Canadian farmers. Because of the Chinese ban on US corn due to a failure to register a genetically modified trait, North American corn prices fell, with Canadian corn producers losing some C$30 million (T.G. Schmitz 2018). As more genetic engineering of crops occurs, trade disputes will likely increase.

8.5.1   Dairy Supply Management: Economic Framework

The key to supply management is the use of import quotas and domestic production controls (Vercammen and Schmitz 1992). These policy instruments are modelled in Figure 8.7. Do-mestic demand is given by the curve D_0 and domestic supply is given by S. Under free trade, the domestic border price is Pb, domestic production is Q_1, and domestic consumption is Q_2. Imports total $Q_2 - Q_1$. Only an agreed-upon quantity of imports, the Minimum Access Com-mitment or tariff rate quota (TRQ), is given tariff-free access to the Canadian market. Imports are restricted to $Q_2 - Q_1''$ (Figure 8.7). Now domestic producers face the demand curve D'.

Because of the nature of demand, the pricing structure for milk is much more complicated than that presented in Figure 8.7. For example, there are many demands for milk, including fluid milk by households and industrial milk by processors. An expanded version of Figure 8.7 should include at least two demand curves: one that is inelastic (demand for fluid milk) and one that is elastic (demand for milk products such as cheese or yogurt). Producers will maximize profit for

Figure 8.7. Framework for analysing supply management (quota) regime

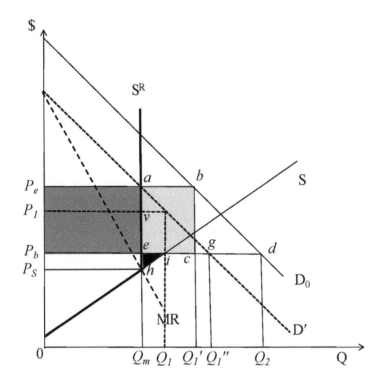

any given level of output by practising price discrimination in different markets (as occurs and is permitted in the US dairy sector). Because of the nature of demand and the allocation of the output to various markets, conflicts often arise between producers and industrial processors.

For the domestic producers to maximize profits, the production of quota is set where the marginal revenue curve MR equals the supply curve S, which results in domestic production Q_m – that is, supply management leads to the vertical supply curve S^R. Producers gain ($P_eP_b ea$ – ehi), the relatively dark shaded rectangle area minus the black-shaded triangle. The quota value for any producer will be the discounted value of (P_e – P_S) per unit of quota. The total approximate quota value for the industry will be the discounted value of ($P_eP_S ha$).

In Figure 8.7, consumers lose ($P_eP_b db$) and importers gain ($aecb$). The availability of import quotas gives importers (many of whom are also domestic food retailers) incentives for rent-seeking behaviour, because import quotas have a value equal to [$P_eP_b db$ – ($P_eP_b ea$ + $aecb$)]. This area plus ehi represents the net cost of the supply management program. The smaller the deadweight loss (DWL), the greater is the efficiency with which income can be transferred from consumers to producers. Thus, the size of the income transfer can be large, while the deadweight loss triangle can be small. The burden of supply management thereby falls on consumers, with the poorest hurting the most.

Table 8.3. Cross-border price comparisons for selected products under supply management and products not under supply management, various regions, 2018 (C$)[a]

Product	Units	Vancouver	US State of WA	Winnipeg	US State of ND	South Ontario	US State of NY	Average Premium/ Discount (%)[d]
Products under Supply Management (Chicken, Eggs, and Dairy Products)								
Whole chicken	$/kg	8.99	4.55	8.99	5.34	8.49	4.27	88
Chicken thigh	$/kg	13.82	8.39	13.82	8.39	13.83	8.39	65
Grade A eggs[b]	$/dzn			2.82	1.52	2.93	2.79	45
Grade AA eggs[b]	$/dzn	2.84	1.26					125
Milk, generic[c]	$/4 L	4.47	3.27	4.58	3.89	4.27	2.72	37
Milk, alternate[c]	$/4 L	4.47	4.43	4.58	4.63	4.27	4.23	0
Milk, other[c]	$/4 L	4.47	3.92	4.58	4.41	4.27	2.55	28
Ice cream	$/L	2.98	2.69	2.98	2.72	2.98	1.94	25
Cheddar cheese	$/kg	11.29	12.08	11.29	12.08	12.82	9.79	6
Processed cheese	$/450 g	3.67	4.48	3.67	4.48	3.67	2.42	5
Butter	$/454 g	6.18	4.21	5.16	4.21	5.16	3.06	46
Products Not under Supply Management								
Lean ground beef	$/kg	9.92	10.37	9.92	10.37	9.92	10.37	−4
Pork chops	$/kg	11.11	13.40	11.11	11.97	11.11	10.21	−5
Bacon	$/kg	7.92	13.13	8.99	13.13	7.92	12.14	−35
Apples	$/kg	4.02	3.44	4.02	4.24	3.29	2.81	10
Oranges	$/kg	3.17	3.17	3.17	3.49	3.17	3.21	−3
Bananas	$/kg	1.46	1.47	1.70	1.58	1.22	1.31	0
White bread	$/kg	2.75	3.39	2.75	3.39	2.43	2.47	−13
Plain flour	$/kg	2.35	1.99	2.35	1.99	2.15	1.87	17
Peanut butter	$/kg	3.77	5.01	3.77	5.01	3.27	2.93	−13
Ketchup	$/L	3.47	4.64	3.47	4.64	3.47	3.46	−17

Source: Adapted from Cardwell, Lawley, and Xiang (2018)
[a] Using an exchange rate of C$1 = US$0.77
[b] Grade refers to US grade
[c] Generic/alternate/other refer to Walmart's Great Value and alternate brands or milk from other stores
[d] Extent to which Canadian prices exceed US averaged over the local area differences

That the burden falls on consumers is shown in Table 8.3, where prices for basic food commodities in various regions/cities in Canada are compared with those in nearby US states or cities. While Canadian prices of basic foods that are not under supply management are comparable or even slightly lower than those in the United States, foods produced under supply management, including chicken, eggs, milk, and butter, are substantially higher than the same product in the United States (Cardwell, Lawley, and Xiang 2015, 2018; Doyon, Bergeron, and Tamini 2018). The data in Table 8.3 also support the theoretical arguments of Figure 8.7.

Van Kooten (2019) uses the theoretical model in Figure 8.7 to estimate the annual quota rent (dark shaded rectangle), the quasi-rent (P_1P_bev) component of the quota rent, the deadweight loss triangle (*ehi*), and the net loss to dairy producers (P_eP_bea) should supply management end. This

Table 8.4. Annual quota rent, quasi-rent component, DWL triangle, and net loss if supply management ended: dairy sector, Canada, various scenarios (C$ million)

Year	Quota Rent	Quasi-Rent	DWL Triangle	Net Potential Loss Should Quota Regime End
2010	2,422.0	373.5	18.7	354.8
2011	2,332.4	346.4	17.4	329.0
2012	2,587.3	398.0	19.7	378.3
2013	2,050.5	252.6	13.6	239.0
2014	2,051.8	254.0	13.6	240.3
2015	2,106.5	263.2	14.0	249.1
2016	936.5	60.0	3.7	56.3
Average	**2,069.6**	**278.2**	**14.4**	**263.8**

Source: Adapted from van Kooten (2019).

information (Table 8.4) is given for each of the years 2010 through 2016 (because the wedge between P_e and P_b differs across years). The value of quota depends on the rate used to discount the annual quota/monopoly rent. If there is a high risk that the dairy supply management system will be reformed (see below), the rate used to discount future benefits from quota will be high. If it is assumed to be a moderate 20 per cent, then the average total quota rent C$2,069.6 million will result in a quota value to Canadian dairy producers of C$10.35 billion; if the rate is 40 per cent, the quota has a value of only C$5.17 billion.

8.5.2   Dairy Supply Management: Operation and Pitfalls

The government supports the prices of butter fat and skim milk powder (SMP), buying and disposing of excess product at those prices. The dairy producer receives a blend of the two prices depending on the butter fat content of their milk. Demand for butter fat is robust and because quotas are measured in terms of butter fat, Canada exports the excess non-fat component as SMP; such exports are currently limited under WTO rules and, unless Canada removes its support price for SMP, will be prohibited after 2020.

CANADA-UNITED STATES TRADE: NAFTA AND USMCA

In early 2020, the United States, Mexico, and Canada signed into law a new free trade agreement (USMCA). One sticking point in reaching an agreement between the United States and Canada was over the limited importation by Canada of US dairy products (see Figure 8.7). In addition to Canada's high tariffs (averaging more than 250 per cent) applied to US imports above the tariff rate quota (TRQ), the United

States disagreed with Canada's response to increasing US imports of milk-based protein. Wisconsin milk processors had developed an ultra-fine filtered milk protein isolate (MPI), which was classified in the Canadian tariff schedule as a "protein" rather than as a dairy product, and thus outside supply management. In response, the Canadian Dairy Commission created a new class of milk protein products meant to compete with Wisconsin imports but implicitly subsidized by the supply-managed marketing regime.

Under WTO rules, Canada's total TRQ on dairy products was 20,412 tonnes (t). Under the Comprehensive Economic and Trade Agreement (CETA) between Canada and the European Union and the USMCA trade deals, the low-duty or duty-free TRQs in dairy were increased to 3.25 per cent and 3.59 per cent of the market, respectively. By the sixth year of USMCA, additional quota would be allowed: fluid milk, 50,000t; cheese, 12,500t; cream, 10,500t; SMP, 7,500t; butter and cream powder, 4,500t; yogurt and buttermilk, 4,135t; concentrated and condensed milk, 1,380t; and other dairy products, 4,660t. These amounts are to increase at 1 per cent annually for thirteen years thereafter. (If the market were to grow by more than 1 per cent annually, the US share of the Canadian dairy market would actually decline over time.) Tariffs on milk protein concentrate and SMP from Europe and the United States were also eliminated. Since the MPI market is only a subset of the non-fat market, Canada has some ability to maintain the domestic price above the world price (as high tariffs on above-TRQ amounts remain in place). However, given robust demand for butter fat, Canada must accept the world price for SMP or restrict production of butter fat, even importing butter, to support the farm gate price of milk, which is based on target prices for butter fat and SMP and a producer's milk protein and fat content.

In addition to the quota rents earned by farmers, Canadian dairy programs also provided subsidies of over C$200 million annually over the period 1981–2002. Subsidies continue in the form of the Dairy Farm Investment Program and Dairy Processing Investment Fund; the former provides dairy producers with C$250,000 (one time over the period 2018–23) to invest in their operation, while the latter provides dairy processing firms upward of C$10 million (with an additional C$250,000 for consulting, R&D, and other services) to invest in technological processes. These programs seek to make dairy producers and processors more efficient, enabling processors to replace aging plants and compete in the ultra-fine filtered MPI market. Canadian dairy producers always have the option to participate in BRM programs.

8.5.3   Supply Management in Other Sectors

The Farm Products Agency Act of 1972 is also the enabling legislation for poultry and eggs. Under the Act, marketing plans may be developed, and federal-provincial agreements may be set up to govern the creation and operation of national agencies. Output levels must be approved by the National Farm Products Council (NFPC) and are decided by agencies made up largely of provincial representatives. The NFPC reports to the minister of Agriculture and Agri-Food Canada (AAFC), but pricing jurisdiction for poultry and eggs remains at the provincial level.

The NFPC approves national production levels, but it must be satisfied that plant production is adequate to protect the interests of consumers as well as producers. Beyond monitoring and its supervisory role, the NFPC is charged with conducting the process under which new plans may be established There is an important difference between dairy and poultry in terms of the governance structure, however. The poultry agency is governed by directors who are usually elected by producers in each member province. In contrast, the Canadian Dairy Commission (CDC) is a federal Crown corporation with members appointed by the AAFC federal minister. As such, the CDC members have no particular geographical constituency in the same sense as do the provincial directors of the poultry agencies.

What are the consequences of this structural difference? The approach underlying the poultry and egg systems, while more democratic in terms of producer input, is also more rigid and less capable of change, particularly when it comes to adjusting provincial production shares (Skogstad 1993). Moreover, the necessity for a federal-provincial agreement will lead some provinces to view poultry and dairy as instruments of regional economic development. If provinces sign on to the production plan, they will expect a piece of the action in return.

REFORMING QUOTA REGIMES

Supply management (SM) is an impediment to efficient production and results in income transfers from consumers to farmers and, increasingly, processors. Economists have long opposed the use of quotas to restrict supply. SM has already been eliminated in tobacco (US, Canada), peanuts (US), dairy (Australia, EU), and sugar (EU). There are economic analyses of the tobacco buyouts in the United States and Ontario (Canada), and a peanut buyout program in the United States (A. Schmitz and T.G. Schmitz 2010; A. Schmitz, Haynes, and T.G. Schmitz 2016a, 2016b). In the United States, compensations for peanut producers and tobacco producers were US$264 million and US$9.6 billion, respectively. The tobacco buyback program in Ontario based payments on a producer's basic production quota rather than total marketing quota (actual production), where the latter was significantly lower than the former (although based on it). Almost all farmers participated in the voluntary buyout, receiving C$275,000 each and costing government C$286 million; but the enabling legislation did not prevent tobacco farming, with production increasing after the buyout. The researchers found that producers were generally overcompensated. In the case of Canada's dairy quota regime, van Kooten (2019) argues that proposed compensation exceeds the theoretical level of compensation by an order of magnitude.

8.6   FUTURE TRENDS IN CANADA'S AGRICULTURAL SUPPORT POLICIES

Canada has significantly reduced its agricultural support since the late 1980s. Producer support as a share of gross farm receipts fell sharply between 1986–8 and 1995–7, in large part because producer support payments to the grains industry were discontinued in 1995. The decline in the level of support since then has been more gradual because there have not been any significant policy changes to support measures for dairy, poultry, and eggs. Lower levels of disaster payments in recent years and a shift of budgetary expenditures towards general service support to agriculture since the mid-1990s have resulted in lower farm income support overall. Based on producer support estimates (PSE), Canada's overall support to agricultural value added is now below that of the OECD average, and below that of the EU-28, Japan, Norway, Russia, and China, but above that of the United States. Total support to agriculture as a share of GDP has declined significantly over time. Nonetheless, as a result of rent seeking by the supply-managed sector, the Government of Canada has declared that changes to SM are non-negotiable. International pressure for Canada to open its markets, especially in dairy, continues to be quite strong, although bilateral trade agreements have slowly reduced some of the large income transfers from consumers to producers.

RENT SEEKING BY DAIRY PRODUCERS

The main reason supply management survives in Canada is rent seeking by dairy producers. The dairy producers argue that, since it only serves the domestic market, it should not be considered in trade negotiations. At a political level, the House of Commons unanimously passed a motion in 2005 asking the government not to give up any protection for the SM sectors in international trade negotiations. This stance was reaffirmed in the government's 2011 Speech from the

Throne (Busby and Schwanen 2013). Yet, under the CETA trade agreement with the EU, the industry gave up 2 per cent of its domestic market, followed by another 3.25 per cent under the Trans-Pacific Partnership (TPP). During the renegotiation of NAFTA, which led to the USMCA, dairy farmers lobbied the prime minister and, again, all parties in Parliament resolved to protect SM. Despite this stance, the negotiators gave US producers greater access to Canada's dairy market. Clearly, rent seeking by farmers and acquiescence by politicians characterize SM and its continuance.

Unlike the AgriInsurance and AgriRecovery components of agricultural support, AgriInvest and AgriStability have been modified to benefit smaller farms. Initially, farmers received an indemnity from AgriStability that covered 70 per cent of their revenue loss when the realized gross margin was between 70 and 85 per cent of the reference margin, but 80 per cent of their loss when it was less than 70 per cent; participants paid no premiums. Later, farmers were not covered until their loss exceeded 30 per cent (smaller losses were to be covered by AgriInvest) and they had to pay premiums. A reference margin limit was also imposed for calculating indemnities – the reference margin was set at the lesser of the historic average program margin and the historical average of allowable expenses used to calculate the reference margin. Under the present Canadian Agricultural Partnership, a late participation mechanism was introduced to ensure that all producers could access AgriStability support should a significant decrease in revenue threaten the viability of their farm, although there would be a 20 per cent reduction in the payout. A trend in BRM is the desire for greater participation by the private sector and the development of new insurance products, particularly index-based insurance. Greater emphasis on business risk management led some to argue that Canadian agricultural food policy has taken a different direction than in the past (Mussell, Hedley, and Bilyea 2019).

8.7   SUMMARY AND CONCLUSIONS

- From the 1970s to the 1990s, Canadian agricultural policies sought to respond to those of the United States and the European Union by providing farmers with sizeable subsidies.
- Subsidies were capitalized in farmland prices, leading to even more pressure to support farmers.
- By the end of the 1990s, Canada had shifted its farm programs from direct payments to the subsidization of agricultural business risk programs.

- State trading by the Canadian Wheat Board (CWB) ended in 2012. Western Canadian farmers were no longer required to sell wheat and certain other grains only to the CWB, which had held a monopsony position.
- The successful conclusion of trade negotiations with the European Union (CETA) and the United States (USMCA) led to freer trade in dairy products.
- The supply management program established for dairy, poultry, and eggs in the early 1970s has strong political support and is a major component of Canadian agricultural policy.
- Canada's agricultural programs also focus on business risk management. Such programs include crop yield insurance, protection against large downward variation in net revenues, and a number of smaller programs to promote marketing of all sorts of products, research and development, and investments in farm equipment and downstream processing of agricultural commodities. Unlike supply management, these programs are subsidized by the federal and provincial governments.

CHAPTER NINE

European Union Agricultural Policy and Reforms

9.1 BACKGROUND

The European Union (EU) began life in 1951 as the European Coal and Steel Community (ECSC), with the objective of pooling the raw materials required by industry in Germany, France, and the Benelux countries (Belgium, Netherlands, and Luxembourg), thereby lessening the chances of another world war. The ECSC was followed by the Treaties of Rome (1957), which consisted of two separate treaties: one established the European Economic Community (EEC) and the other created the European Atomic Energy Community (Euratom). Thus, beginning in 1958, what was to become the European Union consisted of three separate communities plus guidelines for developing future policies.

The objective of the EEC was to reduce customs duties among member states, leading to an eventual customs union. This would be accomplished by creating a single market for goods, labour, services, and capital. Further, the Treaty Establishing the EEC proposed development of common policies related to agriculture, transportation, and social welfare, as well as a European Commission (Brunet-Jailly, Hurrelmann, and Verdun 2018). During negotiations on how the EEC Treaty would be implemented, the Common Agricultural Policy (CAP) was struck. The CAP would protect EEC farmers from outside competition, thereby facilitating exports of higher-cost French agricultural products into the large German market. Indeed, to protect its farmers from British competition, France vetoed the application of the United Kingdom (UK) to join the EEC on two occasions (1963 and 1967). The United Kingdom finally joined the EEC in 1973, along with Denmark and Ireland (Table 9.1).

The treaties that followed sought greater integration of the member states comprising the EEC. For example, the Schengen Treaty and Convention (1985) permits people to move freely without border controls (but only among countries that are party to "Schengen"); the Treaty on

Table 9.1. Expansion of the European Union

Year	EU Members
1958	Belgium, France, Germany, Italy, Luxembourg, Netherlands
1973	Denmark, Ireland, United Kingdom
1981	Greece
1986	Portugal, Spain
1989	East Germany (integrated into Germany)
1995	Austria, Finland, Sweden
2004	Cyprus, Czech Republic, Estonia, Hungary, Latvia, Lithuania, Malta, Poland, Slovakia, Slovenia
2007	Bulgaria, Romania
2013	Croatia

European Union, or Maastricht Treaty (1992), led to a single currency (euro); and the Lisbon Treaty (2007) founded the European Union as a legal structure.[1] A major expansion of the European Union that had particular relevance for agricultural policy occurred in 2004 when ten additional countries, primarily from Central and Eastern Europe, joined the European Union (Table 9.1). Government outlays under the CAP were increased significantly to accommodate these countries. The European Union was further enlarged to include Bulgaria and Romania in 2007, and Croatia in 2013, bringing the total number of member states to twenty-eight (EU-28). Lastly, as a result of a 23 June 2016 referendum, Britain exited the European Union in January 2020.

In the next sections, we examine the origins and problems of the CAP, discuss how the CAP was subsequently reformed, illustrate the economic implications of reforms, and examine the consequences of the UK decision to leave the European Union, known as Brexit.

9.2   THE COMMON AGRICULTURAL POLICY (CAP)

After World War II, it was easy to establish an agricultural policy regime that provided farmers with large transfer payments. Three main reasons for this can be identified: (1) the desire to avoid future food shortages; (2) a large proportion of the population was rural and dependent on agriculture, giving the agricultural constituency political clout; and (3) European governments promoted and supported protection of agriculture. The result was the establishment of the CAP in 1962 by the six founding members of what later became the European Union. High levels of agricultural support have continued under the CAP to the present day, despite large costs to consumers and taxpayers and a declining farm population. Major reasons include rent seeking by agricultural producers and food safety concerns on the part of the public

From a historical perspective, Articles 38–47 of the 1957 Treaty Establishing the EEC (Treaties of Rome) defined five general objectives that a CAP should have: (1) increase productivity by promoting technical progress and ensuring optimum use of the factors of production, especially labour; (2) ensure a fair standard of living for the agricultural community; (3) stabilize markets; (4) secure availability of supplies; and (5) provide consumers with food at reasonable prices. Three general objectives of the CAP that then emerged at the Stresa Conference (1958) were (1) market unity, (2) community preference, and (3) financial solidarity (Ackrill 2000). Agriculture was thereby included in the Common Market, with member states required to remove quantitative restrictions and tariffs on intra-Europe trade and erect a common external tariff. A mechanism for supporting farmers' incomes was also established.

In 1962 the European Agricultural Guidance and Guarantee Fund (EAGGF) was created to provide payments to farmers, although a Council of Ministers subsequently laid the groundwork for price support policy, border taxes and subsidies, production quotas, direct income support, and Common Market Organizations (CMOs). The Council of Ministers (now Council of the European Union) is meant to oversee the European Commission on behalf of the first ministers (leaders of countries). An ensuing CMO established for cereals included (1) target prices, (2) intervention prices (domestic floor price), (3) threshold prices (minimum import prices) supported by variable import levies on grain, (4) export restitution payments, and (5) tariffs on food for consumption. Different intervention prices were established for cereal crops. High intervention prices led to overproduction of cereal crops, and the European Union shifted from being a major importer of cereals to a major exporter in 1984, remaining so ever since.

The original overarching theme of the CAP was to provide price protection to domestic producers, with farmers receiving direct payments to grow commodities such as oilseeds, wheat, and olive oil. Initially, the system was expected to provide positive net returns, with revenues from import levies expected to exceed the cost of farm payments. But as early as 1968, the EU Agricultural Commissioner, Sicco Mansholt, recognized that CAP would result in overproduction and the need to store or export surplus products. However, the costs of export refunds were greater than the revenue from tariffs on imported commodities (Tracy 1996), and there were increasing costs of storing commodities such as butter and skim milk powder. Reforms were clearly required.

The main decision-making body for CAP affairs is the Agriculture Council in Brussels, which includes the agricultural ministers from each member state or their representatives. Since CAP redistributes income among member states, each country has an incentive to lobby for policies that benefit its own farmers. Agricultural policy includes such things as price support levels and direct acreage payments. Once a policy is approved by the Agriculture Council, it must also be approved by the Council of Ministers. Regulations approved by the Council of Ministers have direct force of law in all member states and require no further national approval. However, Council directives have to be translated into national legislation. The formal decision-making procedure within the Council of Ministers is the qualified majority vote; the European Union strives to achieve near consensus to avoid small states outvoting the large member states, although this often results in the marginalization of some smaller member states. Farmers in all countries lobby their ministers to ensure high levels of protection, and countries with strong farm lobbies (particularly France) exert undue influence over both the Agriculture Council and Council of Ministers. Since agricultural reforms can be difficult to implement, individual countries have some leeway over their own farm policies.

DIRECT PAYMENTS

Direct payments replace price supports and other subsidies that incentivize greater production. They are made to farmers regardless of how much they produce. In 2008, the European Union provided famers with a crop-specific direct payment, with countries able to choose one of the following approaches for determining a producer's reference yields:

- Historic: entitlements depend on farm-specific historical reference yields.
- Regional: entitlements depend on a region's outcomes for establishing reference yields.
- Hybrid: a combination of the historic and regional approaches.

While the European Commission preferred the regional approach, most countries opted for the historical one. Only lands growing specific crops were considered eligible for fixed payments (€/hectare [ha]) that varied by crop based on historic 2000–2 or, for recent member states, 1995–9 yields. Payments were based on farm-specific entitlements, so their size differed significantly by type of farm and across farms. Further, they depended on cross-compliance measures linked to (1) food safety, (2) animal welfare, and (3) environmental standards. This made direct payments eligible for the World Trade Organization's (WTO's) Blue Box (see section 4.6). However, the Agriculture Council did not reduce the level of intervention prices for cereal crops even though reducing price supports was a significant part of the original reform agenda (Daugbjerg and Swinbank 2007). Then, after the 2013 reforms, farmers received a direct payment – a single-farm payment – regardless of what and how much they produced. The only requirement was that a farm commodity was produced.

9.3 REFORMING THE COMMON AGRICULTURAL POLICY

The Common Agricultural Policy has changed over time (see discussion in Chapter 7, A. Schmitz et al. 2010). Changes included Mansholt's 1968 plan to reform agriculture by

Figure 9.1. Agricultural budget and components of total EU budget

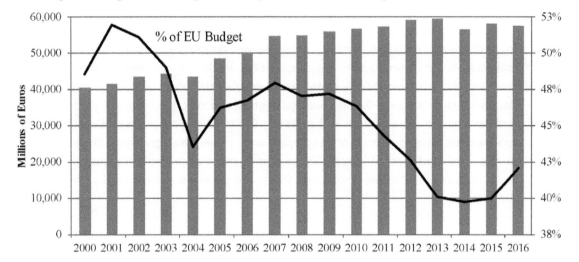

consolidating small farms to increase farm size and take advantage of economies of scale, and reducing payments to smaller producers.

Beginning in the 1990s, agricultural reforms became intertwined with the politics of EU enlargement and greater integration. Reforms were driven by four factors: (1) the high, and increasing, costs of CAP at a time when politicians wished to allocate more of the EU budget to other programs; (2) pressure for reform emanating from trade negotiations, particularly as a result of the WTO 1995 Agreement on Agriculture that required the eventual elimination of export subsidies; (3) the integration of new members with EU expansion; and (4) increased environmental concerns (Buckwell 2017).

Agricultural expenditures grew rapidly after the establishment of CAP in 1962. By 1970, payments to the agricultural sector from EAGGF accounted for nearly 90 per cent of the total EU budget. While payments increased, the proportion of the EU budget going to agriculture decreased. High levels of subsidization eventually harmed trade negotiations while negatively impacting farmers in developing countries – by lowering global agricultural prices, producers in poor countries were at a competitive disadvantage. The evolution of the EU agricultural budget (2000 through 2016) is illustrated in Figure 9.1.

One of the earliest CAP reforms was the transfer of income from farm support to regional development. The reforms began with the MacSharry Reform (1992), which moved the European Union from a market intervention system to direct compensation to individual farmers (Buckwell 2017), while also facilitating the eventual creation of the WTO in 1995.

REFORMING THE CAP – THE MACSHARRY REFORM (1992)

The 1992 MacSharry Reform lowered EU prices towards world prices and provided for direct compensation to farmers. Compensation was provided because policy-makers assumed that reductions in support prices would reduce revenues. In the crop sector, direct payments were area-based and fixed in value (€/ha); they were determined as a five-year, Olympic average (highest and lowest removed) of yields and the area sown to cereals over the period 1986 to 1990. Beef cattle producers received enhanced payments on a complex array of per-head premiums based on the number of beef cattle kept. The area payment scheme also embraced oil-seeds and certain other field crops, and sheep and goats were also brought into the package.

Additional reform measures initiated in 1999, known as Agenda 2000, set the stage for increasing EU membership while building on the MacSharry Reform by further lowering support prices. The scope of EU enlargement is shown in Table 9.2. For example, the number of farms increased from 3.3 million to 14.5 million, and the number of farm workers increased from 3.1 million to 12.6 million. As a result, EU members based direct payments to farmers in the Central and Eastern European Countries (CEEC) on yields and area cropped during the period 1995–9, not 2000–2, which reduced overall payments to CEECs. Further, eligibility for full direct farm payments was phased in over a period of years, beginning with 25 per cent in 2004; direct payments were phased in by 2013 for the ten members entering in 2004, by 2015 for Romania and Bulgaria, and 2022 for Croatia. Overall, the direct payments provided to agricultural producers in CEECs varied from €300 for small farms in Poland to €40,000 for large farms in Hungary and the Czech Republic. Although average payouts per farm were significantly lower in the CEECs than in the EU-15 member states, the original EU-6 member states contributed more to agricultural support payments than they received in benefits (Table 9.3).

AGENDA 2000 (1999)

The Agenda 2000 reform addressed the EU enlargement planned for 2004 and the need to further reduce intervention prices. In the short term, the CAP budget was limited to €40.5 billion and intervention prices were lowered; half of the price reductions were compensated by direct payments. Yet, EU prices remained above world prices.

Table 9.2. Population and agricultural statistics, EU groupings, 2008

Grouping	Population (million)	Farmland (million hectares)	# of farms (thousands)	Farmworkers (thousands)
Original Six	214.7	60.4	3,334.00	3,116.30
EU-15	336.8	129.4	5,845.00	6,244.40
EU-25	410.9	162.8	9,691.00	9,468.40
EU-27[a]	440.1	182.1	14,482.00	12,564.10

[a] Excludes Croatia, as it was added in July 2013.

Table 9.3. Agricultural payouts by EU groupings, 2008 (€)

Grouping	Contribution per Citizen	Payout per Citizen	Payout per Hectare	Payout per Farm
Original Six	126.4	99.6	353.7	6,411.20
EU-15	145.4	138.8	361.0	7,995.00
EU-25	126.9	128.7	324.9	5,457.80
EU-27[a]	120.0	120.2	290.5	3,652.80

[a] Excludes Croatia, as it was added in July 2013.

As the EU expanded to include new member states, especially those of the CEEC, the supply and demand conditions for commodities within all the EU member states were altered (Banse 2003). Policymakers were mainly concerned with budget implications. To include new member states whose agricultural sectors were quite large, politicians increased the EU budget for agriculture from 1 per cent of total GDP to 1.05 per cent.

There was also a concern about governance due to less-developed accounting practices and corruption in the CEECs. The addition of several countries with large agricultural sectors, most notably Hungary, Poland, and the Czech Republic, and later Romania and Bulgaria, would likely aggravate trade negotiations under the WTO.

Agenda 2000 revised the payment structure of the CAP by creating two pillars:

- "Pillar 1" provides market and income support measures (direct payments to farmers and market-related subsidies, such as intervention prices, variable import levies, export restitution, public storage, and surplus disposal schemes).
- "Pillar 2" constitutes rural development measures and environmental services, providing assistance to difficult-to-farm areas, promoting food quality and safety, and improving animal welfare.

The reallocation of farm program payments from Pillar 1 to Pillar 2 is termed "modulation," with reforms shifting more of the focus towards the second pillar.

A Mid-term Review (also known as the Fischler Reform) occurred in 2003, followed in 2008 by the "Health Check." The Mid-term Review used direct payments to decouple subsidies from production. Farmers received a per hectare payment for producing a particular crop regardless of how much of that crop they produced. This reduced the incentive for more intensive production (e.g., greater use of fertilizer) to increase yields, thereby allowing farmers to adapt their planting intentions to market signals. This made CAP more WTO-friendly.

MID-TERM REVIEW, A.K.A. FISCHLER REFORM (2003)

This reform introduced the *Single Payment Scheme* (SPS) that was gradually implemented during 2005 and 2006. The main aims were to (1) allow farmers the freedom to respond to market forces; (2) promote environmentally and economically sustainable farming; (3) simplify CAP applications for farmers and administrators; and (4) strengthen the European Union's position in the WTO's agricultural trade negotiations. Crop-specific direct payments were decoupled from production but linked to eligible farmland. However, states were able to allocate payments in ways that incentivized production, leading to undesirable and unpredictable outcomes at the EU level, even though this type of coupling was removed by the "Health Check." The SPS distorted land use because payments differed across crops, thereby causing farmers to prefer the land uses in place in the 2000–2 (1995–9) reference period. Finally, the reforms also required an accounting standard, which some states could not attain; some of the more recent entrants to the European Union lacked the institutions and qualified accountants to handle the reforms due to corruption and less-than-desirable rule of law.

Agricultural reforms in 2013 focused on removing incentives that caused farmers to produce more domestically consumable products. The main approach was to provide farmers with direct payments that were independent of quantity and type of crop produced. Consequently, it was assumed in accordance with economic theory that farmers would respond solely to market signals. Unfortunately, the 2013 reforms also took a major step backwards, because they reintroduced the use of coupled payments by introducing a greening component.

PROTECTING THE ENVIRONMENT AND THE 2013 CAP REFORMS

The 2013 CAP reforms introduced a single-farm payment scheme (SFPS) that eventually provided the same level of support to every hectare of farmland in a region, independent of the type of farm or crop grown. The reforms included new environmental requirements for farmers; producers were to be compensated for providing public goods in the form of environmentally friendly farming practices – a so-called *greening component* added to the SFPS if farmers were in compliance. The greening component imposes a set-aside requirement referred to as the Ecological Focus Area (EFA). Farmers were also compensated for actions that improved animal welfare and food safety. Although the European Parliament and European Commission wanted a mandatory cap, countries were only required to limit annual payouts to €275,000 per farm.

CAP spending remains the largest item in the European Union's long-term budget for 2014–21. In 2016, CAP expenditures were about €38 billion, with €29 billion in direct payments to farmers. The objective of long-term budget plans is to reduce the disparity in payments made to farmers, while shifting funds from the agricultural sector to provide greater funds for expenditures on things such as the environment and social programs. Modulation from Pillar 1 to Pillar 2 is not sufficient to satisfy all of these desires.

VOLUNTARY COUPLED SUPPORT (VCS)

According to EU Regulation 1307–2013, member states are allowed to use part of their national envelope for direct payments for coupled support in certain clearly defined cases. VCS should be limited to specific sectors or regions in a member state where specific agricultural activities are particularly important for economic, environmental, or social reasons, including incentives to maintain current levels of output. Member states are allowed to employ up to 8 per cent of their national *de minimis* ceilings for coupled support. However, countries can increase support by up to 2 per cent to specifically support the production of protein crops. The VCS policy option has been widely used to support various farm commodities by all states except Germany. The extent to which countries have employed coupled support is shown in Table 9.4.

VCS constitutes a direct payment for each hectare allocated to a crop in question. The payment effectively operates as a price subsidy, the value of which is equal to the per hectare payment divided by the crop yield. Expressed as a price equivalent, the VCS subsidy induces additional production that is likely to have a downward impact on market prices, thereby counteracting the VCS incentive. The extent of these shifts can only be determined numerically, although they would likely increase competitiveness, putting some countries at an advantage relative to others depending on the VCS rates employed.

Table 9.4. Impact of the 2013 CAP reform on the importance of coupled payments by EU member states: Total direct support and proportion of added coupled support

Country	Total Direct Support	Share Provided by Coupled Payments	
(ISO designation)	2013 (€ million)	2013 (%)	2015 (%)
Austria (AT)	706.4	11.1	2.1
Belgium (BE)	566.8	16.1	17.0
Bulgaria (BG)	494.4	5.5	15.0
Croatia (HR)	–	–	15.0
Cyprus (CY)	43.8	7.5	7.9
Czech Republic (CZ)	824.2	3.8	15.0
Denmark (DK)	939.1	1.4	2.8
Estonia (EE)	91.9	1.3	4.2
Finland (FI)	531.9	9.0	20.0
France (FR)	7,967.5	11.5	15.0
Germany (DE)	5,254.0	0.0	0.0
Greece (EL)	2,282.3	12.0	7.4
Hungary (HU)	1,203.3	3.8	15.0
Ireland (IE)	1,250.3	1.8	0.2
Italy (IT)	3,959.6	3.2	11.0
Latvia (LV)	132.9	3.8	14.0
Lithuania (LT)	345.5	3.8	15.0
Luxembourg (LU)	33.7	0.0	0.5
Malta (MT)	4.8	0.0	57.0
Netherlands (NL)	822.9	2.0	0.5
Poland (PL)	2,769.5	3.8	15.0
Portugal (PT)	648.8	31.8	21.0
Romania (RO)	1,086.9	3.5	12.0
Slovakia (SK)	354.4	3.3	13.0
Slovenia (SI)	130.2	6.0	15.0
Spain (ES)	5,237.3	13.5	12.0
Sweden (SE)	689.3	0.4	13.0
United Kingdom (UK)	3,205.9	0.6	1.7
European Union (EU)	41,658.3	6.8	10.0

Source: Adapted from Matthews (2015).

9.3.1   The Future of CAP and Direct Payments

Over time, direct payments have become capitalized in land prices, resulting in higher costs for new entrants purchasing land and higher rental payments for tenant farmers. There has also been a high leakage of benefits to non-farm groups, such as non-farmer landowners. Further, direct payments made to farmers for doing nothing are not always politically acceptable, nor do they stabilize farm incomes in sectors with high risk, such as horticulture, with direct payments made regardless of whether farm gate prices are good or bad – direct payments do not reduce income volatility. Eventually, the next CAP reform should replace direct payments with policies designed to better equip farmers in the future.

In a 2017 policy document (*The Future of Food and Farming*), the European Commission (2017) proposed to retain direct payments but cap them at between €60,000 and €100,000 per farm, in an effort to focus on family farms. However, such policies often incentivized larger farms to subdivide their operations while still de facto functioning as a single entity. Another major proposed change regards individual member states being given greater responsibility over CAP programs. Decentralization of CAP programs raises issues of governance and potential corruption, although the Commission is confident that it can ensure *credible performance reporting* and spending. While such a move is generally seen as an improvement as decentralization does take into account local conditions and needs, and can reduce transaction costs, there is no co-responsibility for spending on direct payments.

Other challenges to further reforming the CAP relate to the environment (reduced pollution from agricultural activities), the provision of public goods, climate change, and sustainable development (European Commission 2017). While the agricultural sector plays an important role in achieving environmental and development goals, placing the burden for achieving these goals primarily on agriculture may be difficult. There are insufficient instruments currently available to agricultural policymakers to achieve these goals while still maintaining food security. Many instruments are already being used, including cross-compliance measures such as set-asides, land retirement, and reduced use of chemicals. Under Pillar 2, agricultural producers are also already incentivized to provide public goods that include animal welfare measures, enhanced food safety procedures, and more wildlife habitats. However, Pillar 2 funds could be spent more efficiently by introducing subsidiary fiscal responsibility. For example, if EU funds are spent to protect a bird species, the European Union might contribute up to 100 per cent of the program costs, but if the primary beneficiaries of a Pillar 2 program are domestic citizens of an individual country, the European Union might contribute less than 50 per cent of the program costs. Unfortunately, if a country were unwilling to contribute funds, the program would not be undertaken. This is an aspect of credible performance.

9.4   ANALYSIS OF CAP REFORMS IN SPECIFIC SECTORS

The economics of CAP policies, such as the price support regime for cereals, are discussed using the generally accepted principles of welfare analysis (T.G. Schmitz, A. Schmitz, and Dumas 1997; R.E. Just, Hueth, and Schmitz 2004). Table 9.5 illustrates the allocation of agricultural land uses across member states. In most member states, cereal crops dominate land use, followed by oilseeds and protein crops (peas, beans, lentils). Combined, cereal, oilseeds, and protein crops account for more than half of the arable land use in all member states, except Malta (0 per cent), the Netherlands (35 per cent), Greece (42 per cent), and Ireland (49 per cent); they exceed 90 per cent in Hungary, Luxembourg, and Slovakia.

Table 9.5. Agricultural land allocated by use, EU member states, 2013 (thousand hectares [ha])

Member State	Cereals	Oilseeds & Protein Crops	Other Crops	Horticulture	Total Arable	Other Use	Total Agric. Land
Austria	821.6	394.2	579.4	1.8	1,797.0	929.9	4,523.9
Belgium	332.5	44.1	280.6	3.9	661.1	646.8	1,969.0
Bulgaria	2,015.6	2,882.6	1,100.9	3.8	6,002.9	0.0	12,005.7
Croatia	590.9	345.8	421.7	1.2	1,359.6	211.6	2,930.8
Cyprus	31.3	14.6	15.7	0.7	62.2	47.1	171.6
Czech Rep.	1,428.9	870.5	296.1	0.0	2,595.5	896.0	6,087.0
Denmark	1,434.8	684.2	384.1	1.9	2,504.9	114.4	5,124.3
Estonia	311.0	305.5	93.2	0.3	710.0	247.6	1,667.5
Finland	1,163.3	874.6	317.3	5.1	2,360.2	0.0	4,720.4
France	9,623.2	7,579.5	2,985.7	38.8	20,227.2	7,512.3	47,966.6
Germany	6,533.7	3,604.7	2,150.8	8.8	12,297.9	4,401.6	28,997.5
Greece	1,001.8	536.0	2,119.4	14.1	3,671.4	1,185.4	8,528.2
Hungary	2,437.6	2,506.1	458.4	9.8	5,411.8	0.0	10,823.7
Ireland	307.8	258.1	590.4	1.6	1,157.9	3,801.5	6,117.4
Italy	3,503.1	2,228.3	2,399.7	72.7	8,203.8	3,895.1	20,302.7
Latvia	583.5	620.5	326.7	0.3	1,531.0	346.8	3,408.7
Lithuania	1,216.1	1,189.4	279.7	2.7	2,687.9	173.4	5,549.1
Luxembourg	29.1	4.0	2.9	0.0	36.0	95.1	167.0
Malta	0.0	0.0	2.9	0.1	3.0	7.9	13.9
Netherlands	210.2	29.6	430.7	12.1	682.5	1,165.0	2,530.1
Poland	7,479.5	3,853.4	2,688.8	58.4	14,080.1	329.8	28,489.9
Portugal	301.6	151.9	373.0	5.1	831.6	2,810.0	4,473.2
Romania	5,266.3	4,722.6	3,291.1	10.3	13,290.2	0.0	26,580.5
Slovakia	770.6	639.8	123.1	1.8	1,535.2	366.4	3,436.9
Slovenia	99.2	35.3	43.5	0.4	178.5	307.3	664.2
Spain	6,408.9	6,803.4	3,401.1	60.9	16,674.3	6,625.9	39,974.6
Sweden	989.3	656.8	482.8	1.5	2,130.3	905.6	5,166.3
UK	3,048.9	2,957.5	3,686.3	15.1	9,707.8	7,388.4	26,804.0

Source: European Union (2017) and authors' calculations.

9.4.1   EU Policy in Cereals, Oilseeds, and Protein Crops

Three policy instruments were used to maintain the CAP price support regime for cereals prior to the reforms described in section 9.3. First, producers were guaranteed an *intervention price* that was usually considerably higher than the world price. Intervention prices are those at which intervention agencies will purchase domestically produced commodities, creating a floor price. Second, the intervention price was enforced by imposing variable import levies (tariffs) to keep foreign sellers from taking advantage of the internal intervention price. These import levies were adjusted weekly due to fluctuating world prices and were set at a level equal to the difference between the intervention price and the world market price. This reduced imports to zero, except under rare market conditions. Third, to eliminate excess production, the European Union provided export restitution payments equal to the difference between the intervention price and the world price. Export refunds were managed by a Management Committee for Cereals of the European Commission. In cases where the world price rose above the intervention price, the variable import levy was set to zero, export restitution payments were suspended, and producers may have been forced to pay an export tax equal to the difference between the (higher) world market price and the (lower) intervention price.

Figure 9.2 represents EU cereal markets under average historical prices and illustrates the three main policy instruments discussed above (intervention prices, import levies, and export subsidies). The aggregate supply curve for cereals in all EU countries is represented by S and the demand curve by D. The world market price for cereals is P_F, which is below the intersection of the supply and demand curves. Under average market conditions, in the absence of CAP, the European Union would be a net importer of cereals (as it was prior to 1984). Therefore, in the absence of CAP, if the free trade price is P_F, the European Union will produce Q_F^S, but EU consumers will purchase Q_F^D, and the difference I_F will be imported.

Consider what happens when the intervention price is set at P_1, which lies above the intersection point of the domestic (EU-level) supply and demand curves. P_1 is the actual intervention price that EU cereal farmers receive under the CAP and, at this support price, the European Union will produce Q_1^S while EU consumers purchase only Q_1^D. The European Union maintains a variable import levy equal to $(P_1 - P_F)$ to block potential imports. To eliminate overproduction, the difference between production and consumption, X_1, is exported at the world price P_F and producers receive government payments equal to the difference $(P_1 - P_F)$.

If CAP did not exist, producers would receive a total dollar amount equal to $(P_F 0g)$, consumers would receive $(aP_F f)$ in the form of consumer surplus, and the EU government would pay nothing. However, since CAP does exist at a price support level of P_1, producers receive $(P_1 0c)$ as producer surplus (quasi-rent) while consumers receive consumer surplus equal to $(aP_1 b)$. Perhaps most importantly, the government (taxpayers) must pay $(bhdc)$ as export restitution payments to producers, who gain $(P_1 P_F gc)$ under the CAP at the expense of both consumers and taxpayers. Consumers lose $(P_1 P_F f)$ because of higher prices. Additionally, taxpayers lose $(bhdc)$ because they must ultimately pay the bill for the export restitution payments. The European Union loses $(bhf + gdc)$ in total welfare – the European Union loses (egf) twice because, while both consumers and taxpayers lose (egf), producers never receive it. Essentially, producers receive a direct transfer of $(P_1 P_F geb)$ from consumers and (bec) from taxpayers. However, consumers lose $(P_1 P_F fb)$ and taxpayers pay $(bhdc)$ to fund this transfer. Essentially, for every euro spent by the European Union on CAP price support for cereals, only $(P_1 P_F fb) / [(P_1 P_F fb) + (bhdc)]$ is transferred to producers; the remainder is a deadweight loss.

Unlike grains, there was no price support mechanism for oilseeds, although compensatory payments were made to rapeseed, sunflower, and soybean growers. The subsidized oilseed production area was limited by the US-EU Blair House Agreement. Except for small producers, oilseed producers were required to set aside a certain portion of their land to qualify for

Figure 9.2. EU price support policies in cereals

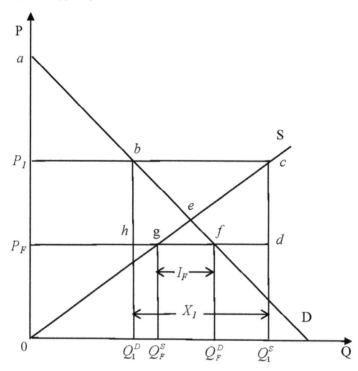

payments. There were no tariffs on imports of oilseeds and meal, and a low or nominal tariff on vegetable oils other than olive oil.

When intervention prices, import levies, and export subsidies were abandoned in the grain and oilseed sectors, individual countries still could employ their VCS option to provide support in addition to the basic payment. In 2015, the proportion of the European Union's VCS funds for crops was 10.7 per cent for protein crops, 2.1 per cent for cereal crops, and 1.7 per cent for olive oil crops; oilseed crops received no support beyond the basic payment.

9.4.2   EU Sugar Policy

The European Union's intervention and export regimes for beef, dairy products, sugar, and fruits and vegetables are similar to those used for cereals: producers sell the product either directly on the market or through intervention. The decision to sell directly depends on whether the market price (generally the world price) is greater than the intervention price. Intervention purchases are made only when market prices fall below the intervention price net of deductions for shipping and handling; thus, intervention purchases are made at roughly 94 per cent of the intervention price.

The EU sugar regime was introduced in 1968 and targeted sugar beet growers, becoming one of the most trade-distorting sugar programs in the world (A. Schmitz 2002). The EU sugar policy had a major impact on the world sugar market, with some studies indicating that, in the absence of the EU sugar policy, world sugar prices would have approached US internal price support levels (Roningen and Dixit 1989; A. Schmitz and Vercammen 1990, 1995). Burrell and Pearce (1999) estimated that in the absence of both EU and US sugar policies, world sugar prices would increase by about 30 per cent. Freeman and Roberts (1999) estimated that, even if the European Union did not liberalize its sugar policy while other countries did, global prices would increase by roughly 25 per cent; if the European Union also reformed, the world price would rise by over 40 per cent. Rather, the EU sugar policy reduced world sugar prices by roughly 20 per cent (Koo 2002).

Until the end of 2017, the European Union used country-level quotas to maintain sugar prices at levels well above world sugar prices. Prior to 2006, the European Union employed three types of quotas: the A-quota accounted for approximately 95 per cent of the domestic market and received the highest price; the price of the B-quota was historically about 69 per cent of the price of the A-quota; and the C-quota received the world price. Under special trade agreements, developing countries were provided access to the EU market through a duty-free tariff rate quota of about 1.3 million tonnes. The program was self-financing, paid for by a levy of 2 per cent on A-quota holders, with consumers paying the remaining costs in the form of higher prices. Earnings on A-quotas and B-quotas subsidized exports (C-quotas) – in essence, EU consumers subsidized exports.

Trade negotiations led to major reforms, with the WTO ruling that rents accruing to A-quotas and B-quotas constituted a subsidy to out-of-quota exports (Powell and Schmitz 2005). Policy reform began in 2006 with the B-quota eliminated, public storage limited, reference prices for sugar reduced by more than 30 per cent, and limits imposed on the C-quotas (exports). Steps were then put in place to decouple EU support payments to sugar beet farmers from production. Thus, after 2017, all sugar quotas were eliminated, and producers were provided the same basic payment as other farmers. By abolishing the sugar quota, the European Union fell from second largest sugar exporter in the world to seventh largest (USDA/FAS 2017a, 2017b).

Recall that countries could use their VCS payments to provide aid to crop producers, including sugar beet growers. While the shift from classical price support to direct payments during the 2014–20 CAP reforms resulted in support that was largely decoupled from production, the option for member states to establish VCS went against the philosophy of greater market orientation. Coupled support can distort the level playing field between farmers and the processing sectors (supply chains), especially when support is granted unevenly across the European Union. This is precisely what happened in the sugar sector. VCS payments have varied between €81 and €784 per hectare. The impact of eliminating the sugar quota and implementing VCS can be examined with the aid of Figure 9.3. It is assumed that there are no export subsidies as these were ruled out by the WTO.

Figure 9.3. Elimination of sugar quota and use of voluntary coupled support in sugar beet sector

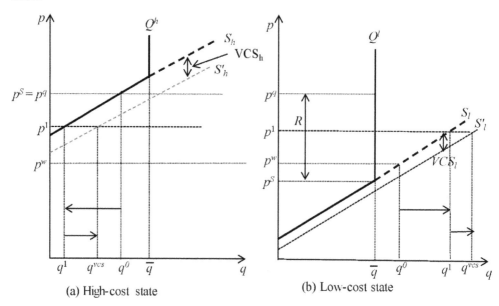

(a) High-cost state   (b) Low-cost state

Source: Authors.

Some member states were unable to meet their EU-assigned quota. This scenario is depicted in Figure 9.3 as high-cost member states (high-cost state) and low-cost producing member states (low-cost state). The respective supply functions for the high-cost and low-cost producing states are S_h and S_l. Under the quota regime, the level of assigned quota is given by $\overline{q}$, which may or may not be the same level in each state, while the EU-level price is p^q. A high-cost state will produce $q^0 < \overline{q}$ in panel (a); that is, it produces less than its allowable quota and there is no quota rent as the marginal cost of growing beets, given by p^S, is equivalent to the marginal revenue given by p^q. The low-cost state will produce its quota $\overline{q}$ plus an amount $q^0 - \overline{q}$ to sell at the world price p^w, thus earning a quota rent of R for each unit of quota produced.

As a first step in the adjustment to a free market, the European Union lowered the price of sugar and compensated growers with a basic payment. Assume that the intervention price was set at p^1. In that case, the high-cost state reduces production from $\overline{q}$ to q^1 in panel (a) while the low-cost state increases production as indicated in Figure 9.3b. Seeing the decline in production, policymakers in a high-cost state have an incentive to provide VCS payments (over and above the basic payment) to sugar beet growers, perhaps to ensure the survival of local sugar producers. This will shift the supply function from S_h to S_h' so that output increases from q^1 to q^{vcs} in panel (a); however, unless the level of VCS is sufficiently large so that the vertical intercept of S_h lies below p^w, the member state will cease to produce sugar beets when the reform is completed. Since the low-cost state in Figure 9.3b exported sugar under the quota regime, it will continue to export sugar when markets are totally freed. In this case, VCS will increase exports even more.

9.4.3   EU Dairy Policy

The EU dairy policy was originally formulated in 1968 under CAP Regulation 804/68. Quotas on milk production were introduced in 1984, but the basic mechanism of public regulation has remained unchanged since 1968. Policy instruments include support prices for butter and skim milk powder (SMP), import tariffs and tariff rate quotas (TRQs), export refunds, production and consumption subsidies, intervention buying of surpluses, and a marketing quota on milk.

As indicated in Table 9.6, the European Union dominates the export market for dairy products, both in terms of quantity and value. Within the European Union, the largest dairy producers are Germany and France, followed by Poland, the Netherlands, and Italy. The largest dairy exporters are Germany, France, and the Netherlands. Among the EU member states, the Netherlands is considered the most efficient producer of dairy products.

Beginning with the 2003 Mid-term Review, the European Union began to phase out the dairy quota system by reducing intervention prices for some products and increasing quotas for the member states (Jongeneel and Tonini 2009; Jongeneel, Burrell, and Kavallari 2011). Only butter and SMP were considered eligible for public intervention because these products could be stored. As illustrated in Table 9.7, there were limits as to how much the European Union would purchase – 109,000 tonnes of SMP over the period from 2004 until the quota system ended. Using butter as an example, a maximum of 70,000 tonnes would be purchased in 2004, but the amount would decline by 10,000 tonnes annually until it levelled off at 30,000 tonnes per year from 2008 onward, but the Commission could purchase more in emergencies (Jongeneel, Burrell, and Kavallari 2011).

The dairy quota regime was eliminated in 2015, with producers receiving a basic payment (equal to single-farm payment). The EU dairy policy from establishment of the quota regime in 1984 through its demise in 2015 can be analysed with reference to Figure 9.4. Price and quantity in the absence of trade are given by P^* and q^*, respectively, in panel (b). With trade, EU producers face demand D_T, which is the sum of domestic demand function (D_E) and excess demand by rest of the world (ED_R). Abstracting from shipping and handling costs, the world price would be P^W with trade, q^{wd} would be consumed domestically, and the difference $q^W - q^{wd}$ in panel (b) exported to the rest of world – with equivalent imports indicated for P^W in panel (a).

When the EU dairy farmers face support price P^S, they produce q^S but only q^D would be consumed within the European Union at that price. Thus, the European Union must either store the excess production or subsidize exports. The cost of purchasing the overproduced dairy products (butter and SMP) is given by the area bounded by (eq^Dq^Se'). Since excess production

Table 9.6. Milk production and exports, EU member states, United States, Australia, and New Zealand[a]

Country	Milk Production (thousand tonnes)	Exports (thousand tonnes)				Exports (US$ million)			
		Butter	Cheese	SMP	Fresh	Butter	Cheese	SMP	Fresh
Austria	3,493.9	1.8	75.9	3.0	609.5	10.1	446.6	15.7	378.4
Belgium	3,689.4	91.3	120.2	142.0	542.0	458.1	667.2	521.8	337.4
Bulgaria	1,102.7	1.0	23.1	4.5	5.3	2.3	103.6	17.5	3.9
Croatia	711.4	1.9	1.8	0.0	14.8	8.4	7.5	0.0	12.7
Cyprus	164.6	0.0	11.8	0.0	0.0	0.0	103.0	0.0	0.0
Czech Rep	2,933.5	4.1	41.6	14.7	667.1	19.1	205.8	59.1	341.5
Denmark	5,191.1	38.2	289.3	26.0	208.2	236.3	1,556.3	105.3	150.1
Estonia	804.8	2.5	20.4	1.1	201.5	13.3	91.3	4.7	95.8
Finland	2,400.0	24.2	29.4	20.1	13.0	136.2	148.1	79.0	12.6
France	25,332.5	59.4	632.7	164.6	681.4	325.9	3,582.7	631.7	471.9
Germany	32,395.0	124.7	1,073.4	286.7	1,792.6	613.3	4,781.4	1,091.7	1,108.2
Greece	769.1	0.3	52.8	0.4	1.0	1.4	393.9	1.1	1.2
Hungary	1,875.7	0.9	12.2	0.1	331.7	4.0	63.5	0.3	178.4
Ireland	5,816.2	156.4	179.9	42.5	188.5	738.9	845.6	138.8	101.4
Italy	11,044.1	7.2	317.0	4.4	20.7	36.0	2,712.9	20.0	20.3
Latvia	968.9	4.3	15.3	7.6	244.8	21.7	67.8	30.6	110.5
Lithuania	1,791.1	5.8	71.7	22.1	111.0	31.4	354.6	88.1	70.6
Luxembourg	317.0	2.5	44.2	0.1	157.2	19.0	309.6	0.2	81.3
Malta	42.8	0.0	0.1	0.0	0.0	0.0	0.5	0.0	0.0
Netherlands	12,473.0	120.3	654.8	88.8	359.9	606.2	3,659.8	362.0	227.9
Poland	12,985.5	29.9	159.8	61.0	200.5	147.1	723.1	238.0	142.7
Portugal	1,940.1	14.2	8.1	3.5	200.2	69.0	44.8	12.8	112.6
Romania	4,533.6	0.3	10.1	1.9	21.5	1.3	42.6	2.6	16.0
Slovakia	933.9	2.2	17.6	2.8	222.8	11.6	103.9	6.1	133.8
Slovenia	616.6	0.1	3.3	0.1	269.5	0.5	15.6	0.3	147.6
Spain	6,786.0	19.1	64.7	8.3	106.5	67.2	387.2	19.8	100.2
Sweden	2,973.0	3.6	18.9	27.3	37.3	17.0	93.0	108.3	23.8
UK	15,050.0	44.6	107.1	54.1	498.4	226.2	597.9	126.8	263.4
EU-28	159,135.5	760.7	4,057.0	987.8	7,706.7	3,821.6	22,109.6	3,682.1	4,644.1
Australia	9,542.0	40.9	151.0	121.0	94.4	170.3	646.8	478.8	113.4
NZ	21,317.0	461.1	255.6	392.0	89.9	1,823.6	1,060.9	1,621.8	92.0
US	93,460.9	84.0	299.1	554.8	80.5	317.7	1,280.4	2,050.1	58.4

Source: FAO (2017b).
[a]Data are for latest available year: milk production data are for 2014, and export data are for 2013.

equals ee' (= dd'), this is then used to establish the foreign price based on D_T, because amount ed is not sold at P^S. That is, the correct price in foreign markets is P_0 and not P_1, so that the export subsidy equals $(ekk'e') < (eq^D q^S e')$.

To avoid accumulating stocks of dairy products or the high costs of export subsidies while still supporting prices, the European Union employed a quota beginning in 1984. Assume the quota was initially set at R_0. A dairy farmer would produce q^{R0} and receive a price (P^S) greater than the marginal cost of production (c), thereby capturing a rent equal to ($P^S cbx$). EU

Table 9.7. Reductions in intervention prices on butter and skim milk powder, €/100 kg[a]

Year[a]	Butter	Skim Milk Powder (SMP)
2003/4	328.20	205.52
2004/5	305.23	195.24
2005/6	282.44	184.97
2006/7	259.52	174.69
2007/8	246.39	174.69
2008 onwards	246.39	169.80

Source: Jongeneel, Burrell, and Kavallari (2011).
[a] The agricultural year begins 1 April and ends 31 March.

consumers still pay P^S, so amount *ex* must be exported. Assuming for the convenience of explanation that $ed (= e'd') = R_1 - R_0$, the price foreigners pay would be P'' and the European Union would still be subsidizing exports by $ex \times (P^S - P'')$ in Figure 9.4b. As a consequence of the WTO's Agreement on Agriculture, the European Union needed to eliminate the quota regime.

To eliminate the quota, the support price is initially removed while the quota remains. The price falls from P^S to P', with farmers provided an annual deficiency payment equal to the level of their initial individual quota (i.e., reference quantity) multiplied by the price difference (or milk premium), with the total deficiency payment equal to $(P^S P'yx)$. The quota is then increased in steps to the level that would lead to the free-market trade outcome, price P^W and output q^W. In the first step, the quota is increased to R_1, which causes price to fall from P' to P''. The milk premium paid to dairy producers increases from $P^S - P'$ to $P^S - P''$ (or by $P' - P''$). Thus, the total milk premium rises by the darker shaded area. In the next steps (but shown as one step in the figure), the quota is increased to R_2 ($= q^{R2}$), but the total milk premium paid to producers is equal to the light-shaded area, which is only a proportion of the total decline in producer rent. That is, as the quota is slowly increased, the milk premium becomes a declining proportion of the fall in price. Increases beyond q^W are not needed as this is where price equals the marginal cost.

9.4.4 Fruits and Vegetables

The CAP includes most of the fruits and vegetables grown in EU countries. The European Union supports its fruit and vegetable (F&V) sector though its market-management scheme (part of the "common market organization" in agriculture). The policies have four broad objectives: (1) a more competitive, market-oriented sector; (2) reduced crisis-type fluctuations in producers' incomes; (3) greater consumption of fruits and vegetables in the European Union; and (4) increased use of eco-friendly cultivation and production techniques (European Commission 2014). As in most countries, the F&V sector does not garner the same support as cereals, oilseeds, protein crops, and livestock.

Figure 9.4. Europe's dairy regime and its demise

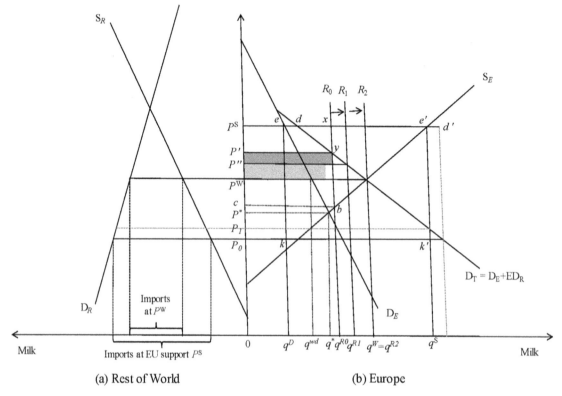

(a) Rest of World   (b) Europe

Source: van Kooten (2017).

As a result of reforms in 1996, common market organizations (CMOs) became the cornerstone of the EU regime for the F&V sector. CMOs were meant to blunt the marketing power of downstream processors, plus serve as a conduit for addressing environmental concerns related to the production and marketing of F&Vs. Through the CMOs, the sector was able to access EU funds for implementing EU programs. Subsequent reforms in 2007 strengthened the power of CMOs by encouraging their merger and the formation of associations of CMOs in order that the sector could better deal with crises. This reform also removed export refunds and decoupled aid for fruit destined for processing but requiring a minimum level of spending by CMOs on environmental activities. Since environmental spending falls under Pillar 2, this meant that member states were required to contribute 40 to 50 per cent of any funding support for CMOs.

From 2003 to 2010, EU farmland devoted to fruits and vegetables fell by 6 per cent, while the number of F&V enterprises declined by 39.1 per cent (compared with a 20 per cent decline in total EU agricultural holdings), thus being indicative of increasing concentration in the sector. Not surprisingly, there was a rise in average F&V enterprise holdings by 1.9 hectares in the EU-27 and 3.0 hectares in the EU-15 as a result of the concentration of production in fewer farms. There was also a 3 per cent reduction in the volume of F&V output in 2008–10 compared to 2004–6, although the value of production rose by 6.5 per cent as a result of somewhat higher prices. While the European Union will continue to provide some support to the F&V sector in the future, particularly through Pillar 2 with its focus on regional development and the environment, there is likely to be increased interest in agricultural business risk management programs (Jongeneel et al. 2019).

9.4.5   Brexit

On 23 June 2016, a majority of UK residents voted to leave the European Union, thereby triggering negotiations to determine what trade relations would look like after 2019, when the British Exit (Brexit) process was scheduled to be completed. After pushback on the vote, a referendum, and initial negotiations, the United Kingdom officially left the European Union on 31 January 2020. Further negotiations will cover the status of Northern Ireland, industry, banking, finance, and agriculture.

THE IRISH BACKSTOP ISSUE

Northern Ireland, which is part of the United Kingdom, shares an open border with Ireland, which retains EU membership and use of the euro. The border creates a problem for Brexit because goods arriving from EU states cannot be allowed across the border without inspection. Northern Ireland opposes this development, so a political solution needs to be put in place to facilitate acceptance by citizens in Northern Ireland and Ireland. Finding such a solution has proved difficult during negotiations and will continue to be a subject of contention in the future.

The overall impact of Brexit on agriculture is difficult to determine and depends upon the terms of the final trade relation between the United Kingdom and the EU-27. In anticipation of Brexit, the United Kingdom passed a 2019–20 agricultural bill that outlines the method for replacing CAP, shifting away from CAP's direct payments based upon the amount of farmland managed and instead focusing on production of "public goods." Under the bill, UK farmers will receive payments to produce public goods in an effort to meet the requirements of the United Kingdom's twenty-five-year Environmental Plan and Clean Growth Strategy. New environmental land management contracts will determine how funds are dispersed in the United Kingdom.

To determine the overall potential impact on agricultural trade, two potential scenarios have been investigated (Jongeneel, van Berkum, and Vrolijk 2016; van Berkum et al. 2018):

1 The United Kingdom and EU-27 enter into a free trade agreement (FTA) that does not grant the United Kingdom the same access as a single market. No tariffs are applied on bilateral trade, but border arrangements to identify country of origin will be required, and this will increase transaction costs. The United Kingdom would also accord most favoured nation (MFN) status to extra-EU nations (e.g., Norway, Iceland) included under the European Union's Common Custom Tariff.
2 There is the default WTO position, whereby the United Kingdom and EU-27 trade on MFN terms, as well as with extra-EU nations. However, the European Union's import concessions under tariff rate quotas would no longer apply so that less is imported and UK prices for those products would increase.

Jongeneel, van Berkum, and Vrolijk (2016) point out that the United Kingdom contributes about €7.9 billion to the CAP budget, whereas its farmers receive only €3.8 billion. They estimate that Brexit would reduce the United Kingdom's expenditure on agriculture between €4.1 billion and €7.3 billion, depending on the extent to which the UK agricultural policy would continue to subsidize farmers. While this amount has yet to be determined, given that the United Kingdom sought to reform the CAP by reducing direct payments to farmers under Pillar 1, the United Kingdom will likely reduce payments to its farmers under the new environmental land management contracts. As to Pillar 2 (rural development), Britain has well-established policies related to rural development, provision of public goods on agricultural lands, and animal welfare.

An indication of the importance of agricultural trade between the EU-27 and the United Kingdom is provided in Table 9.8. UK agricultural trade with the European Union is less important than agricultural trade with countries outside the European Union; 69.8 per cent of UK exports go to countries other than the EU-27 and 65 per cent of imports come from outside the European Union. The Netherlands, Ireland, Germany, France, and Spain are the major suppliers of agricultural commodities to the United Kingdom and could be harmed the most by Brexit, although little is known about the effects that Brexit might have on bilateral trade between the United Kingdom and individual EU states.

Studies suggest that the impacts of Brexit-related changes in trade on EU-27 countries are likely to be small and may not all be negative; the same is true with respect to the United Kingdom (Jongeneel, van Berkum, and Vrolijk 2016; van Berkum et al. 2018). As an illustration, projections of the changes in UK production and prices are provided in Table 9.9 under the two scenarios identified above. Changes in the EU-27 are expected to be smaller due to the difference in size between the United Kingdom and EU-27 and because much of the UK agricultural trade is with countries outside the European Union. The impact on both UK and EU farmers' incomes depends as much on decisions regarding domestic agricultural policy

Table 9.8. UK agricultural exports and imports by category, 2016 (% of total)

Item	UK Exports			UK Imports		
	Intra-EU	Extra-EU	World	Intra-EU	Extra-EU	World
Propagation materials	3	2	2	3	1	2
Unprocessed products	10	7	8	8	8	8
Semi-processed products	28	21	25	22	30	24
Final products, not fresh	58	70	63	55	38	50
Final products, fresh	2	1	2	12	23	15
Total (€ billions)	€16.5	€10.8	€27.3	€42.2	€18.1	€60.3

Source: van Berkum et al. (2018).

Table 9.9. Estimated changes in UK prices and production under free trade agreement and default WTO scenarios, % change in 2025 relative to 2016 baseline

Agricultural Product	Free Trade Agreement		Default WTO	
	Price Change (%)	Production Change (%)	Price Change (%)	Production Change (%)
Wheat	4	2	25	10
Barley	−5	−3	−4	−19
Sugar beet	5	2	8	1
Tomato	3	0	6	0
Beef	5	−1	46	12
Pig meat	5	1	27	6
Poultry	5	2	11	8
Milk	4	1	26	11
Butter	5	0	74	20
Cheese	5	0	15	−9
Skim milk powder	5	17	24	426
Whole milk powder	6	15	49	464

Source: van Berkum et al. (2018).

(e.g., level of direct payments) as it does on the future trade relationship between the United Kingdom and the EU-27. For example, Jongeneel, van Berkum, and Vrolijk (2016) find that horticultural, poultry, and hog producers are likely beneficiaries overall, while grain producers lose or gain depending on final negotiations and domestic agricultural policy.

9.5   SUMMARY AND CONCLUSIONS

- Brexit: the United Kingdom was a member of the European Union from 1973 to 2020.
- The European Union's Common Agricultural Policy (CAP) has affected the evolution of the EU farm sector and global agricultural markets in addition to EU governance structure and movement towards greater integration of EU markets.

- In the future, the EU agricultural sector is expected to take on more responsibility for the European Union's mission to achieve sustainable development goals, climate mitigation, and environmental improvement.
- Initially, high levels of support through the EU CAP led to significant productivity increases in European agriculture. As a result, the European Union has shifted from being a net importer of food prior to 1970 to one of the world's largest net exporters of wheat, sugar, beef, poultry, and dairy products. This led to overall food price increases for EU consumers.
- Although large outlays from the EU budget are necessary to support agriculture, spending has shifted away from Pillar 1 (direct support for agriculture) to Pillar 2 (regional development, environment, and other objectives).
- The European Union moved from payments tied to commodities to direct income support payments that now have been converted into single-farm direct payments. As such, decoupling farm support from production permits markets to function more freely.
- Direct payments will likely prove unsustainable, mainly because of leakage (benefits accruing to those not in agriculture) and because such payments quickly get capitalized in land values, thereby benefiting only those landowners in place at the time the basic payment was made.
- Thus, many direct payment benefits do not benefit tenant farmers or those purchasing new land.
- When decoupled from production, the basic direct payment increases production costs. Therefore, direct payments must be temporary.
- Rent-seeking on the part of the agricultural sector, farmers, handlers, and processors will cause politicians to continue support of agriculture. Therefore, to replace direct payments, the European Union is looking towards greater use of agricultural business risk programs like those used in Canada and the United States (van Asseldonk et al. 2019). For example, they might create subsidies for crop revenue insurance premiums.

CHAPTER TEN

Insurance Mechanisms in Agriculture

10.1 INSURANCE AND RISK IN AGRICULTURE

Risk has been endemic to farming throughout history. A field of wheat affected by drought would reduce the expected yield below the cost of harvest – a fact that became painfully obvious to the farmers in the US Great Plains during the Dust Bowl era. The same is true for crops lost to pests: for instance, the earliest record of pest control dates back to 2500 BCE when Sumerians used sulphur compounds to kill insects. To some extent, these risks have been limited by the advancement of new technologies. Historically, the United States has responded to widespread disasters, such as drought, with a variety of disaster assistance programs. These programs have aided farmers affected by agricultural catastrophes by providing loans at extremely low interest rates. Since 1996, agricultural policy in the United States has attempted to replace these programs with insurance products. The concept is that when farmers pay for insurance, they must anticipate and meet the potential cost of these disasters in their business model. Even with this shift towards insurance, some disaster programs, such as the 2017 Wildfires and Hurricanes Indemnity Program (WHIP), are still offered in extreme circumstances.

The most recent US crop insurance program is a hybrid public-private partnership. Crop insurance is sold and indemnities are paid by private insurance providers; however, the prices are set according data from the USDA's Risk Management Agency. In general, these data (and the statistical formulations used to estimate the premiums) are set so that the insurance premiums are actuarially sound (i.e., the price of the insurance is roughly equal to the expected payout or indemnity). The overall demand for crop insurance is then increased by a subsidy that varies by the level of coverage. For example, if the producer chooses a 55 per cent coverage level, the federal government will provide a subsidy of 64 per cent of the price of the insurance policy for corn. The insurance providers also receive support in that the government subsidizes a share of the administrative cost for writing crop insurance and access to a reinsurance pool where they can sell a portion of their riskiest insurance policies.

10.2   EVOLUTION OF CROP INSURANCE IN CANADA

In 1960, the Manitoba provincial government was the first to introduce a federal-provincial crop insurance program. The program was rather slow to catch on. By 1965, only 828,000 seeded acres out of a possible thirty million acres in Canada were insured. Most of the insured acres at that time were in the Canadian Prairie provinces of Alberta, Saskatchewan, and Manitoba. One cause for the low participation level in the crop insurance program was caused by the low subsidy offered by the program. Low participation also reflected the relative newness of the concept of crop insurance (Sigurdson and Sin 1994). Further, even in the Prairies, crop insurance was not available to all farmers. Federal legislation stipulated that 25 per cent of the farmers, or 25 per cent of the farmland in an area, must be registered for crop insurance before insurance could be implemented, which restricted the areas in which the provinces could introduce the program. Moreover, protection offered under the crop insurance program insured only 60 per cent of long-term yields.

In 1966, the Federal Crop Insurance Act was amended in an attempt to increase farmer participation in the program. The insurance yield-coverage level available to farmers was increased from 60 per cent to 80 per cent of the long-term, average-area yield. The federal contribution of premiums also increased, from 20 per cent to 25 per cent. In 1970, minor amendments were made to allow for the expansion of crop insurance coverage to include all losses resulting from a farmer's inability to seed a crop due to weather conditions.

One could reasonably argue that this program was created primarily for Prairie grain farmers. In 2000, the majority of Canadian land covered by the crop insurance program was still located in the Prairies; Saskatchewan had the most acres in the program, followed by Alberta and Manitoba. Other Canadian farmers received much less benefit from the program, partly because their yields were less variable than those on the Prairies. Further, crop insurance participation within the provinces varies by region. For example, farmers in regions with a higher yield variance, which were generally the drier regions, tended to participate more in crop insurance because they expected to receive a payout more frequently.

Participation in the program increased dramatically in 1973, when federal and provincial governments added hail spot-loss coverage and increased their combined share of the premiums from 25 per cent to 50 per cent. Participation in the Canadian crop insurance program increased from 14.6 million acres in 1974 to 30.6 million acres in 1981. During the 1980s, the provinces of Quebec and Ontario extended their participation to 1.8 million and 1.1 million acres, respectively. By 1998, the per-province percentage of eligible acres enrolled in Canada's crop insurance program was as follows: Newfoundland (13.8 per cent), Prince Edward Island (12.9 per cent), Nova Scotia (27.6 per cent), New Brunswick (55.4 per cent), Quebec (50 per cent), Ontario (46 per cent), Manitoba (81.1 per cent), Saskatchewan (63.5 per cent), Alberta (51.2 per cent), and British Columbia (52.4 per cent).

10.3   EVOLUTION OF CROP INSURANCE IN THE UNITED STATES

The US government has administered a crop insurance program since the Federal Crop Insurance Corporation (FCIC) was created in 1938. The first crop insurance contracts were issued in 1939 for wheat (Gardner 1994).

US FEDERALLY SUBSIDIZED MULTIPLE-PERIL CROP INSURANCE PROGRAM

Since the 1930s, federally subsidized multiple-peril crop insurance has been a principal means of managing the risk associated with crop losses. The FCIC administers the crop insurance program. Over time, this program has grown from covering a few crops and areas to covering most crops and areas. In addition, Congress has periodically appropriated funds for disaster assistance to farmers when farming areas have suffered widespread crop losses because of weather conditions, such as drought or flooding.

Between 1980 and 1998, the United States Department of Agriculture (USDA) expanded the availability of crop insurance from thirty to sixty-seven crops, and from about one-half of the nation's counties to virtually all counties. Participation, measured in terms of the per cent of eligible acres insured, increased from about 10 per cent in 1980 to about 40 per cent in the early 1990s. Under the Federal Crop Insurance Reform Act and the Department of Agriculture Reorganization Act of 1994, Congress required farmers wishing to participate in other USDA farm programs to purchase a minimum amount of crop insurance. This requirement helped increase participation to over 70 per cent of eligible acres (GAO/RCED 1998, 15).

From the very beginning, the FCIC was confronted with two problems. First, there was low participation in the crop insurance program. Even though the premiums for crop insurance were subsidized by the government, few farmers purchased the insurance. Second, the loss ratio was large. That is, the indemnities paid by the FCIC to cover the crop losses divided by the premiums received from farmers and the government were greater than one. So, the government had to make up the additional shortfall in the program over and above the government subsidy on the crop insurance premiums.

The low participation and the high loss ratio were caused by adverse selection. Farmers joined the program when a payout was likely, and they stayed out of the program when the likelihood of a payout was low. Clendenin summarizes this phenomenon: "in counties and years when soil moisture was lacking, insurance sold freely, [but] in those same counties, the number of contracts dropped as much as 75 per cent when soil-moisture conditions presaged a good crop" (Clendenin 1942, 249).

An additional reason for low participation was thought to be the introduction of disaster payments in the Agriculture and Consumer Protection Act of 1973, which essentially gave farmers free insurance for wheat, rice, feed grains, and cotton if they joined the price support program. Gardner (1994) argues this was not the case; rather, he argues, multiple-peril crop insurance was open to farmer manipulation because of the design of the crop insurance program.

The Federal Crop Insurance Act (FCIA) of 1980 was intended to improve the crop insurance program so it would generate greater farmer participation. The FCIA made four improvements to the existing US crop insurance program: (1) the government subsidy on premiums could be as high as 30 per cent; (2) crop insurance coverage could be expanded to new counties and new commodities; (3) private firms could be authorized to sell FCIC crop insurance; and (4) crop insurance premiums could be reduced for those farmers who purchase additional hail or fire insurance. All these measures failed to increase participation in the crop insurance program or to reduce its cost to the government. In 1996, the government took a new direction and began to offer insurance to farmers based on a futures price. It should be noted that all crop insurance contracts guarantee a price (often a specific-grade price, such as the price of #2 dark northern spring wheat in the United States).

10.4   THEORY OF CROP INSURANCE

The essence of the insurance problem is that some factors of production are either partially or completely beyond the decision maker's control. For example, while farmers can control the level of nitrogen applied per acre, the quantity of rainfall is beyond their control. Furthermore, the overall quantity of rainfall occurring over the crop year is largely unknown at the time the decision maker has to make several important decisions (e.g., the share of each crop to plant or the level of nitrogen fertilizer to apply). Yet there is an interaction between the appropriate choice of controllable factors and the ultimate level of the uncontrollable input. If farmers know the rainfall is adequate, they will apply more nitrogen than they will if the level of rainfall is inadequate.

There are several ways to reduce or eliminate this source of uncertainty. For example, the decision maker can invest in irrigation equipment to supplement soil moisture in low-rainfall events. In this scenario, the farmer can make better decisions with regard to levels of nitrogen and crop selection, but profitability is still dependent on rainfall because the farmer has to incur the additional expense of irrigation during periods of low rainfall. However, the investment in irrigation technology is only one approach to controlling risk. Another approach is to write a contract that pays the farmer an agreed upon payment (indemnity) for the occurrence of a bad outcome (e.g., low rainfall). In this section, we explain the economic consequences of such a contract from perspective of both the farmers, who demand these contracts, and the insurers, who supply these contracts. As in any other market, we assume that a market equilibrium exists, whereby the price will equate the supply of insurance contracts with the demand for insurance contracts. However, in the case of insurance contracts, this equilibrium is complicated by the terms of the contract (i.e., the definition of a bad outcome such that a payment will be made).

10.4.1   Pricing Crop Insurance Policies – Art and Science

The theoretical development of the price of crop insurance presented in Appendix 10 simplifies the estimation of crop insurance price by focusing on two events – a high-rainfall event and a low-rainfall event. In practice, the distribution of yields tends to be more continuous, as depicted in Figure 10.1. The distribution depicted in Figure 10.1 is an updated version of the corn distribution function estimated by Moss and Shonkwiler (1993). As a starting point, one of the basic questions in constructing insurance policies for crop yields under the most recent farm bill is the determination of the coverage level – selection of the insured yield. Table 10.1 presents the typical coverage levels available to most crops. The average yield for the data presented in Figure 10.1 is 198.75 bushels per acre (bu/acre) while the standard deviation (std dev) is 10.87 bu/acre. Given this average yield, we could select a coverage rate of 85 per cent – or 168.9 bu/acre. At this coverage rate, the subsidy rate is 38 per cent, implying that the farmer will pay 62 per cent.

So, how much is the premium? First, let us assume that the premium will be set at the actuarial value of the policy. To develop this actuarial value, consider the indemnity line presented in Figure 10.1. Specifically, if the yield falls below 168.9 bu/acre, the insurance contract will pay the difference. For example, if the yield were 160.0 bu/acre, the insurance contract would pay a market price times 8.9 bu/acre (e.g., p_c (168.90 – 160.00), where p_c is some agreed upon price of corn). Taking the expected value of this payment over all possible corn yields and assuming a corn price of US$3.60/bu yields a value of US$1.40/acre. Based on the rates in Table 10.1, the government pays US$0.53/acre of the premium. To examine the sensitivity of these results, Table 10.1 also presents insurance premiums and subsidy rates for a similar distribution with 1.25 times the original standard deviation (e.g., holding the average yield constant). To evaluate the relative size of this subsidy, let us consider an 80 per cent coverage product written on the 1.25 times the original standard deviation scenario. Under this scenario, the insured yield is 159.00 bu/acre, the actuarial value of the insurance policy is US$ 3.22/acre, and the

Figure 10.1. Distribution of corn yields and payoff insurance based on 85 per cent coverage

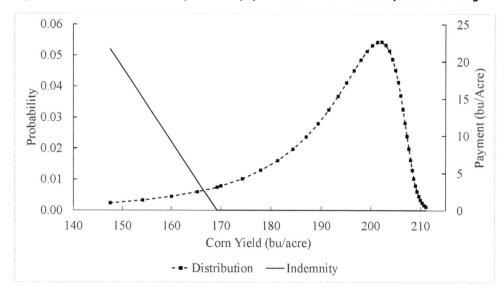

Table 10.1. Coverage, subsidy, and insurance payments

Coverage Rate (share of yield covered)	Subsidy (share of insurance paid)	Farmer (share of insurance paid)	Coverage Yield (bu/acre)	Original Std Dev		1.25 Times Std Dev	
				Insurance (US$/ acre)	Subsidy (US$/ acre)	Insurance (US$/ acre)	Subsidy (US$/ acre)
50	67	33	99.4	0.0593	0.0397	0.4783	0.3205
55	64	36	109.3	0.0883	0.0565	0.6552	0.4193
60	64	36	119.2	0.1322	0.0846	0.8928	0.5714
65	49	41	129.2	0.2003	0.0981	1.2160	0.5958
70	59	41	139.1	0.3093	0.1825	1.6631	0.9812
75	55	45	149.1	0.4908	0.2699	2.2961	1.2628
80	48	52	159.0	0.8084	0.3880	3.2196	1.5454
85	38	62	168.9	1.4006	0.5322	4.6227	1.7566

subsidy is US$1.54/acre. How big is this subsidy? Let us start by assuming that a farmer in Fayette County, Ohio, farms five sections (3,840 acres) – half of which (1,920 acres) is planted in corn. In that example, an 80 per cent coverage yields an insured yield of 305,280 bushels for the corn crop. The actuarial cost of this policy would be US$6,182 for the farm, of which the government pays US$2,967.

Consider the impact of the crop insurance subsidy. In this scenario, the US$2,967 would probably not be considered large compared to price loss coverage or agricultural risk coverage payments. However, as discussed in Appendix 10A, the subsidy may be distortionary.

Table 10.2. US crop insurance programs for corn

Insurance Program	Description
Yield Protection (YP)	Only protects against production loss. The harvest price is not used.
Revenue Protection (RP)	Protects against loss of revenue due to production loss, change in price, or a combination of both.
Revenue Protection with Harvest Price Exclusion (RPHPE)	RPHPE is based on the expected price at harvest; it does not insure price fluctuations.
Supplemental Coverage Option (SCO)	The Supplemental Coverage Option (SCO) is a crop insurance option that provides additional coverage for a portion of the underlying crop insurance policy deductible.
Area Risk Protection Insurance (ARPI)	Offers three insurance plans based on previous experience from an area, generally a county, rather than actual yield. Replaces Group Risk Protection and Group Risk Income Protection. Coverage availability varies by county.
Area Yield Protection (AYP)	Indemnifies the insured in the event the final yield falls below the trigger yield.
Catastrophic Coverage (CAT)	Pays 50% of average yield and 55% of the projected price. CAT has no premium but does have a US$300 administrative fee per crop per county.
Margin Protection (MP)	An area-based plan that protects against an unexpected decrease in operating margin. Can be purchased by itself or in conjunction with YP or RP plans with the same insurance company. Sales closing date for MP is 30 September.
Margin Protection with Harvest Price Option (MP-HPO)	Whenever the harvest price exceeds the projected price, the expected revenue used in setting the trigger margins is reset based on the harvest price.

Specifically, the subsidy could lead to increased input levels. Further, the subsidies for crops like corn or soybeans may draw planted acres away from crops with less profitable insurance programs (one example may be hay crops). In addition, subsidizing insurance typically leads to direct producer gains from risk reduction.

The foregoing insurance contract is referred to as yield protection; however, several types of insurance (Table 10.2) are offered under the crop insurance program. For our purposes, two variations merit additional discussion. First, the revenue protection program insures both declines in yield and reductions in prices. Second, the payments for Area Risk Protection Insurance (ARPI) are based on outcomes at the county level. Table 10.3 presents the number of policies sold, total liabilities under those policies, total premium received, subsidy, indemnity, and loss ratio for corn for four US states in 2018 (Arkansas, Florida, Indiana, and Ohio). The data indicate that the most popular products for corn are ARP (area revenue protection), RP (revenue protection), and YP (yield protection). Further, catastrophic protection (YP [CAT]) is somewhat popular in all US states. The loss ratios tend to be higher outside the corn belt, although this may simply be the "luck of the draw" for 2018.

In addition to depicting the distribution of values for different insurance options, Table 10.3 also provides information about the ex ante/ex post nature of crop insurance subsidy. For

Table 10.3. USDA/Risk Management Agency insurance information, selected US states, 2018

	Acres (number)	Policies Sold (number)	Liabilities (US$)	Total Premium (US$)	Subsidy (US$)	Indemnity (US$)	Loss Ratio (indemnity/ premium)
			Arkansas				
RP	3,010	1,113	98,480,120	13,078,452	9,061,621	14,782,777	1.13
RPHPE	6	0	0	0	0	0	0.00
SCO-RP	2	0	0	0	0	0	0.00
SCO-YP	1	0	0	0	0	0	0.00
YP	2,325	1,025	79,730,451	6,545,787	4,424,555	9,711,468	1.48
YP(CAT)	1,529	542	24,289,465	735,331	735,311	344,600	0.47
Total	6,873	2,680	202,500,036	20,359,570	14,221,487	24,838,845	1.22
			Florida				
RP	574	108	9,730,500	712,504	452,017	540,624	0.76
YP	188	59	4,897,003	221,207	108,647	108,351	0.49
YP(CAT)	125	44	2,903,445	31,221	31,221	0	0.00
Total	887	211	17,530,948	964,932	591,885	648,975	0.67
			Indiana				
ARP	1,379	1,040	211,962,314	13,493,025	5,998,758	0	0.00
ARP-HPE	31	25	3,971,179	221,178	97,566	0	0.00
AYP	305	206	33,968,978	1,300,998	671,409	0	0.00
AYP (CAT)	2	2	366,751	5,867	5,867	0	0.00
MP	49	44	16,437,961	728,719	321,521	0	0.00
MP-HPO	824	662	166,669,847	13,023,843	5,735,820	0	0.00
RP	23,273	17,434	2,137,029,069	162,582,113	94,600,952	18,875,237	0.12
RPHPE	314	242	37,226,676	1,252,946	708,261	108,448	0.09
SCO-RP	42	29	515,426	141,216	91,796	0	0.00
SCO-YP	1	0	0	0	0	0	0.00
YP	1,025	754	49,503,891	1,957,797	1,108,708	420,289	0.21
YP (CAT)	183	115	5,557,908	92,758	90,370	694	0.01
Total	27,428	20,553	2,663,210,000	194,800,460	109,431,028	19,404,668	0.10
			Ohio				
ARP	392	283	42,337,086	3,633,547	1,608,975	0	0.00
ARP-HPE	3	3	239,902	1,705	7,482	0	0.00
AYP	123	88	5,357,530	278,248	145,150	0	0.00
MP	28	15	3,417,344	173,954	76,690	0	0.00
MP-HPO	278	239	37,065,547	3,258,190	1,438,140	0	0.00
RP	21,010	15,257	1,376,385,017	100,300,707	61,557,465	14,194,258	0.14
RPHPE	123	105	13,147,310	677,279	410,704	21,082	0.03
SCO-RP	3	3	66,471	18,076	11,750	0	0.00
YP	1,400	865	27,615,678	1,226,621	750,257	257,957	0.21
YP (CAT)	110	77	4,004,369	55,526	56,526	9,882	0.17
Total	23,470	16,935	1,509,636,254	109,623,853	66,063,139	14,483,179	0.00

example, Ohio receives US$66 million in insurance subsidies but only receives US$14 million in insurance indemnities. This is much different from Arkansas, which received US$14 million in insurance subsidies and US$24 million in insurance indemnities. If we view the insurance policies as an input subsidy, Ohio clearly received a higher subsidy than Arkansas; however, corn producers in Arkansas received a higher payment ex post.

10.4.2 Other Provisions of US Crop Insurance

Up to this point, our discussion on pricing crop insurance has focused on the actuarial price (e.g., the value of the yield lost under an insured event). The cost of providing insurance may be complicated by several factors. First, insurance companies that insure agriculture in a relatively small geographic region may face significantly higher risks if crop yields are highly correlated within that region. One response is to diversify across regions by swapping a portion of that company's insurance portfolio with a portion of another company's insurance portfolio for another region (i.e., one where the crop yields are less correlated with the original company's geographic region). Alternatively, the company may seek participation with other entities that have much different insurance portfolios (e.g., auto insurance companies), or even lines of business outside of the insurance industry. Within the limits, these contracts become *reinsurance* contracts – agreements where outside entities participate in the insurance contracts made by the insurance firm.

To date, the United States Department of Agriculture's Risk Management Agency (USDA/RMA) provides reinsurance through the private insurance company's participation in two funds: the Assigned Risk Fund, where the company retains 20 per cent of the risk (and premium) and assigns the remainder to the FCIC; and the Commercial Fund, where the insurance company retains 35 per cent of the risk. The reinsurance agreement provides for a sharing of the losses and gains between the insurance company and the USDA/RMA based on the terms of the fund (e.g., Assigned Risk and Commercial) and state-level adjustments. Table 10.4 presents the gains and losses for the reinsurance contracts for the four selected states highlighted in this textbook. As reported in Table 10.4, crop insurance companies in Indiana placed US$246 million in insurance liabilities in the Assigned Risk Fund and US$4.6 billion in the Commercial Fund. In the case of the Assigned Risk Fund, these companies received US$19 million in premiums and paid US$9 million in indemnities. Abstracting from the indemnity and premium retained by the originating firms, the FCIC made US$328,749 on underwriting this insurance activity, meaning that the amount of premium received by the USDA/RMA's reinsurance fund exceeded the indemnity payments by this amount. Notice that there are significant reinsurance losses in Florida. Despite such losses, in total, the USDA/RMA's reinsurance program made US$2.6 billion in 2017.

Table 10.4. US crop insurance: Reinsurance gains and losses, 2017 (US$)

	Fund	Gross Liability	Gross Premium	Gross Indemnity	Retained Liability	Retained Premium	Retained Liability	Net Gain
AR	Assigned risk	272,238,292	28,630,258	49,234,877	50,908,560	5,353,860	5,616,290	−262,430
AR	Commercial	1,318,891,163	105,566,792	106,166,998	1,233,163,237	98,704,951	92,472,831	4,820,507
FL	Assigned risk	186,728,518	22,147,309	35,712,647	34,918,234	4,141,546	4,155,252	−148,891
FL	Commercial	2,580,337,547	86,868,050	294,014,567	2,412,615,606	81,221,627	111,333,619	−30,514,853
IN	Assigned risk	246,401,518	19,643,578	9,830,677	46,077,085	3,673,349	1,795,211	328,749
IN	Commercial	4,602,503,519	363,247,278	110,785,533	4,303,340,790	339,636,205	103,584,473	112,844,357
OH	Assigned risk	64,552,694	5,589,884	4,752,622	12,071,354	1,045,308	737,498	51,947
OH	Commercial	3,179,623,024	263,044,752	88,521,477	2,972,947,527	245,946,843	82,746,140	100,619,633

Table 10.5. Florida early orange yield and revenue by age of tree

Tree Age	Per Tree		127 Trees per Acre	
Years	Boxes	US$	Boxes	US$
3	0.855	6.69	108.60	849.70
4	0.927	7.26	117.76	921.39
5	1.004	7.85	127.46	997.24
6	1.084	8.48	137.68	1077.18
7	1.169	9.14	148.40	1161.10
8	1.257	9.83	159.61	1248.82
9	1.349	10.55	171.28	1340.12
10	1.444	11.30	183.37	1434.71
11	1.542	12.06	195.84	1532.24
12	1.643	12.85	208.63	1632.32
13	1.746	13.66	221.69	1734.51
14	1.850	14.47	234.96	1838.32
15	1.956	15.30	248.37	1943.23
16	2.062	16.13	261.85	2048.72
17	2.168	16.96	275.33	2154.22
18	2.274	17.79	288.75	2259.19
19	2.378	18.61	302.03	2363.09
20	2.481	19.41	315.11	2465.42
21	2.582	20.20	327.92	2565.68
22	2.680	20.97	340.42	2663.44
23	2.776	21.72	352.54	2758.31
24	2.868	22.44	364.26	2849.93
25	2.957	23.13	375.52	2938.03
26	3.042	23.80	386.30	3022.38
27	3.123	24.43	396.58	3102.81
28	3.200	25.03	406.34	3179.20
29	3.272	25.60	415.58	3251.48
30	3.341	26.14	424.29	3319.64

In addition to reinsurance, the Standard Reinsurance Agreement (SRA) provides additional payments to crop insurance companies. First, the actuarial price of insurance developed in Appendix 10 does not represent the full cost of providing insurance, because it excludes administrative costs, such as the cost of writing policies, the cost of determining whether an insurable event has occurred, the cost of paying claims, etc. With many insurance contracts, these expenses are written into the insurance contract under the term *expense loading*. In the case of US crop insurance policies, this load has been replaced by a USDA subsidy to insurance companies to cover *administrative and operating* (A&O) *expenses*. These terms are included in the SRA.

10.4.3   Insuring Florida Citrus

Specific types of crop insurance are available for specialty crops, such as citrus in Florida. For Florida citrus, the Risk Management Agency offers two coverages. First, RMA provides insurance for the yield loss within a given crop year (i.e., for damages from wind, freeze, or hurricane). Second, RMA insures against the loss of the trees themselves. To develop the consequences of both types of insurance, we must remember that the yield for each tree is a function of the tree's bearing volume (within the tree's canopy). As the tree ages, this volume approaches a limit as the tree crowds its neighbours. Table 10.5 depicts the boxes of Florida early oranges produced per tree as the tree ages, as well as the total yield of Florida early oranges per acre based on a 127 trees/acre set. Table 10.5 also presents the total value produced at US$7.824/box (the average value of Florida early oranges in 2019).

First, the insurance for the loss of oranges involves the selection of a coverage level as in the case of field crops. The choices of coverage level and the subsidy for each level of coverage are the same as for other crops presented in Table 10.1. In this case, we assume that the citrus grower chooses a 60 per cent coverage level on a ten-year-old grove. Based on the yields and revenues, the reference revenue for the ten-year-old grove is US$1,434.71/acre. The stated coverage level for this grove is then US$860.83/acre (i.e., 0.60 x 1,434.71). Next, we assume that an insurable event occurs – the revenue of the grove drops to 55 per cent of base revenue (i.e., US$789.09/acre). Following the Risk Management Agency's Fact Sheet for Citrus Fruit in the 2019 crop year, the percentage of adjusted damages is computed as:

	Damage Percentage
0.55	Per cent damage
– 0.40	Per cent deductible (100 – 60 = 40%)
0.15	Per cent damage
÷ 0.60	Coverage level percentage
0.25	Per cent adjusted damage
	Indemnity
1,434.71	Reference revenue
× 0.60	Coverage level
860.83	Amount of insurance
× 0.25	Per cent of adjusted damage
215.21	Indemnity

The Risk Management Agency defines citrus insurance as a revenue insurance based on observed yields and prices. The expectation that citrus tree yields will increase as trees age raises an additional empirical question: how does the variance/riskiness of tree yields change with time?

The second part of the insurance program protects the grower's investment in trees. As depicted in Table 10.5, trees yield more citrus as they age. That is, a ten-year-old tree is worth more to the grower than a newly planted tree that does not produce fruit. However, the Florida Fruit Tree Program nearly covers the replanting cost (at US$85/tree of the US$87/tree actual cost). In this case, assume that the grower has an eighty-acre citrus grove with a planting density of 127 trees/acre, or 10,160 trees. The total value of the grower's trees from a replanting perspective is US$863,600. Again, assume that the grower chooses a coverage level of 0.60, implying an insurance level of US$518,160. For this level of insurance, the deductible is computed as:

10,160	Orange trees
× 87	Price per tree
883,920	
0.40	Deductible (100 − 60 = 40%)
353,568	Unit deductible

Assume that a freeze occurs, and the grower loses half of the trees. The indemnity received by the grower would be:

10,160	Orange trees
0.50	Per cent of trees
5,080	Destroyed trees
87	Dollars per tree
441,960	Value of destroyed trees
353,568	Less the deductible
88,392	Indemnity for trees lost

The majority of citrus tree loss in Florida in the twentieth century was due to weather, with four freeze events (1981, 1983, 1985, and 1989). So far in the twenty-first century, the most pernicious cause of citrus tree loss has been Huanglongbing disease (citrus greening).

10.4.4 Insuring Popcorn

Three types of insurance exist for popcorn produced in Indiana: Yield Protection, Revenue Protection, and Revenue Protection with Harvest Price Exclusion. Each of these products is based on actual production history (APH, in the RMA vernacular). Following the RMA's example, assume that the producer has a proven yield (APH) of 4,000 pounds per acre and plants 50 acres of popcorn. Assuming a projected harvest price of US$0.1968 per pound and a coverage level of 0.75, the guaranteed yield can be computed as:

4,000	APH yield pounds per acre
0.75	Coverage level
3,000	Pounds guaranteed
50	Acres
150,000	Pounds guaranteed
$0.1968	Projected price
$29,520	Insurance guarantee

As another example, assume that the yield is 2,250 pounds per acre. Under a yield protection contract, the guaranteed yield can be computed as:

2,250	Actual yield in pounds per acre
50	Coverage level
112,500	Pounds produced
0.1968	Projected price
22,140	Value of production
29,520	Guaranteed value
22,140	Value of production
7,380	Final payment

Hence, the 43.75 per cent reduction in yield results in a final payment of US$7,380.

10.5 INFORMATION COSTS ASSOCIATED WITH CROP INSURANCE PROGRAMS

When signing an insurance contract between an insurer and a farmer, information about the farmer is needed. This information is expensive and, in some cases, may be impossible to obtain. The insurer needs two pieces of information that the farmer may not want to reveal. First, if we assume all individuals in the insurance pool do not represent equal risk for the insurer (i.e., riskiness is different across individuals), the high-risk farmers will not want to reveal their identities, which could lead to adverse selection. Following our previous discussion, if farmer i is riskier than farmer j, the actuarially sound premium will be higher for farm i than farm j, and the riskier farmer has reason to misrepresent his or her true probability of a bad outcome. Second, the behaviour of an individual may change after the insurance contract is signed, the result of which could lead to moral hazard. This implies that the actual insurance price will not follow the actuarially fair insurance price.

10.5.1 Adverse Selection

Nobel laureate George Akerlof's classic paper "The Market for 'Lemons'" (1970) demonstrates adverse selection. He argues that the lack of information regarding a product may destroy the market for that product. He uses the example of the market for used cars. Suppose we have two types of used cars: good used cars and poor used cars. If a potential buyer of a good used car cannot distinguish it from a poor used car, the buyer is unwilling to pay the price for a good used car. Therefore, no one will be prepared to offer good used cars for sale, and the market for good used cars will not exist.

This is an example of the type of adverse selection that can affect crop insurance. The lack of information about the product characteristics in the market means other market participants cannot be sure of the quality of the product. This type of information problem arises in many markets and is of special concern in insurance markets in which the risk characteristics of individuals must be determined.

Adverse selection is the result of hidden information about the risk level associated with an individual who buys an insurance contract. Each farmer joins the program independently, thus, a farmer considers the expected value of insurance by using personal farm-yield distribution and comparing this with the premium level when deciding whether to participate in the crop insurance program. Meanwhile, the insurer considers an aggregate distribution of yields and premiums and is concerned with the final aggregate outcome. When the distribution of yields differs among farmers in ways that are not taken into account in the insurance premiums, adverse selection occurs because farmers who are more likely to collect indemnities are more likely to participate in the insurance program. The participation of high-risk farmers further raises the premiums and discourages low-risk farmers from joining the crop insurance program.

Not all farmers have the same attitude towards risk. Ex ante, insurers may be unable to identify a farmer's risk when claiming an indemnity, so the problem of the market for "lemons" may result (i.e., if farmers are willing to pay a higher price for insurance, they are signalling that the crop is riskier), implying there will be no market for risk. Thus, one problem insurers must overcome is to distinguish the high-risk farmers from the low-risk farmers and to use this knowledge to target the contract accordingly.

If the insurer knows the yield history of an individual farm, adverse selection will not be a problem because those who are at higher risk can be charged higher premiums. However, this is not always possible, because collecting an accurate yield history on individual farmers is difficult. This lack of data can lead to adverse selection and, potentially, to more expensive crop insurance coverage. Those farmers with a lower mean or larger variance in yield have a greater incentive to participate in the program simply because they will expect a more frequent and larger indemnity payment from the crop insurance program. Whatever the cause, this asymmetry of information between the farmer and the insurance company is the fundamental cause of adverse selection. The potential for adverse selection is increased when heterogeneity between/among the risk areas is high. In an attempt to deal with adverse selection, in Canada, for example, farmers' insurance indemnities are based on their own individual yields and not on the area average.

Adverse selection can also be caused by differences in management abilities that may not be discernible to the insurer. R.E. Just, Calvin, and Quiggin (1999) separate the three effects – risk aversion, subsidy incentive, and asymmetric information – for US farmers who decide to

Table 10.6. Effects of crop insurance on US farmers' net income from corn production (per acre mean and variance), using the high-price option

Insured Yield Level for Corn	Uninsured Farmers		Insured Farmers	
	Mean[a]	Variance	Mean[b]	Variance
50%	−0.54*	−986.37*	3.502 [2.11]**	−2,721.88
65%	−0.65*	−1,610.61*	0.95 [1.41]***	−1,981.21
75%	−3.69*	−2,184.91*	3.93 [3.85]*	−3,624.60

Source: R.E. Just, Calvin, and Quiggin (1999).
[a] The asterisks are significance indicators of the population mean and variance effects estimated by the farmer. * = 1%; ** = 2%; *** = 10%.
[b] The numbers in square brackets are t statistics for testing the equivalence of means between insured and uninsured farmers.

purchase crop insurance for corn (Table 10.6). First, each of the three levels of yield coverage available provides an incentive for farmers to participate in the program. In each level, the incentive to participate occurs because the mean income is greater and the variance lower for insured farmers when compared with uninsured farmers.

Second, the reduction in risk is greater for higher levels of coverage. Assuming both groups have the same level of risk aversion, the risk-aversion incentive is greater for those who participate than it is for those who do not (i.e., uninsured farmers have a lower variance).

R.E. Just, Calvin, and Quiggin (1999) estimate the effects of subsidies and asymmetric information on whether farmers decide to participate in crop insurance and find that subsidized premiums encourage farmers to join the program (an indication of adverse selection). They also find that the asymmetric information incentive is negative for both groups (ibid.). The yield distribution used by the insurer lags the yield distribution perceived by the farmer (i.e., yields are increasing over time rather than constant), which acts as a deterrent for the farmer to buy insurance. Thus, any added information reserved by farmers about their actual yields does not benefit their participation in crop insurance. Just, Calvin, and Quiggin draw the strong conclusion that crop insurance is heavily influenced by rent-seeking activity; thus, the risk-aversion incentive from crop insurance is small. Rather, farmers participate in crop insurance mainly to receive subsidies or for adverse selection possibilities, so the merits of crop insurance as a welfare-enhancing policy are debatable.

10.5.2 Moral Hazard

Moral hazard is where farmers alter their farming practices after insuring their crops. There are at least two ways in dryland crop production that a farmer can alter input decisions that affect indemnity payments. Both of these practices depend on the farmer expecting that a problem will occur, while the insurance company expects simultaneously that average moisture conditions will occur at the time the premium and price are determined. First, a farmer may apply less than the optimal non-insured input level (i.e., the level used in the absence of an insurance contract) for fertilizer, pesticides, or seed. Second, a farmer may increase the number of acres insured by planting more acres of the insured crop. Take, for instance, the case of drought, since no indemnity will be received until yield falls below 60 or 70 per cent of normal, which usually occurs in a drought situation. The insurance of crops against drought may change the incentives that motivate farmers who participate in the program.

Using the expected utility equation, moral hazard results because the insurer cannot observe farmers' input level x, and the insurer cannot determine whether farmers changed their input level because of the insurance contract. For the insurer to charge fair premiums, the insurer must know the behaviour of a farmer after the contract is signed. If the ex post value of x is not known by the insurer, then the insurer will not know the exact conditional distribution of revenue.

A farmer receives indemnity payments from the insurer in the form of a cash settlement whenever the crop yield is below the guaranteed level. The insurer sets the price for the crop in the spring before the realized crop price is known; therefore, the insurer must use an expected price. If the crop price moves upward during the growing year, farmers will have no incentive to practise moral hazard. However, if the crop price moves downward during the crop growing year, farmers may have an incentive to practise moral hazard. The magnitude of the incentive to practise moral hazard depends on the extent of the price decline. Because insurers know that indemnity payments are sensitive to the price set, the insurers will choose the insurance price carefully. One case in which the expected price used by the insurer differed from the market price was the price set for barley by the Saskatchewan Crop Insurance Corporation (SCIC) in 1996. The market price for barley fell during the spring. The SCIC set their price in early spring before the change in price was known. The price difference was more than C$30 per tonne from the time the farmers signed the contracts until they planted their crops. Thus, farmers had the incentive to collect indemnities on their barley production by changing their use of inputs.

One effect of moral hazard is to increase the size of the payout when a payout is anticipated (e.g., by bringing more acreage into production during a period of drought). Coble et al. (1997) find that Kansas wheat farmers will increase the size of the payout they hope to collect from the insurer if they are convinced that an insurance payout will occur. That is, farmers do not respond to the adverse incentives every time, but once they do respond, they attempt to increase the size of the payout. The crucial point is that moral hazard, while always present, does not increase program costs every year (Vercammen and van Kooten 1994). Because insurance companies adjust premiums and coverage levels depending on individual payouts, it often does not benefit the farmer to practise moral hazard.

10.6   DEALING WITH ADVERSE SELECTION AND MORAL HAZARD

Nothing short of the total monitoring of farmers' decisions will completely prevent moral hazard and adverse selection. Of course, total monitoring is impossible (or prohibitively expensive). Therefore, governments have tried to create incentives to minimize these difficulties by adjusting premium and coverage levels.

Crop insurance companies use two policies to reduce moral hazard. First, most crop insurance companies have moved from area average-yield coverage to individual yield coverage. Individual yield coverage means that farmers can obtain yield insurance up to a proportion, usually 70 or 80 per cent, of their own ten-year average yield. Thus, if a farmer practises moral hazard that results in a yield loss, the yield loss will lower the farmer's future crop insurance coverage level. A second policy used by insurance companies to reduce moral hazard is to provide farmers who do not claim crop insurance with an opportunity to increase their level of crop insurance coverage at a lower cost. What this means is that farmers can both increase the coverage level up to the maximum (say, 120 per cent) of their ten-year average yields and reduce their premiums to as low as 50 per cent of the risk-area premium.

10.7   CROP INSURANCE COVERAGE FALLS AS PRICES FALL

Farming is a risky business. Both price and yield fluctuate, and both can be unpredictable. For many years, farmers in the United States and Canada wanted insurance that would protect them from the uncertainty of price and yield changes. Historically, crop insurance has provided some yield protection, but it has never provided price insurance. The crop price used by crop insurance entities to calculate indemnity payments is a function of the world market price; thus the price changes as the supply and demand conditions in the world market change.

10.8   CROP INSURANCE COMPARED WITH MORE TRADITIONAL PROGRAMS

Recalling our discussion of the agricultural risk coverage (ARC) and the Margin Protection Program for Dairy (MPP) in Chapter 7, the similarity between these commodity programs and crop insurance is undeniable. Likewise, the similarity between revenue insurance and ARC is striking (see Appendix 10B for further discussion). In fact, ARC has been referred to as a "shallow loss" revenue protection program (because the payment under ARC is limited to

10 per cent of the benchmark revenue). However, as described in Appendix 10B, even traditional programs such as the price floor provided by the loan rate can be reformulated as a free price insurance program. This possible linkage may portend a future unification of traditional commodity programs and the array of crop insurance instruments available from the current federal/private partnership.

10.9   SUMMARY AND CONCLUSIONS

- Crop insurance is designed to provide farmers with all-risk crop insurance because the private sector is unable or unwilling to provide such coverage at prices that farmers are able and willing to pay. The governments of the United States and Canada, for example, subsidize crop insurance.
- While the overall policy objectives of crop insurance are well understood, the overall market for insurance in agriculture is less well developed. This chapter presents a model of the insurance firm that incorporates critical aspects often ignored in the existing agricultural literature.
- Crop insurance coverage falls as commodity prices fall. For example, low farm incomes for grain farmers are positively correlated with low revenue coverage from crop insurance.
- While crop insurance can avoid disasters at the level of the individual farm, it cannot support collective farm income to any major degree during periods of depressed prices.
- Problems of moral hazard and adverse selection demonstrate that asymmetric information between the farmer and the insurer can add costs to insurance programs.
- The interaction between the application of inputs and the demand for crop insurance is complex. Some inputs increase production-associated risk, while other inputs do not. More research is required to understand these interactions (Moss 2009).
- In the 1996 US Farm Bill, the US government introduced a revenue insurance plan for grain farmers that became costly to the US government.
- Agricultural trade generally considers crop insurance to be a Green Box program under the World Trade Organization (WTO); that is, it does not distort production. However, the conclusions of R.E. Just, Calvin, and Quiggin (1999) regarding asymmetric information and subsidy incentives call this assumption into question.
- In the United States, farmers must participate in crop insurance to collect subsidies, at least at the catastrophic risk protection level (CAT). This raises the question as to whether or not crop insurance in the United States is a PEST (political-economic-seeking transfer) or a PERT (political-economic-resource transaction).
- US crop insurance is not confined to just grain and oilseed crops. Insurance is now available for other crops such as citrus and popcorn.

APPENDIX 10A: VALUE OF INSURANCE UNDER RISK AVERSION

To develop the value of insurance, we start with the standard assumption that farmers attempt to maximize profit by choosing the level of a variable input (i.e., the choice of the level of nitrogen in the production of corn). However, unlike the basic production scenario, we assume that the production function is stochastic. Mathematically, we define the production function of corn as a function of the level of rainfall (ω)

$$f(x) = \begin{cases} f_1(x) = 4.5097x - 0.0407x^2 \ if \ \omega = \omega_1 \ and \ P[\omega_1] = 0.50 \\ f_2(x) = 4.4258x - 0.0338x^2 \ if \ \omega = \omega_2 \ and \ P[\omega_2] = 0.50 \end{cases} \tag{10.A1}$$

where x is the level nitrogen applied to corn, and where rainfall can take on two values: ω_1, which is a low-rainfall event and ω_2, which is a high-rainfall event. Thus $P[\omega_1]$ and $P[\omega_2]$ are the probabilities of the low- and high-rainfall events, respectively. In much of our discussion here, we will assume that the high and low-rainfall events are equally likely (i.e., $P[\omega_1] = P[\omega_2] = 0.5$). Given the stochastic production function, the profit maximization specification can then be specified as

$$\pi_0 = \max_x 0.5[(4.5097x - 0.0407x^2)p_y - p_x x] + 0.5[(4.4258x - 0.0338x^2)p_y - p_x x],$$

where π_0 is the profit per acre, p_y is the output price that we take to be the corn price of US\$3.50 per bushel, and p_x is the price of the input (a nitrogen price of US\$0.125 per pound). This problem can be simplified by taking the weighted average of the two production functions. Specifically, the profit maximization problem becomes

$$\pi_0 = \max_x [4.4678x - 0.0372x^2]3.50 - 0.125x. \tag{10.A2}$$

Solving this problem, the profit maximizing solution is $\pi^* = 461.41$ by using $x^* = 59.4904$ pounds of nitrogen per acre.

Next, we consider the introduction of an insurance policy that pays for any reduction in yield below y^*. Under this contract, the farmer receives a payment

$$\phi(x, p_y) = Max(y^* - f(x), 0)p_y = \begin{cases} (y^* - f(x))p_y \ if \ f(x) < y^* \\ 0 \ if \ f(x) if \ f(x) \geq y^*, \end{cases} \tag{10.A3}$$

where $\phi(.)$ is the indemnity payment in dollars, $Max(a,b)$ is the maximum function such that $Max(a,b) = a$ if $a > b$, and $Max(a,b) = b$ if $a \leq b$, (this is different than the $max_x f(x)$ function that returns the maximum value of the function $f(x)$ obtainable for all possible values of x). If we define $y^* = 125$ in the foregoing example, the insurance policy will pay US\$2.364 per acre

(0.675 bushel per acre at a price of US$3.50 per bushel of corn) in the event of low rainfall. From a slightly different perspective, the farmer receives

$$R(y^*, x, p_y) = Max(y^*, f(x))p_y = \begin{cases} y^* p_y \ if \ f(x) \le y^* \\ f(x)p_y \ if \ f(x) > y^*, \end{cases}$$

(10.A4)

where $R(.)$ is the revenue function. The revenue function in Equation 10.A5 is the result of adding the indemnity payment in Equation 10.A4 to the profit function for each state. Specifically,

$$f(x)p_y + \phi(x, p_y) = \begin{cases} f(x)p_y + (y^* - f(x))p_y = y^* p_y \ if \ f(x) < y^* \\ f(x)p_y + 0 = f(x)p_y \ if \ f(x) \ge y^* \end{cases}$$

(10.A5)

Thus, the firm's problem becomes

$$\pi_1 = \max_x 0.5[Max(4.5097x - 0.0407x^2, 125)3.50 - 0.125x] +$$
$$0.5[Max(4.4258x - 0.0338x^2, 125)3.50 - 0.125x] - \Psi,$$

(10.A6)

where π_1 is the profit per acre with the insurance policy in place and ψ is the cost of the insurance policy. Solving this optimization problem yields a profit of US$461.81 per acre based on an application of 64.414 pounds of nitrogen per acre.

Assuming that the farmer has constant absolute risk aversion following the negative exponential utility function, the optimal application rate for nitrogen is derived from the utility maximization problem

$$\max_x - \theta exp(-\rho[(b(\omega_1)x + c(\omega_1)x^2)p_y - p_x x])$$
$$-(1 - \theta)exp(-\rho[(b(\omega_2)x + c(\omega_2)x^2)p_y - p_x x])$$

(10.A7)

where p is the Arrow-Pratt absolute risk-aversion coefficient. Starting with $p = 0.0025$, the optimal amount of nitrogen applied becomes 59.0806 pounds, which is somewhat smaller than the profit-maximizing solution of 59.4904 pounds. If the farmer becomes more risk averse so that the risk aversion coefficient increases to $p = 0.0050$, the optimal quantity of nitrogen will decrease to 58.6940 pounds.

The actuarial (or fair) price of insurance can be expressed as

$$\psi^*(\theta, x, y^*) = p_y(\theta Max (y^* - f_1(x), 0) + (1 - \theta)Max(y^* - f_2(x), 0))$$

(10.A8)

where θ is the probability of the low-rainfall event ($P[\omega_1] = \theta$ in Equation 10.A1). The actuarial price of the insurance policy then will increase if the gap between the insured yield level

Figure 10.A1. Stochastic and average production function

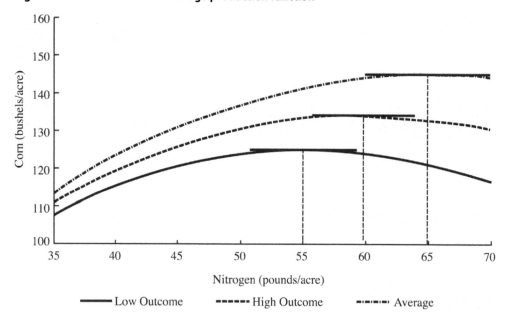

Low Outcome ——— High Outcome ------ Average ·—·—·

and the quantity produced increases at the margin. As depicted in Figure 10.A1, the marginal physical product (or slope of the total physical product) in the low-yield state is negative around the optimum point from Equation 10.A2. Hence, as the level of input applied increases, the actuarially fair price of crop insurance will increase.

Next, we introduce the optimal insurance contract into the utility maximization problem to yield

$$\max_{x} -\theta \exp(-\rho[Max(b(\omega_1)x + c(\omega_1)x^2, y^*)p_y - p_x - \psi^*(\theta, x, y^*)])$$
$$-(1-\theta)\exp(-\rho[Max(b(\omega_2)x + c(\omega_2)x^2, y^*)p_y - p_x x - \psi^*(\theta, x, y^*)]) \tag{10.A9}$$

which yields an optimal amount of 59.2620 pounds of nitrogen applied for a risk-aversion coefficient of 0.0025, and 59.0216 pounds for a risk-aversion coefficient of 0.0050 (such that the insured yield is 125 bushels). Hence, when farmers are risk averse, the introduction of even actuarially sound insurance policies will increase the amount of nitrogen applied for any set of prices and will shift the supply curve to the right.

As a final modification, we consider the effect of insurance subsidies on the production decision. As discussed in the text, the current US crop insurance program includes a percentage subsidy on crop insurance. For example, in Table 10.1, the government pays 64 per cent of the cost of crop insurance for a coverage of 60 per cent. We introduce a subsidy share of S into the utility maximization problem developed in Equation 10.A9, yielding

$$\max_{x} -\theta \, exp(-\rho[Max(b(\omega_1)x + c(\omega_1)x^2, y^*)p_y - p_x x - (1-S)\psi^*(\theta, \tilde{x}, y^*)])$$
$$-(1-\theta)exp(-\rho[Max(b(\omega_2)x + c(\omega_2)x^2, y^*)p_y - p_x x - (1-S)\psi^*(\theta, \tilde{x}, y^*)]) \qquad (10.A10)$$

where $\tilde{x}$ is the input level without subsidy. Fixing the optimal insurance policy where $\tilde{x} =$ 59.2620 (e.g., the solution of Equation 10.A9) and setting the subsidy at 0.25, the optimal level of nitrogen is 64.3137. To further explore the implications of subsidizing insurance, consider the results for the solutions for Equations 10.A9 and 10.A10 presented in Table 10.A1 (unsubsidized versus subsidized). Following the implications of the stochastic production function in Equation 10.A1, using more nitrogen results in a "spreading" of the output. The yield in the low-rainfall state declines from 124.316 to 121.690, while the yield in the high-rainfall state increases from 143.577 to 144.834. Under our specific set of assumptions, the average yield falls slightly with subsidized insurance. The story for profits is somewhat different. Specifically, the profit in the low-rainfall state falls slightly (with the difference being made up by an increase in the payoff from insurance), while profit in the high-rainfall state increases by US$3.89/acre.

Given the mathematical results presented in Table 10.A1, the question becomes: what is the net economic benefit of subsidizing crop insurance? There are several ways to formulate this question. First, Table 10.A1 includes the certainty equivalent (e.g., the certain amount that the producer would be willing to take in place of the risky opportunity). The certainty equivalent with the subsidy is US$1.684/acre higher than the certainty equivalent without the subsidy. Given the cost of the subsidy as US$0.299/acre, the net gain appears to be US$1.385/acre. However, this computation may not tell the whole story. Specifically, subsidizing the insurance premium results in different corn yields. Given the ex ante nature of welfare economics, we focus on the effect of subsidizing crop insurance on the expected yield (or average yield). For our current formulation, subsidizing the insurance premium actually produces a small decrease in expected yield; however, alternative specifications of the stochastic production function may actually lead to increases in the expected yield. Under these scenarios, the supply of the crop will shift to the right with a subsidy in crop insurance. Further, several authors, such as Yu and

Table 10.A1. Effect of subsidizing insurance (unsubsidized versus subsidized)

Effect on Yields			
Low Rainfall	High Rainfall	Average	Variance
124.316	143.577	133.946	9.630
121.690	144.834	133.262	11.572

Effect on Profits				
Low Rainfall	High Rainfall	Average	Variance	Certainty Equivalent
428.895	493.914	461.405	32.5092	460.085
428.384	497.803	463.094	34.7099	461.769

Sumner (2018), note that insurance subsidies may cause shifts in cropping decisions. For example, if crop insurance for corn is subsidized but there is no crop insurance for hay, the insurance will cause producers to increase the amount of corn planted and reduce the planting of hay.

APPENDIX 10B: CONVERGENCE OF INSURANCE AND GENERAL AGRICULTURAL POLICY

The idea that support mechanisms in the 2018 Farm Bill are parallel to crop insurance is most evident in the agricultural risk coverage (ARC) alternative in the current farm bill (section 7.4). Following the logic of ARC, the farmer receives a payment when the gross revenue for a crop falls below 86 per cent of a benchmark revenue. The terms of this program exactly follow the construction of a revenue insurance program

$$\pi^R(R^*) = \int_{\underline{P}}^{\bar{P}} \int_0^{y_M} \text{Max } R^* - py, 0] \, f(p,y) dp dy \tag{10.B1}$$

where R^* is the insured level of revenue, $\underline{P}$ is the lowest possible price (i.e., zero), $\bar{P}$ is the highest possible price (p), y_m is the maximum yield (y), and $f(p,y)$ is the joint probability density function for prices and yields. Equation 10.B1 defines the actuarially fair price for a fairly general insurance policy. Modifying the policy slightly, the payoff under ARC becomes

$$\pi^{ARC}(R) = \int_{\underline{P}}^{\bar{P}} \int_0^{y_M} \text{Min}\left[\text{Max}[0.86\,R - py, 0], 0.10\,R\right] f(p,y)\, dp dy \tag{10.B2}$$

However, we must note that the insurance provided in Equation 10.B2 is free under the 2018 Farm Bill. In this legislation, the farmer has a choice between receiving ARC payments or participating in the more traditional price loss coverage (PLC) program that provides a payment when the market price is lower than the reference price.

This shift from "traditional" price-based agricultural programs towards insurance or risk-based programs is mirrored in the shift of dairy programs from two-price policies reinforced by government purchases of fluid milk for the production of government cheese and butter to the Margin Protection Program for Dairy, which is also a form of revenue insurance.

The big question is then whether this shift from price-based instruments to revenue-based instruments is a dramatic change in direction or a slight shift in course. To analyse this question, it is important to realize that many of our traditional price-based programs can be reformulated as insurance-based contracts. To demonstrate this, we start with the most traditional program: the loan rate. As a starting point for this discussion, consider the "payoff" under the loan rate program depicted in Figure 10B.1 where the loan rate for corn is set at US\$2.20/bu under the 2018 Farm Bill. Next, we assume that the market price falls to US\$2.00/bu. Under

Figure 10.B1. Loan rate as a put option

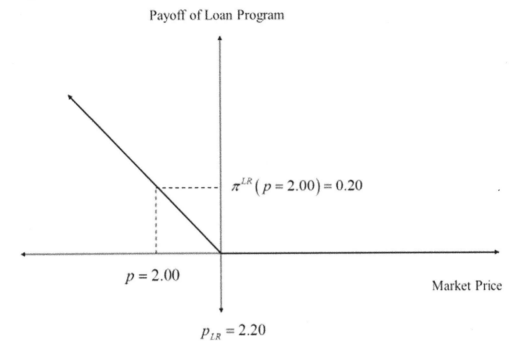

Payoff of Loan Program

$\pi^{LR}(p = 2.00) = 0.20$

$p = 2.00$

Market Price

$p_{LR} = 2.20$

this scenario, the farmer received US$2.20 by placing the crop under loan. Another way to look at the problem is that the agricultural policy paid the farmer US$0.20/bu. The advantage of the latter approach is that the historical agricultural policy can be reformulated as a put option. Further, there is an implicit parallel between options and insurance.

Moving from the payoff formulation in Figure 10.B1 into a market framework in Figure 10.B2, we assume that the expected demand for corn is $D^*(p)$ and that the supply of corn is $S(p)$. The market equilibrium then follows the option formulation in Figure 10.B1: the market price is US$2.00/bu, but under the loan rate policy the farmer receives US$2.20/bu. Implicitly, the "option" paid US$0.20/bu. The "expansion" of the formulation, as in our discussion of ARC, is the fact that the demand curve is stochastic – it has some degree of randomness. In Figure 10.B2, this randomness is depicted by the lower bound of the demand for corn and the upper bound for the demand of corn $\left[\underline{D}(p)\right]$. Under this scenario, the loan rate program is a function of the randomness of the demand curve $\left[\bar{D}(p)\right]$.

To develop the value of the loan rate policy under this scenario, consider all the possible loan rate payouts for q_{LR}. The interaction between the randomness in the corn market and value of the loan rate program is depicted in Figure 10.B3. Panel (a) of Figure 10.B3 depicts the possible market prices that could result from the farmer's decision to supply q_{LR}. As depicted in

Figure 10.B2. Loan rate and stochastic demand

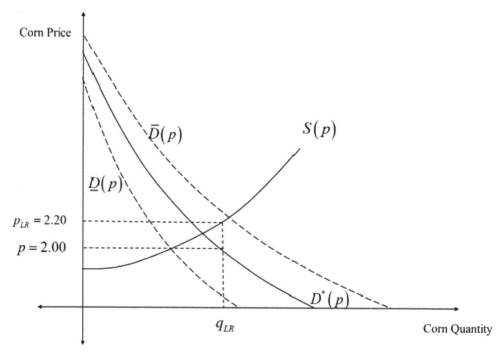

this panel, the price of corn could range from a low of $\underline{P}$, set as US$1.35/bu in panel (b), to a high of $\bar{P}$ per bushel, US$2.30 in panel (b). Panel (b) of Figure 10.B3 then presents the probability of each outcome and the payoff of the loan rate program given a loan rate of US$2.20/bu.

$$\pi^{LR}(p_{LR} = 2.20) = \int_{\underline{P}}^{\bar{P}} Max\,[p_{LR} - p, 0]f(p)dp = 0.2541 \qquad (10.B3)$$

or US$0.25/bu for every bushel marketed under the loan program. Considering the randomness of demand, the value of the loan rate program is higher than the simple formulation in Figure 10.B1 because of the probability that market prices could be much lower than US$2.00/bu. This linkage between the loan program and insurance is actually strengthened by the loan deficiency payment where the payment is actually made without going through the loan mechanism.

Based on the above discussion, the loan rate program can be viewed as a free price insurance program. Similar derivations would show that the PLC program is another form of free price insurance provided through the commodity program. These results raise questions about whether any significant differences exist between traditional commodity programs and multi-peril crop insurance in any form (e.g., yield protection or revenue protection). The fact

Figure 10.B3. Valuing the loan rate program

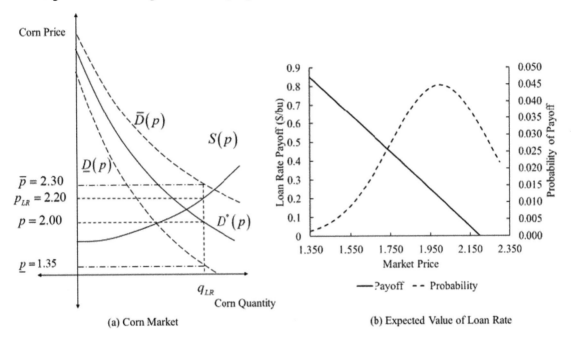

(a) Corn Market

(b) Expected Value of Loan Rate

that traditional commodity programs have been free is only a matter of scale, because crop insurance programs in the United States have tended to be highly subsidized. In addition, the formulation of traditional commodity programs to insurance products yields a meaningful comparison between the two approaches to agricultural programs.

CHAPTER ELEVEN

Agricultural Productivity and R&D Policy

11.1 INVESTING IN AGRICULTURAL RESEARCH

In this chapter we highlight the importance of R&D in the growth and development of the agricultural economy. We explore how agricultural productivity has changed over time and we discuss the role of science and agricultural policy in the achievement of productivity growth. We scrutinize the institutional and regulatory frameworks for R&D and observe how the creation and adoption of new technology is affected by R&D. Finally, we analyse the costs and benefits of investments in R&D under various market conditions and regulations.

One of the major sources of economic growth in the agricultural sector is R&D (Schultz 1953). Since there is a limited amount of land that can be brought into agricultural production, increasing the food supply will depend more on new and improved technology. Economic growth results from a shift in the production function (which maps inputs into output space) or the production possibility frontier (which shows the maximum product output attainable from given inputs). The inputs used in production either produce more output with the same level of inputs or the same output with less input. In either case, productivity increases.

Growth in agricultural productivity is important for a number of reasons. First, some countries export much of their agricultural produce, and the prices received for most of these commodities are set in the world marketplace. Less productive farmers may be forced out of the market and experience a loss of income (assuming no subsidies are given for exports or domestic production). Second, food is a considerable expense for many households and consumers are sensitive to the price they pay for food. Agricultural research is an important factor in lowering the cost of food and increasing the quality and choice of food to consumers. Third, in those countries in which agriculture makes up a large portion of the gross national product (GNP), growth in agriculture frees up resources such as labour for other sectors of the economy.

11.2   MEASURING PRODUCTIVITY AND PRODUCTIVITY GROWTH

Productivity is the ratio of output produced to input used within the production process. Change in productivity is that part of growth in output that cannot be explained by the increased use of inputs, and for this reason Abramovitz (1956) calls productivity growth *residual output growth*. The measure of residual output growth is obtained by subtracting the weighted increase in the quantity of inputs from the observed increase in output. The residual output growth may be attributed to various factors, including technological change, economies of scale, efficiency improvements, and increases in capital stock. Econometric analysis is used to estimate technological change, which is the most commonly cited source of productivity growth.

Ruttan (1997) lists three theories that can be used to explain growth in agricultural productivity: (1) induced technological change, (2) evolutionary theory, and (3) path dependence. The literature on induced technological change explains growth through demand-pull models (Griliches 1957), stability in factor shares, and a microeconomic model of changing relative factor prices. The evolutionary model is based on the work of R.R. Nelson and Winters (1982), who suggested that when innovators adopt new technologies, they use a satisfying objective function rather than a profit-maximizing objective function (i.e., innovators do not try to get the most profit possible from the innovation). The path dependence model assumes that firms innovate along a given trajectory and, once they are locked into one technology, they will not easily change to a completely different technology (de Janvry 1973).

INVESTING IN RESEARCH AND DEVELOPMENT (R&D)

The policy followed by most developed countries to achieve economic growth in agriculture is to invest in R&D. Canada, the United States, and the European Union have budgets (i.e., taxpayer funds) to invest in research. Investment in agricultural research (both private and public) is the major policy tool that governments and private firms use to explore ideas or develop new agricultural products to solve problems that do not always benefit everyone (P.M. Romer 1993).

11.3   RESEARCH EXPENDITURES IN AGRICULTURE

Prior to 1990, agricultural research in the United States, Canada, and the European Union was largely accomplished through public sector expenditures. Since 1990, some government expenditures are declining. (Whether or not the government is investing adequately in agricultural research depends on the rate of return to research investment, which is discussed later.)

The trend in agricultural research expenditures and the growth in agricultural productivity are correlated. Most economic analyses conclude that the rate of return on this expenditure is considerable and is well above the market rate of return. But even with a high rate of return on agricultural research, given the competing needs for public resources, it is difficult to convince policymakers that research investment in agriculture is a beneficial public expenditure, especially for farm subsidies when there is no shortage of food. Some argue that there is a greater need for health-related research than for agriculture-related research. Perhaps this explains why, in the United States, the National Institutes of Health (NIH) receives more budget funds for health research than the US Department of Agriculture (USDA) receives for agricultural research.

11.3.1   Private Sector Research

Unlike the growth in public expenditures on R&D, the growth in private sector research, especially in the United States, has increased dramatically. Private expenditures now exceed public expenditures (Alston, Pardy, and Smith 1999). This pattern is consistent with the increase in biotechnology research and the development of patent protection. (In the biotechnology field, most research investment worldwide is completed by large multinational corporations, such as Monsanto.)

11.3.2   Check-Off Research

Farm organizations invest in research through check-off programs placed on various commodities – these are public-private-producer partnerships (Alston and Gray 2013). By deducting an amount of money from each commodity sold to fund R&D, check-off programs enable producers to maximize profits and minimize risk. Most grain produced in the United States and Canada has a small research check-off that is invested through the commodity organization. For example, in Canada, through check-off money the Western Grains Research Fund supports research for the enhancement of wheat and barley yields.

INTERNATIONAL R&D
International donors, such as the United States and the European Union, fund the Consultative Group on International Agricultural Research (CGIAR) system. Given that hunger is still a real concern in the world, why is support for CGIAR-type agricultural research declining? First, it may be that international donors have lost interest in never-ending support of research in developing countries. Second, cutbacks on government expenditures reduce support to international development. Third, developed countries prefer exporting their agricultural products, rather than funding

the agricultural production in developing countries. Fourth, with declining trade barriers for agricultural commodities, developing countries are viewed as competition to developed countries. This change in R&D funding represents a major shift in policy on the part of donor countries. The policy shift is consistent with the notion of rent-seeking behaviour on the part of agriculture in developed countries. Increased crop yields reduce the export opportunities for international donor countries.

11.3.3 Joint Public-Private Research

There are increasing numbers of joint public-private ventures in agricultural research. In such cases, the private sector invests money alongside the public sector to create public-private partnerships (PPPs) for research innovations in agriculture. In one case study, Ulrich, Furtan, and Schmitz (1986) confirm that for malt barley breeding in Canada, universities and maltsters, who invested jointly in breeding new malt barley varieties, received a high rate of return from their investments.

11.4 EVALUATION OF RESEARCH EXPENDITURES

Economic research shows that the rates of return to public expenditures on agricultural research are high. Griliches (1957) estimated the return on investment in hybrid corn research to be in the range of 700 per cent. This was followed by studies duplicating his approach that had similar results. These results are summarized by Ruttan (1982) and by Alston, Norton, and Pardy (1995). In view of the high rates of return to research, the question still remains as to why public expenditures for agricultural research have declined. Some argue that even though the rates of return to agricultural research are high in absolute value, they may be low relative to what could be obtained if public funds were invested in other areas.

11.4.1 A Basic Model for Evaluating Research Expenditures

Consider the case in which we have only public investment in research that results in a new technology available to the public. Assume, for example, that the public invests in research. After a period of time, a new technology is made available to farmers that shifts the supply curve to the right from S_0 to S_1 (Figure 11.1). There are two effects of this investment: (1) an increase in consumer surplus (P_0P_1ba), and (2) a change in returns to the fixed factors of production, or producer surplus ($P_1cb - P_0da$).

Figure 11.1. Supply shift due to a change in technology

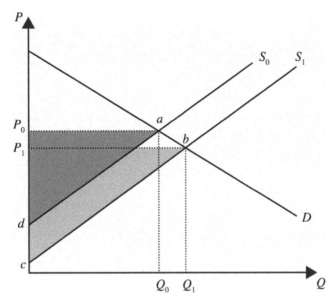

Most research in agriculture is an ongoing process and cannot be adequately described as a one-time investment. In such a case, the net present value (NPV) formula is used to estimate the rate of return on the investment

$$NPV = \sum_{i=1}^{A} \frac{(B_i - C_i)}{(1+r)^i},$$ (11.1)

where B_i is the return in period i, and C_i is the cost incurred in period i, given a total of A periods. Also, the technology developed may decay or depreciate over time, which implies that the benefits and costs need to include a depreciation allowance (Alston, Norton, and Pardy 1995). The internal rate of return on the investment can be calculated from the above NPV equation by solving for value of r that makes the NPV = 0. The value of r that makes the NPV = 0 for any given stream of net revenue is called the internal rate of return. It is this estimate of r that is compared with the market rate of return.

11.4.2   Returns to Joint Public-Private Agricultural Research

The focus of joint public-private research was highlighted in a study on malting barley in Canada (Ulrich, Furtan, and Schmitz 1986). To estimate the rate of return to joint public-private investment in research, it is necessary to distinguish between private and social rates of return that stem from different types of investment (including public, private, and joint investment). Ulrich, Furtan, and Schmitz define the average social rate of return (public sector plus private benefits) from such an investment as

$$r_s = \frac{\sum_{i=0}^{n} \Delta C_i + \sum_{i=1}^{n} \Delta \pi_i}{Is + \sum_{i=0}^{n} Ip_i},$$
(11.2)

where ΔC_i = change in consumer surplus in industry i, the industry in which the R&D investment occurs; $\Delta \pi_i$ = change in producer surplus or quasi-rents in industry i; Is = amount of public investment; Ip_i = amount of investment from industry; and n = number of industries experiencing a change in quasi-rents or producer surplus as a result of R&D.

Similarly, the private rate of return to the ith industry r_{ppi} can be defined as

$$r = \frac{\Delta \pi_i}{Ip_i},$$
(11.3)

and the private rate of return on public investment r_{psi} is

$$r = \frac{\Delta \pi_i}{Is}.$$
(11.4)

There are three cases in which the rates of return to agricultural research can be calculated:

$Ip_i = 0$, $Is > 0$ for pure public investment.

$Is = 0$, $Ip_i > 0$ for some I, or pure private investment.

$Is = 0$, $Ip_i > 0$, n > 1 for joint private-public investment.
(11.5)

Research is conducted jointly among governments, universities, and private industry. Agriculture and Agri-Food Canada used the Matching Investment Initiative (MII) in the 1990s to encourage joint research between the public and private sectors. In some projects the investments and benefits are not equally distributed. Ulrich, Furtan, and Schmitz (1986) estimate returns from jointly funded agricultural research and find that only a small amount of private investment is needed to induce large public expenditures. Thus, through joint public-private research ventures, private firms are able to capture the benefits from the public investment. Malla and Gray (1999) argue that the rate of return to agricultural research will be overestimated if private expenditures are not adequately taken into account. When these market conditions are integrated, the conclusion that research expenditures result in high rates of return does not always hold.

11.5   ESTIMATED RETURNS TO AGRICULTURAL RESEARCH

The returns to agricultural research have been estimated for many countries and many commodities. They have been found to be well above the market rate (Ruttan 1982). The estimates of the rate of return are within the 21 to 96 per cent range, as reported in Table 11.1.

Table 11.1. Selected economic returns to agricultural research

Commodity	Study	Rate of Return (%)	Country
Aggregate agriculture	Evenson, Waggoner, and Ruttan (1979)	65	United States
Barley	Ulrich, Furtan, and Schmitz (1986)	31–75[a]	Canada
Beef	Widmer, Fox, and Brinkman (1987)	61.5	Canada
Canola	Ulrich, Furtan, and Downey (1984)	51	Canada
Hybrid corn	Griliches (1957)	35–40	United States
Poultry	Peterson (1967)	21–5	United States
Rice	Scobie and Posada (1978)	79–96	Colombia
Tomatoes	A. Schmitz and Seckler (1970)	≥50	United States
Wheat	Zentner and Peterson (1984)	38	Canada

Source: Studies shown above.
[a] $r_s = 31$, $r_p = 75$; r_s = social rate of return; r_p = private rate of return.

11.6 EFFECTS OF GOVERNMENT SUBSIDIES AND TRADE ON R&D

The above economic models used to estimate the rates of return to agricultural research have ignored trade and market distortions caused by government subsidies. What are the effects of international trade and government subsidies on the estimates of returns to agricultural research? Many of the international markets for agricultural products are subsidized, so it is important to incorporate these effects in the measure of returns (Edwards and Freebairn 1984; Murphy, Furtan, and Schmitz 1993).

The domestic supply and demand schedules are S_0 and D, respectively, in Figure 11.2a. The corresponding excess supply schedule is ES_0, in Figure 11.2b, while the excess demand curve facing the country is ED. The free trade price is P_t and exports are Q_t^e. In the domestic market, the production level is Q_s^e and domestic consumption is Q_d. Because of technological change the domestic supply curve shifts from S_0 to S_1, and domestic production increases to Q_s. The corresponding excess supply in Figure 11.2b will shift from ES_0 to ES_1, and the resulting world price and quantity traded will be P_t' and Q_t'.

Domestic consumers gain $\left(P_f P_f' ca\right)$, while producers gain $\left(m_0 m_1 ed - P_f P_f' db\right)$ from the new technology (Figure 11.2a). Producers and consumers both benefit from the new technology. In other countries, there is a net gain equal to $\left(P_t P_t' hg\right)$ (Figure 11.2b).

If the government subsidizes exports, then the cost of the subsidy must be accounted for when determining the gross annual research benefit from the cost-reducing agricultural research. In 1999 most developed countries used some form of agricultural subsidy for exported commodities. A. Schmitz, Sigurdson, and Doering (1986) demonstrate that the cost of the domestic subsidy may be larger than the additional benefits gained from the adoption of cost-reducing research. Murphy, Furtan, and Schmitz (1993) develop a mathematical model to compare the benefits from research with and without farm subsidies

Figure 11.2. Research returns under trade for the large-country case

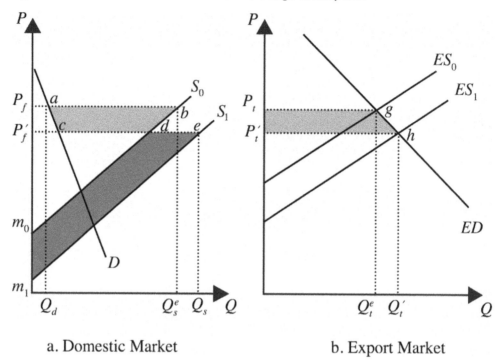

a. Domestic Market   b. Export Market

(Appendix 11A). They reach the strong conclusion that, when farm subsidies are taken into account, the rates of return to society can be negative. Chambers and Lopez (1993) reach a similar conclusion.

One assumption made in the above analysis is that the technology adopted in the domestic market is not adopted by other exporters (Edwards and Freebairn 1984). If technology is adopted and this factor is not taken into account, the rate of return to research in the home country is overestimated. This is shown in Figure 11.3, where the total excess supply is initially the horizontal sum of the excess supply curves from country A and country B ($ES_T^0 = ES_A^0 + ES_B^0$). Given the excess demand ED, the equilibrium price is P_w. Suppose that the new technology is only adopted in country A, which shifts country A's supply curve in a parallel fashion from ES_A^0 to ES_A'. The new excess supply curve will be ES_T' and the new equilibrium price will be P_w'. Finally, suppose the new technology developed in country A is fully adopted in country B. The new total excess supply curve will be ES_T''. In this case, the price falls to P_w''. The benefits to producers in country A depend on the elasticities of demand and supply in each country and on the market share of each country.

Figure 11.3. Returns to research with multiple exporters

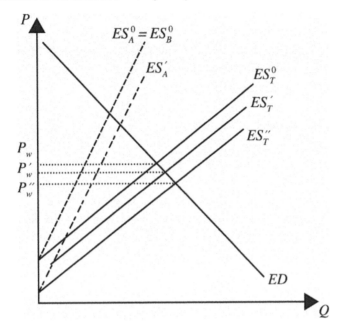

11.7   AGRICULTURAL RESEARCH: WHO BENEFITS?

Beneficiaries of R&D include consumers, processors, and owners of the fixed factors of production. One justification for public R&D is to help raise the income of family farmers. In the past, agricultural productivity has increased because of R&D, but farm incomes have not increased accordingly.

Consumers and producers can both benefit from agricultural research, but the distribution of benefits depends on the relative demand and supply elasticities and on the type of innovation. Consumers benefit from lower commodity prices. Producers benefit when there is an increase in producer surplus (producers do not always benefit; in fact, there are many cases in which producers become worse off). Many suggest that R&D was one of the causes of low farm incomes and record low farm commodity prices in 2000.

Landowners can also benefit from technological change. Output and the demand for land increase as agricultural profits increase from production cost reductions. If land is the most limiting resource, the price of land will increase until all the profits gained from technological change have been dissipated (W.W. Cochrane 1958). For example, Moss (2006) estimates the relationships between the stock of agricultural R&D expenditures that capture agricultural productivity, the return to agricultural assets, and the value of agricultural assets. He finds a positive relationship between the research stock and total factor productivity (TFP). The benefits from increased productivity accrue to the consumer through lower food prices and/or to processors and wholesalers. It is questionable whether the increased TFP leads to higher agricultural farm incomes. Later in this chapter, we discuss investments in mechanization, which have also yielded positive rates of return.

11.7.1   R&D and Processor Benefit

Often-neglected beneficiaries of R&D are the processors and marketers beyond the farm gate. In Figure 11.4 the demand curve facing the farmer is D and the farm level supply curve is S_0. If the margin required by the processors is $(P_0 - P_1)$, the processor gross margin will be (P_0P_1ab) and quantity Q_0^e will be produced on the farm. If the farm supply curve shifts to S_1 due to technological change and processors require the same per unit margin, the farm price will fall to P_3. In this case, the processor profit will increase by $(P_2P_3cd - P_0P_1ab)$ and the net gain (loss) to farmers is $(P_3m_1c - P_1m_0a)$.

Major inroads have been made into making processing more efficient. This has an impact on both processors and producers. The added efficiency can easily be incorporated into the above framework. The farm supply curve S_0 need not change due to these added efficiencies, but the per unit cost of processing will drop.

11.7.2   Market Structure

The price farmers pay for new technology is a function of market structure. How does a monopoly supplier of a new agricultural technology, such as new crop varieties, affect farmers? Suppose the demand curve for seed D_S in the input market (Figure 11.5) is based on the cost of fertilizer and chemicals needed in conjunction with the seed to produce a crop. If the supply of seed is perfectly elastic at P_0, then the farmer will demand quantity X_0 of the input. If the supply curves of all the inputs (except for land used by the farmer) are perfectly elastic, the output supply curve will be S_0 in the output market (Figure 11.5b). In this case, the demand curve for the output is assumed to be perfectly elastic. The resulting producer surplus from using these inputs is (P_wnb).

If a new seed that reduces the amount of herbicide used becomes available at the same cost P_0, the demand for the seed will shift outward from D_S to D_S' (Figure 11.5a). The farmer plants more acreage of that crop, and the output supply curve shifts from S_0 to S_1 (Figure 11.5b). The resulting producer surplus will increase by $(nycb)$.

In the place of the competitive seed industry, suppose that the government grants monopoly rights for new seed varieties. The seed company then charges producers P_2 for the seed instead of P_0. This will result in a monopoly rent of (P_2P_0ba) that goes to the seed company and shifts the supply curve in the output market from S_0 to S_2. Producer welfare will be reduced by $(myca)$.

Figure 11.4. Agricultural R&D and its impact on processors

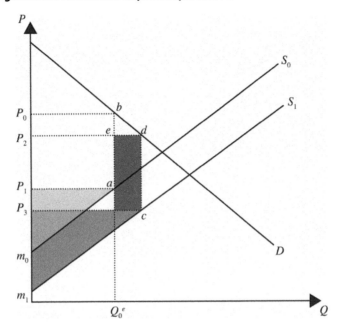

11.7.3   R&D and Demand Characteristics

Most of the studies on R&D focus on cost savings to producers while ignoring the effect on consumer demand and product quality. If product quality is improved due to R&D, one will underestimate the rate of return to research. Consider Figure 11.6 where S and D exist prior to R&D. Suppose that R&D shifts the supply schedule from S to S'' and shifts the demand schedule from D to D'. In this case, the total gain to R&D will be ($abcdef$). If demand is ignored, the net gain from R&D will become $[(P_2bg) - (P_1af)]$ and will be underestimated by $[(abcdef) - (P_2bg - P_1af)]$.

11.7.4   Economics of Yield Maintenance

In many of the studies discussed earlier, there is little attention paid to the role of R&D in yield maintenance. Many commodities would show a decline in yield over time had it not been for an investment in new crop varieties. This is clearly demonstrated with reference to productivity changes in Florida sugar cane production. A. Schmitz and Zhu (2017) show impressive sugar cane yields over time due to R&D, which take into account the R&D that was needed for yield maintenance. A. Schmitz and Zhang (2019) highlight the changes in the adoption of new sugar cane varieties over time. There have been numerous new sugar varieties used in sugar cane production.

Figure 11.5. Effects of R&D on input markets

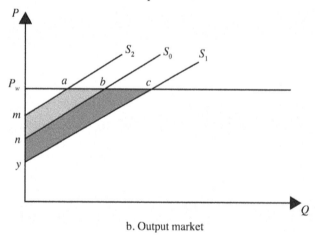

a. Input market

b. Output market

FLORIDA SUGAR CANE YIELDS, R&D, AND YIELD MAINTENANCE

A. Schmitz and Zhu (2017) show that there have been impressive yield increases in sugar cane production in Florida. Impressive rates of return due to new varietal development exist even though part of the R&D is needed to maintain stable yields. Generally, there can be a high rate of return to R&D investment in new crop varieties even though yields may not show a positive increase. The payoff to investing in new crop varieties may be understated if the payoff to crop maintenance is not taken into account.

Figure 11.6. Agricultural R&D and product quality

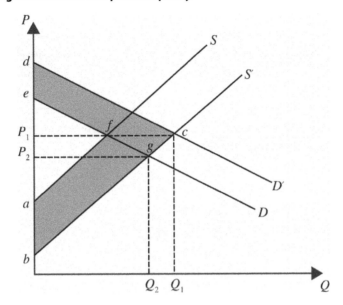

11.7.5   New Crop Varieties and Mechanization

Even though there is a tendency to attribute yield increases to new crop varietal development, the importance of mechanization cannot be ignored. A. Schmitz and Zhang (2019) show impressive rates of return to plant breeding efforts for Florida sugar cane. However, in addition, at least 30 per cent of the yield increases are due to mechanization. As late as the mid-1980s, sugar cane in Florida was hand harvested, and harvesting was totally mechanized by 1993.

> **THE IMPORTANCE OF MECHANIZATION AND CROP YIELDS**
> A. Schmitz and Zhang (2019), along with Edmé et al. (2005), suggest that improvements in mechanization contribute to about 35 per cent of the yield increases in sugar cane. Mechanical harvesters equipped with vertical pickup augers are capable of harvesting flat sugar cane stalks (A. Schmitz and Moss 2015).

11.7.6   Labour Displacement and Mechanization

There are relatively few studies that focus on the impact of mechanization on farm labour displacement. A. Schmitz and Seckler (1970) demonstrated that there was a significant displacement of farm labour due to the mechanical tomato harvester. This type of rate of return research study has not been carried out for the mechanization of sugar cane or cotton, for example. The majority of sugar cane was hand harvested in Florida until the mid-1980s. For cotton, mechanization that began in the 1950s displaced thousands of farm workers. (Mechanization not only displaced farm workers but was a factor in the increase in farm size.) An interesting point with mechanization is the extent to which farm workers were compensated when they were displaced as a result of mechanized harvesting. In this regard, it is interesting to point out that in the buyout of the US and Canadian tobacco programs, little mention was made of the extent to which the farm workers involved were compensated even though farmers and landowners received compensation.

HAND HARVESTING FLORIDA SUGAR CANE

In *Sugar* (1953), the hand harvesting of sugar cane was discussed: "Cutting crews move into the fields about November 1 and continue harvesting until the middle of April. Each man cuts two rows of cane, two cutters combining their efforts into a single row of cut stalks between them" (Anonymous 1953). Although in the United States, sugar cane is now mechanically harvested, this is not the case in many major sugar-producing areas in the world, such as Brazil, India, and Indonesia.

11.7.7   Greenhouse Technology

To highlight the importance of mechanization, greenhouse technology (GHT) now has a prominent place in agricultural production and international trade, especially in fruits and vegetables. Consider, for example, tomatoes. The emergence of GHT has changed the pattern of trade in tomatoes significantly. Mexico and Canada have adopted GHT, but few Florida producers have done so. In 2018, GHT tomato shipments from Mexico totalled roughly 2000 million pounds (F. Zhang 2019).

GREENHOUSE TECHNOLOGY

Some countries encourage the adoption of greenhouse technologies (GHT) through the use of subsidies. Consider Mexico, which has made significant inroads into GHT. The US tomato industry has been in a decline since 2000. It accounts for only 40 per cent of the total domestic demand for fresh-market tomatoes; the rest of the demand is met by imports from other countries. This downward trend is expected to continue as the result of increases in foreign competition and domestic land values.

Figure 11.7. Florida tomato production and imports from Mexico, 2000–15

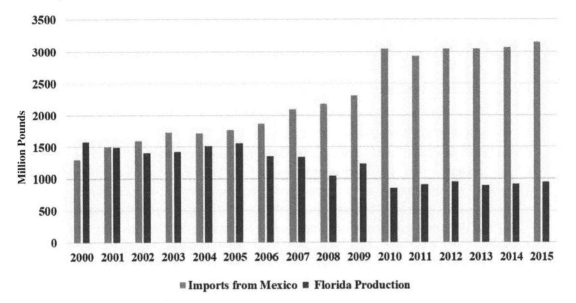

Source: Guan, Biswas, and Wu (2017); data taken from USDOC.

The US tomato industry might consider changing its production strategy to increase its market share in the global market. Mexico, a major competitor in the fresh-market tomato industry heavily subsidizes protected production practices such as greenhouse technology. The Ministry of Agriculture in Mexico (SAGARPA) provides millions of dollars annually to subsidize greenhouse tomato production, which allows Mexican producers to supply fresh-market tomatoes year-round. Overall, Mexico and Canada supply 98 per cent of the imported greenhouse tomatoes to the United States.

Unlike these countries, the United States depends on traditional field technology, which is more seasonal, with California supplying fresh tomatoes in the summer and Florida in the winter. As an example of foreign competition, Figure 11.7 illustrates the widening disparity between tomato production in Mexico and Florida between 2000 and 2015 using data from the United States Department of Commerce (USDOC).

11.7.8 CRISPR Technology

Within the chromosomes of every cell of a living organism is the DNA molecule that contains a long string of chemical letters. This genome contains millions of letters (e.g., about two billion for a corn plant). Conventional breeding requires trial and error to identify regularly spaced repeats of DNA sequences, but this is no longer the case with clustered regularly interspaced short palindromic repeats (CRISPR) technology (also see Chapter 18).

> **THE CRISPR REVOLUTION**
> "Genome editing advances plant and animal breeding, promising to change the agricultural landscape in the 21st Century" (Houghton 2018, 10).

11.7.9   R&D: Developed and Less-Developed Countries

> **PIONEER HI-BRED OPENS RESEARCH CENTRES**
> Pioneer Hi-bred, a DuPont business, opened two new seed research centres in Hungary and Italy. The new research centres are part of a large increase in R&D across Europe. The Hungarian research centre is analysing corn germ plasms for corn rootworm resistance, ear mould tolerance, drought stress tolerance, and end-use characteristics. The Italian research centre is developing and testing corn hybrids with high yield potential combined with native European corn borer tolerance and is developing products to combat stalk and root lodging and ear moulds (Fatka 2008).

As the natural logarithm of income increases, the proportion of the consumer's income spent on food decreases (Working 1943). Using a slightly more complex form of Working's model derived by Moss and Seale (1993), the price elasticity of demand is a function of the natural logarithm of income

$$\varepsilon(w,\phi,\beta,Y) = \phi \frac{\left(w + \beta \ln[Y]\right)}{w}[1 - (w - \beta \ln[Y])], \tag{11.6}$$

where $\varepsilon(.)$ is the elasticity of demand for agricultural outputs, ϕ is the income flexibility, w is the consumer's average budget share for agricultural outputs, β is the estimated Working's coefficient, and $\ln[Y]$ is the natural logarithm of income.

Normalizing income by dividing by the US income and assuming $\beta = -0.134$, $w = 0.125$, and $\phi = -0.05$, we can compare the elasticity of demand for agriculture in the United States (i.e., $\ln[1] = 0$) with the elasticity of demand for a less-developed economy (i.e., $\ln[0.5] = -0.693$, so that the income level in the less-developed economy is one-half that in the US economy). The elasticity of demand in the United States is -0.0438, while the elasticity of demand for the less-developed economy is -0.0739. We assume that the aggregate investment in R&D will lead to a lower agricultural price as supply shifts to the right (computed given the elasticities above). Thus, these elasticities imply that the relative increase in consumption for the United States will be smaller than the increased demand will be in the less-developed countries. This can be seen in Figure 11.8 where D_d is demand by the United States (Figure 11.8a) and D_1 is demand by the less-developed countries (Figure 11.8b). To derive the initial demand for agricultural output for the United States, we multiply the budget share by the normalized income (1.0 x 0.3 = 0.3).

Figure 11.8. Distributional effect of technological change

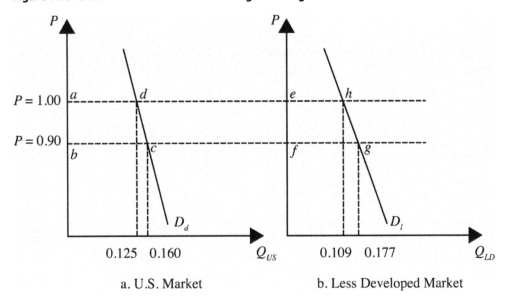

a. U.S. Market   b. Less Developed Market

The initial demand for the less-developed country can be derived as (0.5 x 0.218 = 0.109). As a starting point, we assume the initial price is US$1.00, which falls to US$0.90 with the investment in R&D. As the price falls from US$1.00 to US$0.90, the quantity demanded in the US market will increase to 0.160, while the quantity demanded in the less-developed country will also increase to 0.177. Thus, the increase in demand will be relatively larger in the low-income country. Further, (*abcd*) in Figure 11.8a is the increase in welfare in the United States, while (*efgh*) in Figure 11.8b is the increase in consumer surplus in the less-developed country. Numerically, the increase in surplus is larger for the less-developed country (US$0.0177) compared with the increase in welfare in the United States (US$0.0160). The gain in surplus as a percentage of each country's original expenditure is 0.059 for the less-developed country (i.e., 0.0177/0.30) and 0.016 for the United States (i.e., 0.0160/1.0). Hence, the welfare gain will be 3.68 times larger in relative terms for the less-developed country. This result gives added support to investment in R&D through CGIAR, which focuses on less-developed countries.

11.8   REGULATION AND AGRICULTURAL RESEARCH

The regulation of scientific research is a difficult and contentious policy issue facing governments in the twenty-first century. First, no department of government has sole jurisdiction over the management of science. There is no all-encompassing government policy with the mandate to balance the need for technological innovation with the need to protect producers and consumers. The claim has often been made that the regulation of science has blocked the adoption of new technology. One case frequently cited is the regulation of grain varieties, which comes under the Canada Grain Act. In Canada, all new wheat and barley varieties must be visually identifiable from other classes of wheat and barley before they can be licensed. For example, if a new wheat variety is to be licensed in the Canadian Western Red Spring (CWRS) bread-wheat class, then an individual must be able to see the difference between it and other wheat varieties of that class. In the case of barley, feed barley must be visually identifiable from varieties of malting barley. This visual identification requirement restricted the release of potentially higher-yielding varieties of feed barley in Canada (Thompson [Gibney] and Furtan 1983).

Ulrich, Furtan, and Schmitz (1986) examine the question of introducing high-yielding wheat varieties into western Canada, and they show that the return to changing the licensing regulation has been 50 to 80 per cent. Carter, Loyns, and Ahmadi-Esfahani (1986) report a similar result for other wheat varieties in Canada.

Food safety is a concern when considering new technology. One example is recombinant bovine somatotropin (rBST) in the dairy industry. This new technology has been adopted by US farmers, but has not yet been licensed for use in Canada or the European Union because of questions surrounding how rBST affects animal and human health. Why is rBST considered safe in the United States but not in Canada? In Canada, dairy producer groups have lobbied to restrict the use of rBST. They have not wanted a new technology that could potentially increase supplies of milk without making dairy farmers any better off. Dairy farmers have seen all the potential benefits of using rBST going to the input suppliers and to the consumers. The case of not licensing rBST for use in Canada seems to be more a result of rent-seeking behaviour by Canadian dairy farmers than one of concern for animal and human health.

The rBST example raises an important question for policymakers on the regulation of new agricultural technologies. As biotechnology is becoming more ubiquitous, how do governments balance the needs of consumers, producers, and the private business sector? If governments allow food regulations to be determined by special interest groups that oppose large biotechnology firms, it is unlikely the private sector will be interested in making large investments in agricultural technology.

11.9   RESEARCH INSTITUTIONS AND INTELLECTUAL PROPERTY RIGHTS

Property rights are central to the question of research expenditures and productivity growth. When a new technology is developed, it is important to know who has the property rights to the technology and how, or if, property rights are to be enforced. If a firm develops a new technology but cannot exclude others from using or selling the technology, the firm will have a limited incentive to make initial investments. In economics, we distinguish between technology that is embodied and technology that is disembodied. Embodied technology is incorporated into the product to be sold, (e.g., new metallurgy in tractor engines). Disembodied technology is not part of a particular good that is easily priced by the market (e.g., the optimal depth to plant seed). It is generally easier to exclude others from using embodied technology than it is to exclude others from using disembodied technology that is easier to share. For example, once a farmer knows the optimal depth to plant seeds, that information technology is easy to share with others.

A simple process to protect property rights is through hybridization. Plants in which hybrid

---

PROTECTING TECHNOLOGY RIGHTS

Many countries have laws to protect technology rights. These laws encourage private investment to generate new ideas. If a company develops a new technique or product, it can apply for a patent which, when granted, means other companies may use the new technology only if they pay the owner of the patent for its use. All patents are in force for a limited time, after which anyone may use the invention at no cost. If a country does not enforce patent laws, companies will not invest in the development of new technologies, and they may even refuse to sell their products. For some new agricultural products, like new crop varieties, it is almost impossible to protect them from being sold among farmers, and this discourages the development of new varieties (hybrids are the exception). For this reason, most of the initial plant breeding has been done by the public, with new varieties released free of charge to producers. However, with governments wanting to encourage private investment in agricultural R&D, governments have introduced legislation that provides patent protection for new agricultural technologies.

---

vigour can be developed are attractive to private investors because, by making the product excludable, companies can protect their property rights to the technology. To make the product excludable, companies simply have to keep the genetics of the parent plants or animals (i.e., the F1 generation) confidential. Corn was one of the first field crops to be adapted to this type of research, and today almost all corn research is done in the private sector. Over time, scientists have employed hybrid technology on other crops, such as vegetables and flowers. Hybrid technology is also being used when breeding animals and the result is the same: research investment is now made by the private sector.

The protection of intellectual property rights is a transaction cost that firms must pay when investing in agricultural research. Minimizing these costs depends on the cost of enforcement, type of technology developed, and the institutional structure of the country. Governments have introduced policies to minimize such expenses, like speeding up the patent process.

However, the price to protect intellectual property remains an entry barrier to the marketplace for many firms.

Another important issue surrounding property rights is the transfer of technology among countries. For example, two countries, such as Canada and the United States, have similar crop-growing regions, in this case Manitoba and North Dakota, so it is expected that the technology used in one country will be easy to adopt for the other. This is often the case. However, if the technology has been protected through patents in one country but not the other, then the lack of an appropriate institutional structure can block the technology transfer between the countries. This is why many new trade agreements, like the North American Free Trade Agreement (NAFTA), and trade organizations, like the World Trade Organization (WTO), are concerned about the protection of intellectual property rights.

One of the most promising areas of agricultural research is biotechnology. This research deals almost exclusively with life forms (plant and animal) and is very powerful in the type of changes it can introduce. New technologies include improved drugs and crop varieties, and modifications to animal genetics. There are at least two parts to biotechnology that are worth protecting for a private company: (1) the technique used when making the transfer of genetic material, and (2) the material itself (McHughen 2000). Techniques that move genetic material from one organism to another are patentable. Genetic materials are also patentable. For example, the gene that makes crops resistant to herbicides, like Roundup, is a patented gene.

PROPERTY RIGHTS

The control of genetic material, which is the basis for the development of many new agricultural technologies, is particularly problematic. The material used for genetic manipulation is not invented but discovered by individuals. Other individuals, such as producers, have often made use of these genetic properties without specific knowledge of the science behind them, and they feel they should not have to pay for using these genetic properties in the future. Thus, there is the question of who really holds the property rights to genetic material that is being used by farmers.

11.10   SUMMARY AND CONCLUSIONS

- Increases in agricultural productivity result in part from investment in research and development (R&D), with investment in R&D yielding impressive rates of return.
- While farmers generally benefit from productivity gains, consumer gains often outweigh those gains.
- Public expenditures on agricultural R&D have been declining globally, but private R&D is increasing. This increases the potential rents that can be earned by input suppliers such as seed companies.

- R&D impacts the degree of mechanization and farm size. This results, in some cases, with the displacement of farm workers and gains to processors and handlers.
- Patents help to protect intellectual property rights, and they allow private firms to capture benefits from innovation.
- Many of the new technologies involve biotechnology, a powerful tool for scientific innovation. These technologies have public policy implications, such as concerns about how new technologies affect food safety, the environment, and the long-term sustainability of the resource base.
- While most of the literature has focused on R&D and its effect on crop yields, R&D has also generated significant returns from mechanization that replaces farm workers.
- The effects of R&D are increased in the presence of agricultural subsidies.
- Greenhouse production is among new technologies that influence the pattern of trade.

APPENDIX 11: GAINS FROM RESEARCH UNDER DISTORTED TRADE

In Appendix Figure 11.A1, the domestic supply and demand schedules are S^0 and D, respectively. The corresponding excess supply schedule is ES^0, while the excess demand curve facing the country is ED, giving a free trade price of P_f and exports of Q_x^f. The effect of an internal price supported at P_S by means of export refunds (subsidies) is to increase exports to Q_x^0 and cause the export price to fall to P_w^0.

The cost of the export refund is ($abcd$). Suppose supply shifts to S^1 because of R&D, causing the excess supply curve to shift to ES^1. In the domestic market, the increase in producer surplus ΔPS is ($m^0 m^1 ld$). Since exports increase to Q_x^1, the cost of export refunds rises to ($ahkl$). Thus, the increase in export refund payments ΔER is ($dcbhkl$). The conditions that give rise to zero gains from research can be assessed by setting $\Delta PS = \Delta ER$.

Let the intercept change for the domestic supply curve be represented by

$$P_s - m^1 = \delta(P_s - m^0), \delta > 1 \qquad (11.A1)$$

where m^0 and m^1 are the pre- and post-research intercepts, respectively. It also follows that, since S^1 and S^0 are parallel, ($Q^1 = \delta Q^0$) and the increase in supply is $(\delta - 1)Q^0$. Then

$$\Delta PS = \frac{1}{2}(\delta^2 - 1)Q^0(P_s - m^1). \qquad (11.A2)$$

The increase in export subsidies can be viewed in two parts. The first allows for the rise in quantity exported but holds the world price at its initial level P_w^0. The extra subsidy cost in that case in given by ($dcvl$). This is equal to

$$\Delta P_w Q_x^0 = \Delta Q P_w^0 f \qquad (11.A3)$$

Figure 11.A1. Gains from research under distorted trade

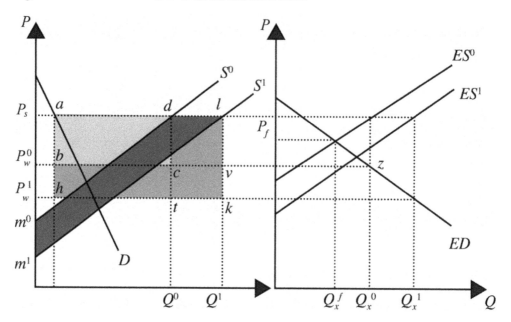

The second is represented by the (*bhkv*), which results from the drop in P_w. The latter can be written as

$$\Delta P_w = \frac{\Delta Q}{Q_x^0} P_w^0 f \tag{11.A4}$$

where Q_x^0 is the original quantity exported, P_w^0 is the original export price, and f is the world price flexibility coefficient measured at point z on the excess demand curve *ED*. Rearranging (11.A4) gives

$$\Delta P_w Q_x^0 = \Delta Q P_w^0 f \tag{11.A5}$$

If ΔP_w and f are treated as positive values, the left-hand side of Equation 11.A5 is equivalent to (*bhtc*). Expanding this by the proportion Q_x^1 / Q_x^0 gives the (*bhkv*)

$$dvkl = \Delta Q P_w^0 f Q_x^1 / Q_x^0 = (\delta - 1) Q^0 P_w^0 f \delta^1 \tag{11.A6}$$

where δ^1 is the proportionate increase in exports ($= Q_x^1/Q_x^0$) and δ is as defined above. Setting $\Delta PS = \Delta ER$ for zero gains in research gives (11.A2) = (11.A3) + (11.A6); that is,

$$\frac{1}{2}(\delta - 1)Q^0(P_s - m^0) = (\delta - 1)Q^0(P_s - P_w^0) + (\delta - 1)Q^0 P_w^0 f \delta^1 \tag{11.A7}$$

Noting that $[(\delta^2 - 1) = (\delta + 1)(\delta - 1)]$ and dividing through by $(\delta - 1)Q^0$ gives

$$\frac{1}{2}(\delta - 1)Q^0(P_s - m^0) = P_s - P_w^0(1 - f\delta^1) \qquad (11.A8)$$

Since $[\delta(P_s - m^0) = P_s - m^1]$ (see Equation 11.A1 above), the left-hand side is equivalent to $(P_s - M)$, where M is the average of m^0 and m^1. Thus the break-even point is where

$$M = P_w^0(1 - f\delta^1) \qquad (11.A9)$$

or

$$\frac{P_w^0}{M} = \frac{1}{1 - f\delta^1} \qquad (11.A10)$$

Positive returns to research will be obtained if

$$P_w^0(1 - f\delta^1) > M \qquad (11.A11)$$

This condition is likely to be met if P_w^0 is high relative to M and/or the export demand curve exhibits low price flexibility. On the other hand, the lower P_w^0, or the higher the f is, the greater the export subsidy bill, and negative returns will be reached if

$$P_w^0\left(1 - f\delta^1\right) < M \qquad (11.A12)$$

Since $f = 1/\delta_d$, where δ_d is the price elasticity of ED in absolute terms and evaluated at P_w^0, then Equation 11.A12 can also be written as

$$\varepsilon_d / \varepsilon_s = \delta^1. \qquad (11.A13)$$

If the ratio of the two elasticities exceeds δ^1, positive returns to research will be achieved.

CHAPTER TWELVE

Policy and Land Markets

12.1   FARM PAYMENTS AND LAND VALUES

Land is a major input in world agriculture. One of the largest agricultural producers is the United States where farmland used for agricultural purposes totals over one hundred million acres. Historically, farmland has accounted for roughly 70 per cent of all agricultural assets since the Second World War. Therefore, the well-being of the agricultural sector is heavily influenced by the value of farmland. The effect of agricultural policy must be considered when seeking to understand land prices. In countries such as Canada, the United States, and the European Union, agricultural policies provide a major source of farmer income. For example, in 1988 over 80 per cent of net farm income for North Dakota came from direct US government payments. Furthermore, in 2000 and 2001 direct US government payments accounted for over 50 per cent of net farm income. The 2002 US Farm Bill – the US Farm Security and Rural Investment Act (FSRI) – provided record subsidies to US farmers.

CAPITALIZATION OF FARM PAYMENTS
To what extent do farm payments get capitalized into land values? Tweeten (1986), a well-known policy analyst, argues that the main beneficiaries of farm programs are landowners. However, considerable controversy still exists on this topic. Interestingly, in farm states like Illinois, land values and cash rents both reached an all-time

high in 2001 in the presence of some of the lowest commodity prices in history. This illustrates that subsidies are ultimately transferred, at least in part, to farmland owners through various mechanisms. These mechanisms include adjustments in cash-rental rates and other farmer-tenant crop share agreements.

Apart from the impact of returns to farmland, including government payments, farmland markets in the United States are influenced increasingly by urbanization. There are many cases in which the price of farmland is a result of its potential sales value for housing and for real estate development. On these types of land, agriculture eventually disappears because the income from agriculture cannot support the high price of land, especially in parts of California and Florida, where land has extremely high values due to urban pressures.

Many studies have been conducted on the factors that influence farmland markets, although some models are only modestly successful at tracking land values. For example, A. Schmitz (1995a) finds that land values during boom-bust cycles are positively correlated with interest rates. However, more consistent with the model suggested by R.E. Just and Miranowski (1993) and models of earlier capitalization, we show in this chapter that land values over time bear a relationship to net farm income; both are influenced by farm policy. We do so by comparing land values among selected Canadian provinces and by comparing Canadian land values with those of the northern United States.

This chapter provides the theory of land markets along with an empirical counterpart. We discuss the impact of urban growth and trade on land values and show how comparative-advantage principles affect land markets. The boom-bust nature of land markets is discussed along with factors associated with the solvency of the US agricultural sector. We conclude the chapter with a discussion of the impact of politics on land values. Since the land value collapse of the mid-1980s, US land values have risen consistently over time. To prevent a decline in land values and to avoid another land market crash and its disastrous consequences, US farmers lobby governments through rent-seeking activities.

12.2   US LAND VALUES

US agricultural land values are given in Table 12.1. With the exception of a small drop during the financial crisis of 2008, and a 1.7 per cent drop from 2015 to 2017, the price of land has increased every year since 1997. On a longer timeline, land prices have more than tripled between 1997 and 2019.

Table 12.1. US agricultural land values, 1997–2019 (US$/acre)

Year	Land Value	Year	Land Value
1997	1270	2009	2640
1998	1340	2010	2700
1999	1400	2011	2980
2000	1460	2012	3350
2001	1510	2013	3810
2002	1590	2014	4090
2003	1660	2015	4100
2004	1750	2016	4040
2005	2060	2017	4030
2006	2300	2018	4050
2007	2530	2019	4100
2008	2760		

Source: USDA/NASS (2019).

There was an interesting period in US history (the financial crisis of the 1980s) where the agriculture industry ran into financial difficulty. Land values declined significantly and dropped roughly by half between 1980 and 1985 (Figure 12.1).

12.3   THE THEORY OF LAND MARKETS

Land is an important input in agricultural production. As a fixed factor, it is assumed that land garners most of the producer surplus (R.E. Just and Hueth 1979). Theory suggests that land prices vary with future agricultural earnings. For example, a simple land price model follows the capitalization framework

$$V_t^A = \sum_{i=0}^{\infty} \delta^i E_t(Y_{t+i}),$$

(12.1)

where V_t^A is the value of farmland at time t; $E_t(Y_{t+i})$ is the per acre net rental rate for farmland at time $(t+i)$ expected at time t; and δ is a discount factor.

Farmland often has alternative uses that include recreation and urban development. The model in Equation 12.1 can be expanded to include alternative uses. Assuming conversion to recreation or to urban development is an irreversible decision, a model with alternative uses may follow

Figure 12.1. Farmland values, US and selected US states, 1960–2007

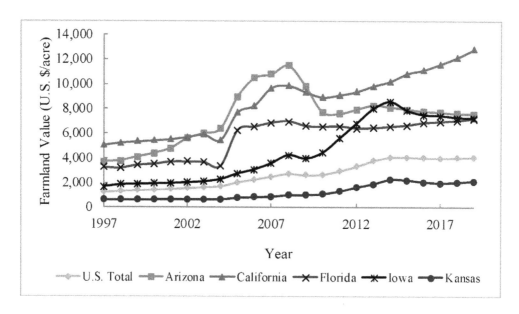

$$V_t^D = \max_n \left\{ \sum_{i=0}^{n} \delta^i E_t (Y_{t+i}) + \sum_{i=n+1}^{\infty} \delta^i E_t (R_{t+i}) \right\}, \tag{12.2}$$

where V_t^D is the value of farmland considering its development potential, n is the year farmland is converted to recreation or urban development, and $E_t(R_{t+i})$ is the rental rate from land that has been converted to recreation or to urban development at time $(t + i)$, expected at time t. Clearly, the value of land considered to be of development potential in Equation 12.2 is higher than the value of land for agricultural purposes in Equation 12.1, $(V_t^D \geq V_t^A)$.

In Figure 12.2 we consider the relationship between product market prices and land rental rates. Equilibrium price and quantity (P_e, Q_e) in the product market (Figure 12.2a) corresponds to the equilibrium price and quantity (W_e, X_e) in the land and other input markets (Figure 12.2b). Suppose the final output price decreases as a result of a change in agricultural policy. Production will then fall to Q^1 in the product market (Figure 12.2a) given supply S_0 (P, W_e) and land utilized for production will decrease to X^1 (Figure 12.2b). In turn, the associated decrease in the rental rate for land will lower the cost of production of the final good and will shift the supply curve from S_0 (P, W_e) to S_1 (P, W^1) (Figure 12.2a), which increases production at P^1 to Q^2. The resulting supply curve, $S^*(P)$, includes land market adjustments (i.e., it does not consider the land market as fixed), and intersects (P, Q_e) and (P^1, Q^2) at a and c, respectively. The change in producer surplus in Figure 12.2a of $(P_e P^1 ca)$ will be exactly equal to the change

Figure 12.2. Product market prices and land rental values

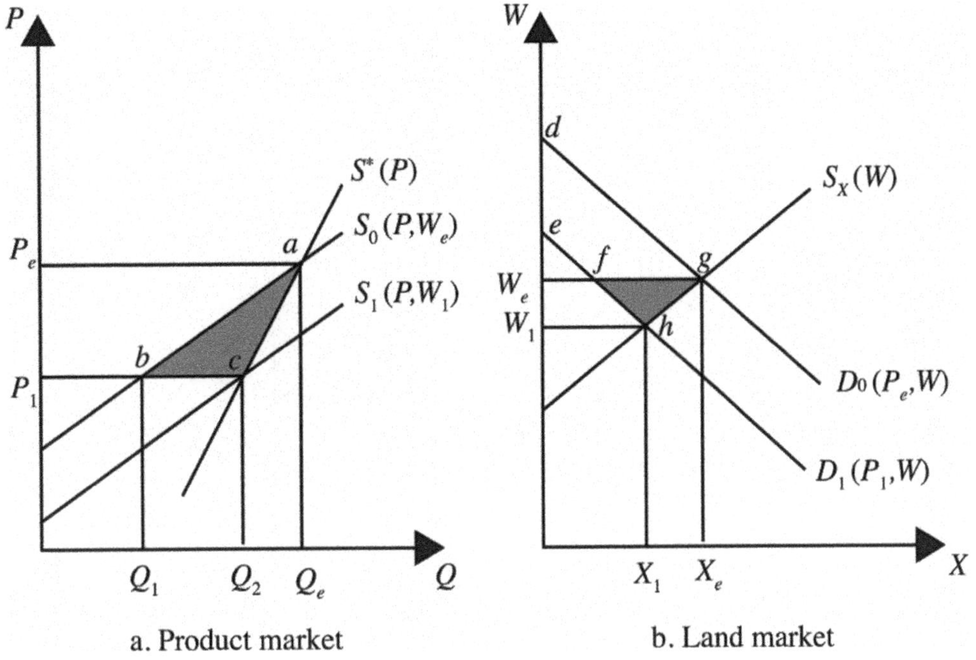

a. Product market

b. Land market

in total economic surplus in Figure 12.2b of (*dehg*). In cases in which farmers rent their land, the welfare loss for the farmer in Figure 12.2a is ($P_e P^1 ca$), which is equivalently measured by (*defg*) in Figure 12.2b. The welfare loss for the landowner in the product market is (*abc*), which is equivalently measured by (*fhg*) in Figure 12.2b. For farmers who own their land, the producer is both the consumer and the supplier in the market for land (R.E. Just, Hueth, and Schmitz 1982).

Consider the extreme case in which all farmers produce on rented land (Figure 12.3). Assume that rents are paid on a cash basis and the supply of land for rent is perfectly inelastic. Initial equilibrium is again at (P_e, Q^1) in Figure 12.3a and at (W_e, X_e) in Figure 12.3b. Suppose a support price of P^S is introduced in Figure 12.3a. Ignoring for simplicity the possible increased use of other production inputs, as in the case of fixed-proportions production, output does not increase because additional land is not brought into production. The demand for land increases from $D^0(P_e, W)$ to $D^1(P^S, W)$ in Figure 12.3b, but this only causes the rental rate for land to increase because no more land is drawn into use. Production does not increase, rather the supply of output shifts from S to S^1 in Figure 12.3a due to the higher cash rents the farmers must pay. The equilibrium supply corresponding to $S^*(P)$ accounts for land-market adjustments that become perfectly inelastic at Q^1. Thus, the tenant pays the landlord the increased

Figure 12.3. Inelastic land supply and output price subsidies

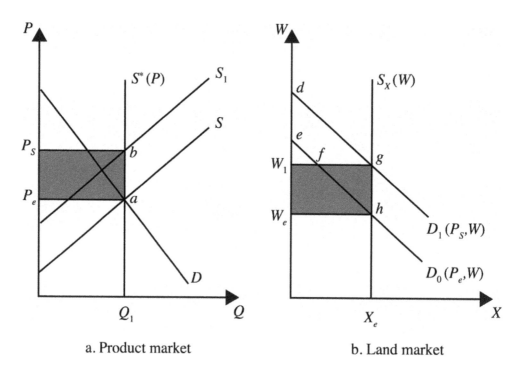

a. Product market   b. Land market

revenue generated by price supports. In this extreme of inelastic land supply and fixed-proportions production, landowners rather than farmers collect all the extra rent (P^SP_eab) due to price supports because landowners command a higher rent from their renters for their land.

Using this same analysis, we assume that inelastic land supply and fixed-proportion agricultural production can be relaxed to show that a farmer can receive a proportion of the increased benefits from his or her subsidized output prices. But the proportion of the benefits received by farmers is lower with more inelastic land supply and with more inelastic supply of other inputs. Even though land may have urban development alternatives, the one-way and permanent nature of farmland conversion likely causes farmland supply to be highly inelastic in the short run. And while agricultural production is not restricted to fixed proportions, the fixed-proportions assumption has approximated reality sufficiently that linear programming models are used widely when modelling farm production. Thus, a large share of the benefits of an agricultural subsidy goes to the landowner.

From the perspective of farmers and landowners, farm size has increased with more and more of the farmland being cash rented (Table 12.1). As an example, in the US state of Iowa, the proportion of cash-rented farmland increased from 21 per cent in 1982 to 35 per cent in

1997, while the proportion under crop-share lease increased from 21 per cent to 24 per cent. At the same time, the proportion of land operated solely by the owner decreased from 54 per cent to 31 per cent. As a result, if land values increase due to farm programs, many of the benefits will not flow to the producer. Instead, landowners who do not farm will capture a large share of the program benefits through the rents they receive from their renters.

12.4 EMPIRICAL BACKGROUND

A number of studies have tested variations of the land market model found in Equation 12.1 and Equation 12.2. Although a correlation between farm income and land price has been found, it is not the only, or even the major, determinant of farmland values. For example, although farmland values and incomes in the United States were closely linked from 1910 to 1950, in the 1960s and 1970s, farmland prices increased while farm incomes decreased (Shalit and Schmitz 1982). In addition, Melichar (1979) questions the use of net farm income as a proxy for expected income and believes that only expected income from farmland should be considered. Since this finding, most studies have used net rent as a proxy for expected income from farmland. Alston (1986) tests the hypothesis of the association between farmland values and inflation rates. He also tests the hypothesis of whether or not the ownership of land acts as a hedge against inflation. He finds almost no evidence to support the hypothesis. In contrast, A. Schmitz (1995a) finds that inflation was a major factor driving land prices up in the late 1970s and early 1980s. Moss (1997) finds that the majority of the variation in land values at the state level from 1960 through 1996 is explained by changes in inflation rates.

Land models are not easy to estimate empirically. Many factors other than net farm income and interest rates affect land values. Studies by both Pope (1985) and J.S. Clark, K.K. Klein, and Thompson (1993) find that farm income alone is incapable of explaining the level of land value. Robison, Lins, and VenKataraman (1985) find that the demand for land in non-farm use has a significant effect on farmland prices. For example, the price of farmland near large cities is driven more by urban expansion and the demand for open space than it is by net farm income. Also, capital gains taxes impact farmland values (Gilbert and Akor 1988).

Because of the large number of variables that affect farmland prices, simple regression models focusing on one or a few aspects of the problem can yield misleading results. For example, in Table 12.2, we present ordinary least squares (OLS) for Florida in which both pastureland prices and developed land prices are regressed against interest rates and cattle prices. The interest rate variable is inconsistent with the theoretical model on farm debt variable (i.e., increases in the interest rates should reduce the value of farmland). Models that omit part of the explanation for land prices may be misleading about the estimated impacts of other variables. A common problem in econometric studies that have many independent variables is the lack of identification of individual coefficients due to multicollinearity, particularly when most variables have a high

Table 12.2. Ordinary least squares of the land market in Florida[a]

Dependent Variable	Price of Unimproved Land in Florida		Price of Improved Land in Florida	
	Model 1	Model 2	Model 3	Model 4
Constant term	−1577.06	960.97	−2802.00	1441.17
	(−3.10)**	(−1.76)*	(−3.58)**	(−1.94)*
Interest rate on farm debt	157.15	188.82	265.45	274.59
	(3.88)**	(3.70)**	(4.11)**	(3.79)**
Price of steers	24.78		43.15	
	(5.66)***		(6.16)***	
Price of calves		10.67		17.60
		(4.22)**		(5.04)**
R^2	0.7267	0.6077	0.7565	0.6807
Adjusted R^2	0.6903	0.5554	0.7241	0.6381
F value	19.94	11.62	23.30	15.99
Probability > F	0.0001***	0.0009**	0.0001***	0.0002**

Source: Moss (2009).

[a] Significance is indicated by * at the 0.05 level, by ** at the 0.01 level, and by *** at the 0.001 level. Values in parentheses are t ratios.

positive correlation naturally, as in the case of land prices. The R.E. Just and Miranowski (1993) solution to the identification problem is to use economic theory to determine the relative role of the various economic variables, in which case econometric estimation is required only to determine a few absolute impact coefficients. Their model estimates: (1) both the plausible impacts of income from farming and the plausible effects of government payments; (2) inflation; (3) risk associated with farm income that includes government payments; (4) taxation of current income, capital gains, and land; and (5) credit availability and interest rates.

12.5   CANADIAN AND US LAND VALUES

The following illustrates how policy impacts land markets and how these markets are influenced by the rapid increase in the demand for land for urban and recreational uses.

12.5.1   Canadian Land Values

Land markets are influenced by government policy and by other factors, including the demand for open space. Supply management commodities, including dairy and poultry, dominate agriculture in both Quebec and Ontario. Supply management has afforded a significant degree of protection for these commodities. On the other hand, government policies play a much

Figure 12.4. Changes in Canadian land values 1971–2018

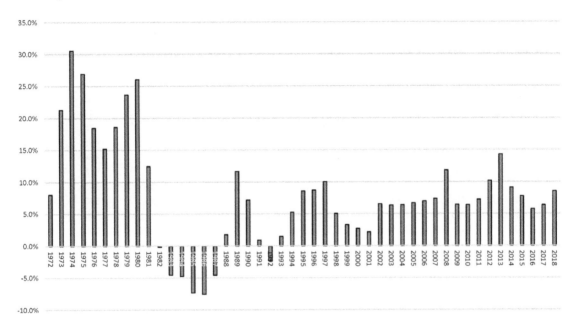

smaller role in the Prairie agricultural sector and these government payouts have declined over time (A. Schmitz, Furtan, and Baylis 2002). Also, the Agricultural Income Disaster Assistance (AIDA) government program that was introduced to compensate for low farm incomes in the late 1990s benefited the major hog producers in Quebec and Ontario at the expense of the farmers of the Prairie provinces. Because of intensive livestock production in Quebec and Ontario, farmers are purchasing additional land for manure disposal, which is driving up the price of farmland. Unlike the Prairie provinces of Alberta, Manitoba, and Saskatchewan, Quebec and Ontario have also had significant population and urban growth, which also drives up the price of farmland.

Land values for Canada and selected provinces are given in Table 12.3 for the years 1981 through 2018. Per acre values are highest for Ontario, followed by British Columbia and Quebec. Note that except for Saskatchewan, where the price for farmland was fairly stagnant from 1988 through 1995, land values elsewhere have been rising sharply since 1988. Net farm income in Quebec and Ontario is less variable than in provinces such as Saskatchewan and has risen more rapidly over time. Also, the urban demand for land inclusive of the demand for open space has been rising steadily in Quebec and Ontario. In addition to demand for land for urban purposes and open space, the demand for farmland to deal with the waste from intensive livestock operations has been increasing steadily because of environmental pressures.

Table 12.3.   Per acre value of farmland, Canada and selected provinces, 1981–2018 (C$/acre)

Year	PQ	ON	MB	SK	AB	BC	Canada
1981	666	1,695	410	382	600	1,191	615
1982	690	1,659	380	413	592	1,083	614
1983	707	1,542	380	405	543	1,091	586
1984	690	1,509	367	393	493	1,035	558
1985	659	1,402	359	357	453	961	517
1986	662	1,288	344	332	407	884	478
1987	697	1,288	325	298	386	833	456
1988	727	1,489	304	286	374	873	464
1989	781	1,908	328	286	411	962	518
1990	859	2,147	359	284	432	1,083	555
1991	918	2,303	357	265	414	1,190	560
1992	943	2,184	360	255	405	1,242	547
1993	977	2,144	373	253	413	1,399	555
1994	1,031	2,134	388	271	450	1,589	584
1995	1,114	2,188	413	299	515	1,767	634
1996	1,220	2,384	443	314	553	1,890	689
1997	1,428	2,671	483	329	611	2,010	758
1998	1,572	2,813	501	333	658	2,016	796
1999	1,696	2,900	510	334	690	2,012	822
2000	1,789	2,964	518	336	721	2,029	844
2001	1,856	3,028	525	337	747	2,044	862
2002	2,017	3,248	547	345	806	2,158	918
2003	2,126	3,466	581	360	863	2,297	976
2004	2,211	3,712	605	371	931	2,496	1,038
2005	2,302	3,938	636	381	1,012	2,774	1,107
2006	2,379	4,201	664	391	1,095	3,191	1,184
2007	2,436	4,443	706	411	1,203	3,653	1,271
2008	2,635	4,750	804	463	1,381	4,355	1,421
2009	2,875	5,036	890	517	1,426	4,602	1,512
2010	2,979	5,461	981	551	1,514	4,765	1,608
2011	3,128	5,985	1,035	624	1,592	4,988	1,724
2012	3,375	7,013	1,140	720	1,706	4,898	1,899
2013	4,175	8,087	1,395	872	1,893	4,886	2,170
2014	4,624	8,705	1,596	1,026	2,025	4,951	2,367
2015	5,032	9,289	1,767	1,134	2,185	5,083	2,550
2016	5,320	9,580	1,919	1,210	2,354	5,321	2,696
2017	5,660	9,997	2,034	1,287	2,541	5,744	2,867
2018	6,087	11,358	2,112	1,454	2,683	5,674	3,111

Source: Authors' compilation from Farm Credit Canada (FCC) data.

The per cent change in farmland values in Canada between 1971 and 2018 is given in Figure 12.4. Prior to 2002, the annual growth in land values was highly variable (Farm Credit Canada [FCC] 2020). However, farmland values have been increasing at a rate between 6 and 15 per cent since 2002.

Figure 12.5. US land values, selected corn belt states, 1960–2007

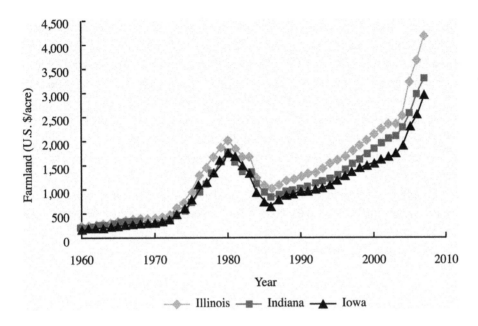

Figure 12.6. US land values, selected Great Plains states, 1960–2007

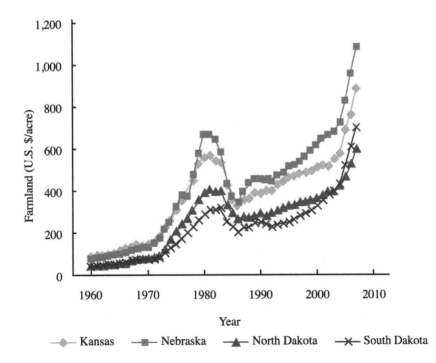

12.5.2   US Land Values

We plot US land value data for selected US corn belt states in Figure 12.5 and for selected Great Plains states in Figure 12.6 for 1960 to 2007. Generally, these land values are highly correlated and have increased steadily since 1986. Land values are influenced by many factors, including urban growth. Recall from Table 12.2 that farmland values in Florida are not related to traditional economic variables such as cattle prices and interest rates. Florida land values bear little relationship to land values in the corn belt states (e.g., Iowa). Nor do Florida land values resemble those in the Great Plains states (Kansas, Nebraska, North Dakota, and South Dakota). For the latter, land values are determined largely from income generated from agriculture.

   Land values and cash rental rates are highly correlated. In Indiana, for example, land values reached near record highs in the year 2000 despite rock-bottom commodity prices. Even so, average cash rents reached their peak from 1998 to 2000. In Indiana, the correlation between average rent and average land value was 0.91.

12.5.3   Land Values in Perspective

In the mid-1990s, for some US states (e.g., North Dakota), up to 86 per cent of net cash farm income was represented by government subsidies, while for Canadian provinces this proportion reached a high of only 42 per cent (in the case of Manitoba; Table 12.4). Canadian farm programs for western Prairie grain and oilseed producers are very different from those programs in the United States (see discussion in Chapter 1). The producer subsidy equivalents between 1980 and 2008 are roughly twice as high in the United States as those in Canada.

   As a result of these differences in government support and program structure, land values in Saskatchewan follow a different pattern than they do in the neighbouring US states. For example, in Saskatchewan, 19 per cent of net farm income is from government payments over the years 1995 to 1999 (Table 12.4). In North Dakota, 86 per cent of net farm income is made up of government payments. Since 1997 Saskatchewan land values have fallen, but this is not the case with the northern US states. The correlation between Montana and North Dakota land values is 0.81 (Table 12.5). The correlation between North Dakota land values and those in Saskatchewan is substantially lower, at 0.68, and between Montana and Saskatchewan the correlation is even lower, at 0.38. Saskatchewan land values dipped in the early 1990s. Simultaneously, the land values in the Great Plains states increased with the expansion of federal support for crop insurance in the United States in the early 1990s.

   A land value comparison between North Dakota and Saskatchewan is given in Figures 12.7 and 12.8. Between 2004 and 2008, land values in North Dakota increased by roughly 50 per cent while those in Saskatchewan increased by roughly 20 per cent.

Table 12.4. Government payments as proportion of net cash farm income, selected US states and Canadian provinces, 1995–8

State	Percentage	Province	Percentage
Minnesota	38.7	Ontario	16.2
North Dakota	85.9	Manitoba	41.5
Montana	68.6	Saskatchewan	19.0
		Alberta	13.1

Source: A. Schmitz, Furtan, and Baylis (2002).

Table 12.5. Land value correlations for North Dakota, Montana, and Saskatchewan, 1981–2000

State/Province	North Dakota	Montana	Saskatchewan
North Dakota	1.00	0.81	0.68
Montana	0.81	1.00	0.38
Saskatchewan	0.68	0.38	1.00

Source: Authors' calculations.

In Table 12.6 we give additional information on the relationship between land values in Indiana, Iowa, and Kansas compared with land values in Quebec and Saskatchewan. As emphasized earlier, farm programs heavily influence land values. High levels of subsidies exist for farmers in states like Indiana and provinces like Quebec, but in Saskatchewan the subsidy levels are low. (Also, the levels of farm subsidies have moved together over time for Indiana and Quebec.) Note the high positive correlation of land values between Indiana and Quebec and the negative correlation of land values between Indiana and Saskatchewan. There is also a low correlation between land values in Iowa and Kansas as compared with those in Saskatchewan.

Table 12.6. Land values correlations between selected US states and Canadian provinces, 1981–2001

US State	Quebec	Saskatchewan
Indiana		
With exchange rate adjusted	0.73	−0.14
Without exchange rate adjusted	0.82	0.21
Iowa		
With exchange rate adjusted	0.59	0.09
Without exchange rate adjusted	0.63	0.31
Kansas		
With exchange rate adjusted	0.43	0.27
Without exchange rate adjusted	0.48	0.47

Source: Authors' calculations.

Figure 12.7. Changes in Saskatchewan land values

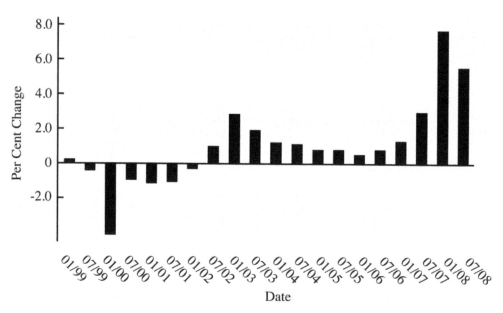

Figure 12.8. Changes in North Dakota land values

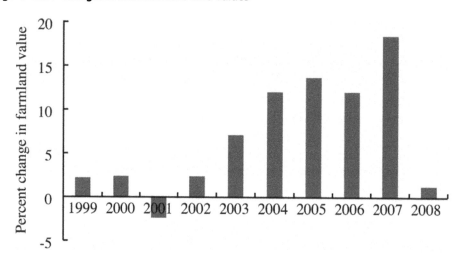

12.6   BOOM-BUST CYCLES AND FARMER WEALTH

Historically, farmland prices have shifted significantly over time, and so has the wealth of those who own farmland. Fluctuations in farmland values and the associated variations in wealth are akin to the rise and fall of the stock market. A drastic reduction in stock market prices represents a reduction of household wealth. In his Waugh lecture on "Boom/Bust Cycles and

WEALTH AND FARM INCOME

"Critical to understanding the boom-bust phenomenon are the dynamic changes in wealth as distinguished from net realized farm income. During the North American agricultural boom that peaked in 1981–2, the value of farm real estate in the United States exceeded US$800 billion – more than double the 1974 value – only to drop in 1987 to US$597 billion. The changes in Saskatchewan, Canada, were even more dramatic. Between 1972 and 1982 the value of land and buildings increased by a factor of roughly 7.0, from C$3.6 billion to C$27.1 billion. The value of implements and machinery increased six-fold between 1972 and 1986. Realized net farm income, however, did not grow nearly as rapidly as did asset values. Interestingly, Kansas and Montana, two large wheat-growing states, did not experience the same degree of escalation and depreciation in land values that Saskatchewan did, even though US farm programs provided much more income insurance than did Canadian programs, especially during the boom phase of the cycle. The US government wrote off proportionately more farm debt than did the Canadian government" (A. Schmitz 1995a, 1110–11).

Ricardian Rent," A. Schmitz (1995a) emphasizes the volatile nature of land markets and the significance of wealth changes. He distinguishes between changes in wealth from net realized farm income and cases in which farmland prices increase even though net farm income decreases.

12.7 URBAN GROWTH AND FARMLAND VALUES

In some regions, land has many competing uses both within agriculture and from urban growth. In certain US states, the latter has caused land values to rise and wealth of landowners to skyrocket to the point at which farmland is bid out of agricultural use. The rate of urbanization is higher for several counties in California that produce high-value crops such as vegetables and citrus. Livanis et al. (2006) examine whether increased urban pressure has had a positive effect on agricultural output by increasing farmers' access to urban markets. As urban centres encroach on agricultural areas, Livanis et al. (2006) hypothesize that farmers switch to higher-valued crops, including fresh fruits and vegetables. In addition, they find that a 1 per cent increase in accessibility (defined by the number of people who could drive to a location in a fixed period of time) is associated with a 0.101 per cent increase in the median house value at the county level and that a 1 per cent increase in median house values within a county is associated with a 0.404 per cent increase in farmland values.

Moss and Schmitz (2008) estimate the relationship between farmland values and housing prices and find generally that they are positively correlated. From the last quarter of 2007 through the first quarter of 2008, the residential housing market in the United States softened significantly. Moss and Schmitz (2008) examine whether the onset of this slump negatively affects the farm sector. Using aggregate data for the United States, Moss and Schmitz estimate Equation 12.3, a linear relationship between farmland values, V_t, average house prices, H_t, returns to agriculture, R_t, and the cost of capital, r_t.

$$V_t = -5244.676 + 0.0163H_t + 14.532R_t - 52454.87r_t,$$
$$(0.0054)\ (10.692)\ (9440.73)$$

(12.3)

where the numbers in parentheses are standard errors of the estimate. The coefficients for H_t and r_t are statistically significant. The estimated relationship is consistent with the conjecture that a slumping residential housing market exists along with a slumping farmland market. At the state level, Moss and Schmitz (2008) find that while the housing market weakened in Arizona, California, and Florida, house values continued to increase in Illinois, Indiana, Iowa, and Texas. Furthermore, they find that farmland values in Illinois, Indiana, and Iowa benefited from increasing commodity prices (primarily corn). Thus, the effect of the weakening home market can be mitigated by the impact of increasing commodity prices (recognizing that in late 2008 commodity prices plummeted).

DAIRYING IN CALIFORNIA

"In a capitalist society with fee-simple ownership, few controls on property use, and a 'free market' in land, rapid urbanization creates real estate booms ... In the 1950s, Los Angeles (L.A.) County added almost 2 million people to its total and in the next decade, [it added] another million. Between the late 1950s and late 1970s, it lost nearly 16,000 farm acres. Land prices were US$8,000 per acre to US$30,000 per acre, occasionally reaching US$90,000 per acre. Dairy owners with 15 acres to 20 acres sold their land for development and for windfall profits ... Some of the former L.A. dairy owners moved to the rural southern San Joaquin Valley. But most went only to the western tips of neighbouring San Bernardino and Riverside Counties, to an area called the Chino Valley ... The dairy operators purchased 10 acres to 80 acres of farmland, built state-of-the-art dairies, and constructed lavish new homes beside the facilities. Finally, with the remaining capital, they were still able to enlarge their herds, which often doubled or tripled their size ... It was through these cycles of urbanization, relocation, and expansion that industrial dairying was born. The windfall of urban prices for farmland, combined with the Dutch 'dairy culture' of Southern California, enabled the capitalization of large-scale dairying. A case study sums up the process: One farmer relates that he bought his first dairy farm in Artesia [southeast of L.A.] in 1950 at a price of 12 acres for US$12,000. He sold the land for subdivision for US$300,000 and bought 30 acres in Dairy Valley, now Cerritos. In 1970 he again sold to sub-dividers for US$1.3 million and moved to Chino" (Gilbert and Akor 1988, 64–5).

12.8 LAND VALUES AND THE SOLVENCY OF THE FARM SECTOR

The significance of real estate to the equity of domestic agriculture can be documented. In 1950 real estate represented 62 per cent of all agricultural asset values. By 1981 the significance of real estate increased to 78 per cent of all agricultural assets. In 1981 farm real estate values stood at US$783 billion. By 1986 real estate fell to US$542 billion, or to 69 per cent of its 1981 value, which represents an annual decline of 7 per cent. Hence, 88 per cent of the total decline in agricultural asset values between 1981 and 1986 was due to downturns in real estate compared with 2 per cent from reductions in livestock and poultry investments, 8 per cent from reductions in machinery investment, and 5 per cent from reductions in crop inventories. From 1986 through 2007, total farm assets in the United States increased from US$722 billion to US$1,979 billion (90 per cent of this increase was from increased real estate values, compared with 3 per cent from livestock investments and investments in machinery). Thus, the swings in the balance sheet can be traced primarily to changes in real estate values (USDA/ERS 2009).

Several previous studies have noted the significance of the relationship between farmland values and farm equity. Shalit and Schmitz (1982) develop a model where farmers use farmland as a store of value that allows farmers access to the credit market. DeBoer-Lowenberg and Boehlje (1986) suggest that increases in commodity prices in the 1970s, coupled with tax considerations, generated incentives for farm expansion. These incentives caused farmland to appreciate in value, which in turn increased the value of agricultural collateral and the demand for debt capital. The financial stress experienced by US agriculture in the 1980s was a result of the combined effects of capital losses from falling commodity prices and the financial risk (from increased debt) that farms took on to finance expansion. Lence and Miller (1999, 257) state that "the aforementioned boom-bust cycles in farmland prices have triggered noticeable wealth changes for the farm sector as a whole." In their analysis of the potential impact of the US Federal Agriculture Improvement and Reform (FAIR) Act of 1996, Lamb and Henderson (2000) link the potential impact of agricultural policy to farmland values primarily through subsidies on corn production, and infer that these impacts could have dramatic consequences for the sector's solvency. It is conjectured by de Fontnouvelle and Lence (2002, 549) that "because land has become a major source of collateral in agricultural lending, large drops in land values have typically been accompanied by substantial reductions in the availability of credit to the sector."

To model the linkage between farmland values and solvency in the sector, we start with the accounting identity

$$E(t) + D(t) = L(t)p(t) + k(t) + C(t), \tag{12.4}$$

where $E(t)$ is the equity in the farm sector, $D(t)$ is the level of debt, $L(t)$ is the acres of farmland, $p(t)$ is the price of farmland, $K(t)$ is the level of intermediate assets, and $C(t)$ is the level of current assets, all valued at time t. Differentiating this equality yields

$$dE(t) + dD(t) = dL(t)p(t) + L(t)dp(t) - \delta(t)K(t) + I(t) + dC(t), \qquad (12.5)$$

where we substitute $[dK(t) = -\delta(t) K(t) + I(t)]$; $\delta(t)$ is the depreciation for intermediate assets; and $I(t)$ is the investment in new intermediate assets. Next, we assume that intermediate assets are in steady state, or that $[dK(t) = -\delta(t) K(t) + I(t) = 0]$. Thus,

$$dE(t) = [dL(t)p(t) + L(t)dp(t) + dC(t)] - dD(t), \qquad (12.6)$$

where the change in equity is determined by the change in the level of farmland, the price of farmland, and the change in current assets less the change in debt level. To refine this measure, let the change in current assets be defined as the profit from operations less consumption

$$dC(t) = r_0 (t)[L(t)p(t) + K(t) + k(t) + C(t)] - c(t), \qquad (12.7)$$

where $r_0(t)$ is the operating return on assets (i.e., the return not including capital gains) and $c(t)$ is the level of consumption that must be supported from operating returns or increases in the level of debt, since $dC(t)$ must be chosen such that $C(t) \geq 0$. Mathematically,

$$c(t) \leq dD(t) + r_0(t)[L(t)p(t) + K(t) + C(t)] \ni : C(t) \geq 0. \qquad (12.8)$$

In essence, capital gains cannot be consumed directly, but must be converted into increased debt (see Chapter 14). Theoretically, the change in level of debt is an endogenous variable that can be modelled using a variety of mechanisms. Following Ramirez, Moss, and Boggess (1997), we can use an optimal debt formulation for $dD(t)$, which makes the change in debt a function of the expected rate of return on agricultural assets (including both the operating return and the expected rate of capital gains), the riskiness of those returns, and the decision maker's risk-aversion coefficient. Alternatively, we can view the change in debt as rationed externally because of credit market failures such as asymmetric information (Stiglitz and Weiss 1981). However, for the purposes of this study, we focus on the linkage between farmland values and equity. Specifically, given that the total quantity of farmland in US agriculture is relatively constant over time, changes in farm equity are affected primarily by changes in farmland prices over time.

This linkage between agricultural equity and farmland values can be problematic from a policy perspective. As noted by A. Schmitz (1995a), farmland values are subject to boom-bust cycles. Schmitz's findings indicate that farmland values appear to be appropriately priced in the long run but may exhibit systematic and sustained departures from this equilibrium in the short run. Similar support for the boom-bust cycle behaviour of farmland values is presented by Featherstone and Moss (2003) using a stochastic trend model. Their findings suggest that a large portion of the annual fluctuations in farm returns are transitory and should not contribute to fluctuations in farmland values. However, their results do reproduce the boom-bust cycles observed in US farmland values during the 1980s and 1990s.

Table 12.7. Transition land values, Southeast Miami-Dade County, Florida, 1994–2001 (US$/acre)

Year	<5 miles to a major town	>5 miles to a major town
1994	25,166	15,000
1995	28,500	16,200
1996	30,167	17,375
1997	28,400	19,000
1998	28,000	20,600
1999	32,063	21,953
2000	34,000	22,917
2001	40,000	26,250

Source: Reynolds and Dorbecker (2002).

12.9   LAND VALUES, URBAN DEVELOPMENT, AND TRADE

The price for agricultural land will be much higher if the land is sold for urban real estate than it will be if the land is considered exclusively for agricultural purposes. Consider tomato production in Miami-Dade County, Florida. Farmland prices for tomato land in southeast Miami-Dade County are given in Table 12.7 for the years 1994 through 2001. Land situated less than five miles from a major town is priced at US$40,000 per acre in 2001. At a 5 per cent interest rate, the annual per acre land rental payment will be US$2,000. It is clear that the per acre income generated from tomatoes cannot support farmland that costs US$40,000 an acre. The price of farmland in Miami-Dade County remains high because of its potential for urban development.

Cases such as these, which can be found around most major cities, raise questions about what role land values play in comparative-advantage arguments in trade. In the tomato case over the long term, US Miami-Dade County tomato production cannot compete with that of Mexico if new or existing US farmers have to pay US$40,000 per acre for farmland.

Often, trade barriers affect land prices in the same manner as increased urbanization, and at times both forces work together to prop up land values. We consider first the impact of trade on land values. The US supply curve for tomatoes is S_Q in Figure 12.9a, while domestic demand is D_Q. Under a free trade scenario, price is P^0 and imports are $(Q^1 - Q^0)$. The land market is modelled in Figure 12.9b. The supply curve for farmland is S_x and DP^1 is the derived demand curve for farmland, given the tomato price, P^0. In Figure 12.9b, if the land for tomato production is used only for agriculture, the rent is (e^0X^1f).

Now suppose producers lobby the government to impose an import quota with the effect of raising the commodity price to P^*, causing domestic output to increase to Q^* (Figure 12.9a). Producer rents increase by (P^*P^0hi) as the demand curve for land shifts to D^*. In Figure 12.9b, what if instead of an import quota, the government imposes a deficiency

Figure 12.9. Land rent, urban development, and trade barriers

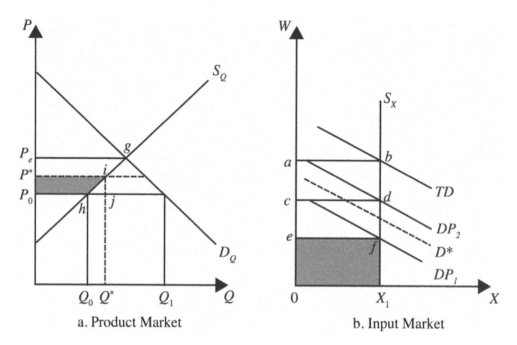

a. Product Market   b. Input Market

payment scheme supporting producer prices at P^* (Figure 12.9a). The deficiency payment to producers is (P^*P^0ji). Note that producer rents are the same under either an import quota or a deficiency payment scheme because (ihj) is lost to the increasing marginal cost of production. If producers lobby for the complete elimination of imports, their rents will increase by (P^eP^0hg), which is equal to rent $(cefd)$ in Figure 12.9b. The derived demand for farmland thereby shifts to DP^2.

Studies often correlate land values with producer deficiency payment levels but ignore the effects of hidden subsidies (e.g., import quotas). This is a problem in cross-country comparisons in which one country uses hidden subsidies while another country uses direct subsidies to protect its producers. As shown above, either type of subsidy can have a similar effect on producer rents and land values.

Now consider the case in which urban development has pushed the derived demand for farmland outward to demand TD (Figure 12.9b). The so-called urban demand rent is $(acdb)$. If the farmer continues to use this land for tomato production, this rent will be a lost opportunity for increased income from the sale of the property. Alternatively, if the farmer chooses to continue farming in the anticipation that the appreciation of his or her land will be equal to or greater than the additional urban-demand rent, these economic rents will not be realized until the land is sold for development purposes. Under these circumstances, new entrants will not purchase the land for growing tomatoes unless the land is zoned solely for agricultural use. If the agricultural land is zoned residential, new entrants will probably not enter into tomato production, and eventually the existing viable farmers may be able sell their land to developers.

It is difficult to assess the meaning of cost of production when the demand from urban growth is present. If governments subsidize producers to cover the full costs of production, then huge subsidies will be needed where land is valued at a much higher urban opportunity cost. Furthermore, subsidizing farmers for foregone urban rents may offer them a windfall if the land continues to appreciate at a high rate due to increasing urban development opportunities. Policymakers are having a difficult time coming to grips with these urban-rural interface issues. At one extreme, some groups argue that prime agricultural land should be zoned such that it cannot be sold for urban development. If this were done, will the producers be compensated for their loss in land value due to lost urban development opportunities? If they are reimbursed, how much remuneration will they receive? The answer to these questions involves legal arguments surrounding both property rights and economic compensation.

12.10   PRODUCTIVITY AND FARMLAND VALUES

Apart from traditional factors such as government payments and international competition, farmland prices are affected by more and more technological change and urban pressure. For example, from 1960 through 2000 in Florida, agricultural productivity increased at an annual rate of 2.01 per cent (Moss 2006). This increase was largely the result of increased output of farm commodities that grew at an annual rate of 2.65 per cent while agricultural input use remained constant at an annual rate of 0.65 per cent. Moss (2006) compares this growth in productivity with agricultural income and land values in Florida from 1960 to 2002 to examine whether rents from increased productivity are bid into farmland values. In general, productivity leads to neither higher net farm cash income nor higher farmland values through time (Figure 12.10). While these results may be specific to Florida, Moss conjectures that the competitive nature of agriculture may imply that most of the gains to research are captured by consumers and not by producers through either increased incomes or increased farmland values.

12.11   US LAND VALUES AND DECOUPLED FARM PROGRAMS

Many argue that farm programs generally cannot be decoupled from production and that farm program payments impact the price of farmland (Tweeten and Martin 1966; Shalit and Schmitz 1982; J.S. Clark, K.K. Klein, and Thompson 1993). The degree of decoupling present

Figure 12.10. Florida's total factor productivity (TFP), net cash income (total asset values), and farmland values, 1995–2000

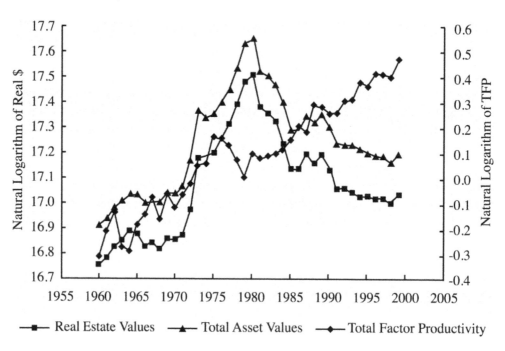

in farm programs is at the heart of the World Trade Organization's (WTO's) classification of trade-distorting policies. There is a mixture of programs that affect producer welfare. Under the 2002 and 2008 US Farm Bills, there are both target prices and loan rates for wheat and corn, along with drought-relief assistance and crop insurance subsidies. It is possible that one of the elements of the farm program is not decoupled while others are.

FARMLAND PRICES AND POLICY

"When comparing US and Canadian real estate values, we see that in the 1990s land prices increased in Montana and North Dakota but remained relatively constant in Saskatchewan (though in some areas of Saskatchewan, land values have fallen sharply). Since input costs, crop yields, and crop prices are similar in the three regions, the remaining explanation for the difference in land values is government policy. The producer subsidies for grain and oilseed production are much higher in the United States. Many of these subsidies are not decoupled, which partially explains why US land values remain high. The old saying still remains: Many of the benefits of farm programs get capitalized into land values" (A. Schmitz and Gray 2001, 474).

Figure 12.11. Decoupled programs and land rents

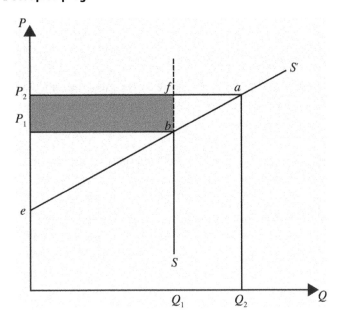

A great deal of confusion exists about the decoupling of farm programs and the relationship of such programs to land values. A program can be decoupled in a production sense but can still cause land values to increase. Consider the case in which supply is S (Figure 12.11). In this case, a price support of P^2 is decoupled from production because output does not change in response to a price support. But rents go up by an amount (P^2P^1bf) due to the price support. Thus, even though a program is decoupled with respect to production, it may generate rents. In this case, the increased rents would be bid into land prices. For a program to be decoupled it would have to be one that affects neither production nor the rents earned on assets.

WORLD TRADE ORGANIZATION (WTO) AND AGREEMENT ON AGRICULTURE

- *Green Box* subsidies must not distort trade or cause minimal distortions. They have to be government funded (i.e., supply management is not permitted as the burden falls on consumers) and must not involve price supports. Subsidies cannot target particular products but may provide direct income support for farmers if decoupled from current production levels or prices. Subject to certain conditions, environmental protection and regional development programs can be subsidized without limits.

- *Amber Box* subsidies include all domestic support measures considered to distort production and trade and are not included in the other boxes. These include measures to support prices or subsidies directly related to production quantities. There are limits to support; *de minimis* (minimal) levels of support, referred to as aggregate measure of support (AMS), are 5 per cent of the agricultural production value for developed countries and 10 per cent for developing countries. Because Amber Box subsidies are trade distorting, countries are to reduce or eliminate them.
- *Blue Box* subsidies may be considered as "Amber Box with conditions" – conditions designed to reduce distortions. Any support that would normally be in the Amber Box is placed in the Blue Box if the support also requires farmers to limit production. Thus, agricultural programs that require farmers to set aside land for conservation use to be eligible for subsidies (cross compliance) are included, as are production-limiting programs, such as supply restrictions that might adversely affect trade. There are no limits on spending on Blue Box subsidies.

Under existing WTO rules and as argued by the United States, direct payments to agricultural producers fall into the Green Box because they do not incentivize production nor distort trade. There is no limit on what a country can spend on Green Box subsidies. Subsidization of crop insurance premiums, which can affect output, are trade distorting. The United States recognizes that its yield and revenue insurance programs must be classified as Amber Box subsidies.

The objective of trade negotiations is to reduce or eliminate Amber Box subsidies, while Green Box programs continue to be exempt from trade reduction commitments. Blue Box programs are tolerated but could be targeted by other countries for modification (e.g., supply management regimes have been singled out). Even so, some countries want to retain the Blue Box as it is because they see it as a crucial means of moving away from distorting Amber Box subsidies without causing too much hardship.

In Figure 12.12, we further extend the discussion on farm program decoupling. The supply and demand schedules are S and D in the absence of farm programs. The free trade price is P^1 and exports total $(Q^1 - Q^2)$. Suppose that, due to a change in international conditions, price falls to P^2. Without government involvement, the price decline causes output to fall to Q^3 and exports also fall. Total producer revenue declines by $[(P^1 - P^2)(Q^1 - Q^3)]$.

Figure 12.12. Decoupled payments

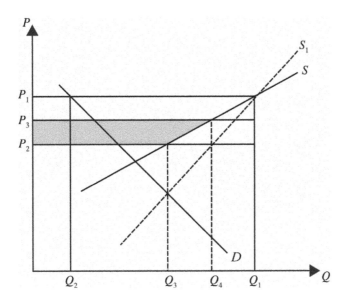

What happens if the government responds to a price decline by subsidizing farmers' income with a supposedly decoupled payment to make up for the lost revenue? If the program is truly decoupled, then output responds only to price P^2 and remains at Q^3. If output increases beyond Q^3 in response to government payments, then the program is not decoupled. Suppose, for example, that production increases from Q^3 to Q^4 as a result of the government payments. Then the program is only partially decoupled. In essence, government payments create a new supply curve S^1. (Note that the supply curve S^1 is drawn with reference to price P^2.) Alternatively, output Q^4 corresponds to price P^3 on the original supply curve, S. Accordingly, trade increases by the same amount as if output price were raised to P^3. The corresponding Ricardian rents from the farm program are given by the shaded area in Figure 12.12. Hence, the effects are the same as if a non-decoupled program were imposed to restore only part of the lost revenues. Thus, to the extent that programs are not truly decoupled, farm payments will be bid into rents and, in turn, into the price of land.

12.12   MULTINATIONALS: CAPITAL MOVEMENTS AND PRODUCT TRADE

Land markets are influenced by agricultural and trade policies. Likewise, the location of production is influenced by policy and by such factors as increased urbanization. More and more of the importation of products into a country, such as the United States, is done by multinationals.

Figure 12.13. Agricultural production and trade, locating abroad

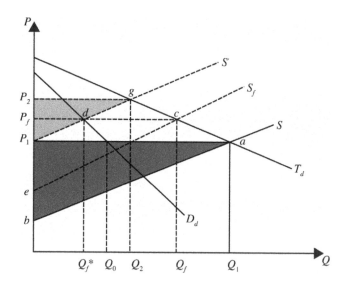

American capital (human and physical) moves from the United States to produce goods abroad. The goods, in turn, are shipped back to the United States and to third markets. The trend towards increased capital movements and product trade (where they are complements), has risen sharply (A. Schmitz and Helmberger 1973). Examples abound and include US companies that once produced in Florida but now produce in Mexico, Costa Rica, and Belize, and ship farm products back to the United States and elsewhere (Moss, T.G. Schmitz, and A. Schmitz 2007).

A model of the complementary nature of product trade and foreign direct investment is given in Figure 12.13. US demand is D_d, total demand is T_d, and US supply is S. At price P_1, the US exports $(Q_1 - Q_0)$ of the goods and sells q_0 domestically.

Now assume that because of such factors as increased urbanization, land taxes, and regulation, the US supply curve shifts to S'. In the absence of international capital flows, price rises to P_2 and production falls to Q_2. Producers lose $(P_1ba - P_1gP_2)$.

Suppose that by investing abroad, US firms can produce more cheaply abroad than they can in the United States. Consider supply, S_f, which is now the supply curve for producing the product abroad. The equilibrium price is P_f. Now the US firms located abroad export the amount to the US market and to third markets. This is a much-preferred position for US firms since their rents under the umbrella of foreign investment of (P_fec) will exceed rents of (P_1P_2g), where the latter are the rents if the good is produced in the United States.

In the context of Figure 12.10, it is easy to show the effect of tariff policy on the outcome. For example, a US tariff on the good will reduce incentives to produce abroad. Likewise, tax incentives by the host country will favour investing abroad. Also, a major component in the production of fruits and vegetables, for example, is farm labour. Wage rates are generally much lower for workers located abroad than, for example, in the United States. Differences in labour costs partly determine the position of S_f and S' in Figure 12.13.

12.13   SUMMARY AND CONCLUSIONS

- In some key agricultural states, over 50 per cent of farmed land is rented. This makes designing policy difficult, since a primary beneficiary of farm subsidies is the landowner and not necessarily those who farm rented land.
- Differences in agricultural support are reflected in differences in farmland values worldwide.
- US farm policy has enhanced farm income significantly. Whether these transfers are merely redistributive in nature or whether they create inefficiencies in resource use is uncertain. Policy support levels around the world account for a portion of the differences in farmland values.
- While the theory of land values is well developed, estimating these models empirically is difficult.
- Because of the wealth that land represents, farmers lobby governments for farm policies. Landowners try to avoid a collapse in land values and the accompanying decrease in wealth that occurred in the mid-1980s. Because of the increasing separation between farm operators and landowners, more and more farm subsidies will end up in the hands of landowners than they will in the hands of farm operators.
- Farm owners may rely on equity from capital appreciation to augment consumption when cash income declines.
- Urban growth drove up the price of land significantly in the urban-rural fringe until the financial crisis of 2007, which collapsed the urban land market but not the farmland market. Thus, in the United States, a dual land market has emerged.
- Farmland values have increased dramatically since 2010. For many parts of the United States and Canada, farmland values have more than doubled. Thus, the agricultural debt-to-asset ratios have declined.

CHAPTER THIRTEEN

The Economics of Biofuels

13.1 GAS PRICES AND BIOFUELS

Sharply rising oil prices at the beginning of the twenty-first century significantly contributed to the interest in biofuel production. Policies that promote biofuel production, at least in the United States, are for energy self-sufficiency. Starting with the energy crisis in 1973, US reliance on oil imports from the Middle East has been a growing policy concern. Figure 13.1 presents the US monthly production, importation, and consumption of oil in thousands of barrels from April 1993 through November 2018 along with the domestic production of ethanol. Between August 2008 and September 2018, US oil production increased 121.6 per cent, from 155,403 thousand barrels to 343,750 thousand barrels, while US ethanol production increased 52.9 per cent, from 20,059 thousand barrels to 30,667 thousand barrels. Oil imports reached a maximum of 455,595 thousand barrels in August 2006. Total crude oil consumption peaked at 671,658 thousand barrels in August 2005. The overall consumption of oil declined slightly from August 2005 to October 2013. Since the passage of the US Energy Independence and Security Act of 2007, the relative use of ethanol has steadily increased. In September 1995, ethanol represented 0.50 per cent of total oil consumption in the United States. By August of 2008, ethanol use had risen to 3.36 per cent of oil consumption, and to 5.37 per cent by February 2018.

Ethanol is a major component of biofuels. From April 1993 to October 2006, the ethanol and gasoline prices remained fairly similar. After October 2006, ethanol prices became systematically lower than gasoline prices because ethanol generates relatively less energy than does gasoline (Figure 13.2). The policy mechanism for regulating the amount of ethanol used in domestic fuels (both gasoline and diesel) has changed over time. From 2007 to 2012, the use of ethanol was encouraged through a Volumetric Ethanol Excise Tax Credit (VEETC) of US$0.51

Figure 13.1. US monthly domestic oil production, oil imports, oil consumption, and ethanol production, April 1993 through November 2018

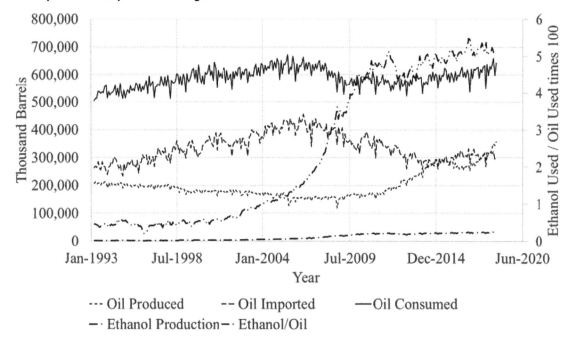

per gallon. Since 2012, refiners and importers are required to blend ethanol with domestic fuels. This requirement is enforced through Renewable Identification Numbers (RINs).

Biofuels are produced from many sources, including corn, sugar, wheat, soybeans, and canola. Some countries, such as France, Germany, Spain, and Sweden, have made significant inroads in promoting biofuel production, while others, such as India and Southeast Asia, have not. Countries that pursue biofuel production offer significant incentives to do so. For example, Brazil is a major producer of ethanol from sugar using hidden subsidies, including refinery subsidization (T.G. Schmitz, A. Schmitz, and Seale 2003). The United States promotes ethanol production through several means, including tax credits and import duties.

13.2   THE ECONOMICS OF BIODIESEL

In the United States, the emergence of biodiesel has been much slower than the growth in ethanol. Biodiesel is produced from oil crops such as soybeans. According to the US Department of Energy, biodiesel production increased from 204 million barrels in 2001 to 11,691 million barrels in 2007. Comparing this with the ethanol production of 42,028 million barrels in 2001 and 154,416 million barrels in 2007, biodiesel production lags behind that of ethanol. Differences in growth can

Figure 13.2. Gasoline and ethanol prices (US$/gallon), April 1993 through November 2018

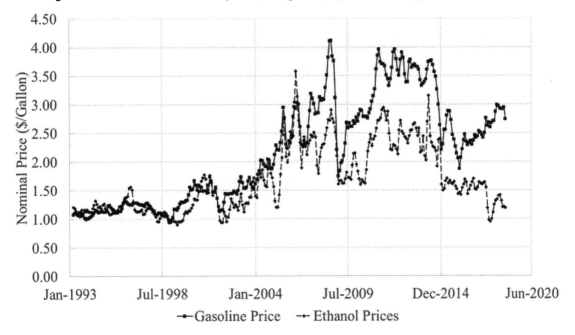

be attributed to the conversion efficiency between the two biofuels and the relative price of production inputs. In the United States, corn is less expensive than soybeans and each bushel of corn produces 2.8 gallons of ethanol, while each bushel of soybeans produces 1.49 gallons of biodiesel.

13.3   THE ECONOMICS OF ETHANOL

WINNERS AND LOSERS

"A standard argument in international trade is that while most trade arrangements have winners and losers, successful agreements are so beneficial to the winners that they create enough surplus to help the losers adjust and adapt. An interesting policy question concerns whether the long list of positives associated with the expansion of corn ethanol production is sufficient to offset the shorter list of negatives" (Elobeid et al. 2006, 11).

The model below focuses on US ethanol production and explicitly takes into account the inter-relationships between direct subsidies to corn producers under the US farm program and the indirect subsidies to ethanol processors via the US government ethanol tax credit. Empirically, we show the conditions under which government outlays to ethanol producers are less than government payments to corn producers (which fall in the presence of ethanol tax credits). However, while corn producers may gain from ethanol production, even with a reduction in farm payments, society as a whole may not gain from subsidization.

13.3.1 Modelling the Derived Demand for Corn for Ethanol Production

To model the impact of ethanol on the agricultural sector, we need to specify the demand for ethanol. We assume that ethanol is used in the production of other goods and services in the economy. Following this specification, businesses select the level of outputs that maximize profit defined as

$$\max \pi = p'y - C(w,y) \tag{13.1}$$

where π is the profit accruing to firms, p' is a vector of output prices, y is a vector of output levels, and $C(w, y)$ is the cost of producing that vector of outputs given the vector of input prices w. Solving the optimization problem yields a vector of optimal output levels y^* and an implied level of input demands conditional on those optimal output levels. $\left[x_i^* \left(y, w \right) = \partial C \left(w, y \right) / \partial w_i \right]$

From the consumer perspective, households choose the vectors of goods (x) that maximize their utility function for a specified price vector w

$$\begin{aligned} max\, U(x) \\ s.t. \ \ w'x \leq I, \end{aligned} \tag{13.2}$$

where I is the level of consumer income. This specification yields a consumer demand for each good of $\bar{x}_i \left(w, I \right)$. Following the arguments of Diewert (1971), the level sets for each demand function can be retrieved from optimization behaviour. Starting from the cost function, we can derive the level sets by

$$M(y) = [x : w'x \geq C(w,y) \ \text{ for all } p >> 0, \ x \geq 0] \tag{13.3}$$

Thus, we can represent the selection of inputs that minimize the cost of production (to maximize profit), as well as the selection of consumption goods that maximize utility, as convex sets in x space.

The top panel of Figure 13.3 presents both the cost minimization problem for the firm and the utility maximization problem of the individual based on the tradeoff between ethanol x_1 and gasoline x_2. The corner solution, a, represents the point where no ethanol is produced or consumed. This solution will hold as long as the ratio of the price of ethanol w_1^0 to the price of gasoline w_2^0 is greater than some observed constant k_0. Different scenarios could lead to a deviation from this corner solution. The price of gasoline could increase (as the price of crude

Figure 13.3. Optimal combination of ethanol and gasoline, and ethanol market

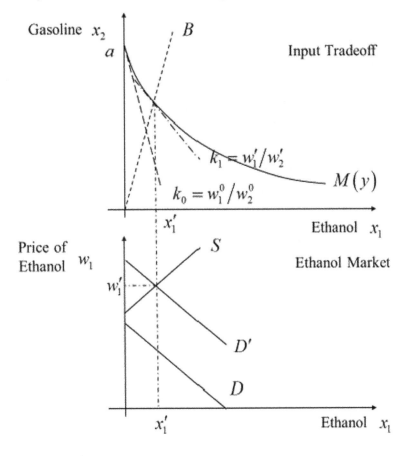

oil rises) or the cost of producing ethanol could decrease (as corn prices drop or investments in ethanol increase). Essentially, the corner solution acts as a choke point for the derived demand curve for inputs used in ethanol production. If the price of gasoline w_2^0 is greater than $-w_1^0/k_0$, no ethanol will be produced and the derived demand for corn used in ethanol production will be zero. However, if the price of gasoline increases to the point where $(w_w' > w_1'/k_1)$ fuel producers demand a non-zero quantity of ethanol and the derived demand for corn in ethanol production will become positive.

The bottom panel of Figure 13.3 depicts the increase in gasoline price on the ethanol market. Originally, the price ratio between ethanol and gasoline yields the corner solution in the top panel (i.e., the price ratio k_0). At this ratio, the supply curve for ethanol (S) and the demand curve for ethanol in the production of fuel (D) do not cross. In this equilibrium, no ethanol is bought or sold for use in the creation of fuel. However, if the price of gasoline relative to ethanol rises to $(w_2' > w_1'/k_1)$, the amount of ethanol used to produce automotive fuel increases to x_1'.

Figure 13.4. Effect of volumetric ethanol excise tax credit on ethanol/gasoline decision

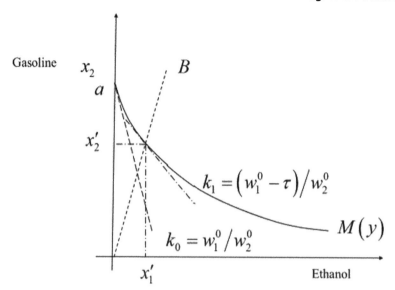

Figure 13.3 depicts concave level sets, but the technology supports more linear level sets (at least in the economically relevant range). Most of our results are based on the assumption that 1.5 gallons of ethanol can be used to replace 1.0 gallon of gasoline (or that the slope of the input requirement set is –2/3). As more ethanol is added, however, technological changes to vehicular carburetors may make the level set surface in Figure 13.2 less convex, implying a non-linear trade-off between gasoline and ethanol.

The foregoing discussion assumes that market changes give rise to increased demand for ethanol. The increased ethanol demand since 2007 has been driven more by policy interventions than changes in the relative ethanol/gasoline price ratio. Consider a slight reformulation of the level set formulation in the top panel of Figure 13.2 presented in Figure 13.4. In Figure 13.4 we hold the price of gasoline constant at w_2^0, but we have reduced the price of ethanol by subtracting a "subsidy" (τ). As described in the introduction to this chapter, this subsidy represents the Volumetric Ethanol Excise Tax Credit (VEETC) of US$0.51 per gallon. The VEETC causes ethanol production to increase. At first glance, the reduction in ethanol prices relative to gasoline in Figure 13.2 would appear inconsistent; however, our analysis holds all other inputs constant. Hence, the lower price can be explained in part by the significant investment in distilleries producing ethanol for fuel.

As described above, a mandated fuel blend replaced the VEETC in 2012 (represented by the ray B in Figures 13.3 and 13.4). The "subsidy" for the use of ethanol was realized by a reduction in the tax liability of corporations purchasing ethanol for blending. While a tax credit is a "dollar-for-dollar" concept (each dollar of tax credit reduces the tax liability by one dollar),

Figure 13.5. Ethanol direct and indirect subsidies

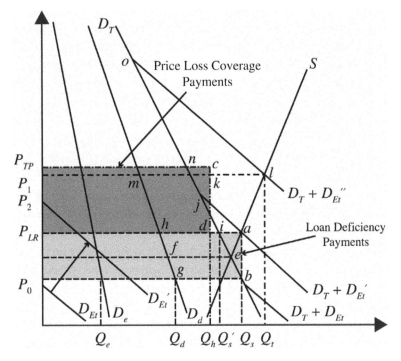

Source: A. Schmitz, Moss, and T.G. Schmitz (2007).

different corporations may have different tax situations. Further, it is unlikely that a US$0.51 per gallon tax credit returned the desired blend level.

13.3.2   US Agricultural Commodity Programs

With reference to Figure 13.5, we discuss the economics of ethanol production in the context of US agricultural policy. For the US corn market, S is the supply schedule and D_T is the total demand. Under the loan rate provisions of the Agricultural Improvement Act of 2018, farmers receive a price of P_{LR} for each bushel of corn produced q_S. Given a domestic demand curve D_d and an export demand curve of D_e, the total demand curve is D_T. These demand curves result in a market clearing price of p^0. With this market clearing price, q_d is consumed domestically and q_e is exported. At this equilibrium, the loan deficiency payments (LDPs) paid to farmers based on the level of production are represented by $(P_{LR}P_0ba)$. In addition, farmers receive a price loss coverage (PLC) payment based on their historical level of production q_h, (typically 85 per cent of historical yields) and the reference price P_{TP}. This payment is depicted by $(P_{TP}P_{LR}dc)$. The net cost of the subsidy program from the US perspective is (*fgbea*), of which (*fgbe*) is a gain to importers (the *slippage effect*).

In the original equilibrium in Figure 13.5, we assume that the market clearing price p_0 is less than the choke price for the derived demand curve for corn used to produce ethanol D_{Et}. Thus, given the total demand curve for both food and ethanol use $(D_T + D_{Et})$ in this situation, no ethanol is produced. Next, we assume that increases in the price of gasoline shift the derived demand for corn used to produce ethanol outward to D'_{Et}. This changes the shape of the total demand curve to $(D_T + D'_{Et})$. This rightward shift in the derived demand for corn from ethanol producers is sufficient to raise the equilibrium price of corn to the loan rate, which will eliminate the loan deficiency payments to farmers. Thus, there are no direct subsidies based on production, but there are indirect subsidies to corn producers via ethanol tax credits. However, farmers continue to receive price loss coverage payments (PLCs) that are unaffected by production decisions.

Starting from D'_{Et} (which assumes a fixed oil price), a sufficiently large increase in corn prices above p_2 chokes off the demand for corn to produce ethanol. This point represents the corner solution in Figure 13.2. However, if one assumes an increase in oil prices for a given price of corn, the derived demand curve for corn will shift to the right. From a theoretical perspective, the demand for corn for ethanol production could be positive without a tax credit. At least two factors affect ethanol production: (1) the favourable oil-to-corn price ratio, and (2) a tax credit for ethanol production.

In the first case, we assume that ethanol demand has no impact on producers, even though corn prices rise. This is because the LDPs no longer exist (the PLCs remain unchanged). Also, an important result is derived from the observation that market clearing prices rise from p_0 to P_{LR}, causing both domestic and export demand to fall for those components making up demand, D_T. Domestic consumers now pay a higher price for corn and related products, given demand Dd. Likewise, foreign importers pay a higher price for the corn they import.

In the model, (1) producers are unaffected by ethanol demand, (2) domestic consumers lose $(P_{LR}P_0gh)$, (3) foreign importers lose $(hgbi)$, (4) the reduced government loan deficiency payments are $(P_{TP}P_{LR}dc)$, (5) the consumers of ethanol gain (jia), and (6) there are government cuts from the indirect subsidy on ethanol production. Extreme caution should be used when interpreting (jia) as this area represents a gain to the consumers of fuel. We calculate this effect by incorporating ethanol into the total demand for fuel in a general equilibrium framework.

To calculate the *net effect* of ethanol, consider (1) the net welfare gain of $(aefgb)$, (2) the consumer gain from the introduction of ethanol of (jia), and (3) the cost of the indirect ethanol subsidy. The first two components are positive while the third component is negative. Ethanol subsidies replace direct subsidies, which affects consumers because the price of corn increases. Production costs are now covered, so direct subsidies are no longer binding.

To further show the interrelationship between ethanol production and government payments to corn farmers, we assume that the derived demand for corn used to produce ethanol shifts farther outward to D''_{Et}. This increased derived demand causes the total demand for corn to shift outward to $(D_T + D''_{Et})$, increasing the market equilibrium price to p_1 and the equilibrium quantity to q_t. Comparing this equilibrium with the equilibrium at the loan rate, producers gain $(p_1P_{LR}al)$. However, part of this gain $(p_1P_{LR}dk)$ is offset by reductions in the countercyclical payments to farmers. Thus, the net producer gain is $(kdal)$. This shift results in an economic loss to domestic consumers of $(p_1P_{LR}hm)$ and a loss to foreign consumers of $(mhdn)$. Also, ethanol producers gain from the ethanol tax.

If the demand for ethanol shifts even farther to the right than D''_{Et}, all government payments (including price loss coverage payments) are eliminated. Thus, there is a direct linkage between tax credits to ethanol and farm program payments.

13.3.3   Overall Impacts

Several researchers have calculated the impacts of US biofuel policies. Among these are the notable researchers Taheripour, Cui, and Tyner (2019). Their results complement the findings presented below.

13.3.4   Price Impacts

Our estimations of the effect of ethanol on corn prices are lower than those of Gardner (2002), Elam (2008), and Tokgoz et al. (2008) (Table 13.1). The market equilibrium price of corn increases from US$2.05 per bushel to US$2.46 per bushel for a difference of US$0.41 per bushel. This brings about changes in the relative components of demand. The food, alcohol, and industrial uses increase from 2,015.9 million bushels to 3,578.5 million bushels, while the demand for corn used in feed decreases from 5,762.5 million bushels to 5,236.74 million bushels and exports decrease from 1,895.6 million bushels to 1,848.37 million bushels. Further, PLCs decrease from US$4.67 billion to US$1.36 billion. As expected, if we increase the magnitude of the demand to 2.0 billion bushels of corn for ethanol, the price of corn will increase (to US$2.56 per bushel), which will almost eliminate PLCs to producers (US$0.58 billion).

13.3.5   Welfare Impacts

The welfare effects associated with ethanol production are presented in Table 13.2. Given a supply elasticity of 0.5, as the equilibrium corn prices shift from US$2.05 per bushel to US$2.46 per bushel (Table 13.1), consumers will lose US$0.82 billion on the food, alcohol, and industrial component, US$2.26 billion on the feed component, and US$0.77 billion on the export component. The industrial component includes the effect of increased corn prices on the high fructose corn syrup (HFCS) market. The HFCS market accounts for roughly 20 per cent of the corn marketed in the United States. As corn prices increase, so does the cost of producing HFCS, which translates into higher HFCS prices and products using HFCS. Sweetener users

Table 13.1. Ethanol production: levels and composition of corn supply and demand

	Supply Elasticities			
	0.4	0.5	0.6	0.7
	Base Scenario (million bushels)			
Corn price (US$/bu)	2.06	2.05	2.04	2.03
Total demand	9,677.39	9,694.31	9,707.53	9,718.15
Food/alcohol/industrial use	2,014.47	2,015.93	2,017.06	2,017.97
Seed use	20.33	20.30	20.28	20.26
Feed/residual use	5,748.25	5,762.46	5,773.58	5,782.50
Exports	1,894.35	1,895.62	1,896.62	1,897.42
CCPs (million $)	4,580.46	4,665.04	4,729.97	4,781.05
	Shift Based on 2006 Market Conditions (million bushels)			
Corn price (US$/bu)	2.53	2.46	2.41	2.36
Total demand	10,580.57	10,684.89	10,766.43	10,831.91
Food/alcohol/industrial use	3,569.52	3,578.46	3,585.46	3,591.07
Seed Use	21.49	21.32	21.19	21.08
Feed/residual use	5,149.08	5,236.74	5,305.26	5,360.29
Exports	1,840.49	1,848.37	1,854.53	1,859.47
CCPs (million $)	814.88	1,364.43	1,792.77	2,135.71
	2.0 Billion-Bushel Shift in Demand (million bushels)			
Corn price (US$/bu)	2.64	2.56	2.49	2.44
Total demand	10,795.06	10,920.13	11,017.89	11,096.40
Food/alcohol/industrial use	3,938.81	3,949.53	3,957.92	3,964.65
Seed use	21.77	21.56	21.40	21.28
Feed/residual use	5,006.79	5,111.89	5,194.05	5,260.02
Exports	1,827.70	1,837.14	1,844.53	1,850.46
CCPs (US$ million)	0.00	580.60	1095.25	1,507.50

Source: A. Schmitz, Moss, and T.G. Schmitz (2007).
CCPs = countercyclical payments; bu = bushels.

lose from both higher HFCS and sugar prices, while sugar producers gain as the price of the substitute sweetener (HFCS) increases.

The effect of ethanol expansion on corn producers is somewhat more complicated. Overall, the market income of producers increases by US$4.19 billion ($p_1 P_{LR}al$) in Figure 13.3. However, part of this gain (US$3.30 billion in Table 13.2) represents lost countercyclical payments ($p_1 P_{LR}dk$) in Figure 13.4. The net gain to producers (producer welfare impact) is US$0.88 billion (US$4.19 billion minus US$3.30 billion in lost countercyclical payments in Table 13.2). Increasing the demand shift from 1.6 billion bushels to 2.0 billion bushels produces similar results.

There is an aggregate net welfare cost of between US$1.82 and US$1.97 billion associated with the US shift to the ethanol program, based on 2006 market conditions (Table 13.2). However, from a US perspective, the loss is reduced, ranging between US$0.95 million and US$1.35 million, where the losses to importers are not considered. For an ethanol demand of

Table 13.2. Welfare impacts of shifts in corn demand (US$ million)[a]

	Supply Elasticities			
	0.4	0.5	0.6	0.7
	Shift Based on 2006 Market Conditions			
Food/alcohol/industrial use	−928.66	−816.96	−729.24	−658.52
Seed use	9.79	8.55	7.59	6.82
Feed/residual use	−2,550.52	−2,258.79	−2,026.70	−1,837.73
Exports[b]	−874.14	−768.86	−686.22	−619.61
Producer welfare impact	975.80	884.45	808.20	743.89
Reduction in direct payments	3,765.57	3,300.61	2,297.20	2,645.34
Increased ethanol tax credits[c]	−2,220.60	−2,231.30	−2,239.67	−2,246.39
Aggregate net gain, excluding new product effect[d]	−1,822.76	−1,882.31	−1,928.84	−1,966.20
Net gain to United States, excluding product effect	−949.00	−1,113.00	−1,246.00	−1,346.00
	2.0 Billion-Bushel Shift in Demand			
Food/alcohol/industrial use	−1,144.99	−1,007.73	−899.85	−812.82
Seed use	18.08	15.80	14.03	12.61
Feed/residual use	−3,544.50	−3,094.13	−2,745.21	−2,466.95
Exports[b]	−1,135.93	−993.18	−882.29	−793.67
Producer welfare impact	1,349.01	1,154.26	1,057.06	974.53
Reduction in Treasury cost	4,580.46	4,084.44	3,634.72	3273.55
Increased ethanol tax credits[c]	−2,747.94	−2,761.19	−2,771.54	−2,779.86
Aggregate net gain, excluding new product effect[d]	−2,625.82	−2,601.74	−2,593.09	−2,592.61
Net gain to United States, excluding product effect	−1,490.00	−1,609.00	−1,711.00	−1,799.00

Source: A. Schmitz, Moss, and T.G. Schmitz (2007).
[a] Ignoring the impact of ethanol on the gasoline market.
[b] We present numbers on how importers are affected from rising corn prices. While this is a loss to importers, the effect for the United States was taken into account by the reduction in net farm program payments due to increased ethanol.
[c] Ethanol tax credits are computed at US$0.51 for each gallon based on 2.8 gallons of ethanol for each bushel of corn.
[d] The bounded area between the total corn demand with and without ethanol ranges from between US$3.1 billion and US$3.9 billion. As shown in Table 13.4, this estimate is roughly comparable to the net gain estimate of the effect of ethanol in the context of the total fuels market.

2.0 billion bushels of corn, the net welfare cost to the United States ranges from US$1.49 billion to US$1.80 billion. In terms of distributional effects, the largest loss occurs in the feed and residual market. There is also a loss to importers. There is a producer gain along with a reduction in the direct payment cost. However, there is also an ethanol tax credit cost.

13.3.6   Ethanol Processors and Tax Credits

Our previous models did not account for profitability for ethanol processors. The profitability of ethanol production depends on many factors, including the price of corn and the price of

Figure 13.6. Ethanol processor profitability

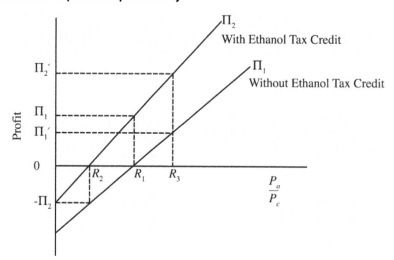

fossil fuels. The lower the price of corn and the higher the price of oil, the greater the profitability for using corn to produce ethanol. There is some combination of oil and corn prices where ethanol production will be economically feasible, even in the absence of ethanol tax credits. Further, there is some combination of oil and corn prices where ethanol production would be profitable even in the absence of direct corn subsidies.

Consider Figure 13.6 where the profits of the processing of the ethanol sector are graphed against the ratio of the price of oil to the price of corn (P_o / P_c). At ratio R_1, there are only positive processing profits, π_1, with the ethanol tax credit in place. At R_3, profits for the processing sector are positive regardless of the subsidy. However, at R_2, profits are zero even in the presence of subsidies but negative in the absence of the ethanol tax credit. Implicit in Figure 13.6 is the choice between direct ethanol subsidies through tax credits and indirect subsidies through farm commodity payments. Clearly, in the absence of ethanol credits, there is still the possibility of subsidizing ethanol production through subsidies for corn producers.

Figure 13.7 illustrates the relationship between ethanol production and the gasoline-to-corn price ratio. As the ratio increases, so does ethanol production. At a ratio of 0.20, ethanol production is about 40,000 billion barrels. Production increased by approximately a factor of 4, at a ratio of 1.0. We regress the level of ethanol production q in million barrels on the ratio of the gasoline price P^G to corn price P^C. The result is given as

$$q_t^E = -31,697.05 + 132,896.4 \left(P_t^G \Big/ P_t^C \right) + \varepsilon_t$$
$$(24,279.00)\ (33,926.4)$$

(13.4)

Figure 13.7. Relationship between ethanol production and relative ethanol price ratio

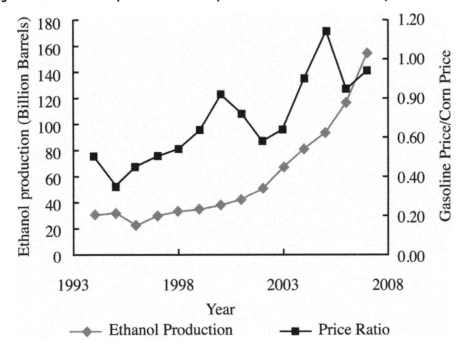

where the numbers in parentheses denote standard errors of the estimated parameters. As hypothesized, a change in the relative price of gasoline to corn affects US production of ethanol.

13.3.7 Ethanol in the Broader Energy Picture

Earlier we discussed the interface between the ethanol market and the oil and gas market and raised the question of whether the emergence of ethanol represents a new product or simply competes with existing fossil fuel products. It is possible that ethanol production could exist under a free market situation with no direct payments to corn farmers or tax credits to ethanol producers. Figure 13.8 presents a more general equilibrium picture where ethanol is integrated into the overall fuels market consistent with the earlier theoretical model. Figure 13.8a presents the equilibrium in the crude oil market. The domestic supply curve for crude oil, S_f^c, when added to the foreign supply curve for crude oil, S_T^c, gives the total supply of crude oil in the fuels market, S_T^c, in Figure 13.8b. The addition of the marginal cost of refining crude oil into gasoline yields the supply curve of gasoline, S_T^g. Consider the original demand curve for gasoline in the United States as D_g. The corresponding price of gasoline will be P_g with q_g gallons of gasoline consumed. At the equilibrium price of oil of (P_c, q_d^c) barrels of oil are

Figure 13.8. Effect of ethanol on the oil market

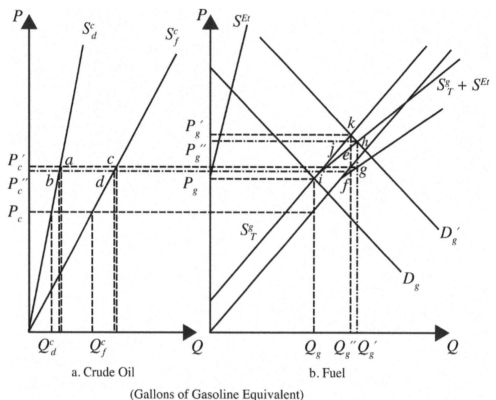

a. Crude Oil   b. Fuel

(Gallons of Gasoline Equivalent)

produced domestically and q_f^c barrels of crude oil are supplied by foreign producers (Figure 13.8a). Next, assume that the demand for gasoline shifts outward to D_g' (Figure 13.8b). At this equilibrium, the price of gasoline is p_g' and the resulting price of crude oil is P_c' (Figure 13.8a). However, we assume that this increase in gasoline prices results in the expansion of ethanol supply along the supply curve S^{Et}. This supply shifts the total supply of gasoline (in combination with gasohol) outward to $(S_T^g + S^{Et})$. This expansion in supply reduces the market price of fuel down to P_g'' and reduces the price of crude oil to P_c''. Hence, the net welfare loss to domestic crude oil producers from the production of ethanol is $(P_c'abP_c'')$. The net welfare loss to foreign suppliers of crude oil is $(P_c'cdP_c'')$ and the economic loss to fuel refiners is $(efgh)$ (Figure 13.8b). However, this loss is partially offset by gains to ethanol processors of (iej). In addition, fuel consumers in the domestic fuel market gain a surplus of $(P_g'P_g''hk)$.

Rather than attempting to calculate the bounded area between the total demand for corn with and without ethanol, we calculate the welfare gains and losses from ethanol directly in the overall fuels market. We calculate the market demand for gasoline to be

Table 13.3. US ethanol and the broader fuels market

	Supply Elasticities (Corn)			
	0.4	0.5	0.6	0.7
	Shift Based on 2006 Market Conditions			
Gasoline market price ($/gal)	2.969	2.969	2.969	2.969
Gasoline market quantity (billion gal)	139.726	139.730	139.733	139.733
Gain in consumer surplus (billion $)	4.369	4.390	4.411	4.411
Loss to gasoline & oil producers (billion $)	−4.358	−4.378	−4.399	−4.399
Loss to foreign producers (billion $)	−3.042	−3.057	−3.071	−3.071
Loss to domestic producers (billion $)	−1.307	−1.314	−1.320	−1.320
Gain to ethanol producers (billion $)	0.046	0.046	0.046	0.046
Net welfare gain (billion $)	3.107	3.122	3.138	3.138
	2.0 Billion-Bushel Shift in Demand			
Gasoline market price ($/gal)	2.961	2.961	2.961	2.961
Gasoline market quantity (billion gal)	139.897	139.904	139.907	139.907
Gain in consumer surplus (billion $)	5.397	5.439	5.460	5.460
Loss to gasoline & oil producers (billion $)	−5.379	−5.421	−5.442	−5.442
Loss to foreign producers (billion $)	−3.753	−3.782	−3.797	−3.797
Loss to domestic producers (billion $)	−1.614	−1.626	−1.633	−1.633
Gain to ethanol producers (billion $)	0.069	0.070	0.071	0.071
Net welfare gain (billion $)	3.852	3.883	3.898	3.898

Source: A. Schmitz, Moss, and T.G. Schmitz (2007).

139.28 billion gallons (USDE 2007), assuming that each bushel of corn yields 2.8 gallons of ethanol and that 1.5 gallons of ethanol are required to yield the same energy as 1.0 gallon of gasoline (Table 13.3). An increase of 2.1 billion bushels of corn will yield 3.92 billion gallons of gasoline-equivalent fuel in the domestic market, which will generate a 2.82 per cent increase in gasoline equivalents. An increase in the gasoline supply by 2.82 per cent from the introduction of ethanol will lower the price of gasoline by US$0.043 per gallon, assuming a -0.50 elasticity of demand for gasoline. For an elasticity of -0.25, the impact will be US$0.06 per gallon.

In Table 13.3 we show the results of the impact of increased ethanol production. The gain to consumers ranges from US$4.4 billion to US$5.5 billion. The gain to ethanol processors is roughly US$50 million, which is somewhat lower than that obtained by Gardner (2007). The loss to gasoline and oil producers is roughly of the same magnitude. When one excludes the loss to oil exporters, the net welfare gain for ethanol ranges from US$3.10 billion to US$3.90 billion.

There is considerable debate over the impact ethanol has on gasoline prices. For example, using an econometrics approach, Elam (2008) argues there is no relationship between ethanol production and gasoline prices. However, Du and Hayes (2008) show that increased ethanol production has depressed US gasoline prices by between US$0.29 and US$0.40 per gallon.

Table 13.4. Summary of welfare costs and benefits of US ethanol production (US$ million)[a]

Category	Gains	Losses	Gains	Losses
		$e_s = 0.5$		$e_s = 0.7$
Food/alcohol/industrial use		−1,008		−813
Feed/residual use		−3,094		−2,466
Producer impact	1,154		975	
Treasury costs	4,084		3,274	
Ethanol tax credit		−2,761		−2,780
Change in surplus in fuel market	3,883		3,898	
Other	16		13	
Total	9,137	−6,863	9,447	−6,059
Net gain (domestic)	+2,274		+3,388	
Foreign net cost (grain market)		−993		−794
Net gain (global)	+1,281		+2,594	

Source: A. Schmitz, Moss, and T.G. Schmitz (2007).
[a] Corn demand from ethanol totals 2 billion bushels.
E_s = excess supply.

ETHANOL PRODUCTION AND GASOLINE PRICES

"Increasing US ethanol production is having no effect on US gasoline prices or re-fining margins. Crude oil prices, gasoline inventories, crude oil inventories, refinery utilization rates, seasonal demand patterns, and temporary gasoline supply issues of 2005–7 have been the drivers of the gasoline prices and margins" (Elam 2008, 16).

13.3.8   Overall Impact of Ethanol

Table 13.4 gives an overview of the welfare costs and benefits of US ethanol production. We present the net gains from both a domestic and global perspective. When the cost to those outside the United States is not taken into account, the net benefit from ethanol production exceeds US$2.27 billion. However, if we exclude the gasoline market, there are net costs from ethanol production. There are net costs to corn importers from ethanol production, but these are gains to the United States in terms of reduced subsidy payments to corn farmers. From a global perspective, the net gains from ethanol production range between US$1.28 billion and US$2.60 billion. Even though there are net losses to importers from US ethanol production, corn producers in importing countries gain while their consumers lose.

13.3.9   Treasury Costs with and without Ethanol

An often-neglected element is the impact of ethanol on US government farm payments. Table 13.5 presents the relative Treasury cost under the price loss coverage payments and the

Table 13.5. Comparison of CCPs with an ethanol tax credit

	Elasticity of Corn Supply			
	0.4	0.5	0.6	0.7
	Shift Based on 2006 Market Conditions			
Increased corn production (million bu)	1,555.04	1,562.54	1,568.40	1,573.10
Decreased countercyclical payment (million $)	3,765.57	3,300.61	2,937.20	2,645.34
Increased tax credit on ethanol (million $)	2,220.60	2,231.30	2,239.67	2,246.39
	2.0 Billion–Bushel Shift in Demand			
Increased corn production (million bu)	1,924.33	1,933.61	1,940.86	1,946.68
Decreased countercyclical payment (million $)	4,580.46	4,084.44	3,634.72	3,273.55
Increased tax credit on ethanol (million $)	2,747.94	2,761.19	2,771.54	2,779.86

Source: A. Schmitz, Moss, and T.G. Schmitz (2007).

tax credits to ethanol. For a 0.5 corn supply elasticity scenario, the 1.6 billion-bushel shift in the food, alcohol, and industrial demand for corn implies an increase of 1.56 billion bushels of corn, which accounts for the price responsiveness of demand. This shift, coupled with the increased price of corn, results in a US$3.30 billion decrease in CCPs under US agricultural policy. However, assuming that each bushel of corn produces 2.8 gallons of ethanol, and that each gallon of ethanol implies a tax credit of US$0.51, there is a Treasury cost of US$2.23 billion. Hence, the overall Treasury cost decreases by US$1.07 billion.

13.3.10 Mandate and Renewable Identification Numbers

The ethanol policy in the United States is a subset of the US Energy Policy implemented through the US Environmental Protection Agency (USEPA). As discussed earlier, the Energy Independence and Security Act (EISA) of 2007 increased the policy emphasis on ethanol as a renewable fuel. This Act established the series of volumetric standards or goals (Table 13.6). In setting forth these goals, the USEPA set up four categories of renewable energy:

1 Biomass-based diesel must meet a 50 per cent lifecycle greenhouse gas (GHG) reduction.
2 Cellulosic biofuel must be produced from cellulose, hemicellulose, or lignin and must meet a 60 per cent lifecycle GHG reduction.
3 Advanced biofuel can be produced from qualifying renewable biomass (except corn starch) and must meet a 50 per cent GHG reduction.
4 Renewable (or conventional) fuel typically refers to ethanol derived from corn starch and must meet a 20 per cent lifecycle GHG reduction threshold.

A variety of policies were implemented to meet these targets, but from our perspective the most significant intervention was the VEETC. While the Energy Policy Act of 2004 and the

Table 13.6. EISA volumetric standards

Year	Cellulosic Biofuel	Biomass-Based Diesel	Advanced Biofuel	Total Renewable Fuel	"Conventional" Biofuel
2009	NA	0.50	0.60	11.10	10.50
2010	0.10	0.65	0.95	12.95	12.00
2011	0.25	0.80	1.35	13.95	12.60
2012	0.50	1.00	2.00	15.20	13.20
2013	1.00	—*	2.75	16.55	13.80
2014	1.75	—*	3.75	18.15	14.40
2015	3.00	—*	5.50	20.50	15.00
2016	4.25	—*	7.25	22.25	15.00
2017	5.50	—*	9.00	24.00	15.00
2018	7.00	—*	11.00	26.00	15.00
2019	8.50	—*	13.00	28.00	15.00
2020	10.50	—*	18.00	33.00	15.00

* The statute sets a one billion gallon minimum, but the EPA may raise the requirement.
Source: USEPA (2020).

Energy Independence and Security Act (EISA) of 2007 modified the VEETC, its basic provisions were introduced as Section 301 of the American Jobs Creation Act of 2004.

As previously discussed, a renewable fuels mandate enforced through Renewable Identification Numbers (RINs) replaced the VEETC in 2012. In the current Renewable Fuel Standard Program, the process starts with the creation of unblended gasoline. As depicted in Figure 13.9, the production or importation of unblended gasoline creates a Renewable Volume Obligation (RVO). To offset this RVO, the fuel refinery or importer must purchase the right to buy a quantity of renewable fuel (i.e., cellulosic biofuels [RIN types D3/D7], biomass-based diesel [RIN type D4], advanced biofuels [RIN type D5], and ethanol [RIN type D6]). This right to purchase ethanol is created by the production of one of the biofuel types. As depicted in Figure 13.9, when biofuel producers create a biofuel, they generate an RIN (RINs can be separated from the biofuel and sold in a secondary market). Following the fuel through the market, the fuel refinery sells the fuel along with the right to purchase biofuel to blenders who combine the gasoline with ethanol purchased on the open market. When the biofuel is blended with non-renewable fuel, the RIN is fulfilled, and the RIN is retired with the USEPA.

To develop the consequences of this blend wall, consider an extension of the fuel blender's model in Equation 13.1

$$max\ \pi^* = pf(x_1, x_2, x_3) - w_1 x_1 - w_3 x_3$$
$$s.t. \frac{x_1}{x_2} = R \tag{13.5}$$

where x_1 is the level of ethanol used and w_1 is the price of ethanol, x_2 is the level of gasoline used and w_2 is the price of gasoline, x_3 is the quantity of another input such as labour and w_3

Figure 13.9. Renewable identification number system

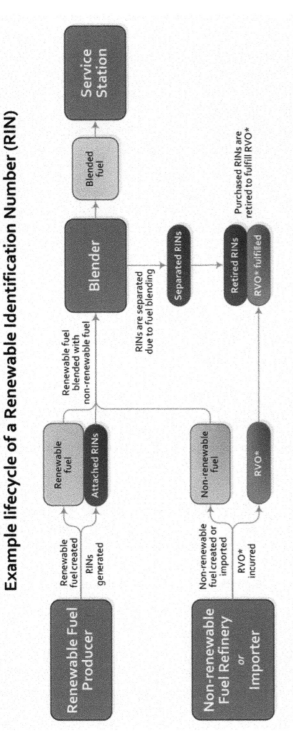

Example lifecycle of a Renewable Identification Number (RIN)

* RVO = Renewable Volume Obligation

is the price, and R is the mandated blend ratio (gallons of ethanol required for each gallon of gasoline, the ray B in top panel of Figure 13.3).

Transforming the profit maximization problem slightly, and forming the Lagrange yields

$$L = p f(x_1, x_2, x_3) - w_1 x_1 - w_2 x_2 - w_3 x_3 + \lambda(x_2 R - x_1) \tag{13.6}$$

where λ is the Lagrange multiplier for the rewritten constraint (i.e., $[R - x_1 / x_2 \Rightarrow x_2 R - x_1]$). The first-order conditions for this Lagrange formulation becomes

$$\frac{\partial L}{\partial x_1} = p \frac{\partial f}{\partial x_1} - \lambda - w_1 = 0$$

$$\frac{\partial L}{\partial x_2} = p \frac{\partial f}{\partial x_2} + \lambda R - w_2 = 0$$

$$\frac{\partial L}{\partial x_2} = p \frac{\partial f}{\partial x_3} - w_3 = 0 \tag{13.7}$$

$$\frac{\partial L}{\partial \lambda} = x_1 R - x_2 = 0$$

For our current purposes, let us focus on the first and second conditions. Taking the first condition, we can derive the value of the Lagrange multiplier

$$\lambda = p \frac{\partial f}{\partial x_1} - w_1. \tag{13.8}$$

In equilibrium, the value of the marginal product of ethanol equals the price of ethanol. If the blending constraint is not binding, the Lagrange multiplier's value at optimal is zero. Substituting this result into the second Lagrange condition yields

$$p \frac{\partial f}{\partial x_2} + \left[p \frac{\partial f}{\partial x_1} - w_1 \right] R - w_2 = 0. \tag{13.9}$$

Again, notice that if the amount of ethanol is consistent with the unconstrained solution, the optimal level of gasoline is also consistent with the unconstrained amount. However, given that the current policy involves constraining the ethanol use above its free market solution

$$p \frac{\partial f}{\partial x_2} - w_1 \ll 0 \tag{13.10}$$

the marginal value product for ethanol at the point of production will be less than its price. Hence, $\left[p \partial f / \partial x_1 - w_1 \right] R \ll 0$ or the price of gasoline is implicitly increased by the requirement that an increase in gasoline must be accompanied by proportional increase in a less productive input.

Figure 13.10. Market clearing ethanol and RIN prices under mandate

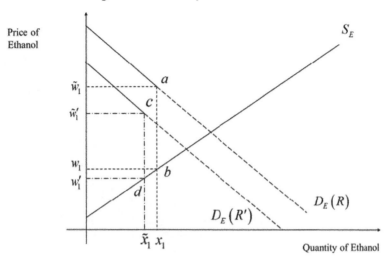

Thus, a mandated blend ratio increases the amount of ethanol used in the creation of fuel by its very nature. However, this increase in the amount of ethanol decreases the amount of gasoline used at any set of prices (that is for any fixed combination of fuel price, gasoline or oil prices, ethanol prices, and other input prices). This decrease reduces the amount of fuel produced – shifting the supply curve for fuel upward. If the demand curve for fuel is fixed, this results in higher fuel prices. While the effect of the mandate on gasoline/oil prices is somewhat uncertain, it is clear that the price of ethanol will be higher than without the mandate.

Given the implications of the mandated blend on supply of fuel, we turn to how the RINs affect the ethanol market. Figure 13.10 provides a graphical depiction of the supply and demand equilibrium in the ethanol market. Let us focus first on an original mandated blend ratio R. Given this blend ratio and the optimal decisions of fuel producers, there is a maximum amount of ethanol that fuel producers wish to use ($x_1 = {}_{\text{Rx2}}$). The demand curve for any level of ethanol above this amount is essentially zero. At this restricted level, the value of ethanol in the production of fuel is $\tilde{w}_1$ (where $\tilde{w}_1 = p\partial f / \partial x_1 - \lambda$ from the fuel producer's problem); however, at this quantity the ethanol producers only demand a price of w_1. The concept is that RIN price is then set as the difference between the fuel producer's willingness to pay and the ethanol producer's willingness to accept ($P'_{RIN} = \tilde{w}'_1 - w'_1$). The rent accruing to the ethanol producers from the RIN market is then $\tilde{w}_1 abw_1$.

As a slight extension, consider what happens as the mandate declines from R to R'. As the mandate declines, the demand curve for ethanol under the mandate shifts inward and the point of discontinuity on the demand curve for ethanol shifts to the left. Hence, the

Figure 13.11. Ethanol market prices for RINs, 2010–19

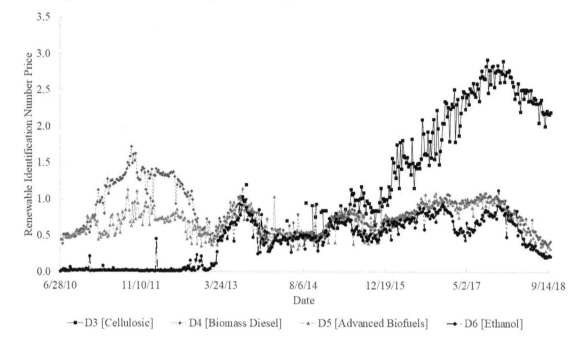

amount that fuel producers are willing to pay declines from $\tilde{w}_1$ to w_1'. While the price ethanol producers are willing to accept for ethanol declines from w_1 to w_1', the price of the RIN falls to $\left(P_{RIN}' = \tilde{w}_1' - w_1' \right)$.

Figure 13.11 presents the market prices for RINs from 2010 through 2019. In general, the price for ethanol RINs (D6) was zero until 2012, when VEETC ended. Afterward, RIN increased to US$0.50 per gallon in 2017, before falling to around US$0.20 per gallon at the end of 2018.

13.3.11   Effect of Ethanol Programs on Food Prices

Often, the impact of biofuels production on corn and food prices is overstated. The initial impact of increased energy prices will be a widening of the margin between consumer prices and farm prices. In Figure 13.12, D_c is the consumer demand for food items produced using agricultural outputs, and D_F is the farm level demand for those agricultural outputs. The difference between the curves is the marginal cost of transforming agricultural outputs into consumer products. Rising energy prices increase the cost of transforming agricultural outputs into consumer goods. Thus, the farm-level demand curve shifts to the left from D_F to D_F' due to the increased marginal cost. In addition, rising energy prices increase the cost of agricultural

Figure 13.12. Effect of increased energy prices on farm and food prices

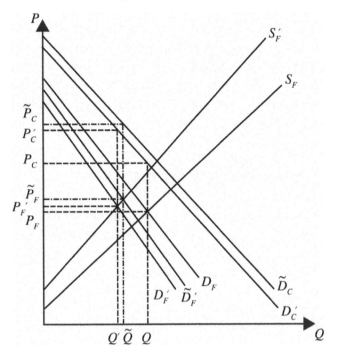

production, shifting the farm supply curve to the left, from S_F to S_F'. The combination of supply and demand effects results in a decline in agricultural output, from Q to Q'. Farm-level prices increase from P_F to P_F'. However, regardless of the effect of rising fuel prices on farm-level prices, rising prices result in increased consumer prices, from P_C to P_c'. Without considering the impact of biofuel demand, rising fuel prices lead to increased consumer food prices.

Next, to model the impact of biofuel demand on food prices, we shift the demand for products made from agricultural outputs (e.g., ethanol from corn) in Figure 13.12 to the right, from D_c to $\tilde{D}_c$ (the demand curve for products produced from agricultural output is the horizontal summation of the demand for each product; it shifts to the right as the demand curve for biofuels increases). In this scenario, the price paid by consumers shifts upward from P_c' to $\tilde{P}_c$ as the total quantity of agricultural output processed increases from Q' to $\tilde{Q}$ (a portion of this increase is the increased use of corn to produce biofuel). In addition, farm-level prices increase from P_F' to $\tilde{P}_F$. While the price of agricultural commodities is higher after the advent of biofuel than it is with the increased energy price alone, the net impact of the two shocks (increased energy prices and increase in biofuel demand) may cause agricultural prices to increase or decrease from the initial equilibrium, P_F, depending on the impact of energy prices on the cost of transforming agricultural outputs into consumer goods.

We do not estimate the impact of ethanol production from corn on retail food prices. A study by Tokgoz et al. (2007) estimates that a 30 per cent increase in the price of corn and the associated increases in the price of wheat and soybeans will increase egg prices by 8.1 per cent, poultry prices by 5.1 per cent, pork prices by 4.5 per cent, beef prices by 4.1 per cent, and milk prices by 2.7 per cent. For all food consumed at home, average prices would increase by 1.3 per cent. For food consumed away from home, average prices were estimated to increase by 0.9 per cent. So, across all food consumed, a 30 per cent higher corn price will increase all average food prices by 1.1 per cent (Tokgoz et al. 2007).

13.4   IMPACT ANALYSIS: LIMITATIONS

First, the above results are overstated with respect to the price impact from ethanol production since we have not included the production of distillers grain (DG) as a by-product of ethanol production. As a result, the welfare costs to US consumers are also overstated. Seventeen pounds of distillers grain are produced from fifty-six pounds of corn (Tokgoz et al. 2007). Therefore, from 1.6 billion bushels of corn, roughly 500 million bushels of distillers grain are produced. If distillers grain is priced in a manner similar to corn, the gross sales of distillers grain will range from US$1.0 billion to US$1.5 billion (although there will be little agreement as to the price of distillers grain). Distillers grain is sold as a by-product from the ethanol processors. Second, a critical assumption is that the increase in demand for corn for ethanol is entirely due to the ethanol tax credit. If this is not the case, then the welfare gains from the ethanol tax credit will be overstated. Third, our estimates of the savings and direct subsidies are somewhat higher than reported by Babcock (2008); however, like Babcock, we show that the direct payments essentially will fall to zero in the presence of ethanol production. For example, in Babcock's analysis, annual direct payments to corn producers will fall from US$2.1 billion to US$6 million in 2008. Fourth, over the estimation time period, corn prices rose because of increased ethanol demand and rising fuel prices as the supply curve of corn shifted leftward due to rising input costs. Fifth, there is considerable debate on the environmental impacts of ethanol production. Elam (2007) argues that there are large environmental costs associated with ethanol. Fatka (2007) contends that biofuels harm water quality and create water supply problems. Babcock, Rubin, and Feng (2007) raise questions as to whether corn ethanol is a low-carbon fuel. We have not factored these costs into our analysis, nor have we factored in positive environmental benefits from ethanol production. Sixth, as the price of corn increases because of ethanol production, there is a shift in acreage to corn away from crops such as soybeans (Tokgoz et al. 2007). These general equilibrium effects should be recognized in cost-benefit analyses. Seventh, we have not factored in the protection offered ethanol from the high US ethanol tariffs on imports.

13.5   FOOD CONCERNS: NO FREE LUNCH

Part of the controversy over the use of food commodities such as corn for the production of ethanol is because corn prices rise due to ethanol production. This, in turn, affects food prices. Those who oppose ethanol production argue that it is unethical to inflict harm (due to rising food costs) on low-income consumers by promoting the US ethanol production, especially when subsidies have been used to do so. Often newspaper headlines have titles similar to "biofuels forcing world to ration food aid." According to D.T. Avery and A.A. Avery (2008), US ethanol production from corn has doubled and tripled world food prices. As a result, countries such as China are blocking further expansion of their biofuel programs due to the food inflation rate.

> **FOOD SHORTAGES**
> Oxfam has pointed out that the poor in developing countries often spend 60–80 per cent of their incomes on food, so any price increase drastically threatens their well-being, especially due to food shortages in the household (D.T. Avery and A.A. Avery 2008).

Given the global production of ethanol from food stocks, the effect of ethanol programs worldwide has to be considered when addressing the impact of biofuel production on food shortages (Moss and Schmitz 2019). The impact of biofuels on poor people is much greater than the effects on the wealthy.

> **ETHANOL IN BRAZIL**
> In Brazil, roughly 40 per cent of the automotive fuel/gasoline consumed is in the form of ethanol produced from sugar cane. Also, subsidies in Brazil, often in a hidden form, have a major positive impact on ethanol production in Brazil (T.G. Schmitz, A. Schmitz, and Seale 2003). Further, relative to corn, sugar cane produces much more energy than is required to produce it. The gross domestic product (GDP) of the sugar and alcohol sectors of Brazil accounts for 6.91 per cent of total GDP for Brazil (Loures and Tavares 2018).

13.6   SUPPORT FOR AND OPPOSITION TO BIOFUELS

In view of the complex modelling needed to determine the gainers and losers from ethanol production, there is little wonder that there is disagreement on whether subsidizing ethanol production is a winner. Economists are divided on investments in biofuels, especially given the complex nature of the interrelationships between energy used for corn production and ethanol produced from corn. In addition, one has to take into account the impact of ethanol tax credits, the potential for producing ethanol under free market conditions, and the degree to which subsidies on ethanol offset the direct subsidy to corn producers.

Using the economic framework along the lines of R.E. Just, Hueth, and Schmitz (2004), Gardner (2007), A. Schmitz, Moss, and T.G. Schmitz (2007), and Hochman, Sexton, and Zilberman (2008) examine theoretically and empirically the impacts of ethanol production. Gardner's results show that there can be sizeable net costs from subsidizing ethanol production in the United States. A. Schmitz, Moss, and T.G. Schmitz show that this can be the case unless ethanol production causes a drop in gasoline prices. Hochman, Sexton, and Zilberman are more positive on the net benefits of ethanol and biofuels generally.

13.7   SUMMARY AND CONCLUSIONS

- The United States has seen a significant increase in the production of ethanol from corn. This increase will likely continue along with the production of biofuels, an industry that some argue has unlimited growth potential.
- The increase in biofuels supply has added to the growth in domestic US energy production. This has reduced the US reliance on energy imports.
- Opinions differ about whether using food to produce ethanol is a sound economic policy.
- Our models raise some important issues with regard to general equilibrium effects versus partial analysis. While we provide empirical estimates on the distributional impacts of producing ethanol from corn, future research should extend our explicit modelling of the fossil fuels market in conjunction with the ethanol market. Results from estimates using the new product market approach should be compared with estimates obtained from the gasoline market.
- The biofuels industry has experienced financial difficulties, which have triggered a high degree of industry consolidation.
- One solution might be a new type of program for ethanol production. A tax credit for ethanol production would be a function of the oil-corn price ratio where the subsidy would be triggered only when the ratio reaches a certain level.
- Because of political pressures, incentives for biofuel production will continue, but perhaps with a decrease in emphasis on ethanol production. Biodiesels will add to the overall energy supply.
- One thing is clear: the debate over biofuels as an energy source is unlikely to be resolved quickly or easily. Even so, growth in the biofuels industry is likely to continue.

CHAPTER FOURTEEN

Climate Change and Agriculture

14.1 INTRODUCTION

There is intense global debate on climate change and what might be the impacts. In 2015 the Paris Agreement of the United Nations (UN) Framework Convention on Climate Change was signed. Its aim was "to strengthen the global response to the threat of climate change by keeping a global temperature rise in this century well below 2 degrees Celsius above pre-industrial levels and to pursue efforts to limit the temperature increase even further to 1.5 degrees Celsius. Additionally, the agreement aims to strengthen the ability of countries to deal with the impacts of climate change" (United Nations Climate Change 2018). The 2015 Paris Agreement has not been without controversy. A major player, the United States, withdrew from the Paris Agreement in 2020, and then rejoined under President Biden.

WHAT IS CLIMATE?
The Merriam-Webster dictionary defines climate as "the average course or condition of the weather at a place usually over a period of years as exhibited by temperature, wind velocity, and precipitation." Climate consists of all these aspects – heat units during the growing season, the amount and timing of rainfall, and the timing and intensity of winds. In contrast, climate change refers mainly to the mean global surface temperature, but its determination is suspect as there is no statistically agreed upon means for aggregating surface temperature readings from weather monitoring stations across the globe (van Kooten 2013, 16–35). The best temperature data come from satellites, which have been available only since 1979.

Considerable uncertainty surrounds the international climate change agenda. Scientists disagree regarding (1) the extent to which average global temperatures are likely to increase (Lewis and Curry 2015; Hourdin et al. 2017; Millar et al. 2017; McKitrick and Christy 2018); (2) the regional changes in climate that might be expected (Lomborg 2007; Pielke 2018b); and (3) human-based versus nature-based contributions to global warming (de Laat and Maurellis 2004, 2006; Khilyuk and Chilingar 2006; McKitrick and Michaels 2004, 2007; McKitrick and Nierenberg 2010; Lewis 2018).

The water is also muddy regarding any potential damages from future climate changes, as well as any potential benefits of mitigating (avoiding) future climate change. This is seen in the controversy over the estimates of the optimal path that carbon taxes should take. The tax is determined by economists as the social cost of carbon, which depends on estimates (in dollars) of the expected economic damages from global warming (Nordhaus 2013; Pindyck 2013; van Kooten 2013; Tol 2014; Dayaratna, McKitrick, and Kreutzer 2017; Auffhammer 2018). For instance, many estimates of potential economic damages from climate change are related to goods and services that are not traded in markets (e.g., wetland services, biodiversity, heat/cold stress, threats to national security). These values are not only difficult to measure, but it is also unclear how they are impacted by changes in climate.

Agriculture is a major sector projected to be, on net, adversely affected by climate change. As our empirical results show, agriculture in some parts of the world could gain from climate change. We note that agricultural land-use practices and greenhouse gas (GHG) emissions from the agricultural sector are major factors in global warming. For example, zero tillage practices (direct drilling – crops sown directly into the soil) are promoted as a means to sequester carbon in soil; reducing meat consumption could reduce GHG emissions since the livestock sector accounts for "14.5% of total anthropogenic greenhouse gas emissions" (FAO 2017a, 9). In this chapter, our focus is on the impact of climate change on crop production and yield. To do this, we emphasize the grain sector, as grains account for the majority of the calories consumed by humans and animals.

INTERNATIONAL CLIMATE ACTION

The Intergovernmental Panel on Climate Change (IPCC) was jointly established in 1988 by the World Meteorological Organization and the United Nations Environmental Program to assess the risk of anthropogenic (human-induced) climate change, along with its potential impacts and how it might be prevented. Natural causes of climate changes and adaptation were not part of the IPCC's mandate. At the Earth Summit in Rio de Janeiro, Brazil, in 1992, countries signed the UN Framework Convention on Climate Change (FCCC). At the third annual Conference of the Parties

(COP) in 1997, held in Kyoto, Japan, countries agreed to the Kyoto Protocol, which required industrialized nations to reduce their emissions of CO_2 by an average of 5.2 per cent from the baseline 1990 emissions by 2008–12 (van Kooten 2004). Success at meeting the Kyoto targets was mixed, with some countries failing to reach their targets, but global emissions of CO_2 continued to rise as China, India, and other developing countries increased emissions dramatically.

A new agreement, known as the Paris Agreement, was struck at COP21 in December 2015. Each country provided its Intended Nationally Determined Contributions (INDCs) towards the global objective to limit the increase in the atmospheric concentration of CO_2 to no more than 450 parts per million (ppm), compared to 560 ppm under the Kyoto Protocol. For comparison, the atmospheric concentration of CO_2 was some 415 ppm in 2019 and 280 ppm in pre-industrial times (circa 1750), with 200 ppm a rough minimum concentration required for crop growth. While the Earth is thought to have already warmed by about 1°C since 1750, the target of 450 ppm would, according to climate models, limit global mean temperature rise to 2°C above pre-industrial levels. Under the Paris Agreement, developed countries indicated they would reduce CO_2 emissions by 30 per cent within the next fifteen years, while aiming to reduce emissions by 80 per cent by 2050 compared to 1990 emissions. Recently, the IPCC reported that it would be necessary to limit the rise in average global temperature to 1.5°C, which would require countries to eliminate all CO_2 and other greenhouse gas emissions by 2050.

The United States removed itself from the Paris Accord as it felt that (1) the costs of meeting targets would be too high; (2) the Agreement threatened to lead to global institutions that would reduce its sovereignty; and (3) computer models were not sufficiently reliable to warrant drastic policy action that would alter the country's entire economy. All other countries remain committed to the Agreement, including large emitters such as China, India, Russia, and the European Union.

Changes in output and the location of crop production can be impacted by climate change and are thus potentially measurable. Adverse weather during any crop season is perhaps the greatest risk to agriculture (R.M. Adams et al. 1995; McCarl, Thayer, and Jones 2016), but it is unclear whether climate change will be accompanied by greater incidences of adverse weather (Pielke 2018a). A more important question relates to the effect of climate change on crop production. Information presented in the climate-damage literature may offer the potential to mitigate climate change through carbon policies, especially through the uptake of carbon in soils and living biomass.

GREENHOUSE GAS EMISSIONS AND EFFORTS TO REDUCE THEM

Emission reductions of as little as 25 per cent would be difficult and costly to achieve, requiring huge investments in nuclear power, massive changes in transportation infrastructures, and impressive technical breakthroughs in everything from biofuels to battery technology. Few countries can afford such costly investments. Without global cooperation, the impact on climate change will be small. Fossil fuels are still abundant, ubiquitous, and inexpensive relative to alternative energy sources so they will continue to be the major driver of economic growth and wealth into the foreseeable future.

There are two particular sticking points in reaching international agreements to reduce CO_2 emissions. First, developing countries argue that rich countries should pay for their past emissions as these are responsible for the current situation. In 2010–11, the United Nations (UN) established a Green Climate Fund (GCF) to which rich countries pledged to contribute US$10.3 billion (US$4.7 billion from the European Union, US$3.0 billion from the United States). The GCF would grow to US$100 billion by 2020 and would compensate developing countries for past CO_2 emissions by developed countries through a redistribution of income. Second, developing countries are unwilling to impede development by controlling their own GHG emissions. China is now the largest user of coal, followed by India, and China's CO_2 emissions exceed those of the United States and the European Union combined.

Climate change and crop yield studies imply that an increase in average global temperatures and CO_2 concentration does not affect all crops in the same way, nor does the increase impact different crop regions in the same way. In general, the positive influence of a higher level of CO_2 concentration in the atmosphere (i.e., a CO_2-fertilization effect, as plants need CO_2 the way humans need oxygen) is limited by increased heat and adequate water supply (Porter, Howden, and Smith 2017). Overall, it could be true that unprecedented global warming may lead to reduced crop yields, but dire warnings that climate change will lead to dangerous reductions in future crop yields and increasing incidence of famines are considered unwarranted on the bases of available evidence.

We focus on one particular issue: Will climate change lead to lesser or greater crop output? Despite concerns that crop yields and net farm income could decline due to climate change, which could increase future food insecurity, global food security may not be under any threat. There is evidence that crop yields could increase despite climate change due to technological changes and other factors. We examine the possible differences in the priorities of policies to adapt to climate change between developed and developing countries.

14.2   CLIMATE CHANGE PROJECTIONS

Climate models assume that human activities are responsible for greenhouse gas emissions and that these have a significant impact on climate. A recent Intergovernmental Panel on Climate Change (IPCC) report attributed the increase in temperatures since pre-industrial times solely to anthropogenic sources (IPCC 2018).[1] Climate models are necessarily complex because they model interactions between two chaotic fluids of different viscosities – the atmosphere and ocean – moving against each other and over the irregular surface of the Earth and its varied ecosystems. Further, many uncertain parameters are used to represent the climate change process, which is full of scientific uncertainty itself. Consequently, outcomes from various climate models differ in many aspects, with no one model considered superior to any other (IPCC 2013).

Climate models can project temperature and precipitation changes at both the global and regional level. Most models agree that global temperatures will gradually increase, but there is uncertainty regarding the projected rise in temperature and any tipping points that may result in a runaway rise in average global temperature. As to uncertainty, IPCC (2013) projected global mean surface temperature to increase 0.3 to 0.7°C by 2035, for example. Precipitation is much harder to predict; fewer models are available, and projections often conflict with each other regarding changes in the pattern and scale of precipitation even at a global level. Many models project an increase in extreme rainfall and snowfall events (Fischer et al. 2014), and higher temperatures are projected to increase evaporation, thereby making droughts more severe, even if overall precipitation increases or remains unchanged (Dai 2013).

Regional projections of future climate scenarios are derived from regional climate models (RCMs) that are downscaled from global climate models (GCMs).[2] The uncertainty in regional projections of temperature and rainfall is larger than that in their corresponding GCMs because regional projections are more sensitive to model design. Hence, conflicting results can be found between GCMs and RCMs or between two RCMs for the same region (Karmalkar 2018; Fernández et al. 2019). RCMs, increasingly used to guide local policies, cannot predict future snowfall, which is an important source of moisture for crop production in some areas.[3]

MITIGATING THE EFFECTS OF CLIMATE CHANGE
Climate change is not a new phenomenon, but concerns have arisen that climate change may accelerate to a point where society's adaptation falls far behind and food security might be compromised at the regional or even global level, especially in the least developed countries (LDCs). Mitigating the adverse impacts from unprecedented warming will require extra efforts from farmers, governments, and international institutions.

Figure 14.1. Five-year moving average of maize yields, selected regions, 1965–2017

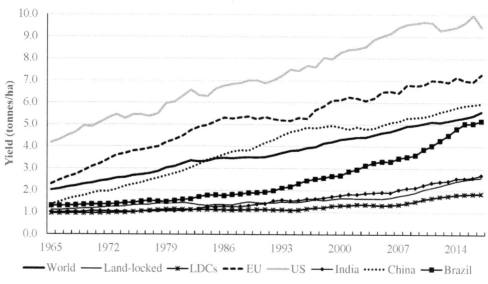

Source: FAO (2019a).

14.3   CLIMATE CHANGE AND CROP YIELDS

While some may argue the case for climate change causing future food insecurity, data (FAO 2019a) show that the crop yields (measured in tonnes per hectare [t/ha]) have been increasing. Over the period 1961–2017, annual average global yields of wheat increased by 2.1 per cent, followed by maize (2 per cent), soybeans (1.7 per cent), rice (1.6 per cent), fresh vegetables (0.9 per cent), and sorghum (0.8 per cent). Specifically, Figures 14.1 through 14.4 provide five-year, moving average yield trends for 1965–2017 (with data beginning in 1961) for four major crops (maize, rice, wheat, and fresh vegetables) for selected regions.

Figures 14.1 through 14.3 show that all yield trends for maize, rice, and wheat are strongly upward. In Figure 14.4, vegetable yields have slowly but steadily increased in South America (mainly Brazil), somewhat less so in Asia, landlocked countries, and the LDCs, while EU vegetable yields have remained relatively flat. The yield data suggest that some fresh vegetables might be more vulnerable to weather conditions. Hence, without further knowledge about the environmental conditions for different vegetables and the use of irrigation, it is difficult to draw further conclusions.

US vegetable yields sharply increased from the late 1980s to the 2000s, which led to yields that exceeded those of any other region by a factor of four or more (which is why US yields are not plotted in Figure 14.4). This suggests that advances in technology can increase the agricultural

Figure 14.2. Five-year moving average of rice yields, selected regions, 1965–2017

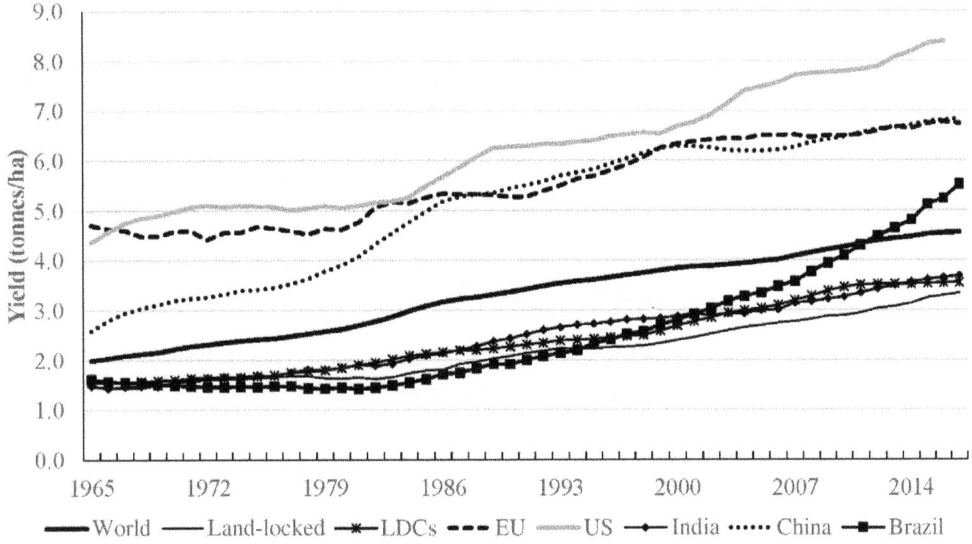

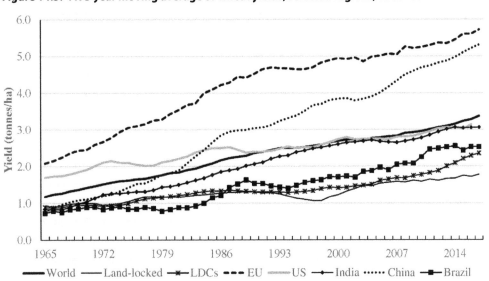

Source: FAO (2019a).

Figure 14.3. Five-year moving average of wheat yields, selected regions, 1965–2017

Source: FAO (2019a).

Figure 14.4. Five-year moving average of fresh vegetable yields, selected regions, 1965–2017

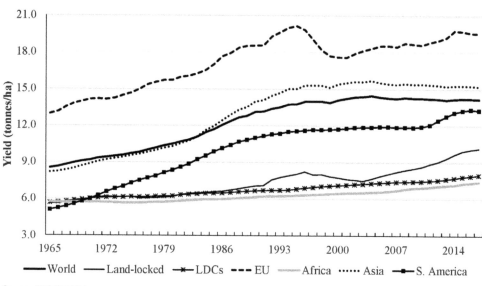

Source: FAO (2019a).

industry's ability to adapt to climate change (Eisenhut and Weber 2019). The LDCs have the lowest crop yields in all categories. This implies that more work is required to improve agricultural production in these countries; conversely, there is great potential for agricultural development.

For historical crop yields, it is difficult to find evidence suggesting that temperature increases have lowered yields. Once adverse weather events are taken into account using a moving average of yields, it is easier to argue that technological improvements combined with rising carbon dioxide (CO_2) levels have actually increased agricultural productivity.

US SUGAR PRODUCTION

Sugar cane is a major crop in the US states of Florida and Louisiana, where yield has increased due to investments in varietal improvements and technology (A. Schmitz and Zhang 2019; A. Schmitz, Kennedy, and Zhang 2020). The increase in US sugar production over the years has been dramatic. Sugar produced from sugar cane grew from 2.9 million short tons, raw value (STRV) in 1980 to 4.0 million STRV in 2018 (USDA/ERS 2019). Sugar cane is also a better source of ethanol (a gasoline substitute) than corn, because production and processing of corn into ethanol releases more greenhouse gases than is the case with sugar cane (Crutzen et al. 2008).

14.4   CLIMATE CHANGE AND WEATHER

As with the projections of climate change, there is conflicting evidence on how crop yields respond to changes in climate.[4] Consider first the impacts of atmospheric concentrations of CO_2. Plants can "derive their own carbon (C) source directly from inorganic CO_2 in the air by chemically fixing it into an organic form" via a multiple-step photosynthesis process (Bueckert 2013, 64). We focus on two of several different C-fixation processes: C3 and C4. The basic pathway is called C3 because the first product of the process is a 3-carbon (3C) molecule. The C4 pathway is different because a 4-carbon (4C) molecule is produced (Bueckert 2013). The most prevalent food crops are C3 plants (e.g., wheat, rice, barley, oats, vegetables, and tree crops such as apples); yields of C3 crops respond more positively to increased atmospheric CO_2 than do C4 crops. The primary C4 crops (i.e., maize, sorghum, and sugar cane) are well suited to produce biofuels (Arunanondchai et al. 2019). There are proportionally more C4 plants among perennial weeds, implying that they do less well under climate change than C3 plants (C3 weeds would develop herbicide resistance more easily than C4 weeds as CO_2 increases). Because crops are mainly C3 and many weeds are C4, C3 crops might outcompete weeds for valuable nutrients as CO_2 levels rise, with genetic engineering potentially able to provide food crops with an additional advantage over controlling weed infestation.

If the concentration of atmospheric CO_2 increases, crop production (yield and biomass) is expected to increase. As evidence of this occurring, the twentieth century increase in atmospheric CO_2 contributed to a 16 per cent increase in cereal crop yields (Idso 2001), and perhaps upward of one-fifth of the yield increases associated with the Green Revolution (Stevenson et al. 2013; Idso et al. 2014). Andresen et al. (2018) attribute rising CO_2 to a 15 per cent increase in biomass productivity in European pasturelands. Overall, there is increasing evidence that crop yields will increase as atmospheric CO_2 levels and temperatures increase.

Numerous studies conclude that crop yields will increase with global warming because higher CO_2 reduces leaf stomatal pores that take in CO_2 and release water vapor (Idso 2001), enabling plants to better withstand drought, higher temperatures, and noxious air pollutants (Morgan et al. 2011). A number of studies have linked higher levels of atmospheric CO_2 to increased crop yields even if precipitation is lower (Long 1991; Bettarini, Vaccari, and Miglietta 1998; Gifford 2004; Long et al. 2004; Goklany 2015). Early studies by Wittwer (1995) found that yields of rice, wheat, barley, oats, and rye could increase by upward of 64 per cent, potatoes and sweet potatoes by as much as 75 per cent, and legumes (including peas, beans, and soybeans) by 46 per cent at higher levels of CO_2. Levitt and Dubner (2009) indicated that there could be a 70 per cent increase in plant growth with a double CO_2 atmosphere.

Prakash et al. (2017) found that wheat yields increased by 44–52 per cent (depending on variety) when CO_2 concentrations went from 335 ppm to 477 ppm (compared to a 2019 level of 410 ppm), while the same increase in CO_2 accompanied by a 1°C increase in average growing season temperature still resulted in an 8–38 per cent increase in yields. Pandey, Lal, and

Vengavasi (2018) found that wheat biomass increased by 73–145 per cent in going from 330 ppm to 700 ppm CO_2, despite limited phosphorous in both situations. Wheat yields can also be increased by warmer temperatures. In a study of winter wheat in China, Hou, Xu, and Ouyang (2018) artificially increased soil temperatures by +2°C, finding that total nitrogen (N) uptake rates rose by 47 per cent and 40 per cent in the conventional and no-till treatments, respectively, leading to respective wheat biomass increases of 14.7 per cent and 13.2 per cent. Both the quantity and quality of the wheat crop increased.

Importantly, "results from 3,586 separate experimental conditions conducted on 549 plant species reveal nearly all plants will experience increases in dry weight or biomass in response to atmospheric CO_2 enrichment" (Idso et al. 2014, 13). Clearly, crop yields are positively correlated with CO_2 levels, which explains why Dutch farmers will grow crops in greenhouses with an atmosphere of 1,000 ppm CO_2 (Idso 2001) and hydroponic operations often run at 1,400 ppm CO_2 (Levitt and Dubner 2009).

RENEWABLE ENERGY

Wind, solar, biomass, and hydroelectricity are the major sources of renewable energy. Environmentalists oppose further development of hydroelectric dams because of their adverse effects on land use and aquatic life. Despite the fact that biomass is the most important source of primary energy in the world, biomass burning releases more CO_2 per unit of heat than coal, oil, or natural gas, leading some to question its use (see Johnston and van Kooten 2015, 2016). However, legislation in most countries treats biomass as carbon neutral because the CO_2 emissions released are eventually removed from the atmosphere by growing trees. Wind and solar are important sources of energy in the electricity sector, but they are unreliable and impose costs on existing generating assets that are not taken into proper account in determining appropriate policies for incentivizing their development (van Kooten and Mokhtarzadeh 2019). As a result, and despite the tremendous growth in the capacity of these renewable energy sources, fossil fuel use still accounts for 80 per cent or more of global energy use. Some argue that carbon neutrality can only come about by decommissioning fossil fuel power plants and replacing them with nuclear power plants (Pielke 2019; van Kooten 2017).

With regard to the effect of climate change on precipitation, the literature contains few quantitative assessments. Generally, the main concern of researchers has focused on the potential increase in extreme events, such as heavy rainfall or severe drought during the growing season. Intense rainfall can lead to soil erosion and water contamination when nutrients, chemicals, or livestock wastes leach or discharge into bodies of water. Low levels of precipitation could worsen the seriousness of water shortages, resulting in reduced crop production (R.M. Adams, Hurd, and Reilly 1999). It is important to stress that climate includes both changes in temperature and precipitation. Accurately modelling the joint effects from changes in temperature and precipitation (rainfall/snowfall) is extremely important as they significantly affect agriculture.

At the regional level, the evidence suggests that agricultural productivity in tropical countries might be under greater threat than that in temperate countries. Challinor et al. (2014) conducted a meta-analysis of 1,048 observations from 66 studies to determine the separate impacts of adaptation, change in temperature, change in CO_2, and change in precipitation on crop yields in tropical and temperate regions. They concluded that with adaptation, wheat, maize, and rice yields would increase in temperate regions and decrease in tropical regions due to higher temperatures – all else remaining constant (*ceteris paribus*). Moore et al. (2017) conducted a meta-analysis using an updated version of the same database as Challinor et al. (2014), with 1,010 published point estimates from 56 studies, to show that crop yields in wheat, maize, rice, and soybeans would decrease with global temperature rises of 1°C and more. They concluded that the impacts on agriculture, as used in integrated assessment models to find the social cost of carbon, increases from net benefits of US$2.7 per tonne of CO_2 (tCO_2) to net costs of US$8.5/$tCO_2$.

The IPCC summarized studies that find climate change reduces crop yields. The IPCC's Fifth Assessment Report (IPCC 2014) reviewed 782 studies, finding a median reduction in crop yields of 4.8 per cent and an average reduction of 5.9 per cent (Porter, Howden, and Smith 2017, 682). Porter, Howden, and Smith write that "The grand mean of the five [Assessment Reports] (-4.0%) and the overall median (-0.92%) shows a worrying change in food production for a range of scenarios of climate change, locations, crops, and levels of adaptation" (ibid., 681).

The US National Climate Assessment report (USGCRP 2018) projects mid-century (2036–65) yields of commodity crops to decline by "5% to over 25% below extrapolated trends broadly across the region for corn, and more than 25% for soybeans in the southern half of the region." Notice that the report does not suggest that crop yields will fall; rather, US crop yields are expected to continue trending upward, but productivity growth will be below what it would be in the absence of climate change.

14.5 ECONOMIC IMPACT OF CLIMATE CHANGE ON AGRICULTURE

Early estimates of potential climate change damages in agriculture employed crop simulation models and assumed that farmers would continue to plant the same crops and variety of crops with the same methods as those employed prior to any changes in climate. This assumption is unrealistic because agricultural researchers and producers improve crop varieties, update management practices, and adopt new technologies to facilitate adaptation to weather uncertainty and, thereby, climate change. Studies that took into account adaptation found that the damages from potentially higher temperatures were significantly lower or negated entirely (Challinor et al. 2014).

Canadian studies by Louise Arthur and her colleagues at the University of Manitoba (Arthur 1988; Arthur and Abizadeh 1988; Mooney and Arthur 1990; Arthur and van Kooten 1992) assumed that, with climate change, the climate characterizing the US corn belt would shift to include parts of Manitoba and Saskatchewan. In that case, the authors found that, even if farmers only adopted crops suited to the changed climate, Canadian farmers could benefit from global warming. For the United States, R.M. Adams (1989), R.M. Adams et al. (1990), and D.M. Adams et al. (1996) used the projected climate from GCMs in crop simulation models for various regions to determine how climate change might impact crop yields and how changes in agricultural output might affect the economy. They concluded that climate change could lead to an overall increase or decrease in wellbeing, but that such changes were generally small. Regardless of the climate models employed, researchers were unambiguous in finding that the distributional impact of climate change is more important than its overall impact (Kaiser et al. 1993a, 1993b).

To further quantify the economic impacts on agriculture, two main methods have been employed to determine climate change damages: a statistical approach and a modelling approach. Both methods are rooted in economic theory. The statistical approach employs the theory of land rents to estimate the potential damages from climate change on agriculture. The second approach uses mathematical programming (MP) models that maximize the net social benefits of agricultural activities subject to biophysical and economic constraints. The following section introduces the background, application, and conclusions from each approach in the context of climate change. The models' technical details are not covered.

14.5.1   Statistical Approach

Rising food prices lead to an expansion of agricultural production onto marginal land that could not be profitably cultivated at a lower price. At the margin, farmers would earn enough to cover all expenses, including an adequate return on the capital they used in crop production. When marginal land is brought into crop production, owners of better land – land that is more fertile, experiences better weather outcomes, or is situated nearer markets – earns a differential rent. The concept of differential land rent can be applied in the context of climate change, as illustrated in Figure 14.5. Assume Figure 14.5 pertains to a particular parcel of farmland, and ignore the crop denoted as "GE grain" for now. The farmer can plant one of three crops (wheat, corn, or sorghum), with the expected number of growing degree days (GDDs) determining differential rent.[5] In the illustration, rents determine the use to which the land is put (i.e., the crop to be planted). As temperature rises, rents to agriculture fall, with farmers switching first from corn to wheat at intensive margin A and then to sorghum at B.

Figure 14.5. Impact of changing heat availability on crop choice

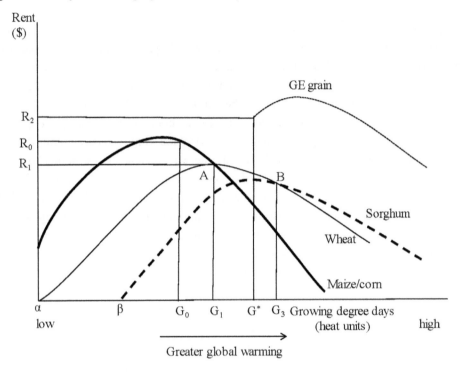

If heat were to increase from G_0 to G_1, for example, the difference $R_0 - R_1$ constitutes a measure of the damage to agriculture that would be associated with climate change. Conversely, if there were a reduction in heat units (as measured by GDDs) from G_1 to G_0 as a result of global warming, then the difference $R_0 - R_1$ would be a measure of the gain. The statistical approach assumes that landowners will adjust input use to maximize rent accruing to the land, choosing the crop best suited to the expected number of GDDs.

Beginning with research by Mendelsohn, Nordhaus, and Shaw (1994), statistical models have been used to estimate the potential impact of weather on agriculture. Such models have become the most widely used approach for determining the costs or benefits from climate change because they rely on actual market data. The statistical approach estimates a land-rent regression model that has the following general functional form (Schlenker and Roberts 2009):

$$Y_{it} = \hat{a}_{1,it}\,\Delta h_{1,it} + \hat{a}_{2,it}\,\Delta h_{2,it} + \ldots + \hat{a}_{n,it}\,\Delta h_{n,it} + \hat{b}_{1,it}\,k_{1,it} + \hat{b}_{2,it}\,k_{2,it} + \ldots + \hat{b}_{m,it}\,k_{m,it},$$

where Y_{it} is the dependent variable, with subscript i (= maize, wheat, etc.) referring to crop type and t to the year the various variables were measured. The dependent variable might consist of actual land sales data, yield data (which is multiplied by price to obtain value), assessed values (used for tax purposes), or even self-reported land values (e.g., the value of land in crop i in year t). Note that the explanatory variables on the right-hand side of the above equation are heat units, h, and control variables k (e.g., soil type, machinery types used, seed quality, slope of cropland). Rainfall is not included in these models because precipitation data are not available at the desired level of disaggregation; it is not available at the farm level nor is there any information on snowfall (if any) or the timing of rainfall during the growing season.

Heat units are measured as the amount of time (e.g., hours or days) during the growing season in year t that crop i is exposed to temperatures that fall within a small interval j denoted Δh_{jit}. There are n such j intervals, where the initial j interval, Δh_1, might be the number of hours the crop is exposed to temperatures $<1°C$; the second interval, Δh_2, would be the hours the crop is exposed to temperatures from $1°C$ to $2°C$, and so on. Control variables might include longitude and latitude, distance to a city, etc. An important variable such as precipitation is generally ignored in such models because rainfall can vary greatly even between neighbouring farms, so instrumental variables such as average regional precipitation or a drought index might be used instead. Finally, ε_{it} represents the error term, which is often assumed to be normally distributed.

Once the parameters of the model ($a_1, \ldots, a_n, b_1, \ldots, b_m$) are estimated, as indicated by the hats ($\wedge$) on the parameters (in which case the ε_{it} should not really be shown), it is possible to forecast the impact of changes in the Δh_j on the dependent variable. The changes in Δh_j are derived from climate forecasts that provide the future pattern of temperatures. If future climate affects one of the k variables, it too will need to be changed to derive a forecast of Y_i.

As an example, assume the dependent variable in the above equation is farmland value. Then, once the model parameters have been estimated for a sample of farms, the results are used first to predict the farmland values across an entire study region or country. Next, the temperature variables are changed to reflect the projected change in climate, with the same model parameters now used to predict farmland values for that region or country under global warming. (Rainfall is addressed via an instrumental variable, as noted above, or simply left unchanged.) The model implicitly assumes that if landowners face different climate conditions, they will choose the agricultural land use (crop and technique) that maximizes their net returns. The differences between farmland values in the current climate state and the projected future climate regime constitute the costs (if overall farmland values fall) or benefits (if values rise) of climate change.

There is no reason to suppose that the estimated parameters will continue to hold under a changed climate regime, however. They are unlikely to hold, for example, if growing conditions under a future climate regime are outside the observed range of values used to estimate the model. Model results might hold for temperature increases of 0–5°C, but not for projections that fall outside the range of data used to estimate the model parameters. Such projections are simply unreliable, partly because they fail to take proper account of precipitation. Likewise, the estimated parameters may no longer apply if technology has changed over time.

For the United States, Mendelsohn, Nordhaus, and Shaw (1994) projected a small increase in US GDP as a result of global warming impacts on agriculture. Subsequently, Schlenker, Hanemann, and Fisher (2005) argued that the Mendelsohn, Nordhaus, and Shaw (1994) model was misspecified: when irrigated areas were accounted for, the earlier conclusions were reversed because climate change would reduce the water available to irrigators. Schlenker, Hanemann, and Fisher (2006) subsequently found that climate change would unambiguously impose net costs upon agriculture, although dryland cropping in the northern US states would benefit. The authors examined the deleterious effects of high temperatures (30°C or more) on crop yields (although yields increased over a broad range of higher temperatures). They further speculated that climate change will impose a net economic cost on agriculture in irrigated counties, whether in the form of higher costs for replacement water supply or lower profits due to reduced water supply. Other econometric studies employing mainly US data also concluded that the overall effect of climate change would be negative (Schlenker and Roberts 2009; Chen, McCarl, and Thayer 2017; Arunanondchai et al. 2019).

In a study of Canadian agricultural land values, Weber and Hauer (2003) found that agricultural landowners could gain substantially as a result of climate change. They projected average gains in land values of more than 50 per cent in the short term (to 2040) and upward of 75 per cent or more in the longer term (to 2060).

Chatzopoulos and Lippert (2015) investigated the impacts of climate change on agricultural land prices based on German farm data. They concluded that temperature and precipitation are important factors determining land prices. Land rent will increase for all types of farms when temperature moderately increases. Meanwhile, land prices increase and then decrease with precipitation.

14.5.2   Modelling Approach

The second class of models uses economic theory to develop a normative mathematical representation of land-use allocation decisions. To obtain sector or input specific (namely land) details requires a regional-level farm management, or land-use, mathematical programming (MP) model that examines the allocation of land across crops. MP models specific to the agricultural sector optimize an economic objective function subject to biophysical, political, and economic constraints. MP models initially replicate observed crop allocations, land use, usage of other inputs, or other primary sector activities. Then they are used to investigate the impacts of exogenous price shocks, introduction of a carbon tax, changes in crop/livestock insurance schemes, entry of new crops or crop varieties (e.g., resulting from genetic engineering), etc.[6] Since these MP models focus solely on agriculture or land use, they can provide detailed information about how climate change affects the agricultural sector. To determine the costs (or benefits) associated with climate change, the calibrated model is solved with current climate conditions, and then is re-solved with projected future climate conditions. Differences between the base-case scenario and the future scenario (or counterfactual) constitute an estimate of the costs or benefits of climate change.

The majority of studies about damages to the agricultural sector are for the United States, Canada, and Europe. The general conclusion from either the statistical approach or the modelling approach is that the US and EU agricultural sectors will likely be slightly harmed by climate change, while Canada's agricultural sector will benefit overall (Darwin et al. 1995; Weber and Hauer 2003; Schlenker, Hanemann, and Fisher 2006).

In a study of the impacts of global warming on individual countries, Cline (2007) concluded that there could be short-term gains but long-term losses to global agriculture. While potential CO_2-fertilization benefits would quickly account for the short-term benefits of climate change, Cline argues that diminishing returns from CO_2-fertilization and adverse effects of excessive warming will inevitably lead to long-term declines in crop yields, but this conclusion is more speculative than scientific.

As to the global welfare impacts of climate change, Darwin et al. (1995) and Schimmelpfennig et al. (1996) used a land-use model linked to a computable general equilibrium (CGE) model to estimate the global welfare impacts of climate change as it affects output in the primary sectors. They found that if landowners were able to adapt their land uses to maximize net returns (as assumed in the statistical models), global GDP would increase by 0.2–1.2 per cent depending on the climate model projections employed.

Another approach for estimating the damages from climate change is to include information from agricultural studies into an integrated assessment model (IAM) of economic growth and determine the social costs via a damage function specified within the model. Moore et al. (2017) felt the damage function used in the IAM employed by the economist Richard Tol would underestimate the potential reduction in crop yields associated with a warmer world. Upon re-parameterizing the damage function, an estimated agricultural sector benefit of US\$2.70/tCO_2 became a cost of US\$8.50/tCO_2, thereby resulting in near doubling of the social cost of carbon (Yang et al. 2018). This research exemplifies the direction that research on damages in the agricultural sector has taken: adverse effects of climate change in the agricultural sector are an important driver of the parameterization of the damage function used in an IAM.

14.6   FOOD SECURITY AND CLIMATE SMART AGRICULTURE

Does climate change lead to greater food insecurity? The above models are somewhat limited in answering this question. Food security might be compromised at the regional level, but not at the global level, or it might be compromised at both scales. As noted, evidence for future crop production is mixed: greenhouse experiments suggest that increasing concentrations of atmospheric CO_2 can improve agricultural productivity, so that crops can better utilize nutrients and be less susceptible to drought. As illustrated in Figures 14.1 through 14.4, crop yields will likely continue to rise in the future. Nonetheless, many scientists believe that at higher temperatures, the adverse effect of heat on crop yields will eventually offset the benefits of CO_2 fertilization. The importance of technological change remains unknown, except that genetic engineering and other developments will likely overturn conclusions regarding threats to future food security.

Climate change and its impact on agriculture is a source of concern for future food security. The agriculture sector's vulnerability, adaptation, and potential contribution to the mitigation of climate change have been addressed in the literature (R.M. Adams, Hurd, and Reilly 1999; McCarl and Schneider 2002; Manley et al. 2005; McCarl, Thayer, and Jones 2016). One approach to implementation of the ideas found in the literature is climate smart agriculture.

At the level of individual countries, food security involves more than economic development. People cannot easily move to another country to avoid food insecurity, nor can income re-distributional tools, such as taxes, be applied internationally to generate subsidies to countries with serious food insecurity. That is, the problem cannot be tackled from the point of view of a global-level social planner (A. Schmitz, Kennedy, and T.G. Schmitz 2017). Addressing food insecurity is complex; there is no easy solution to the problem (Kennedy, Schmitz, and van Kooten, 2018, 2020; A. Schmitz, Kennedy, and T.G. Schmitz, 2015, 2016, 2017; van Kooten, Schmitz, and Kennedy, 2020).

CLIMATE SMART AGRICULTURE

Farmers are by necessity climate smart because the failure to address variations in weather outcomes could lead to personal bankruptcy. At the international level, the climate smart agriculture (CSA) movement seeks to link the challenges of food security, climate change, and agricultural development to integrated approaches and practices for development, adaptation, and mitigation. The Food and Agriculture Organization of the United Nations (FAO) defined and presented the concept of CSA at the Conference on Agriculture, Food Security, and Climate Change held in The Hague in 2010. Since then, the CSA idea has evolved around three main objectives: (1) increasing productivity and income in a sustainable way; (2) building resiliency to adapt to climate change; and (3) reducing greenhouse gas emissions (FAO 2018). The intention of CSA is to organize issues and approaches so that all interested parties in different countries can identify useful strategies that suit their own situations. The CSA approach is comprehensive, covering elements of all agricultural systems (rather than being customized to particular countries or regions).

CSA promotes common practices, such as providing seeds of different crop varieties to farmers. It recommends improving the performance of foreign aid and implementation of private and public policies or schemes that increase farmers' acceptance of new crops and improve their access to herbicides, pesticides, fertilizers, and other inputs. It also finds linking smallholder farmers to high-value markets for agricultural or other commercial products essential, encouraging crop diversification and participation in commercial markets (e.g., opening a local brewery to purchase barley may incentivize a shift from maize to barley plantings). With diversified crops, farmers become more resilient to wider fluctuations in climate and production (AGRA 2014, 2017, 2018).

Table 14.1 reports selected agricultural indicators grouped by income, climate zone, and region, including the median value of an indicator for each subgroup. The proportion of the added value from agriculture to gross domestic product (GDP), the percentage of rural population, and the proportion of employment in agriculture are inversely correlated with income. For example, the median value of employment in agriculture is 67.8 per cent for low-income, Sub-Saharan African countries in the tropical zone. The value of the same indicator for high-income countries in the Middle East and North Africa located in the tropical zone is 3.1 per cent. Hence, impacts of climate change on agriculture will directly affect more incomes in low-income countries than in high-income countries. The priorities of CSA practices in the two groups of countries will thus differ.

Most developed countries have greater capacity to adjust to climate change because they have better access to advanced technologies, a more vibrant private sector that can invest in agriculture, ongoing research and development organizations (e.g., universities, agricultural experiment stations), and private and public sector institutions that provide price supports and facilitate agricultural business risk management. The cost of adaptation is a much lower proportion of total income in developed countries than it is in developing countries.

Likewise, governments in developed countries focus more on guiding practices towards sustainability and environmental protection. For example, US farm bills have environmental protection programs, such as the Conservation Reserve Program (CRP) and the Agricultural Conservation Easement Program, that encourage farmers to protect soil quality and water quality and reduce GHG emissions by paying farmers to idle fragile croplands, grasslands, and wetlands. At the end of 2018, 603,667 CRP contracts were active and 22.44 million acres (9.09 million hectares) of farmland were held by the US Conservation Reserve Program (USDA/FSA 2019).

Most countries in Sub-Saharan Africa depend on agriculture as the main source of income. While the priority in these countries is to increase productivity and income for smallholder farmers, organizations, such as the World Bank, hinder, rather than promote, economic growth by providing funds for climate-based policies rather than infrastructure-based policies. Shifting from subsistence agriculture to commercial agriculture will be difficult without significant restructuring of agriculture to take advantage of economies of scale.

Table 14.1. Global 2015 selected agricultural indicators grouped by income and climate zone[a]

Income Group	Climate Zone	Region	No. of Countries	Ag. Area (%)	Agric. (% of GDP)	Arable Land (ha)	Rural Pop. (%)	Ag. Labour (%)	Cereal Yield (kg/ha)
Low	Subtropics	EU/ Central Asia	1	34.2	21.9	0.09	73.3	51.8	3,261
		South Asia	2	43.4	25.0	0.15	78.3	66.7	2,439
	Tropical	Latin America	1	66.8	17.1	0.10	47.6	42.6	995
		Mid-East/ N. Africa	1	44.6	10.3	0.05	65.2	34.7	784
		Sub-Saharan Africa	24	50.4	29.6	0.22	65.2	67.8	1,323
Lower middle	Subtropics	Mid-East/ N. Africa	3	64.8	11.4	0.23	39.2	25.8	2,141
		South Asia	3	47.0	16.7	0.13	64.0	42.7	3,309
		Sub-Saharan Africa	1	75.0	5.0	0.13	73.1	11.0	587
	Temperate	East Asia/ Pacific	1	72.7	13.4	0.19	31.8	28.5	554
		EU/ Central Asia	5	62.9	12.2	0.21	49.3	29.3	2,999
	Tropical	East Asia/ Pacific	8	28.2	17.3	0.11	68.5	41.5	3,607
		Latin America	4	38.4	11.2	0.18	36.9	28.3	2,094
		Mid-East/ N. Africa	1	73.4	1.8	<0.01	22.6	30.7	1,908
		South Asia	2	52.1	12.2	0.09	74.5	36.2	3,351
		Sub-Saharan Africa	9	38.5	14.8	0.12	45.9	42.5	1,611
Upper middle	Cold zone	EU/ Central Asia	1	13.3	4.1	0.85	26.0	6.7	2,391
	Subtropics	East Asia/ Pacific	1	56.2	8.8	0.09	44.5	19.5	5,982
		EU/ Central Asia	2	61.0	8.1	0.31	38.0	14.6	2,208
		Latin America	1	54.9	3.2	0.18	20.7	13.5	3,470
		Mid-East/ N. Africa	5	21.3	4.7	0.14	26.6	13.1	2,231
		Sub-Saharan Africa	1	79.8	2.1	0.23	35.2	5.6	3,537
	Temperate	EU/ Central Asia	11	46.2	6.3	0.29	42.6	18.0	3,544
	Tropical	East Asia/ Pacific	5	23.9	9.4	0.17	52.3	31.0	2,959
		Latin America	15	33.8	6.3	0.08	36.6	15.9	4,076
		South Asia	1	26.3	5.7	0.01	61.5	8.0	2,168
		Sub-Saharan Africa	5	41.9	3.2	0.17	32.8	26.9	1,269
High	Cold zone	EU/ Central Asia	4	7.5	1.9	0.31	14.1	3.1	4,801
	Subtropics	East Asia/Pacific	3	17.8	2.1	0.03	14.3	3.6	6,091
		EU/ Central Asia	3	40.4	2.1	0.11	33.1	7.5	4,085
		Latin America	4	37.8	4.5	0.39	10.6	6.4	6,045
		Mid-East/ N. Africa	6	17.9	0.8	0.01	6.7	1.4	4,714
		North America	1	44.4	1.1	0.47	18.3	1.7	7,431
	Temperate	East Asia/ Pacific	1	42.2	5.5	0.13	13.7	6.1	8,027
		EU/ Central Asia	21	48.0	2.0	0.22	29.5	3.8	6,027
	Tropical	East Asia/ Pacific	3	2.7	0.1	<0.01	0.0	0.6	1,404
		Latin America	4	26.3	1.1	0.03	40.0	3.4	2,591
		Mid-East/ N. Africa	2	4.7	1.2	0.01	16.5	3.1	16,661

Source: World Bank (2019) and DSPL (n.d.).

[a] Data are for 2015. The countries and regions with missing data are not included. Except for the "# of countries" column, the values in each cell represents the median of the corresponding subgroup.

Three other factors also need consideration. First, evidence from some developing countries located in the tropical zone indicates that an upper-middle income country can have crop yields comparable to those in Europe or North America (Table 14.1). Fifteen upper-middle income countries in Latin America and the Caribbean experienced average cereal yields of 4.1 tonnes per hectare. This group includes Brazil, which has become an agricultural superpower due to large investments in technology and farmland; it has become increasingly competitive with the United States in agricultural export markets. For countries vulnerable to climate change, Brazil's experience provides hope that food security can be achieved through good government policies and proper institutions (including agricultural research stations, extension programs, etc.). Figures 14.1 and 14.2 show that the rate of growth in maize and rice yields in Brazil has been faster than that in other countries since the 1990s. Further, Brazil is now the world's largest exporter of sugar, coffee, beef, and poultry; the second largest exporter of soybeans; the third largest exporter of corn; and the fourth largest exporter of cotton. These statistics lead to an important question: can other tropical countries duplicate Brazil's success? For example, with temperatures in tropical regions projected to rise more slowly under climate change than temperatures in higher latitudes, does this suggest that the Brazilian experience can be extended to African countries? What implication would this have for their food security?

Second, the potential impact of research and development on improving crop yields in the presence of climate change should not be underestimated. Standard crop breeding and genetic engineering (GE) have the ability to take advantage of higher atmospheric CO_2 and greater growing season heat. Consider again Figure 14.5. If heat, as measured by GDDs, exceeds G_3, sorghum would be a better crop choice than would maize. Suppose research results in the development of a genetically modified crop, denoted here as "GE grain," that is better suited to higher temperatures. Then, if available heat during the growing season exceeds G^*, farmers will adopt GE grain over maize or sorghum – more rent is available by growing the new crop. An adaptation of this sort is ignored in statistical land rent models. Technological developments related to crop varieties can improve food security even in the presence of climate change.

Other technologies also improve crop production. For example, drones are increasingly used to identify weed patches within planted fields or in places where more fertilizer is needed to promote the growth of plants that are lagging behind the rest of the field. Drone data are used by a mechanical spreader to release herbicide or fertilizer precisely at the location identified by the drone. This reduces input use and associated GHG emissions while increasing crop yields.

Third, global food security depends on both the production of and demand for food. The Shared Socioeconomic Pathways project provides twenty-five different scenarios (van Vuuren et al. 2011; Riahi et al. 2017). The average population growth over the period 2010–2100 is 30 per cent, with only two scenarios indicating a slight decline in population over this period. However, recent research by Bricker and Ibbitson (2019), among others, suggests that there could be a significant decline in population by 2100 (including a possible reduction in China's population by half). If this is the case, future food security is unlikely to be a problem.

14.7   SUMMARY AND CONCLUSIONS

> **CLIMATE CHANGE COMPLEXITIES**
>
> First, climate change will affect water quality and availability. Confronting drought is a major problem facing world agriculture. Will it get worse if temperatures rise? Second, while climate change is partly responsible for rising sea levels, the magnitude of its impact on agriculture is unclear. Third, aquaculture is an industry often overlooked in damage assessment models. Aquatic species are a major food source that would be negatively affected if seas and oceans are warming due to climate change. Fourth, the effects of climate change on forestry are tied to the magnitude of deforestation (which is often due to the need for land for agriculture), the degree to which forests sequester CO_2, and the role of forestry activities in mitigating climate change (including bioenergy with carbon capture and storage [BECCS]). In general, a great deal of further research is still needed.

The consensus that climate change will have a negative effect on agriculture – that crop yields will decline (Moore et al. 2017) – is fraught with uncertainty because it ignores data on the positive effects of increased atmospheric CO_2 and higher temperatures for crop production.

- Investments in crop breeding and genetic engineering could lead to crop varieties that withstand drought, grow better in a concentrated CO_2 atmosphere, and protect against pests and disease. Crops may also mature more quickly in a warmer atmosphere, creating the potential to grow more than one crop during the year.
- Technological improvements related to machinery and management methods, including greater use of artificial intelligence, irrigation, and financial instruments that protect farms against harmful vagaries in temperatures and precipitation (e.g., weather-indexed insurance) can help farmers adapt to climate change while increasing yields.
- Climate models do not accurately model precipitation. Due to the uncertainty regarding future temperatures and precipitation, the impact on crop yields and food security is difficult to assess.
- To mitigate the effect of climate change, future agricultural policies should be more adaptive of innovative technologies (genetic engineering, micropropagation, water harvesting, etc.) to ensure adequate food supplies in the future.
- Policies that encourage planting energy crops for transportation (ethanol, biodiesel) and using biomass for generating electricity do very little if anything to reduce the concentration of CO_2 in the atmosphere and may even increase it because they promote

environmental damage by expanding cultivation at the extensive margin (into wild spaces) and expanding chemical use at the intensive margin.

- Incentives to increase the production of energy crops have one major benefit: by increasing energy crop prices, they reduce the costs to the Treasury for farm program payments. Once these added benefits are capitalized in land values, however, farmers will again need agricultural programs that protect them from production and price shocks. The unwanted consequences are that land prices increase and some lands are diverted away from growing food towards energy production, thereby increasing food costs that harm the poorest in the global society.

- The priorities of agronomic practices to address potential climate change differ across regions and income groups. For developed countries and large corporations, sustainability and long-term environmental protection are important for adapting to climate change. For low- and lower-middle income countries and their small-scale farmers, a more urgent task is to increase productivity and incomes to prevent risks of food insecurity. Financial aid and efforts to retain small-scale agricultural enterprises cannot lead to the required agricultural transformation needed to address food security. Although some envision the development of a holistic approach involving both government and the private sector – especially small-scale participants – a more fruitful route may be to encourage economies of scale through larger agricultural enterprises and the movement of much of the rural population to urban centres to encourage economic development.

- This chapter's assessment of the effects of climate changes on agriculture is merely a glimpse into the issue's complexities. First, we do not consider the livestock sector, which is responsible for one-seventh of the total anthropogenic greenhouse gas emissions. An alternative approach to mitigation policies that reduce meat consumption is to integrate livestock into a sustainable agricultural system (FAO 2018). Intensive feeding operations will incur additional costs due to rising temperatures. To the extent that climate change negatively affects precipitation, it will also negatively affect livestock producers who rely on grains and grassland as inputs. Second, generalizations concerning the impact that warming will have on the fruit and vegetable sector are made difficult by shifts in consumer preferences on the demand side and technological advances (e.g., related to greenhouse growing technologies) on the supply side. Third, we do not address the land-use conflict between forestry and agriculture. This is a significant omission because "bioenergy with carbon capture and storage (BECCS)" is considered to be a major, if not the major, focus of policy to achieve carbon dioxide removals, thereby limiting the rise in temperatures to 1.5°C (IPCC 2018, 16). The primary source for BECCS is forest biomass, with the forest-land area required for BECCS exceeding 700 million hectares (ha); this is more than double Canada's forested area of 347 million ha. This problem is indicative of the severity of the issue.

CHAPTER FIFTEEN

Multifunctionality in Agriculture: Externalities and Non-traded Goods[1]

15.1 INTRODUCTION

This chapter discusses externalities in conjunction with multifunctionality. Multifunctionality uses negative externality arguments to justify the use of tariff and non-tariff barriers in trade. Externalities are goods for which no markets exist. The lack of a market may be the result of misspecified or non-existing property rights. For example, once a pollutant is in a waterway, to whom does it belong? An externality causes the private demand or supply curve to be different from the social demand or supply curve. This inequality can result in a market that produces equilibrium prices and quantities that are not Pareto optimal.

Agricultural activities generate many benefits to society, but there are also costs. Air and water quality can be negatively impacted by farm operations. Nitrogen (N) leaching into groundwater could result in blue baby syndrome, while N runoff into surface waters causes eutrophication, thereby harming marine life. Carbon dioxide (CO_2) emissions from machinery operations and degrading soils, and methane (CH_4) from livestock production both increase the potential for global warming. Other externalities include noise, smell, and other nuisances that may be considered harmful.

> **EXTERNALITIES**
> There are both positive and negative externalities that are neglected or not properly accounted for in determining the overall contribution that agriculture makes to society. Consideration of these externalities is important in countries where industrial

agriculture and exports dominate. In countries such as the Netherlands, which is the second largest exporter of agricultural commodities by value in the world, the externality costs and benefits need to be balanced against value added to get a sense of whether the agricultural sector provides an overall benefit to society. However, if negative externality costs exceed value added, this does not imply that agriculture should be abandoned entirely. Rather, when the cost of negative externalities exceeds value added, this may indicate that society should cut back somewhat on the intensity of agricultural production to reduce the externality costs in relation to other value-added factors.

15.2   ARGUMENTS FOR PROTECTIONISM

The farm sector produces a variety of outputs, some of which are marketable (or tradable) and others of which are not. Protectionism, under the guise of multifunctionality, is then justified to support the non-marketed dimensions of the agricultural sector. In international trade negotiations, countries have introduced the concept of the multifunctionality of agriculture, in which they argue that non-marketed externalities and the public goods that agriculture produces jointly with marketable food and fibre must be taken into account. These arguments are made in order to protect agricultural sectors from international competition. This position is taken primarily by the European Union (EU) and Japan but has met stiff resistance from the United States and the Cairns Group (a coalition of agricultural exporters).

ACTIVITY-ORIENTED CONCEPT

"Multifunctionality refers to the fact that an economic activity may have multiple outputs and, by virtue of this, may contribute to several societal objectives at once. Multifunctionality is thus an activity-oriented concept that refers to specific properties of the production process and its multiple outputs" (OECD 2001, 11).

The term *multifunctionality* refers to any unpriced spillover benefits that are additional to the provision of food and fibre. Claimed benefits include environmental values, rural amenities, cultural values, rural employment, and rural development. Multifunctionality is a form of protectionism and is applied to both import- and export-competing commodities and associated non-traded goods. The Organisation for Economic Co-operation and Development (OECD) (2001) examines multifunctionality within a theoretical framework. In this chapter we extend this analysis by more formally incorporating multifunctionality arguments into standard welfare economics. We also include a discussion on multifunctionality as it relates to property rights. (Unfortunately, there is little empirical work to parallel these theoretical constructs.) For those interested in this topic, the OECD report is an excellent background piece on the subject.

NET WELFARE COSTS

Many of the agricultural policies around the world result in net welfare costs (A. Schmitz, Furtan, and Baylis 2002; R.E. Just, Hueth, and Schmitz 2004). However, studies on the costs and benefits of farm programs implicitly assume that there is no divergence between the private and social marginal costs of production. It is difficult to quantify the presence of externalities (i.e., divergence between private and social costs and benefits) in multifunctionality arguments.

15.3 EXTERNALITIES

Externalities are discussed with reference to Figure 15.1. MC_P is the private marginal cost and MC_S is the social marginal cost, which is higher because of the production of a negative by-product (e.g., pollution). For each unit of production, some fixed quantity of pollution results. If the market determines the exchange price, then producers will produce at the point where their marginal cost MC_P is equal to price P_P. However, the socially optimal point of production is Q_S along with price P_S. The presence of a cost that is not captured by the market (thus an externality) causes a socially non-optimal level of production. In this case, governments could levy a per unit tax equal to the difference between private and social costs (i.e., $MC_S - MC_P$) to move society back to its optimal level of production Q_S. This tax is known as a Pigouvian tax (Pigou 1932).

MULTIFUNCTIONALITY: THE CASE OF ITALY'S GARFAGNANA REGION

The Garfagnana region of Tuscany has witnessed a resurgence in the small-scale farming sector based on a historical practice of multifunctional agriculture. This includes revalorizing native livestock breeds and promoting agroecological practices (Treakie 2019).

Figure 15.1. Social versus private marginal cost

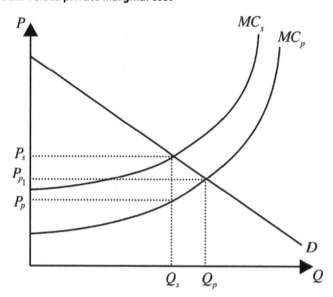

15.3.1 Externalities in Agriculture: Theory and Measurement

The discussion of externalities is expanded further (Figure 15.2). The MC_P is the private marginal cost and MC_S is the social marginal cost, which is higher because of the production of a negative by-product (e.g., pollution). For each unit of production, some fixed quantity of pollution results. If the market determines the exchange price, then producers will produce at the point where their marginal cost MC_P is equal to the price P_{P1}. However, the socially optimal point of production is Q_S along with price P_S. The presence of a cost that is not captured by the market (thus an externality) causes a socially non-optimal level of production. In this case, governments could levy a per unit tax equal to the difference between private and social costs (i.e., $MC_S - MC_P$) to move society back to its optimal level of production Q_S. This tax is often referred to as a Pigouvian tax.

15.3.2 Negative Externalities

The theory of externalities in agriculture can be extended even further with the aid of Figure 15.2. In the absence of incentives to address externalities, the agricultural sector (whether livestock or crop) will produce an amount Q^* at price P^* (Figure 15.2a). One can view the demand function as the marginal willingness to pay (WTP) for agricultural output and the supply function as the private marginal cost ($MC_{private}$) of producing it.

Figure 15.2. Measuring externality costs in agriculture

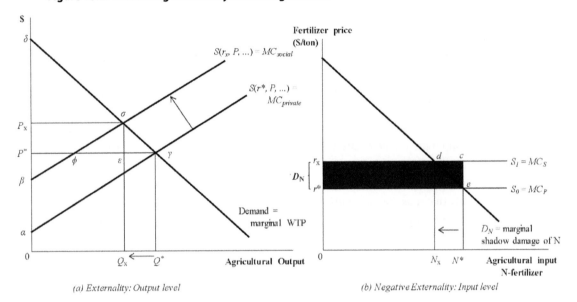

(a) Externality: Output level   (b) Negative Externality: Input level

The private marginal cost function does not take into account negative externalities, if they exist, associated with agricultural activities. The social marginal cost (MC_{social}) takes into account the private costs of farming plus their (negative) social impacts. In this case, the social equilibrium quantity is Q_x, while the corresponding price is P_x.

What constitutes the proper measure of the external costs? If externality costs are ignored, consumers of agricultural commodities realize a consumer surplus given by area ($\delta P^* \gamma$), while producers realize a quasi-rent (producer surplus) to set against fixed costs that is given by ($P^* \alpha \gamma$). After correcting for the externality, the new consumer surplus is area ($\delta P_x \sigma$), while the quasi-rent is ($P_x \beta \sigma$). That is, consumers are worse off by ($P_x P^* \gamma \sigma$), while agricultural producers gain ($P_x P^* \phi \sigma$), which is a transfer from consumers, but lose area ($\beta \alpha \gamma \phi$). The net loss to the agricultural sector is given by ($\beta \alpha \gamma \sigma$) – the area between the MC_{social} and $MC_{private}$ functions bounded by the demand function. This is the cost to society of reducing agricultural externalities to their socially desirable level. Of course, the benefits to society of reducing these externalities presumably exceed these costs, although this is something to be settled in the political realm.

How does one measure these costs given we do not have all the information to determine the demand and supply functions in Figure 15.2a? To do so, we must first realize that agricultural externalities occur upstream from the market for agricultural commodities. It occurs at the farm level where too many inputs are employed than is socially desirable; that is, the farm sector uses too much fertilizer, pesticides, herbicides, and land. It is the intensity of input use that causes negative externalities.

Consider the market for nitrogen (N) fertilizer in Figure 15.2b. The demand function for fertilizer is derived from the demand for fertilizer by the agricultural sector. The supply function for fertilizer is assumed to be infinitely elastic (horizontal supply), which is identical to assuming that the agricultural sector is a price taker in the (international) market for fertilizer.[2] If no action is taken to address negative externalities, N^* amount of fertilizer will be applied, but then excessive nitrogen is considered to enter ground and surface water. An appropriate way to incentivize farmers to consider negative externalities is to tax chemical pollutants or greenhouse gas emissions, thereby shifting $S = MC_P$ (private MC) upward to $S = MC_S$ (social MC), increasing the input price of N fertilizer from r^* to r_x, and reducing fertilizer use from N^* to N_x.

Given that government supports farm incomes, taxes at the farm level are difficult to implement. Instead, the authority will regulate the use of certain chemicals or specify a standard for water quality that must be met, with a failure to meet the standard addressed using fines or stringent on-farm (best-practice) requirements. However, the result is the same: fertilizer use is limited to N_x, with the use of tradable permits one option for ensuring that the restricted quantity is optimally allocated. Whatever mechanism is used, the marginal shadow damage resulting from fertilizer use equals $r^* - r_x$, which represents the cost of the externality. This cost can be measured using a non-market or contingent valuation method.

An increase in the price of fertilizer causes the supply function in the agricultural output market to shift upward and to the left, as indicated in Figure 15.2a. Indeed, if excessive use of the fertilizer input was the sole cause of agricultural spillovers, then the increase in fertilizer price alone would reduce farm output from Q^* to Q_x.[3] Importantly for measurement purposes, the reduction in quasi-rent in the agricultural commodity market can be measured in the fertilizer market by the reduction in consumer surplus; that is, area ($P_x P^* \phi \sigma$) minus ($\beta \alpha \gamma \phi$) in panel (a) is identical to area ($r_x r^* ed$) in panel (b). If there were more inputs responsible for negative externalities in the agricultural sector, then it would be the sum of the lost consumer surplus areas in the various input markets that would equal the lost quasi-rent in the market for agricultural commodities.

The welfare measure used in the UK environmental studies by Pretty et al. (2000, 2001, 2005) and O'Neill (2007) is given by the shaded area in Figure 15.2b, or ($r_x r^* ec$). This area is equal to the shadow cost/price of fertilizer (D_N) multiplied by the amount of fertilizer applied in the absence of policy to address the externality (N^*). This overstates the loss in quasi-rent by triangle (dec). Further, it neglects the loss in consumer surplus in the market for agricultural commodities; that is, it ignores the negative impact on consumers of an increase in food prices. If consumer surplus is ignored, the net loss to the agricultural sector is identical to the reduction in quasi-rent (or net value added), which is identical to ($r_x r^* ed$), and is (over) estimated by shaded area (dec) in panel (b). This implies infinite elasticity of demand so that consumers are price takers, and only the change in producers' welfare or quasi-rent needs to be measured. This is illustrated in Figure 15.3, where the demand function is horizontal rather than downward sloping as in Figure 15.2a. Area ($wxyv$) in Figure 15.3 equals ($r_x r^* ed$) in panel

Figure 15.3. Measuring externality costs in agriculture at output level, infinite demand elasticity

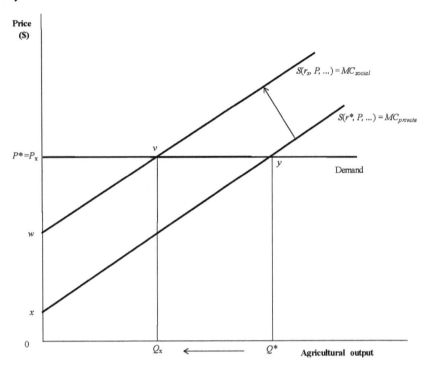

(b) of Figure 15.2. This then is the theoretically correct estimate of the cost to society of reducing agricultural externalities to their socially desirable level.

15.3.3   Positive Externalities

With positive externalities, too little of the input is employed (e.g., too little lime might be applied to lands that are acidic). The social benefit from expanding the use of the input (e.g., lime) is given in Figure 15.3. If the private marginal cost lies above the social marginal cost, the shift in the private supply function to the right generates a positive externality of area (*wxyv*).

In addition to the demand for food, citizens are willing to pay directly for some positive externalities – the benefits that spill over from agricultural activities and for which they do not pay. These include visual amenities provided by the farm landscape (e.g., livestock grazing in a field, rapeseed in bloom) and wildlife habitats. In Figure 15.4, the horizontal axis measures environmental amenities, with E^* equal to the environmental amenities associated with the level of agricultural output Q^* in Figure 15.3. Private demand for environmental services equals D_0, while society's demand is given by D_1. At the private provision E^*, society's marginal value of

Figure 15.4. Agricultural production and environmental services, positive externalities

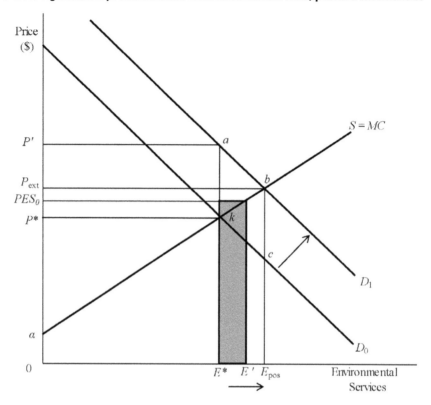

the environmental services equals P', while the cost of producing them equals P^*. Society is willing to pay for more environmental services from the agricultural land. In the absence of other considerations, it would be socially optimal to incentivize farmers to increase production of environmental services to E_{pos}. In that case, the added cost to agricultural producers is given by the area bounded by points $(kE^*E_{pos}b)$, while the benefit to society from expanding agricultural activities is given by $(aE^*E_{pos}b)$. The net benefit to society in this case is measured by the triangle (akb). This area represents a measure of the welfare loss – the loss in society's wellbeing – of producing at Q^*.

Farmers would need to be subsidized to produce more environmental amenities. The government can pay agricultural landowners to modify their practices to provide certain environmental services. Some examples include incentivizing farmers to protect wetlands and not drain them, delay mowing hayfields to facilitate breeding of certain meadow birds, plant trees to sequester carbon, and practise zero-till agriculture to prevent soil erosion and also store carbon. Payments for ecosystem services (PES) are increasingly used to incentivize landowners to take into account the willingness to pay (WTP) of citizens for environmental amenities or services. Of course, society should require farmers to implement certain environmental practices in return for farm payments (known as cross compliance), thereby obtaining desirable levels of ecosystem services, as is done in the EU and the United States.

Society's WTP for positive externalities (Figure 15.4) is generally unknown and difficult to assess. One way around the measurement issue is to assume that the political process reflects society's preferences. Suppose the authority incentivizes the landowner with a payment for the environmental service equal to PES_0, which causes environmental services to increase from E^* to E'. An estimate of the benefit to society is then given by the shaded area in Figure 15.4, although, with the exception of the shaded triangle lying above MC (which constitutes a quasi-rent or surplus to the producer), the payment essentially equals the cost of providing the service.[4] Society's value exceeds PES_0 as society would prefer more than E' (indeed, preferring E_{pos}).[5]

15.3.4   Export Goods: Positive and Negative Externalities

The multifunctionality arguments revolve around positive externalities, in which case the market underestimates the benefits from government intervention. Several cases are considered in A. Schmitz and Moss (2005). We now consider one case in which the extent of the externality depends on the commodity price.[6] In Figure 15.5, S is the private marginal cost curve and S_S is the social marginal cost curve. Total demand is D_t and domestic demand is D_d. At the price support P_S, the market clearing price is P_C. At this price, too much of the good is produced by an amount ($q_2 - q_1$). In this case, the cost of the price support policy is even greater than ($cdeab$) when there is no divergence between the private and social marginal cost curves.

However, consider a lower price support of P_S'. Now the social marginal cost curve lies to the right of the private marginal cost curve, in which case there exist positive externalities from price supports. In this case, price supports can result in net benefits to society. Note that regardless of whether externalities are positive or negative, producers always gain from price supports.

An interesting discussion on externalities that switch between positive and negative is presented by Rude (2008), who argues that a positive by-product of protectionism may become a negative by-product. For instance, low-intensity agriculture may promote positive environmental benefits, but intensive agriculture may lead to environmental degradation. Rude also discusses the externality of landscape effects and argues that the promotion of agricultural production can foster a scenic pastoral landscape, but at some point the landscape effect will be lost when large buildings and silos are erected and marginal marsh and/or forest areas are brought into intensive production.

It is obvious why producers in certain regions, such as Japan and the EU, lobby for the multifunctionality approach in trade negotiations. They clearly gain from protectionism and argue that society as a whole benefits. One could argue that the United States also uses a multifunctionality

Figure 15.5. Positive and negative externalities

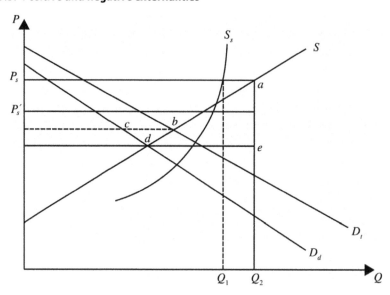

approach to agricultural policy in which part of the emphasis has been on conservation and environmental protection. Even though the United States eliminated its use of land set-asides as a supply control measure in 1996, various programs that are based on an environmental protectionism rationale remained in the 2008 US Farm Bill, including the Conservation Reserve Program (CRP), the Wetland Reserve Program (WRP), and the Grassland Reserve Program (GRP). US farm programs, such as the Environmental Quality Incentives Program (EQIP), in which producers are rewarded for enhancing a variety of environmental outcomes, consolidate a number of existing subsidy programs, with the goal of maximizing environmental programs for dollars spent. The 1996 US Farm Bill gave cost-share and incentive programs a directive to efficiently address agro-environmental degradation (Clayton and Ogg 1999). There are parallel examples in the EU, which previously had supply control programs for only dairy and sugar, but these programs were extended to arable crops with a voluntary land set-aside in 1992. These types of programs create positive externalities that are not output increasing, rather they are output decreasing. For example, CRP land has limited agricultural use and provides habitats for wildlife.

In the context of multifunctionality, there are several important points to keep in mind. First, the use of price supports and trade instruments (e.g., tariffs) results in increased production. Producers gain from these policy instruments, which is why producers generally support agricultural policy intervention. Second, externalities are tied to production whether they are positive, negative, or non-existent. This is a crucial point in the discussion of the use of multifunctionality arguments to support protectionism. Third, the area between the private marginal cost curve and social marginal cost curve modelled above represents society's *willingness to pay* for the positive externality generated through added production by protectionism. However, we are not aware of empirical studies that have estimated society's willingness to pay for these benefits. Fourth, there is a relationship between multifunctionality and decoupling of farm output. Protectionism under multifunctionality leads to the production of output beyond competitive levels. It is the increased production associated with trade barriers that gives rise to the (supposedly) positive benefits for which the public is willing to pay. (The supporters of multifunctionality are suggesting that protectionist policies are coupled to production.) However, as countries move towards more World Trade Organization (WTO) Green Box policies, arguments weaken for the multifunctionality approach to trade liberalization. Of course, if policies are totally decoupled from production, they are no longer protectionist policies nor do they distort trade.

15.3.5   Property Rights

Externalities can be created by misspecified (or absent) property rights that are inherent in certain products such as public goods. This is the case when land is privately owned while wildlife is a public good. Land use decisions made by private individuals produce the externality (e.g., the quantity and quality of wildlife habitat). For instance, private landowners do not protect wildlife habitats, and this results in an overall reduction of wildlife habitats available. However, this need not be the case if property rights are redefined.

PROPERTY RIGHTS AND PRODUCTION

Property rights influence production decisions. For example, some countries allow farmers to charge for the right to hunt on their land while others do not. Property rights influence land use in that they determine whether land must be used for agriculture or for other uses. These other uses (if permitted) may well generate a higher value per acre than will land used for agriculture. Also, the so-called positive externality may be greater for land used for non-agricultural purposes than for agriculture. Changing property rights may well bring about a more desired outcome in terms of generating positive externalities than they will under price supports and other protectionist instruments.

Consider Figure 15.6a in which S is both the private and marginal social cost curve. The total demand for good x is D_t, while domestic demand for good x is D_d. Under free trade, the price of x is P_f and the free trade output is q_f. If a price support of P_S is introduced, output will increase to q_S, but there is an associated net welfare cost of ($cdeab'b$).

Suppose the property rights are changed, allowing for alternative uses of the land. If higher valued uses are available, the production of x will be reduced and some new output y will be

Figure 15.6. Resource use and property rights

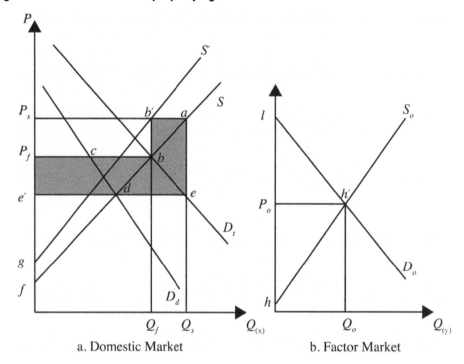

a. Domestic Market   b. Factor Market

created (Figure 15.6b). The supply for x shifts to S' (Figure 15.6a) while the supply and demand for y becomes S_0 and D_0.

In the above context, the impact of price supports will depend on the assignment of property rights. (The change in property rights will change the nature of the supply and demand for x and y.) In Figure 15.6a, the Treasury outlay is much less under the new assignment of property rights ($P_s aee'$) versus ($P_s b' P_f$). Consumers pay a higher price for x, but there is a net saving of ($cbed$). However, there is a net loss to producers of ($fgb'a$). The net effect is therefore ($b'bcdea - gfab'$). However, while producers lose in the production of good x, they will gain ($P_0 h'h$) in the production of good y. There is an additional societal gain of ($P_0 h'1$). Clearly, ($P_0 h'h$) would have to be greater than ($gfab'$) for there to be production of good y

15.4   NON-TRADED GOODS

One benefit cited for agricultural production, especially small-scale agricultural production, is the maintenance of the scenic beauty of rural areas. Additional support can be found for maintaining rural employment opportunities. Many of these attributes are not tradable, and these amenities will not be imported if agriculture loses to trade pressures. The contention in multifunctionality arguments is that these non-traded goods are produced jointly with traded goods. As a result, the change in the price relationship between traded goods associated with free trade will distort the market for the non-traded goods.

To develop a more formal model of this relationship between traded and non-traded goods, we begin by assuming that each of two countries' preferences for agricultural outputs can be modelled as the optimizing behaviour of a single consumer. A country chooses the consumption level for three goods (two traded and one non-traded) as the basis for its negotiating position. In autarky, in the presence of positive externalities, society selects the level of the non-traded good associated with production. However, once trade is allowed, the availability of non-traded goods will change.

Graphically, we show in Figure 15.7a the trade-off between these three goods, where x_1 and x_2 are traded goods; a mathematical treatise on the effect of non-traded goods can be found in Thornsbury, Moss, and Schmitz (2003). The market manifests this trade-off by an equilibrium price ratio that balances the benefits of each good against the cost of production, $(-p_2 / p_1)$. However, the optimizing choice of outputs x_1^* and x_2^* implies a set of production possibilities for the non-traded good x_3 (Figure 15.7b). The optimal amount of the non-traded goods consumed is determined by the production possibility frontier for the non-traded good, which is determined by the level of x_1 and x_2 produced and by society's preferences for the non-traded good. Based on these production possibilities, the economy chooses the level of the non-traded good to consume.

Figure 15.8 adds trade to the model of non-traded goods. In Figure 15.8a, the feasible consumption set increases over the closed market scenario. The economy produces x_1^p of agriculture and x_2^p of manufacturing, while $\hat{x}_1$ and $\hat{x}_2$ are consumed. This implies that the economy imports $\left(\hat{x}_1 - x_1^p\right)$ and exports $\left(x_2^p - \hat{x}_2\right)$. Note that the change in production also changes the availability of non-traded goods. The change in production associated with the emergence of trade reduces the production possibility frontier of the non-traded good associated with agricultural production. This reduced output yields less consumption of the non-traded good, which declines from x_3^* to $\hat{x}_3$ to in Figure 15.8b and lowers overall welfare from $U(x_3|x_1^*, x_2^*)$ to $U(x_3|\hat{x}_1\hat{x}_2)$. The effect of increased trade on welfare depends on the size of the positive externality. Also, this model does not imply autarky, which is important to recognize since many view multifunctionality as a no-trade solution.

The effect of increased trade on non-traded goods outlined above extends beyond the comparison of agriculture and manufacturing. For example, we could examine the interaction between export-oriented agriculture and import-competing agriculture. In such cases, increased agricultural trade will actually increase social welfare by increasing the amount of non-traded goods available for consumption. However, in most countries that support multifunctionality, the import sector is prominent.

Tariffs can be used to reduce the impact of trade on non-traded goods. If a tariff τ is imposed on good x_1, then the price ratio under trade will become $(-p_2 / p_1 + \tau)$. The result of this

Figure 15.7. Market equilibrium between traded and non-traded goods

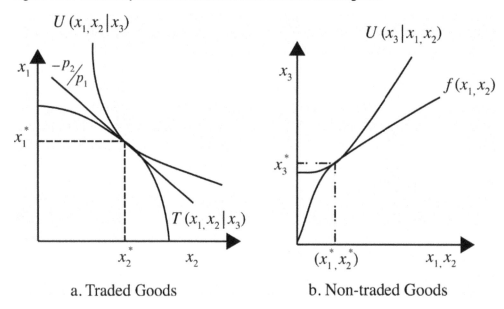

a. Traded Goods   b. Non-traded Goods

tariff is an increase in x_1 produced domestically and a reduction in x_2 consumed domestically, which will yield an increase in the production of the non-traded good.

The model in Figure 15.8 implies that protectionism could be used to increase social welfare by increasing the quantity of non-traded goods produced and consumed. One argument regarding the multifunctionality of agriculture is that agricultural policies in some countries support small farms because this structure generates a multitude of benefits (e.g., scenic countryside, rural employment, and environmental stewardship). However, the expansion of trade will change the composition of agriculture. Small farms may vanish or, at least, produce a different combination of crops. These changes will then cause a shift in these non-market benefits generated by the agricultural sector. This model does not consider the possible improvements to overall welfare from targeted policy interventions aimed directly at the externality problem.

15.5   IDENTIFYING POSITIVE AND NEGATIVE EXTERNALITIES

Negative externalities include environmental damage such as chemical and animal effluent leaching into water supplies, increased salinity, and loss of vegetation. Furthermore, there is considerable evidence that negative spillovers are made worse by protecting agriculture (USEPA 1990; Mahé and Ortalo-Magné 1999). Subsidizing agriculture means that production and inputs used in subsidizing countries are higher than would be the case in the

Figure 15.8. Open market equilibrium between traded and non-traded goods

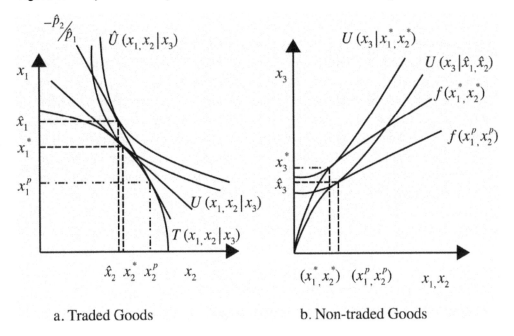

a. Traded Goods   b. Non-traded Goods

absence of protectionism. This, in turn, leads to the production of more negative spillovers from the greater amounts of inputs used. For example, the maintenance of high levels of industry protectionism in the EU under the Common Agricultural Policy has resulted in intensified input use and the deterioration of rural environments and natural resources (Mahé and Ortalo-Magné 1999, 99).

Gunasekera, Rodriguez, and Andrews (1992) analyse the impact of trade liberalization in the EU on the contamination of water from increased use of nitrate fertilizers. They find that reducing protectionism in the EU will lead to a reduction in EU farm production and a significant decrease in farm input use, including the use of nitrogenous fertilizers. This translates into a substantial reduction in the negative environmental spillovers from excessive input use.

Using the Global Trade Analysis Project (GTAP) model, Hertel (1997) estimates that removal of agricultural protectionism in the EU will reduce the use of variable inputs such as fertilizers, chemicals, and fuel by 18 per cent. With reduced protectionism, producers will use far lower amounts of production inputs, and will probably produce fewer negative spillovers.

While there is qualitative evidence, the claims that positive externalities are tied to production have generally not been empirically demonstrated. For example, we know of no study quantifying the utility that people will receive from viewing corn fields in Iowa, cotton fields in Texas, or sugar beet fields in Europe as opposed to viewing grassland parks.

THE DEMISE OF RURAL TOWNS

Related to multifunctionality, many rural towns in America are dying despite government support for agriculture. They are dying in part because of technological change, that is, capital-intensive farming in which farm size is being dictated by such factors as equipment availability. The adoption of technology is not necessarily a function of the level of profitability in agriculture. In this regard, questions have been raised about the extent to which US farm policy has saved or fostered rural communities. The evidence is that, if anything, US farm policies have had a negative impact on rural communities. The positive impact through price supports has fostered larger-scaled agriculture that has had a negative impact on rural towns, which has reduced the scenic impact of the rural countryside.

PLACE-BASED MULTIFUNCTIONALITY IN CENTRAL ITALY

As opposed to the demise of rural towns in America, a 2019 study (Treakie) examined how new forms of multifunctional agriculture are fostering a *"place-based"* food and agriculture system in the Garfagnana region of central Italy and how this approach can be expanded to strengthen family farming and rural communities. Three small-scale family farms that participate in a variety of multifunctional activities were evaluated on the extent of their multifunctional practices and their ties to local and regional society. Some of the multifunctional practices include ecological sustainability and creation of environmental capital; socio-ecological relations and territorial embeddedness; engagement with local government systems; and productivity, diversification, and relation to markets. For example, one of the farms engaged in biodynamic farming practices and another focused on maintaining a small and sustainable herd size as determined by the local geography. From a geographic territorial perspective, one of the farms focused on returning value to a native sheep breed and began to promote somewhat of a regional Garfagnana brand.

Farm production and marketing can also lead to multifunctionality, especially on a small-scale level, when small farms choose to diversify production (one of the farms revitalized a variety of territorial wild fruits) and market to local food systems rather than large national or global markets. One of these farms also created social capital and engagement through local agricultural educational outreach (Treakie 2019).

GEOGRAPHY OF MULTIFUNCTIONALITY

Importantly, farms in areas that are geographically disadvantaged to agricultural production are more likely to engage in positive multifunctional practices as a type of adaptive strategy. Moreover, while place-based and multifunctional practices can support the socio-economic vitality of both small-scale farms and their surrounding communities, these strategies unfortunately do not automatically provide a buffer against competition from large-scale productivist models. If positive and place-based multifunctional practices are to succeed and primarily serve their local communities, they will require support from local institutions to sustain production against global concentration and production trends (Treakie 2019).

In the United States, the Conservation Reserve Program takes land out of intensive agricultural production. However, this is associated with both positive and negative externalities. Catering to activities such as hunting on CRP land rather than using the land for intensive farming reduces employment in rural areas and has a negative impact on rural communities.

It has been argued that people enjoy the beauty of observing dairy cattle grazing on rolling hills. If this is true, then production is truly coupled to positive externalities. The benefits to viewing dairy cattle contrast with recent technological advances in dairy production in states like Arizona, California, and Florida, where production is managed intensively, creating negative externalities associated with manure disposal and odour.

One example of a positive externality coupled with production is the scenic value of grape and wine production areas in Napa Valley, California. But wine production has little to do with US farm programs. However, consider the case of negative externalities generated, for example, from intensive hog production. Farm programs have an indirect effect through the provision of cheaper feed grains than under a free market setting.

The United States generally does not support the notion of multifunctionality when imposing tariff and non-tariff trade barriers. Consider the state of Florida, which produces many import-competing commodities such as tomatoes, citrus, and sugar cane. The latter is protected by tariff rate quotas. To our knowledge, no study uses positive externalities as an argument for protectionism. If anything, those who support free trade argue that negative externalities are associated with increased production from protectionism.

15.6   REGULATIONS

In many instances, agriculture in the United States and worldwide has become increasingly regulated, which suggests that increased production is often associated with negative externalities. Dairy operations must file environmental plans to manage manure, some site locations of hog operations are controlled in watersheds, and buffer strips are required for crop production in the United States (A. Schmitz, Boggess, and Tefertiller 1995; Casey et al. 1999). Agricultural production when unchecked can create negative externalities, but it is important to keep in mind that regulations apply to both program and non-program commodities. Empirically, an assessment of the importance of externalities associated with production should separate those commodities that are influenced by protectionist policies and those that are not.

15.7   TARGETING EXTERNALITIES

In theory, at least, there may be better ways to deal with positive externalities than through domestic price supports and standard trade policy instruments. These include redefining property rights and targeting externalities directly with separate policy instruments. Dealing with positive externalities through multifunctionality arguments results in a second-best outcome. According to Freeman and Roberts (1999) and Anderson (2000), there are significant threats to agricultural trade reform if agricultural protectionism is sanctioned as a means of achieving multifunctionality policy initiatives under the WTO. Using agricultural protectionism in one country under the umbrella of multifunctionality lowers the benefits from agriculture elsewhere. For example, employment in agriculture, which is the occupation of more than one-half of the population in many developing countries, is threatened by European subsidies that distort world prices and production.

According to Anderson (2000) and Rude (2000), providing agricultural support is an indirect, high cost, and ineffective way to achieve enhanced spillover benefits from agriculture. Many of the benefits put forward by supporters of multifunctionality as a basis for agricultural protectionism are related indirectly to agricultural production. As a result, subsidizing agricultural production is unlikely to enhance positive spillovers because the subsidy is not targeted at the spillovers themselves. In other cases, secondary benefits could be enhanced by targeting non-market benefits directly, rather than using agricultural protectionism to maintain or increase agricultural production. Such an approach avoids the negative spillovers that agricultural protectionism has for the national economy and for farmers in developing countries. The details of targeting specific spillovers are provided by Baumol and Oates (1988), Cornes and Sandler (1996), and Rude (2000). Payments linked explicitly to specific non-market benefits will be more effective in attaining the desired secondary effects than direct support to protect agriculture. The provision of direct payments should be made conditional on achieving the desired outcome (e.g., payments for maintaining hedgerows should be made only where hedgerows are properly maintained).

One example of a frequently cited multifunctionality spillover benefit of agriculture is enhanced rural employment. While agricultural industries are located in rural areas, rural economies are not necessarily dominated by agriculture. In some heavily populated industrialized countries, many rural areas are adjacent to urban areas and have numerous non-farm as well as farm activities. For example, European farm households often earn the largest part of their income from non-farm activities (Mahé and Ortalo-Magné 1999, 93). If rural employment is a desired social policy, a more efficient and lower-cost option will be to redirect agricultural support payments specifically to rural or regional employment programs.

Another example in which positive externalities could be targeted more directly and at a lower cost is flood-mitigation benefits and erosion-prevention benefits in Japan (Anderson 2000). Cultivating paddy fields is unlikely to be the only way of providing these environmental benefits. If cultivated paddy fields are the most direct and least-cost form of providing flood-mitigation benefits, the most efficient policy will be to pay farmers based on their capacity to maintain specific paddy fields as a water buffer. Payments can be directly related to the contribution of the fields to flood mitigation and will be made only to growers who provide flood-control spillover at a payment rate based on the degree of water buffering provided by paddy maintenance or alternative activities. This means that not all farmers will be subsidized at the same rate. The key difference between this and the broadly based support measure is that the payments farmers receive will be decoupled from production and from price support measures for rice. Under this system, producers will receive only the world price for rice. This will minimize both the distortion to the allocation of resources domestically and the international spillover effects on rice producers in other countries.

EFFICIENT POLICIES

More efficient policies aimed directly at preserving spillover benefits in rural areas already exist in some countries. For example, the Countryside Stewardship Scheme in the United Kingdom offers direct payments to conserve, restore, and/or maintain a range of landscape, wildlife, and historical features (MAFF 2021). The scheme is targeted to where the greatest public benefits can be gained, and individuals other than farmers are also eligible to apply. Over the 1991 to 1996 period, farmers represented 75 per cent of the Countryside Stewardship Scheme applicants, with the remainder included non-farming landowners and tenants, local authorities, and voluntary bodies (Mahé and Ortalo-Magné 1999).

A program targeted to the explicit provision of spillover benefits is the Countryside Access Scheme in England and Wales under which money is paid to farmers to set aside suitable farmland for hedgerows, which are valued by people as defining the character of the English landscape because they provide a habitat for animals and plants, and they act as corridors for the movement of some species. However, support under the EU's Common Agricultural Policy to promote cereal production has encouraged farmers to replace pastures with crops. Modern cropping technologies require large areas unimpeded by obstacles such as hedgerows. Indeed, until 1989, farmers were actually paid a subsidy to remove hedges. It is estimated that the length of hedgerows in Britain has shrunk by more than one-half since the mid-1940s (Conniff 1997). More efficient policies have been introduced that directly seek to preserve the benefits that people in the United Kingdom derive from the remaining hedgerows. For example, the Countryside Stewardship Scheme provides payments to farmers and other land managers to restore hedgerows at rates of £2 to £4 per metre for hedge laying, coppicing, and planting (MAFF 2021).

15.8 MEASURING EXTERNALITIES IN AGRICULTURE: EXAMPLES

Below, we give additional studies that empirically estimate the extent of externalities. Most studies, though limited in number, find significant negative externalities associated with agriculture, but very few find positive externalities.

15.8.1 Micro Studies

The Florida Everglades restoration project has drawn significant attention. The Florida Everglades and its deterioration has been a controversial subject since the 1980s. Many arguments have been made that the quality of the Everglades is deteriorating in part because of fertilizer runoff from sugar production. At the same time, millions of dollars have been spent to restore the Everglades. Such projects include the buyout of sugar lands in order to create water treatment facilities and restore water flow.

> **FLORIDA EVERGLADES NATIONAL PARK**
> The Everglades National Park is a 1.5-million-acre wetlands preserve in south Florida. The Everglades is made up of coastal mangroves, sawgrass marshes, and pine flatwoods that are home to hundreds of animal species. Among the Everglades' abundant wildlife are the endangered leatherback turtle, American crocodile, Florida panther, and West Indian manatee.

In 2010, the US Sugar Corporation sold sugar acreage for the Everglades restoration. Even though the buyout of the US sugar lands involved 26,000 acres (which was far less than the originally proposed 187,000 acres), less than half of this land has been used for Everglades restoration. In their study on the issue, A. Schmitz, Kennedy, and Hill-Gabriel (2012) employed the concept of an Environmental Equivalent (EE), which is the dollar amount of environmental benefits needed from the Save the Everglades project to generate net positive benefits from removing the negative externalities created by both agriculture and urban development. Their analysis found that the originally proposed 187,000-acre project would have resulted in a net welfare loss between US$1.0 billion and US$1.3 billion while the 26,800-acre project would have resulted in between US$0.5 billion and US$0.8 billion in net welfare losses.

However, when calculating the EE needed to generate benefits greater than costs, the EE approach to program implementation can be undermined by noneconomic arguments. For example, often policies are introduced within the context of public choice theory, in which a Political Lobbying Equivalent or a Political Corruption Equivalent plays a key role. Although most analyses do not determine where EE benefits will occur, they are expected to accrue through tourism, job creation, and sustaining resources for both natural and built environments (A. Schmitz, Kennedy, and Hill-Gabriel 2013).

EPA AND THE EVERGLADES RESTORATION

In 1988, the United States filed suit against the state of Florida, claiming that the levels of phosphorus flowing into federally controlled lands in Everglades National Park and the Arthur R. Marshall Loxahatchee National Wildlife Refuge violated the Clean Water Act (*United States v South Florida Water Management District*, 847 F. Supp 1567 (S.D. Fla 1992)). After several years of litigation, the parties entered into a settlement agreement in 1991 that was implemented by a Consent Decree in 1992. Some of the residential measures included a commitment by the South Florida Water Management District (SFWMD) to construct Stormwater Treatment Areas (STAs) to filter phosphorus before it reaches the federal lands in the Everglades, and the establishment of a regulatory program to require permits for water discharging from the Everglades Agricultural Area (EAA).

Removing phosphorus and improving water quality addresses only one challenge facing the Everglades, and many ecological benefits will only come from completing restoration projects that reconnect water flow throughout the Everglades.

15.8.2   Macro Studies

In studies of agricultural spillovers in the United Kingdom, Pretty et al. (2000, 2001, 2005) and O'Neill (2007) state that the total externality costs of agriculture were calculated to be £233 million annually, or 89 per cent of average net farm income, in 1996. To encourage farm activities that would result in positive externalities, which are under-provided in the market-place, subsidies and regulatory measures were recommended, whereas regulation and economic instruments (levies/taxes) were recommended to correct negative externalities. For the United States, the external costs of agricultural activities were estimated to range from US$5.7 billion to US$16.9 billion annually. Based on 168.8 million hectares of cropland in the United States, the external costs could vary from US$29.44 to US$95.68 per hectare, which appears quite dramatic. Note that the studies estimate the negative externalities associated with agriculture. But were there any positive externalities?

In reviewing empirical studies, one might ask: what constitutes agricultural externalities, negative or positive? Both livestock operations and crop production impose external costs. Both have a negative impact on the soil. In many developed countries, there are regions where manure from livestock is spread on the land, causing excessive deposits of nitrogen (N) that get converted to nitrates (NO_3) and phosphates (P), and that can carry zoonotic diseases (diseases that are transferable from animals to humans), while crop production employs pesticides and fertilizers that negatively impact the soil. These forms of chemical pollution of soil adversely affect plant and animal biodiversity. Likewise, changes in land use and how land is managed also impact the composition of the soil, thereby affecting its future productivity and biodiversity. (In developing countries, however, manure is used to promote crop growth, as fertilizers are often applied at suboptimal rates or not at all; indeed, sometimes manure and other nutrients, such as crop residues, are removed from the land and used for cooking purposes.) Finally, certain land-use practices (e.g., planting of trees, zero tillage, and permanent grasslands) can sequester carbon from the atmosphere, thereby mitigating climate change.

Livestock enterprises and arable farms have an impact on water quality, primarily because chemicals that first enter the soil subsequently leach into groundwater or runoff into surface water. P and N can adversely affect lakes, making them less suitable for supporting aquatic ecosystems, while polluted water can have a negative effect on biodiversity more generally. Chemicals in ground (and surface) water can also affect human health. To improve water quality involves costs, with an estimate of these costs providing information about the negative externality effects of agricultural activities.

Livestock operations emit methane (CH_4), CO_2, nitrous oxide (N_2O), sulphur dioxide (SO_2), and ammonia (NH_3) to the atmosphere, while arable farms emit CO_2 and nitrogen. Emissions of N_2O and SO_2 are a concern because N_2O rapidly oxidizes to become nitrogen dioxide (NO_2), which results in smog, while SO_2 leads to acid rain. CH_4 and CO_2 emissions from agricultural activities are important contributors to global warming (see Chapter 14). The impacts of CH_4 and CO_2 can be measured using information on the shadow price of carbon and knowledge about emissions of these gases from livestock operations and crop production.

The impacts of agriculture go beyond the traditional environmental impacts on soils, water quality, and the atmosphere. They also concern biodiversity, wildlife habitat, landscapes, animal welfare, food security, and human health. Farming reduces habitat for some animals (e.g., large ungulates), but creates habitat for others (e.g., meadow birds); it destroys some amenities (wooded areas that store carbon), while providing new ones (visually appealing landscapes); it eliminates some wetlands that function to filter water and mitigate flooding, although the in-filling of such wetlands destroys mosquito habitat, thereby improving human health. Agricultural policies affect land management and use, thereby incentivizing activities that have both negative and positive externality effects.

15.9   SUMMARY AND CONCLUSIONS

- In countries where the agricultural sectors will suffer serious consequences from trade liberalization, support for a multifunctionality approach to agricultural policy is on the rise. Trade liberalization will create both gainers and losers, with agriculture in many parts of the world suffering in the absence of compensation. The spillover benefits from agriculture are being put forward as a reason to maintain or even increase agricultural protectionism.

- Essentially, multifunctionality arguments refute the standard gains from trade arguments, where externalities are generally not taken into account. There are strong arguments against the multifunctionality approach, insofar as it implies increased agricultural protectionism.

- Multifunctional arguments create distortions to world markets and damage efficient agricultural producers elsewhere, including developing countries.

- Subsidizing agricultural production has been shown to increase negative spillovers from agriculture, including causing ongoing damage to rural environments. As the OECD recognizes, a more efficient and potentially more effective approach to achieving multifunctionality objectives is to use specific policy instruments that are targeted at providing the multifunctionality outcome. Indeed, targeted policies aimed explicitly at achieving some of the spillover benefits claimed under the banner of multifunctionality already exist. However, the agricultural sector will lose because of decreased protectionism, even though society as a whole will gain.

- The potential benefits of multifunctionality alone cannot justify use of multifunctionality arguments in trade negotiations. First, no empirical estimates exist of the value of existing or potential positive externalities associated with agriculture anywhere in the world. (Most economists agree that the theory of externalities has a solid foundation, but whether externalities exist in the real world is a different question.) Further research on this topic should attempt case studies on externality issues using the willingness-to-pay framework that has been applied to many sectors outside of agriculture. Questions will need to be addressed, such as: Who is willing to pay for these amenities? Will it be only rural people, urban populations, tourists, or some combination of these groups? Poor people in urban areas, for example, may be more motivated by cheaper food prices than they are by the beauty of the countryside. Without resolving these issues, arguments that support multifunctionality lack empirical content and compromise further discussions of the multifunctionality approach to trade negotiations. Second, if positive externalities exist, the current thinking on economic policy will be to deal with these externalities directly, including potentially changing property rights. For now, economic theorists commonly hold that using a trade instrument such as a tariff is not the most efficient way to deal with the externality problem. Instead, payments must target the positive (or negative) externality directly.

- Multifunctionality arguments are used by countries that have relatively high costs of production (e.g., Switzerland and Japan). Because they are high-cost producers, their agricultural sectors will suffer losses from increased trade under liberalization. As a result, some representatives from the agricultural sector in these economies will continue rent-seeking behaviour for protectionism and will add multifunctionality arguments to support their position, while others will not. This is not surprising when cast in public-choice theory. From a national perspective, agricultural policy formulation is not only about protecting agricultural producers, but about human rights as well.

- The OECD recognizes that price supports and standard trade instruments that weaken the arguments for protectionism are not efficient ways of dealing with positive and negative externalities. Generally, one cannot use multifunctionality arguments to support protectionism if the externalities can be targeted efficiently with other policy instruments. Moreover, if externalities are targeted directly, the argument for protectionism becomes even less convincing. Farmers and agribusinesses may need to come up with a different argument to support protectionism than the use of the multifunctionality approach.

CHAPTER SIXTEEN

Food Quality and Safety

16.1   FOOD QUALITY AND SAFETY

Agricultural policy for countries such as the United States takes into account food quality and safety, including foodborne illnesses, diseases, and allergies. Illnesses caused by pathogens such as Campylobacter, Salmonella, and E. coli have affected foodstuffs from peppers to peanut butter; similarly, diseases such as bovine spongiform encephalopathy (BSE, or mad cow disease) and foot-and-mouth disease also have clear implications for animal husbandry and agricultural policies. Problems associated with genetically modified organisms (GMOs) have food safety implications as well, such as the Cry9C protein found in tortillas made with StarLink corn, which raised concerns about allergic reactions in humans. A significant debate surfaced in California with the failed "Big Green" Proposition 128, which would have limited the use of pesticides in fruit and vegetable production to prevent possible health consequences from pesticide residues. Apart from concerns about possible food contamination, consumers have expressed concerns about the inherent health consequences of food itself, for example, the burgeoning incidence of obesity and the possible role of trans-fats in the human body. These are but a few samples of policy debates over food quality and safety.

FOODBORNE DISEASES: WHICH ARE THE MOST COMMON?
The most commonly recognized foodborne diseases are those caused by the bacteria Campylobacter, Salmonella, and E. coli O157:H7, and by a group of viruses called Caliciviruses, also known as the Norwalk and Norwalk-like viruses.

Campylobacter is a genus of bacterial pathogens that causes fever, diarrhoea, and abdominal cramps. It is the most commonly identified bacterial cause of diarrhoeal illness in the world. These bacteria live in the intestines of healthy birds, and most raw poultry meat has Campylobacter on it. Eating undercooked chicken, or other food that has been contaminated with juices from raw chicken, is the most frequent source of this infection.

Salmonella is also genus of bacterium that is widespread in the intestines of birds, reptiles, and mammals. It can spread to humans via a variety of different foods of animal origin. The illness it causes – salmonellosis – typically includes fever, diarrhoea, and abdominal cramps. In persons with poor underlying health or weakened immune systems, it can invade the bloodstream and cause life-threatening infections.

E. coli O157:H7 is a bacterial pathogen that affects cattle and other similar animals. Human illness typically follows consumption of food or water that has been contaminated with microscopic amounts of cow feces. The illness it causes is often severe, with bloody diarrhoea and painful abdominal cramps, but without much fever. In 3 to 5 per cent of cases, a complication called haemolytic uremic syndrome (HUS) can occur several weeks after the initial symptoms. This severe complication includes temporary anaemia, profuse bleeding, and kidney failure, and in rare cases can be fatal to those with weakened immune systems.

Caliciviruses, such as Norwalk virus, are an extremely common cause of foodborne illness, although they are rarely diagnosed because the laboratory test is not widely available. They cause acute gastrointestinal illness, usually with more vomiting than diarrhoea, which resolves within two days. Unlike many foodborne pathogens that have animal reservoirs, evidence indicates that Norwalk-like viruses spread primarily from person to person. Restaurant workers whose hands are infected with the virus can contaminate food during food preparation; infected fishermen can contaminate oysters as they harvest them.

Some common diseases are occasionally foodborne, even though they are usually transmitted by other routes. These include infections caused by Shigella, Hepatitis A viruses, and the parasites Giardia lamblia and Cryptosporidium. Even Streptococcal pharyngitis (strep throat) can be transmitted occasionally through food.

In addition to disease caused by direct infection, some foodborne diseases are caused by toxins produced by microbes in foods. For example, the bacterium Staphylococcus aureus can grow in some foods and produce a toxin that causes intense vomiting. The rare but deadly disease botulism occurs when the bacterium Clostridium botulinum grows and produces a powerful paralytic toxin in foods.

These toxins can produce illness even if the microbes that produced them are no longer there. Other toxins and poisonous chemicals can cause foodborne illness. People can become ill if a pesticide is inadvertently added to a food, or if naturally poisonous substances are used to prepare a meal. For example, people can become ill from consuming naturally poisonous foods, such as certain mushrooms or fish (USDHHS/CDC 2009).

16.2   GOVERNMENT INVOLVEMENT IN DOMESTIC FOOD SAFETY

Food safety concerns can have a huge economic impact. In certain cases, only a government has the scope of power needed to properly address matters of food safety regulation. Further, the form of these regulations is often industry-wide preventive policies rather than case-by-case responses after the fact. Two main forces behind current food safety policies include the impacts of food safety on the market and historical patterns of government-level agricultural policy interventions.

16.2.1   Consumer and Market Factors

Van Ravenswaay and Hoehn (1996) describe consumer responses to foodborne contamination. For example, consumers may respond by avoiding a product or switching brands until after the problem is resolved (e.g., in the case of Salmonella outbreaks). Each option implies a different impact on the market. Product avoidance may be more likely when the product is largely undifferentiated (e.g., the consumption of fresh meats under the threat of BSE). Brand switching may deliver a premium price if one producer incurs the cost of delivering a safe product. The aggregate demand for the commodity in question will undoubtedly decline due to the added cost or reduced value associated with the contaminated product. Both farmer profits and consumer welfare suffer. Thus, the mere possibility of foodborne illness affects consumer demand.

Food markets are complex. Most countries have decentralized marketing due to the wide array of participants involved. For example, meat packers sell to wholesalers who then sell to retailers, such as supermarkets and restaurants. Given the myriad market participants, standardized marketing is necessary to reduce transaction costs, especially for lower income consumers (Working 1943). Governments in developed countries often impose regulations (e.g., standardizing weights and volumes or mandatory food safety and grade restrictions) on the food market to minimize transaction costs.

16.2.2   Historical Contexts for Government Food Regulation

Food safety regulations have been in existence for thousands of years. For example, there are biblical admonitions against certain foods (Leviticus 11) and against the consumption of blood (Leviticus 17). Hutt and Hutt (1984) describe the basis for modern food safety in Roman law. Specifically, the adulteration of food was an offence called *stellionatus* (a fraud not distinguished by a special name and not defined by written law), which would be comparable to a civil offence in current legal systems. Tampering with food safety was comparable to fraud "where anyone has substituted some article for another; or has put aside goods which he was obliged to deliver, or has spoiled them" (ibid., 5). Of course, in that system "a substantial portion of the Roman civil law was designed to assure a sufficient supply at reasonable prices" (ibid., 5). Following this principle, the Code of Justinian (issued in 527 CE by Emperor Justinian) controlled the potential monopolization of the supply of food.

Governments have long been involved in enforcing standards of quality as a component of food regulations. The use of standards can be traced back to the Theodosian Code (issued in 438 CE by Theodosius II, emperor of the Eastern Roman Empire), which allowed for distinguishing between different qualities of bread (e.g., "coarse bread" and "fine bread"). False labelling was considered fraud: "The transfer of step bread from one step to another shall be prohibited, and the office of the prefect of Annona shall know that the severest punishments threaten them if they shall further permit such transfers to be made throughout the steps" (Hutt and Hutt 1984, 8).

The Roman common laws for food standardization found their way into English common and statutory laws. One of the earliest instances of food labelling can be traced to the English requirement that bakers impose a mark (or label, much like a brand) onto each loaf of bread, denoting the quality of the bread and the name of the baker. The law then provided for punishments for selling a lower quality of bread in place of a "finer" quality.

FOOD SAFETY IN ENGLISH COMMON LAW

"(1) If any corrupted wine be in town, or such as is not wholesome for man's body ... Also if there be any that sell by one measure, and buy by another. Also if any do use false ells, weights, or measures; (2) If any butcher does sell contagious flesh, or that died of Murren; [and] (3) Also they shall enquire of cooks that seethe flesh or fish with bread or water, or any otherwise, that is not wholesome for man's body, or after that they have kept it so long that it loseth its natural wholesomeness, and then seethe it again, and sell it" (Henry III Stat 6 [1266], qtd. in Hutt and Hutt 1984, 14). In addition to setting prices for bread, wine, and ale, and punishments for any offence, these statutes required that "every Baker shall have a mark of his own for his Bread" and provided strong punishment for the sale of "unwholesome Flesh" (ibid.).

Early food safety regulations in the United States followed English common law until the economic dynamics spawned by the Industrial Revolution increased the political visibility of food safety. Many pre-industrial populations lived in farm communities and were either directly involved in the production of foodstuffs (e.g., as farm households) or transacted directly with farmers to acquire foodstuffs. As they moved away from rural communities, following industrial job opportunities into urban centres, they became more distant from the source of food products. The loss of this direct market was further complicated as technological advances and specialization made it more difficult for consumers to judge the quality of food themselves (Law 2003). While a consumer could visually inspect the quality of fresh meat, canned meats could be inspected only after the can was purchased and opened. Moreover, the development of pickling and other processing methods created opportunities to disguise the presence of, for example, spoiled meat. The possibility of these illegal acts was brought to public attention by literature such as Upton Sinclair's *The Jungle,* which highlights labour strife and the possibility of monopoly pricing by large meat packers, in addition to food safety concerns. Taken together, these factors contributed to the passage of the US Meat Inspection Act and the Pure Food and Drug Act of 1906.

EVERYTHING BUT THE SQUEAL

There have been many exposés on safety violations in the food industry, such as those in the meat-packing industry. One example is Upton Sinclair's description of meat-packing in *The Jungle*: "With one member trimming beef in a cannery, and another working in a sausage factory, the family had a first-hand knowledge of the great majority of Packingtown swindles. For it was the custom, as they found, whenever meat was so spoiled that it could not be used for anything else, either to can it or else to chop it up into sausage. With what had been told them by Jonas, who had worked in the pickle-rooms, they could now study the whole of the spoiled-meat industry on the inside, and read a new and grim meaning into that old Packingtown jest – that they used everything of the pig except the squeal" (Sinclair [1906] 2006, 147).

Ultimately, human health should be a concern for any government. Governments become involved in the regulation of agriculture and food because the food industry has not been successful at self-regulation. One argument for the self-regulation of the food industry states that product safety can be assured by liability and the threat of lawsuits, but this may not hold true in the case of food safety (Viscusi 1989). For the threat of a lawsuit to effectively ensure product safety, several conditions need to hold: (1) court costs must be less than anticipated benefits; (2) the product must be linked to the damage (e.g., illness); and (3) the producers must have the funds to pay for the damage. In the case of food, all three of these conditions are rarely met (Antle 1996). For all of these reasons, government inspection, grading, and other standards are the most common methods of maintaining food safety.

16.3   INSPECTION AND GRADING

Many governments are involved in grading, inspecting (both domestic and imported goods), licensing, labelling, and setting standards for various agricultural products. The regulation of the agriculture and food industry is complex, involving numerous agencies at all levels of state/provincial, municipal, and federal governments. For example, in the United States, the Department of Agriculture, the Food and Drug Administration, the Environmental Protection Agency, and the Department of Health and Human Services are involved at the federal level.

16.3.1   Jurisdiction in the United States

US food safety falls under the jurisdiction of both state and federal governments. Food safety regulation began with the Pure Food and Drug Act and the Meat Inspection Act of 1906 (Hutt and Hutt 1984). These were initially under the administration of the US Department of Agriculture (USDA). In 1940 the Food and Drug Administration was removed from the USDA's jurisdiction because of the perceived conflict of interest. Since then, food safety regulation has resided in the US Department of Health and Human Services. The Food and Drug Administration handles all inspection responsibilities except those regarding meat and poultry (Knutson, Penn, and Flinchbaugh 1998). Pesticide regulation is under the auspices of the US Environmental Protection Agency.

16.3.2   Jurisdiction in Canada

The Canadian federal government has streamlined the agencies involved with food health and safety regulations. The Canadian Food Inspection Agency (CFIA) was created in 1997. All inspection and quarantine services formerly provided by Agriculture and Agri-Food Canada, Health Canada, Industry Canada, and the Department of Fisheries and Oceans now fall under the Canadian Food Inspection Agency. The CFIA is mandated to harmonize food safety standards that cover, for example, dairy, meat, poultry, and transportation across provinces and municipalities throughout Canada.

Governments are encouraging private firms to be more directly involved in food inspection. For example, the United States in 1996 began to switch its meat inspection from organoleptic procedures (i.e., procedures that rely solely on sight, smell, and touch) to a hazard analysis critical control point (HACCP) scheme. The HACCP plan is the method of inspection recommended in the Codex Alimentarius, an international set of standards discussed further in section 16.6.1. The goal of the HACCP is to identify points in the food-production and food-processing systems that are critical for food quality and safety. Firms are required to pursue a plan to control possible hazards at these critical points. In some cases, HACCP has led to a trace-back system, allowing industry or government to identify what end products have resulted from which inputs. In effect, the goal of the government is to create a health paper trail that runs from consumer to processor and, ideally, back to the farmer (Spriggs and Isaac 1999).

16.3.3   Meat Inspection and Grading

Prior to 1996 the USDA Food Safety and Inspection Service (FSIS) was required to inspect slaughterhouses; meat-, food-, and poultry-processing plants; and egg-packing and egg-processing plants. The early inspection process used organoleptic methods that were incapable of detecting microorganisms or chemical contamination. The process was labour intensive. For example, every carcass that passed through a slaughtering facility had to be inspected. In addition, this inspection procedure failed to consider changes in production technology associated with new drugs and environmental contaminants (Antle 1996).

In 1996 the United States moved to a hazard analysis critical control point (HACCP) management system of meat and poultry inspection. The initial HACCP proposal required each plant to develop a plan for each animal species and process and to perform microbiological testing for salmonella on every slaughter class and species of ground meat each day. A major criticism of the proposal was that this placed relatively high costs on smaller (low-volume) plants that slaughtered a number of species or that produced a wide variety of products (e.g., processing plants producing specialty meats). The regulations were then changed to require more frequent testing for *E. coli* and to require only one comprehensive HACCP plan per plant.

THE HACCP SYSTEM:

1 Conduct a hazard analysis.
2 Identify critical control points (CCPs) for physical, biological, and chemical hazards.
3 Establish critical limits for preventive measures associated with each critical control point.
4 Establish CCP monitoring requirements.
5 Determine and perform corrective actions.
6 Establish record-keeping systems.
7 Conduct verification procedures.

Table 16.1. Total estimated US benefits over twenty years (US$ billion) of the HACCP plan for meat inspections

Pathogen-Reduction Scenario (%)	LS (3%)[a]	VOSL (3%)[b]	LS (7%)	VOSL (7%)
30	3.7–13.7	15.7–71.3	2.4–8.9	10.2–46.1
60	7.4–27.5	31.5–142.6	4.8–17.7	20.3–92.1
90	11.0–41.2	47.2–213.9	7.1–26.6	30.5–138.2

[a] LS = Landefeld and Seskin; LS estimates of value based on a hybrid human capital/willingness-to-pay approach.
[b] VOSL = value of a statistical life; VOSL is assumed to be US$5 million.
Source: T. Roberts, Buzby, and Ollinger (1996).

T. Roberts, Buzby, and Ollinger (1996) note that the cost assumptions made by the Economic Research Service Division of the United States Department of Agriculture (USDA/ERS) are relatively conservative, except for the assumption that the HACCP is able to achieve a 90 per cent reduction of illnesses. The USDA Food Safety and Inspection Service estimated that the proportion of illness reduction ran from 10 per cent to 100 per cent and found that for all levels higher than 10 per cent, the benefits of HACCP exceeded its costs (Table 16.1).

16.3.4   Cost Recovery

A key change affecting meat inspection is the move by the Canadian government to a system of cost recovery. When producers, rather than taxpayers, have to pay for inspection, the number of inspections may decline because producers will bear neither the full cost of non-inspection nor the full benefits of complete inspection. To self-insure against problems of food quality, firms may increase the expenditure on quality control as a substitute for costly inspection. These alternatives include an HACCP-type system with a trace-back program that may allow processors to provide incentives to farmers to improve the quality of their products and to lower the overall cost of producing safe products.

16.4   GREATER ROLE FOR THE PRIVATE SECTOR

Collectively, the meat industry is becoming increasingly involved in the promotion of products. The Canadian Beef Grading Agency (CBGA) was created when the government privatized its beef-grading activities in 1996. The CBGA developed a grading system based on the objectives and scientific standards of meat quality on a cost-recovery basis. Meat-packing plants must be federally inspected to be graded, and graders can refuse to grade carcasses that appear abnormal (Spriggs and Isaac 1999).

The Canadian Cattle Identification Agency (CCIA) was created in 1998 to trace live-stock activities in the meat industry. The National Beef Identification System (NBIS) traces cattle at processing plants back to the original herd, while the Canadian Livestock Tracking System (CLTS) traces cattle through the supply chain from producer to dealer, including third parties.

In Australia, co-regulation for meat was introduced in 1997. Under this system, private companies take responsibility for food inspection, while the government plays an overseer's role. Private companies, which perform the inspections, must file reports with the government for auditing the system.

16.5   REGULATION OF GENETICALLY MODIFIED FOODS

The introduction of genetically modified organisms (GMOs) has further complicated the de-bate over who decides what food is acceptable and what is not (Chegini and A. Schmitz 2021). Food production using recombinant genes has raised concerns about the safety of genetically modified foods and the effect of GMOs on the environment. Some countries are demanding that imported food products meet their own domestic regulations, regardless of regulations in the exporting country. This demand has raised the argument that domestic regulation is sim-ply a barrier to trade. Most countries follow two very different basic approaches to regulating GMOs: the North American approach, based on the concept of substantial equivalence, and the European Union (EU) framework, based on the precautionary principle (Table 16.2). (For details on GMOs, see Chapter 18.)

The EU has a more stringent approach to regulating GMOs than does either the United States or Canada. All products produced using biotechnology are subject to regulation in the EU, and they must be proven to be safe before being allowed into the market. If or when they enter the market, they must be labelled as potentially containing GMOs. In North America, GM food products that are viewed as essentially equivalent to conventionally produced goods are deemed to be safe, and labelling is not mandatory.

16.6   INTERNATIONAL INSTITUTIONS FOR FOOD REGULATION

Harmonizing food inspection standards among countries can reduce the transaction costs associated with international trade. If a food processor needs to gear its production process to meet only a single set of standards and needs only to go through one inspection, its costs of exporting to multiple markets will decrease dramatically. Several mechanisms have been created to set international standards for food regulation, including those set forth by the Food and Agriculture Organization of the United Nations (FAO). Institutions and trade agreements

Table 16.2. Competing regulatory processes for genetically modified (GM) organisms

Characteristics of Regulatory System for GM Food	North American Approach	EU Approach
Trigger for regulation	Novel product attributes	Use of biotech processes
Precautionary principle	Essential equivalence: product equivalent to non-GM products deemed safe	Certainty
Access to system	Closed to interest groups	Open to interest groups
Labelling	Discretionary	Mandatory

Source: Isaac and Phillips (1999).

attempt to set a benchmark for domestic standards, both to encourage harmonization and to reduce the use of standards as a non-tariff barrier to trade.

16.6.1   Codex Alimentarius

The Codex Alimentarius Commission implemented the joint FAO/World Health Organization (WHO) Food Standards Programme to protect the health of consumers and to ensure fair practices in the food trade (FAO 1999). Adopted in 1985, the Codex is a series of international food standards and guidelines. For example, it contains guidelines on food labelling that include the maximum amounts of certain substances in a product for it to be considered as low-fat or fat-free and defines what qualifies as a polyunsaturated fatty acid.

Codex standards are set by members of the Codex Committee, which is made up of member countries of the United Nations. The Codex Committee meets at least annually to set up new guidelines or to revise the old ones. Subcommittees can be created to handle specific concerns such as the labelling of GM foods. Codex regulations have become more important since the 1995 implementation of the General Agreement on Tariffs and Trade (GATT), which uses the Codex as the international measuring stick to determine whether domestic regulations are illegally restricting trade.

Other international agreements set out acceptable actions for countries to use to limit the risks of food to plant and animal health. The International Plant Protection Convention (IPPC), like the Codex Alimentarius, is a multilateral agreement administered through the FAO. The IPPC is an attempt to harmonize plant protection measures, such as controlling the introduction of pests. The IPPC was updated in 1997 to create the institutional framework for setting international standards; in 2019 the IPPC convention included 183 member countries (FAO 2019b). In addition, there is an international agreement to harmonize animal health standards: the Office International des Epizooties (OIE), also known as the World

Organisation for Animal Health. This intergovernmental organization was created in 1924; between 1999 and 2019 its membership grew from 152 member countries to 182 (OIE 2020). Along with the Codex, these agreements have become more important since their inclusion in the GATT.

16.6.2   The Sanitary and Phytosanitary Agreement

The Uruguay Round of GATT negotiations set regulations surrounding the health and safety of food, food production, and the various standards of product quality. The Sanitary and Phytosanitary (SPS) Agreement of the GATT sets out rules for food safety and standards for animal and plant health (WTO 1999a, 1999b). Although countries want the right to protect the health of their consumers and agriculture, GATT signatories have concerns that countries may use health and safety regulations to block trade. To address these concerns, the SPS Agreement encourages countries to use existing international standards (e.g., the Codex, IPPC, and OIE) and requires scientific justification for standards that are higher.

16.6.3   Excessive Regulations

When are regulations excessive? First, GATT agreements dictate that sanitary (human and animal health) and phytosanitary (plant health) regulations must be applied to domestic and international products equally. Second, the agreement states that if there are several measures that can be used, the least trade-restricting measure will be taken. For example, countries with concerns about protecting their cattle from a disease can either completely block imports from a country known to have cattle affected by that disease or they can demand certification that the animals imported have been vaccinated against the disease. Although the latter route is less trade restricting, it also has higher monitoring costs.

The most controversial aspect of the SPS Agreement is the requirement that regulations in excess of international standards are based on scientific risk assessment. Prior to the SPS Agreement, if a country had a certain health standard, the onus was placed on the importer to ensure the product met the standard. Until the country determined the product was safe, the importation of the product was blocked. If a country bars an import, its challenge may be to show scientific proof that indicates the possible health problems caused by the import. This challenge is made only if the country bans a product that is already allowed in other countries, or if the product meets international safety standards. This raises an interesting question regarding liability. If a country is forced to allow the import of a certain product and the product is later found to cause health problems, the importing country's own regulatory system may be liable.

THE SPS AGREEMENT AND TRADE

In April 1997, the United States filed a complaint with the WTO regarding Japanese measures to block imports of US apples, cherries, nectarines, and walnuts until the United States showed that quarantine measures were effective to protect Japan's domestic agricultural industry and environment. The US complaint rested on the fact that Japan blocked all varieties of the products while it decided if the quarantine was effective, and the United States argued that if the measure was shown to be effective for one variety, it should be assumed to be equally effective for similar products. The United States argued that the Japanese process violated Articles 2, 5, and 8 of the SPS Agreement, covering basic rights and obligations, the appropriate level of SPS protection, and control procedures, respectively. In November 1997, the Dispute Settlement Board of the WTO organized a panel of scientific experts from various countries to hear the US complaint. The panel found that the Japanese system contradicted Art. 2.2, which states: "Members shall ensure that any sanitary and phytosanitary measure is applied only to the extent necessary to protect human, animal, or plant life or health, is based on scientific principles, and is not maintained without sufficient scientific evidence" (WTO 1999b [SPS Agreement, 2]), and Art. 5.6, that states: "Members shall ensure that [SPS measures] are not more trade-restricting than required" (WTO 1999b [SPS Agreement, 4]). In November 1998, Japan appealed, and in February 1999, the Appellate Body upheld the original decision (WTO 1999c).

16.6.4   Technical Barriers to Trade

The Uruguay Round of GATT also introduced a new agreement on technical barriers to trade (TBT). Like the SPS Agreement, the TBT Agreement aimed to sort out acceptable safety, information, and quality requirements, and to identify barriers to trade for products not covered in the SPS. In the Tokyo Round of GATT negotiations (1974 to 1979), a TBT Agreement was reached, beginning the process of harmonizing standards across countries. In its original form, the agreement included regulations surrounding plant and animal health that were strengthened and developed into the SPS Agreement.

Like the SPS Agreement, the TBT Agreement requires that countries treat imported products the same as they treat domestic products in terms of quality, information, and safety requirements. The TBT Agreement is less strict about requiring adherence to international standards. Whereas the SPS Agreement demands scientific justification if a country sets requirements higher than the international standard, the TBT Agreement may allow these requirements for a number of reasons, including differences in technologies and geography (WTO 1999a).

16.7   REGULATIONS AND INFORMATION

What happens if no regulations exist to govern the quality of food? Many more contaminated foods will be allowed into the market. A problem arises should the consumer wish to know which products are of high quality and have a lower probability of bacterial contamination and which are of low quality and have a higher probability of contamination. A number of economic theories explain the outcome. For example, asymmetric information between the producer and consumer could lead to a theory known as the market for "lemons" (Akerlof 1970).

MARKET FOR "LEMONS"

Akerlof (1970) shows that if goods of two qualities are produced, and if consumers lack the information on their quality ex ante (before purchase), only low-quality goods will be produced. If consumers are uncertain about differences in product quality, they will only pay the low price associated with the lower-quality goods, driving the higher-quality goods out of the market.

Firms could find providing information about product quality to be in their own best interest. This information might come in the form of demonstrations, guarantees, or the reputation of the product. If a firm earns a reputation by producing differentiated higher quality products, it will be able to earn a premium for quality.

MEAT INSPECTION REGULATION IN PACKINGTOWN

"The people of Chicago saw the government inspectors in Packingtown, and they all took that to mean that they were protected from diseased meat; they did not understand that these hundred and sixty-three inspectors had been appointed at the request of the packers, and that they were paid by the United States government to certify that all the diseased meat was kept in the state. They had no authority beyond that; for the inspection of meat to be sold in the city and state the whole force in Packingtown consisted of three henchmen of the local political machine! And shortly afterward one of these, a physician, made the discovery that the carcasses of steers which had been condemned as tubercular by the government inspector, and which therefore contained ptomaines, which are deadly poisons, were left upon the platform and carted away to be sold in the city; and so he insisted that these carcasses be treated with an injection of kerosene – and was ordered to resign the same week! So indignant were the packers that they went further, and compelled the mayor to abolish the whole bureau of inspection; so that since then there has not been even a pretense of any interference with the graft" (Sinclair [1906] 2006, 103–4).

The timing of information may have significant implications for the economic cost of a food safety event. Consider the 1982 discovery that milk in Hawaii was potentially contaminated with Heptachlor (a highly toxic pesticide used on pineapples). R.E. Just, Hueth, and Schmitz (2004) describe four stages of the contamination: (1) the period where the contamination continued in ignorance; (2) the period of the dissemination of information about the contamination; (3) the period of psychological cost associated with uncertainty regarding the ultimate health effect of consuming the contaminated milk; and (4) the eventual adverse health effects on the population. Most information costs emphasize the second period, focusing on the loss in producer and consumer surplus as individuals react to an outbreak of foodborne illness such as Heptachlor.

16.8   REPUTATION EFFECT

Firms that attempt to differentiate their product and guarantee the product's quality may be able to create a reputation for supplying only high-quality products. For this reputation effect to be worthwhile, consumers must be willing and able to pay a premium for quality, and the firm must be able to capture that quality premium as a rent for its reputation (B. Klein and Leffler 1981). The quality premium must be greater than the extra costs associated with producing the higher-quality product to motivate a firm to invest in building a reputation and to turn down the one-time excess profits associated with dropping their quality without dropping their price (Shapiro 1983). Lynch et al. (1986) show that the reliance on reputation does not fully remove the problem of the market for "lemons." Leland (1979a, 1979b) illustrates that in markets where asymmetric information exists the quality will be suboptimal. Thus, the reputation effect is less efficient than a market that has perfect information (Carlton and Perloff 2000).

Without regulation, consumers may face high search costs, and they may be forced to pay premiums (above cost) for goods of high quality. Some high-quality products may not even be available because of the "lemons" problem. This, at least in part, is a market failure, which the government seeks to solve through supplying information.

Information does not have to reveal the quality characteristics of goods. It can also be directed to consumers regarding how they themselves can affect the quality of goods purchased. In the case of food safety, for example, some information provided by the government relates to food preparation methods used to minimize contamination. Thus, there are actions that consumers can take to decrease the likelihood of contamination. Moreover, insurance theory predicts that consumers may change their behaviour and be less vigilant in their own food handling if there are strict government standards (van Ravenswaay and Hoehn 1996).

16.9   COSTS AND BENEFITS OF REGULATION

Government regulation of food products has both costs and benefits. For one example, Brinkman et al. (1985) document the costs and estimate the benefits of apple and potato grading in Canada from 1979–80 to 1983–4 (Table 16.3). In both cases, the benefits outweigh the costs. Because of the competitive nature of these industries, Brinkman et al. (1985) state that the benefits are not captured by the producer; rather, they are passed through to the consumer. Economic efficiency dictates that the groups capturing the benefits, whether they are consumers or processors, should pay for the inspection.

16.9.1   Information on Quality

We have shown that asymmetric information can lead to market failure and to the call for regulation. Now, we need to ask: (1) Why is information asymmetric? and (2) Why do consumers lack knowledge about product quality?

Carlton and Perloff (2000) describe five reasons for limited consumer knowledge:

1 Information varies in reliability among groups.
2 The process of collecting information is costly.
3 Consumers have limited ability to store and recall information.
4 Information may not be fully processed because processing information is costly. Caswell and Padberg (1992) find that consumers choose up to two-thirds of their food products while in the store, where they spend about an hour a week shopping. Therefore, especially for food products, if information takes a long time to process, it will not likely be used in the decision.
5 Consumers may not have the resources to fully process the information. For example, look at the list of ingredients on a container of cheap ice cream. Many people (including the authors) have difficulty correctly pronouncing many of the names of the additives, and they certainly do not understand the nutritional implications of consuming them.

Table 16.3. Costs and benefits of grading apples and potatoes (C$ million)

Benefits	Apples	Potatoes	Costs	Apples	Potatoes
	(C$ million)			(C$ million)	
Increased value	34.6	33.6	Federal inspection	3.8	19.9
Lower storage and handling costs	9.4	5.7	Provincial inspection	1.8	5.5
Reduced product loss from receivers	15.9	24.1	Industry compliance	0.9	3.8
Facilitation of offshore exports	16.1	30.4	Related costs of R&D	1.4	6.4
Total	76.0	93.8		7.9	35.6

Source: Brinkman et al. (1985).

16.9.2   Information Attributes

Consumer goods can be split into three groups based on their information attributes: (1) search goods, (2) experience goods, and (3) credence goods (Tirole 1988). A search good is one whose quality a consumer can tell ex ante (e.g., a bouquet of cut flowers). An experience good is one that a consumer must experience or consume before knowing its quality (e.g., a restaurant meal). A credence good is one whose quality a consumer may never determine (e.g., the harmful effects of pesticide residue). Most goods have some combination of these characteristics. Consider a tomato. Some characteristics can be determined visually, such as lack of bruising or approximate ripeness (search good). Some characteristics, such as taste, can be determined only after consumption (experience good). Some characteristics may not be determined, such as pesticide or herbicide residue on the tomato or the tomato's ability to resist disease (credence good).

16.9.3   Making Credence "Concrete"

Information (such as food labels) can transform credence qualities into search attributes. Consider organic produce. If the credence quality of the good (i.e., it was produced without chemical herbicides or pesticides) becomes known ex ante via a certified organic label, it becomes a search attribute. In other words, if products are labelled organic and if that label is trustworthy, consumers can tell easily which produce is organic and which is not.

16.9.4   Standards

Standards can help solve information problems associated with experience goods and credence goods. Standards can be set by either the industry or a third party, such as the government (Carlton and Perloff 2000). The Organisation for Economic Co-operation and Development (OECD) lists three types of standards: (1) target, (2) performance, and (3) specification (OECD 1997a, 1997b).

Target standards detail what is unacceptable in a product and leave it to the individual firm to find ways to comply. For example, the United Kingdom has a standards test that states it is an offence to sell food unfit for human consumption. Although target standards allow the firm some flexibility, they may lead to uncertainty due to their broad nature (e.g., what is defined as unfit?). To ensure against being in violation, firms may set their own quality standards well above those required by law. Because of their uncertainty, these standards are more costly to enforce (e.g., how does the government prove that a certain product is unfit?).

Performance standards are the flip side of target standards in that they set the safety standards that products must meet, but they allow firms to choose their own mechanism to ensure these standards. The costs of implementing performance standards may be greater than the costs of implementing target standards because the restrictions are greater.

Specification standards are the most restrictive set of standards, applying both to the end product and to the production process, either by limiting certain activities and outcomes or by insisting on certain product characteristics and processes. This type of regulation has the least amount of flexibility, but also the least amount of uncertainty. Thus, these regulations may be easier to enforce (although production standards whose effects are not identifiable in the end product will imply higher monitoring costs). Because of their restrictive nature, specification standards must also be changed frequently as production technology advances (OECD 1997a).

Quality assurance may be considered a public good, and it would be underproduced if left to the private market. Governments or the participatory sector, through consumer organizations, may be better able to provide quality assurance than can the private sector (Tirole 1988). In food inspection, for example, governments or industry groups, rather than individual firms, undertake food inspection because the benefit is captured by the entire industry. Consider organic produce. The industry has organized a certification procedure to test the method of production used by farmers who want to be certified as organic farmers. The rationale behind having an industry-wide body (or government) regulate the organic produce industry is that it will allow this higher-valued market to exist. If consumers pay a premium for a product they believe is organic, only to later find that it was produced using conventional farming methods, the credibility of the organic label will erode. Thus, consumers will no longer be willing to pay a premium for organic foods, which will lower the returns for all organic producers, not just for the firm misrepresenting its product. Another example in which labelling is being used to differentiate products is ecolabelling.

ECOLABELLING

More than twenty countries and the EU have adopted public ecolabelling systems to encourage production methods with less environmental impact. A number of non-profit ecolabelling programs operate in the United States and Canada as well (e.g., Green Seal, Scientific Certification Systems, and Environmental Choice). The labels identify products that cause the least amount of environmental damage (or products that meet certain environmental guidelines) compared with their substitutes. The degree of environmental impact is based on a third-party assessment that includes the production, consumption, and disposal of the product.

Ecolabelling is voluntary. For ecolabelling to work, target consumers must be concerned or affected by the environmental externalities caused by the production, consumption, or disposal of the commodity. A 1997 study by the Food Marketing Institute (FMI 1997) found that a significant number of consumers reported that environmental friendliness was a factor when choosing among brands, but they were not willing to pay more for the products. They also found that only 10 per cent of consumers will pay a premium for environmentally friendly food. Part of the problem may be the lack of consumer awareness about which products are environmentally friendly. More consumers are aware of the USDA organic label than they are of the Green Seal label.

The costs of ecolabelling are difficult to determine, partly because of the variation in standards. For example, some ecolabels on agricultural products require that producers use integrated pest management (IPM) systems, which minimize pesticide use. Earning and maintaining certification as environmentally friendly is also associated with negotiation and monitoring costs. As the programs become larger and the inspection systems become more exact, these costs may decrease. Moreover, with increased recognition, consumers may be more willing to pay an increased premium for environmentally friendly products, and ecolabelling could provide a way to capture consumers' preferences for environmental benefits associated with production (van Ravenswaay and Blend 1999).

16.10   A POSITIVE VIEW OF BIOTECHNOLOGY

ECONOMICS OF GM CANOLA

GM canola, developed in the mid-1990s, is engineered to be resistant to certain herbicides that kill all other growing plant material in the canola fields. Using GMOs allows producers to use less herbicides due to the need for only one application of herbicides to the field during the growing season. While GM canola has a higher yield rate, some consumers (and countries) refuse to purchase GM-canola oil and are willing to pay a premium for non-GM vegetable oils.

Table 16.4. Loss in Canadian canola profits resulting from wild mustard infestation[a]

Infestation (plants/m2)	Yield Loss (%)	Economic Loss Given Yield (C$/acre)			
		18 bu/acre	22.78 bu/acre	27 bu/acre	32 bu/acre
2	5	5.53	6.99	8.29	9.82
4	10	11.05	13.98	16.58	19.65
5	15	16.58	20.98	24.87	29.47
10	22	24.31	30.77	36.47	43.20
15	27	29.84	37.76	44.76	53.05
20	32	35.36	44.76	53.05	62.87

[a] Canola price is assumed to be C$6.14/bushel (bu).
Source: Mayer and Furtan (1999).

Mayer and Furtan (1999) examined the economic effect of introducing herbicide-tolerant (HT) canola into the crop rotation of farmers in western Canada. Canola is an economically important crop to Canadian Prairie producers. The authors' focus was on two issues that affect farmers who use HT canola. First, farmers may reduce the amount of herbicide usage because at least one less herbicide application is required each crop year. Second, gene introgression (the transfer of genes from one species to another) could lead to increased weed infestation. While the benefits of herbicide usage are easily measurable, the potential effects of gene introgression are more complex.

The economic loss that will occur from increased weed infestation is illustrated in Table 16.4. The calculations show that at a breakeven point of C$5 to C$8 per acre, any infestation of herbicide-resistant (HR) wild mustard above two plants per square metre will reduce the benefits of HT canola to below zero. If one assumes Canadian canola production has no effect on canola prices (open economy case), then infestation levels can reach four plants per square metre before the benefits of herbicide tolerance will be reduced to zero.

16.11   NUTRITION, OBESITY, AND AGRICULTURAL POLICY

Apart from food safety and the availability of affordable foods, the nutritional content of food has increasingly become an important dimension of the food policy debate. Most governments have developed dietary standards for nutrition. Despite these standards, obesity is becoming a global problem. There is considerable discussion on the health problems created by obesity and how this is linked to dietary standards and to government involvement in the food system.

OBESITY IN THE UNITED STATES

In the United States, the rate of obesity is increasing for both adults and children. Following the typical American eating and activity patterns (caloric intake plus caloric expenditure) often leads to food consumption in excess of energy requirements. In the energy balance equation, caloric expenditure needs to be balanced by caloric intake to maintain body weight and must exceed caloric intake to achieve weight loss. To reverse the obesity trend, Americans need to eat fewer calories, be more active, and make wiser food choices (USDHHS 2009).

Obesity looms as a major global problem. Food sufficiency and food security in most developed and developing economies are no longer significant policy concerns. One way that obesity levels are determined is the body mass index (BMI), which is based on height and weight. As an example, Table 16.5 illustrates the body mass guidelines for the United States.

THE LINK BETWEEN DIET AND HEALTH

In defining a healthy diet, Dorfman, Samuelson, and Solow (1958) demonstrated with linear programming the amount of resources needed for a healthy diet. They concluded that the resources used to produce unhealthy foods popular with consumers exceed those for healthy foods. (For examples of a healthy diet that meets certain quality specifications, see Chapter 17.)

Using a model similar to that proposed in Dorfman, Samuelson, and Solow (1958), known as the household production model (Appendix 16), we investigate the implications of agricultural policy on nutrition. The equilibrium relationship (Equation 16.1) between high- and low-calorie inputs is derived considering the relative impacts on health

$$k = \frac{p_2 - p_1}{p_3}. \tag{16.1}$$

Here k is the adverse effect of the consumption of the high-calorie good x_1 on health, p_2 is the price of the relatively healthier food (i.e., the consumption of the good with no health consequences, x_2), p_1 is the price of the high-calorie food, and p_3 is the price of health. Starting with the equilibrium implicit in Equation 16.1, we introduce an agricultural policy which subsidizes the high-calorie good,

Table 16.5. US Department of Health and Human Services body mass guidelines

BMI/	Healthy		Overweight		Obese	
	19	24	25	29	30	35
Height	Weight in Pounds					
4'10"	91	115	119	138	143	167
5'	97	123	128	148	153	179
5'2"	104	131	136	158	164	191
5'4"	110	140	145	169	174	204
5'6"	118	148	155	179	186	216
5'8"	125	158	164	190	197	230
5'10"	132	167	174	202	209	243
6'	140	177	184	213	221	258
6'2"	148	186	194	225	233	272

BMI = Body Mass Index. Height is measured in feet (') and inches (").
Source: USDHHS (2009).

$$k > \frac{p_2 - (P_1 - \tau_1)}{p_3}, \qquad (16.2)$$

where τ_1 is the subsidy payment to the production of the high-calorie good. Based on this relationship, consumers expand the consumption of the high-calorie good. Intuitively, the original (optimal) relationship could be recovered by adjusting the price of the health good

$$k = \frac{p_2 - (P_1 - \tau_1)}{p_3 - \tau_3}, \qquad (16.3)$$

where τ_3 is a subsidy payment for health (e.g., subsidized health club memberships).

The impact of this substitution on aggregate health is not readily apparent. Specifically, the shift to high-calorie foods (due to lower prices) has an income effect. That is, as the price of the high-calorie food falls, less income will be used to purchase the same quantity of food, and more income will be available for the purchase of the healthy good. Hence, the net impact of subsidizing high-calorie food is a function of the income elasticity of food and the price elasticity of the healthy good.

16.12 ANIMAL RIGHTS AND HUMANE SLAUGHTER

Another dimension related to food safety is the growing interest in animal rights. This interest has resulted in more people adopting a vegetarian or vegan diet despite the debate over what constitutes a healthy diet. Public opinion on animal agriculture practices has led to a growing trend to regulate animal agriculture based on animal rights and unethical, inhumane practices. In the future, animal rights will become more important in the agricultural policy agenda.

INTEGRATING ANIMAL RIGHTS CONSIDERATIONS

The animal rights movement is evolving, with the expectation of it becoming more influential in the future of agriculture. Issues of the confinement of livestock (e.g., cattle, pigs, and poultry) in small pens/cages and overcrowded buildings are starting to be addressed. Future farm bills could ease the transition from inhumane to humane treatment of agriculture animals by providing financial incentives to end unethical agricultural practices. As part of its evolution, the animal rights movement is spreading beyond the boundaries of agriculture. For example, some oppose certain types of wildlife trapping and the use of animals for testing cosmetics.

To develop an economic model of animal rights, we return to the basic utility function formulation. Assume that consumers' utility is a function of three goods: (1) x_1 is meat consumption or the consumption of a good that impinges directly or indirectly on animal welfare; (2) x_2 is other commodities that do not directly affect animals; and (3) x_3 is the individual's demand for animal welfare. The animal welfare variable raises the issue of exclusionary versus non-exclusionary consumption in that expenditures intended to guarantee animal rights may generate non-exclusionary output that benefits everyone.

A more significant point in agricultural policy may be the indirect nature of the pricing of the animal-rights good. Specifically, the standard derivation of the Marshallian demand curves for each commodity assumes that the cost of consumption is directly proportional to the quantity of the good consumed:

$$\max_{x_1,x_2,x_3} U(x_1,x_2,x_3)$$
$$s.t.\, p_1 x_1 + p_2 x_2 + p_3 x_3 \leq Y, \tag{16.4}$$

where p_1 is the price of the consumption good that affects animal welfare, p_2 is the price of the consumption good that does not affect animal welfare, p_3 is the direct price of animal welfare, and Y is the consumer's income. Conversely, when developing a model of the demand for animal welfare in the food sector, recognize that the consumer does not pay for animal welfare directly, but pays for animal welfare through regulations that raise the cost of certain foods. Thus, the utility maximization model becomes

$$\max_{x_1,x_2,x_3} U(x_1,x_2,x_3)$$
$$s.t.\, [p_1 + \tau_1(x_3)]x_1 + p_2 x_2 \leq Y, \tag{16.5}$$

where $\tau_1(x_3)$ denotes the effect that increased levels of animal welfare have on the cost of meat consumption. Forming the Lagrange multiplier and taking the first-order conditions yields

$$\frac{\partial L}{\partial x_1} = \frac{\partial U}{\partial x_1} - \lambda[p_1 + \tau_1(x_3)] = 0$$

$$\frac{\partial L}{\partial x_2} = \frac{\partial U}{\partial x_2} - \lambda p_2 = 0 \qquad (16.6)$$

$$\frac{\partial L}{\partial x_3} = \frac{\partial U}{\partial x_3} - \lambda \frac{\partial \tau_1(x_3)}{\partial x_3} x_1 = 0.$$

Taking the ratio between the first and third first-order conditions yields

$$\frac{dx_3}{dx_1} = \frac{\partial U / \partial x_1}{\partial U / \partial x_3} = \frac{p_1 + \tau_1(x_3)}{\partial \tau_1(x_3) / \partial x_3 \, x_1} = \frac{p_1^*(x_3)}{p_3^*(x_3, x_1)}, \qquad (16.7)$$

where $p_1^*(x_3)$ is the effective price of x_1 subject to the level of animal welfare, and $p_3^*(x_3, x_1)$ is the effective price of animal rights given the individual's consumption of animal products.

Note that as long as the cost imposed by animal safety is positive (i.e., $\tau_1(x_3) > 0$ for all x_3), the demand for animal welfare reduces the consumption of animal products. Furthermore, there is a linkage between the individual demand for animal welfare and the consumption of animal products as long as the cost of increasing animal welfare is positive (i.e., $\partial \tau_1(x_3) / \partial x_3 > 0$) and the level of consumption of meat products is positive (i.e., $x_1 > 0$). Hence, the presence of animal welfare will shift the demand curve for meat products inward.

THE HUMANE METHODS OF SLAUGHTER ACT OF 1978
The Humane Methods of Slaughter Act (HMSA), Sections 1901, 1902, and 1906, states that the slaughtering and handling of livestock are to be carried out only by humane methods. In that Act, Congress determined (among other things) that: "[T]he use of humane methods in the slaughter of livestock prevents needless suffering; results in safer and better working conditions for persons engaged in the slaughtering industry; brings about improvement of products and economies in slaughtering operations; and produces other benefits for producers, processors, and consumers which tend to expedite an orderly flow of livestock and livestock products in interstate and foreign commerce. It is therefore declared to be the policy of the United States that the slaughtering of livestock and the handling of livestock in connection with slaughter shall be carried out only by humane methods" (USDA/FSIS 2003).

16.13   SUMMARY AND CONCLUSIONS

- Governments have long played a part in regulating and monitoring food safety.
- Outbreaks of foodborne illnesses raise new concerns about market-regulated food safety.
- Most food labelling laws targeted at guaranteeing food safety and nutritional content reduce transaction costs by increasing consumer welfare, consumer confidence, and producer profits. These economic benefits help explain government involvement in food labelling.
- Food safety regulations could potentially be used to reduce market access, generating increased profits for domestic producers.
- The emergence of genetically modified crops has added a new dimension to food safety concerns.
- Animal rights are influencing the future of agriculture.
- The animal rights movement argues that animals have legal rights, which further complicates the debate.
- Obesity is a growing worldwide policy concern.

APPENDIX 16: THE HOUSEHOLD PRODUCTION MODEL AND FOOD DEMAND

The household production approach recognizes that in many cases the consumer does not actually purchase the final product. Instead of purchasing sandwiches, the consumer purchases bread, meat, lettuce, and tomatoes, and then combines these inputs with labour to produce a sandwich. In most cases, the net effect of this complication is small. Specifically, if production can be represented by a fixed factor proportion production function (e.g., the production of one sandwich requires two slices of bread, one or more pieces of meat, a leaf of lettuce, and a slice of tomato) and the amount of labour required is small, the implementation of the household production approach yields little additional insight. However, if the proportion of factors used to produce the consumption item or labour use become significant considerations, the household production approach can be used to address some significant issues. For example, an emerging issue in agricultural policy may be the implications of two-income households on the demand for agricultural outputs. Under this scenario, consumers shift away from the production of food towards the consumption of processed foods because of the value of household labour. Thus, the value added in the agribusiness channel may shift increasingly to providing labour services (pre-cut salads, TV dinners, and the like). In addition, the household production approach can be used to address the effect of food-labelling issues such as country of origin labelling (COOL) and the effect of agricultural policy on food nutrition.

In its most general form, the household production formulation of consumption can be written as

$$\max_{z,x,L} U(z)$$
$$s.t. G(z,x,L) = 0$$
$$p'x \leq Y - w(L_T - L) \tag{16.A1}$$

where $U(z)$ is the standard quasi-concave utility function defined on a set of consumption goods. $G(z,x,L)$ is an implicit production function that depicts the technology by which inputs x and labour L can be combined to produce the consumption goods. The income constraint specifies that the spending on inputs P_x' in which p is a vector of prices is less than the fixed income level Y plus earned income $w(L_T - L)$, where w is the wage rate and L_T is the total quantity of labour available to the household. Simplifying the specification in Equation 16.A1 by taking the first-order Taylor series expansion of the production technology and solving for the production of two inputs yields

$$\max_{z_1,z_2,x_1,x_2,x_3} U(z_1,z_2)$$
$$s.t. z_1 \leq g_{11}x_1 + g_{12}x_2 + g_{13}x_3$$
$$z_1 \leq g_{21}x_1 + g_{22}x_2 + g_{23}x_3$$
$$p_1x_1 + p_2x_2 + p_3x_3 \leq Y \quad, \tag{16.A2}$$

where three inputs are used to produce two outputs (or consumption goods). In each formulation in this chapter, z_1 represents the consumption of an aggregate food good (i.e., meals consumed), and z_2 is a health good. Given non-satiation in each consumption good, we can form the Lagrange multiplier for Equation 16.A2 as

$$L = U(g_{11}x_1 + g_{12}x_2 + g_{13}x_3, g_{21}x_1 + g_{22}x_2 + g_{23}x_3) + \lambda (Y - p_1x_1 - p_2x_2 - p_3x_3), \tag{16.A3}$$

where λ is the Lagrange multiplier representing the marginal utility of income.

Starting with the general formulation in Equation 16.A3, we construct the food labelling problem by letting x_1 be food from one source (i.e., domestic production), x_2 be food from another source (i.e., foreign production), and x_3 be the purchase of a health good (such as a mitigation agent in van Ravenswaay and Hoehn, 1996). To simplify the specification, we assume that $g_{11} - g_{12} = 1$ and $g_{13} = 0$. The effect of each food input on health is then modelled as a probabilistic event of a foodborne illness ($g_{21} = \varepsilon_1$ and $g_{22} = \varepsilon_2$). ε_1 and ε_2 are uncorrelated Bernoulli random variables

$$\varepsilon_1, \varepsilon_2 = \begin{cases} -1, P[\Omega_j] = \theta_j \\ 0, P[\tilde{\Omega}_j] = 1 - \theta_j \end{cases} j = 1,2, \tag{16.A4}$$

so that in each case $\varepsilon_j = -1$ is the outcome where the foodborne illness occurs (with probability $P[\Omega_j] = \theta_j$), and $\varepsilon_j = 0$ denotes the event where foodborne illness does not occur.

Modifying the formulation in Equation 16.A3 to focus on the maximization of expected utility yields

$$L = E[U(x_1 + x_2, x_1\varepsilon_1 + x_2\varepsilon_2 + x_3)] - \lambda(Y - p_1 x_1 - p_2 x_2 - p_3 x_3),$$ (16.A5)

where $E[\ ]$ denotes the expectation operator. The Kuhn-Tucker conditions for Equation 16.A5 become

$$\frac{\partial L}{\partial x_1} x_1 = \left\{ E\left[\frac{\partial U}{\partial z_1}\frac{\partial z_1}{\partial x_1} + \frac{\partial U}{\partial z_2}\frac{\partial z_2}{\partial x_1}\right] - \lambda p_1 \right\} x_1 = 0$$

$$\frac{\partial L}{\partial x_1} x_2 = \left\{ E\left[\frac{\partial U}{\partial z_1}\frac{\partial z_1}{\partial x_2} + \frac{\partial U}{\partial z_2}\frac{\partial z_2}{\partial x_2}\right] - \lambda p_2 \right\} x_2 = 0$$

$$\frac{\partial L}{\partial x_3} x_3 = \left\{ E\left[\frac{\partial U}{\partial z_2}\frac{\partial z_2}{\partial x_3}\right] - \lambda p_3 \right\} x_3 = 0.$$ (16.A6)

This formulation allows the examination of the possible corner solutions (i.e., where $x_1 \geq 0$ and $x_2 = 0$ or $x_1 = 0$ and $x_2 \geq 0$). As a starting point, we solve for the case where both $x_1 > 0$ and $x_2 > 0$ and by solving for the term inside the { } of the first two equations in Equation 16.A6, which are equal to zero. Taking a first-order approximation of each expression yields

$$E\left[\frac{\partial U}{\partial z_1}\right] - E\left[\frac{\partial U}{\partial z_2}\right]\theta_1 - \lambda p_1 = 0$$

$$E\left[\frac{\partial U}{\partial z_1}\right] - E\left[\frac{\partial U}{\partial z_2}\right]\theta_2 - \lambda p_2 = 0.$$ (16.A7)

Subtracting the second equation of Equation 16.A7 from the first and rearranging yields

$$E\left[\frac{\partial U}{\partial z_2}\right](\theta_2 - \theta_1) = \lambda(p_1 - p_2).$$ (16.A8)

From the third condition in Equation 16.A6 (assuming that $x_3 > 0$), we get $E[\partial U/\partial z_2] = \lambda p_3$. Substituting this expression into Equation 16.A8 and rearranging yields

$$\theta_2 - \theta_1 = \frac{p_1 - p_2}{p_3}.$$ (16.A9)

Thus, if the difference in probability of foodborne illness ($\theta_2 - \theta_1$) is greater than the implicit price of health, $[(p_1 - p_2) / p_3]$, the consumption of the foreign good is equal to zero, ($x_2 = 0$), and only the domestic good is consumed. However, if the difference in probability of food-borne illness is less than the price of health, then the consumption of the domestic good will be equal to zero and only the foreign good will be consumed.

Reformulating the problem in Equation 16.A3 to address nutrition, consider the case where expanding the consumption of one of the goods in the area around the optimum is deleterious to health. For example, once all calorie requirements are met, increased consumption of carbohydrates, sugars, or fats contributes to obesity, which is detrimental to health. Thus, assume that good x_1 is a commodity with high caloric content while x_2 does not contribute to obesity. The formulation in Equation 16.A3 is altered so that

$$g_{11} = 1, g_{21} = -k, g_{12} = 1, g_{22} = 0, \text{ and } g_{23} = 1 \text{ or}$$

$$L = U(x_1 + x_2, -kx_1 + x_3) + \lambda(Y - p_1 x_1 - p_2 x_2 - p_3 x_3). \tag{16.A10}$$

This yields the Kuhn-Tucker conditions

$$\frac{\partial L}{\partial x_1} x_1 = \left[\frac{\partial U}{\partial z_1} - k \frac{\partial U}{\partial z_2} - \lambda p_1 \right] x_1 = 0$$

$$\frac{\partial L}{\partial x_2} x_2 = \left[\frac{\partial U}{\partial z_1} - \lambda p_2 \right] x_2 = 0$$

$$\frac{\partial L}{\partial x_3} x_3 = \left[\frac{\partial U}{\partial z_2} - \lambda p_3 \right] x_3 = 0. \tag{16.A11}$$

In this formulation $-k$ is the deleterious effect on health z_2 resulting from the consumption of the first consumption good. Again, solving for the point where each good is consumed (implicitly that price ratio where x_2 replaces x_1), the second condition in Equation 16.A11 implies

$$\frac{\partial U}{\partial z_1} = \lambda p_2, \tag{16.A12}$$

while the third condition in Equation 16.A11 implies

$$\frac{\partial U}{\partial z_2} = \lambda p_3. \tag{16.A13}$$

Substituting both of these results back into the first condition of Equation 16.A11 and solving for k yields

$$k = \frac{p_2 - p_1}{p_3}. \tag{16.A14}$$

If the actual k is less than this value, the consumer will maximize utility by consuming the high-calorie good, but he or she will be paying to offset the health effect. However, if k is greater than this amount, the consumer will purchase the low-calorie product and will reduce the consumption of the health good.

CHAPTER SEVENTEEN

Food Pyramids and Nutritional Guidelines

17.1 NUTRITION

Nutrient availability and intake are challenges for any society, and they only intensify as a population continues to grow and resources become increasingly scarce. The world faces a food paradox caused by two forms of malnutrition: overnutrition and undernutrition. Overnutrition is caused by overconsumption of food and can lead to obesity and negative health outcomes such as heart disease, stroke, and diabetes. Undernutrition is caused either by an inadequate supply of or access to food, or by a physical inability of the body to absorb available nutrients that results in deficiencies in macronutrients (e.g., carbohydrates, fat, and protein) and micronutrients (e.g., vitamins and minerals). Morbidity and mortality occur more often with undernutrition (Blössner and De Onis 2005). Malnutrition is strongly affected by economics, diet, and physical health (Fulgoni et al. 2011; Martins et al. 2011).

This chapter places malnutrition within the context of food pyramids and dietary guidelines in the United States and Canada (in the European Union, each member country has its own dietary guidelines; more information on EU guidelines can be found online). Despite government efforts to encourage healthful eating, following the dietary guidelines is at the discretion of individuals (healthy eating cannot be mandated or enforced). As an example, consider obesity. Worldwide obesity rates have more than doubled since 1980. In 2014, more than two billion adults worldwide were classified as overweight or obese. Using the example of the United States and Canada, 65 per cent of Americans (Lakkakula 2018) and 53.6 per cent of Canadians are classified as overweight or obese (S.J. Clark et al. 2019).

17.2   US DIETARY GUIDELINES, 1890–2015

The US government has issued guidance regarding optimal dietary intake for over a century. The pressing dietary concerns of Americans, public health officials, and health care workers have evolved considerably over time. In the early 1900s, dietary guidelines were issued by the US government through the United States Department of Agriculture (USDA) at various stages, in a variety of ad hoc formats. The USDA dietary guidelines have a long history, with government recommendations evolving due to advances in knowledge about diet and nutrition. Recommendations are of interest to many food and agricultural groups, who often lobby to have their type of food product represented in the dietary guidelines. Thus, conversations regarding these recommendations bring many groups to the table, with some voices being more influential than others. Unfortunately, for consumers who attempt to follow the USDA Dietary Guidelines, the dynamic nature and inherent complexities of the recommendations can cause confusion.

In 1980, the content of dietary guidance was clarified and streamlined, and the first Dietary Guidelines for Americans (DGA) was published. The National Nutrition Monitoring and Related Research Act of 1990 (Public Law 101-445) required that the DGA be reviewed, revised, and published every five years. The most recent US dietary guidelines were issued by the USDA in 2015 (USDHHS/USDA 2015). According to the United States Department of Health and Human Services (USDHHS), "the Dietary Guidelines are an important part of a complex and multifaceted solution to promoting health and preventing diet-related chronic diseases including cardiovascular disease, type 2 diabetes, some cancers, and obesity" (USDHHS/USDA 2015). The sections below summarize each phase of the US dietary guidelines' evolution.

17.2.1   US Dietary Guidelines, 1890–1909

In 1894, W.O. Atwater, the first director of the USDA Office of Experiment Stations, published the first general dietary guidance by the USDA in the form of a farm bulletin. Since specific minerals and vitamins had not yet been identified at that time (C. Davis and Saltos 1999), he suggested diets for American males based on the content of protein, carbohydrate, fat, and mineral matter (ash) (Atwater 1894). Through this bulletin, Atwater introduced the basis for relating the composition of food intake to health. In a follow-up bulletin in 1902, he recognized the potential health effects that could arise from a poor diet, remarking that "[t]he evils of overeating may not be felt at once, but sooner or later they are sure to appear, perhaps in an excessive amount of fatty tissue, perhaps in general debility, perhaps in actual disease" (Atwater 1902). Atwater's early work provided the framework for the future official dietary guidelines that translated recommended nutrient intake into recommended food intake.

17.2.2   US Dietary Guidelines, 1910–29

In 1917, the USDA issued its first set of official dietary guidelines, called "How to Select Foods" (Hunt and Atwater 1917) and "Food for Young Children" (Hunt 1916). These guides established the initial food-group format by organizing food into five categories: fruits and vegetables; meats and other protein-rich foods (including milk for children); cereals and other starchy foods; sweets; and fatty foods. While these guides were intended to help guide consumers on purchases, the authors did not recommend any specific combination of foods nor did they suggest restricting or limiting intake of one group in favour of another (McFadden and Schmitz 2017). The USDA expanded the guidelines in the early 1920s to include recommended amounts of weekly food purchases for differing family sizes (C. Davis and Saltos 1999), and also emphasized the diversity of food production in the United States and the necessity of a wholesome diet (Hunt 1923).

17.2.3   US Dietary Guidelines, 1930–9

Due to the economic constraints of the Great Depression, the USDA's recommended dietary allowances and food planning for families were based upon differing income levels (Stiebling 1933). The intention was to provide guidance for families in different income groups. The policy of differentiating dietary advice based on income continued into the 1980s.

17.2.4   US Dietary Guidelines, 1940–9

In 1940, the Food and Nutrition Board was established by the US National Academy of Sciences. In 1941, President Franklin D. Roosevelt held the National Nutrition Conference for Defense, where the committee created Recommended Dietary Allowances (RDAs) that established standards for daily intake of calories and nine essential nutrients (C. Davis and Saltos 1999). Since that time, recommendations have been updated every five to ten years, with the most recent revision developed in 2015.

In 1942, federal pamphlets encouraged Americans to eat foods from eight groups daily (ODHWS 1942) that combined meat, eggs, fish, and beans into one group, while placing milk into a separate category, and retaining fats and sugars as separate groups (Nestle 2007). In 1943, the USDA issued a National Wartime Nutrition Guide that included the *basic seven* (USDA 1943), in which a plate was divided into seven equally sized food groups (Figure 17.1). This wartime version of dietary guidelines was intended to help people maintain proper nutrition while coping with food rationing (C. Davis and Saltos 1999).

Following the end of World War II, when food rationing was no longer necessary, the USDA began to encourage increased food consumption and actively promoted consumption of fats and sweets for adults and children, which coincided with the increasing import quotas of sugar coming into the United States (McFadden and Schmitz 2017). In 1946, the National Wartime

Figure 17.1. The basic seven food groups (1943–56)

Note: (1) green and yellow vegetables; (2) oranges, tomatoes, grapefruit (or raw cabbage or selected greens); (3) potatoes and other vegetables and fruits; (4) milk and milk products; (5) meat, poultry, fish, or eggs (or dried beans, peas, nuts, or peanut butter); (6) bread, flour, and cereals (natural whole grain); and (7) butter and fortified margarine (with added vitamin A).
Source: USDA (1943).

Nutrition Guide was amended to become the National Food Guide. Because of decreased rationing, the new guidelines assumed consumers would include additional foods in their diet beyond the recommendations to satisfy their full calorie and nutrient needs beyond the basic seven food groups (USDA 1946).

17.2.5 US Dietary Guidelines, 1950–69

Due to the complexity and lack of serving size information contained in the basic seven, the USDA released the *basic four* in 1956 (Page and Phipard 1956), which introduced specific recommendations regarding portions and serving sizes (McFadden and Schmitz 2017). In 1958, the Institute of Home Economics issued a four-page leaflet entitled "Food for Fitness: A Daily Food Guide" based on the basic four food groups, emphasizing family meal and cost plans for the following broad categories: (1) vegetable/fruit, (2) meat, (3) bread/cereal, and (4) milk (USDA 1958). The new guide recommended four or more servings from both the vegetable/fruit and bread/cereal group; two or more servings of meat; and the equivalent of two or more cups of milk for adults, three to four cups of milk for young children, and four or more cups of milk for adolescences (McFadden and Schmitz 2017). These guidelines remained in place until the 1970s (C. Davis and Saltos 1999).

17.2.6 US Dietary Guidelines, 1970–89

In 1970, the US White House held a conference called "Food, Nutrition, and Health" (White House 1970). This conference, along with a series of hearings that followed, led to concerns that overconsumption of certain types of food would increase the risk for cancer, cardiovascular disease, and obesity. In response, in 1977, the US Senate Select Committee on Nutrition and Human Needs published "Dietary Goals for the United States," which provided six different goals in the attempt to shift the focus from consuming sufficient nutrients to avoiding food components that led to disease (C. Davis and Saltos 1999; McFadden and Schmitz 2017). The first goal was to increase carbohydrate consumption to 60 per cent of caloric intake. The next three goals called for a 30 per cent reduction in calories from fat, a 10 per cent reduction in calories from saturated fat, and a 15 per cent reduction in calories from sugar. The final two goals were to reduce cholesterol to three hundred milligrams per day and reduce salt intake to three grams per day. Meeting these goals would require increasing the consumption of fruit, vegetables, whole grains, fish, poultry, and low-fat milk while simultaneously decreasing the consumption of red meat, eggs, butterfat, sugar, salt, and whole milk. The release of these goals caused cattle ranchers, egg and sugar producers, and the dairy industry to register strong protests with Congress (Nestle 2007).

Due to the substantial differences between the basic four and the goals of the 1977 senate committee, the USDA did not begin to address the roles of fat, sugar, and sodium until 1979 when they published "Hassle Free Guide to a Better Diet." This guide modified the basis four to include a fifth group of fats, sweets, and alcoholic beverages to be consumed in moderation (C. Davis and Saltos 1999).

Due largely to political pressure from various industry groups, the dietary guidelines were revised four times before the USDA and USDHHS jointly released "Nutrition and Your Health: Dietary Guidelines for Americans" (USDHHS/USDA 1980). Throughout the 1980s, a new advertising campaign was launched that focused on intake of essential nutrients while maintaining recommended body weight and moderation of other dietary constituents.

17.2.7   US Dietary Guidelines, 1990–9

In the early 1990s, the Dietary Guidelines Advisory Committee (DGAC) determined that while food and nutrition professionals generally agreed that reducing total fat and saturated fat consumption was the most effective dietary change to reduce the risk of chronic diseases, many consumers wanted more specific guidance in terms of numerical goals and strategies to modify food consumption behaviour (C. Davis and Saltos 1999). Taking these results into account, the 1992 "Food Guide Pyramid" provided a graphic representation of the food guide with the goal of conveying key concepts of variety, proportionality, and moderation.

The final version of the Food Guide Pyramid was released by the USDA in 1992 (Figure 17.2). In the final version of the food pyramid, the recommendations for servings per food category consisted of six to eleven servings of bread, cereal, rice, and pasta; three to five servings of vegetables; two to four servings of fruit; two to three servings of milk, yogurt, and cheese; and two to three servings of meat, poultry, fish, dry beans, eggs, and nuts. In addition, the USDA recommended that fats, oils, and sweets were to be used sparingly. The 1992 USDA pyramid resulted in new food stamp regulations and a myriad of other nutrition programs.

In 1994, a revised version of the pyramid – the Harvard Healthy Eating Pyramid – was released to help the public decide exactly where certain ambiguous food items should be placed within the Food Guide Pyramid (Thomas 1995). The Healthy Eating Pyramid (Figure 17.3) was offered as an alternative that more closely followed recommendations of modern nutritionists (Reedy and Krebs-Smith 2008).

HARVARD HEALTHY EATING PYRAMID

In the Healthy Eating Pyramid, daily exercise and weight control were placed at the bottom, while vegetables and fruits, healthy fats and oils, and whole grains were placed in the second tier. Nuts, seeds, beans, tofu, fish, poultry, and eggs were placed in the third tier. Dairy (one to two servings) was placed near the top. Fats, oils, and sweets (the top of the pyramid) was replaced with red meat, butter, refined grains, potatoes, sugary drinks, sweets, and salt. On the left side of the pyramid there was also a recommendation for alcohol in moderation (not for everyone) and a daily multivitamin plus extra vitamin D (for most people).

Figure 17.2. The Food Guide Pyramid (1992–2005)

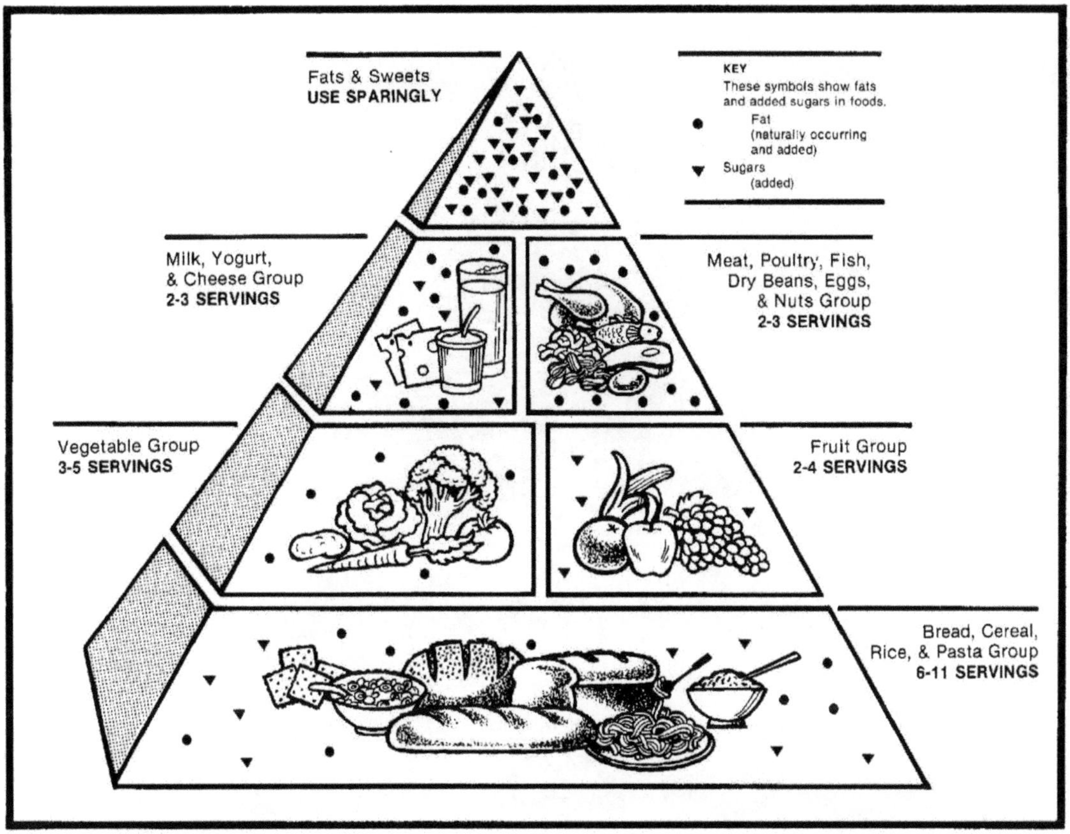

Fats & Sweets
USE SPARINGLY

KEY
These symbols show fats
and added sugars in foods.
● Fat
(naturally occurring
and added)
▼ Sugars
(added)

Milk, Yogurt,
& Cheese Group
2-3 SERVINGS

Meat, Poultry, Fish,
Dry Beans, Eggs,
& Nuts Group
2-3 SERVINGS

Vegetable Group
3-5 SERVINGS

Fruit Group
2-4 SERVINGS

Bread, Cereal,
Rice, & Pasta Group
6-11 SERVINGS

Source: USDA/FNS (1992).

17.2.8 US Dietary Guidelines, 2000–14

In 2005, a new set of guidelines was created, and the USDA issued "MyPyramid" (Figure 17.4). The new design added a person climbing a flight of stairs to encourage more physical activity and removed the hierarchy of food choices that were such an integral part of the original pyramid. Portions were simplified and reorganized into six different coloured strips that extended vertically from the bottom to the top. Reading left to right, the bands came in different widths according to recommended portions: grains (orange), vegetables (green), fruits (red), oils (yellow), dairy/milk (blue), and meats and beans (purple). The number of suggested servings was removed from the graphic and users logged online onto the MyPyramid website (http/www.mypramid.gov) to obtain a personalized dietary plan based on gender, age, activity, and one of twelve calorie levels (Nestle 2007).

Figure 17.3. Harvard Healthy Eating Pyramid

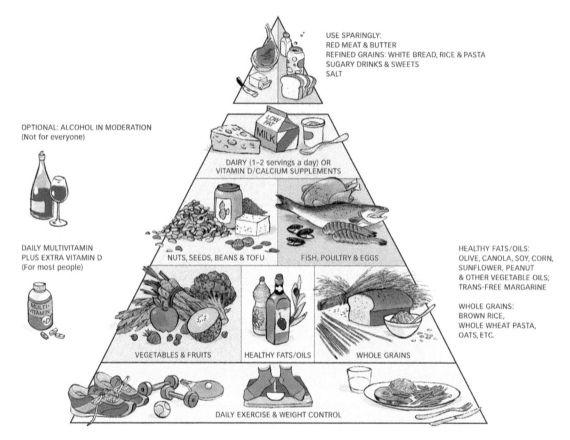

USE SPARINGLY:
RED MEAT & BUTTER
REFINED GRAINS: WHITE BREAD, RICE & PASTA
SUGARY DRINKS & SWEETS
SALT

OPTIONAL: ALCOHOL IN MODERATION
(Not for everyone)

DAIRY (1–2 servings a day) OR
VITAMIN D/CALCIUM SUPPLEMENTS

DAILY MULTIVITAMIN
PLUS EXTRA VITAMIN D
(For most people)

NUTS, SEEDS, BEANS & TOFU   FISH, POULTRY & EGGS

HEALTHY FATS/OILS:
OLIVE, CANOLA, SOY, CORN,
SUNFLOWER, PEANUT
& OTHER VEGETABLE OILS;
TRANS-FREE MARGARINE

WHOLE GRAINS:
BROWN RICE,
WHOLE WHEAT PASTA,
OATS, ETC.

VEGETABLES & FRUITS   HEALTHY FATS/OILS   WHOLE GRAINS

DAILY EXERCISE & WEIGHT CONTROL

Source: Harvard T.H. Chan School of Public Health (1995).

In 2011, ChooseMyPlate was created (Figure 17.5) to replace the food pyramid scheme altogether. It resembles a large computer icon consisting of a plate divided into four roughly equal portions of fruits, vegetables, grains, and protein, with a smaller circle representing a glass for dairy. The ChooseMyPlate website (choosemyplate.gov) includes detailed information on many aspects of different foods.

17.2.9   US Dietary Guidelines, 2015

In 2015, a new set of dietary guidelines was released by the USDA. After reviewing the 2010 DGA, the 2015 Dietary Guidelines Advisory Committee (DGAC 2015) identified six overarching themes associated with US food consumption (McGuire 2016).

Figure 17.4. MyPyramid (2005–11)

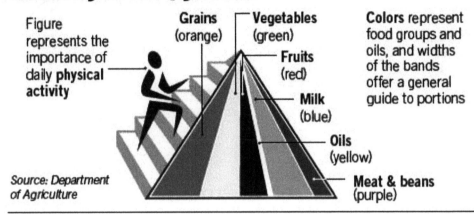

Anatomy of the pyramid

Figure represents the importance of daily **physical activity**

Grains (orange)

Vegetables (green)

Fruits (red)

Milk (blue)

Oils (yellow)

Meat & beans (purple)

Colors represent food groups and oils, and widths of the bands offer a general guide to portions

Source: Department of Agriculture

Associated Press

Source: USDA/FNS (2005).

SIX THEMES ASSOCIATED WITH US FOOD CONSUMPTION

The Problem: About half of US adults have more than one chronic disease related to poor diet and lack of exercise. More than two-thirds of adults and nearly one-third of children in America are overweight. This trend does not appear to be subsiding, resulting in an ethos of medical treatment rather than prevention.

The Gap: Food consumption patterns typical to the US diet are poor, characterized by excessive intake of calories and unhealthy foods. Poor dietary patterns result in inadequate consumption of essential macronutrients and micronutrients.

The Dietary Patterns: There is no one-size-fits-all diet. While individuals do not need to eliminate any particular food to stay healthy, they should follow a diet that includes moderation and balance in eating a variety of foods to promote good health.

The Individual: Individuals should rely upon a variety of proven tools, resources, and educational strategies to achieve a healthy lifestyle through diet and exercise.

The Population: Policy changes and environmental initiatives that involve families, schools, retail outlets, and health care institutions are effective in changing diet and exercise patterns for the better.

The Long-Term View: Initiatives should be enacted to improve human health and create a sustainable, healthy environment. To that end, evidence shows that a more plant-based, lower-calorie diet is healthier for humans.

Figure 17.5. MyPlate (2011–15)

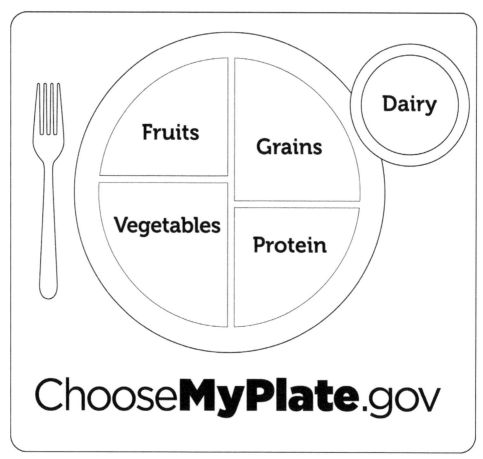

Source: USDA (2011).

To address these six themes, the DGAC recommended a healthier pattern of eating: (1) a variety of vegetables; (2) fruits, especially whole fruits; (3) grains, at least half of which are whole grains; (4) dairy, including milk, yogurt, and cheese; (5) a variety of protein foods, including seafood, lean meats and poultry, eggs, legumes (beans and peas), nuts, and seeds; and (6) healthy oils. The DGAC also included specific limits on the percentage of daily intake from the following sources: (1) less than 10 per cent of calories per day from added sugars; (2) less than 10 per cent of calories per day from saturated fats; (3) less than 2,300 milligrams per day of sodium; and (4) moderation in alcoholic beverages, with a limit of one drink per day for women and two drinks per day for men (USDHHS/USDA 2015).

Although the goal of the USDA Dietary Guidelines is to assist consumers in choosing healthy eating patterns, consumers do not always follow the guidelines (Carlson and Frazão

2014). Moreover, since no clear evidence proves that the guidelines have improved the US diet, a more comprehensive approach is needed (Krebs-Smith, Reedy, and Bosire 2010).

Consumers do not follow USDA dietary guidelines for many reasons often related to the inherent complexities of the 2015 USDA Dietary Guidelines. For example, consumers report confusion caused by the volume and ambiguity of information in the recommendations, including caveats indicating that the document's intended audience is dietary professionals rather than the general public (Martinez 2016).

17.3   US SUPPLEMENTAL NUTRITION ASSISTANCE PROGRAM (SNAP)

The USDA included several nutrition and food assistance programs in the 2018 US Farm Bill. The largest food assistance program is the Supplemental Nutrition Assistance Program (SNAP), known as the Food Stamp Program (FSP) prior to 2009. The FSP began during the Great Depression and has been described as "the cornerstone of the nation's nutrition safety net" (Landers 2007). Figure 17.6 provides a timeline of FSP/SNAP from 1970 through 2016, including the average annual participation rate and total annual cost. The FSP was added to the US Farm Bill in 1973 and has been reformed several times. The Food Stamp Act of 1977 ended the requirement that people purchase a minimum number of stamps before they are able to receive more for free and removed the requirement that households must have access to cooking facilities. Both requirements had been a barrier to participation for many, especially the homeless (Landers 2007). Significant welfare reforms were made in the 1996 US Farm Bill and eligibility rules were eased in both the 2002 and 2008 US Farm Bills.

The 2008 US Farm Bill (FB2008) increased the benefits and expanded the eligibility. In 2009, the FSP was renamed SNAP. FB2014 and FB2018 revised SNAP funding. With an annual budget of US$85 billion in 2015, SNAP is the largest US program that provides assistance to families in need, providing nutritional support to more than forty-six million participants in twenty-two million households (D.R. Just and Gabrielyan 2018). SNAP recipients can use the SNAP benefit only to purchase food. With SNAP, participants purchase food using electronic benefit transfer (EBT) machines rather than food vouchers.

In a related matter, a growing body of literature suggests that many factors beyond food costs lead to unhealthy food choices (Okrent and Alston 2011; Todd and ver Ploeg 2015). Challenges in certain neighborhoods include lack of knowledge regarding proper nutrition and limited access to grocery stores (commonly referred to as food deserts). Also, researchers have noted that behavioural nudges may encourage healthier eating behaviour to combat obesity (D.R. Just and Gabrielyan 2018). D.R. Just and Garbrielyan (2018) proposed a series of five behavioural principles – some of which have proven successful in school lunch programs – that could be used to nudge healthier choices among SNAP participants.

Figure 17.6. Supplemental Nutrition Assistance Program (SNAP) participation and costs

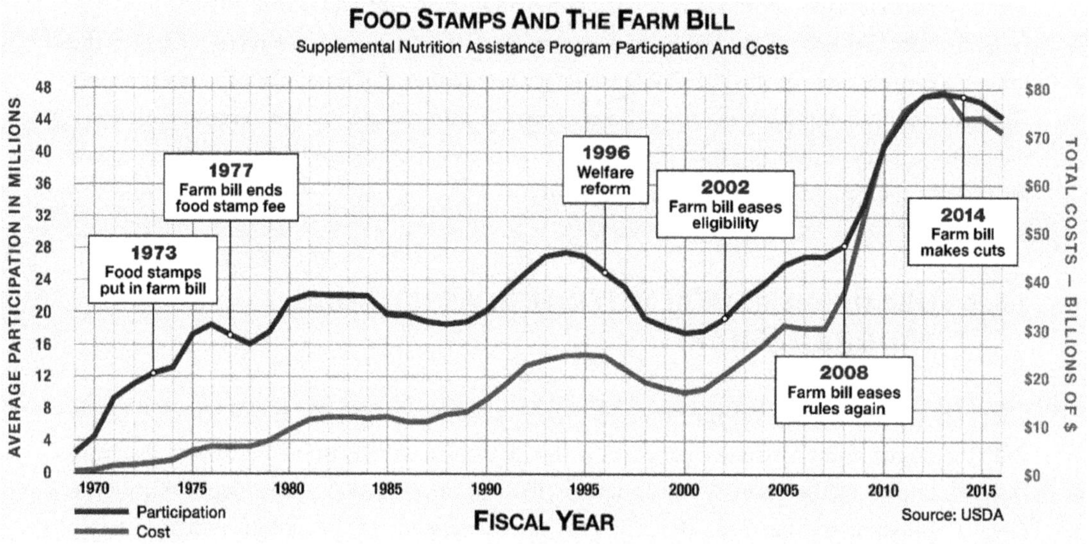

Source: USDHHS/USDA (2015).

FIVE PRINCIPLES OF FOOD NUDGES FOR BETTER FOOD CHOICES

1 Very small differences in the level of convenience, such as positioning food at convenient reaching heights on grocery shelves, can have a significant impact on selection.
2 Social norms can be used to influence food selection.
3 Increased visibility can influence consumers to make better food choices, since many items are purchased on impulse.
4 Wider aisles in the produce section can encourage better food choices, so that shoppers avoid mindless walking through the grocery store.
5 Consumer's hedonic expectations related to taste and preference can be significantly influenced through different strategies, such as offering food samples to expose shoppers to healthier foods.

17.4   US SCHOOL LUNCH PROGRAMS

Modelled after European programs, the first US school lunch programs for poor children in urban areas were launched in the 1850s. Rural school programs were less successful due to lack of infrastructure for food preparation. The Depression years of the 1930s deepened the concern over hunger and malnourishment among school children, and many US states and municipalities adopted legislation, and in some cases appropriations, to enable schools to serve their students a noonday meal. Although both state and local legislations authorized local school districts to provide meals for children through various means, many local governments and school district boards were clearly unable to provide the funds necessary to carry the increasing load. Supplementary contributions by charitable organizations and individuals did not suffice, so federal aid became inevitable.

The earliest federal aid for school lunches came from the Reconstruction Finance Corporation in 1932, which granted loans to cover the labour costs of preparing and serving school lunches. Such federal assistance was expanded to other areas beginning in 1933 under the Civil Works Administration and the Federal Emergency Relief Administration, which covered thirty-nine US states. The changes made to federal aid during World War II and into the 1960s demonstrated a positive relationship between nutrition and child development.

In 1966, the Child Nutrition Act, providing federal funding to subsidize the school lunch program for poor children, extended the program to include a school breakfast program and provided federal funds for non-food items required for a successful school lunch program. The school lunch program continued to grow as an integral part of the total educational experience, despite claims that it was just another way to subsidize agricultural producers.

Over time, the US school lunch program has come under scrutiny for providing less healthful options that contribute to the increase in child obesity. In 2010, President Barack Obama introduced the Healthy, Hunger-Free Kids Act (HHFKA) to fight obesity in schools. This law reformed the National School Lunch Program (NSLP), which provides meals to millions of children. The HHFKA expanded the number of children eligible for meal subsidies and set national nutrition standards for school vending machines (Guenther et al. 2009). There have been criticisms over the influence of some lobby groups, such as allowing pizza (with tomato sauce) and French fries to qualify as healthy vegetables. Some school districts have implemented policies that are more stringent than the HHFKA (R. Paarlberg 2013), while other school districts are requesting more flexibility to make food substitutions (USDA/FNS 2020).

17.5   SUSTAINABLE FOOD SYSTEMS

Historically, recommendations contained in the USDA Dietary Guidelines have mainly been limited to nutrition, but this is beginning to change. For example, the DGAC included a chapter on food sustainability and safety for the first time in 2015 due to the significant impact of food production on the environment. The DGAC defined sustainable diets as eating patterns that promote good health and provide environmentally sustainable food security. After reviewing recommendations from other developed countries, the DGAC concluded that environmentally sustainable dietary guidelines should focus on decreasing meat and non-sustainable seafood consumption, eating more plants and plant-based products, limiting energy intake, and reducing food waste. A Johns Hopkins University opinion poll found that 74 per cent of Americans surveyed agreed with the DGAC report's sustainability measures (Johns Hopkins Center for a Livable Future 2015), so future DGAC reports will likely stress more environmentally sustainable diets.

HEALTHIER, MORE SUSTAINABLE FOOD SYSTEM

In 2009, one hundred leading experts in health, nutrition, sustainable agriculture, economics, business, marketing, and public policy convened at a conference in Virginia to discuss how the United States can move towards a healthier and sustainable food system. The experts recognized that concerns about our food supply include social and environmental issues related to food (how it is produced and distributed) and to agricultural systems that are too resource-intensive and not sustainable (Story, Hamm, and Wallinga 2009).

These same experts recommended a food systems approach to sustainability that accounts for the complexity of the supply chain from farm to fork and acknowledges the contribution of various factors to overall health. Story, Hamm, and Wallinga (2009, 223) define a sustainable food system as one that provides healthy food while maintaining a healthy ecosystem that "can provide food for generations to come, with minimal negative impact to the environment; encourages local production and distribution infrastructures; makes nutritious food available, accessible, and affordable to all; is humane and just – protecting farmers and other workers, consumers, and communities."

Most consumers do not comply with USDA Dietary Guidelines. Even if consumers wanted to comply with the guidelines, there is not a sustainable supply of all food groups to meet demand. While meat and grain supplies meet the demand, supplies of vegetables, fruit, and milk are insufficient (Krebs-Smith, Reedy, and Bosire 2010). This has been an ongoing situation. It has been estimated that to meet USDA Dietary Guidelines, harvested fruit and vegetable acreage would have to more than double, dairy supplies would have to grow by almost 50 per cent, and milk production would have to increase by more than 100 billion pounds per year (Buzby, Wells, and Vocke 2006). Meat is a relatively resource-intense source of energy, and in order to supply projected future consumption, the required increases in production would have implications for land use, food security, and sustainability.

The variety, quality, and quantity of food available in the food supply chain reflects the economic balance between agriculture and economic policies. The USDA uses the Loss-Adjusted Food Supply Data to monitor the potential of the food supply to meet the nutritional needs of the US populations, translate nutrition goals for Americans into food production and supply goals, and evaluate the effects of marketing practices over time. The data suggest it may be unrealistic to expect an increase in consumer demand that would be sufficient to influence the food supply through distribution channels. Instead, deliberate efforts on the part of policymakers and industry may be necessary to provide a supply of food consistent with nutrition recommendations and make healthy choices available to all (Krebs-Smith, Reedy, and Bosire 2010).

Evidence of the community food environment's effect on USDA Dietary Guidelines compliance is conflicting. Several studies have found that the community food environment does affect fruit and vegetable consumption (Morland, Wing, and Roux 2002; Rose and Richards 2004; Zenk et al. 2009), while other studies have found that such access does not create significant impacts (Pearson et al. 2005; Pearce et al. 2008; Ding et al. 2012). However, research examining the impact of access to healthier food on overall dietary quality has concluded that improved access does not improve overall dietary quality (An and Sturm 2012; Shier, An, and Sturm 2012), and when distance to a grocery store is significantly associated with obesity, the significance diminishes after accounting for prices (Sturm and Datar 2005).

In summary, food systems are complex and involve complicated interactions among humans and nature. As noted by Auestad and Fulgoni (2015, 19): "Consistent and credible science that brings together agriculture, food systems, nutrition, public health, environment economics, culture, and trade is needed to identify synergies and trade-offs and to inform guidance on vital elements of healthy, sustainable diets."

17.6   EVOLUTION OF CANADA'S FOOD GUIDE, 1942–2019

Canada's first food guide, entitled "The Official Food Rules," was published in July 1942 and updated in 1944. The main purpose of the original food guide was to prevent nutritional deficiencies and to improve the health of Canadians during times of wartime food rationing. Canada's food rules, as approved by the Canadian Council on Nutrition, advised consumers to eat healthy food and drink plenty of water. The Council divided daily healthy food consumption into five categories (Figure 17.7).

Figure 17.7. Canada's Food Guide, 1944.

I. CANADA'S FOOD RULES

Approved by the Canadian Council on Nutrition

THESE ARE THE FOODS FOR HEALTH. EAT THEM
EVERY DAY. DRINK PLENTY OF WATER

1. *Milk*—Adults, ½ to 1 pint. Children, 1½ pints to 1 quart.

2. *Fruit*—One serving of citrus fruit or tomatoes or their juices; *and* one serving of other fruit.

3. *Vegetables*—At least *one* serving of potatoes; at least *two* servings of other vegetables, preferably leafy, green or yellow, and frequently raw.

4. *Cereals and Bread*—One serving of a whole-grain cereal *and* at least four slices of Canada Approved Vitamin B bread (whole wheat, brown or white) *with butter.*

5. *Meat and Fish*—One serving of meat, fish, poultry or meat alternates such as beans, peas, nuts, eggs or cheese. Also use eggs and cheese at least three times a week each, and liver frequently.

A fish liver oil, as a source of vitamin D, should be given to children and expectant women, and may be advisable for other adults.

Iodized salt is recommended.

Source: Health Canada (2019a).

Canada's Food Guide has been revised several times over the years (Health Canada 2019c). In 1977, 1992, 2007, and 2019, major revisions to the food guide have reflected the latest scientific evidence on healthy food choices (Health Canada 2019d, 2019b). In 1977, food was divided into four equally proportioned food groups: fruits/vegetables, meat/eggs, dairy, and grains (Figure 17.8). Between 1992 and 2007, more emphasis was placed on fruits/vegetables, followed by grains, dairy, and meat/eggs in descending order (Figure 17.9). In 2019, food was divided into three groups consisting of fruits/vegetables, grains,

Figure 17.8. Canada's Food Guide, 1977.

Source: Health Canada (2019a).

and protein (meat and dairy combined), with fruits/vegetables receiving an even greater emphasis (Figure 17.10).

17.7   CONSUMER RESPONSE AND BEHAVIOUR

Despite years of dietary guidance in the United States and Canada, there has been no substantial shift in consumer dietary consumption. This lack of change in consumer behaviour is a multifaceted

Figure 17.9. Canada's Food Guide, 2007.

Source: Health Canada (2019a).

problem that is difficult to measure due to many factors, such as cultural and individual food preferences, access and availability to healthy food options, and lack of time or skills for food preparation (Webb and Byrd-Bredbenner 2015). Compounded with the fact that making conscious sustainable changes to ingrained daily habits is difficult, many consumers find the changing content and lack of specificity of dietary guidelines confusing. Time has proved the difficulty in changing overall consumer behaviour through education and marketing alone (Global Panel 2017).

Some groups have tried to regulate healthy food consumption through food taxes. For example, Lakkakula and Schmitz (2019) examined the effect of tax rates on sweetened beverages.

Figure 17.10. Canada's Dietary Guidelines, 2019.

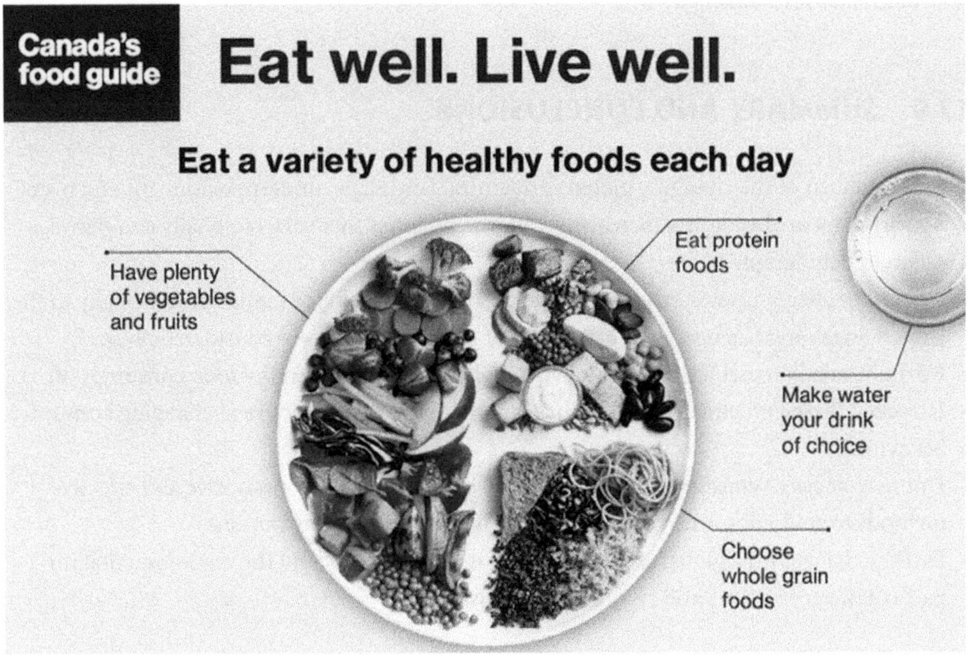

Source: Health Canada (2019c).

They determined the input tax rate on all types of sweeteners (not just sugar or high fructose corn syrup) required to reduce consumer intake to the recommended levels in different regions. This method could be expanded to discourage consumption of other unhealthy foods.

17.8   THE FUTURE OF DIETARY GUIDELINES

Governments are becoming increasingly aware of the need to deliver dietary guidelines in a manner that resonates with consumers in order to create lasting changes to the overall health of their respective nations. Therefore, future solutions must make information clear and concise in terms that consumers can easily interpret and provide the reasoning behind the next iteration of changes. A simple example of this may be reformatting serving size recommendations away from ounces and cups and towards whole food measures (e.g., one large egg). On a broader scale, future proposals should provide recommendations on both individual and regulatory levels (such as programs that influence consumer choice through industry regulation) to support sustainable and quantifiable long-term changes with methods for proper tracking and evaluation of results. Further, future changes to dietary guidelines must expand the scope of responsibility from beyond individual consumers to include agricultural production and environmental sustainability.

17.9   SUMMARY AND CONCLUSIONS

- In the context of the changing global agricultural landscape, undernourishment and over-nourishment are becoming increasingly prevalent issues that vary regionally and between different demographics.
- Obesity has become an increasingly large problem in developed countries, especially in the United States and Canada, where over half of the populations are considered obese.
- US and Canadian dietary guidelines have evolved to address healthy food consumption. However, these guidelines are often unclear and may not be effective at changing consumer behaviour.
- Future changes to consumer dietary guidelines must find more innovative and effective methods to shift consumer behaviour towards choosing healthy options.
- Further changes on a global level must address sustainability and the environmental impacts of dietary choices and recommendations.

CHAPTER EIGHTEEN

Biotechnology and GMOs

18.1 DIFFERENT PLANT SPECIES

Two recent innovations have affected global agriculture: the genetic modification of crops and the birth of genomics, an interdisciplinary field of biology focused on the structure, function, evolution, mapping, and editing of genomes, which is different from the science of GMOs. Genetically modified organisms (GMOs) are created in the laboratory by recombining DNA molecules from different species into a new gene. This new gene is then implanted into an organism that will possess genetic traits of both species. Since the 1980s, agriculture has seen the introduction and rapid adoption of genetically modified (GM) crops for food (e.g., corn and soybeans) and fibre (e.g., cotton). Since 2010, genomics has become an integral part of biotechnology. In the interim, the global area planted to GMOs increased rapidly (ISAAA 2006), and by 2006, an estimated 10.3 million farmers worldwide grew GMOs in twenty-two countries (Table 18.1). The United States is the world leader in land areas planted to GMO crops, with 54.6 million hectares under cultivation. The eleven developing countries planting GMOs account for 40 per cent of biotech crop acreage, a proportion that has been increasing steadily. It is to be noted that two important traded crops – wheat and rice – are not GMOs.

First-generation GMOs are made by splicing genes from different types of crops to increase crop resistance to pests or herbicides and to increase production (Moss, A. Schmitz, and T.G. Schmitz 2006). Examples of first-generation GMOs include Roundup Ready corn, soybeans, and canola that are resistant to the Roundup herbicide, and Bacillus thuringiensis (Bt) cotton that is resistant to specific insects.

Second-generation GMOs are made by mixing the DNA of crops or animals with the DNA of other species to produce better-tasting varieties and to enhance vitamin content. Examples of second-generation plant GMOs include CalGene's FLAVR SAVR tomato (later acquired by

Table 18.1   Countries growing 50,000 hectares or more of genetically modified (GM) crops, 2006

Rank	Country	Land Area in GM Crops (million ha)	GM Crops Grown
1	United States	54.6	Soybean, maize, cotton, canola, squash, papaya, alfalfa
2	Argentina	18.0	Soybean, maize, cotton
3	Brazil	11.5	Soybean, cotton
4	Canada	6.1	Canola, maize, soybean
5	India	3.8	Cotton
6	China	3.5	Cotton
7	Paraguay	2.0	Soybean
8	South Africa	1.4	Soybean, maize, cotton
9	Uruguay	0.4	Soybean, maize
10	Philippines	0.2	Maize
11	Australia	0.2	Cotton
12	Romania	0.1	Soybean
13	Mexico	0.1	Cotton, soybean
14	Spain	0.1	Maize
15	Colombia	<0.1	Cotton
16	France	<0.1	Maize
17	Iran	<0.1	Rice
18	Honduras	<0.1	Maize
19	Czech Republic	<0.1	Maize
20	Portugal	<0.1	Maize
21	Germany	<0.1	Maize
22	Slovakia	<0.1	Maize

Source: ISAAA (2006).

Monsanto), Ingo Potrykus's Golden Rice with enhanced vitamin A, and Syngenta's Golden Rice II. An example of second-generation animal GMOs included Atlantic salmon. In the United States, second-generation GMOs are dwarfed by first-generation GMOs.

Third-generation GMOs (not intended for use as food or feed) are organisms (plants and animals) used as "factories" to produce pharmaceuticals for humans and animals, and materials for research and industry. When plants are used as factories, third-generation GMOs are also referred to as plant-made pharmaceuticals (PMPs). Either food plants (e.g., corn or rice) or non-food plants (e.g., tobacco or algae) can be used to produce PMP products. Examples of PMPs undergoing open field trials include rice (used to extract milk proteins as anti-diarrhoeal additives for infant oral rehydration formula); insulin extracted from safflower; cystic-fibrosis treatment extracted from corn; ovarian cancer treatment extracted from tobacco; and monoclonal antibodies extracted from duckweed. An example of using animals as factories is xenotransplantation, which is any procedure that involves the transplantation of living cells, tissues, or organs from one species to another.

Considerable controversy surrounds the use and adoption of GMOs in food production (Moss, A. Schmitz, and T.G. Schmitz 2006). Anti-biotech activists believe that engineered foods hold health and environmental dangers; pro-biotech enthusiasts wax eloquent regarding better, cheaper, and more environmentally friendly GM crops. Certain consumer groups have labelled GM products as "Frankenfoods" and have raised long-term health concerns regarding the consumption of GM products. Some non-governmental organizations (NGOs) have been successful in anti-GM campaigns, helping lead to decisions such as the United States and Canada not adopting GM wheat varieties and Aventis terminating the production of StarLink corn.

This chapter provides an economic assessment of the issues surrounding first-generation GMOs in agriculture. It includes a theoretical discussion of the economic impacts of the introduction of GM commodities and an empirical synopsis of several case studies of GM crops. In Appendix 18A, we present a more rigorous assessment of the adoption of GM corn and soybeans.

18.2   REGULATORY FRAMEWORK

GM foods have been increasingly regulated by governments but without a unified framework of regulation. Indeed, "the current approval procedures and labeling regulations covering GM foods differ widely across OECD [Organisation for Economic Co-operation and Development] countries, with a large and visible gap between North America and European Union (EU) approaches" (Carter and Gruère 2006, 459). In general, biotech regulations in the United States are more friendly towards GMOs than they are in the EU, which explains partly why GMOs are more widespread in the United States. Other countries, such as New Zealand and Australia, seem to have combined portions of the regulatory frameworks utilized by the United States and that of the EU when formulating their own policies with respect to GMOs.

Prior to the adoption of a GM food product in a country, the appropriate regulatory bodies must (1) ensure that GM foods are safe for human consumption, and (2) provide consumer choice and information about the GM food products. For food safety purposes, a company's application for authorization to sell a GM food product in a country often requires the completion of standardized safety tests. The results of these safety tests are reviewed by public authorities and are compared with the results of similar analyses conducted by public scientific authorities.

GM products are referred to as novel foods. The safety assessment and food-labelling procedures for GM products vary widely across countries, partly because of differing definitions of what a novel food is. Regulation procedures regarding GMOs can be formulated using either a product-related standard or a process-related standard. Product-related standards are based on the specific characteristics of the final product by comparing GMO output with traditional food products. Process-related standards are based on the characteristics of the technology used to create the product.

As Carter and Gruère state, "The *novelty criterion* is important in that it triggers a series of administrative steps required to obtain pre-marketing food safety approval" (2006, 460). In countries outside the United States, biotech companies applying for pre-marketing approval must submit a scientific assessment of the potential safety risks of the product. In the United States, however, the approval process is voluntary for GM foods generally recognized as safe. While assessment is similar around the world, risk management is not:

> The scientific assessment procedures tend to have similar features across developed countries: they follow the general approach defined in the OECD consensus report written in 2000, in collaboration with experts from the World Health Organization (WHO) and the United Nations Food and Agriculture Organization (FAO). Safety assessment is commonly based on the concept of *substantial equivalence*, as defined by the OECD in 1993, and endorsed by the FAO/WHO joint consultation in 1996.
>
> Although scientific risk assessments are similar across countries in many ways, the risk management steps differ in important ways. In some countries, all GM food varieties have to be approved by different legislative bodies; in some others the system does not require legislative approval. (Carter and Gruère 2006, 462)

The regulatory framework in the United States and Canada is founded on the premise that GM food is not significantly different from food produced using conventional methods as long as the characteristics of the final GM product do not differ significantly from similar non-GM products. This implies that "foods produced with biotechnology do not necessarily present any new or greater risk than traditional foods. This approach is based on the concept of *substantial equivalence*" (Carter and Gruère 2006, 463).

The regulatory framework in the United States relies on four principles: "(i) existing laws are adequate, (ii) regulations should be based on product not process, (iii) GMOs are not fundamentally different from conventional crops, and (iv) oversight authority is exercised only when there is evidence of risk that would make it unreasonable to introduce the product" (Carter and Gruère 2006, 466). The responsibility of enforcing these US product acceptance regulations rests with three governmental agencies: the Environmental Protection Agency (EPA), the Department of Agriculture (USDA), and the Food and Drug Administration (FDA).

In contrast, "the EU has built its safety system under the premise that GM food may present specific risks and thus should be treated separately from conventional foods" (Carter and Gruère 2006, 463). Derived from Article 7 of the EU General Food Law (Byrne 2004), GM foods in the EU are subject to the concept of the precautionary principle, which states that biotech food may contain unknown risks. Therefore, the regulatory authorities in EU countries believe they should take appropriate measures to limit the development of unknown future food risks and to limit the development of changes to the environment that may be caused by the introduction of GM foods into their countries.

The EU approach is precautionary and process-related, and includes a mandatory labelling requirement (i.e., any product potentially containing GM materials must be labelled as such). The US food and biotechnology industry is opposed to a mandatory labelling system (Muth, Mancini, and Viator 2003). As a result of mandatory labelling, it is difficult to find GM food products in the EU and certain other countries: "Labeling and approval regulations in major developed countries have affected international trade in all GM crops except cotton (because most cotton products are not edible and thus not subject to food safety and labeling requirements). In particular, regulations in the EU and Japan – two large importers of these crops – have impacted trade. Furthermore, the choice of regulations in the EU and Japan has discouraged the development of new GM food varieties and at the same time encouraged third countries to adopt labeling requirements similar to those in the EU" (Carter and Gruère 2006, 473).

EU LABELLING
The EU labelling system has discouraged the use of any GM food ingredients in food products. Food processors have switched to non-GM ingredients while farmers have been discouraged from adopting GM crops (Carter and Gruère 2006).

18.2.1   Consumer Confidence

At the heart of the GMO controversy is consumer confidence. Why do US consumers eat GM corn while GM corn is not part of EU consumption? Are GM products inferior, equivalent, or in some cases superior to non-GM products? Should the answers to questions surrounding GMOs be based on science or consumer perception? Interestingly, Gerber Foods announced that starting in 1999, its baby food products would no longer use ingredients from GM crops. As Kershen (2000) stresses, Gerber may have unintentionally increased the health risk for its baby food consumers because non-GM ingredients are more prone to contamination by mycotoxins, which are poisons produced by fungus. In another such case, Monsanto developed a potato containing a Bt gene to control the Colorado potato beetle that was combined with another transplanted gene to control a virus from aphids. From 1994 to 1999 potato growers who planted the GM variety reduced their use of chemicals and subsequently increased their yields. These transgenic potatoes appeared to be environmentally and economically superior to the previous potato varieties. Even so, companies such as McDonald's, Burger King, and Wendy's no longer accept transgenic potatoes for use in their French fry preparations because of fears about GM foods. Yet researchers such as Kershen (2000) have shown that non-GM potatoes are more of a risk to health than are GM potatoes.

Kershen (2000) argues that food companies should use science when making decisions on whether or not to use GM foods. GM food products should not be removed from grocery shelves based only on consumer opposition to these products. Rather, the food companies should educate consumers on the scientific facts about GM food product safety.

Consumers in many countries likely know very little about GMOs. Hallman et al. (2004) find that the US population is generally ignorant about the health risk of GM foods. Less than half of the people interviewed by Rutgers University were aware that GM foods had even been sold in supermarkets.

Producer and environmental groups in many countries, especially import-competing countries, oppose GM crops. This is especially true in the EU. In some cases, certain producer groups may play on consumer fears over the health risks of GMOs in order to create or maintain non-tariff barriers to protect their domestic industry. Domestic producers competing against foreign imports can participate in rent-seeking behaviour – that is, the behaviour of individuals seeking profits through political action (A. Schmitz, Furtan, and Baylis 2002) – to ban imports so that producers can keep the domestic price for their product at high levels.

> **HEALTH RISK**
> In the debate over the long-term health risks from the consumption of GM commodities, it is important to keep in mind that: "Seven academies of science issued a report ... expressing the overwhelming scientific consensus that, in order to feed the people of the world, scientific discoveries and new technologies (including transgenic plants) must be used. Specifically, these seven scientific academies state: foods can be produced through the use of GM technology that are more nutritious, stable in storage, and in principle health promoting – bringing benefits to consumers in both industrialized and developing nations" (Kershen 2000, 643–4).

As with the debate over GM commodities described above, consumer perception rather than science determines the impact of regulatory change in other areas. For example, in the case *City of Santa Fe* v. *Komis*, the court adopted the view that the government entity must pay damages if it is shown that fear of danger exists and that fear affects market value (Gregory and von Winterfeldt 1996, 206). Furthermore, the court concluded that whether the transportation of hazardous nuclear materials actually is or is not safe is irrelevant; the issue is whether public perception of those dangers has a depressing effect on the value of the property (ibid.). In another case that involved the public's apprehension of living near high-voltage power lines, the court found that "in accordance with *San Diego Gas & Electric Co.* v. *Daley* (205 Cal. App. 3d

1334, 1988), the jury was instructed that it was not to decide on the 'scientific controversy' over the health effects of EMFs (electro-magnetic fields) but only on whether public fear of EMFs could diminish property values" (ibid.).

18.2.2 Producer Profitability

Producer profitability depends on many factors, including the savings on overall inputs from GMO adoption and the impact of commodity prices that depend on consumer acceptability. Then there is the issue of adopters and non-adopters of GM products. Generally, non-adopters of GM products lose because of lower commodity prices when, in aggregate, the industry adopts GM varieties.

18.3 ECONOMIC FRAMEWORK

Several factors are at play when developing economic models that measure the impact of GMO adoption: (1) for many commodities in which GM varieties are available, a sizeable number of non-GM producers remain; (2) for many GM commodities, there is an excess supply of their non-GM counterpart needed to satisfy non-GM consumer demand for which no significant price premium is paid; and (3) the rate of adoption of GM varieties depends critically on consumer perception of the GM product.

Three scenarios describe the potential impact of the introduction of GM varieties: (1) the GM variety is viewed by the consumer as equivalent to conventional crops; (2) the GM variety is viewed as inferior to conventional varieties; or (3) the GM variety is viewed as superior to traditional crops.

First, if GM commodities are perceived to be identical to non-GM commodities, they will be perfect substitutes for each other, and the analysis of the economics of GMOs will be straightforward. The model of hybrid corn applies (Griliches 1957, 1958, 1960). In the case of hybrid corn, Griliches estimates the rates of return to public investment and assumes that consumers are indifferent between the new hybrid corn varieties and traditional corn varieties. Consumers, either directly through consumption or indirectly through livestock production, are better off because they have increased access to more and cheaper corn. In the mechanized agriculture case, A. Schmitz and Seckler (1970) estimate the rates of return from investment in the mechanical tomato harvester. However, unlike Griliches, they assume the quality of tomatoes deteriorates as a result of mechanization. These studies estimate that there are sizeable societal gains from the introduction of new technology, but in agriculture these benefits are captured largely by consumers.

Second, consumers may perceive that first-generation GMOs are inherently inferior to non-GM commodities. Thus, non-GM products may sell at a premium to GM goods, and in certain instances there may be no demand for GM commodities, even at a zero price. However, if the premium merely offsets the costs of segregating the two products, the non-GM producers will bear the cost of this segregation and will bear the additional marketing cost of maintaining separate market channels to guarantee GM-free product, and it will be a negative externality brought about by the GM market (Gray, Moss, and Schmitz 2004). Society may benefit from the introduction of the GM varieties, but these gains will not be as large as in the first scenario.

Third, apart from its agronomic impact, the GM innovation may provide health benefits for consumers. In this case, the innovators must pay the various identity preservation costs in order to exploit the consumers' willingness to pay for the improved attribute. This imperfect substitutability in demand necessitates the need for market segmentation, which is the tailoring of market channels to cater to consumers who have different preferences for GM content.

In aggregate, we express the net gains to society from the introduction of GM varieties as

$$\Delta W = (\Delta CS_{NG} + \Delta CS_G) + (\Delta PS_{NG} + \Delta PS_G) - T, \tag{18.1}$$

in which ΔW is the change in aggregate welfare; ΔCS_{NG} is the change in consumer surplus, that is, the willingness to pay for the consumption of the commodity above the market price paid by non-GM consumers (R.E. Just, Hueth, and Schmitz 2004); ΔCS_G is the change in consumer surplus for GM consumers; ΔPS_{NG} is the change in producer surplus, that is, profit generated from the sale of the commodity in excess of the production cost; ΔP_G is the change in producer surplus for GM producers; and T is the segregation cost after the introduction of GM varieties. Non-adopters who wish to sell GM-free commodities bear the segregation costs in addition to the negative price consequences of an increase in supply (Figure 18.A1).

To account for international trade, the previous model needs to be expanded:

$$\Delta W = (\Delta CS_{NG} + \Delta CS_G + \Delta CS_{INT}) + (\Delta PS_{NG} + \Delta PS_G + \Delta PS_{INT}) - T - \Delta GP, \tag{18.2}$$

in which ΔCS_{INT} is the change in foreign consumer surplus accruing through international trade; ΔPS_{INT} is the change in foreign producer surplus from international trade; and ΔGP is the change in government payments. The introduction of new GM varieties will affect government support payments if GM varieties reduce the market-clearing price below the target price.

The adoption of GMOs can affect international trade and the welfare of importers and exporters. If an exporter adopts a GMO, importers will benefit, but producers in the importing country will lose as prices fall. Thus, the introduction of new GM varieties can provide an opportunity for rent-seeking behaviour through trade policy (A. Schmitz, Furtan, and Baylis 2002). Countries have banned the importation of GM commodities, alleging concerns over the long-term health consequences of GM commodities, but these actions may represent protectionist rent-seeking behaviour on the part of the import-competing producers. In addition, the refusal of shipments of commodities because of allegations of GM content can represent a risk and a cost to producers. These allegations can be motivated by an opportunistic desire to renegotiate the price through (1) political activity that can use international relations as leverage, or (2) corruption (e.g., bribery by alternative suppliers). Banning the importation of GM commodities can increase producer welfare in the importing country and can reduce producer welfare in the exporting country. The possible intrusion of rent-seeking behaviour is increased by the use of different food safety criteria among nations.

Much of the work on the adoption of GM crops focuses on the potential gains to producers and consumers (see Appendix 18B). But market risks exist; for example, consumers may reject commodities with GM content regardless of the scientific data on the safety of GM technologies and products. These market risks are deliberated by politicians and the media rather than being predicated by science-based determinations about the safety of GM commodities. Future research on the economics of GM crops should assess these market risks. The case study on wheat in section 18.4.1 below begins to address potential market risk. Of the five first-generation GM crops (wheat, soybeans, corn, cotton, and canola), only GM wheat has not been introduced into either the US or Canadian food market chain.

WILL GM FOOD EVER BE ON EUROPE'S MENU?
The attitude of EU member states towards the adoption of GM products remains controversial. New laws about GM products require a positive evaluation from the European Food Safety Authority (EFSA). The EFSA was established in 2002 and even though it was modelled after the Food and Drug Administration of the United States, it is very different in that it is not a regulatory body. Its function is to provide scientific advice to the European Commission. When an application is cleared by EFSA, the European Commission places it before a regulatory committee made up of EU member states. Approval requires a qualified majority vote, which has rarely happened (Byrne 2004).

18.4   CASE STUDIES

Economic studies have determined the economic significance of commodities such as GM wheat, cotton, canola, soybeans, and corn. These studies are discussed in detail in A. Schmitz et al. (2010). We provide a brief summary:

18.4.1   Wheat

The United States and Canada have resisted the adoption of GM wheat despite efforts by Monsanto to have GM varieties licensed. Some economists support GM wheat while others do not. A major difference in opinion revolves around how researchers deal with the demand characteristics of GM versus non-GM wheat. There is little scientific evidence that GM wheat is inferior to non-GM wheat. However, because certain importers perceive GM wheat to be of lower quality, they are likely to purchase their wheat from countries that do not produce GM wheat. In addition, food processors such as General Mills in the United States fear a negative backlash from using GMO crops such as wheat.

18.4.2   Cotton

The introduction of the Bt microbe into cotton seeds benefits producers by inducing the production in the plant of the Cry1Ac protein, which is toxic to the various species of bollworm (Falck-Zepeda, Traxler, and R.G. Nelson 2000; Qaim and Zilberman 2003). According to Qaim and Zilberman (2003), the introduction of the Bt cotton varieties in India, for example, has had sizeable benefits due to yield advantages. Similar findings were made regarding the adoption of Bt cotton in China (Pray et al. 2002).

Falck-Zepeda, Traxler, and R.G. Nelson (2000) estimate that the gains from the introduction of Bt cotton in the United States include (1) US farmers capture average yearly gains of US$140 million of producer surplus from GM varieties; (2) Monsanto benefits by only US$49 million; and (3) Delta and Pine Land, who market the cottonseed, obtain US$13 million. Falck-Zepeda, Traxler, and Nelson also find that while US producers are made better off by the introduction of the Bt cotton, producers in the rest of the world are worse off. This can be attributed to several factors. Only a small share of cotton is consumed as a foodstuff for humans and animals (e.g., a small amount of cottonseed oil is used as a protein supplement). Thus, the introduction of GM cotton varieties does not require separate market channels because GM cotton has generally the same ginning quality as non-GM cotton.

18.4.3   Canola

Canola is a trademarked variety of rapeseed developed in Canada for both human and livestock consumption (Gray and Malla 2001). Traditional varieties of rapeseed produce high levels of erucic acid, which causes myocardial lesions on the heart tissue of animals. In 1978, canola was registered as a trade name by the Western Canadian Oilseed Crushers Association to designate varieties of rapeseed that contained 5 per cent or less erucic acid. The market for canola oil in the mid-1980s expanded with the finding that it is low in polyunsaturated fatty acids. In addition, genetic modification increased herbicide tolerance. While Roundup Ready canola does not provide health benefits beyond traditional varieties, it reduces producer costs in certain cases.

Two improvements in canola occurred simultaneously during the 1990s. First, the yield of traditional varieties was increased through the introduction of high-yielding (HY) traits.

At the same time, herbicide-tolerant (HT) traits were introduced to make some varieties Roundup Ready. Thus, while canola yields increased steadily over this period, it is difficult to disentangle the canola-yield effects of the new high-yielding varieties from the introduction of GM characteristics. In 2018 and 2019, over 90 per cent of the canola planted in Canada were GMO varieties.

18.4.4   Soybeans

Roundup Ready, or herbicide tolerant, varieties are the most frequently used type of GM soybean seed. GM soybeans produced in the United States accounted for 92 per cent of all soybean acres nationwide in 2008. The introduction of these GM technologies has the potential to segment the market channel, resulting in price premiums for the producers of non-GM products. However, the emergence of a premium depends on the level of identity preservation (IP) costs and also on government price supports, such as the loan deficiency program (LDP) or target prices. Sufficiently large identity preservation costs, coupled with price supports, result in the loss of market segmentation opportunities.

A. Schmitz, Moss, and T.G. Schmitz (2004) estimate the costs and benefits from the introduction of GM soybeans in the United States and finds that US consumers are the largest gainers from GM soybeans. The introduction of GM soybeans had little effect on producer price because the LDP for soybeans essentially established a floor on the price US soybean producers received. When GM varieties cause market prices to fall to low levels, the government pays for the difference between the floor price and the lower market price (i.e., government program payments increase when market prices fall). Crucial to their analysis is the observation that the demand for non-GM soybeans is small relative to the potential supply of non-GM output because the largest percentage of soybeans is consumed through livestock feed. Furthermore, their results apply only when US soybean prices are so low that farmers receive subsidies under the LDP program.

The introduction of GMOs can lead to a segmentation of the soybean market in the United States. However, even if it exists, market segmentation alone may not result in a price premium for non-GM soybeans. For a price premium to emerge, the demand for non-GM soybeans must be greater than the supply of non-GM soybeans at the original price equilibrium. This analysis is complicated by agricultural policies.

When an excess supply of non-GM soybeans exists in the marketplace, non-GM soybeans can be substituted for GM soybeans in all uses, since there will be no price premium at the producer level. However, consumers of non-GMOs will have to pay a price premium over GMOs due to the imposition of identity preservation costs in the grain-handling system. In addition, US price supports, when binding, affect the final price realized by producers of both GM and non-GM soybeans.

There has been worldwide resistance to GM soybeans, especially by the EU. The EU imports soybeans largely in processed form rather than as raw soybeans because the EU contends that processed products produced using GM soybeans are less likely to contain modified proteins. Thus, the EU ban on the importation of raw soybeans is consistent with the precautionary principle.

18.4.5   Corn

Corn is a major crop with many uses, including food, feed, ethanol, and high fructose corn syrup (HFCS). In 2008 approximately 80 per cent of all corn seed in the United States was genetically modified. However, most genetic modifications made to corn address problems regarding specific pests in specific regions. The US adoption of GM corn is more prevalent in the western corn belt where Bt corn is planted to combat the European corn borer. Other types of GM corn in the United States include Ht corn and rootworm-resistant corn, but Bt corn is the most prevalent (Alston et al. 2002).

For producers to sell their corn as GM-free corn, a segregated market channel must be established. The implicit assumption is that marketing non-GM corn yields a price premium for the quantity demanded by GM-free corn users (e.g., Gerber). There are processing firms in the United States such as Frito Lay and Taco Bell that buy only GM-free corn. However, the possibility of a price premium for non-GM corn is closely linked to the segregation costs required to meet the GM-free corn demands (see Appendix 18C).

NON-GM DEMAND
Because the demand for non-GM corn is small relative to its supply, no premium for non-GM corn can be generated in excess of the segregation costs. An outward shift in the supply of corn resulting from the adoption of GM varieties has a greater impact on aggregate welfare than do the segregation costs required to satisfy the GM-free demand. A 10 per cent increase in the aggregate supply of GM corn increases aggregate welfare by more than US$250 million. However, non-adopters of GM corn lose while adopters can gain or lose depending on the nature of the aggregate demand curve for US corn.

NON-ADOPTERS
The adoption of GM technology can adversely affect non-adopters and non-consumers of the GM product. Biotechnology redefines the agricultural output. Corn is no longer corn, but it is potentially a GM crop. This shift in definition then imposes an economic cost on non-adopters and non-consumers. Without the requirement to

segregate their product, the producers of GM crops do not have to prove that their crops are genetically modified, but the producers of non-GM crops now must prove that their crops are not genetically modified. In essence, the adoption of a new technology has changed the property rights of the non-adopter, causing the producer of non-genetically modified crops to bear an additional cost.

Demand for corn in the United States can be specified as two separate demand curves: GM and GM-free corn. Non-GM corn that is destined for GM-free markets must be tested at several points along the marketing channel. If non-GM corn contains GM material above a specified tolerance level at any of these delivery points, that corn will be diverted into the GM market. The theoretical model discussed below incorporates the additional segregation costs associated with non-GM corn destined for GM-free markets and with estimating the economic impact of GM corn on the US corn market.

Details of the empirical estimates on the impact of GM corn are given in Moss, A. Schmitz, and T.G. Schmitz (2009, 419–21). US society as a whole has benefited from GM corn, largely due to the positive impact on the livestock industry, in which corn is a major feed stock.

SEGREGATION COSTS

Changes in segregation costs have a minor impact on overall producer and consumer welfare, even though gains can accrue to users of GM corn in the presence of segregation costs. Also, premiums for non-GM corn in the United States cannot be large because of the excess of non-GM corn that is actually produced. When the presence of GM corn causes the US corn supply curve to shift, the overall welfare impact from GM corn can be large and positive, but there are both losers and gainers. In many cases, both non-GM corn producers and GM corn producers lose from the adoption of GM corn, while the large beneficiaries are users of GM corn. However, under different demand elasticities, GM corn adopters gain while those producers not adopting GM varieties lose. The overall welfare impact from supply responses due to GM corn is much larger than under the imposition of segregation costs alone.

18.4.6   Japanese and Chinese Corn Embargoes

The use of StarLink corn highlights the role the regulatory framework plays in the adoption of GMOs. Aventis Crop Science introduced StarLink corn in the United States in the late 1990s, even though the US Environmental Protection Agency had not approved it for human consumption (T.G. Schmitz, A. Schmitz, and Moss 2004; T.G. Schmitz, A. Schmitz, and Moss 2005b). Japan, a major corn importer, blocked imports of US corn because they discovered the existence of StarLink contamination. StarLink is a first-generation GMO containing the Cry9C protein that offers protection against the European corn borer. StarLink was not approved for human consumption because some research showed a link between the Cry9C protein and food allergies in humans. Due to the food allergy risk, Archer-Daniels-Midland started testing corn deliveries at its elevators for the presence of Cry9C in 2000. The discovery of the Cry9C protein caused US corn exports to Japan to decline (T.G. Schmitz, A. Schmitz, and Moss 2005b). Much of this reduction was replaced by increased imports of corn from other countries. US corn producers would have lost up to US\$1.5 billion in revenue if they had not received subsidies under the LDP. This essentially dampened the effect of the StarLink event on US producers because the majority of the burden was borne by the US government.

In 2009, Syngenta created two insect-resistant corn varieties (Agrisure Viptera and Agrisure Duracade), containing the MIR162 biotechnology-enhanced genetic trait. MIR162 has been engineered to produce its own insecticidal protein within the corn plant. Unlike with StarLink, these varieties were approved for commercial release in North America. On 20 November 2013, China imposed an embargo on corn imports from North America because of its zero-tolerance policy for unapproved genetic traits in imported crops. A detailed analysis on estimating the impact of StarLink corn can be found in A. Schmitz et al. (2010, 422–3) and in Carter and Smith (2007). For the Chinese corn embargo case, see T.G. Schmitz (2018).

18.5   GMOs – DEMAND ATTRIBUTES

One factor that is often neglected during the assessment of GMOs' impact is their effect on consumer demand and product quality. Often, the demand schedule for a GMO is presumed to be identical to the non-GMO that it replaced, but as we have seen, a GMO can be superior, identical, or inferior to a non-GMO. As noted in section 18.4.3, GMO canola fits the superior category. Consider Figure 18.1, where S and D exist prior to the introduction of a GMO. Suppose that a GMO shifts the supply schedule from S to S' and shifts the demand schedule from D to D'. In this case, the total gain from the introduction of a GMO will be ($abcdef$). If demand is ignored, the net gain from the introduction of the GMO will become $[(P_2bg) - (P_1af)]$. The effect of R&D that produces a GMO can be large depending on the magnitude of the demand shifts. The effect will be underestimated by the amount $[(abcdef) - (P_2bg - P_1af)]$.

There is a separate body of literature that estimates the effect of product advertising and promotion (F. Zhang 2019). In cases that examine demand shifts over time, researchers generally attribute the shift to advertising and promotions. The difficulty with reaching this conclusion, however, is that other factors contribute to demand changes over time. As shown

Figure 18.1. GMOs and product quality

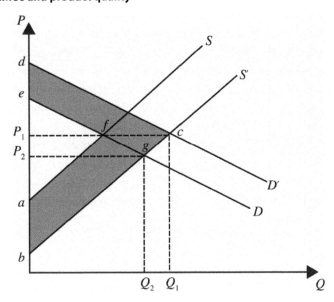

above, the demand shift for a product has nothing to do with advertising and promotion, but rather with genetic engineering. Therefore, this has to be separated using advanced econometric techniques so one does not over-calculate the benefits from either advertising/promotions or genetic engineering that brings about new product varieties.

18.6   GMO AND NON-GMO LIKE PRODUCTS

Can GMO and non-GMO varieties coexist? This question has no clear answer. Consider sugar: the varieties of sugar cane grown in the United States are non-GMO; however, certain varieties of sugar beets grown in the United States are GMO. Kennedy, Lewis, and Schmitz (2017) and Kennedy, Schmitz, and Lewis-Lelong (2019) find that sugar beet GMO varieties outyield non-GMO varieties.

How is it that the sugar produced from both GM and non-GM plants is GMO-free? Confusion arises over the health impacts of GMOs because the significant difference between GMOs and non-GMOs is not well understood. The following example of GMO sugar beets and non-GMO sugar cane sheds light on what is and is not a GMO. As discussed earlier, the EU, for example, generally blocks imports of GMO products. Refined sugar derived from GM sugar beets is identical to refined sugar derived from non-GM sugar cane (J. Klein, Altenbuchner, and Mattes 1998). In fact, no traces of GM DNA can be found in refined sugar originating from GM sugar beets, which means that sugar consumed from non-GM sugar cane and sugar consumed from GM sugar beets are identical. Consumable sugar (e.g., bagged sugar, sugar used as an ingredient in soft drinks) is refined and, by definition, refined sugar does not have any detectable DNA or protein; therefore, refined sugar derived from GM seeds is molecularly identical to refined sugar derived from non-GM seeds (J. Klein, Altenbuchner, and Mattes 1998; Zilberman et al. 2019). Thus, bagged sugar and sugar in soft drinks originating from GM sugar beets and non-GM sugar cane are nutritionally identical, as are the tastes of the sugars (J. Klein, Altenbuchner, and Mattes 1998; Zilberman et al. 2019).

In the context of food labelling, many non-GMO foods contain a non-GMO label. However, this is not the case for GMO foods; rarely does one find a GMO product labelled as GMO. GMO labelling is not required as such because the term "GMO" has a negative connotation. Including a voluntary GMO label would decrease product demand and make GMO products less desirable.

18.7   GMOs AND PLANT DISEASE

From an agricultural perspective, investment in GMO varietal development to prevent the destruction of certain agricultural industries is ongoing. One example is the millions of dollars of damage that citrus greening (HLB) and citrus canker diseases have cost the Florida citrus industry. As Florida's largest orange production competitor, Brazil is set to monopolize the market, so developing a GMO orange variety that is resistant to citrus greening is viewed as an answer to the problem (Grosser and Dutt 2017). According to Dr. Jude Grosser (pers. comm., Dec. 2017), though HLB can be solved by both biotechnology-facilitated conventional breeding and by a transgenic solution, there remains a significant problem with consumer acceptance of a GMO solution. Tropicana is owned by PepsiCo, and Minute Maid/Simply Orange is owned by Coca Cola. Both of these international companies support GMO research in order to remain competitive in the world market but may hesitate to commercialize a GMO solution due to resistance in the EU to GMO products. Looking towards the future, both companies are experimenting with transgenic engineering involving citrus products.

18.8   GENOMICS

Considerable attention is now given to genomics, in which genome editing is not a GMO technology (W.A. Kerr 2017). The new technology, CRISPR, is exciting because it is efficient, versatile, and inexpensive. Like GMOs, this new technology is not without controversy. Some argue that this technology should be subject to the same regulatory framework as GMOs. This is consistently the stance of the EU.

GENOMICS

Genomics is an interdisciplinary field of biology focused on the structure, function, evolution, mapping, and editing of genomes, which is different from the science of GMOs. Rather than being transgenic, genome editing alters a plant's DNA without introducing foreign genes. In 2012, scientists introduced a new method (CRISPR/Cas9) to cut and paste genes in a plant's genome.

18.9   SUMMARY AND CONCLUSIONS

- Eleven developing countries account for 40 per cent of global biotech crop acreage, a percentage that has been steadily increasing.
- Wheat and rice, two major crops, are non-GMO.
- Some consumers have been reluctant to accept GM technologies because they associate GM commodities with negative long-term health implications.
- Science contends that GMO foods are safe. Marketing decisions influenced by rent-seeking behaviour are based more on consumer perceptions than on scientific evidence.
- Moreover, economists are not in the position to judge the science surrounding food product quality and food product safety.
- EU regulations concerning GMOs are much more stringent than those in the United States. The EU uses the precautionary principle, which states that biotech foods may contain unknown risks, whereas US regulations allow biotech foods that do not show evidence of risk.
- In the economic modelling of the impact of GMOs, economists often make strong assumptions about the demand characteristics of GM versus non-GM products that affect their models' results. This uncertainty is magnified for ex ante analyses of new GM events.
- Some argue that GMO companies, such as Monsanto, are non-competitive and that they overcharge farmers for GM seeds. Under this premise, these parties oppose the adoption of GM varieties. However, non-competitive behaviour is not a reason for blocking the adoption of GM varieties. Rather, it is a basis for antitrust regulation.
- Some argue that GMOs are necessary to solve the world's food problems.
- Farmers using biotechnology have seen worldwide yield increases, cost reductions, better crop management, and sustainable agriculture. Even so, many oppose the adoption of GMOs.

Figure 18.A1. Adopters of GMOs and non-adopters of GMOs

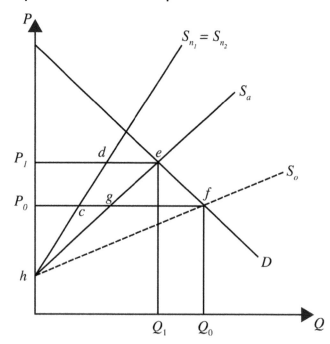

APPENDIX 18A: GMOs: NON-ADOPTERS

The introduction of GMOs can have both negative and positive effects. Consider Figure 18.A1, where prior to the introduction of a GMO output, Q_1 is produced at a price P_1. Assume that there are two producing regions with supply curves S_{n1} and S_{n2} that are identical. These sum to S_o.

With the introduction of GMOs, the supply shifts from S_a to S_o, and price falls to P_0 and output increases to Q_0. Now suppose that for technical reasons, region 1 does not adopt the GMO, but region 2 does. As a result, region 1 loses by ($P_1 P_0 cd$). The gain (or loss) to producers in region 2 is ($ghf - dcge$).

APPENDIX 18B: MODELLING MARKET SEGREGATION FOR CORN

To justify combining the firm-level expenditures on segregation or identity preservation costs with the marketing cost, we begin with the firm-level model proposed by Hudson and Jones (2001):

$$\max_{q} \pi = p(Q-q)+(p+k)q-C(Q-q)-K(q) \tag{18.C1}$$

where π is the firm-level profit; p is the price of undifferentiated or generic output; Q is the total quantity of output produced, which includes both undifferentiated US corn and identity preserved US corn; q is the quantity of segregated output produced; k is the price premium for segregated output; $C(.)$ is the cost of production for undifferentiated output; and $K(.)$ is the cost of production for identity-preserved output. In this formulation, the cost of production for undifferentiated and segregated output is separable (the level of production of undifferentiated output does not affect the cost of production of identity-preserved production). To demonstrate this, we substitute $q_T = Q = q_1 + q_2$ into Equation 18.C1, where q_1 is the production of undifferentiated output and q_2 is the production of identity-preserved output. The firm-level optimization model then becomes

$$\max_{q_1, q_2} \pi = [pq_1 - C(q_1)] + [(p+k)q_2 - K(q_2)]. \tag{18.C2}$$

We modify this formulation slightly to focus attention on the firm's expenditures on identity preservation

$$\max_{q_1, q_2} \pi = pq_1 + (p+k)q_2 - \tilde{C}(q_T) - \tilde{K}(q_2), \tag{18.C3}$$

in which $\tilde{C}(q_T)$ is the cost of producing the commodity (e.g., corn) and $\tilde{K}(q_2)$ is the expenditure on inputs required to meet the requirements of identity preservation. The Kuhn-Tucker conditions for this formulation are

$$\frac{\partial \pi}{\partial q_1} q_1 = \left[p - \frac{\partial \tilde{C}(q_T)}{\partial q_T} \frac{\partial q_T}{\partial q_1} \right] q_1 = 0$$

$$= \left[p - \frac{\partial \tilde{C}(q_T)}{\partial q_T} \right] q_1 = 0$$

$$\frac{\partial \pi}{\partial q_2} q_2 = \left[p + k - \frac{\partial \tilde{C}(q_T)}{\partial q_T} \frac{\partial q_r}{\partial q_2} - \frac{\partial \tilde{K}(q_2)}{\partial q_2} \right] q_2 = 0 \tag{18.C4}$$

$$= \left[\left(p + k - \frac{\partial \tilde{K}(q_2)}{\partial q_2} \right) - \frac{\partial \tilde{C}(q_T)}{\partial q_T} \right] q_2 = 0.$$

The equilibrium condition in Equation 18.C5 yields the equilibrium for GM-free corn:

$$D_N'(P) = D_N(P) - \left(M(P) + \frac{\partial \tilde{K}(q_2(P))}{\partial q_2(P)} \right), \tag{18.C5}$$

in which $D_N(P) - M(P)$ represents the price premium consumers are willing to pay for GM-free corn net of segregation costs incurred above the farm level $M(P)$ (k in Equation 18.C4) and $D'_N(P)$ is the effective demand for GM-free corn net of the segregation costs incurred at the firm level. In addition, we assume that the marginal cost of segregation at the farm level is constant $\{a\tilde{K}[q_2(P)] / \partial q_2(P) = \tilde{K}\}$.

CHAPTER NINETEEN

Conclusions and Future Directions

19.1 GOALS AND OBJECTIVES OF POLICY

One of the most difficult aspects of formulating agricultural policy is setting goals and objectives for the agricultural sector. This is understandable when policy is analysed within the context of rent-seeking behaviour. Without a clear set of goals and objectives, the development of policy will be muddled and confusing. One main goal of agricultural policy is to stabilize farm incomes. Governments have invested vast sums of money to stabilize agriculture, but many analysts disagree with the approach governments take. As this is the case, we present a summary of a vast literature dealing with the use of stocks to create stability; however, theory in general does not accord with the policy instruments that are actually used. For example, in the United States, storage has not been used as a prime instrument to create stability; rather, stock accumulation in past periods was the outcome of commodity price support programs. Stabilizing farm income ex ante through a planning exercise can be very different from stabilizing farm income when the actual events unfold.

A major change in North American agriculture is the significant increase in farm size, which has been facilitated by farm technology and rental arrangements, thus complicating assessments of who benefits from farm programs. For example, in the early twentieth century, less than 10 per cent of farmland in the Canadian Prairies was rented, while today in the early twenty-first century, between 40 and 45 per cent of the farmland is rented. Because farm programs help support land values, landowners may receive more benefits from farm programs than the actual farm operators do. In addition, whether intended or not, many of the policy benefits go to the larger farmers, not only in the form of direct government payments, but also because the larger farmers are better able to cope with environmental regulations.

19.2 PUBLIC CHOICE AND RENT-SEEKING BEHAVIOUR

The rent-seeking activities that drive agricultural policy can be both productive and non-productive from society's standpoint, where productive rent-seeking leads to improved economic efficiency. Differences in rent-seeking behaviour create variations in support for farmers across the United States, Canada, and the European Union (EU). The difference in the rent-seeking ability of American and Canadian farmers, for example, was best illustrated in 2000, when grain production was at record highs while grain incomes were at record lows in both the United States and Canada. That year, the US government injected over US$20 billion into the farm economy, while the Canadian government put C$1 billion into farm safety nets, most of which went to pre-existing programs such as crop insurance.

The theory of public choice helps explain, for example, the widespread practice of logrolling, as strong alliances form between different commodity groups that support farm programs. For example, in the United States, the American Sugar Alliance is made up of many farm interests and includes corn producers and sugar beet and sugar cane producers along with high fructose corn syrup manufacturers. Very seldom does lobbying take place by one commodity group independently of others.

In addition, new groups have formed that support the broadening of farm policy to include more than traditional program crops. In the United States, the National Association of the State Departments of Agriculture (NASDA) supports the expansion of the scope of farm program legislation. NASDA's policy recommendations include cost of production insurance, countercyclical assistance, and provision for specialty crops.

19.3 LAMENT FOR DYING COMMUNITIES

Future work on agricultural policy should add the *community dimension* to our welfare economics framework. Under the Republican government in the United States in the 1980s, US farmers received unprecedented farm subsidies. At that time, President Ronald Reagan stated that if money could solve the farm problem, it would have been easily solved. Perhaps that president's frustration was linked to the criticism levied against farm programs by many economists: that policy generally has not come to grips with the viability of rural communities. In one such example, the Conservation Reserve Program, policy has contributed to the demise of rural communities. However, even under a different policy framework, rural communities on the Canadian Prairies have suffered declines at the same rate as those in the United States. The EU, under the rubric of multifunctionality, contends that EU policy has added to the viability of rural communities. However, the empirical evidence supporting this claim is lacking thus far.

19.4 THE OPIOID AND COVID-19 EPIDEMICS AND AGRICULTURAL POLICY

The opioid crisis is a major worldwide problem. It is growing and drug-related suicide rates are at an all-time high. The USDA is increasing resources to find solutions through policy intervention. Specifically, it is funding research into determining the location and causes of the epidemic in rural America. The seriousness of this epidemic is regionally specific, where agricultural labour is negatively impacted. Also, the increased concentration in meat packing plants negatively impacts the well-being of the agricultural labour supply. The COVID-19 outbreak has only added to the seriousness of the opioid crisis.

19.5 VERTICAL AND HORIZONTAL MARKETS AND AGRIBUSINESS

Further work on policy assessment is necessary within vertical and horizontal market structures since policy is influenced by special interest groups that includes producers. Often, policy analysis does not take into account the market structure that exists from producers through to the final retailing of the product. The models presented in this text seek to overcome this shortcoming by showing the link between policy and agribusiness that includes farmers, but more research is needed along these lines. As we have emphasized, policy affects not only producers, but also other agribusiness entities, such as marketing firms and processors. Some economists have commented that the biggest beneficiaries from agricultural programs are probably processors and not farmers. This is especially true when farm policy encourages production beyond competitive levels. New models have to be developed that take into account the widespread benefits to all parties involved.

One thing seems clear: markets will continue to become more and more integrated beyond basic production through both the contracting and producer ownership of various marketing channels. The new institutional economics (NIE) provides insights into why increased integration is occurring. The NIE focuses on the transaction costs of doing business. Understanding the dynamics of change in market structure is critical to future policy design.

19.6 TARGETING SUPPORT

Debate continues about whether farm support should be targeted to farmers according to income levels and include caps at lower levels. Currently, a small proportion of US farmers receive the largest percentage of government payouts because they produce the greatest output. As report after report contends that there are too many farmers in agriculture, given the demand for farm products and existing production technology, debate has also arisen around whether added support should be given to those who have to exit farming because of financial difficulties. In Canada, agricultural programs have been set up to help farmers exit the agricultural sector.

It is interesting to speculate what the future holds for agriculture. Currently, it is unclear whether the EU agricultural policy is more targeted than either Canadian farm programs or US agricultural policy. Our approach of farm disaggregation according to farm size and type could help future policy work assess how targeting affects agriculture.

19.7 COSTS AND BENEFITS OF AGRICULTURAL PROGRAMS

In this book we focus on many aspects of agricultural policy, including economic costs and benefits. We emphasize that a given policy can be efficient when transferring income to the farm sector and to agribusiness. But even efficient policies may lead to arguments over the optimal distribution of income. Many complain that subsidies are directed towards wealthy farmers (both alive and deceased) instead of towards smaller farmers. Our book provides a framework for discussing these issues.

The theory of applied welfare economics, which is the basis for our book, provides a powerful approach to empirical applications, especially for cost-benefit analyses of agricultural policies and programs. Regarding Canadian agricultural programs, there is relatively little empirical analysis on the grain and oilseeds sectors compared to supply management. For the European Union and the United States, given the size of their agricultural sectors, more empirical studies are needed to analyse the distributional and efficiency effects of their agricultural programs.

Very few studies quantify the impact of farm programs on the red meat sector. In North America, cattle and pork numbers continue to decline, even though for many years US farm policy provided cheap feed grains for this sector. Some argue that one major reason is that effective rent-seeking for government programs is lacking on the part of livestock producers, but since many livestock groups are free enterprisers, this may be by choice.

For the grains and oilseed sectors in the United States, studies generally find that while there are net costs associated with farm policies, these costs are small. However, particular groups, including processors and input suppliers, receive handsome awards from agricultural programs. The net costs of farm programs appear to be getting smaller, at least in the United States; however, this cannot be said for US cotton policy, where the welfare costs can be significant. Studies that have looked at the impact of the US sugar, dairy, tobacco, and peanut programs conclude that the net costs of farm programs for these sectors can be large. Perhaps this is why the US tobacco and peanut programs were terminated.

Totally decoupled farm programs are very efficient when transferring income from government to producers. Some studies argue that the US programs are decoupled, and therefore the deadweight losses are minimal. Government policies that generate small net costs are possible when aimed at redistributing farm income in an efficient manner. However, many observers have reservations about the claim that US farm programs are decoupled.

19.8 THE PARETO AND COMPENSATION PRINCIPLES

Both the Compensation Principle and the Pareto Principle are fundamental when sorting out the impact of government programs. For example, considerable debate took place in Canada over eliminating the Crow transportation subsidy, where the railroads received government transportation subsidies. Thus, farmers did not pay the full cost of transporting grain. When the Crow was eliminated, not all sectors of society benefited, as full compensation was not paid to grain producers who suffered significant losses. Discussion continues about whether or not governments should buy out production quotas in areas with supply management. In one such example, in early 2000, the US tobacco and peanut programs were dramatically altered as the US government bought out production quotas. Often first-best policies cannot be put in place unless one adheres to the Pareto Principle, where no one loses from a policy change.

19.9 GMOS, BIOFUELS, AND THE ENVIRONMENT

Countries are struggling over the adoption of genetically modified organisms (GMOs). While in certain instances biotechnology has added to the producer's bottom line and has the potential of even greater promise, many consumers are not convinced that biotechnological products (i.e., products made with biotechnology) are safe. This raises the question of consumer labelling and of segregating markets by creating separate pools for GM and non-GM grains.

We have highlighted the different types of concerns over GM food products. With the example of StarLink corn, we showed that the concern is over human health and non-compliance with the regulatory system. The failure of StarLink corn is that the product was introduced into the US human food chain when it was licensed only for livestock feed. In the second example, we showed that Roundup Ready canola has raised no health concerns in the United States and Canada. The canola case is all about property rights – who owns the rights to seeds that are genetically modified? Furthermore, some argue that GMOs are bad for the environment, but this has not been scientifically proven. The conclusion is that there are concerns over GMOs that have to do with issues beyond health.

The growth in biofuels, especially ethanol, has been phenomenal in both Brazil and the United States. Those who argue against the production of biofuels do so on the grounds that ethanol causes higher food prices and is not environmentally friendly. Policy plays a direct role in the costs and benefits of biofuel production. For example, in Brazil, hidden subsidies are partly responsible for the rapid growth of ethanol production from sugar cane. In the United States, ethanol tax credits and tariff protection provide incentives for ethanol production. However, the impact on corn prices has been such that US government farm payments have been reduced.

19.10 INTERNATIONAL TRADE CONCERNS

Trade agreements have constrained domestic agricultural stabilization programs. The World Trade Organization (WTO) does not require the removal of farm programs, but it does place a limit on the amount of money that can be paid to producers if a program is determined to be trade distorting. In Canada, the Crow subsidy was removed because it had a large impact on production, and hence was deemed to be a trade-distorting program. In addition, the Net Income Stabilization Account (NISA) and Agricultural Income Disaster Assistance (AIDA) have been justified on the grounds that they fall within the so-called Green Box (policies that are neither production nor trade distorting) category as put forward by the WTO. The EU and the US argue that their programs also fall within the Green Box category and do not distort trade. However, in this context, the United States has been unsuccessful in arguing that the US cotton policy falls within the WTO guidelines. In addition, partly because of pressure from the WTO, the EU single-farm payment scheme was a move towards policy decoupling.

19.11 INTERFACE BETWEEN AGRICULTURE, FOOD POLICY AND TRADE

The relationships between agriculture, food policy, and trade are critical in analysing and determining policy. Quotas, subsidies, and tariffs can all have positive and negative effects on international trade in particular. Subsidies can outperform tariffs, yielding net benefits to exporting countries, while importing countries see an inverse result. We have examined several examples of these forces in the absence and presence of trade to demonstrate the complexity of those interrelationships. These include the impact of corn ethanol tax credits on corn production, prices, and trade.

19.12 FOOD SAFETY AND LABELLING

Food security has become a global concern, with many countries pursuing initiatives to improve the safety of food supplies. Proposals include creating trace-back systems for all food production from retailer to farmer, and registering all the players (all food processors, transporters, distributors, handlers, etc.) to keep track of everyone in the agricultural marketing system. Identity preservation has moved from being a luxury to a necessity. But problems remain, especially food contamination from products produced around the world.

Food security issues take on increasing importance in international markets. Increased border inspection is necessary, which has made it easier to argue for increasing barriers to international trade. As we have demonstrated, adding transaction costs to deal with food security and food safety generally raises consumer prices, which often has a negative impact on farmers. This increases the support for broad agricultural policy measures to ensure farmers, along with processors and others in the marketing chain, have the means to provide safe food to consumers at reasonable prices. Increased emphasis will be placed on the assessment of risk in the context of policy choices.

Country of origin labelling (COOL), which was introduced into the US farm legislation to protect US consumers from contaminated imported foods, was later eliminated due to a WTO ruling. Even so, US grocery stores continue to sell meat labelled "Product of the United States." COOL acted as a non-tariff trade barrier to the benefit of US farmers even when the cost of segregation and labelling is taken into account. US farm groups, unlike many packers and processors, lobbied intensively for COOL. Little ex ante analysis was conducted on consumer perception of imported food safety under the COOL requirements nor on the effect of COOL on the livestock and poultry sectors.

What does food safety really entail? One of the major problems in the twenty-first century is obesity. It is usually not the food itself, but the type of diet that is unhealthy (e.g., highly processed foods containing high quantities of sugar, salt, fats, and artificial food products). Agricultural policy has contributed to the obesity problem by providing inexpensive food year-round.

19.13 CLIMATE CHANGE AND AGRICULTURE

There is intense debate around climate change and its economic impact. There is disagreement about what the impact of the changing climate might be on agriculture. Most studies find that global average temperature is climbing, creating droughts and wildfires worldwide. The impact on agriculture varies by country and the nature of the commodity grown.

19.14 FOOD PYRAMIDS, DIETARY PROGRAMS, AND OBESITY

We present a historical progression of food pyramids and dietary programs in the United States and Canada. Undernutrition and overnutrition remain problems due to imprecise and ineffective dietary guidelines. We examine the role of obesity and outline the need for future work to create more effective, usable guidelines and resources to help encourage healthy food choices.

19.15 AGRICULTURE AND TECHNOLOGY

Technological developments are not only affecting crop-level shifts but impacting trade as well. For example, CRISPR technology allows genetic modification to eliminate abnormal or infected genes and protect the health of the organism. This technology may help preserve crops that are underperforming, and in the examples of highly imported and exported crops such as chocolate or oranges, this can create a major impact on trade patterns and policies.

19.16 FUTURE POLICY OPTIONS

Agricultural policy will be around for many years to come. Canada, the United States, and the European Union have made major policy changes since 2001. The United States passed a new farm bill in 2018, Canada introduced the Growing Forward Program, and the European Union introduced a single-farm payment scheme. All of these policy changes are aimed at improving resource efficiency and making farm programs less production and trade distorting. Even so, economists argue that further policy reform is needed.

In this book, we discuss agricultural policy in a much broader framework than most other treatises on this topic. As we emphasize, policymakers need to come to grips with such problems as obesity, which can be addressed in part through changes in agricultural policy. Likewise, issues regarding climate change are linked to agricultural policy. Debate also continues on the best use of farmland from a societal perspective. Some argue that more farmland should be diverted to trees, which would have a positive impact on global warming. Professionals must perform cost-benefit analyses on various proposals so that politicians are at least aware of what is at stake. We must remember, however, that politicians do not necessarily adopt policies that have high benefit-to-cost ratios. Rent-seeking takes its toll and can create wide divergence between first-best policies and those that are adopted, which often fall into second-rate and third-rate categories.

Notes

Chapter Four

1 This section is taken largely from A. Schmitz (2000).

Chapter Six

1 Material in this section and the next is based on Johnston and van Kooten (2014) and van Kooten (2014).

Chapter Nine

1 Although the term "European Union" did not emerge until 2007, we will employ it throughout the remainder of this chapter rather than distinguish between EU and EEC according to dates.

Chapter Fourteen

1 Summary for Policymakers states that "human activities are estimated to have caused approximately 1.0°C of global warming above pre-industrial levels, likely ranging from 0.8°C to 1.2°C. Global warming is likely to reach 1.5°C between 2030 and 2052 if it continues to increase at the current rate (high confidence)" (IPCC 2018, 6).
2 The acronym "GCM" initially referred to a general circulation model, but as models became more complex, the more generic term "global climate model" was employed. A climate model can be a simple energy balance model with one or more "boxes" to account for heating of oceans, or a more complicated atmosphere-ocean coupled model to which a terrestrial component may have been added. Climate model outcomes turn out to be extremely sensitive to various parameterizations (Lewis and Curry 2015; Hourdin et al. 2017).
3 Many weather stations located in Canada's Prairie region no longer collect separate data on snowfall, yet this information is key for Canadian farmers making decisions regarding what crops to plant, particularly whether to plant more or fewer drought-resistant crops or varieties.

4   The www.co2science.org website provides an inventory of studies that find positive impacts of higher atmospheric CO_2 levels and greater heat on crop production.

5   GDD =, $\sum_{j=1}^{N} (T_j - 5^\circ C)$, where T_j is the average temperature on day j and N is total days in the growing season.

6   The importance of new crops and crop varieties should not be understated, especially since genetic engineering can potentially increase food production beyond what is currently envisioned (Eisenhut and Weber 2019).

Chapter Fifteen

1   This chapter relies heavily on A. Schmitz and Moss (2005).

2   This is a crucial assumption for measurement because, if the supply function for inputs is upward sloping, changes in upstream markets (e.g., petroleum refining, transportation, machinery production) will also need to be considered. This is avoided by the assumption of infinitely elastic supply functions in agricultural input markets.

3   Supply in the commodity market is a function of the input price. Thus, the increase in the price of fertilizer shifts the supply curve in the commodity market upward from $S(r^*, \dots)$ to $S(r_x, \dots)$.

4   Notice that suppliers of environmental services always earn a producer surplus (quasi-rent) when they receive a payment for environmental services, but this payment is required to cover fixed costs.

5   The concern with this approach is the assumption that, if the political process leads to an increase in the availability of some environmental amenity, the benefit will exceed the expenditure required to achieve it. This is blatantly not true because environmental lobbying could lead to greater provision of environmental amenities than is socially optimal.

6   We thank Richard Gray for this possibility. See also Rude (2000).

References

Abramovitz, M. 1956. *Resource and Output Trends in the United States Since 1870*. National Bureau of Economic Research. https://www.nber.org/books-and-chapters/resource-and-output-trends-united-states-1870

Ackrill, R.W. 2000. *The Common Agricultural Policy*. Sheffield, UK: Sheffield Academic Press.

Adams, D.M., R.J. Alig, J.M. Callaway, B.A. McCarl, and S.M. Winnett. 1996. *The Forest and Agricultural Sector Optimization Model (FASOM): Model Structure and Policy Applications*. Portland, OR: USDA Pacific Northwest Research Station.

Adams, R.M. 1989. Global climate change and agriculture: An economic perspective. *American Journal of Agricultural Economics* 71(5): 1272–9. https://doi.org/10.2307/1243120

Adams, R.M., R.A. Fleming, C.-C. Chang, B.A. McCarl, and C. Rosenzweig. 1995. A reassessment of the economic effects of global climate change on U.S. agriculture. *Climatic Change* 30(2): 147–67. https://doi.org/10.1007/BF01091839

Adams, R.M., B.H. Hurd, and J. Reilly. 1999. *A Review of Impacts to U.S. Agricultural Resources*. Arlington, VA: PEW Center on Global Climate Change.

Adams, R.M., C. Rosenzweig, R.M. Peart, J.T. Richie, B.A. McCarl, J.D. Glyer, R.B. Curry, J.W. Jones, K.J. Boote, and L.H. Allen, Jr. 1990. Global climate change and U.S. agriculture. *Nature* 345(6272): 219–24. https://doi.org/10.1038/345219a0

Agriculture and Agri-Food Canada (AAFC). 2017. *Growing Forward 2: A Federal-Provincial-Territorial Framework Agreement on Agriculture, Agri-Food and Agri-Based Products Policy*.

Agriculture and Agri-Food Canada (AAFC). 2021a. *AgriStability: Fact Sheets*. https://agriculture.canada.ca/en/agricultural-programs-and-services/agristability/resources/agristability-fact-sheets

Agriculture and Agri-Food Canada (AAFC). 2021b. *Business Risk Management Programs*. https://agriculture.canada.ca/en/agricultural-programs-and-services/business-risk-management-programs

Agriculture and Agri-Food Canada (AAFC). 2021c. *Expired Programs and Services*. https://agriculture.canada.ca/en/agricultural-programs-and-services/expired-programs-and-services

Agriculture and Agri-Food Canada (AAFC). 2021d. *Agricultural Programs and Services*. https://agriculture.canada.ca/en/agricultural-programs-and-services

Akerlof, G.A. 1970. The market for "lemons": Quality uncertainty and the market mechanism. *Quarterly Journal of Economics* 84(3): 488–500. https://doi.org/10.2307/1879431

Allen, R., C. Dodge, and A. Schmitz. 1983. Voluntary export restraints as protection policy: The U.S. beef case. *American Journal of Agricultural Economics* 65(2): 291–6. https://doi.org/10.2307/1240876

Alliance for a Green Revolution in Africa (AGRA). 2014. *Africa Agriculture Status Report 2014: Climate Change and Smallholder Agriculture in Sub-Saharan Africa*. Nairobi: Alliance for a Green Revolution in Africa.

Alliance for a Green Revolution in Africa (AGRA). 2017. *Africa Agriculture Status Report 2017: The Business of Smallholder Agriculture in Sub-Saharan Africa*. Nairobi: Alliance for a Green Revolution in Africa.

Alliance for a Green Revolution in Africa (AGRA). 2018. *Africa Agriculture Status Report 2018: Catalyzing Government Capacity to Drive Agricultural Transformation*. Nairobi: Alliance for a Green Revolution in Africa.

Alston, J.M. 1986. An analysis of growth of U.S. farmland prices, 1963–82. *American Journal of Agricultural Economics* 68(1): 1–9. https://doi.org/10.2307/1241644

Alston, J.M., and R.S. Gray. 2013. Wheat research funding in Australia: The rise of public-private-producer partnerships. *EuroChoices* 12(1): 30–5. https://doi.org/10.1111/1746-692X.12017

Alston, J.M., J. Hyde, M.C. Marra, and P.D. Mitchell. 2002. An ex ante analysis of the benefits from the adoption of corn rootworm resistant transgenic corn technology. *AgBioForum* 5(3): 71–84. https://doi.org/10.22004/ag.econ.57828

Alston, J.M., G.W. Norton, and P.G. Pardy. 1995. *Science under Scarcity: Principles and Practice for Agricultural Research Evaluation and Priority Setting*. Ithaca, NY: Cornell University Press.

Alston, J.M., P.G. Pardy, and V.H. Smith, eds. 1999. *Paying for Agricultural Productivity*. Baltimore: Johns Hopkins University Press.

An, R., and R. Sturm. 2012. School and residential neighborhood food environment and diet among California youth. *American Journal of Preventive Medicine* 42(2): 129–35. https://doi.org/10.1016/j.amepre.2011.10.012

Anderson, K. 2000. Agriculture's "multifunctionality" and the WTO. *Australian Journal of Agricultural and Resource Economics* 44(3): 475–94. https://doi.org/10.1111/1467-8489.00121

Anderson, K., and T. Josling. 2007. *The EU's Common Agricultural Policy at Fifty: An International Perspective*. CEPR: Centre for Economic Policy Research Policy Insight No. 13. http://www.cepr.org/pubs/PolicyInsights/PolicyInsight13.pdf

Anderson, K., W. Martin, and D. van der Mensbrugghe. 2006. Market and welfare implications of Doha reform scenarios. In *Agricultural Trade Reform and the Doha Development Agenda*, ed. K. Anderson and W. Martin, 333–400. Washington, DC: World Bank.

Anderson, K., and S. Nelgen. 2013. *Updated National and Global Estimates of Distortions to Agricultural Incentives, 1955 to 2011*. Washington, DC: World Bank.

Anderson, K., G. Rausser, and J. Swinnen. 2013. Political economy of public policies: Insights from distortions to agricultural and food markets. *Journal of Economic Literature* 51(2): 423–77. https://doi.org/10.1257/jel.51.2.423

Andresen, L.C., N. Yuan, R. Seibert, G. Moser, C.I. Kammann, J. Luterbacher, M. Erbs, and C. Müller. 2018. Biomass responses in a temperate European grassland through 17 years of elevated CO_2. *Global Change Biology* 24(9): 3875–85. https://doi.org/10.1111/gcb.13705

Anonymous. 1953. Sugar empire in the Everglades. *Sugar* (September): 36–9.

Antle, J.M. 1996. Efficient food safety regulation in the food manufacturing sector. *American Journal of Agricultural Economics* 78(5): 1242–7. https://doi.org/10.2307/1243500

Arthur, L.M. 1988. The implications of climate change for agriculture in the prairie provinces. *Climate Change Digest* 88:1–13.

Arthur, L.M., and F. Abizadeh. 1988. Potential effects of climate change on agriculture in the prairie region of Canada. *Western Journal of Agricultural Economics* 13(2): 215–24. https://doi.org/10.22004/ag.econ.32107

Arthur, L.M., and G.C. van Kooten. 1992. Climate change impacts on agribusiness sectors of a prairie economy. *Prairie Forum* 17: 97–109. https://inis.iaea.org/search/search.aspx?orig_q=RN:25006892

Arunanondchai, P., C. Fei, A. Fisher, B.A. McCarl, W. Wang, and Y. Yang. 2019. How does climate change affect agriculture? In *Routledge Handbook of Agricultural Economics*, ed. G.L. Cramer, K.P. Paudel, and A. Schmitz, 191–210. London: Routledge.

Asche, F., J.L. Anderson, and T.M. Garlock. 2019. Food from the water – fisheries and aquaculture. In *Routledge Handbook of Agricultural Economics*, ed. G.L. Cramer, K.P. Paudel, and A. Schmitz, 134–58. London: Routledge.

Asci, S., J.L. Seale, G. Onel, and J.J. VanSickle. 2016. U.S. and Mexican tomatoes: Perceptions and implications of the renegotiated suspension agreement. *Journal of Agricultural and Resource Economics* 41(1): 138–60. https://doi.org/ DOI:10.22004/ag.econ.230780

Atwater, W.O. 1894. *Foods, Nutritive Value, and Cost*. Washington, DC: United States Department of Agriculture (USDA).

Atwater, W.O. 1902. *Principles of Nutrition and Nutritive Value of Food*. Washington, DC: Government Printing Office (GPO).

Auestad, N., and V.L. Fulgoni. 2015. What current literature tells us about sustainable diets: Emerging research linking dietary patterns, environmental sustainability, and economics. *Advances in Nutrition* 6(1): 19–36. https://doi.org/10.3945/an.114.005694

Auffhammer, M. 2018. Quantifying economic damages from climate change. *Journal of Economic Perspectives* 32(4): 33–52. https://doi.org/10.1257/jep.32.4.33

Avery, D.T., and A.A. Avery. 2008. Biofuels forcing world to ration food aid. *Feedstuffs* 80(11): 8.

Azzam, A., and S. Dhoubhadel. 2021. COVID-19, beef price spreads, and market power. *Journal of Agricultural and Resource Economics* (forthcoming). https://doi.org/10.22004/ag.econ.313309

Babcock, B.A. 2008. Distributional implications of U.S. ethanol policy. *Review of Agricultural Economics* 30(3): 533–42.

Babcock, B.A., C.A. Carter, and A. Schmitz. 1990. The political economy of U.S. wheat legislation. *Economic Inquiry* 28(2): 335–53. https://doi.org/10.1111/j.1465-7295.1990.tb00820.x

Babcock, B.A., O. Rubin, and H. Feng. 2007. Farm programs, fuel mandates, and agricultural prosperity. *Iowa Ag Review* 13(4): 1–3.

Banse, M. 2003. CAP and EU enlargement. Paper presented at the USDA Agricultural Trade Conference: WTO – Competing Policy Issues and Agendas for Agricultural Trade, September 2003, Washington, DC.

Barichello, R., J. Cranfield, and K. Meilke. 2009. Options for the reform of supply management in Canada with trade liberalization. *Canadian Public Policy/Analyse de politiques* 35(2): 203–17. https://doi.org/10.3138/cpp.35.2.203

Baumol, W.J. and W.E. Oates. 1988. *The Theory of Environmental Policy*. Cambridge: Cambridge University Press.

Becker, G.S. 1983. A theory of competition among pressure groups for political influence. *Quarterly Journal of Economics* 98(3): 371–400. https://doi.org/10.2307/1886017

Benedict, M.R. 1953. *Farm Policies of the United States, 1790–1950: A Study of Their Origins and Development*. New York: Twentieth Century Fund.

Bettarini, I., F.P. Vaccari, and F. Miglietta. 1998. Elevated CO_2 concentrations and stomatal density: Observations from 17 plant species growing in a CO_2 spring in central Italy. *Global Change Biology* 4(1): 17–22. https://doi.org/10.1046/j.1365-2486.1998.00098.x

Blössner, M., and M. De Onis. 2005. *Malnutrition: Quantifying the Health Impact at National and Local Levels*. Geneva: World Health Organization.

Boadway, R.W. 1997. Public economics and the theory of public policy. *Canadian Journal of Economics* 30(4A): 753–72. https://doi.org/10.2307/136268

Boadway, R.W., and N. Bruce. 1984. *Welfare Economics*. Oxford: Blackwell.

Borrell, B., and D. Pearce. 1999. *Sugar: The Taste Test of Trade Liberalisation*. Canberra and Sydney: Center for International Economics.

Brannan, M. 1949. *The Brannan Plan as Presented by Secretary Brannan in 1949, in the U.S. Congress, House Committee on Agriculture, General Farm Program, Hearings, Part 2., April 7, 11, 12, 25, and 26*. Washington, DC: US Congress.

Bredahl, M.E., A. Schmitz, and J.S. Hillman. 1987. Rent seeking in international trade: The great tomato war. *American Journal of Agricultural Economics* 69(1): 1–10. https://doi.org/10.2307/1241300

Bricker, D.J., and J. Ibbitson. 2019. *Empty Planet: The Shock of Global Population Decline*. New York: Crown.

Brinkman, G., N. Brown, L. Martin, and R. Osbourne. 1985. *An Assessment of the Benefits and Costs of Fresh Apple and Table Potato Grade Inspection*. Ottawa: Agriculture Canada.

Brunet-Jailly, E., A. Hurrelmann and A. Verdun, eds. 2018. *European Union Governance and Policy Making: A Canadian Perspective*. Toronto: University of Toronto Press.

Buchanan, J.M., and G. Tullock. 1974. *The Calculus of Consent: Logical Foundations of Constitutional Democracy*. Ann Arbor: University of Michigan Press.

Buckwell, A. 2017. Twenty years after the Carpe (Buckwell) report: Impacts and remaining challenges? *Agriregionieuropa* 13(50): 1–7.

Bueckert, R.A. 2013. Photosynthetic carbon fixation and crops. *Prairie Soils and Crops* 6: 64–77.

Busby, C., and D. Schwanen. 2013. *Putting the Market Back in Dairy Marketing*. Toronto: C.D. Howe Institute.

Buzby, J.C., H.F. Wells, and G. Vocke. 2006. *Possible Implications for U.S. Agriculture from Adoption of Select Dietary Guidelines*. Washington, DC: United States Department of Agriculture/Economic Research Service (USDA/ERS).

Byrne, D. 2004. The regulation of food safety and the use of traceability/tracing in the EU and USA: Convergence or divergence? *Seedquest*, 19 March 2004. https://www.seedquest.com/News/releases/2004/march/8114.htm

Cambell, D.R., P. Comtois, J.C. Gilson, D.L. McFarlane, and D.H. Thain. 1969. *Canadian Agriculture in the Seventies*. Report of the Federal Task Force on Agriculture. Cat. no. A21-15. Ottawa: Queen's Printer.

Cardwell, R., C. Lawley, and D. Xiang. 2015. Milked and feathered: The regressive welfare effects of Canada's supply management regime. *Canadian Public Policy/Analyse de politiques* 41(1): 1–14. https://doi.org/10.3138/cpp.2013-062

Cardwell, R., C. Lawley, and D. Xiang. 2018. Milked and feathered: The regressive welfare effects of Canada's supply management regime: Reply. *Canadian Public Policy/ Analyse de politiques* 44(3): 278–88. https://doi.org/10.3138/cpp.2018-025

Carlson, A., and E. Frazão. 2014. Food costs, diet quality, and energy balance in the United States. *Physiology and Behavior* 134(July): 20–31. https://doi.org/10.1016/j.physbeh.2014.03.001

Carlton, D.W., and J.M. Perloff. 2000. *Modern Industrial Organization*, 3rd ed. Reading, MA: Addison-Wesley Longman.

Carter, C.A., and G.P. Gruère. 2006. International approval and labeling regulations of genetically modified food in major trading countries. In *Regulating Agricultural Biotechnology: Economics and Policy*, ed. R.E. Just, J.M. Alston, and D. Zilberman, 459–80. Boston: Springer.

Carter, C.A., and R.M.A. Loyns. 1996. *The Economics of Single Desk Selling of Western Canadian Grain*. Report to Alberta Agriculture. Edmonton: Government of Alberta.

Carter, C.A., R.M.A. Loyns, and Z.F. Ahmadi-Esfahani. 1986. Varietal licensing standards and Canadian wheat exports. *Canadian Journal of Agricultural Economics* 34(3): 361–77. https://doi.org/10.1111/j.1744-7976.1986.tb02218.x

Carter, C.A., and A. Schmitz. 1979. Import tariffs and price formation in the world wheat market. *American Journal of Agricultural Economics* 61(3): 517–22. https://doi.org/10.2307/1239439

Carter, C.A., and A. Smith. 2007. Estimating the market effect of a food scare: The case of genetically modified StarLink corn. *Review of Economics and Statistics* 89(3): 522–33. https://doi.org/10.1162/rest.89.3.522

Casey, F., A. Schmitz, S. Swinton, and D. Zilberman, eds. 1999. *Flexible Incentives for the Adoption of Environmental Technologies in Agriculture*. Boston: Kluwer.

Caswell, J.A., and D.I. Padberg. 1992. Toward a more comprehensive theory of food labels. *American Journal of Agricultural Economics* 74(2): 460–8. https://doi.org/10.2307/1242500

Challinor, A.J., J. Watson, D.B. Lobell, S.M. Howden, D.R. Smith, and N. Chhetri. 2014. A meta-analysis of crop yield under climate change and adaptation. *Nature Climate Change* 4: 287–91. https://doi.org/10.1038/nclimate2153

Chambers, R.G., and R. Lopez. 1993. Public investment and real-price supports. *Journal of Public Economics* 52(1): 73–82. https://doi.org/10.1016/0047-2727(93)90105-3

Chambers, R.G. and D.C. Voica. 2017. "Decoupled" farm program payments are really decoupled: The theory. *American Journal of Agricultural Economics* 99(3): 773–82. https://doi.org/10.1093/ajae/aaw044

Chatzopoulos, T., and C. Lippert. 2015. Adaptation and climate change impacts: A structural Ricardian analysis of farm types in Germany. *Journal of Agricultural Economics* 66(2): 537–54. https://doi.org/10.1111/1477-9552.12098

Chegini, C., and A. Schmitz. 2021. GMOs: The past and the future. *Journal of Biotechnology and Bioresearch* 2(5): 000547.

Chen, J., B.A. McCarl, and A. Thayer. 2017. Climate change and food security: Threats and adaptation. In *World Agricultural Resources and Food Security: International Food Security*, ed. A. Schmitz, P.L. Kennedy, and T.G. Schmitz, 70–84. Bingley, UK: Emerald.

Clark, J.S., K.K. Klein, and S.J. Thompson. 1993. Are subsidies capitalized into land values? Some time series evidence from Saskatchewan. *Canadian Journal of Agricultural Economics* 41(2): 155–68. https://doi.org/10.1111/j.1744-7976.1993.tb03740.x

Clark, S.J., L.O. Dittrich, S.M. Law, D. Stará, and M. Barták. 2019. Food prices, taxes, and obesity in Canada and its implications for food taxation. *Economics and Management* 22(1): 22–34. https://doi.org/10.15240/tul/001/2019-1-002

Clayton, A., and A.C.W. Ogg. 1999. Evolution of EPA programs and policies that impact agriculture. In *Flexible Incentives for the Adoption of Environmental Technologies in Agriculture*, ed. F. Casey, A. Schmitz, S. Swinton, and D. Zilberman, 27–41. Norwell: Kluwer.

Clendenin, J.C. 1942. Federal crop insurance in operation. *Wheat Studies* 18(6): 229–90.

Cline, W.R. 2007. *Global Warming and Agriculture: Impact Estimates by Country*. Washington, DC: Center for Global Development and Peterson Institute for International Economics.

Clouser, R.L., R. Muraro, L. Racevskis, C. Moss, and A. Morris. 2009. *2008 Florida Land Value Survey: Farmland Prices Down*. EDIS FE798. Gainesville: University of Florida.

CME Group. 2021. *Lean Hog Futures and Options*. https://www.cmegroup.com/markets/agriculture/livestock/lean-hogs.quotes.html#

Coase, R.H. 1937. The theory of the firm. *Economica* 4(16): 386–405. https://doi.org/10.1111/j.1468-0335.1937.tb00002.x

Coble, K.H., T.O. Knight, R.D. Pope, and J.R. Williams. 1997. An expected-indemnity approach to the measurement of moral hazard in crop insurance. *American Journal of Agricultural Economics* 79(1): 216–26. https://doi.org/10.2307/1243955

Cochrane, N., *and* N.R. Seeley. 2004. EU Enlargement: Implications for New Member Countries, the United States, and World Trade. Report WRS04-05-01. Washington, DC: United States Department of Agriculture/Economic Research Service (USDA/ERS).

Cochrane, W.W. 1958. *Farm Prices, Myth, and Reality*. Minneapolis: University of Minnesota Press.

Cochrane, W.W. 1959. Some further reflections on supply control. *Journal of Political Economy* 67(3): 697–717.

Cochrane, W.W. 2000. A food and agricultural policy for the 21st century. Institute for Agriculture & Trade Policy. https://www.iatp.org/sites/default/files/Food_and_Agricultural_Policy_for_the_21st_Cent.htm

Cochrane, W.W., and C.F. Runge. 1992. *Reforming Farm Policy: Toward a National Agenda*. Ames: Iowa State University Press.

Cochrane, W.W., and M.E. Ryan. 1976. *American Farm Policy, 1948–1973*. Minneapolis: University of Minnesota Press.

Commission on Twenty-First Century Production Agriculture. 2001. *The Role of Government in the Support of Production Agriculture*. Report to President George W. Bush. Washington, DC: Government Printing Office (GPO).

Conniff, R. 1997. Can Britain save its hedgerows? *International Wildlife Magazine*, July/August 1997.

Conte, S.D. 1965. *Elementary Numerical Analysis: An Algorithmic Approach*. New York: McGraw Hill.

Cornes, R., and T. Sandler. 1996. *The Theory of Externalities, Public Goods, and Club Goods*, 2nd ed. Cambridge: Cambridge University Press.

Crutzen, P.J., A.R. Mosier, K.A. Smith, and W. Winiwarter. 2008. N_2O release from agro-biofuel production negates global warming reduction by replacing fossil fuels. *Atmospheric Chemistry and Physics* 8(2): 389–95. https://doi.org/10.5194/acp-8-389-2008

Currie, J.M., J.A. Murphy, and A. Schmitz. 1971. The concept of economic surplus and its use in economic analysis. *Economic Journal* 81(324): 741–99. https://doi.org/10.2307/2230317

Dai, A. 2013. Increasing drought under global warming in observations and models. *Nature Climate Change* 3: 52–8. https://doi.org/10.1038/nclimate1633

Darwin, R., M.E. Tsigas, J. Lewandrowski, and A. Raneses, 1995. *World Agriculture and Climate Change: Economic Adaptations*. Washington, DC: United States Department of Agriculture/Economic Research Service (USDA/ERS).

DataSet Publishing Language (DSPL). n.d. *Countries.csv*. https://developers.google.com/public-data/docs/canonical/countries_csv

Daugbjerg, C., and A. Swinbank. 2007. The politics of CAP reform: Trade negotiations, institutional settings, and blame avoidance. *Journal of Common Market Studies* 45(1): 1–22. https://doi.org/10.1111/j.1468-5965.2007.00700.x

Davis, C., and E. Saltos. 1999. Dietary recommendations and how they have changed over time. In *American Eating Habits: Changes and Consequences*, ed. E. Frazão, 33–50. Washington, DC: United States Department of Agriculture/Economic Research Service (USDA/ERS).

Davis, J.H., and R.A. Goldberg. 1957. *A Concept of Agribusiness.* Boston: Graduate School of Business Administration, Harvard University.

Dayaratna, K., R. McKitrick, and D. Kreutzer, 2017. Empirically constrained climate sensitivity and the social cost of carbon. *Climate Change Economics* 8(2): 1750006. https://doi.org/10.1142/S2010007817500063

DeBoer-Lowenberg, J., and M. Boehlje. 1986. The impact of farmland price changes on farm size and financial structure. *American Journal of Agricultural Economics* 68(4): 838–48. https://doi.org/10.2307/1242130

De Fontnouvelle, P., and S.H. Lence. 2002. Transaction costs and the present value "puzzle" of farmland prices. *Southern Economic Journal* 68(3): 549–65. https://doi.org/10.2307/1061717

De Janvry, A. 1973. A socioeconomic model of induced innovations for Argentine agricultural development. *Quarterly Journal of Economics* 87(3): 410–35. https://doi.org/10.2307/1882013

De Laat, A.T.J., and A.N. Maurellis. 2004. Industrial CO_2 emissions as a proxy for anthropogenic influence on lower tropospheric temperature trends. *Geophysical Research Letters* 31(5): L05204. https://doi.org/10.1029/2003GL019024

De Laat, A.T.J., and A.N. Maurellis. 2006. Evidence for influence of anthropogenic surface processes on lower tropospheric and surface temperature trends. *International Journal of Climatology* 26(7): 897–913. https://doi.org/10.1002/joc.1292

Devadoss, S. and J. Luckstead. 2019. A synopsis of trade theories and their applications. In *The Routledge Handbook of Agricultural Economics*, ed. G.L. Cramer, K.P. Paudel, and A. Schmitz, 301–26. London: Routledge.

Dietary Guidelines Advisory Committee (DGAC). 2015. *Scientific Report of the 2015 Dietary Guidelines Advisory Committee.* Washington, DC: United States Department of Agriculture/ United States Department of Health and Human Services (USDA/USDHHS).

Diewert, W.E. 1971. An application of the Shephard duality theorem: A generalized Leontief production function. *Journal of Political Economy* 79(3): 481–507. https://doi.org/10.1086/259764

Ding, D., J.F. Sallis, G.J. Norma, B.E. Saelens, S.K. Harris, J. Kerr, D. Rosenberg, N. Durant, and K. Glanz. 2012. Community food environment, home food environment, and fruit and vegetable intake of children and adolescents. *Journal of Nutrition Education and Behavior* 44(6): 634–8. https://doi.org/10.1016/j.jneb.2010.07.003

Dohlman, E., and J. Livezey. 2005. *Peanut Backgrounder.* Electronic Outlook Report CS-05i-01. Washington, DC: United States Department of Agriculture/Economic Research Service (USDA/ERS).

Dorfman, R., P.A. Samuelson, and R.M. Solow. 1958. *Linear Programming and Economic Analysis.* New York: McGraw-Hill.

Downs, A. 1957. *An Economic Analysis of Democracy.* New York: Harper and Row.

Doyon, M., S. Bergeron, and L.D. Tamini. 2018. Milked and feathered: The regressive welfare effects of Canada's supply management regime: A comment. *Canadian Public Policy/Analyse de politiques* 44(3): 272–7. https://doi.org/10.3138/cpp.2017-044

Du, X., and D.J. Hayes. 2008. *The Impact of Ethanol Production on U.S. and Regional Gasoline Prices and Regional Gasoline Prices and on the Profitability of the U.S. Oil Refinery Industry.* Working Paper 08-WP 467. Ames, IA: CARD.

Dupuit, J. 1844. On the measurement of the utility of public works. *Annales des Ponts et Chausees.* 2nd series. London: Macmillan.

Edmé, S.J., J.D. Miller, B. Glaz, P.Y.P. Tai, and J.C. Comstock. 2005. Genetic contribution to yield gains in the Florida sugarcane industry across 33 years. *Crop Science* 45(1): 92–7. https://doi.org/10.2135/cropsci2005.0092

Edwards, G.W., and J.W. Freebairn. 1984. The gains from research into tradable commodities. *American Journal of Agricultural Economics* 66(1): 41–9. https://doi.org/10.2307/1240614

Eisenhut, M., and A.P.M. Weber. 2019. Improving crop yield. *Science* 363(6422): 32–3. https://doi.org/10.1126/science.aav8979

Elam, T. 2007. Grain-based ethanol: Ten inconvenient facts. *Feedstuffs* 79(33): 8.

Elam, T. 2008. Does ethanol affect gas prices? *Feedstuffs* 80(48): 16.

Elobeid, A., S. Tokgoz, D. Hayes, B. Babcock, and C. Hart. 2006. *The Long-Run Impact of Corn-Based Ethanol on the Grain, Oilseed, and Livestock Sectors: A Preliminary Assessment.* CARD Briefing Paper 06-BP 49. Ames, IA: CARD.

European Commission. 2014. *Implementation of the Provisions Concerning Producer Organisations, Operational Funds, and Operational Programmes in the Fruit and Vegetables Sector since the 2007 Reform.* http://eur-lex.europa.eu/legal-content/en/ALL/?uri=CELEX:52014DC0112

European Commission. 2017. *The Future of Food and Farming.* http://www.arc2020.eu/cap-communication-leak-full/

European Commission. 2021. *Annual EU Budget.* https://ec.europa.eu/info/strategy/eu-budget/annual-eu-budget/all-annual-budgets_en

European Union. 2017. *Agricultural Statistics.* https://ec.europa.eu/agriculture/statistics_en

Evenson, R., P.E. Waggoner, and V.W. Ruttan. 1979. Economic benefits from research: An example from agriculture. *Science* 205(4411): 1101–7. https://doi.org/10.1126/science.205.4411.1101

Falck-Zepeda, J.B., G. Traxler, and R.G. Nelson. 2000. Surplus distribution from the introduction of a biotechnology innovation. *American Journal of Agricultural Economics* 82(2): 360–9. https://doi.org/10.1111/0002-9092.00031

Farm Credit Canada (FCC). 2020. *Farmland Values.* https://www.fcc-fac.ca/fcc/resources/2020-historic-farmland-values-report-e.pdf

Fatka, J. 2007. Biofuels could spell water issues. *Feedstuffs* 79(43): 1, 5.

Fatka, J. 2008. *Pioneer* opens research centers. *Feedstuffs* 80(35): 3.

Featherstone, A., and C. Moss. 2003. Capital markets, land values, and boom-bust cycles. In *Government Policy and Farmland Markets: The Maintenance of Farmer Wealth*, ed. C. Moss and A. Schmitz, 159–78. Ames: Iowa State University Press.

Feder, G., R.E. Just, and A. Schmitz. 1980. Futures markets and the theory of the firm under price uncertainty. *Quarterly Journal of Economics* 94(2): 317–28. https://doi.org/10.2307/1884543

Feldstein, M. 1980. Inflation, portfolio choices, and the prices of land and corporate stock. *American Journal of Agricultural Economics* 62(5): 910–16. https://doi.org/10.2307/1240283

Ference & Company Consulting Ltd. 2016. *Business Risk Management Survey.* Technical Report. Vancouver: Ference & Company.

Fernández, J., M.D. Frías, W.D. Cabos, A.S. Cofiño, M. Domínguez, L. Fita, M.A. Gaertner, M. García-Díez, J.M. Gutiérrez, P. Jiménez-Guerrero, G. Liguori, J.P. Montávez, R. Romera, and E. Sánchez. 2019. Consistency of climate change projections from multiple global and regional model intercomparison projects. *Climate Dynamics* 52(1/2): 1139–56. https://doi.org/10.1007/s00382-018-4181-8

Fischer, E.M., J. Sedláček, E. Hawkins, and R. Knutti. 2014. Models agree on forced response pattern of precipitation and temperature extremes. *Geophysical Research Letters* 41(23): 8554–62. https://doi.org/10.1002/2014GL062018

Food and Agriculture Organization of the United Nations (FAO). 1999. *Codex Alimentarius*. Rome: FAO.

Food and Agriculture Organization of the United Nations (FAO). 2009. *How to Feed the World in 2050*. Rome: FAO.

Food and Agriculture Organization of the United Nations (FAO). 2017a. *Climate-Smart Agriculture Sourcebook. Summary*, 2nd ed. Rome: FAO.

Food and Agricultural Organization of the United Nations (FAO). 2017b. *FAOSTAT*. http://www.fao.org/faostat/en/#data

Food and Agriculture Organization of the United Nations (FAO). 2018. *The State of Agricultural Commodity Markets. Agricultural Trade, Climate Change and Food Security*. Rome: FAO.

Food and Agriculture Organization of the United Nations (FAO). 2019a. *FAOSTAT Database*. Rome: FAO.

Food and Agriculture Organization of the United Nations (FAO). 2019b. *International Plant Protection Convention*. Rome: FAO.

Food Marketing Institute (FMI). 1997. *The Greening of Consumers: A Food Retailer's Guide*. Washington, DC: FMI.

Fowke, V.C. 1957. *The National Policy and the Wheat Economy*. Toronto: University of Toronto Press.

Freeman, F., and I. Roberts. 1999. Multifunctionality: A pretext for protection. *ABARE Current Issues: Australian Bureau of Agricultural and Resource Economics* 99(3): 1–6.

Fulgoni, V.L., D.R. Keast, R.L. Bailey, and J. Dwyer. 2011. Foods, fortificants, and supplements: Where do Americans get their nutrients? *The Journal of Nutrition* 141(10): 1847–54. https://doi.org/10.3945/jn.111.142257

Fulton, M.E., K.A. Rosaasen and A. Schmitz. 1989. *Canadian Agricultural Policy and Prairie Agriculture*. Ottawa: Economic Council of Canada.

Fulton, M.E., A. Schmitz, and R.S. Gray. 2000. *Niskasan-Style Canadian Wheat Board*. Working Paper. Saskatoon: University of Saskatchewan.

Gardner, B.L. 1981. *The Governing of Agriculture*. Lawrence: The Regents Press of Kansas.

Gardner, B.L. 1983. Efficient redistribution through commodity markets. *American Journal of Agricultural Economics* 65(2): 225–34. https://doi.org/10.2307/1240868

Gardner, B.L. 1987. Causes of U.S. farm commodity programs. *Journal of Political Economy* 95(2): 290–310.

Gardner, B.L. 1994. Crop insurance in U.S. farm policy. In *Economics of Agricultural Crop Insurance: Theory and Evidence*, ed. D.L. Hueth and W.H. Furtan, 18–44. Boston: Kluwer.

Gardner, B.L. 1996. The political economy of the export enhancement program for wheat. In *The Political Economy of Trade Protection*, ed. A.O. Krueger, 61–70. Chicago: University of Chicago Press.

Gardner, B.L. 2002. *North American Agricultural Policies and Effects on Western Hemisphere Markets since 1995, with a Focus on Grains and Oilseeds*. Working Paper WP-02-12. College Park: University of Maryland.

Gardner, B.L. 2007. Fuel ethanol subsidies and farm price support. *Journal of Agricultural and Food Industrial Organization* 5(2): Article 4. https://doi.org/10.2202/1542-0485.1188

Gardner, B.L., and D.A. Sumner. 2007. *U.S. Agricultural Policy Reform in 2007 and Beyond*. https://www.aei.org/articles/u-s-agricultural-policy-reform-in-2007-and-beyond/

Gifford, R.M. 2004. The CO_2 fertilising effect – does it occur in the real world? *New Phytologist* 163(2): 221–5. https://doi.org/10.1111/j.1469-8137.2004.01133.x

Gilbert, J., and R. Akor. 1988. Increasing structural divergence in U.S. dairying: California and Wisconsin. *Rural Sociology* 53: 56–72.

Global Panel on Agriculture and Food Systems for Nutrition. 2017. *Policy Actions to Support Enhanced Consumer Behaviour for High-Quality Diets.* London: Global Panel on Agriculture and Food Systems for Nutrition.

Goklany, I.M. 2015. *Carbon Dioxide. The Good News.* London: Global Warming Policy Foundation.

Government of Canada. 2021. Canadian Agricultural Partnership. Ottawa: Government of Canada.

Grant, W. 1997. *The Common Agricultural Policy.* New York: Macmillan.

Gray, R., and S. Malla. 2001. The evaluation of the economic and external health benefits from canola research. In *Agricultural Science Policy*, ed. J.M. Alston, P.G. Pardey, and M.J. Taylor, 211–37. Baltimore: Johns Hopkins University Press.

Gray, R, C.B. Moss, and A. Schmitz. 2004. Genetically modified organisms: Rights to use commodity names and the lemons problem. *Journal of Agricultural and Food Industrial Organization* 2(2): Article 7. https://doi.org/10.2202/1542-0485.1057

Greenville, J. 2017. *Domestic Support to Agriculture and Trade: Implications for Multilateral Reform.* Geneva: International Centre for Trade and Sustainable Development (ICTSD).

Gregory, R., and D. von Winterfeldt 1996. The effects of electromagnetic fields from transmission lines on public fears and property values. *Journal of Environmental Management* 48(3): 201–14. https://doi.org/10.1006/jema.1996.0073

Greider, W. 2000. Antitrust issues in the new food system. Paper presented at Policy Issues in the Changing Structure of the Food System, American Agricultural Economics Association (AAEA) Preconference Workshop, June 2000, Quebec City, QC.

Griliches, Z. 1957. Hybrid corn: An exploration in the economics of technological change. *Econometrica* 25(4): 501–22. https://doi.org/10.2307/1905380

Griliches, Z. 1958. Research costs and social returns: Hybrid corn and related innovations. *Journal of Political Economy* 66(5): 419–31. https://doi.org/10.1086/258077

Griliches, Z. 1960. Hybrid corn and the economics of innovation. *Science* 132(3422): 275–80. https://doi.org/10.1126/science.132.3422.275

Grosser, J., and M. Dutt. 2017. Genetic engineering "fastest method" to save Florida citrus industry from greening disease. *Citrus Industry*, 7 November 2017. https://geneticliteracyproject.org/2017/11/07/genetic-engineering-fastest-method-save-floridas-citrus-industry-greening-disease/

Guan, Z., T. Biswas, and F. Wu. 2017. *The US Tomato Industry: An Overview of Production and Trade.* FE1027. Gainesville, FL: University of Florida.

Guenther, P.M., W. Juan, M. Lino, H.A. Hiza, T.V. Fungwe, and R. Lucas, R. 2009. Diet quality of low-income and higher-income Americans in 2003–2004 as measured by the Healthy Eating Index–2005. *The FASEB Journal* 23:540–5.

Gunasekera, H.D.B.H., G.R. Rodriguez, and N.P. Andrews. 1992. World market implications of taxing fertilizer use in EC agriculture. *Agriculture and Resources Quarterly* 4(3): 389–96.

Hallman, W.K., W.C. Hebden, C.L. Cuite, H.L. Aquino, and J.T. Lang. 2004. *Americans and GM Food: Knowledge, Opinion, and Interest in 2004.* RR-1104-007. New Brunswick, NJ: Rutgers University.

Harberger, A. 1971. Three basic postulates for applied welfare economics: An interpretative essay. *Journal of Economics Literature* 9(3): 785–97.

Harl, N.E. 1990. *The Farm Debt Crisis of the 1980s.* Ames: Iowa State University Press.

Harvard T.H. Chan School of Public Health. 1995. *Healthy Eating Pyramid.* Cambridge: Harvard Medical School. http://www.hsph.harvard.edu/nutritionsource

Health Canada. 2019a. *Canada's Dietary Guidelines.* https://food-guide.canada.ca/en/guidelines/

Health Canada. 2019b. *Canada's Dietary Guidelines for Health Professionals and Policy Makers*. Ottawa: Health Canada.

Health Canada. 2019c. *History of Canada's Food Guides from 1942 to 2007*. Ottawa: Health Canada.

Health Canada. 2019d. *Revision of Canada's Food Guide*. Ottawa: Health Canada.

Hertel, T., ed. 1997. *Global Trade Analysis: Modeling and Applications*. Cambridge: Cambridge University Press.

Hicks, J.R. 1939. The foundation of welfare economics. *Economics Journal* 49(196): 696–712. https://doi.org/10.2307/2225023

Hochman, G., S.E. Sexton, and D.D. Zilberman. 2008. The economics of biofuel policy and biotechnology. *Journal of Agricultural and Food Industrial Organization* 6(2): Article 8. https://doi .org/10.2202/1542-0485.1237

Hoppe, R.A., R. Green, D. Banker, J. Kalbacher, and S. Bently. 1996. *Structural and Financial Characteristics of US Farms, 1993: 18th Annual Farm Report to Congress*. AIB 728. Washington, DC: United States Department of Agriculture/Economic Research Service (USDA/ERS).

Hou, R., X. Xu, and Z. Ouyang, 2018. Effect of experimental warming on nitrogen uptake by winter wheat under conventional tillage versus no-till systems. *Soil and Tillage Research* 180:116–25. https://doi.org/10.1016/j.still.2018.03.006

Houghton, D. 2018. The CRISPR revolution. *The Furrow* (September/October):10–13.

Hourdin, F., T. Mauritsen, A. Gettelman, J. Golaz, V. Balaji, Q. Duan, D. Folini, D. Ji, D. Klocke, Y. Qian, F. Rauser, C. Rio, L. Tomassini, M. Watanabe, and D. Williamson. 2017. The art and science of climate model tuning. *Bulletin of the American Meteorological Society* 98(3): 589–602. https://doi .org/10.1175/BAMS-D-15-00135.1

Hudson, D., and T. Jones. 2001. Willingness to plant identity preserved crops: The case of Mississippi soybeans. *Journal of Agricultural and Applied Economics* 33(3): 475–85. https://doi.org/10.1017/ S1074070800020940

Hunt, C.L. 1916. *Food for Young Children*. Washington, DC: United States Department of Agriculture (USDA).

Hunt, C.L. 1923. *Good Proportions in the Diet*. Washington, DC: United States Department of Agriculture (USDA).

Hunt, C.L., and H.W. Atwater. 1917. *How to Select Foods: What the Body Needs*. Washington, DC: United States Department of Agriculture (USDA).

Hutt, P.B., and P.B. Hutt, II. 1984. A history of government regulation of adulteration and misbranding of food. *Food, Drug, and Cosmetic Law Journal* 39:2–73.

Idso, C.D. 2001. Earth's rising atmospheric CO_2 concentration: Impacts on the biosphere. *Energy and Environment* 12(4): 287–310. https://doi.org/10.1260/0958305011500797

Idso, C.D., S.B. Idso, R.M. Carter, and F. Singer. 2014. *Climate Change Reconsidered II: Biological Impacts*. Chicago: Heartland.

Ingersoll, B. 2000. Glut of sugar, corn, soybeans: This fall to fuel farm-price woes, debate on aid. *Wall Street Journal*, 14 August 2000, B6.

Innis, H.A. 1956. *Essays in Canadian Economic History*. Toronto: University of Toronto Press.

Intergovernmental Panel on Climate Change (IPCC). 2013. *Climate Change 2013: The Physical Science Basis*. Cambridge: Cambridge University Press.

Intergovernmental Panel on Climate Change (IPCC). 2014. *Climate Change 2014: Impacts, Adaptation, and Vulnerability. Part A: Global and Sectoral Aspects*. Cambridge: Cambridge University Press.

Intergovernmental Panel on Climate Change (IPCC). 2018. *Global Warming of 1.5°C. Summary for Policymakers*. Geneva: IPCC.

International Service for the Acquisition of Agri-Biotech Application (ISAAA). 2006. *ISAAA Brief 35-2006: Executive Summary*. Ithaca, NY: ISAAA.

Isaac, G., and P.W.B. Phillips. 1999. Market access and market acceptance for agricultural biotechnology products. Paper presented at the ICABR Conference: The Shape of the Coming Agricultural Biotechnology Transformation – Strategic Investment and Policy Approaches from an Economic Perspective, June 1999, Tor Vergata, Italy.

Jeffrey, S.R., D.E. Trautman, and J.R. Unterschultz. 2017. Canadian agricultural business risk management programs: Implications for farm wealth and environmental stewardship. *Canadian Journal of Agricultural Economics* 65(4): 543–65. https://doi.org/10.1111/cjag.12145

Johns Hopkins Center for a Livable Future. 2015. *Public Support for Food Sustainability*. Baltimore: Johns Hopkins University.

Johnson, D.G. 1973. *World Agriculture in Disarray*. London: Macmillan.

Johnson, G.L. 1958. Supply functions – some facts and notions. In *Agricultural Adjustment Problems in a Growing Economy*, ed. G.L. Johnson, 5–20. Ames: Iowa State University Press.

Johnson, M.A., and E.C. Pascur. 1982. An opportunity cost view of fixed asset theory and the overproduction trap. *American Journal of Agricultural Economics* 63(1): 1–7. https://doi.org/10.2307/1239806

Johnson, P.R. 1965. The social cost of the tobacco program. *Journal of Farm Economics* 47(2): 242–55.

Johnson, T. 2000. Future prospects for rural communities. Paper presented at the AAEA Policy Issues in the Changing Structure of the Food System Conference, July 2000, Tampa, FL.

Johnston, C.M.T., and G.C. van Kooten, 2014. *Modelling Bi-lateral Forest Product Trade Flows: Experiencing Vertical and Horizontal Chain Optimization*. Working Paper 04. Victoria: University of Victoria.

Johnston, C.M.T., and G.C. van Kooten. 2015. Back to the past: Burning wood to save the globe. *Ecological Economics* 120: 185–93. https://doi.org/10.1016/j.ecolecon.2015.10.008

Johnston, C.M.T., and G.C. van Kooten. 2016. Global trade impacts of increasing Europe's bioenergy demand. *Journal of Forest Economics* 23(1): 27–44. https://doi.org/10.1016/j.jfe.2015.11.001

Jongeneel, R., A. Burrell, and A. Kavallari. 2011. *Evaluation of CAP Measures Applied to the Dairy Sector. Final Deliverable*. Wageningen: Wageningen University.

Jongeneel, R., and A. Tonini. 2009. The impact of quota rent and supply elasticity estimates for EU dairy policy evaluation: A comparative analysis. *Agrarwirtschaft* 58(5/6): 269–78. https://doi.org/10.22004/ag.econ.134880

Jongeneel, R., M. van Asseldonk, G.C. van Kooten, and J. Cordier. 2019. Agricultural risk management in the European Union: A proposal to facilitate precautionary savings. *EuroChoices* 18(2): 40–6. https://doi.org/10.1111/1746-692X.12230

Jongeneel, R., S. van Berkum, and H. Vrolijk. 2016. Brexit: Breaking away – would it pay? *EuroChoices* 15(2): 26–33. https://doi.org/10.1111/1746-692X.12130

Josling, T. 2008. External influences on CAP reforms: An historical perspective. In *The Perfect Storm: The Political Economy of the Fischler Reforms of the Common Agricultural Policy*, ed. J. Swinnen, 57–75. Brussels: Centre for European Policy Studies (CEPS).

Just, D.R., and G. Gabrielyan. 2018. Influencing the food choices of SNAP consumers: Lessons from economics, psychology, and marketing. *Food Policy* 79: 309–17. https://doi.org/10.1016/j.foodpol.2018.03.003

Just, R.E., L. Calvin, and J. Quiggin. 1999. Adverse selection in crop insurance: Actuarial and asymmetric information incentives. *American Journal of Agricultural Economics* 81(4): 834–49. https://doi.org/10.2307/1244328

Just, R.E., and D.L. Hueth. 1979. Welfare measures in a multimarket framework. *American Economic Review* 69(5): 947–54.

Just, R.E., D.L. Hueth, and A. Schmitz. 1982. *Applied Welfare Economics and Public Policy*. Upper Saddle River, NJ: Prentice-Hall.

Just, R.E., D.L. Hueth, and A. Schmitz. 2004. *The Welfare Economics of Public Policy: A Practical Approach to Project and Policy Evaluation*. Cheltenham, UK: Elgar.

Just, R.E., D.L. Hueth, and A. Schmitz. 2008. *Applied Welfare Economics*. Cheltenham, UK: Elgar.

Just, R.E., and J.A. Miranowski. 1993. Understanding farmland price changes. *American Journal of Agricultural Economics* 75(1): 156–68. https://doi.org/10.2307/1242964

Kaiser, H.M, S.J. Riha, D.S. Wilks, D.G. Rossiter, and R. Sampath. 1993a. A farm-level analysis of economic and agronomic impacts of gradual climate warming. *American Journal of Agricultural Economics* 75(2): 387–98. https://doi.org/10.2307/1242923

Kaiser, H.M, S.J. Riha, D.S. Wilks, and R. Sampath. 1993b. Adaptation to global climate change at the farm level. In *Agricultural Dimensions of Global Climate Change*, ed. H.M. Kaiser and T.E. Drennen, 136–52. Delray Beach, FL: St Lucie Press.

Kaldor, N. 1939. Welfare propositions of economics and interpersonal comparisons of utility. *Economic Journal* 49(195): 549–52. https://doi.org/10.2307/2224835

Karmalkar, A.V. 2018. Interpreting results from the NARCCAP and NA-CORDEX ensembles in the context of uncertainty in regional climate change projections. *Bulletin of the American Meteorological Society* 99(10): 2093–106. https://doi.org/10.1175/BAMS-D-17-0127.1

Kennedy, P.L., K.E. Lewis, and A. Schmitz. 2017. Food security through biotechnology: The case of genetically modified sugar beets in the United States. In *World Agricultural Resources and Food Security*, ed. A. Schmitz, P.L. Kennedy, and T.G. Schmitz, 35–52. Bingley, UK: Emerald.

Kennedy, P.L., A. Schmitz, and K. Lewis-Lelong. 2019. Biotechnology and demand concerns: The case of genetically modified U.S. sugar beets. *AgBioForum* 22(1): 1–13.

Kennedy, P.L., A. Schmitz, and G. van Kooten. 2018. Food security and food storage. In *Reference Module in Food Science*. Amsterdam: Elsevier.

Kennedy, P.L., A. Schmitz, and G. van Kooten. 2020. The role of storage and trade in food security. *Journal of Agricultural and Food Industrial Organization* 18(1): 20190056. https://doi.org/10.1515/jafio-2019-0056

Ker, A., B. Barnett, D. Jacques, and T. Tolhurst. 2017. Canadian business risk management: Private firms, Crown corporations, and public institutions. *Canadian Journal of Agricultural Economics* 65(4): 591–612. https://doi.org/10.1111/cjag.12144

Ker, W.A. 2017. Genomics, international trade, and food security. *The Estey Journal of International Law and Trade Policy* 18(2): 63–7. https://doi.org/10.22004/ag.econ.262480

Kershen, D.L. 2000. The risks of going non-GMO. *Oklahoma Law Review* 53(4): 631–52.

Kesmodel, D., L. Etter, and A.O. Patrick. 2008. Grain companies' profits soar as global food crisis mounts. *Wall Street Journal*, 30 April 2008, A1.

Khilyuk, L.F., and G.V. Chilingar. 2006. On global forces of nature driving the earth's climate. Are humans involved? *Environmental Geology* 50: 899–910. https://doi.org/10.1007/s00254-006-0261-x

Klein, B., and K.B. Leffler. 1981. The role of market forces in assuring contractual performance. *Journal of Political Economy* 89(4): 615–41. https://doi.org/10.1086/260996

Klein, J., J. Altenbuchner, and R. Mattes. 1998. Nucleic acid and protein elimination during the sugar manufacturing process of conventional and transgenic sugar beets. *Journal of Biotechnology* 60(3): 145–53. https://doi.org/10.1016/S0168-1656(98)00006-6

Knutson, R.D., J.B. Penn, and B.L. Flinchbaugh. 1998. *Agricultural and Food Policy*, 4th ed. Upper Saddle River, NJ: Prentice-Hall.

Koo, W.W. 2002. U.S. sugar and alternative trade liberalization options. In *Sugar and Related Sweetener Markets: International Perspectives*, ed. A. Schmitz, T.H. Spreen, W.A. Messina, and C.B. Moss, 357–78. London: Centre for Agriculture and Bioscience International (CABI).

Kotz, N. 1976. Agribusiness. In *Radical Agriculture*, ed. R. Merrill, 41–55. New York: Harper.

Krebs-Smith, S.M., J. Reedy, and C. Bosire. 2010. Healthfulness of the U.S. food supply: Little improvement despite decades of dietary guidance. *American Journal of Preventive Medicine* 38(5): 472–7. https://doi.org/10.1016/j.amepre.2010.01.016

Krueger, A.O. 1974. The political economy of the rent-seeking society. *American Economic Review* 64(3): 291–303.

Krueger, A.O. 1980. The political economy of the rent-seeking society. In *Toward a Theory of the Rent-Seeking Society*, ed. R.D. Tollison and G. Tullock, 51–70. College Station: Texas A&M University Press.

Krugman, P.R., and M. Obstfeld. 1991. *International Economics: Theory and Practice*, 2nd ed. New York: Harper Collins.

Lakkakula, P. 2018. Potential impact of sweetener input tax on public health. *Applied Health Economics and Health Policy* 16(6): 749–51. https://doi.org/10.1007/s40258-018-0428-0

Lakkakula, P., and A. Schmitz. 2019. U.S. sweeteners: Combating excess consumption with an excise tax? *Agricultural Economics* 50(5): 543–54. https://doi.org/10.1111/agec.12508

Lamb, R.L. 2000. Policy only effective if farm economy is recognized. *Feedstuffs* 72(23): 22.

Lamb, R., and J. Henderson. 2000. FAIR Act implications for land values in the Corn Belt. *Review of Agricultural Economics* 21(1): 102–19.

Landers, P.S. 2007. The Food Stamp Program: History, nutrition education, and impact. *Journal of the Academy of Nutrition and Dietetics* 107(11): 1945–51. https://doi.org/10.1016/j.jada.2007.08.009

Law, M.T. 2003. The origins of state pure food regulation. *Journal of Economic History* 63(4): 1103–30. https://doi.org/10.1017/S0022050703002547

Leland, H.E. 1979a. Quacks, lemons, and licensing: A theory of minimum quality standards. *Journal of Political Economy* 87(6): 1328–46. https://doi.org/10.1086/260838

Leland, H.E. 1979b. Quality standards in markets with asymmetric information. In *Occupational Licensure*, ed. S. Rottenberg, 33–45. Washington, DC: American Enterprise Institute (AEI).

Lence, S.H., and D.J. Miller. 1999. Transaction costs and the present value model of farmland: Iowa, 1900–1994. *American Journal of Agricultural Economics* 81(2): 257–72. https://doi.org/10.2307/1244580

Levins, R.A. 2000. A new generation of power. *Choices* 15(2): 43–5.

Levitt, S.D., and S.J. Dubner. 2009. *Superfreakonomics: Global Cooling, Patriotic Prostitutes, and Why Suicide Bombers Should Buy Life Insurance*. New York: Harper Collins.

Lewis, N. 2018. *Abnormal Climate Response of the DICE IAM – A Trillion Dollar Error?* https://www.nicholaslewis.org/tag/climate-sensitivity/

Lewis, N., and J.A. Curry. 2015. The implications for climate sensitivity of AR5 forcing and heat uptake estimates. *Climate Dynamics* 45:1009–23. https://doi.org/10.1007/s00382-014-2342-y

Liu, S., J. Duan, and G.C. van Kooten. 2018. The impact of changes in the AgriStability program on crop activities: A farm modeling approach. *Agribusiness* 34(3): 650–67. https://doi.org/10.1002/agr.21544

Liu, S., J. Duan, and G.C. van Kooten. 2019. Risk aversion and the calibration of farm management models: Examining the effect of farm cost structure on the allocation of farm program benefits. Paper under review at *Australian Journal of Agricultural and Resource Economics*.

Livanis, G., C.B. Moss, V.E. Breneman, and R.F. Nehring. 2006. Urban sprawl and farmland prices. *American Journal of Agricultural Economics* 88(4): 915–29. https://doi.org/10.1111/j.1467-8276.2006.00906.x

Livestock Price Insurance. 2021. https://lpi.ca

Lomborg, B. 2007. *Cool It. The Skeptical Environmentalist's Guide to Global Warming*. New York: Alfred A. Knopf.

Long, S.P. 1991. Modification of the response of photosynthetic productivity to rising temperature by atmospheric CO_2 concentrations: Has its importance been underestimated? *Plant, Cell and Environment* 14(8): 729–39. https://doi.org/10.1111/j.1365-3040.1991.tb01439.x

Long, S.P., E.A. Ainsworth, A. Rogers, and D.R. Ort. 2004. Rising atmospheric carbon dioxide: Plants FACE the future. *Annual Review of Plant Biology* 55: 591–628. https://doi.org/10.1146/annurev.arplant.55.031903.141610

Loures, A. and I. Tavares. 2018. GDP of the sugar and alcohol sector in Brazil and northeast: An input-output approach. *Revista de Economia e Agronegócio (REA)* 16(3): 422–39. https://doi.org/10.25070/rea.v16i3.7815

Lynch, M., R. Miller, C.R. Plott, and R. Porter. 1986. *Experimental Studies of Markets with Buyers Ignorant of Quality before Purchase: When Do "Lemons" Drive Out High-Quality Products?* Washington, DC: Government Printing Office (GPO).

Macrotrends. 2021a. *Wheat Prices, 1999–2021*. https://www.macrotrends.net/2534/wheat-prices-historical-chart-data

Macrotrends. 2021b. *US Oats Prices, 2000–2021*. https://www.macrotrends.net/2536/oats-prices-historical-chart-data

Macrotrends. 2021c. *US Cotton Prices, 2019–2021*. https://www.macrotrends.net/2533/cotton-prices-historical-chart-data

Mahé, L.P., and F. Ortalo-Magné. 1999. Five proposals for a European model of the countryside. *Economic Policy* 14(28): 89–131. https://doi.org/10.1111/1468-0327.00045

Malla, S., and R.S. Gray. 1999. *The Effectiveness of Research Funding in the Canola Industry*. Regina: Government of Saskatchewan.

Manchester, A. 1983. *The Public Role in the Dairy Economy: Why and How Governments Intervene in the Milk Business*. Boulder, CO: Westview.

Manley, J., G.C. van Kooten, K. Moeltner, and D.W. Johnson. 2005. Creating carbon offsets in agriculture through no-till cultivation: A meta-analysis of costs and carbon benefits. *Climatic Change* 68:41–65. https://doi.org/10.1007/s10584-005-6010-4

Marchildon, G.P. 1998. Canadian-American agricultural trade relations: A brief history. *American Review of Canadian Studies* 28(3): 233–52. https://doi.org/10.1080/02722019809481571

Marshall, A. 1920. *The Principles of Economics*, 8th ed. London: Macmillan.

Martinez, P. 2016. *2015 USDA Dietary Guidelines Cookbook*. Mesa: Arizona State University.

Martins, V.J.B., T.M.M. Toledo Florêncio, L.P. Grillo, M.D.C.P. Franco, P.A. Martins, A.P.G. Clemente, C.D.L. Santos, M.F.A. Vieira, and A.L. Sawaya. 2011. Long-lasting effects of undernutrition.

International Journal of Environmental Research and Public Health 8(6): 1817–46. https://doi.org/10.3390/ijerph8061817

Matthews, A. 2015. Two steps forward, one step back: Coupled payments in the CAP. *CAP Reform* (blog), 16 April 2015. http://capreform.eu/two-steps-forward-one-step-back-coupled-payments-in-the-cap/

Mayer, H., and W.H. Furtan. 1999. Economics of transgenic herbicide-tolerant canola: The case of western Canada. *Food Policy* 24(4): 431–42. https://doi.org/10.1016/S0306-9192(99)00043-3

McCarl, B.A., and U.A. Schneider, 2002. U.S. agriculture's role in a greenhouse gas emission mitigation world: An economic perspective. *Review of Agricultural Economics* 22:134–59.

McCarl, B.A., A.W. Thayer, and J.P.H. Jones. 2016. The challenge of climate change adaptation for agriculture: An economically oriented review. *Journal of Agricultural and Applied Economics* 48(4): 321–44. https://doi.org/10.1017/aae.2016.27

McCutcheon, M.L., and E. Goddard. 1992. Optimal producer and social payoff from generic advertising: The case of the Canadian supply managed egg sector. *Canadian Journal of Agricultural Economics* 40(1): 1–24. https://doi.org/10.1111/j.1744-7976.1992.tb03674.x

McFadden, B.R. and T.G. Schmitz. 2017. The nexus of dietary guidelines and food security. In *World Agricultural Resources and Food Security: International Food Security*, ed. A. Schmitz, P.L. Kennedy, and T.G. Schmitz, 19–31. Bingley, UK: Emerald.

McGuire, S. 2016. Scientific report of the 2015 Dietary Guidelines Advisory Committee. *Advances in Nutrition* 7(1): 202–4. https://doi.org/10.3945/an.115.011684

McHughen, A. 2000. *Pandora's Picnic Basket: The Potential and Hazards of Genetically Modified Foods.* Oxford: Oxford University Press.

McKitrick, R., and J. Christy. 2018. A test of the tropical 200- to 300-hPa warming rate in climate models. *Earth and Space Science* 5(9): 529–36. https://doi.org/10.1029/2018EA000401

McKitrick, R.R., and P.J. Michaels. 2004. A test of corrections for extraneous signals in gridded surface temperature data. *Climate Research* 26(2): 159–73. https://doi.org/10.3354/cr026159

McKitrick, R.R., and P.J. Michaels. 2007. Quantifying the influence of anthropogenic surface processes and inhomogeneities on gridded global climate data. *Journal of Geophysical Research: Atmospheres* 112(D24): D24S09. https://doi.org/10.1029/2007JD008465

McKitrick, R.R., and N. Nierenberg. 2010. Socioeconomic signals in climate data. *Journal of Economic and Social Measurement* 35(3–4): 149–75. https://doi.org/10.3233/JEM-2010-0336

McLean, R. 2020. Tyson Foods warns that "the food supply chain is breaking" as plants close. *CNN Business*, 27 April 2020.

Melichar, E. 1979. Capital gains versus current income in the farming sector. *American Journal of Agricultural Economics* 61(5): 1085–92. https://doi.org/10.2307/3180381

Mendelsohn, R., W.D. Nordhaus, and D. Shaw. 1994. The impact of global warming on agriculture: A Ricardian approach. *American Economic Review* 84(4): 753–71.

Messina, W.A., and J.L. Seale. 1993. U.S. sugar policy and the Caribbean Basin Economic Recovery Act: Conflicts between domestic and foreign policy objectives. *Review of Agricultural Economics* 15(1): 167–80.

Millar, R.J., J.S. Fuglestvedt, P. Friedlingstein, J. Rogelj, M.J. Grubb, H.D. Matthews, R.B Skeie, P.M. Forster, D.J. Frame, and M.R. Allen. 2017. Emission budgets and pathways consistent with limiting warming to 1.5°C. *Nature Geoscience* 10:741–7. https://doi.org/10.1038/ngeo3031

Ministry of Agriculture, Forestry and Fisheries (MAFF). 2021. *Countryside Stewardship Scheme.* https://www.gov.uk/government/collections/countryside-stewardship

Mooney, S., and L.M. Arthur. 1990. The impacts of climate change on agriculture in Manitoba. *Canadian Journal of Agricultural Economics* 38(4): 685–94. https://doi.org/10.1111/j.1744-7976.1990.tb03503.x

Moore, F.C., U. Baldos, T. Hertel, and D. Diaz. 2017. New science of climate change impacts on agriculture implies higher social cost of carbon. *Nature Communications* 8(1): 1607. https://doi.org/10.1038/s41467-017-01792-x

Morgan, J.A., D.R. LeCain, E. Pendall, D.M. Blumenthal, B.A. Kimball, Y. Carrillo, D.G. Williams, J. Heisler-White, F.A. Dijkstra, and M. West. 2011. C_4 grasses prosper as carbon dioxide eliminates desiccation in warmed semi-arid grassland. *Nature* 476(11): 202–5. https://doi.org/10.1038/nature10274

Morland, K., S. Wing, and A.D. Roux. 2002. The contextual effect of the local food environment on residents' diets: The atherosclerosis risk in communities study. *American Journal of Public Health* 92(11): 1761–8. https://doi.org/10.2105/AJPH.92.11.1761

Moschini, G. 1984. Quota values and price uncertainty. *Canadian Journal of Agricultural Economics* 32(1): 231–4. https://doi.org/10.1111/j.1744-7976.1984.tb02014.x

Moss, C.B. 1997. Returns, interest rates, and inflation: How they explain changes in farmland values. *American Journal of Agricultural Economics* 79(4): 1311–18. https://doi.org/10.2307/1244287

Moss, C.B. 2006. Valuing state-level funding for research: Results for Florida. *Journal of Agricultural and Applied Economics* 38(1): 169–83. https://doi.org/10.1017/S1074070800022148

Moss, C.B. 2009. *Risk, Uncertainty, and the Agricultural Firm.* Hackensack, NJ: World Scientific.

Moss, C.B., and A. Schmitz. 2000. *Comparing Farm Income Support Levels in Canada and the United States.* Gainesville: University of Florida.

Moss, C.B., and A. Schmitz. 2008. *Will the Troubles in the Housing Market Affect Farmland Values?* Gainesville: University of Florida.

Moss, C.B., and A. Schmitz. 2013. Positive and negative externalities in agricultural production: Case of Adena Springs Ranch. *Journal of Agricultural and Applied Economics* 45:1–9. https://doi.org/10.1017/S1074070800004934

Moss, C.B. and A. Schmitz. 2019. Distribution of agricultural productivity gains in selected Feed the Future African countries. *Journal of Agribusiness in Developing and Emerging Economies* 9(1): 78–90. https://doi.org/10.1108/JADEE-01-2018-0009

Moss, C.B., A. Schmitz, and T.G. Schmitz 2006. First generation genetically modified organisms in agriculture. *Journal of Public Affairs* 6(1): 46–57. https://doi.org/10.1002/pa.41

Moss, C.B., T.G. Schmitz, and A. Schmitz. 2007. Intellectual property rights in the multinational firm: The case of high valued agriculture. Paper presented at the NC-1034 Conference, March 2007, Berkeley, California.

Moss, C., T.G. Schmitz, and A. Schmitz. 2009. Segregating genetically modified and nongenetically modified corn in a marketing channel. *Applied Economics* 40(21): 2765–74. https://doi.org/10.1080/00036840600970336

Moss, C.B., and J.L. Seale. 1993. *An allocation model of government outlays: A differential approach.* Paper presented at the Joint Canadian Agricultural Economics Association and Western Agricultural Economics Association Conference, July 1993, Edmonton, Canada.

Moss, C.B., and J.S. Shonkwiler. 1993. Estimating yield distributions using a stochastic trend and nonnormal errors. *American Journal of Agricultural Economics* 75(4): 1056–62. https://www.jstor.org/stable/1243993

Moyer, H.W., and T. Josling. 2002. *Agricultural Policy Reform – Politics and Process in the European Union and United States in the 1990s*. London: Ashgate.

Murphy, J.A., W.H. Furtan, and A. Schmitz. 1993. The gains from agricultural research under distorted trade. *Journal of Public Economics* 51(2): 161–72. https://doi.org/10.1016/0047-2727(93)90082-5

Mussell, A., D. Hedley, and T. Bilyea. 2019. *Shifting Geo-Politics and Trade Policy: Wither Canadian Agri-Food Policy?* Guelph, ON: Agri-Food Economic Systems.

Muth, M.K., D. Mancini, and C. Viator. 2003. U.S. food manufacturer assessment of and responses to bioengineered food. *AgBioForum* 5(3): 90–100.

Nasdaq. 2021. *US Feeder Cattle Price*. https://www.nasdaq.com/market-activity/commodities/gf

Nelson, R.R., and S.G. Winters. 1982. *An Evolutionary Theory of Economic Change*. Cambridge, MA: Harvard University Press.

Nestle, M. 2007. *Food Politics: How the Food Industry Influences Nutrition and Health*. Berkeley: University of California Press.

Niskanan, W.A. 1968. The peculiar economics of bureaucracy. *American Economic Review* 58(3): 298–305.

Nordhaus, W.D. 2013. Integrated economic and climate modeling. In *Handbook of Computable General Equilibrium Modeling*, Volume 1A, ed. P. Dixon and D. Jorgenson, 1069–131. Dordrecht: Elsevier.

North, D.C. 1981. *Structure and Change in Economic History*. New York: Norton.

Office International des Epizooties/World Organisation for Animal Health (OIE). 2020. *OIE: 182 Member Countries*. Paris: OIE.

Office of Defense, Health, and Welfare Services (ODHWS). 1942. (1) *U.S. Needs Us Strong*, and (2) *When You Eat Out: Food for Freedom*. Washington, DC: Bureau of Home Economics.

Offutt, S. 2000. Can the farm problem be solved? *M.E. John Lecture Seminar*. University Park: Pennsylvania State University.

Ohlin, B. 1933. *Interregional and International Trade*. Cambridge, MA: Harvard University Press.

Okrent, A.M., and J.M. Alston. 2011. *Demand for Food in the United States: A Review of Literature, Evaluation of Previous Estimates, and Presentation of New Estimates of Demand*. Davis: University of California-Davis.

Olper, A. 1998. Political economy determinants of agricultural protection levels in EU member states: An empirical investigation. *European Review of Agricultural Economics* 25(4): 463–87. https://doi.org/10.1093/erae/25.4.463

O'Neill, D. 2007. *The Total External Environmental Costs and Benefits of Agriculture in the UK*. London: Environment Agency.

Ontario Ministry of Agriculture, Food, and Rural Affairs (OMAFRA). 2016. *Farm Statistics for Canada, 1996–2016*. Guelph, ON: OMAFRA. http://www.omafra.gov.on.ca/english/stats/census/number.htm

Organisation for Economic Co-operation and Development (OECD). 1997a. *Costs and Benefits of Food Safety Regulations: Fresh Meat Hygiene Standards in the United Kingdom*. Paris: OECD.

Organisation for Economic Co-operation and Development (OECD). 1997b. *Vertical Coordination in the Fruit and Vegetable Sector: Implications for Existing Market Institutions and Policy Instruments*. Paris: OECD.

Organisation for Economic Co-operation and Development (OECD). 1998. *Main Economic Indicators*. Paris: OECD.

Organisation for Economic Co-operation and Development (OECD). 2000. *Producer and Consumer Subsidy Equivalents Database, Directorate for Food, Agriculture, and Fisheries*. Paris: OECD.

Organisation for Economic Co-operation and Development (OECD). 2001. *Multifunctionality: Towards an Analytical Framework*. Paris: OECD.

Organisation for Economic Co-operation and Development (OECD). 2005. *Decoupling – Policy Implications*. Paris: OECD.

Organisation for Economic Co-operation and Development (OECD). 2018. *Producer and Consumer Support Estimates Database*. Paris: OECD.

Paarlberg, D. 1964. *American Farm Policy: A Case Study of Centralized Decision Making*. New York: Wiley.

Paarlberg, D. 1984. *Purpose of Farm Policy*. Washington, DC: American Enterprise Institute (AEI).

Paarlberg, R. 2013. *Food Politics: What Everyone Needs to Know*, 2nd ed. Oxford: Oxford University Press.

Page, L., and E.F. Phipard. 1956. *Essentials of an Adequate Diet. Facts for Nutrition Programs*. Washington, DC: United States Department of Agriculture (USDA).

Pandey, R., M.K. Lal, and K. Vengavasi. 2018. Differential response of hexaploid and tetraploid wheat to interactive effects of elevated $[CO_2]$ and low phosphorus. *Plant Cell Reports* 37: 1231–44. https://doi.org/10.1007/s00299-018-2307-4

Pappi, F.U., and C.H.C.A. Henning. 1999. The organization of influence on the EC's common agricultural policy: A network approach. *European Journal of Political Research* 36(2): 257–81. https://doi.org/10.1111/1475-6765.00470

Pearce, J., R. Hiscock, T. Blakely, and K. Witten. 2008. The contextual effects of neighbourhood access to supermarkets and convenience stores on individual fruit and vegetable consumption. *Journal of Epidemiology and Community Health* 62(3): 198–201. https://doi.org/10.1136/jech.2006.059196

Pearson, T., J. Russell, M.J. Campbell, and M.E. Barker. 2005. Do "food deserts" influence fruit and vegetable consumption? A cross-sectional study. *Appetite* 45(2): 195–7. https://doi.org/10.1016/j.appet.2005.04.003

Peterson, W.L. 1967. Return to poultry research in the United States. *Journal of Farm Economics* 49(3): 656–69.

Pielke Jr., R. 2018a. *The Rightful Place of Science: Disasters and Climate Change*, 2nd ed. Tempe: Arizona State University.

Pielke Jr., R. 2018b. Tracking progress on the economic costs of disasters under the indicators of the sustainable development goals. *Environmental Hazards* 18(1): 1–6. https://doi.org/10.1080/17477891.2018.1540343

Pielke Jr., R. 2019. Net-zero carbon dioxide emissions by 2050 requires a new nuclear power plant every day. *Forbes*, 30 September 2019.

Pigou, A.C. 1932. *The Economics of Welfare*. London: Macmillan.

Pindyck, R.S. 2013. Climate change policy. What do the models tell us? *Journal of Economic Literature* 51(3): 860–72. https://doi.org/10.1257/jel.51.3.860

Pope, C.A., III. 1985. Agricultural productive and consumptive use components of rural land values in Texas. *American Journal of Agricultural Economics* 67(1): 81–6. https://doi.org/10.2307/1240826

Porter, J.R., M. Howden, and P. Smith. 2017. Considering agriculture in IPCC assessments. *Nature Climate Change* 7: 680–3. https://doi.org/10.1038/nclimate3404

Powell, S., and A. Schmitz. 2005. The cotton and sugar subsidies decisions: WTO's dispute settlement system rebalances the agreement on agriculture. *Drake Agricultural Law Journal* 10(2): 287–330.

Prakash, V., S.K. Dwivedi, S. Kumar, J.S. Mishra, K.K. Rao, S.S. Singh, and B.P. Bhatt. 2017. Effect of elevated CO_2 and temperature on growth and yield of wheat grown in sub-humid climate of Eastern Indo-Gangetic Plain (IGP). *Mausam* 68:499–506.

Pray, C., J. Huang, R. Hu, and S. Rozelle. 2002. Five years of Bt cotton in China – the benefits continue. *Plant Journal* 31(4): 423–30. https://doi.org/10.1046/j.1365-313X.2002.01401.x

Pretty, J.N., A.S. Ball, T. Lang, and J.I.L. Morison. 2005. Farm costs and food miles: An assessment of the full cost of the UK weekly food basket. *Food Policy* 30(1): 1–19. https://doi.org/10.1016/j.foodpol.2005.02.001

Pretty, J.N., C. Brett, D. Gee, R.E. Hine, C.F. Mason, J.I.L. Morison, H. Raven, M.D. Rayment, and G. van der Bijl. 2000. An assessment of the total external costs of UK agriculture. *Agricultural Systems* 65(2): 113–36. https://doi.org/10.1016/S0308-521X(00)00031-7

Pretty, J.N., C. Brett, D. Gee, R.E. Hine, C.F. Mason, J.I.L. Morison, M.D. Rayment, G. van der Bijl, and T. Dobbs. 2001. Policy challenges and priorities for internalizing the externalities of modern agriculture. *Journal of Environmental Planning and Management* 44(2): 263–83. https://doi.org/10.1080/09640560123782

Public Law 71-10. 1929. *US Agricultural Marketing Act of 1929 (PL 71-10, 46 Stat. 11).* United States Code, Washington, DC.

Public Law 73-10. 1933. *US Agricultural Adjustment Act of 1933 (PL 73-10, 48 Stat. 31).* United States Code, Washington, DC.

Public Law 75-430. 1938. *US Agricultural Adjustment Act of 1938 (PL 75-430, 52 Stat. 31).* United States Code, Washington, DC.

Qaim, M., and D. Zilberman. 2003. Yield effects of genetically modified crops in developing countries. *Science* 299(5608): 900–2. https://doi.org/10.1126/science.1080609

Quigley, L. 2000. Agriculture's fate compared to the almighty Titanic. *Feedstuffs* 72(31): 1.

Ramirez, O.A., C.B. Moss, and W.G. Boggess. 1997. A stochastic optimal control formulation of the consumption/debt decision. *Agricultural Finance Review* 57: 29–38.

Rausser, G.C. 1992. Predatory versus productive government: The case of U.S. agricultural policies. *Journal of Economic Perspectives* 63(3): 133–57. https://doi.org/10.1257/jep.6.3.133

Reed, M. and S. Saghaian. 2019. Macroeconomic issues in agricultural economics. In *The Routledge Handbook of Agricultural Economics,* ed. G.L. Cramer, K.P. Paudel, and A. Schmitz, 327–56. London: Routledge.

Reedy, J., and S.M. Krebs-Smith. 2008. A comparison of food-based recommendations and nutrient values of three food guides: USDA's MyPyramid, NHLBI's Dietary Approaches to Stop Hypertension Eating Plan, and Harvard's Healthy Eating Pyramid. *Journal of the Academy of Nutrition and Dietetics* 108(3): 522–8. https://doi.org/10.1016/j.jada.2007.12.014

Reynolds, J.E., and H. Dorbecker. 2002. *Agricultural Land Values – Miami-Dade County.*

Riahi, K., D.P. van Vuuren, E. Kriegler, J. Edmonds, B.C. O'Neill, S. Fujimori, N. Bauer, K. Calvin, R. Dellink, O. Fricko, W. Lutz, A. Popp, J.C. Cuaresma, K.C. Samir, M. Leimbach, L. Jiang, T. Kram, S. Rao, J. Emmerling, K. Ebi, T. Hasegawa, P. Havlik, F. Humpenöder, L.A. Da Silva, S. Smith, E. Stehfest, V. Bosetti, J. Eom, D. Gernaat, T. Masui, J. Rogelj, J. Strefler, L. Drouet, V. Krey, G. Luderer, M. Harmsen, K. Takahashi, L. Baumstark, J.C. Doelman, M. Kainuma, Z. Klimont, G. Marangoni, H. Lotze-Campen, M. Obersteiner, A. Tabeau, and M. Tavoni. 2017. The Shared Socioeconomic Pathways and their energy, land use, and greenhouse gas emissions implications: An overview. *Global Environmental Change* 42: 153–68. https://doi.org/10.1016/j.gloenvcha.2016.05.009

Ricardo, D. (1817) 1963. *Principles of Political Economy and Taxation*. Homewood, IL: Irwin.

Ritson, C., and D.R. Harvey. 1997. *The Common Agricultural Policy*, 2nd ed. Wallingford, UK: Centre for Agriculture and Bioscience International (CABI).

Roberts, I., G. Love, H. Field, and N. Klijn. 1989. *US Grain Policies and the World Market*. ABARE Policy Monograph 4. Canberra: Australian Bureau of Agricultural and Resource Economics.

Roberts, T., J.C. Buzby, and M. Ollinger. 1996. Using benefit and cost information to evaluate a food safety regulation: HACCP for meat and poultry. *American Journal of Agricultural Economics* 78(5): 1297–1301. https://doi.org/10.2307/1243510

Robison, L.J., D.A. Lins, and R. VenKataraman. 1985. Cash rents and land values in U.S. Agriculture. *American Journal of Agricultural Economics* 67(4): 794–805. https://doi.org/10.2307/1241819

Romer, P.M. 1993. Idea gaps and object gaps in economic development. *Journal of Monetary Economics* 32(3): 543–73. https://doi.org/10.1016/0304-3932(93)90029-F

Roningen, V.O., and P. Dixit. 1989. *Economic Implications of Agricultural Policy Reforms in Industrial Market Economics*. Washington, DC: United States Department of Agriculture/Economic Research Service (USDA/ERS).

Rose, D., and R. Richards. 2004. Food store access and household fruit and vegetable use among participants in the U.S. Food Stamp Program. *Public Health Nutrition* 7(8): 1081–8. https://doi.org/10.1079/PHN2004648

Rude, J. 2000. Overview of multifunctionality: An examination of the issues and remedies. In *Globalization and Agricultural Trade Policy*, ed. H. Michelmann, J. Rude, J. Stabler, and G. Storey. Boulder: Lynne Rienner.

Rude, J. 2008. Production effects of the European Union's Single Farm Payment. *Canadian Journal of Agricultural Economics* 56(4): 457–71. https://doi.org/10.1111/j.1744-7976.2008.00141.x

Ruttan, V.W. 1982. *Agricultural Research Policy*. Minneapolis: University of Minnesota Press.

Ruttan, V.W. 1997. Induced innovation, evolutionary theory and path dependence: Sources of technical change. *Economic Journal* 107(444): 1520–9. https://doi.org/10.1111/j.1468-0297.1997.tb00063.x

Schimmelpfennig, D., J. Lewandrowski, J. Reilly, M. Tsigas, and I. Parry. 1996. *Agricultural Adaptation to Climate Change: Issues of Long-Run Sustainability*. Washington, DC: United States Department of Agriculture/Economic Research Service (USDA/ERS).

Schlenker, W., M.H. Hanemann, and A.C. Fisher. 2005. Will U.S. agriculture really benefit from global warming? Accounting for irrigation in the hedonic approach. *American Economic Review* 95(1): 395–406. https://doi.org/10.1257/0002828053828455

Schlenker, W., M.H. Hanemann, and A.C. Fisher. 2006. The impact of global warming on U.S. agriculture: An econometric analysis of optimal growing conditions. *Review of Economics and Statistics* 88:113–25. https://doi.org/10.1162/rest.2006.88.1.113

Schlenker, W., and M.J. Roberts. 2009. Nonlinear temperature effects indicate severe damages to U.S. crop yields under climate change. *Proceedings of the National Academy of Sciences* 106(37): 15594–8. https://doi.org/10.1073/pnas.0906865106

Schmitz, A. 1995a. Boom/bust cycles and Ricardian rents. *American Journal of Agricultural Economics* 77(5): 1110–25. https://doi.org/10.2307/1243332

Schmitz, A. 1995b. Supply management and GATT: The role of rent seeking. *Canadian Journal of Agricultural Economics* 43(4): 581–6. https://doi.org/10.1111/j.1744-7976.1995.tb00064.x

Schmitz, A. 2000. The millennium round of multinational trade negotiations. *Journal of Agricultural and Applied Economics* 32(2): 215–20. https://doi.org/10.1017/S1074070800020307

Schmitz, A. 2002. The European Union's high-priced sugar-support regime. In *Sugar and Related Sweetener Markets: International Perspectives*, ed. A. Schmitz, T. Spreen, W. Messina, and C. Moss, 193–214. London: Centre for Agriculture and Bioscience International (CABI).

Schmitz, A. 2018a. Commodity price stabilization under unattainable stocks. *Theoretical Economic Letters* 8(5): 861–5. https://doi.org/10.4236/tel.2018.85061

Schmitz, A. 2018b. Producers' preference for price instability? *Theoretical Economics Letters* 8(10): 1746–51. https://doi.org/10.4236/tel.2018.810114

Schmitz, A., W.G. Boggess, and K.T. Tefertiller. 1995. Regulations: Evidence from the Florida dairy industry. *American Journal of Agricultural Economics* 77(5): 1166–71. https://doi.org/10.2307/1243341

Schmitz, A., and D. Christian. 1993. The economics and politics of U.S. sugar policy. In *The Economics and Politics of World Sugar Policies*, ed. S. Marks and K.E. Maskus, 49–78. Ann Arbor: University of Michigan Press.

Schmitz, A., R.S. Firch, and J.S. Hillman. 1981. Agricultural export dumping: The case of Mexican winter vegetables in the U.S. market. *American Journal of Agricultural Economics* 63(4): 645–54. https://doi.org/10.2307/1241207

Schmitz, A., and H. Furtan. 2000. *The Canadian Wheat Board: Marketing in the New Millennium*. Regina: Canadian Plains Research Center.

Schmitz, A., H. Furtan, and K. Baylis. 2002. *Agricultural Policy, Agribusiness, and Rent-Seeking Behaviour*. Toronto: University of Toronto Press.

Schmitz, A. and R.S. Gray. 2001. The divergence in Canada-U.S. grain and oilseed policies. *Canadian Journal of Agricultural Economics* 49(4): 459–78. https://doi.org/10.1111/j.1744-7976.2001.tb00319.x

Schmitz, A., D.J. Haynes, and T.G. Schmitz. 2016a. Alternative approaches to compensation and producer rights. *Canadian Journal of Agricultural Economics* 64(3): 439–54. https://doi.org/10.1111/cjag.12085

Schmitz, A., D.J. Haynes, and T.G. Schmitz. 2016b. The not-so-simple economics of production quota buyouts. *Journal of Agricultural and Applied Economics* 48(2): 119–47. https://doi.org/10.1017/aae.2016.5

Schmitz, A., and P. Helmberger. 1973. Factor mobility and international trade: The case of complementarity. *American Economic Review* 60(4): 761–7.

Schmitz, A., P.L. Kennedy, and J. Hill-Gabriel. 2012. Restoring the Florida Everglades through a sugar land buyout: Benefits, costs, and legal challenges. *Environmental Economics* 3:74–89.

Schmitz, A., P.L. Kennedy, and J. Hill-Gabriel. 2013. Accounting for externalities in benefit-cost measures: An analysis of a land buyout and associated projects to save the Everglades. *Journal of Agricultural and Applied Economics* 45(3): 421–33. https://doi.org/10.1017/S1074070800004958

Schmitz, A., P.L. Kennedy, and T.G. Schmitz, eds. 2015. *Food Security in an Uncertain World: An International Perspective*. Bingley, UK: Emerald.

Schmitz, A., P.L. Kennedy, and T.G. Schmitz, eds. 2016. *Food Security in an Uncertain World: An Individual Country Perspective*. Bingley, UK: Emerald.

Schmitz, A., P.L. Kennedy, and T.G. Schmitz, eds. 2017. *World Agricultural Resources and Food Security*. Bingley, UK: Emerald.

Schmitz, A., P.L. Kennedy, and F. Zhang. 2020. Sugarcane and sugar yields in Louisiana (1911–2018): Varietal development and mechanization. *Crop Science* 60(3): 1303–12. https://doi.org/ https://doi.org/10.1002/csc2.20045

Schmitz, A., and C.B. Moss. 2005. Multifunctionality in agriculture: Externalities and non-traded goods. *International Journal of Agricultural Resources, Governance and Ecology* 4(3/4): 327–43. https://doi.org/10.1504/IJARGE.2005.007460

Schmitz, A., and C.B. Moss. 2015. Mechanized agriculture: Machine adoption, farm size, and labor displacement. *AgBioForum* 18(3): 278–96.

Schmitz, A., C. Moss, and T.G. Schmitz. 2007. Ethanol: No free lunch. *Journal of Agricultural and Food Industrial Organization* 5(2): Article 3. https://doi.org/10.2202/1542-0485.1186

Schmitz, A., C.B. Moss, T.G. Schmitz, H.W. Furtan, and H.C. Schmitz. 2010. *Agricultural Policy, Agribusiness, and Rent-Seeking Behaviour*, 2nd ed. Toronto: University of Toronto Press.

Schmitz, A., and T.G. Schmitz. 1994a. Supply management: The past and future. *Canadian Journal of Agricultural Economics* 42(2): 125–48. https://doi.org/10.1111/j.1744-7976.1994.tb00013.x

Schmitz, A., and T.G. Schmitz. 1994b. Tariffs and trade. In *Encyclopedia of Agricultural Science*. 4 vols. New York: Academic Press.

Schmitz, A., and T.G. Schmitz. 2010. Benefit-cost analysis: Distributional considerations under producer quota buyouts. *Journal of Benefit-Cost Analysis* 1(1): 1–15. https://doi .org/10.2202/2152-2812.1002

Schmitz, A., T.G. Schmitz, and F. Rossi. 2006. Agricultural subsidies in developed countries: Impact on global welfare. *Review of Agricultural Economics* 28(3): 416–25. https://www.jstor.org/stable/3877188

Schmitz, A., J.L. Seale, and C. Chegini. 2019. Japanese beef tariffs: Beef quality, farm programs, and producer compensation. *Journal of Agricultural and Food Industrial Organization* 17(2): 1–15. https://doi.org/10.1515/jafio-2019-0001

Schmitz, A., J.L. Seale, and T.G. Schmitz. 2003. Sweetener-ethanol complex in Brazil, the United States, and Mexico: Do prices matter? *International Sugar Journal* 105(1259): 505–13.

Schmitz, A., J.L. Seale, and T.G. Schmitz. 2006. The optimal processor tariff under the Byrd Amendment. *International Journal of Applied Economics* 3(2): 9–20.

Schmitz, A., and D. Seckler. 1970. Mechanized agriculture and social welfare: The case of the tomato harvester. *American Journal of Agricultural Economics* 52(4): 569–77. https://doi. org/10.2307/1237264

Schmitz, A., and I. Sheldon. 2019. Trade, policy, and development. In *The Routledge Handbook of Agricultural Economics*, ed. G.L. Cramer, K.P. Paudel, and A. Schmitz, 327–56. London: Routledge.

Schmitz, A., D. Sigurdson, and O. Doering. 1986. Domestic farm policy and the gains from trade. *American Journal of Agricultural Economics* 68(4): 820–7. https://doi.org/10.2307/1242128

Schmitz, A., and J. Vercammen. 1990. *Trade Liberalization in the World Sugar Market: Playing on a Level Field?* Berkeley: University of California-Berkeley.

Schmitz, A., and J. Vercammen. 1995. Efficiency of farm programs and their trade distorting effects. In *GATT Negotiations and the Political Economy of Policy Reform*, ed. G.C. Rausser and P.G. Ardeni, 35–64. New York: Springer.

Schmitz, A., and R.O. Zerbe. 2008a. *Applied Benefit-Cost Analysis.* Cheltenham, UK: Elgar.

Schmitz, A., and R.O. Zerbe. 2008b. Scitovsky reversals and efficiency criteria in policy analysis. *Journal of Agricultural and Food Industrial Organization* 6(3): Article 3. https://doi .org/10.2202/1542-0485.1235

Schmitz, A., and F. Zhang. 2019. The dynamics of sugarcane and sugar yields in Florida: 1950–2018. *Crop Science* 59(5): 1880–6. https://doi.org/10.2135/cropsci2018.11.0674

Schmitz, A., and M. Zhu. 2017. The economics of yield maintenance: An example from Florida sugarcane. *Crop Science* 57(6): 2959–71. https://doi.org/10.2135/cropsci2017.01.0067

Schmitz, A., M. Zhu, and D. Zilberman. 2017. The Trans-Pacific Partnership and Japan's agricultural trade. *Journal of Agricultural and Food Industrial Organization* 15(1): 1–18. https://doi.org/10.1515/jafio-2017-0001

Schmitz, T.G. 2018. Impact of the Chinese embargo against MIR162 corn on Canadian corn producers. *Canadian Journal of Agricultural Economics* 66(4): 571–86. https://doi.org/10.1111/cjag.12185

Schmitz, T.G., and K. Lewis. 2015. Impact of NAFTA on U.S. and Mexican sugar markets. *Journal of Agricultural and Resource Economics* 40(3): 387–404. https://doi.org/10.22004/ag.econ.210546

Schmitz, T.G., C.B. Moss, and A. Schmitz. 2004. Segmentation of GMO and non-GMO soybean markets under identity preservation costs and government price supports. In *The Regulation of Agricultural Biotechnology*, ed. R.E. Evenson and V. Santaniello, 201–10. Cambridge: Centre for Agriculture and Bioscience International (CABI).

Schmitz, T.G., and A. Schmitz. 2014. International trade. In *Encyclopedia of Agriculture and Food Systems*. New York: Elsevier.

Schmitz, T.G., A. Schmitz, and C. Dumas. 1997. Gains from trade, inefficiency of government programs, and the net economic effects of trading. *Journal of Political Economy* 105(3): 637–47. https://doi.org/10.1086/262086

Schmitz T.G., A. Schmitz, and C.B. Moss. 2004. Did StarLink reduce import demand for corn? *Journal of Agricultural and Food Industrial Organization* 2(2): Article 6. https://doi.org/10.2202/1542-0485.1067

Schmitz, T.G., A. Schmitz, and C.B. Moss. 2005a. E-commerce and other marketing channel outlets in Florida's cattle market. In *E-Commerce in Agribusiness*, ed. T.G. Schmitz, C.B. Moss, A. Schmitz, A. Kagan, and B. Babcock. Longboat Key: Florida Science Source.

Schmitz T.G., A. Schmitz, and C.B. Moss. 2005b. The economic impact of StarLink corn. *Agribusiness: An International Journal* 21(3): 391–407. https://doi.org/10.1002/agr.20054

Schmitz, T.G., A. Schmitz, and J. Seale. 2003. Brazil's ethanol program: The case of hidden sugar subsidies. *International Sugar Journal* 105(1254): 254–65.

Schmitz, T.G., A. Schmitz, and J.L. Seale. 2009. The optimal Byrd tariff in vertical markets. *International Journal of Applied Economics* 6:1–10.

Schmitz, T.G., and J.L. Seale. 2004. Countervailing duties, antidumping tariffs, and the Byrd Amendment: A welfare analysis. *International Journal of Applied Economics* 1(1): 65–80.

Schmitz, T.G., and J.L. Seale. 2019. USMCA, supply management, suspension agreements, and retaliatory tariffs. Paper presented at the 2019 Allied Social Sciences Annual Meetings, 4 January 2019, Atlanta, GA. Submitted to *Applied Economic Perspectives and Policy*. https://econpapers.repec.org/RePEc:ags:assa19:281174

Schmitz, T.G., M. Zhu, and A. Schmitz. 2016a. Agricultural import tariffs and export restrictions. In *Reference Module in Food Science*. Amsterdam: Elsevier.

Schmitz, T.G., M. Zhu, and A. Schmitz. 2016b. Nontariff distortions in agricultural trade. In *Reference Module in Food Science*. Amsterdam: Elsevier.

Schnepf, R. 2017. *U.S. farm income outlook for 2017*. CRS Report R40152. Washington, DC: US Congressional Research Service.

Schuff, S. 2009. Cellulosic fuel to get jump-start. *Feedstuffs* 81(2): 2–3.

Schuh, G.E. 1974. The exchange rate and U.S. agriculture. *American Journal of Agricultural Economics* 56(1): 1–13. https://doi.org/10.2307/1239342

Schultz, T.W. 1953. *The Economic Organization of Agriculture*. New York: McGraw-Hill.

Schwartz, C.S. 1959. *The Search for Stability*. Toronto: McClelland and Stewart.

Scobie, G.M., and R. Posada. 1978. The impact of technical change on income distribution: The case of rice in Columbia. *American Journal of Agricultural Economics* 60(1): 85–92. https://doi .org/10.2307/1240164

Seale, J., and H. Theil. 1986. Working's model for food in the four phases of the international comparison project. *Economics Letters* 22(1): 103–4. https://doi.org/10.1016/0165-1765(86)90151-5

Shalit, H., and A. Schmitz. 1982. Farmland accumulation and prices. *American Journal of Agricultural Economics* 64(4): 710–19. https://doi.org/10.2307/1240580

Shalit, H., and A. Schmitz. 1984. Farmland price behavior and credit allocation. *Western Journal of Agricultural Economics* 9(2): 303–13.

Shapiro, C. 1983. Premiums for high quality products as returns to reputation. *Quarterly Journal of Economics* 98(4): 659–79. https://doi.org/10.2307/1881782

Shier, V., R. An, and R. Sturm. 2012. Is there a robust relationship between neighbourhood food environment and childhood obesity in the USA? *Public Health* 126(9): 723–30. https://doi .org/10.1016/j.puhe.2012.06.009

Sigurdson, D., and R. Sin. 1994. An aggregate analysis of Canadian crop insurance policy. In *Economics of Agricultural Crop Insurance: Theory and Evidence*, ed. D.L. Hueth and W.H. Furtan, 45–72. Boston: Kluwer.

Simeone, J. and I. Eastin. 2012. Russia's log export tariff and WTO accession. *CITRAFOR News* (Autumn): 2012. http://www.cintrafor.org/publications/newsletter/C4news2012autumn.pdf

Sinclair, U. [1906] 2006. *The Jungle*. New York: Modern Library.

Skogstad, G. 1987. *The Politics of Agricultural Policy-Making in Canada*. Toronto: University of Toronto Press.

Skogstad, G. 1993. *Policy under Siege: Supply Management in Agricultural Marketing*. Toronto: University of Toronto Press.

Smith, A. [1776] 1937. *An Inquiry into the Nature and Causes of the Wealth of Nations*. London: W. Strahan and T. Cadell.

Smith, V.J. 2017. *The U.S. Federal Crop Insurance Program: A Case Study in Rent Seeking*. Arlington, VA: George Mason University.

Spriggs, J., and G. Isaac. 1999. *Developments in the Institutional Arrangements for Meat Safety in Canada*. Saskatoon: University of Saskatchewan.

Statistics Canada. 2007. *Canada Year Book*. Ottawa: Statistics Canada. http://www.statcan.gc.ca.

Statistics Canada. 2018. Agricultural programs, historical data. Ottawa: Statistics Canada.

Stevenson, J.R., N. Villoria, D. Byerlee, T. Kelley, and M. Maredia. 2013. Green Revolution research saved an estimated 18 to 27 million hectares from being brought into agricultural production. *Proceedings of National Academy of Sciences 110(21)*: 8363–8. https://doi.org/10.1073 /pnas.1208065110

Stiebling, H.K. 1933. *Food Budgets for Nutrition and Production Programs*. Washington, DC: United States Department of Agriculture (USDA).

Stigler, G.J. 1971. The theory of economic regulation. *Bell Journal of Economics and Management Science* 2(1): 3–21. https://doi.org/10.2307/3003160

Stigler, G.J. 1975. *The Citizen and the State: Essays on Regulation*. Chicago: University of Chicago Press.

Stiglitz, J., and A. Weiss. 1981. Credit rationing in markets with imperfect information. *American Economic Review* 71(3): 393–410.

Story, M., M.W. Hamm, and D. Wallinga. 2009. Food systems and public health: Linkages to achieve healthier diets and healthier communities. *Journal of Hunger and Environmental Nutrition* 4(3–4): 219–24. https://doi.org/10.1080/19320240903351463

Stratmann, T. 1992. The effects of logrolling on congressional voting. *American Economic Review* 85(5): 1162–76.

Strick, J.C. 1990. *The Economics of Government Regulation*. Toronto: Thompson.

Sturm, R., and A. Datar. 2005. Body mass index in elementary school children, metropolitan area food prices and food outlet density. *Public Health* 119(12): 1059–68. https://doi.org/10.1016/j.puhe.2005.05.007

Sumner, D.A. 1999. Domestic price regulations and trade policy: Milk marketing orders in the United States. *Canadian Journal of Agricultural Economics* 47(5): 5–16. https://doi.org/10.1111/j.1744-7976.1999.tb00233.x

Sumner, D. 2005. *Boxed In: Conflicts between US Farm Policies and WTO Obligations*. Washington, DC: CATO Institute.

Swinnen, J.F.M., ed. 2008a. *The Perfect Storm: The Political Economy of the Fischler Reforms of the Common Agricultural Policy*. Brussels: CEPS.

Swinnen, J.F.M. 2008b. *The Political Economy of the 2003 Reform of the Common Agricultural Policy*. Brussels: LICOS.

Swinnen, J. 2019. The political economy of agricultural and food policies. In *The Routledge Handbook of Agricultural Economics*, ed. G.L. Cramer, K.P. Paudel, and A. Schmitz, 381–98. London: Routledge.

Taheripour, F., H. Cui, and W.E. Tyner. 2019. The economics of biofuels. In *The Routledge Handbook of Agricultural Economics*, ed. G.L. Cramer, K.P. Paudel, and A. Schmitz, 637–57. London: Routledge.

Tangerman, S. 1985. Special features and ongoing reforms of the CAP. In *Confrontation or Negotiation: United States Policy and European Agriculture*, ed. C. Curry, W. Nichols, and R. Purnell, 84–118. Millwood, NY: Associated Faculty Press.

Theil, H., C.-F. Chung, and J.L. Seale. 1989. *International Evidence on Consumption Patterns*. Greenwich, CT: JAI Press.

Thomas, L.F. 1995. Food guide pyramid stimulates debate. *Journal of the Academy of Nutrition and Dietetics* 95(3): 297. https://doi.org/10.1016/S0002-8223(95)00070-4

Thompson (Gibney), S.J., and W.H. Furtan. 1983. Welfare effects of new crop variety licensing regulations: The case of Canadian malt barley. *American Journal of Agricultural Economics* 65(1): 142–7. https://doi.org/10.2307/1240350

Thornsbury, S., C.B. Moss, and A. Schmitz. 2003. Explaining multifunctionality in trade negotiations: Valuing non-traded commodities. Paper presented at the conference Agricultural Policy Reform and the WTO – Where Are We Heading? June 2003, Capri, Italy.

Tirole, J. 1988. *The Theory of Industrial Organization*. Cambridge, MA: MIT Press.

Todd, J.E., and M. ver Ploeg. 2015. Restricting sugar-sweetened beverages from SNAP purchases not likely to lower consumption. *Amber Waves* 1015(2): 30–9. https://doi.org/10.22004/ag.econ.209927

Tokgoz, S., A. Elobeid, J. Fabiosa, D. Hayes, B. Babcock, T.-H. Yu, F. Dong, C. Hart, and J. Beghin. 2007. *Emerging Biofuels: Outlook of Effects on U.S. Grain, Oilseed, and Livestock Markets*. Ames, IA: CARD.

Tol, R.S.J. 2014. *Climate Economics: Economic Analysis of Climate, Climate Change and Climate Policy*. Cheltenham, UK: Edward Elgar.

Tracy, M. 1996. *Agricultural Policy in the European Union and Other Market Economies*. Grenappe-La Hutte: Agricultural Policy Studies.

Treakie, J. 2019. A place-based turn in multifunctional agriculture: The case of Italy's Garfagnana region. *Journal of Agriculture, Food Systems, and Community Development* 9(A). https://doi.org/10.5304/jafscd.2019.091.039

Tullock, G. 1967. The welfare costs of tariffs, monopolies, and theft. *Western Economic Journal* 2(2): 224–32. https://doi.org/10.1111/j.1465-7295.1967.tb01923.x

Tweeten, L. 1970. *Foundations of Farm Policy*. Lincoln: University of Nebraska Press.

Tweeten, L. 1983. Impact of federal fiscal-monetary policy on farm structure. *Southern Journal of Agricultural Economics* 15(1): 61–8. https://doi.org/10.1017/S008130520001596X

Tweeten, L. 1986. A note explaining farmland price changes in the seventies and eighties. *Agricultural Economics Research* 38(4): 25–30.

Tweeten, L., and J.E. Martin. 1966. A methodology for predicting U.S. farm real estate price variations. *Journal of Farm Economics* 48(2): 378–93.

Ulrich, A., W.H. Furtan, and K. Downey. 1984. *Biotechnology and Rapeseed Breeding: Some Economic Considerations*. Ottawa: Science Council of Canada.

Ulrich, A., W.H. Furtan, and A. Schmitz. 1986. Public and private returns from joint venture research: An example from agriculture. *Quarterly Journal of Economics* 101(1): 103–29. https://doi.org/10.2307/1884644

United Nations Climate Change. 2018. *The Paris Agreement*. New York: United Nations.

United States Department of Agriculture (USDA). 1943. *Wartime Nutrition Guide*. Washington, DC: USDA.

United States Department of Agriculture (USDA). 1946. *National Food Guide*. Washington, DC: USDA.

United States Department of Agriculture (USDA). 1958. *Food for Fitness: A Daily Food Guide*. Washington, DC: USDA.

United States Department of Agriculture (USDA). 2011. *MyPlate*. Washingon, DC: USDA.

United States Department of Agriculture (USDA). 2019. *2019 Budget Summary*. Washington, DC: USDA.

United States Department of Agriculture (USDA). 2020. *2020 Budget Summary*. Washington, DC: USDA.

United States Department of Agriculture/Agriculture Marketing Service (USDA/AMS). 2021. *Market Report*. https://www.ams.usda.gov/market-news/weekly-and-monthly-beef-reports

United States Department of Agriculture/Economic Research Service (USDA/ERS). 2008. *Food and Nutrition Assistance*. Washington, DC: USDA/ERS.

United States Department of Agriculture/Economic Research Service (USDA/ERS). 2009. *Farm Balance Sheet: Data Files*. Washington, DC: USDA/ERS.

United States Department of Agriculture/Economic Research Service (USDA/ERS). 2019. *U.S. Sugar Production*. Washington, DC: USDA/ERS.

United States Department of Agriculture/Farm Service Agency (USDA/FSA). 2019. *CRP Contract Summary and Statistics*. Washington, DC: USDA/FSA.

United States Department of Agriculture/Food and Nutrition Service (USDA/FNS). 1992. *The Food Guide Pyramid*. Washingon, DC: USDA/FNS.

United States Department of Agriculture/Food and Nutrition Service (USDA/FNS). 2005. *My Pyramid*. Washingon, DC: USDA/FNS.

United States Department of Agriculture/Food and Nutrition Service (USDA/FNS). 2020. *USDA Announces School and Summer Meals Reforms*. Washington, DC: USDA/FNS.

United States Department of Agriculture/Food Safety and Inspection Service (USDA/FSIS). 2003. *Humane Handling and Slaughter of Livestock*. Washington, DC: USDA/FSIS.

United States Department of Agriculture/Foreign Agriculture Service (USDA/FAS). 2008. *Fact Sheet: Export Enhancement Program*. Washington, DC: USDA/FAS.

United States Department of Agriculture/Foreign Agricultural Service (USDA/FAS). 2017a. *PSD Database Online*. Washington, DC: USDA/FAS.

United States Department of Agriculture/Foreign Agricultural Service (USDA/FAS). 2017b. *Sugar: World Markets and Trade*. Washington, DC: USDA/FAS.

United States Department of Agriculture/National Agricultural Statistics Service (USDA/NASS). 2019. *Agricultural Prices Summary*. Washington, DC: USDA/NASS.

United States Department of Agriculture/National Agricultural Statistics Service (USDA/NASS). 2021. *Corn Prices, 2010–20*. Washington, DC: USDA/NASS.

United States Department of Energy (USDE). 2007. *Annual Energy Outlook 2007 with Projections to 2030*. Washington, DC: USDE.

United States Department of Health and Human Services (USDHHS). 2009. *Dietary Guidelines for Americans*. Chapter 3. Washington, DC: USDHHS.

United States Department of Health and Human Services/Centers for Disease Control and Prevention (USDHHS/CDC). 2009. *Foodborne Illness*. Atlanta: USDHHS/CDC.

United States Department of Health and Human Services/United States Department of Agriculture (USDHHS/USDA). 1980. *Nutrition and Your Health: Dietary Guidelines for Americans*. Washington, DC: USDHHS.

United States Department of Health and Human Services/United States Department of Agriculture (USDHHS/USDA). 2015. *2015–2020 Dietary Guidelines for Americans*, 8th ed. Washington, DC: USDHHS/USDA.

United States Environmental Protection Agency (USEPA). 1990. *Natural Water Quality Inventory, Report to Congress*. Washington, DC: USEPA.

United States Environmental Protection Agency (USEPA). 2020. *Overview for Renewable Fuel Standards*. Washington, DC: USEPA.

United States General Accounting Office, Resources, Community and Economic Development Division (GAO/RCED). 1998. *Crop Revenue Insurance: Problems with New Plans Need to be Addressed*. GAO/RCED-98–111. Washington, DC: GAO/RCED.

United States Global Change Research Program (USGCRP). 2018. *Impacts, Risks, and Adaptation in the United States: Fourth National Climate Assessment, Volume II*. Washington, DC: USGCRP.

Van Asseldonk, M., R. Jongeneel, G.C. van Kooten, and J. Cordier. 2019. Agricultural risk management in the European Union: A proposal to facilitate precautionary savings. *EuroChoices* 18(2): 40–6. https://doi.org/10.1111/1746-692X.12230

Van Berkum, S., R.A. Jongeneel, M.G.A. van Leeuwen, and I.J. Terluin. 2018. *Exploring the Impacts of Two Brexit Scenarios on Dutch Agricultural Trade Flows*. Wageningen: Wageningen University.

Van Kooten, G.C. 2004. *Climate Change Economics: Why International Accords Fail*. Cheltenham, UK: Edward Elgar.

Van Kooten, G.C. 2005. Economics of forest and agricultural carbon sinks. In *Climate Change and Managed Ecosystems*, ed. J.S. Bhatti, R. Lal, M. Apps, and M. Price, 375–95. Baton Roca, FL: CRC Press.

Van Kooten, G.C. 2013. *Climate Change, Climate Science and Economics: Prospects for an Alternative Energy Future*. Dordrecht: Springer.

Van Kooten, G.C. 2014. The benefits of impeding free trade: Revisiting British Columbia's restrictions on log exports. *Journal of Forest Economics* 20(4): 333–47. https://doi.org/10.1016/j.jfe.2014.09.004

Van Kooten, G.C. 2017. California dreaming: The economics of renewable energy. *Canadian Journal of Agricultural Economics* 65(1): 19–41. https://doi.org/10.1111/cjag.12132

Van Kooten, G.C. 2019. Reforming Canada's dairy sector: USMCA and the issue of compensation. *Applied Economic Perspectives and Policy* 42(3): 542–58. https://doi.org/10.1093/aepp/ppy038

Van Kooten, G.C., and C. Johnston. 2014. Global impacts of Russian log export restrictions and the Canada-U.S. lumber dispute: Modeling trade in logs and lumber. *Forest Policy and Economics* 39:54–66. https://doi.org/10.1016/j.forpol.2013.11.003

Van Kooten, G.C., and F. Mokhtarzadeh. 2019. Optimal investment in electric generating capacity under climate policy. *Journal of Environmental Management* 232:66–72. https://doi.org/10.1016/j.jenvman.2018.11.038

Van Kooten, G.C., D. Orden, and A. Schmitz. 2019. Use of subsidies and taxes and the reform of agricultural policy. In *Routledge Handbook of Agricultural Economics*, ed. G.L. Cramer, K.P. Paudel, and A. Schmitz, 355–80. London: Routledge.

Van Kooten, G., A. Schmitz, and P.L Kennedy. 2020. Is commodity storage an option for enhancing food security in developing countries? *Journal of Agricultural and Food Industrial Organization* 18(1): 20190054.

Van Kooten, G.C., and A. Scott. 1995. Constitutional crisis, the economics of environment and resource development in western Canada. *Canadian Public Policy/Analyse de politiques* 21(2): 233–49. https://doi.org/10.2307/3551596

Van Kooten, G.C., and L. Voss, eds. 2021. *International Trade in Forest Products: Lumber Trade Disputes, Models and Examples*. Wallingford, UK: CABI.

Van Ravenswaay, E.O., and J.R. Blend. 1999. Using ecolabeling to encourage the adoption of innovative environmental technologies in agriculture. In *Flexible Incentives for the Adoption of Environmental Technologies in Agriculture*, ed. F. Casey, A. Schmitz, S. Swinton, and D. Zilberman, 119–39. Norwell: Kluwer.

Van Ravenswaay, E.O., and J.P. Hoehn. 1996. The theoretical benefits of food safety policies: A total economic value framework. *American Journal of Agricultural Economics* 78(5): 1291–6. https://doi.org/10.2307/1243509

Van Vuuren, D.P., J. Edmonds, M. Kainuma, K. Riahi, A. Thomson, K. Hibbard, G.C. Hurtt, T. Kram, V. Krey, J.-F. Lamarque, T. Masui, M. Meinshausen, N. Nakicenovic, S.J. Smith, and S.K. Rose. 2011. The representative concentration pathways: An overview. *Climatic Change* 109(5): 1573–80. https://doi.org/10.1007/s10584-011-0148-z

Vercammen, J. 2013. A partial adjustment model of federal direct payments in Canadian agriculture. *Canadian Journal of Agricultural Economics* 61(3): 465–85. https://doi.org/10.1111/j.1744-7976.2012.01268.x

Vercammen, J.A., and A. Schmitz. 1992. Supply management and import concessions. *Canadian Journal of Economics* 25(4): 957–71. https://doi.org/10.2307/135774

Vercammen, J.A., and G.C. van Kooten. 1994. Moral hazard cycles in individual-coverage crop insurance. *American Journal of Agricultural Economics* 76(2): 250–61. https://doi.org/10.2307/1243626

Viscusi, W.K. 1989. Toward a diminished role for tort liability: Social insurance, government regulation, and contemporary risks to health and society. *Yale Journal of Regulation* 6(1): 65–107.

Voiland, A. 2021. *Waiting to Unload*. Earth Laboratory. NASA.gov. October 10, 2021. https://earthlaboratory.nasa.gov/images/148956/waiting-to-unload

Wallace, T.D. 1962. Measures of social costs of agricultural programs. *Journal of Farm Economics* 44(2): 580–99.

Webb, D., and C. Byrd-Bredbenner. 2015. Overcoming consumer inertia to dietary guidance. *Advances in Nutrition* 6(4): 391–6. https://doi.org/10.3945/an.115.008441

Weber, M., and G. Hauer. 2003. A regional analysis of climate change impacts on Canadian agriculture. *Canadian Public Policy/Analyse de politiques* 29(2): 163–80. https://doi.org/10.2307/3552453

White House. 1970. *White House Conference on Food, Nutrition, and Health*. Washington, DC: White House.

Widmer, L., G. Fox, and G. Brinkman. 1987. *The Rate of Return to Beef Cattle Research in Canada*. Ottawa: Agriculture and Agri-Food Canada.

Willig, R.D. 1976. Consumer's surplus without apology. *American Economic Review* 66(4): 589–97.

Wittwer, S.H. 1995. *Food, Climate and Carbon Dioxide. The Global Environment and World Food Production*. Boca Raton, FL: CRC Press.

Working, H. 1943. Statistical laws of family expenditure. *Journal of the American Statistical Association* 38(221): 43–56. https://doi.org/10.1080/01621459.1943.10501775

World Bank. 2019. *Databank*. Washington, DC: World Bank.

World Trade Organization (WTO). 1999a. *Understanding the WTO Agreement on Sanitary and Phytosanitary (SPS) Measures*. https://www.wto.org/english/tratop_e/sps_e/spsund_e.htm

World Trade Organization (WTO). 1999b. *International Plant Protection Convention*. Geneva: WTO.

World Trade Organization (WTO). 1999c. *Overview of the State-of-Play of WTO Disputes*. Geneva: WTO.

Yang, P., Y-F. Yao, Z. Mi, Y-F. Cao, H. Liao, B.-Y. Yu, Q.-M. Liang, D. Coffman, and Y.-M. Wei. 2018. Social cost of carbon under shared socioeconomic pathways. *Global Environmental Change* 53: 225–32. https://doi.org/10.1016/j.gloenvcha.2018.10.001

Yu, J., and D.A. Sumner. 2018. Effects of subsidized crop insurance on crop choices. *Agricultural Economics* 49(4): 533–45. https://doi.org/10.1111/agec.12434

Zenk, S.N., L.L. Lachance, A.J. Schulz, G. Mentz, S. Kannan, and W. Ridella. 2009. Neighborhood retail food environment and fruit and vegetable intake in a multiethnic urban population. *American Journal of Health Promotion* 23(4): 255–64. https://doi.org/10.4278/ajhp.071204127

Zentner, R.P., and W.L. Peterson. 1984. An economic evaluation of public wheat research and extension expenditures in Canada. *Canadian Journal of Agricultural Economics* 32(2): 327–53. https://doi.org/10.1111/j.1744-7976.1984.tb02131.x

Zhang, F. 2019. The Florida Tomato Committee's education and promotion program, 2011–2017: An evaluation. MS thesis, University of Florida, 2019.

Zhang, W., A. Plastina, and W. Sawadgo. 2018. Iowa farmland ownership and tenure survey, 1982–2017: A thirty-five year perspective. Ames: Iowa State University.

Zilberman, D., J. Wesseler, A. Schmitz, and B. Gordon. 2019. Economics of agricultural biotechnology. In *Routledge Handbook of Agricultural Economics*, ed. G.L. Cramer, K.P. Paudel, and A. Schmitz, 670–86. London: Routledge.

Index

www.ingramcontent.com/pod-product-compliance
Ingram Content Group UK Ltd.
Pitfield, Milton Keynes, MK11 3LW, UK
UKHW050442010225
454513UK00007B/226